THE ECONOMICS OF BANKING

The Economics of Banking provides an accessible overview of banking theory and practice. It introduces readers to the building blocks of fundamental theories and provides guidance on state-of-the-art research, reflecting the dramatic changes in the banking industry and banking research over the past two decades.

This textbook explores market failure and financial frictions that motivate the role of financial intermediaries, explains the microeconomic incentives and behavior of participants in banking, examines micro-level market stress caused by economic recessions and financial crises, and looks at the role of monetary authorities and banking regulators to reduce systemic fragility as well as to improve macroeconomic stability. It delivers broad coverage of both the micro and macroeconomics of banking, central banking and banking regulation, striking a fine balance between rigorous theoretical foundations, sound empirical evidence for banking theories at work, and practical knowledge for banking and policymaking in the real world.

The Economics of Banking is suitable for advanced undergraduate, master's, or early PhD students of economics and finance, and will also be valuable reading for bankers and banking regulators.

JIN CAO is Research Economist of Norges Bank. He has taught at the University of Oslo, NTNU, and the University of Munich. His work is published in the *Journal of Financial and Quantitative Analysis*, *Journal of Money, Credit and Banking*, *Journal of Banking and Finance*, and other academic journals and books.

THE ECONOMICS OF BANKING

Jin Cao

LONDON AND NEW YORK

First published 2022
by Routledge
2 Park Square, Milton Park, Abingdon, Oxon OX14 4RN

and by Routledge
605 Third Avenue, New York, NY 10158

Routledge is an imprint of the Taylor & Francis Group, an informa business

© 2022 Jin Cao

The right of Jin Cao to be identified as author of this work has been asserted in accordance with sections 77 and 78 of the Copyright, Designs and Patents Act 1988.

All rights reserved. No part of this book may be reprinted or reproduced or utilised in any form or by any electronic, mechanical, or other means, now known or hereafter invented, including photocopying and recording, or in any information storage or retrieval system, without permission in writing from the publishers.

Trademark notice: Product or corporate names may be trademarks or registered trademarks, and are used only for identification and explanation without intent to infringe.

British Library Cataloguing-in-Publication Data
A catalogue record for this book is available from the British Library

Library of Congress Cataloging-in-Publication Data
A catalog record has been requested for this book

ISBN: 978-0-367-40571-7 (hbk)
ISBN: 978-0-367-40572-4 (pbk)
ISBN: 978-0-429-35677-3 (ebk)

DOI: 10.4324/9780429356773

Typeset in Minion Pro
by codeMantra

CONTENTS IN BRIEF

PART I	**INTRODUCTION**	1
CHAPTER 1	INTRODUCTION	3
PART II	**THE MICROECONOMICS OF BANKING**	25
CHAPTER 2	FRAGILE BANKS	27
CHAPTER 3	INFORMATION FRICTIONS IN BANKING	89
CHAPTER 4	INDUSTRIAL ORGANIZATION OF BANKING	137
CHAPTER 5	SECURITIZED BANKING	175
CHAPTER 6	COMPLEXITY IN BANKING	223
PART III	**THE MACROECONOMICS AND POLITICAL ECONOMY OF BANKING**	273
CHAPTER 7	CENTRAL BANKING	275
CHAPTER 8	THE BANKING-MACRO LINKAGES	339
CHAPTER 9	INTERNATIONAL BANKING	399

CHAPTER 10	POLITICAL ECONOMY IN BANKING	**433**
PART IV	**THE ECONOMICS OF BANKING REGULATION**	**477**
CHAPTER 11	SYSTEMIC RISKS AND MACROPRUDENTIAL REGULATION	**479**
CHAPTER 12	BANKING REGULATION IN PRACTICE	**525**
PART V	**APPENDIX**	**575**
	SOLUTIONS TO SELECTED EXERCISES	**577**

Bibliography   605
Index   625

CONTENTS

List of figures — xvii
Preface — xxv
Acknowledgments — xxvii
Acronyms — xxix

PART I INTRODUCTION — 1

CHAPTER 1 INTRODUCTION — 3
 1.1 What are banks and why are they special? — 4
 1.2 Structure of this book — 20
 1.3 Exercises — 22

PART II THE MICROECONOMICS OF BANKING — 25

CHAPTER 2 FRAGILE BANKS — 27
 2.1 Introduction — 28
 2.2 Bank liquidity creation and bank run — 30
  2.2.1 Liquidity preferences and the need for liquidity insurance — 30
  2.2.2 Baseline result: the planner's solution — 32
  2.2.3 Resource allocation in a decentralized economy — 34
  2.2.4 Bank run: fundamental-driven versus panic-driven — 37
  2.2.5 Fragile banks and policy implications — 40
  2.2.6 Equilibrium refinement and equilibrium selection — 43
  2.2.7 Summary — 45

	2.3	Optimal bank run	45
		2.3.1 Modelling aggregate asset return risks	46
		2.3.2 Optimal risk-sharing with zero liquidation cost	47
		2.3.3 Optimal risk-sharing with positive liquidation cost	54
		2.3.4 Summary	61
	2.4	Fragility and bank liquidity	61
		2.4.1 Model setup: the need for fragility	62
		2.4.2 Constrained efficiency	68
		2.4.3 Market liquidity and funding liquidity	73
		2.4.4 Summary	78
	2.5	Empirical evidence: drivers of bank runs and policy responses	79
	2.6	Exercises	82
CHAPTER 3		**INFORMATION FRICTIONS IN BANKING**	**89**
	3.1	Introduction	90
	3.2	Bank as delegated monitor	93
		3.2.1 Asymmetric information and monitoring	94
		3.2.2 Costly monitoring under direct lending	95
		3.2.3 Bank and delegated monitoring	96
		3.2.4 Summary	99
	3.3	Monitoring and Capital	100
		3.3.1 Model setup	101
		3.3.2 Direct lending	102
		3.3.3 Banking solution	103
		3.3.4 Summary	106
	3.4	Credit rationing	107
		3.4.1 Model setup	109
		3.4.2 Credit rationing in market equilibrium	110
		3.4.3 Adverse selection and lending efficiency	115
		3.4.4 Summary	118
	3.5	Positive selection and excess lending	119
		3.5.1 Market equilibrium under positive selection	120
		3.5.2 Positive selection and excess lending	123
		3.5.3 Summary	125

3.6	Empirical evidence		125
	3.6.1	Relationship banking	125
	3.6.2	Credit rationing	129
3.7	Exercises		131

CHAPTER 4 INDUSTRIAL ORGANIZATION OF BANKING — 137

4.1	Introduction		138
4.2	Price setting of competitive banks		141
4.3	Competition and stability: a static choice		144
	4.3.1	Franchise value hypothesis	144
	4.3.2	Moral hazard hypothesis	146
	4.3.3	Summary	148
4.4	Competition and stability: a dynamic choice		149
	4.4.1	Risk-taking as dynamic decision-making	149
	4.4.2	Risk-taking: short-run gain versus long-run loss	150
	4.4.3	Policy implication	152
4.5	Market entry under asymmetric information		153
	4.5.1	Credit market with imperfect screening	154
	4.5.2	Competition and market outcome	155
	4.5.3	Winner's curse on market entry	157
4.6	Empirical evidence		158
	4.6.1	Measuring the intensity of competition	159
	4.6.2	Identifying the competition effects on bank behavior	163
	4.6.3	Real effects of banking competition	167
4.7	Exercises		169

CHAPTER 5 SECURITIZED BANKING — 175

5.1	Introduction		176
	5.1.1	Risk appetite and securitization	177
	5.1.2	Procedure of securitization	181
	5.1.3	Repo and securitized banking	182
5.2	Loan sale and screening		188
	5.2.1	Modelling loan sale and screening effort	189
	5.2.2	Inefficient screening with loan sales	190
	5.2.3	Summary	191

5.3		Securitized banking and financial instability	192
	5.3.1	Originate-to-distribute and repo	192
	5.3.2	Market equilibrium	193
	5.3.3	Summary	199
5.4		Repo runs	199
	5.4.1	Modelling dynamic collateralized lending	200
	5.4.2	Non-run equilibrium	203
	5.4.3	Run on the repos	206
	5.4.4	Summary	209
5.5		Empirical evidence	210
	5.5.1	Does securitization encourage banks' risk-taking?	210
	5.5.2	Securitization and bank performance	214
	5.5.3	International evidence	217
5.6		Exercises	218

CHAPTER 6 COMPLEXITY IN BANKING **223**

6.1		Introduction	224
	6.1.1	Organizational complexity	224
	6.1.2	Complexity in products	225
	6.1.3	Network complexity	226
	6.1.4	Opacity	226
6.2		Strategic complexity in product	227
	6.2.1	Model setup: agents, preferences, and technologies	228
	6.2.2	Market power and product complexity	230
	6.2.3	Summary	234
6.3		Network complexity	235
	6.3.1	Banking network as a web of claims	235
	6.3.2	Risk sharing through financial networks	238
	6.3.3	Contagion over banking network	243
	6.3.4	Summary	248
6.4		Opacity and banking	249
	6.4.1	Model setup: agents, preferences, and technologies	250
	6.4.2	Market funding, bank funding, and the role of opacity	251
	6.4.3	Summary	261

	6.5	Empirical evidence			262
		6.5.1	Interbank network and contagion		262
		6.5.2	Opacity measures and bank risk		263
	6.6	Exercises			267

PART III THE MACROECONOMICS AND POLITICAL ECONOMY OF BANKING   273

CHAPTER 7   CENTRAL BANKING   275

7.1	Introduction			276
7.2	Central banking in practice			279
	7.2.1	Quantity tools and price tools		280
	7.2.2	Conducting monetary policy in normal times		284
	7.2.3	Conducting monetary policy in financial crises		288
7.3	Monetary policy, liquidity management, and bank lending			296
	7.3.1	Bank lending and liquidity risk exposure		296
	7.3.2	Liquidity management and bank lending channel		299
	7.3.3	Summary		304
7.4	Monetary policy, maturity transformation, and liquidity risks			304
	7.4.1	Maturity transformation in a monetary economy		305
	7.4.2	Central banking and excess liquidity risk		314
	7.4.3	Summary		315
7.5	Risk-taking channels of monetary policy			315
	7.5.1	Modelling banks' risk-shifting incentives		316
	7.5.2	Risk-taking channels		317
	7.5.3	Summary		322
7.6	Empirical Evidence			323
	7.6.1	Identifying bank lending channel		323
	7.6.2	Risk-taking channel of monetary policy		332
	7.6.3	Bank lending under unconventional monetary policy		334
7.7	Exercises			337

CHAPTER 8 THE BANKING-MACRO LINKAGES — **339**

- 8.1 Introduction — 340
- 8.2 Costly state verification and the financial accelerator — 342
  - 8.2.1 Lending under costly state verification — 344
  - 8.2.2 Market equilibrium with no asymmetric information — 347
  - 8.2.3 Market equilibrium with asymmetric information — 348
  - 8.2.4 Summary — 358
- 8.3 Moral hazard and bank lending — 359
  - 8.3.1 Aggregate deposit supply without financial friction — 359
  - 8.3.2 Aggregate deposit demand under financial friction — 362
  - 8.3.3 Summary — 364
- 8.4 Overborrowing and excess volatility — 365
  - 8.4.1 Collateralized lending and borrowing constraint — 366
  - 8.4.2 Binding borrowing constraint and excess volatility — 367
  - 8.4.3 Summary — 370
- 8.5 Risk management and the leverage cycle — 371
  - 8.5.1 Market equilibrium and asset price — 372
  - 8.5.2 VaR, asset price, and the leverage cycle — 375
  - 8.5.3 Summary — 379
- 8.6 General equilibrium effect and the leverage cycle — 380
  - 8.6.1 Agents, time preferences, and technology — 382
  - 8.6.2 Market equilibrium without borrowing — 383
  - 8.6.3 Market equilibrium with borrowing — 385
  - 8.6.4 The business cycle and the leverage cycle — 391
  - 8.6.5 Summary — 395
- 8.7 Exercises — 396

CHAPTER 9 INTERNATIONAL BANKING — **399**

- 9.1 Introduction — 400
  - 9.1.1 The ownership dimension of international banking — 403
  - 9.1.2 The location dimension of international banking — 405

		9.1.3	The currency dimension of international banking	407
	9.2	\multicolumn{2}{l	}{International financial market and global risk-sharing: traditional view}	410
		9.2.1	Global risk-sharing in an endowment economy	410
		9.2.2	Global risk-sharing in a production economy	413
		9.2.3	Summary	417
	9.3	\multicolumn{2}{l	}{Global banks and international transmission of monetary policy}	418
		9.3.1	Model setup: global bank and global balance sheet	418
		9.3.2	International transmission of monetary policy through global banks	420
		9.3.3	Summary	424
	9.4	\multicolumn{2}{l	}{Empirical evidence}	424
		9.4.1	International banking and transmission of monetary policy	424
		9.4.2	International risk-taking channel	428
	9.5	\multicolumn{2}{l	}{Exercises}	429

CHAPTER 10 POLITICAL ECONOMY IN BANKING — 433

10.1	Introduction		434
10.2	Government ownership and banking outcomes		437
	10.2.1	Government ownership and banking: main hypotheses	438
	10.2.2	Modelling government ownership and control rights	439
	10.2.3	Political economy equilibrium	442
	10.2.4	Summary	447
10.3	Political credit cycle		448
	10.3.1	Reelection and credit supply to voters	448
	10.3.2	Credit supply over election cycles	449
	10.3.3	Summary	452
10.4	Empirical evidence		452
	10.4.1	Government ownership and banking outcomes	453
	10.4.2	Legal systems and banking	457
	10.4.3	Political ties and banking outcomes	462

		10.4.4	Political credit cycles	464
		10.4.5	Moral suasion and home bias	468
		10.4.6	Political economy and allocation efficiency	469
	10.5	Exercises		473

PART IV THE ECONOMICS OF BANKING REGULATION 477

CHAPTER 11 SYSTEMIC RISKS AND MACROPRUDENTIAL REGULATION 479

	11.1	Introduction		480
		11.1.1	Why is banking regulation special?	480
		11.1.2	Bank-specific versus systemic risks	481
	11.2	Maturity rat race and excess maturity mismatch		485
		11.2.1	Maturity structure of debt contracts	486
		11.2.2	Debt rollover and maturity rat race	487
		11.2.3	Summary	492
	11.3	Inefficient liquidity buffer and sellers' strike		492
		11.3.1	Model setup	494
		11.3.2	Market equilibrium	495
		11.3.3	Summary	501
	11.4	Contagion in interbank market		502
		11.4.1	Idiosyncratic liquidity shocks and interbank market	502
		11.4.2	Equilibrium outcomes in the interbank market	505
		11.4.3	Contagion through interbank market	510
		11.4.4	Summary	511
	11.5	Macroprudential versus microprudential perspectives		512
	11.6	Empirical evidence: measuring systemic risks		515
		11.6.1	CoVaR	516
		11.6.2	Systemic expected shortfall	517
		11.6.3	SRISK	519
	11.7	Exercises		521

CHAPTER 12	BANKING REGULATION IN PRACTICE		**525**
	12.1 Introduction: banking regulation in principles		526
	12.2 Liquidity regulation		528
	12.2.1 Idiosyncratic and systemic liquidity risks		528
	12.2.2 Lender-of-last-resort policy		532
	12.2.3 Requirements on market liquidity and funding liquidity		537
	12.2.4 Liquidity regulation and monetary policy implementation: a conceptual assessment		540
	12.3 Capital regulation		542
	12.3.1 Bank capital and resilience		542
	12.3.2 Countercyclical capital requirement		544
	12.3.3 Capital requirement and risk-taking: a conceptual assessment		547
	12.3.4 Empirical evidence		550
	12.4 Other issues		556
	12.4.1 Interaction between banking regulation and monetary policy		557
	12.4.2 Bail-in		558
	12.5 Exercises		565
PART V	**APPENDIX**		**575**
	SOLUTIONS TO SELECTED EXERCISES		**577**

Bibliography   605

Index   625

FIGURES

1.1	Sources of bank funding for banks in Europe and US, as percentage of total liabilities, as of 2019Q4	5
1.2	Bank assets to GDP ratio in nine countries, 2019Q4	6
1.3	Bank assets to GDP ratio in the US and Europe, 2007–2019	8
1.4	Market funding versus bank funding in nine economies, 2017	9
1.5	Frequency of systemic banking crises around the world, 1970–2017	11
1.6	Output loss to GDP during systemic banking crises, 1970–2017	12
1.7	Fiscal cost to GDP during systemic banking crises, 1970–2017	13
2.1	A bank's balance sheet in $t = 0$	36
2.2	Optimal solution to the planner's problem	50
2.3	Optimal solution to the planner's problem, with liquidation cost	56
2.4	Optimal solution to the bank's problem, with liquidation cost	59
2.5	The timing of events, normal state	68
2.6	The timing of events, crisis state	68
2.7	A bank's balance sheet in $t = 0$	72
2.8	A bank's balance sheet in $t = 1$, after withdraw	72
2.9	Depositors' expected return	73

FIGURES

3.1	Direct lending	95
3.2	Delegated monitoring with bank	96
3.3	Projects' payoff structure	101
3.4	A bank's balance sheet	104
3.5	Entrepreneurs' access to funding	106
3.6	Entrepreneurs' demand for loans	111
3.7	Depositors' supply of deposits	114
3.8	Competitive equilibrium without credit rationing	115
3.9	Credit rationing	115
3.10	Entrepreneurs' demand for loans	121
3.11	Loan acceptance rates by rating	130
4.1	Market share for the five largest banks in China, Germany, Japan, UK, and US, 1996–2017	138
4.2	A generic bank's balance sheet	141
4.3	Deposit market competition and banks' risk-taking	152
4.4	Number of branches operated by FDIC-insured commercial banks	165
4.5	The dynamic impact of removing intrastate branching restrictions on the Gini coefficient in the US, 1976–1994	169
4.6	Banks and depositors in the circular world	170
5.1	Traditional intermediation chain	176
5.2	Modern intermediation chain	176
5.3	Securitization procedure: pooling and tranching	181
5.4	Traditional banking versus securitized banking	183
5.5	Bi-party repo	183

5.6	Tri-party repo	184
5.7	Repo haircuts on different categories of structured products during 2007–2009 financial crisis	187
5.8	Timing of events without repo runs	202
5.9	Distribution of propensity scores before and after matching	217
6.1	Bank i's balance sheet in $t = 0$	236
6.2	Complete network	241
6.3	Incomplete network (I)	242
6.4	Incomplete network (II)	244
6.5	Regional liquidity shock	244
6.6	Bond market with the early consumer	254
6.7	Global risk aversion and local risk neutrality	258
6.8	Banking solution	259
6.9	Another incomplete network	267
7.1	Creation of banks and their balance sheets	280
7.2	Loan expansion and money creation	282
7.3	Deposit withdraw and rebalancing	283
7.4	A stylized central bank's balance sheet	284
7.5	Supply and demand in the market for reserves	287
7.6	Effective federal funds rate and the corridor system, 01/2005–10/2020	288
7.7	TED spread, 05/2007–12/2009	290
7.8	Monetary policy rates in the US, Euro area, and UK, 01/2005–10/2020	291

FIGURES

7.9	Main components of assets held by the Federal Reserve System, 07/2007–12/2009, in billion US dollars	292
7.10	Spread between 3-month commercial paper and federal funds rate, 05/2007–12/2009	293
7.11	The size (in trillion US dollars) and composition of assets held by the Federal Reserve System, 08/2007–12/2020	295
7.12	Bank's balance sheets	296
7.13	Monetizing the economy in period $t = 0$	306
7.14	Money flows in period $t = 1$	308
7.15	Sequence of money flows in period $t = 2$ following the good state	309
7.16	Sequence of money flows in period $t = 1$ in the bad state	310
7.17	Sequence of money flows in period $t = 2$ following the bad state	311
7.18	Bank's choice on capital ratio k as a function of monetary policy rate r^*	321
7.19	Bank's choice on monitoring effort p as a function of monetary policy rate r^*	322
7.20	Bank-firm relationships	324
7.21	A bank's balance sheet in each period	325
7.22	Khwaja-Mian identification strategy	327
7.23	A generic bank's balance sheet	329
8.1	Capital demand and supply	349
8.2	Funding structure of the economy	355
8.3	Capital supply with financial friction	356
8.4	The banks' balance sheet	361
8.5	Deposit market equilibrium in the absence of moral hazard	362

8.6	Deposit market equilibrium in the presence of moral hazard with high equity	364
8.7	Drop in deposits when moral hazard problem dominates. Black IC is the new demand curve under falling households' initial wealth N	365
8.8	The balance sheets of banks and consumers in $t = 0$	374
8.9	The equilibrium asset price and demand for risky assets	375
8.10	Asset price rises in the boom phase	377
8.11	Equilibrium demand for risky assets	378
8.12	Balance sheet expansion through bank leverage	379
8.13	The virtuous and vicious cycles through bank leverage	379
8.14	The payoff of the risky assets	382
8.15	The equilibrium price and the boundary buyer	385
8.16	The impact of borrowing	388
8.17	The impact of improving fundamentals (I)	390
8.18	The impact of improving fundamentals (II)	391
8.19	The 3-date extension	392
8.20	The leverage cycle and the marginal buyer	394
9.1	Foreign-controlled banks across the world, 2016	403
9.2	Foreign-controlled banks in selected EU countries, 2019	404
9.3	Outstanding cross-border claims through banking sector in trillions of US dollars, by locations of borrowing economies, 1990Q1–2020Q2	405
9.4	Outstanding cross-border claims through banking sector in trillions of US dollars, by borrowing economies, 1990Q1–2020Q2	406

9.5	Percentage share of foreign currency denominated assets/liabilities in total bank assets/liabilities for selected European countries, 2016	407
9.6	Outstanding cross-border claims through banking sector in trillions of US dollars, by currencies, 1999Q1–2020Q2	409
9.7	International financial market and global risk-sharing in an endowment economy	412
9.8	International financial market and global risk-sharing in a production economy	416
9.9	Bank's consolidated balance sheets in $t = 0$	419
10.1	Government-controlled banks across the world, 2016	435
10.2	Control rights and political economy equilibria	445
10.3	Government-controlled banks' share in total bank assets versus GDP per capita, 2016	454
10.4	Government-controlled banks' share in total bank assets and economic growth, 2016	455
11.1	Liquid assets as share of banks' balance sheets, US and UK	483
11.2	Contagion over banking network and network externality	483
11.3	Short-term contract versus long-term contract	486
11.4	Face value, short-term versus long-term debt	490
11.5	Marginal funding cost, short-term versus long-term debt	491
11.6	Bank balance sheet under "wait-and-see" strategy	495
11.7	Bank balance sheet under "getting-ready-before-the-crisis" strategy	496
11.8	Timing of the model without bank run	504
11.9	Timing of the model with bank run	505

FIGURES

12.1	Time consistency problem in LOLR policy implementation	535
12.2	Balance sheet expansion in the boom	544
12.3	Balance sheet contraction in the bust	545
12.4	Composition of Pillar 1 Common Equity Tier 1 (CET1) requirements for Norwegian banks, 2007–2020	546
12.5	Statutory countercyclical capital buffer adjustments in reaction to the COVID-19 pandemic, as of July 2020	547
12.6	Alternative responses to increase in capital requirement	548
12.7	Balance sheet of a bank with CoCo	559
12.8	Balance sheet of a bank with CoCo, after asset price shock	560
12.9	Recapitalization through debt conversion	560
12.10	Balance sheet of a reference bank without CoCo	561
12.11	Bank recapitalization through CoCos versus common equity	561
12.12	The value of CoCos	562
12.13	The value of common equity in a bank with/without CoCos	563
12.14	Bank's balance sheets	570
A.1	Payoffs of projects	581
A.2	Marginal depositors and suppliers of deposits	587
A.3	$r_P(k)$, $r_G(k)$, and $\hat{r}(k)$	589
A.4	Market equilibrium after the shock	593
A.5	Incentive compatibility constraint and participation constraint	600
A.6	Bank risk-taking and bailout	601

PREFACE

In this book, I provide advanced undergraduate and first-year postgraduate students an overview of foundations in the economics of banking as well as recent developments in banking research. I try to strike a balance between coverage and depth: in each chapter, I focus on a few analytical frameworks that address the key issues; across chapters, I try to cover the core issues in banking, as well as issues that are of increasing importance nowadays, such as securitized banking, the role of complexity in banking, linkages between banking and macroeconomics, international banking, and political economy in banking. Furthermore, this book covers new issues in banking regulation after the 2007–2009 global financial crisis. In each of the chapters, I also review related empirical evidence, to reflect both recent progress of applying cutting-edge econometric techniques as well as exciting studies based on newly available data resources in banking research. This book should not be reported as representing the views of Norges Bank. The views expressed are those of the author and do not necessarily reflect those of Norges Bank.

One challenge to write a textbook on banking is that there is no single framework (or a few frameworks) that fits all issues. Even on one specific issue, many analytical techniques and methodologies are available to provide views from different angles. Although this book is organized by topics, and only a few analytical frameworks are presented under each topic, readers should be aware that frameworks discussed in one chapter can often be applied to issues in other chapters. Due to the width and depth of the field, this book is by no means able to include extensive reviews on all issues that are covered. Fortunately, a few books are available that provide in-depth coverage on certain topics in banking, such as Freixas and Rochet (2008), *Microeconomics of Banking, 2nd Edition* on microeconomic foundations of banking, Degryse et al. (2009), *Microeconometrics of Banking: Methods, Applications, and Results* on empirical methods, and Freixas et al. (2015), *Systemic Risk, Crises, and Macroprudential Regulation* on banking regulation. I strongly recommend ambitious readers to refer to these books.

I look forward to constructive critiques from the readers.

Jin Cao
Oslo, Norway
February, 2021

ACKNOWLEDGMENTS

I would like to thank Gerhard Illing, my doctoral advisor and long-term co-author, who encouraged me to explore research questions on banking fifteen years ago. I would like to thank my co-author Valeriya Dinger who always gives me helpful feedback and generous support, and my colleagues in Norges Bank who always inspire me with exciting new ideas. This book is based on several courses on money and banking that I taught at the Ludwig Maximilian University (LMU) of Munich, the University of Oslo, and the Norwegian University of Science and Technology, as well as internal training course at Norges Bank; I owe many, many thanks to the course participants for their constructive comments and suggestions. I would like to thank Routledge Editors, Andy Humphries, Kristina Abbotts, Natalie Tomlinson, Chloe James, and Cathy Hurren. Without their patience, encouragement, and great support over the past five years, this book would not have been available.

ACRONYMS

ABCP	asset-backed commercial paper
ABS	asset-backed security
ACS	American Community Survey
AFS	available-for-sale
AOIC	accumulated other comprehensive income
ATE	average treatment effect
BCBS	Basel Committee on Banking Supervision
BHC	bank holding company
BIS	Bank for International Settlements
bp	basis point
BR	borrowed reserves
BRICS	Brazil, Russia, India, China, and South Africa
BRSS	Bank Regulation and Supervision Survey
CA	current account
CCB	city commercial bank
CCyB	countercyclical capital buffer
CD	certificate of deposit
CDB	China Development Bank

cdf	cumulative distribution function
CDO	collateralized debt obligation
CDS	credit default swap
CEO	chief executive officer
CET1	common equity tier 1
CIP	covered interest parity
CLO	collateralized loan obligations
CoCo	contingent convertible
CoVaR	contingent, conditional value-at-risk
COVID-19	coronavirus disease 2019
CPS	Current Population Survey
CRS	constant return to scale
CS	capital shortfall
CT1	core tier 1
DID	difference-in-differences
DSGE	dynamic stochastic general equilibrium
EBA	European Banking Authority
ECB	European Central Bank
ES	expected shortfall
FDIC	Federal Deposit Insurance Corporation
FICO	Fair Isaac Corporation
FLS	Funding for Lending Scheme
FRED	Federal Reserve Economic Data
FX	foreign exchange

GARCH	generalized autoregressive conditionally heteroscedastic model
GDP	gross domestic product
GSE	government sponsored enterprise
HHI	Herfindahl-Hirschman index
HMDA	Home Mortgage Disclosure Act
HQLA	high-quality liquid asset
HTM	held-to-maturity
IBBEA	Interstate Banking and Branching Efficiency Act
i.i.d.	independent and identically distributed
IMF	International Monetary Fund
IPO	initial public offering
IRB	internal rating based
JCB	joint-stock commercial bank
KfW	Kreditanstalt für Wiederaufbau
LBO	leveraged buyout
LCR	liquidity coverage ratio
LIBOR	London Inter-bank Offered Rate
LLP	loan loss provision
LOLR	lender-of-last-resort
LRMES	long-run marginal expected shortfall
M&A	merger and acquisition
MBHC	multibank holding company
MBS	mortgage-backed security

MES	marginal expected shortfall
MMMF	money market mutual fund
NBR	non-borrowed reserves
NIM	net interest margin
NPL	non-performing loan
NSFR	net stable funding ratio
OE	operating expense
OECD	Organisation for Economic Co-operation and Development
OMT	Outright Monetary Transactions
OTD	*originate-to-distribute*
pdf	probability density function
PPI	promotion pressure index
PSM	propensity score matching
QE	quantitative easing
RBC	real business cycle
RDD	regression discontinuity design
repo	repurchase agreement
ROA	return on assets
ROE	return on equity
RWA	risk-weighted assets
SA	standard approach
SEO	seasoned equity offering
SES	systemic expected shortfall
SIB	systemically important bank

ACRONYMS

SIPP	Survey of Income and Program Participation
SOE	state-owned enterprise
SPV	special purpose vehicle
UIP	uncovered interest parity
VaR	value-at-risk
WTO	World Trade Organization
ZLB	zero lower bound

PART I
Introduction

CHAPTER 1
Introduction

INTRODUCTION

1.1 WHAT ARE BANKS AND WHY ARE THEY SPECIAL?

Banks are among some of the most important yet sometimes the most controversial institutions in an economy. Banks provide socially desirable services for households, firms, and other financial institutions, but bank failure often costs enormously for taxpayers and economic growth. In this chapter, we will take a brief look inside the banking industry, explain terms and jargon that we will use frequently in the rest of this book, and focus on the features in banking that make banks and the economics of banking special.

According to *Encyclopædia Britannica*, a bank is "an institution that deals in money and its substitutes and provides other money-related services. In its role as a *financial intermediary*, a bank accepts deposits and makes loans". That is, a bank provides financial intermediation services between lenders and borrowers, collecting funds from lenders and lending the funds to borrowers; of course, nowadays, we shall also interpret "deposits", "loans", "depositors", and "borrowers" more broadly. In addition, the boundary between banks and other types of financial institutions is becoming more and more blurred, for example, certain financial institutions such as mutual funds also provide financial intermediation services. In the narrow sense, only a financial institution that carries a banking license that is issued by banking authority is legally classified as a bank. However, as many of the issues discussed in this book are applicable to a wide variety of financial intermediation services which do not necessarily take place in these narrowly defined banks, we do not confine ourselves with such narrowly defined banks, and sometimes we use "bank" and "financial intermediary" interchangeably.

Box 1.1 (p.14) presents an anatomy of a highly stylized bank that allows us to see what a typical bank does and how we can measure its banking outcomes and performance. The *balance sheet* in the Box characterizes the sources from which the bank raises funding, i.e., in its *liabilities*, and how these funds are invested, i.e., in its *assets*. Typically, a bank can raise funding from a large variety of entities, for example, from individuals via checking accounts or savings accounts (*retail deposits*), from other banks via interbank lending (*wholesale funding*), from financial markets via issuing bonds or other financial securities, from shareholders, etc. Figure 1.1 shows a decomposition of banks' funding in the US and several European countries. For many developed European countries, retail deposits only account for less than half of total bank liabilities, while funding from other financial institutions, or, wholesale funding, accounts for a larger share. In contrast, retail deposits account for a much larger share in the US. Furthermore, banks are typically highly leveraged institutions, with much higher leverage ratios than non-financial firms. Given the limited liability of a bank, high leverage ratio implies that its shareholders only incur a small share of bankruptcy cost when the bank goes bust; this creates a potential for banks to take excess risks.

Usually, a large share of funds are lent out as loans, to households, firms, financial institutions, etc. Banks are investing in financial assets, too, such as stocks and bonds; investment activities are nowadays of increasing importance for many banks. Banks also hold cash and other "liquid assets" such as government bonds that can be easily converted to

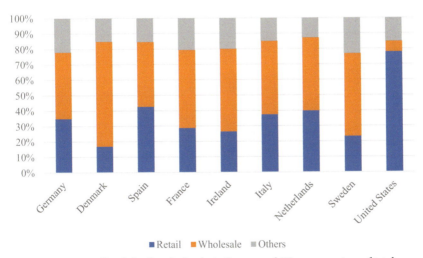

Figure 1.1 *Sources of bank funding for banks in Europe and US, as percentage of total liabilities, as of 2019Q4*

Notes: vertical axis is in percentage points. Sources of bank funding include retail deposits, wholesale funding, and others. Data source: European Central Bank Statistical Data Warehouse, available on https://sdw.ecb.europa.eu/, and FDIC Historical Bank Data, available on https://banks.data.fdic.gov/explore/historical.

cash, often as reserves to meet depositors' withdrawal demand. Overall, through standard intermediation, a bank collects funding from creditors at certain funding cost (for example, interest rate for deposits), and issues loans to borrowers at loan rates that are higher than funding rates. The margin between these two rates is thus the bank's profit.

BANKING SECTOR IS SYSTEMICALLY IMPORTANT

Why are banks special, then? First of all, banks are special and often gain a lot of attention among the general public, researchers, and policy makers because the banking sector is one of the most important sectors in a modern economy. Banks are mobilizing and managing an enormous amount of resources in the economy. Figure 1.2 shows bank assets to

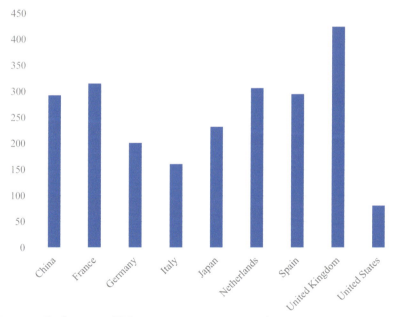

Figure 1.2 Bank assets to GDP ratio in nine countries, 2019Q4

Notes: computed by the author. Vertical axis is in percentage points. Data sources: China Banking and Insurance Regulatory Commission, available on https://www.cbirc.gov.cn/cn/view/pages/tongjishuju/tongjishuju.html; Bank of Japan, available on https://www.boj.or.jp/statistics/index.htm/; European Central Bank Statistical Data Warehouse; Eurostat, available on https://ec.europa.eu/eurostat/; FDIC Historical Bank Data; Federal Reserve Economic Data (FRED) from Federal Reserve Bank of St. Louis, available on https://fred.stlouisfed.org/.

GDP ratio in a number of countries in the world, as of 2019. In many countries, the banking sector accounts for a big share of the economy: on average, total bank assets are around two to four times as large as GDP for countries in Western and Northern Europe; the banking sector is obviously larger, relative to GDP, in financial centers: for example, total bank assets in the United Kingdom are 424% of GDP, and in Luxembourg the number is 1433%, down from 2644% in 2008! In these financial centers, the banking sector also employs a large share of the labor force and makes a major contribution to GDP. On the other hand, the United States is in a stark contrast to the other big economies in the world: as an originating country of the 2007–2009 global financial crisis as well as a number of financial crashes and busts in history, the US does not have an extraordinarily large banking sector compared to the size of the economy.

Figure 1.3 presents the evolution in the size of the banking sector across Europe and the US in 2007–2019. The banking sectors in different countries exhibit clearly different dynamics: in some countries, the banking sector stays relatively "low and stable", such as Italy and the US; in some countries, the banking sector has been in contraction, such as Ireland and the Netherlands, and it seems the larger a country's banking sector was at the run-up to the 2007–2009 global financial crisis, the bigger post-crisis contraction it experienced. The UK, as a financial center, made a strong recovery in its banking sector after the crisis, while the 2016 Brexit referendum seems to trigger a slow outflow of the banking business.

The banking sector is often a major provider of financial resources in an economy, besides other providers offering "market funding". Figure 1.4 presents the relative importance of various funding resources across different countries, measured by the size of a funding resource relative to GDP. Besides funding by bank credit, market funding includes stock market capitalization and bond market capitalization. The bond market is further broken down to private bond market and public bond market that provide funding for public finance through bond securities such as government bonds.

INTRODUCTION

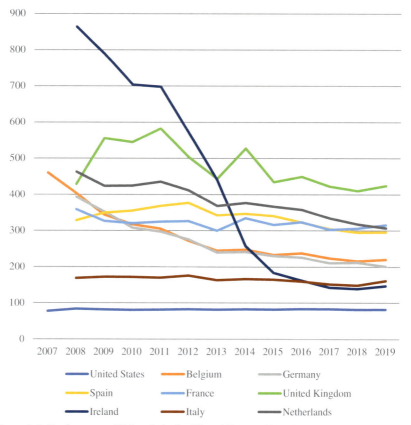

Figure 1.3 Bank assets to GDP ratio in the US and Europe, 2007–2019
Notes: computed by the author. Vertical axis is in percentage points. Data sources: European Central Bank Statistical Data Warehouse, Eurostat, FDIC Historical Bank Data, and Federal Reserve Economic Data (FRED) from Federal Reserve Bank of St. Louis.

There are substantial cross-country variations in funding resources. In terms of relative weight of bank credit versus market capitalization, two features stand out.

1 Market capitalization is far bigger than bank funding in the United States, and the difference between the two is much more distinguishing than most of other countries in the world. For this reason, we may call the US a *market-oriented* economy, as Allen and Gale (2001);

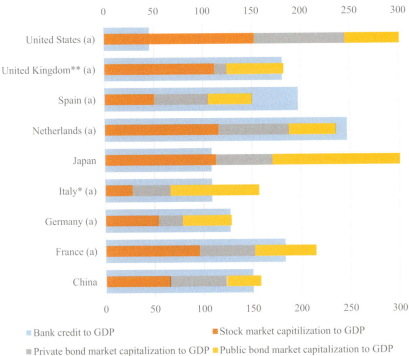

Figure 1.4 Market funding versus bank funding in nine economies, 2017
Notes: computed by the author. Horizontal axis is in percentage points. For each country, the thick bar indicates total bank credit to GDP, and the thin stacked bar indicates market capitalization to GDP. Market capitalization includes stock market capitalization, as well as private and public bond market capitalization. ★ 2014 data for stock market capitalization, ★★ 2012 data for bond market capitalization, (a) 2011 data for bond market capitalization. Data sources: China Banking and Insurance Regulatory Commission, Bank of Japan, European Central Bank Statistical Data Warehouse, Eurostat, FDIC Historical Bank Data, Federal Reserve Economic Data (FRED) from Federal Reserve Bank of St. Louis, World Bank Global Financial Development Database (available on https://www.worldbank.org/en/publication/gfdr/data/global-financial-development-database), and World Bank Financial Structure Database (available on https://www.worldbank.org/en/publication/gfdr/data/financial-structure-database).

2   Bank credit is a substantial funding resource and accounts for around half of total funding in average continental European countries. For this reason, we may call these countries *bank-oriented* economies.

Of course the roles of banks and markets in a country are evolving over time, and heavily shaped by the trajectory of the country's institutions and history. For example, two decades of rising deficit in public finance as a result of long-term economic stagnation and aging population, jointly with the central bank's powerful quantitative easing (QE) effort in Japan left a heavy mark in the capitalization in the public bond market.

In the US, while security markets benefit enormously from US-based global financial centers such as New York, banking in the US was heavily regulated, restricted, and suppressed in most of the 20th century. For example, the 1927 McFadden Act authorized the states over limiting banks' intrastate branching activities. Since then, states only allowed banks to own subsidiaries within states, and some states only allow banks to operate no more than one office to prevent banks from having any branches. Later, the Douglas Amendment to the 1956 Bank Holding Company (BHC) Act effectively barred interstate branching, making it impossible for bank holding companies to operate outside the states where their headquarters were located. These branching restrictions were only mostly removed in 1997, after the passage of the Reigle-Neal Interstate Banking and Branching Efficiency Act (IBBEA) of 1994. The Glass-Steagall Act of 1933 banned commercial banks from investment banking activities, and it was only repealed more than 60 years later, by the Gramm-Leach-Bliley Act of 1999.[1]

Globalization smooths out gaps between countries and results in a convergence of financial institutions. For example, bank credit used to account for an even bigger share of total funding in continental Europe. In the past two decades, the "passporting" or single license concept for European Union's single market allows financial firms that obtain a license from any one of the EU countries to operate in all other EU countries. This has been leading to a more "balanced" bank credit and market funding in Europe. However, recent trends in segregation and decoupling across the world, such as Brexit, may stop or even reverse such convergence.

BANK FAILURE MAY BE COSTLY AND IS NOT RARE

Banks' systemic importance is also revealed when they fail. Actually, bank failure is not rare at all. Figure 1.5 summarizes systemic banking crises

CHAPTER ONE: INTRODUCTION

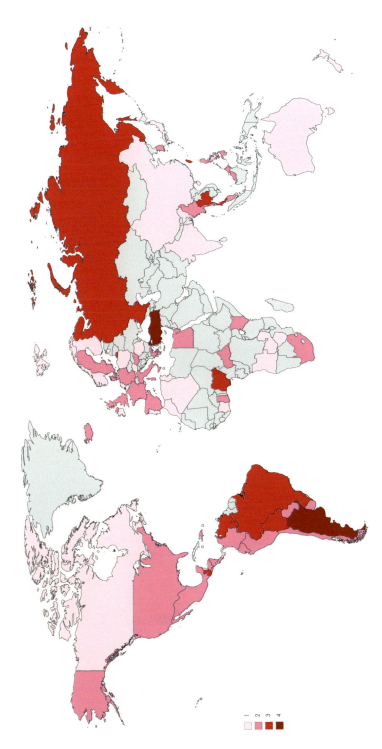

Figure 1.5 Frequency of systemic banking crises around the world, 1970–2017

Notes: map produced by the author. Data source: Global Crises Data by Country, by Carmen Reinhart, Vincent Reinhart, Kenneth Rogoff, and Christoph Trebesch, available on https://www.hbs.edu/behavioral-finance-and-financial-stability/data/Pages/global.aspx. Different colors denote the numbers of instances. Economies in light gray either have zero instance or lack sufficient data.

11

around the world in 1970–2017. Except countries without sufficient data, the world has recorded at least 121 country-level systemic meltdowns, and banking crisis is almost a pandemic that swept over most of sizable economies in the world. For many countries, banking crises are not rare events at all: over just less than 50 years, countries such as Argentina and Turkey have each experienced as many as four nationwide banking crises.

Banking crises may be extremely costly to economies. When a banking system is in a crash and stops functioning, firms and households will be starved for credit and many economic activities will be forced into full stops. Figure 1.6 shows one of the direct impacts of a banking crisis, measured by how much output is lost during each of the episodes since 1970. Although in about 40% of the systemic crises, the output loss was relatively low, lower than 13% of GDP, the sacrifice could be huge for some countries: for example, during its banking crisis in 1997–2000 that was triggered by the 1997 Asian financial crisis, Thailand suffered a total output loss that is larger than its GDP in 1997. Across all the 130 systemic banking crises in the sample, on average each crisis costs around 30.5% of GDP in output; that is why it is not surprising to see many countries suffer from painful recovery and decade-long stagnation in economic growth after banking crises.

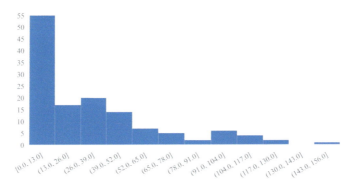

Figure 1.6 Output loss to GDP during systemic banking crises, 1970–2017

Notes: this histogram shows the distribution of output loss to GDP ratio during 130 systemic banking crises, 1970–2017; the horizontal axis contains the bins of percentage ratio, and the vertical axis shows the occurrence frequency in each bin. Data source: Laeven and Valencia (2018), updated from Valencia and Laeven (2012).

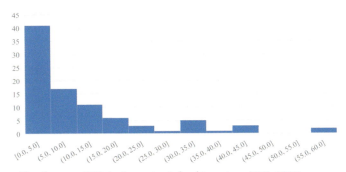

Figure 1.7 Fiscal cost to GDP during systemic banking crises, 1970–2017
Notes: this histogram shows the distribution of fiscal cost to GDP ratio during 134 systemic banking crises, 1970–2017; the horizontal axis contains the bins of percentage ratio, and the vertical axis shows the occurrence frequency in each bin. Data source: Laeven and Valencia (2018), updated from Valencia and Laeven (2012).

National governments are usually forced to step in, by outbreaks of banking crises. Failing systemically important banks need to be bailed out to prevent them from bringing down the entire financial system, and fragile, malfunctioning banks need to be recapitalized to re-assume their role as financial intermediaries allocating financial resources across the economy. Such bailout and recapitalization effort can be costly for taxpayers, too. Figure 1.7 summarizes the fiscal cost of restarting the banking sector, relative to GDP, through 134 systemic banking crises since 1970. On average, the fiscal cost on restructuring the banking sector is equivalent to 11.1% of GDP. The fiscal cost of the late 1990s banking crisis was as high as 56.8% of GDP for Indonesia, 43.8% for Thailand, and 31.2% for South Korea, while the fiscal cost related to bank resolution in the 2007–2009 financial crisis was 37.6% of GDP for Iceland, 8.8% for the UK, and 4.5% for the US.

BANKS ARE LIQUIDITY SERVICE PROVIDERS AND INFORMATION PRODUCERS

One distinguishing feature of the stylized bank's balance sheet, as shown in Box 1.1, is that a bank's funding is often short-term, for example, principle depositors can withdraw from their checking accounts at any

BOX 1.1 INSIDE A STYLIZED BANK

Assume a highly stylized bank operates a balance sheet as follows:

Assets	$	Liabilities	$
Cash *Reserves deposited in the central bank*	1000	On call deposits *Can be withdrawn anytime*	3000
Liquid assets *Safe, e.g. government securities*	1000	Time deposits *"CDs", term deposits*	2500
Investment securities *Risky, e.g. stocks, bonds*	1000	Interbank deposits *Interbank market*	2500
Loans *Risky, e.g. corporate loans, mortgages*	6000	Bonds *Borrowing from financial market*	1000
Fixed assets *"Tangible", such as properties, plants, etc.*	1000	Equity *Shareholders' claims of ownership*	1000
Total	***10000***		***10000***

Suppose in a fiscal year the bank earns

- $800 *interest income* from interest-bearing assets, i.e., assets that generate interest income, such as financial securities and loans in our example;
- $500 *non-interest income*, or fee income from providing financial services;
- $500 *interest expenses*, or, the bank's funding cost that is paid on its funding liabilities such as deposits and bonds;
- $600 *operating expenses* on operating the bank's business.

The bank's *gross profit* is thus computed as its total income (interest and non-interest income) less total cost (interest and operating expenses): $800 + $500 − $500 − $600 = $200.

Several other measures are often used to evaluate performance of the bank:

- *Return on assets* (ROA), as a ratio of gross profit to total assets, reflecting the bank's overall profitability:

$$\text{ROA} = \frac{200}{10000} \times 100\% = 2\%;$$

- *Return on equity* (ROE), as a ratio of gross profit to total equity, reflecting the profitability from bank shareholders' perspective:

$$\text{ROE} = \frac{200}{1000} \times 100\% = 20\%;$$

- *Net interest margin* (NIM), as a ratio of net interest income (interest income less interest expenses) to total interest-bearing assets (total assets less cash and fixed assets that do not generate interest income), reflecting the bank's profitability on financial intermediation:

$$\text{NIM} = \frac{800 - 500}{10000 - 1000 - 1000} \times 100\% = 3.75\%;$$

- *Operating expense* (OE) ratio, as a ratio of operating expenses to total assets, reflecting the bank's cost efficiency:

$$\text{OE} = \frac{600}{10000} \times 100\% = 6\%;$$

- *Leverage ratio*, as a ratio of total assets to total equity:

$$\text{Leverage ratio} = \frac{10000}{1000} = 10.$$

> The inverse of leverage ratio is the bank's *equity ratio*.
>
> Obviously, *ceteris paribus*, ROE increases with leverage ratio: with the same gross profit, ROE doubles when leverage ratio is doubled. However, the bank may become more fragile if its leverage ratio becomes higher, or, when the bank is less capitalized, since lower equity ratio reduces the bank's capability to absorb losses, and bankruptcy thus occurs more likely. A widely-used *z-score*, proposed by Altman (1968), is defined to capture the bank's fragility that is affected by its capitalization and income volatility, as
>
> $$z-\text{score} = \frac{\text{ROA} + \text{equity ratio}}{\sigma_{ROA}},$$
>
> in which σ_{ROA} denotes the standard deviation in ROA. Therefore, the higher volatility in ROA/the lower equity ratio is, the more fragile is the bank, the lower is its z-score.

time,—in other words, the *maturity* of debt liabilities can be as short as almost zero, while banks' investments in assets—for example, mortgage loans or loans to firms—often take much longer to mature and return. That is, banks provide money-like, *liquidity* service for depositors, backed by much more *illiquid* assets. Such *maturity transformation* allows depositors to store and withdraw value according to their consumption schedules, while banks can use the funds to support long-term investments that generate more value-added, facilitating real economic growth. To do so, banks engage in active *liquidity management*: they hold liquid assets as buffers to meet withdrawal demand from outgoing creditors, and they also roll over their liabilities through raising funds from new creditors. However, the *maturity mismatch* also makes banking structure fragile: when banks' capability of liquidity management is impaired by market stress, maturity mismatch will suddenly become a burden for banks when they cannot find incoming creditors to replace outgoing ones and/or when they are unable to generate sufficient cash flow from immature illiquid assets to repay creditors. In this case, banks may fail, and banking crises may break out.

Another distinguishing feature of banking is that banking is an information intensive business. For example, when banks are granting loans, it is difficult to tell, *ex ante*, whether borrowers are credit-worthy and whether borrowers will utilize the funds in banks' interests. Such *asymmetric information* exists almost everywhere in banking activities, and the potential that banks may lend to borrowers with low credit quality or support projects that do not generate positive cash flow exposes banks to *credit risks* so that banks may not recover their lending when the loans default. Therefore, one of the most important elements in banks' *risk management* is to invest in exploring information that reduces default risks, for example, by screening through loan applicants' credit history to judge their credit quality, by monitoring the progress of borrowers' projects to ensure that they behave properly, etc.; in this sense, banks are producers of information and banking business is heavily relying on banks' collected—often proprietary—information. However, as information is probably never perfect, banks often need to impose additional requirements in their lending decisions to reduce their exposure to credit risks, for example, to require collateral from borrowers. This limits banks' credit supply, and restricts financial resources to be allocated to where they are made better use of; the information friction thus has consequences in the real economy.

BANKS HAVE ACCESS TO CENTRAL BANK FACILITIES AND ARE SUBJECT TO STRINGENT REGULATION

One key difference between licensed banks and other financial intermediaries is that banks have access to their accounts in central bank—the monetary authority in an economy that provides banking services for banks—as well as standing facilities provided by central bank. Banks deposit their reserves in their central bank reserve accounts. Such connection provides a channel for central banks to conduct their monetary policy through managing bank reserves via, for example, market operations that inject or withdraw liquidity to or from the banking system, which incentivizes banks to adjust their credit supply to the real economy and hence further influences the real economy outcomes such as households' saving and consumption, firms' production and investment, etc., making such *bank lending channel* an important mechanism for a central bank to fine-tune the economy.

Access to central bank's standing facilities also allows banks to deposit their surplus in reserves in central bank, and borrow from a central bank when they have a deficit in their reserves. Although most banks are able to raise funding and manage reserves through financial markets, the central bank is often committed to be the *lender of last resort* if banks have difficulties in market funding. These standing facilities in the central bank thus provide desirable insurance for banks.

It is probably not surprising that the banking sector is one of the most heavily regulated sectors in an economy, given its strategic position in an economic system and its systemic importance for real economy. As banks are important providers of financial resources to the real economy, banks need to follow the rules of the game, disciplines are necessary to avoid fraud and deceptions, and as firms in other industries, banks need to follow competition rules that prevent them from abusing their market power at the cost of competitors and consumers. As bank failure is often destructive for financial systems as well as the real economy, and public intervention to save the real economy out of banking crises costs taxpayers massively, it is thus also important for banking regulation to increase the resilience of banks *ex ante* by requiring banks to hold sufficient cushions and buffers, instead of fighting the costly last war *ex post*. However, what is more challenging for banking regulation is that banks are closely connected with each other through financial claims so that individual banks' behavior may also affect the stability of the entire banking system; regulation thus also needs to be *macroprudential* and aims at reducing systemic distress, besides maintaining each individual bank's resilience. Furthermore, as new regulatory issues arise from banking sectors' evolution, and banks develop new services and products to get around regulatory rules, banking regulation needs to be regularly updated to catch up with developments in banking.

THE BANKING SECTOR IS DYNAMIC AND EVOLVING

The banking sector can be highly dynamic and evolve quickly. One distinguishing feature in the past few decades is the co-evolution of banks and financial market. Banks and market are not necessarily competitors in providing financial resources to the real economy, they are also deeply integrated in each others' businesses and jointly develop services and products. Such integration does not only happen within those *universal banks* that also provide services such as investment banking, insurance, etc., other than commercial banking, it also happens when banks and other financial institutions make division of labor and specialize in different parts of the intermediation chain between lenders and borrowers. One example is the rising *securitized banking* in which banks originate loans as input for other financial institutions to produce varieties of financial securities, making banking nowadays much different from the financial intermediation in the past.

Of course, banking regulation is often an important driving force behind the evolution in banking. Banks have the incentive to shift their regulated activities to entities—the so-called *shadow banks*—that are out of banking regulators' radar. This may lead to severe consequences that unregulated risks accumulate in less regulated parts of the financial market and bring down the entire financial system someday, just as the lessons that we have learned from the 2007–2009 global financial crisis. Besides banking regulation, technology is also reshaping financial intermediation and banking, as numerous *FinTech* firms are taking off recently. Using modern information technologies, these firms attempt to reduce information friction and improve allocation of financial resources, making revolutions in financial intermediation that may threaten banks' role as financial intermediaries, but they also may spur banks to evolve and adapt. Last but not least, recent trends in (dis-)globalization, such as Brexit, China-United States trade war, may also reshape the geography of banking, as banks often move along with shifts in financial centers and trade flows. All these evolution and trends make issues in banking challenging for regulators and policy makers, but they also make banking an exciting field in economic research.

1.2 STRUCTURE OF THIS BOOK

The main theme throughout this book is financial friction. The reason is simple: should there be no frictions, financial resources would always be allocated to places where they are made the best use of; in such a world, banking would be totally undesirable, as it would produce no value-added besides incurring pure costs. Banks are only desirable when financial frictions prevent efficient resource allocation between lenders and borrowers. In a world of frictions, banks may help reduce frictions through their socially desirable services and products, thus improving social welfare. However, banks themselves are also subject to financial frictions, this may limit banks' efficiency in resource allocation, and even make them fail. As these market failures often cannot be solved by banks themselves, it is thus desirable for regulators to intervene.

Part II of this book focuses on financial frictions in individual banks' behavior as well as banks' interactions. We examine banks' role as liquidity service providers in Chapter 2, and see how banks provide socially desirable liquidity insurance through maturity transmission and how such maturity mismatch makes banking structure fragile. We then examine banks' role as information producers in Chapter 3. The principal-agent problems caused by asymmetric information between lenders and borrowers prevent socially desirable projects from being funded, while banks as experts in monitoring and screening are able to partially overcome such frictions and improve resource allocation. However, banks themselves are subject to these principal-agent problems, too, and this challenges banks' management of credit risks. Chapter 4 investigates the implication of banking competition for banks' risk-taking. Bank competition does not only affect banks' supply and price of services, but also influences how much risk they take; banking competition thus leads to crucial consequences on financial stability. In the past few decades, banks have been migrating towards securitized banking; Chapter 5 analyzes how securitization may reduce certain financial frictions while also increase vulnerability of banks to market stress. In Chapter 6, we discuss reasons why banks, banking services, and banking products become increasingly complex, and how complexity in products, banking networks, and information opacity affect banking outcomes and financial stability.

Part III of this book focuses on how banks interact with macroeconomy and other institutions, under financial frictions. Chapter 7 illustrates how a central bank conducts monetary policy, both in normal times and in crises, through banks to influence the real economy, and how such bank lending channels affect banks' credit supply to the real economy as well as banks' risk-taking. Chapter 8 discusses how financial frictions increase macroeconomic volatility through banks. Under financial frictions, banks' credit supply is limited by various constraints; these constraints may vary with real economy, and the subsequent changes in bank lending thus feed back to real economy, amplifying shocks in real economy. Furthermore, banks' risk-taking incentives also vary with real economic outcomes, which affects macroeconomic stability. Chapter 9 shows how international banking across borders allows real and monetary policy shocks to spill over from one country to another. Chapter 10 presents channels through which governments and politicians may interact with banks, and how political economy affects banking outcomes and resource allocation.

Part IV of this book discusses the need for banking regulation, as well as banking regulation in practice. Chapter 11 investigates the financial frictions that increase systemic fragility, and cause swift comovements of banks, contagion over banking network, and cascading bank failure in banking crises, as well as the motivation for macroprudential regulation. In Chapter 12, we focus on both traditional and new rules in banking regulation, with conceptual assessments on their pros and cons.

1.3 EXERCISES

1 **Understanding the banking sector in your country/region through data**
   There is a growing list of publicly available online resources for consolidated banking statistics and macroeconomic data, including:

   - BIS statistics, Bank for International Settlements, available at https://www.bis.org/statistics/index.htm;
   - European Central Bank Statistical Data Warehouse, available at https://sdw.ecb.europa.eu/;
   - Eurostat, available at https://ec.europa.eu/eurostat/;
   - FDIC Historical Bank Data, available at https://banks.data.fdic.gov/explore/historical;
   - FRED (Federal Reserve Economic Data) from Federal Reserve Bank of St. Louis, available at https://fred.stlouisfed.org/;
   - IMF data, International Monetary Fund, available at https://www.imf.org/en/Data;
   - World Bank Global Financial Development Database, available at https://www.worldbank.org/en/publication/gfdr/data/global-financial-development-database.

   You also have a considerably good chance to find comprehensive banking and macroeconomic data from your national/regional authorities, such as:

   - Central banks or monetary authorities, especially their monetary policy reports and financial stability reports;
   - Bureaus of statistics;
   - Banking regulators, such as financial supervisory authorities.

   Archives of financial newspapers are often good resources for historical data, too.

   Exploring the data sources listed above, try to understand the banking sector in your country/region through—depending on data availability—the following indicators:

(a) Size: total bank assets relative to GDP. How is the size of the banking sector evolving over time?

(b) Types of banks:

   i. How many types of banks are defined by law? How many banks are there in each category? What is the share of each category in total bank assets?

   ii. How many foreign-owned banks are there? What is the share of foreign banks in total bank assets? Among them, how many are foreign subsidiaries and how many are foreign branches?

(c) How important is bank funding, versus market funding? Would you categorize the economy as "market-oriented" or "bank-oriented"?

(d) Bank performance:

   i. How is banks' average return on assets (ROA) evolving over time? How about banks' average return on equity (ROE)?

   ii. How is banks' average net interest margin (NIM) evolving over time?

   iii. Do banks rely more on interest income or non-interest income? How is the dependence evolving over time?

(e) What is the share of retail deposits in banks' total liabilities? What is the share of wholesale funding?

(f) Were there any banking crises, or influential episodes of failed banks in history? What were the causes and major consequences?

2 **Cross-country comparison**

Continue with Exercise 1. Now expand your sample to a group of economies, such as OECD (Organisation for Economic Co-operation and Development) countries, G7, European Union,

Eurozone, BRICS countries (Brazil, Russia, India, China, and South Africa), etc.

(a) Answer the same questions in Exercise 1 for the countries within the same group.
(b) Do you see any similarities, convergence or divergence over time for countries within the same group?

NOTE

1 A timeline of major banking legislation in the US can be found in Mishkin and Eakin (2018), and Kroszner and Strahan (2014) summarize the causes, consequences, and implications of regulation and deregulation in the US banking industry.

PART II
The microeconomics of banking

CHAPTER 2
Fragile banks

2.1 INTRODUCTION

In this chapter, we focus on the role of banks as liquidity providers. We start motivating the needs for liquidity service by a very simple financial friction, that people with investment opportunities—call them "projects" or "assets"—face uncertainties in their preferred timing for consumption. Some investment projects are *liquid*, that they need only a short time to return, and their returns are usually low—for example, putting cash in a safe deposit box. In contrast, some investment projects are *illiquid*, that they need time to mature; if an illiquid project matures, its return is usually higher, but if it is interrupted prematurely, or *liquidated*, its value is much lower. An example for illiquid project is building a house; the house only yields a full return after it is constructed, while the value of an *interrupted, half-finished house is probably much lower*.

The liquid assets are thus more suitable for those who want to consume in the near future, or, with a short notice, so that they can get their funds out of the assets whenever the need to consume. The illiquid assets are more suitable for those who do not need to consume in the near future, so that they have time to wait for the assets to mature and enjoy the higher yields. However, if people's preferred timing to consume is not known when they invest, it will be difficult to allocate their funds: if one needs to consume shortly after her investment is made, then any investment in illiquid assets will be a waste, as she has to liquidate them prematurely for cash at a cost; if one's consumption demand is materialized long after her investment is made, then any investment in liquid assets will be a waste, as she would be better off with investing more in illiquid assets with higher returns.

Such friction implies a need for liquidity insurance, that under these investment opportunities and uncertainties in preferred timing for consumption (so-called *liquidity preferences*), a scheme shall ensure investors to cash out their funds with short notices, and also allow investors who stay longer with the scheme to earn higher yields. Section 2.2 shows that banks, as financial intermediaries, are able to provide such a scheme: by pooling deposits from investors with unknown timing for consumption, or, with liquidity preferences, banks invest in a portfolio that combines liquid and illiquid assets. In this way, banks can fulfill the cash demand for those "impatient" ones who want to consume early by proceeds from liquid assets, and pay those "patient" ones with higher yields from illiquid assets. Banking thus leads to an optimal risk-sharing between people with different liquidity preferences and makes everyone better off.

However, if revealed liquidity preferences are different from expected, banks may have troubles: if cash demand from impatient depositors is higher than proceeds from liquid assets, banks will need to liquidate some illiquid assets to fulfill impatient depositors' cash demand. However, this will reduce the return for patient depositors. If patient depositors fear that proceeds from remaining illiquid assets will be too low, they may demand their cash together with impatient depositors, triggering a *bank run*. A bank run will force a bank into further costly liquidation of illiquid assets, and if the liquidation value of all assets is still not enough to meet depositors' cash demand, the bank will be bankrupted.

The intermediation structure is therefore a double-edge sword for banks: by holding a combination of liquid and illiquid assets, banks conduct *maturity transformation* and liquidity insurance to allow depositors to withdraw with short notices; this also makes banks fragile and exposed to *liquidity risks* that bank runs destroy values in banks. Now the natural questions are: what does such fragility imply for banks? Is such fragility totally undesirable so that regulators should completely eliminate it?

Section 2.3 examines the role of banking fragility in resource allocation under uncertainties in assets' returns. When returns of illiquid assets are uncertain, patient depositors are more likely to run on banks, when a low return is expected—for example, when all banks face a lower yield from illiquid assets in the downturn. Given that bank runs are inevitable, whether banks are able to allocate resources efficiently depends on the liquidation cost arising from bank runs. When there is no liquidation cost, bank run will force impatient depositors to share proceeds from liquid assets with patient depositors, and this may even lead to an optimal risk-sharing among depositors in the downturn. However, when liquidation cost is positive, resource allocation by banks is socially suboptimal, because of costly liquidation in the bank run equilibrium.

Section 2.4 discusses the role of banking fragility as a device for market discipline. Banks' interests do not always align with depositors', so that they have incentives to extort depositors for their own benefit; this may even make bank intermediation break down. The fragility, arising from *demand deposit contract* that allows depositors to withdraw any time, gives depositors a privilege to run on banks and destroy values in banks, once they fear that banks act against their interests. Such a credible threat forces banks to refrain from exploiting depositors and makes bank intermediation feasible. In this sense, fragility may be a necessary evil to discipline banks.

2.2 BANK LIQUIDITY CREATION AND BANK RUN

First, we start with a very simple problem on intertemporal resource allocation for consumers, based on Diamond and Dybvig (1983). The only friction here is that consumers face uncertainty on their *liquidity preferences*, that they do not know what time in the future they will want to consume, when they allocate resources. We will see how banks provide liquidity insurance service and make consumers better off, by pooling consumers' deposits and engaging in a combination of short-term and long-term investments. We will also see how such intermediation structure makes banks vulnerable to destructive bank runs.

2.2.1 LIQUIDITY PREFERENCES AND THE NEED FOR LIQUIDITY INSURANCE

As Diamond and Dybvig (1983) indicate, in a stylized economy, there are two groups of agents: consumers and banks. The economy extends over three periods, $t = 0,1,2$. It is assumed that

1. There is a continuum of *ex ante* identical consumers whose population is normalized to be 1, each of which is endowed with one unit of consumption good in $t=0$. *Ex post*, each consumer learns her true time preference in $t=1$ (call it a liquidity preference shock), such that

    (a) With probability $0 < p < 1$ one consumer turns out to be an impatient consumer so that she only values consumption in $t=1$,—denoted by c_1,—with the periodical utility function being $U = u(c_1)$. Assume that the utility function $u(\cdot)$ is neoclassical such that it is strictly concave and twice differentiable, $u'(\cdot) > 0$, $u''(\cdot) < 0$; in addition, the coefficient of relative risk aversion is assumed to be sufficiently high, such that $-\frac{cu''(c)}{u'(c)} > 1$ (see more discussion on risk aversion in Exercise 2 (a));

    (b) With probability $1-p$ one consumer turns out to be a patient consumer so that she only values consumption in $t=2$, —denoted by c_2,—with the periodical utility function being $U = u(c_2)$.

2. Banks offer demand deposit contracts to the consumers. Banks are financial intermediaries, pooling the deposits from the consumers and investing the funds on different types of assets. In the demand deposit contract issued in $t=0$, a bank promises a fixed return profile (c_1, c_2) for each unit of deposit, in which c_1/c_2 denotes the payment when a depositor withdraws in $t=1/t=2$. There is a perfect competition among the banks in the deposit market so that banks make zero profit from intermediation.

Assume that the types of consumers are private information that is not observable to others. That is, banks only know the probability p over all consumers, but they do not know whether an individual consumer is impatient or patient.

There are two technologies available in the economy:

1. Storage technology. This technology transfers one unit input in t into one unit output in $t+1$. The projects using such technology are called *short assets*, or *liquid assets*;

2. Investment technology. This technology transfers one unit input in $t=0$ into $R>1$ units output in $t=2$. The projects using such technology are called *long assets*, or *illiquid assets*. If the project is terminated ("liquidated") in $t=1$ before it matures, it only yields a poor return $0<c<1$, which is the value recovered from the prematurely terminated project.

There are many reasons in reality why only a lower value can be recovered from a prematurely liquidated project, or, an asset on "fire sale". For example, because of inalienable human capital, as Hart and Moore (1994) state, those who take over projects from their owners do not have the same human capital to properly operate the projects, so that expected returns from these assets are lower, which reduces their market price. Shleifer and Vishny (1997) argue that the market and market participants are often under stress when assets are on fire sale, the "limits of arbitrage" prevent potential buyers from paying the price that reflects the future return of the assets.

2.2.2 BASELINE RESULT: THE PLANNER'S SOLUTION

As a reference for welfare criterion, we start from the social planner's problem which defines the *constrained efficient* allocation in this economy in the presence of liquidity preference shocks. Suppose that the planner chooses the share of the consumers' endowments invested in the liquid assets, denoted by α, and allocates c_1/c_2 consumption goods to an impatient/a patient consumer to maximize social welfare, such that

$$\max_{\{\alpha, c_1, c_2\}} \quad pu(c_1) + (1-p)u(c_2), \tag{2.1}$$

$$\text{s.t.} \quad pc_1 = \alpha, \tag{2.2}$$

$$(1-p)c_2 = R(1-\alpha) \tag{2.3}$$

in which $p/1-p$ is the population of impatient/patient consumers.

The impatient consumers are paid by the return from the liquid assets, as in (2.2), and the patient consumers are paid by the return from the illiquid assets, as in (2.3). The planner's problem is solved by using Lagrangian

$$\mathcal{L} = pu(c_1) + (1-p)u(c_2) + \lambda\left[R(1-pc_1) - (1-p)c_2\right],$$

and the first-order conditions are

$$\frac{\partial \mathcal{L}}{\partial c_1} = pu'(c_1) - \lambda pR = 0,$$

$$\frac{\partial \mathcal{L}}{\partial c_2} = (1-p)u'(c_2) - \lambda(1-p) = 0.$$

Eliminate λ to get the optimal solution to this social planner's problem (2.1), (c_1^*, c_2^*)

$$u'(c_1^*) = Ru'(c_2^*),$$

which implies that $c_1^* < c_2^*$ given that $R > 1$.

Note that consumers' relative risk aversion is assumed to be greater than one, i.e., $-\frac{cu''(c)}{u'(c)} > 1$, which is equivalent to $\frac{d[cu'(c)]}{dc} < 0$—implying that $cu'(c)$ is decreasing in c; therefore, we have $1 \cdot u'(1) > R \cdot u'(R)$ for $R > 1$. Together with the budget constraints (2.2) and (2.3), the first order condition implies that $1 < c_1^* < c_2^* < R$ (see Exercise 1), or, risk-sharing between impatient and patient consumers: should a consumer know her type in $t = 0$, in autarky, an impatient consumer would always invest in liquid assets and consume 1, and a patient consumer would always invest in illiquid assets and consume R; with uncertainty on liquidity preferences, the constrained efficient solution makes consumption of impatient and patient consumers closer to each other, providing a liquidity insurance for consumers. The difference between c_1^* and c_2^* is determined by consumers' risk aversion.

2.2.3 RESOURCE ALLOCATION IN A DECENTRALIZED ECONOMY

Now, without a social planner in reality, will a decentralized economy replicate the constrained efficient allocation? In the following, we discuss the outcomes from various institutional settings.

AUTARKY

Suppose that the economy is under autarky so that every consumer has to take care of herself. Then, for any consumer in $t=0$, without knowing her liquidity preference, she invests $0 \leq \alpha \leq 1$ in liquid assets and the rest in illiquid assets. In $t=1$, after her type is revealed,

- If she turns out to be impatient, she consumes the proceeds from liquid assets and liquidated value of illiquid assets, i.e.,

$$c_1^a = \alpha + (1-\alpha)c \leq 1;$$

- If she turns out to be patient, she will wait till $t=2$, then consume the proceeds from both liquid assets and illiquid assets, i.e.,

$$c_2^a = \alpha + (1-\alpha)R \leq R.$$

Her consumption (c_1^a, c_2^a) is thus different from the constrained efficient solution (c_1^*, c_2^*) with $1 < c_1^* < c_2^* < R$. The autarky economy, therefore, cannot achieve the constrained efficient solution because of impatient consumers' inefficient liquidation.

EXCHANGE MARKET

Suppose, in $t=1$, after the consumers' liquidity preferences are revealed, a market for exchange is opened so that consumers can exchange their assets, and there is a market-clearing price b that exchanges one unit of illiquid assets' return in $t=2$ into b units of liquid assets in $t=1$. Again, for any consumer in $t=0$, without knowing her liquidity preference, she invests $0 \leq \alpha \leq 1$ in liquid assets and the rest in illiquid assets. In $t=1$, after her type is revealed

- If she is impatient, she consumes the proceeds from liquid assets and sales from illiquid assets, i.e., $c_1^e = \alpha + (1-\alpha)Rb$;
- If she is patient, she will exchange her liquid assets for illiquid assets, then wait till $t=2$, consume the proceeds from illiquid assets, i.e., $c_2^e = \frac{\alpha}{b} + (1-\alpha)R$.

We determine the market-clearing price b by guessing:

- Suppose $b > \frac{1}{R}$: in $t=0$, knowing that the return from holding illiquid assets is $bR > 1$, everyone will set $\alpha = 0$ so that there will be no market in $t=1$. Therefore, b cannot be higher than $\frac{1}{R}$;
- Suppose $b < \frac{1}{R}$: in $t=0$, knowing that the return from holding illiquid assets is $bR < 1$, everyone will set $\alpha = 1$ so that there will be no market in $t=1$. Therefore, b cannot be lower than $\frac{1}{R}$.

As a result, the market-clearing price b must be $\frac{1}{R}$ so that consumers are indifferent in holding either type of assets. Correspondingly, consumers' consumption profile is

$$(c_1^e, c_2^e) = (1, R) \neq (c_1^*, c_2^*).$$

Such exchange economy, therefore, cannot achieve the constrained efficient solution.[1]

BANKING SOLUTION

Now suppose we are in a banking economy where banks as financial intermediaries collect deposits from consumers and invest on behalf of them. Banks are engaged in a perfect competition in the market for deposits so that they make zero profit.

Precisely, suppose each bank offers a deposit contract (c_1^*, c_2^*) — c_1^* and c_2^* being the same as in the social planner's solution—for a consumer, such

Assets	Liabilities
Illiquid assets $1 - pc_1^*$	Deposits 1
Reserves pc_1^*	

Figure 2.1 A bank's balance sheet in t = 0

that after depositing in $t = 0$, the consumer who claims to be impatient/patient is entitled to withdraw c_1^*/c_2^* in $t = 1/t = 2$ from the bank. The bank then invests a share of α^*, with $\alpha^* = pc_1^*$ in liquid assets, or, "reserves", and the rest in illiquid assets. Its balance sheet—featured by *fractional reserve banking*—in $t = 0$ is summarized in Figure 2.1.

It is not difficult to see that the deposit contract is *feasible*, *utility maximizing*, and *incentive compatible*:

- **Feasibility:** impatient consumers are repaid by the proceeds from liquid assets $pc_1^* = \alpha^*$, and patient consumers are repaid by the return from illiquid assets, $(1-p)c_2^* = (1-\alpha^*)R$—exactly the same as in (2.2) and (2.3);
- **Utility maximization:** as problem (2.1) states,

$$(c_1^*, c_2^*) = \arg \max_{\{\alpha, c_1, c_2\}} pu(c_1) + (1-p)u(c_2).$$

However, $pu(c_1) + (1-p)u(c_2)$ is also a consumer's expected utility in $t = 0$. Therefore, deposit contract (c_1^*, c_2^*) maximizes consumers' expected utility:

- **Incentive compatibility:** given that the bank cannot observe a consumer's liquidity preference when she withdraws, the deposit contract (c_1^*, c_2^*) is only implementable if consumers self-select the correct timing to withdraw according to their true types, instead of mimicking consumers of the other types. Indeed, $c_1^* < c_2^*$—which is an *incentive compatibility constraint* here—ensures that patient consumers will not mimic impatient consumers to withdraw early, and their liquidity preference ensures that impatient consumers will not mimic patient consumers to withdraw late.

To summarize, the banking solution is able to replicate the constrained efficient solution that is defined in Section 2.2.2, and provides liquidity insurance to consumers who, *ex ante*, do not know their liquidity preferences. To do so, banks invest in a portfolio, as Figure 2.1 shows, that combines liquid assets—reserves pc_1^* that meet the withdrawal demand of impatient consumers in $t = 1$, and high-yield illiquid assets $1 - pc_1^*$ that provide higher return to those who are patient and willing to wait for illiquid assets to mature.

The typical bank balance sheet as in Figure 2.1, arising from the need to provide liquidity services, is featured by *maturity mismatch*: although on the asset side, those illiquid assets take two periods to mature, deposits on the liability side—in principle—can be withdrawn any time after $t = 0$. Note that consumers' liquidity preferences are not observed by banks, and in banking equilibrium they self-select to withdraw in their preferred periods to consume only because of the incentive compatibility constraint $c_1^* < c_2^*$. However, once such constraint cannot be guaranteed, for instance, if there is a negative shock to a bank's illiquid assets' return so that patient consumers who wait until $t = 2$ only receive a return $\tilde{c}_2$ from the illiquid assets which is lower than c_1^*, patient consumers will not be willing to wait any more; instead, they will mimic impatient consumers and demand c_1^* from the bank. As a result, there will be more than expected consumers who demand withdrawal in $t = 1$, which is a *bank run*. Therefore, banks provide liquidity service through balance sheets with maturity mismatch, while such maturity mismatch also exposes banks to *liquidity risks* of bank runs.

2.2.4 BANK RUN: FUNDAMENTAL-DRIVEN VERSUS PANIC-DRIVEN

Although banking solution improves social welfare and achieves constrained efficiency under liquidity preference shocks, the intermediation structure also exposes banks to costly bank runs, that is, under certain circumstances, patient consumers do have the incentive to mimic impatient consumers and withdraw early in $t = 1$, forcing banks into costly liquidation. Such bank runs can either be triggered by fundamentals, or driven by non-fundamental, pure panics.

FUNDAMENTAL-DRIVEN BANK RUN

First, banks are vulnerable to shock to fundamentals which makes the incentive compatibility constraint violated and initiates bank runs. To see this, suppose that in $t=1$, it is known to the public that there is an unexpected negative shock to R that in $t=2$, the realized return on illiquid assets will be $\tilde{R}<R$. As a result, the expected return for patient consumers becomes

$$\tilde{c}_2 = \frac{1-\alpha^*}{1-p}\tilde{R} < c_2^*.$$

If $\tilde{R}$ is sufficiently low, it is possible that $\tilde{c}_2 < c_1^*$.

However, if $\tilde{c}_2 < c_1^*$, patient consumers will not wait any more. Instead, they will mimic impatient consumers and demand the relatively higher repayment, c_1^*. Now with all consumers withdrawing, the total demand c_1^* exceeds banks' total reserves, α^*, forcing them to liquidate illiquid assets. But even if all illiquid assets are liquidated, banks' total supply for resources is only

$$\alpha^* + (1-\alpha^*)c < 1 < c_1^*. \qquad (2.4)$$

As a result of such a bank run, all resources in banks will be depleted and banks are bankrupt in the end. Given that consumers have equal claims on banks' liquidated value, on average, each consumer has a return of $\alpha^* + (1-\alpha^*)c$ which is lower than c_1^*.

PANIC-DRIVEN BANK RUN AND BANK RUN AS A SUNSPOT EQUILIBRIUM

More strikingly, bank runs can be driven by pure panics that have nothing to do with fundamentals, or, return on assets. Suppose, in the beginning of $t=1$, rumor about banks' health makes some patient consumers believe that their expected return in $t=2$ will be low, so that they panic and want to demand c_1^* in $t=1$.

Assume that it is publicly known that a population of f, $f > p$, consumers will withdraw in $t=1$, i.e., a population of $f-p$ patient consumers panic.

As a result, withdrawal demand for banks is larger than banks' liquidity reserves

$$fc_1^* > pc_1^* = \alpha^*.$$

This will force banks to liquidate some illiquid assets, by l, to meet withdrawal demand,

$$\alpha^* + cl = fc_1^*.$$

However, with $c<1$, liquidation is costly and reduces the return of patient consumers, $\tilde{c}_2$, if they wait until $t=2$,

$$\tilde{c}_2 = \frac{1-\alpha^*-l}{1-f}R,$$

and $\tilde{c}_2$ falls with higher f. Therefore, if f is high enough so that $\tilde{c}_2 < c_1^*$, even the non-panicking patient consumers will not wait any more: they will withdraw in $t=1$ and demand c_1^*, too—leading to a bank run that is *self-fulfilling*. If this happens, as (2.4) implies, banks' liquidation value will not be enough to meet the total withdrawal demand and they will be bankrupted: a bank run can be triggered by a rumor and make fundamentally sound banks fail!

Actually, rumor, or panic is only a sufficient but not necessary condition for bank runs, in other words, bank run can be a "sunspot equilibrium" that does not need any trigger: suppose a bank run happens in $t=1$ and all consumers withdraw, then as (2.4) implies, banks will be bankrupted, leaving each consumer a return of $\alpha^* + (1-\alpha^*)c$ from banks' liquidation value. For any individual patient consumer, she cannot be better off if she does not join the run: because if she waits until $t=2$, she will receive nothing from bankrupted banks. In other words, no consumer can make herself better off by unilateral deviation from the bank run, or, bank run is actually another equilibrium of banking solution! In this sense, banking solution is intrinsically fragile. This again shows that bank runs are self-fulfilling; even if banks are fundamentally sound and patient depositors would have been better off with not running on banks, patient depositors will still run on banks once a bank run occurs. In this sense, panic-driven bank run is a result of *coordination failure* of depositors.

2.2.5 FRAGILE BANKS AND POLICY IMPLICATIONS

Although the "good" equilibrium, or non-run equilibrium of banking solution achieves constrained efficiency and is desirable, the existence of "bad" equilibrium, or bank run equilibrium implies that banks' liquidation creation via maturity transformation is fragile and subject to systemic collapse. Therefore, one may think of imposing additional constraint in a banking solution that eliminates the bank run equilibrium. This is not only theoretically interesting, but also crucial for policy makers who attempt to reduce fragility in the banking system. We propose several policy instruments that may serve this purpose.

SUSPENSION OF CONVERTIBILITY

One policy candidate is to impose restrictions on withdrawal—suspend the convertibility of deposits to cash, should bank run break out. Such practice has been taken in history, for example, a "bank holiday" was declared in 1933 during the Great Depression in the United States, requiring banks to be closed until being declared solvent by government auditors. A very recent example is the Greek government's restriction on cash withdrawal in 2015 during the European debt crisis, that each depositor was only allowed to withdraw 60 euros per day.

In the model, such suspension of convertibility means that banks are only allowed to pay out up to $\alpha^* = pc_1^*$ in $t=1$. They will close after α^* is paid, so that illiquid assets will no longer be liquidated. As there is no uncertainty in illiquid assets' return, patient consumers know that they will receive a high return c_2^* for sure, with $c_2^* > c_1^*$, if they wait until $t=2$; as a result, under such convertibility constraint, patient consumers will have no incentive to run on banks, as they will only be worse off with receiving no more than c_1^* if they do so. The bank-run equilibrium is thus eliminated by the policy. Gorton (1985) provides an in-depth analysis on how suspension of convertibility helps prevent bank runs.

However, it is difficult to implement such policy in reality, as the withdrawal demand from truly impatient consumers in $t=1$, pc_1^*, is usually unknown. Suppose the withdrawal limit $\tilde{\alpha}$ is set below the true liquidity demand pc_1^* when a bank run breaks out, then even if patient consumers will be discouraged to run on banks, $\tilde{\alpha} < pc_1^*$ means that some impatient consumers will not be able to consume in $t=1$, reducing social welfare.

DEPOSIT INSURANCE

Another policy candidate is deposit insurance, that banks pay some insurance premium, proportional to their demand deposits, to an insurance scheme; when a bank is not able to meet depositors' withdrawal demand, the insurance scheme will then guarantee the repayments to depositors.

Deposit insurance has been widely implemented around the world, especially during the 20th century. For example, Federal Deposit Insurance Corporation (FDIC) was founded as the insurer for deposits in the US in the aftermath of the Great Depression. As of 2016, over 115 countries have some form of explicit deposit insurance, according to World Bank's Bank Regulation and Supervision Survey (BRSS), compared with 86 in 2010 and 93 in 2013 (Anginer et al. 2019, Anginer and Demirgüç-Kunt 2019).

It is easily seen that deposit insurance eliminates bank-run equilibrium in the model. Knowing that they will be guaranteed with a higher return of c_2^* in $t=2$, patient consumers will have no incentive to withdraw early in $t=1$. Deposit insurance thus works as an equilibrium selection device that ensures patient consumers stay with non-run equilibrium.

However, the Diamond-Dybvig model does not incorporate banks' risk-taking incentives, which complicate implementation of deposit insurance in reality: just as any other insurance scheme, deposit insurance is subject to moral hazard problems that encourage insured banks to take excess risks. With a guarantee on depositors, banks' bankruptcy cost will be borne by the insurance, so that banks will worry less about downside and invest more in risky assets, hoping to reap the higher return on the upside. Such a moral hazard problem may lead to breakdown of the insurance scheme. As a result, in reality, deposit insurance providers have to keep insured banks under careful scrutiny, and they usually offer limited guarantee for each depositor. Such restrictions on deposit insurance may erode its capability to eliminate bank runs.

LENDER-OF-LAST-RESORT POLICY

When banks are under withdrawal pressure, they can also seek liquidity service from a central bank, which is designed as the "lender of last resort" (LOLR) in the banking system. In general, banks can borrow from a central bank, using eligible assets as collateral. Under the settings of the Diamond-Dybvig model, such LOLR policy eliminates bank run.

To see this, suppose a bank is on the brink of a bank run, so that all depositors will withdraw in $t=1$, and withdrawal demand c_1^* exceeds its liquidity buffer α^*, leading to a liquidity shortage of $c_1^* - \alpha^*$. Instead of liquidating illiquid assets, the bank now can borrow from the central bank in $t=1$, using its illiquid assets as collateral, then repay the central bank in $t=2$ out of the proceeds from illiquid assets. Normalize the central bank's gross lending rate to be 1, then the bank can borrow up to the face value of its illiquid assets in $t=2$, $(1-\alpha^*)R$. Given $1 < c_1^* < R$,

$$(1-\alpha^*)R > c_1^* - \alpha^*,$$

so that the bank can meet withdrawal demand by borrowing from central bank, even in a bank run. However, given that the bank does not need to liquidate illiquid assets, a patient consumer is actually better off if she waits until $t=2$ and benefits from the higher return of illiquid assets.

Knowing this, patient consumers will have no incentive to withdraw in $t=1$, so that bank-run equilibrium is eliminated.

However, implementing LOLR policy is challenging in reality. For example, the central bank's providing liquidity insurance through LOLR policy may also suffer from a moral hazard problem that encourages banks to take excess risks, and such concerns may in turn limit the scope and effectiveness of LOLR policy. We will discuss more details on LOLR in Chapter 12.

2.2.6 EQUILIBRIUM REFINEMENT AND EQUILIBRIUM SELECTION

The Diamond-Dybvig model unveils the intrinsic fragility that is deeply rooted in banks' intermediation structure, and reveals that even fundamentally sound banks are vulnerable to destructive runs. However, multiple equilibria also make it difficult to apply the model. From the model itself, it is impossible to predict when bank runs will occur, and banks with what characteristics are more subject to runs, making it difficult to apply the model for policy analysis. Even if certain policy tools as equilibrium selection devices are able to eliminate the bank-run equilibrium, without knowing the actual likelihood for bank runs to happen, it is hard to tell how desirable it is to avoid bank runs, given that implementing policy tools in reality always incurs certain costs. Because of these challenges with multiple equilibria, it is therefore desirable to examine whether one equilibrium is more likely to emerge in certain scenarios, especially under certain mechanisms through which depositors are able to conquer coordination failure and coordinate (not) to run on banks.

For instance, Chen (1999) explores the *information externality* between patient depositors who are differently informed: in an intermediate period, while informed depositors will run on their banks once they know their banks are unhealthy, uninformed depositors can observe the bank runs and make an inference on their own bank's health, too; that is, information spills over from informed to uninformed. Remember that the patient depositors' decision to run on banks depends on their expected return, which is conveyed in the information available about the quality of banks' fundamentals, i.e., returns from illiquid assets. When in the intermediate period, $t=1$, the information about banks' fundamentals is sequentially revealed, the better informed patient depositors will withdraw earlier than the uninformed ones if their private information about the banks is negative. However, the uninformed ones can infer the viability of their own banks by observing the queues in front of the banks that suffer from bank runs, i.e., the private information of the informed depositors generates an externality on uninformed depositors' behavior. If banks' fundamentals are positively correlated, the failure of some banks implies the prospects of the other banks are dull, too. Therefore, the observed bank failures may encourage the uninformed depositors to run on their own banks. If this happens, even the informed depositors in these banks, whose private information about the banks' fundamentals is positive, have to join the run because the so-called "first come, first served" rule in banking means that any depositor who does not join bank runs will only lose out. In this way, the informational externality coordinates both the informed and uninformed depositors, hence a unique bank run equilibrium emerges.

Using the approach of global games, developed by Carlsson and van Damme (1993) and Morris and Shin (2003), Goldstein and Pauzner (2005) suggest that unique equilibrium may arise in the Diamond-Dybvig model, with depositors being coordinated by noisy signals on economic fundamentals. When a patient depositor only receives an imprecise, noisy signal in $t=1$ on the bank's fundamental, i.e., illiquid assets' realized return, whether she will run on the bank or not depends on her speculation on whether other depositors will run. This is important because if other depositors do not run, her running on the bank only makes her worse off. As a result, when the bank's fundamental is above a threshold, for a patient depositor who receives a good signal above this threshold, she will expect that many other depositors will receive good signals above this threshold and will not run on the bank; therefore, she will not run on the bank either, and non-run equilibrium is a unique equilibrium. The reverse also holds, that when the bank's fundamental is below the threshold, bank run is a unique equilibrium. In this sense, fundamental-driven and panic-driven bank runs are separated but also consistent with each other: self-fulfilling bank runs can still be driven by panics, but they only happen when bank fundamentals are below a threshold so that depositors expects others to run on the bank.

2.2.7 SUMMARY

The Diamond-Dybvig model unveils some of the most important insights in banking, on how banks' socially desirable liquidity service is founded on a fragile structure, which is vulnerable to both fluctuations in banks' fundamentals and market sentiment. The Diamond-Dybvig model sheds much light on the sources of fragilities in banking as well as the design of stability policies.

The compact and flexible structure of the Diamond-Dybvig model also enables various extensions that address a wide spectrum of financial frictions in banking, and the model has inspired numerous theoretical and empirical studies in the past decades. For example, a long strand of literature focusing on equilibrium selection attempts to clarify the role of panics and fundamentals in triggering bank runs, which significantly improves policy makers' understanding on systemic instability as well as the efficiency in crisis resolution.

2.3 OPTIMAL BANK RUN

In this section, we further explore the implication of fragility for banks. In Section 2.2.4, we show that banks are vulnerable to *unanticipated* negative shocks to illiquid assets' returns; asset return in the long run is too low so that patient depositors want to withdraw early. However, what will happen if such asset return shocks are anticipated, for example, if in $t=0$ banks know that return from all illiquid assets will be low in some states in the future, due to business cycles? Obviously, bank run will most likely arise when the realized asset return is low, as banks may not be able to honor their deposit contracts. In this case, will banks adjust their deposit contracts in $t = 0$, to avoid costly bank runs in the downturn?

Using a model based on Allen and Gale (1998), we will see that the answers to these questions crucially depend on the cost of bank runs, when bank runs cannot be avoided in the downturn. If there is no cost associated with bank runs, when asset return is low, patient consumers withdraw early and share returns from liquid assets with impatient consumers; this actually leads to optimal risk-sharing among consumers. However, if there is positive cost associated with bank runs, resource allocation will be suboptimal, as early withdrawal of patient consumers leads to costly liquidation and reduces asset return in the long run. In this case, the central bank as the lender of last resort is able to improve efficiency by injecting liquidity to banks to avoid costly liquidation.

2.3.1 MODELLING AGGREGATE ASSET RETURN RISKS

Keep most of the settings the same as in the Diamond-Dybvig model, Section 2.2, except that

1. To simplify the model, assume $p = \frac{1}{2}$, so that half of consumers are impatient and half are patient;
2. Instead of assuming that the illiquid assets return in $t = 2$ with a constant return R, now we assume that R is a non-negative random variable with probability density function (pdf) $f(R)$. Assume the mean of R is $E[R] > 1$ so that consumers are willing to deposit in the banks rather than storing their endowments. Also assume that banks' realized illiquid assets, returns, R is across all banks, are perfectly correlated, i.e., realized R is the same for all banks and banks are subject to *aggregate* instead of idiosyncratic asset return risks. This allows us to focus on risk-sharing among consumers instead of risk-sharing among banks;
3. The distribution, $f(R)$, is publicly known in $t = 0$, the true value of R is revealed as public information in $t = 1$.

2.3.2 OPTIMAL RISK-SHARING WITH ZERO LIQUIDATION COST

We first start with an assumption that there is no liquidation cost when a bank suffers a run, i.e., the illiquid assets cannot be liquidated in $t=1$. As a result, all withdrawal demand in $t=1$ is met only by the proceeds from the liquid assets.

SOCIAL PLANNER'S PROBLEM

Again, as a benchmark, let us start with analyzing the social planner's problem. Under the stochastic return R that is only revealed in $t=1$, the planner's problem involves two stages:

Stage 1 With the knowledge of $f(R)$, in $t=0$ the planner chooses optimal investment α in the liquid assets;

Stage 2 After R is revealed in $t=1$, the planner makes an optimal allocation of resources, c_1/c_2 for impatient/patient consumers.

With the planner's sequential decision-making, we solve the planner's problem by backward induction. First, we start with planner's decision problem in $t=1$, i.e., her optimal decision on c_1/c_2 under a given α that has been chosen in $t=0$; second, we continue with planner's decision problem in $t=0$, i.e., her optimal decision on α, given the optimal c_1/c_2 in $t=1$ as functions of α.

Before we proceed, we further assume, throughout the model, that

$$u'(0) > E[Ru'(R)] \qquad (2.5)$$

to rule out the trivial corner solution $\alpha=0$. To see this, suppose that the social planner invests nothing in liquid assets, $\alpha=0$ so that $c_1=0$ and $c_2=R$. Now instead, the social planner invests a small $\epsilon \to 0$ in liquid assets, this will lead to an increase in impatient consumers' utility by $\epsilon u'(0)$; at the same time, this also reduces investment in illiquid assets by ϵ and reduces impatient consumers' consumption by ϵR, leading to a fall in patient consumers' utility by $E[\epsilon R u'(R)]$. Assumption (2.5) thus means that, by shifting investment from illiquid to liquid assets, the marginal gain in impatient consumers' utility outweighs the marginal loss in patient consumers' utility. Therefore, the optimal α shall be always positive.

Under any given α, after R is revealed in $t=1$, the social planner's problem is then to choose consumption c_1/c_2 for impatient/patient consumers to maximize social welfare

$$\max_{\{c_1, c_2\}} \frac{1}{2}u(c_1) + \frac{1}{2}u(c_2), \tag{2.6}$$

$$\text{s.t.} \quad \frac{1}{2}c_1 \leq \alpha, \tag{2.7}$$

$$\frac{1}{2}c_1 + \frac{1}{2}c_2 = \alpha + (1-\alpha)R. \tag{2.8}$$

Note the difference between the planner's problem here (2.6) and the planner's problem (2.1) in the Diamond-Dybvig model. In the Diamond-Dybvig model, the planner's budget constraints (2.2) and (2.3) are both binding: given that the illiquid assets' return R is always larger than 1, the social planner shall never let patient consumers consume the yields from liquid assets. However, for the budget constraints (2.7) and (2.8) in this model, the realized R can be lower than 1, so that it is not necessarily optimal to prevent patient consumers from sharing the return of liquid assets.

Solve the planner's problem using Lagrangian

$$\mathcal{L} = \frac{1}{2}u(c_1) + \frac{1}{2}u(c_2) + \lambda\left[\alpha - \frac{1}{2}c_1\right] + v\left[\alpha + (1-\alpha)R - \frac{1}{2}c_1 - \frac{1}{2}c_2\right],$$

and the first-order conditions lead to

$$\frac{\partial \mathcal{L}}{\partial c_1} = \frac{1}{2}u'(c_1) - \frac{1}{2}\lambda - \frac{1}{2}v = 0,$$

$$\frac{\partial \mathcal{L}}{\partial c_2} = \frac{1}{2}u'(c_2) - \frac{1}{2}v = 0.$$

Eliminate v to get

$$u'(c_1) = u'(c_2) + \lambda. \tag{2.9}$$

Under inequality constraints, Kuhn-Tucker condition implies that

$$\lambda \begin{cases} = 0 & \text{if } \frac{1}{2}c_1 < \alpha, \\ > 0 & \text{if } \frac{1}{2}c_1 = \alpha, \end{cases}$$

equation (2.9) thus implies that

$$\begin{cases} u'(c_1) = u'(c_2) & \text{if } \frac{1}{2}c_1 < \alpha, \\ u'(c_1) > u'(c_2) & \text{if } \frac{1}{2}c_1 = \alpha. \end{cases}$$

And given that the utility function is strictly increasing and concave so that $u'(\cdot) > 0$ and $u''(\cdot) < 0$, (2.9) implies that

$$\begin{cases} c_1 = c_2 & \text{if } \frac{1}{2}c_1 < \alpha, \\ c_1 < c_2 & \text{if } \frac{1}{2}c_1 = \alpha. \end{cases}$$

Combine with the budget constraints (2.7) and (2.8), this means that

$$\begin{cases} c_1 = c_2 = \alpha + (1-\alpha)R & \text{if } R < \dfrac{\alpha}{1-\alpha}, \\ c_1 = 2\alpha, c_2 = 2(1-\alpha)R & \text{if } R \geq \dfrac{\alpha}{1-\alpha}. \end{cases} \tag{2.10}$$

That is, given α, c_1 and c_2 vary with R. Denote the cut-off value of R as $\hat{R} = \dfrac{\alpha}{1-\alpha}$, the optimal c_1 and c_2 are delineated in Figure 2.2.

When the realized $R = 0$, there is only return of α from liquid assets in the economy, so that the social planner has to equally split the yields between impatient and patient consumers to achieve optimal

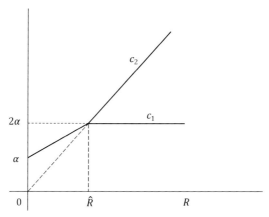

Figure 2.2 Optimal solution to the planner's problem

risk-sharing. When R is slightly larger than 0, the return from illiquid assets is still lower than liquid assets so that optimal risk-sharing requires patient consumers to partially consume from the yields of liquid assets. c_1 and c_2 are equal until $\hat{R}$, when the return from illiquid assets equals liquid assets; when $R > \hat{R}$, patient consumers only consume from the proceeds of illiquid assets, while impatient consumers only consume from the proceeds of liquid assets which is constant at α—the economy is now under *constrained efficiency* that risk-sharing between consumers is imperfect, as impatient consumers only value consumption in $t = 1$ and the planner cannot reshuffle the high yields of illiquid assets to $t = 1$.

With the planner's choice of c_1 and c_2 under certain α, now we can solve for planner's optimal choice of α. To maximize social welfare, the planner solves

$$\max_{\alpha} \underbrace{\int_0^{\hat{R}} u(\alpha + (1-\alpha)R) f(R) dR}_{(A)}$$

$$+ \underbrace{\int_{\hat{R}}^{+\infty} \left[\frac{1}{2} u(2\alpha) + \frac{1}{2} u(2(1-\alpha)R) \right] f(R) dR}_{(B)} \quad (2.11)$$

in which term (A) captures the case when $R < \hat{R} = \dfrac{\alpha}{1-\alpha}$ and $c_1 = c_2 = \alpha + (1-\alpha)R$, and term (B) captures the case when $R \geq \hat{R}$ and $c_1 = 2\alpha$, $c_2 = 2(1-\alpha)R$. The solution to optimal α is left as your exercise (see Exercise 7).

DECENTRALIZED BANKING SOLUTION WITH BANK RUNS

Now let us check to what extent the planner's solution can be replicated in a decentralized economy with banks. Assume that banks are operating the same balance sheets as in Figure 2.1, that they collect deposits from consumers in $t=0$ using deposit contracts that promise a repayment of c_1/c_2 for impatient/patient consumers and invest in a portfolio of both liquid and illiquid assets. Banks engage in perfect competition so that they maximize consumers' utility through deposit contract. Key differences between banks and the social planner are

1. Banks cannot observe the true types of consumers, so that the deposit contract must be incentive compatible so that each consumer is able to self-select the repayment that is designed for her type;
2. Deposit contract is a fixed, demandable contract that consumers' repayments are not totally contingent on the realized R. To capture such rigidity, we assume that in $t=0$ banks promise a fixed repayment d_0 for each impatient consumer in $t=1$; patient consumers are "residual claimants", such that if there is no bank run, after the withdrawal of impatient consumers, patient consumers are paid by whatever is left in banks in $t=2$.

If there is a run on a bank in $t=1$, the liquidation value of the bank is evenly split among all consumers who want to withdraw.

Again we solve a bank's problem as a sequential decision problem: given the bank's choice on α, in $t=0$, then the bank chooses a deposit contract d_0 that promises c_1/c_2 for an impatient/a patient consumer to maximize a consumer's expected utility,

$$\max_{\{d_0, c_1, c_2\}} \frac{1}{2}u(c_1) + \frac{1}{2}u(c_2), \tag{2.12}$$

$$\text{s.t.} \quad \frac{1}{2}c_1 \leq \alpha, \tag{2.13}$$

$$\frac{1}{2}c_1 + \frac{1}{2}c_2 = \alpha + (1-\alpha)R, \tag{2.14}$$

$$c_1 \leq c_2, \tag{2.15}$$

$$c_1 \leq d_0, \text{ and } c_1 = c_2 \text{ if } c_1 < d_0. \tag{2.16}$$

The bank's object function is the same as the planner's, (2.6), so as the budget constraints (2.13) and (2.14). There are two extra constraints:

1. Incentive compatibility constraint (2.15), that patient consumers' payoff cannot be lower than impatient consumers'. Otherwise, a patient consumer can get better off by mimicking the impatient consumer and demanding repayment c_1 in $t=1$;
2. Fixed deposit contract constraint, as in (2.16), that the bank promises a fixed payment d_0 for an impatient consumer in $t=1$. If the bank suffers a run that patient consumers demand repayments in $t=1$, too, the fixed payment d_0 cannot be met and all consumers equally split the bank's liquidation value.

We start by examining these two extra budget constraints to see whether we can simplify the problem. Note that the key question in the fixed deposit contract constraint (2.16) is the choice of d_0. Without early liquidation of the illiquid assets, d_0 is completely paid out of the proceeds from the liquid assets, α, or, $\frac{1}{2}d_0 \leq \alpha$, $d_0 \leq 2\alpha$. Then

- If there is a bank run, that a population f of patient consumers want to withdraw in $t=1$, then they evenly split the proceeds of the bank's liquid assets. Denote the payoff of an early-withdrawing patient consumer as c_{21}, then $c_{21} = c_1 = \dfrac{\alpha}{\frac{1}{2}+f}$; denote the pay-off of a patient consumer who stays until $t=2$ as c_{22}, then $c_{22} = \dfrac{(1-\alpha)R}{\frac{1}{2}-f}$.

Furthermore, it must be that $c_{21} = c_{22} = c_2$, otherwise either more than f patient consumers would join the bank run (if $c_{21} > c_{22}$), or less than f patient consumers would join the bank run (if $c_{21} < c_{22}$). To summarize, if bank run occurs,

$$c_1 = c_2 = \frac{\alpha}{\frac{1}{2} + f} = \frac{(1-\alpha)R}{\frac{1}{2} - f} < d_0. \tag{2.17}$$

Also note that, without early liquidation, budget constraint (2.14) means that consumers' total consumption equals the total proceeds of both liquid and illiquid assets, that is

$$\frac{1}{2}c_1 + \frac{1}{2}c_2 = \alpha + (1-\alpha)R, \text{ or, } c_1 = c_2 = \alpha + (1-\alpha)R. \tag{2.18}$$

- If there is no bank run, then in $t=1$ an impatient consumer withdraws $c_1 = d_0$. After that, if there is remaining yield from liquid assets, $\alpha - \frac{1}{2}d_0$, it will be stored in the bank till $t = 2$ and a patient consumer withdraws $c_2 = 2\left[\alpha - \frac{1}{2}d_0 + (1-\alpha)R\right]$. Furthermore, "no bank run" requires the incentive compatibility condition (2.15) to hold,

$$d_0 \leq 2\left[\alpha - \frac{1}{2}d_0 + (1-\alpha)R\right], \text{ or } R \geq \frac{d_0 - \alpha}{1 - \alpha} = \hat{R}. \tag{2.19}$$

"No-bank-run condition" (2.19) implies that, when R exceeds $\hat{R}$, c_1 is constant at d_0, $c_2 > c_1$ and the gap between c_2 and c_1 is $2\alpha - 2d_0 + 2(1-\alpha)R$. However, for a bank maximizing consumers' expected utility, the concavity of utility function requires the bank to minimize the gap between c_2 and c_1 for optimal risk-sharing. This implies that the optimal choice on d_0 should be $d_0 = 2\alpha$.

Under no-bank-run condition (2.19), the bank's optimal decision problem becomes maximizing (2.12) under constraints (2.13), (2.14), and (2.15), which is similar to the planner's problem except the extra incentive compatibility constraint (2.15). However, the incentive compatibility constraint (2.15), $c_1 \leq c_2$, is naturally guaranteed in the planner's solution, implying that the bank's optimal decision problem yields the same solution as the planner's problem.

To summarize, the bank's optimal decision is to choose $d_0 = 2\alpha$, then

$$\begin{cases} c_1 = c_2 = \alpha + (1-\alpha)R & \text{with bank run under } R < \dfrac{\alpha}{1-\alpha}, \\ c_1 = 2\alpha, c_2 = 2(1-\alpha)R & \text{with no bank run under } R \geq \dfrac{\alpha}{1-\alpha}. \end{cases} \quad (2.20)$$

This is exactly the same as the planner's solution (2.10), as depicted in Figure 2.2.

Why can decentralized banks—even if they suffer from bank runs—replicate the planner's solution? Note that the crucial assumption in the current setting is zero liquidation cost, so that bank run does not destroy the value of bank assets, but rather, it only affects the allocation of resources. When realized R is low and bank run occurs, the early withdrawing patient consumers force the bank to share the proceeds of liquid assets with them, and this achieves the optimal risk-sharing between impatient and patient consumers.

2.3.3 OPTIMAL RISK-SHARING WITH POSITIVE LIQUIDATION COST

Can banks still achieve the planner's solution, if liquidation cost is positive? To model the cost of liquidation in $t=1$, we assume that banks have access to another "reinvestment technology": although, same as before, the return on liquid assets between $t=0$ and $t=1$ is 1, if the bank reinvests in safe assets between $t=1$ and $t=2$, it earns an extra return r, $r>1$. As a result, cashing out from liquid assets in $t=1$ is costly, as it incurs an opportunity cost of $r-1$ from forgoing the reinvestment opportunity; r is thus the liquidation cost when patient consumers withdraw in $t=1$ and cash out from liquid assets, instead of letting the bank reinvest the liquid assets. We further assume that $E[R] > r$, so that the expected return of illiquid assets dominates liquid assets, even if the reinvestment technology is available.

SOCIAL PLANNER'S PROBLEM

Given that the payoff structure of assets is changed, we have to start again with the benchmark social planner's solution. Similarly, under any given α that is chosen in $t=0$, after R is revealed in $t=1$, the social planner's problem is then to choose consumption c_1/c_2 for impatient/patient consumers to maximize social welfare

$$\max_{\{c_1,c_2\}} \frac{1}{2}u(c_1)+\frac{1}{2}u(c_2), \tag{2.21}$$

$$\text{s.t.} \quad \frac{1}{2}c_1 \leq \alpha, \tag{2.22}$$

$$\frac{1}{2}c_2 = \left(\alpha - \frac{1}{2}c_1\right)r + (1-\alpha)R. \tag{2.23}$$

It can be easily seen that the planner's problem degenerates to (2.6), if $r=1$. Using Lagrangian, first-order conditions of the planner's problem lead to

$$\frac{\partial \mathcal{L}}{\partial c_1} = \frac{1}{2}u'(c_1) - \frac{1}{2}\lambda - \frac{r}{2}v = 0,$$

$$\frac{\partial \mathcal{L}}{\partial c_2} = \frac{1}{2}u'(c_2) - \frac{1}{2}v = 0,$$

rearrange to get

$$u'(c_1) = ru'(c_2) + \lambda.$$

By Kuhn-Tucker condition, this corresponds to

$$\begin{cases} u'(c_1) = ru'(c_2) & \text{if } c_1 < 2\alpha, \\ u'(c_1) > ru'(c_2) & \text{if } c_1 = 2\alpha. \end{cases}$$

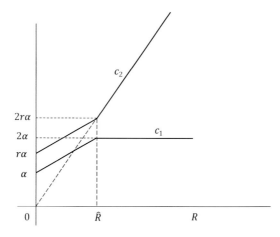

Figure 2.3 *Optimal solution to the planner's problem, with liquidation cost*

The solution to c_1 and c_2 now depends on the functional form of utility. Assuming logarithm-form utility function, $u(\cdot) = \ln u(\cdot)$, the planner's problem can be solved analytically as

$$\begin{cases} c_1 = \dfrac{r\alpha + (1-\alpha)R}{r}, c_2 = r\alpha + (1-\alpha)R & \text{if } R < \dfrac{r\alpha}{1-\alpha}, \\ c_1 = 2\alpha, c_2 = 2(1-\alpha)R & \text{if } R \geq \dfrac{r\alpha}{1-\alpha}. \end{cases}$$

Denote the cutoff value $\hat{R} = \dfrac{r\alpha}{1-\alpha}$, such optimal c_1 and c_2 are delineated in Figure 2.3.

DECENTRALIZED BANKING SOLUTION WITH BANK RUNS

With the additional liquidation cost, in $t = 0$, a bank decides on the fixed deposit contract d_0 for impatient consumers as well as consumption c_1/c_2 for impatient/patient consumers to maximize consumers' expected utility, with an expectation that a population of f patient consumers will withdraw early in the downturn. The bank's problem thus can be specified as

$$\max_{\{d_0,c_1,c_2\}} \frac{1}{2}u(c_1)+\frac{1}{2}u(c_2), \tag{2.24}$$

$$\text{s.t.} \quad c_1 \leq c_2, \tag{2.25}$$

if $f > 0$:

$$c_1 < d_0, \tag{2.26}$$

$$\frac{1}{2}c_1 + fc_2 = \alpha, \tag{2.27}$$

$$\left(\frac{1}{2}-f\right)c_2 = (1-\alpha)R, \tag{2.28}$$

if $f = 0$:

$$c_1 = d_0; \tag{2.29}$$

$$\frac{1}{2}c_2 = \left(\alpha - \frac{1}{2}c_1\right)r + (1-\alpha)R. \tag{2.30}$$

Same as before, inequality (2.25) is the incentive compatibility constraint. Constraints (2.26) to (2.28) characterize what happens if patient consumers of population f run on the bank in $t = 1$: the bank is unable to fulfill the fixed deposit contract d_0 for impatient consumers (constraint 2.26), the early-withdrawing patient consumers split the proceeds of liquid assets together with impatient consumers (constraint 2.27), and the remaining patient consumers share the proceeds of illiquid assets in $t = 2$ (constraint 2.28). Again, in equilibrium, the payoff for early-withdrawing patient consumers should equal the payoff for late-withdrawing patient consumers, that is why we use c_2 for a patient consumer's payoff in both (2.27) and (2.28).

Constraints (2.29) and (2.30) characterize what happens if there is no bank run. Then each impatient consumer withdraws d_0 in $t = 1$ (constraint 2.29), and the patient consumers claim the residuals in $t = 2$ (constraint 2.30).

To solve the bank's problem, we start by examining the budget constraints to simplify the problem. First, notice that, if $f > 0$ and the bank incurs a run in $t = 1$, in equilibrium it must be that $c_1 = c_2$, combine constraints (2.27) and (2.28), we can solve for $c_1, c_2,$ and f

$$\begin{cases} c_1 = c_2 = \alpha + (1-\alpha)R, \\ f = \dfrac{1}{2}\dfrac{\alpha - (1-\alpha)R}{\alpha + (1-\alpha)R} \end{cases} \quad (2.31)$$

with $c_1 < d_0$.

Note that the solution for c_1 and c_2 in (2.31) is exactly the same as the bank run solution in (2.20), when there is no liquidation cost. This is because in both cases, the bank has to liquidate all liquid assets when bank run happens.

Second, if there is no bank run and $f = 0$, $c_1 = d_0$ by (2.29), so that c_2 can be solved from (2.30)

$$c_2 = 2\left(\alpha - \frac{1}{2}c_1\right)r + 2(1-\alpha)R.$$

Incentive compatibility constraint (2.25) requires

$$c_2 = 2\left(\alpha - \frac{1}{2}c_1\right)r + 2(1-\alpha)R \geq c_1, \quad (2.32)$$

if there is no bank run. (2.32) thus implies a "no-bank-run" condition, that R must exceed a threshold $\hat{R}$, which is achieved when the incentive compatibility constraint is just binding, $c_1 = c_2 = d_0$ for (2.32), solve for $\hat{R}$

$$\hat{R} = \frac{(1+r)d_0 - 2\alpha r}{2(1-\alpha)}.$$

To summarize, under no-bank-run condition $R \geq \hat{R}$,

$$\begin{cases} c_1 = d_0, \\ c_2 = 2\left(\alpha - \dfrac{1}{2}d_0\right)r + 2(1-\alpha)R. \end{cases} \quad (2.33)$$

Combining the result from bank run equilibrium, (2.31), and the result from no bank run equilibrium, (2.33). Figure 2.4 depicts the payoffs c_1 and c_2 as functions of R.

CHAPTER TWO: FRAGILE BANKS

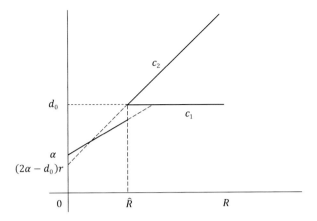

Figure 2.4 Optimal solution to the bank's problem, with liquidation cost

Note that the optimal deposit contract d_0 is still unknown and needs to be solved from the bank's problem (2.24)—if the functional form of utility is given, and optimal d_0 also depends on the values of other variables. However, as we do not need to know the exact value of optimal d_0 for our qualitative comparison, here we will not attempt to solve for d_0. In principle, $d_0 \leq 2\alpha$, as repayments for withdrawing consumers in $t=1$ cannot exceed the liquidation value of liquid assets. Generically, optimal d_0 can be 2α, when r, or liquidation cost, is low; optimal d_0 can also be strictly lower than 2α, when r, or liquidation cost, is higher so that the bank prefers to take some liquid assets over to $t=2$.

What is the difference between the banking solution with costly bank runs and the planner's solution, or, what is the cause of inefficiency in the banking solution, comparing Figure 2.4 to Figure 2.3? First, the payoff for patient consumers in the banking solution is always lower than in the planner's solution: in the planner's solution, even under low R, $R < \hat{R}$, the patient consumers' payoff is r times as much as impatient consumers' payoff; in contrast, as for the banking solution, in the bank run equilibrium under $R < \hat{R}$, the patient consumers' payoff is the same as impatient consumers'. The same also holds for the starting points of c_1/c_2 when R exceeds $\hat{R}$. The reason for such differences between Figure 2.4 and Figure 2.3 is that bank run is costly, as liquidating all liquid assets in

$t=1$ forces the bank to forgo the reinvestment opportunity. With a social planner, under low R and low return from illiquid assets, although patient consumers have to share the proceeds from liquid assets with impatient consumers, the social planner does not need to liquidate all liquid assets in $t=1$; instead, after liquidating just enough liquid assets to repay impatient consumers, the planner can reinvest the remaining liquid assets on behalf of patient consumers and repay them in $t=2$, which allows patient consumers to enjoy the higher return r from the reinvested liquid assets. In contrast, in the banking solution, when a bank run happens under low R, the bank has to liquidate all liquid assets to meet the demand of withdrawing consumers in $t=1$; as a result, the early withdrawing patient consumers cash out from liquid assets and miss the higher return from reinvesting liquid assets.

In this model, as the inefficiency in banking solution arises from costly liquidation during bank runs, any policy intervention that avoids liquidation or eliminates bank runs has the potential to improve efficiency. For example, during a bank run in $t=1$, central bank can step in as the lender of last resort as follows:

1. A bank can borrow an amount of M *fiat money* from central bank in $t=1$ during bank run, and M is equal to the early withdrawal demand of patient consumers. Note fiat money here is just a token of "I owe you" and cannot be used for consumption. Suppose the central bank's gross lending rate is 1;
2. As the early withdrawal demand of patient consumers is fulfilled by borrowed money, after repaying impatient consumers from proceeds of liquid assets, the bank does not need to liquidate more assets so that it can reinvest the remaining liquid assets. As early withdrawing patient consumers do not need to consume in $t=1$, they can just carry the money over to $t=2$;
3. In $t=2$, after collecting proceeds from all remaining assets, the bank can distribute these proceeds evenly among patient consumers who hold money and patient consumers who hold deposit contracts. During the distribution, the bank collects money M from depositors and repays central bank.

In this way, costly liquidation during bank runs is avoided. It is then straightforward to show (as an exercise for readers) that banks are able to restore the efficiency and achieve the same allocation as in the planner's solution, as is characterized by Figure 2.3.

2.3.4 SUMMARY

The Allen-Gale model provides important insights on the role of fragility in banks' resource allocation, when there is uncertainty on asset returns and bank runs are inevitable in equilibrium. As we can see from the model, as long as liquidation cost is low, bank run in the downturn achieves optimal risk-sharing between depositors. Inefficiencies arise when liquidation cost is high, so that bank run leads to destruction of values in the banking system. This implies that policy makers shall not focus on fragility itself and attempt to eliminate fragility altogether, instead, they shall target sources of inefficiencies in bank runs and reduce costly liquidation by providing support on bank liquidity or market asset prices.

2.4 FRAGILITY AND BANK LIQUIDITY

Banks are intrinsically fragile, as is shown in the Diamond-Dybvig model, because deposit contracts are demandable so that depositors can withdraw at any time, and deposit is also fixed, neither renegotiable nor contingent on banks' actual asset returns. On one hand, this is desirable for depositors who have uncertainty in their preferred timing for consumption, so that they can fulfill their liquidity demand at any time from banks that provide deposit contracts as liquidity insurance; on the other hand, such liquidity service exposes banks to liquidity risk arising from maturity mismatch between assets and liabilities, so that when depositors attempt to withdraw more than a bank's liquidity buffer, the bank will be forced to liquidate its illiquid assets at a substantial cost and this may make the bank fail.

However, if such fragility is so detrimental to the banking system, why don't banks or regulators completely eliminate it? Many economists argue that fragility arising from demandable, non-contingent debt is a desirable device for depositors to discipline banks. The reason is that a bank's interest is not necessarily in line with its depositors', and a bank always has the incentive to divert resources for its own benefit and leave the costs to depositors, making depositors worse off. As Calomiris and Kahn (1991) demonstrate, the fragile demandable deposit contract allows depositors to credibly punish such "crooked" banks: should they suspect that their bank acts against their interests, they may run on the bank, demand withdrawal, and destroy the bank. Knowing this, banks will be well-behaved in the first place. The structural fragility thus functions as a *market discipline* on banks' behavior.

In this section, we show how fragility in banking disciplines banks and enables financial intermediation. Based on Cao and Illing (2011), as is demonstrated by Diamond and Rajan (2001), banks have the expertise on managing financial assets and generating high asset returns, but they also have the incentive to abuse this expertise and extort depositors; as a result, without discipline, market breaks down and financial intermediation is not feasible. This dilemma may be solved by demand deposit contract: with the privilege to initiate bank runs, depositors are able to credibly punish their bank by running on the bank, whenever they suspect that their contract will not be honored, destroying all assets of the bank. Knowing this, banks will never abuse their expertise, so that depositors will be willing to deposit. In other words, through using demand deposit contract as a discipline device, banks make financial intermediation feasible by tying their own grabbing hands, making both depositors and themselves better off.

2.4.1 MODEL SETUP: THE NEED FOR FRAGILITY
AGENTS, PREFERENCES, AND TECHNOLOGIES

Consider the following baseline economy with three types of risk-neutral agents: depositors, banks (operated by bank managers), and entrepreneurs. The economy extends over three periods, $t = 0, 1, 2$, and assume that:

1. There are depositors whose population is normalized to be 1, each of them being endowed with one unit of resource in $t = 0$. They will be willing to deposit in banks as long as the real return is no lower than 1. Depositors are impatient: they want to withdraw and consume in $t = 1$; in contrast, banks and entrepreneurs are indifferent between consuming in $t = 1$ and $t = 2$;
2. There are a finite number N of active banks participating in Bertrand competition, so that they compete for depositors' deposits in $t = 0$ and make zero profit. Using these deposits, banks as financial intermediaries can fund the projects of entrepreneurs;
3. There is an infinite number of entrepreneurs, and there are sufficiently many entrepreneurs competing for funds so that bank deposits are scarce. Each of the entrepreneurs borrows one unit from a bank and operates one of two types of projects starting from $t = 0$:

    - Safe projects, each returns early in $t = 1$ with a safe gross return $R_1 > 1$;
    - Risky projects, each yields a higher gross return R_2, with $R_2 > R_1 > 1$. With probability p, risky projects will return in $t = 1$, while the return may be delayed with probability $1 - p$ until $t = 2$. Therefore, in the aggregate, a share p of risky projects will be realized early. The value of p, however, is not known in $t = 0$. It will only be revealed between period 0 and 1 in an intermediate period, call it $t = \frac{1}{2}$.

Both safe projects and risky projects can be liquidated before the mature. When a project is liquidated, the return is c, with $0 \leq c < 1$.

In this model, we are interested in the case of *aggregate* shocks to all risky projects: the value of p can be either p_H or p_L, with $p_H > p_L$. The "good" state, or "normal" state, with a high share $p = p_H$ of risky projects being realized early in $t = 1$ will occur with probability π. Since the "bad" state with $p = p_L$, or, the "crisis" state, is rare, let us assume that π is close to 1. To focus on the relevant case, let us further assume that

$1 < p_S R_2 < R_1$ $(s = H, L)$, so that the risky projects that return early cannot substitute the safe projects, and it is always necessary to invest in safe assets to meet the depositors' withdrawal demand in $t = 1$.

DEPOSIT CONTRACT AND THE NEED FOR FRAGILITY

Banks as financial intermediaries offer liquid deposit contracts redeemable at any time after $t = 0$. In order to understand the role of fragility in bank liquidity creation, instead of simply imposing such deposit contracts as in the standard Diamond-Dybvig model in Section 2.2, we derive bank deposits as outcomes of optimal contracts in the presence of incentive constraints as follows:

Contracting in frictionless matching market We start with a benchmark scenario in which depositors can frictionlessly contract with entrepreneurs directly. Since there is a market demand for liquidity only if depositors' funds are the limiting factor, as we assume, depositors' funds are scarce in the sense that there are more projects of each type of entrepreneurs available than the aggregate endowment of depositors—as a result, all depositors' funds are lent to entrepreneurs in $t = 0$ and depositors have liquidity demand for consumption in $t = 1$. If there were no financial friction, depositors would contract directly with entrepreneurs in a matching market in $t = 0$, and the scarcity of funds would allow them to claim the total surplus of all realized projects. Given that all depositors are impatient and only want to consume in $t = 1$, they would simply invest all their funds in safe projects, and capture the full return, R_1, in $t = 1$. This frictionless matching market outcome is the reference point for our further analysis on the role of liquidity.

Contracting in frictional matching market with hold-up problem In reality, incentive problems prevent the realization of such frictionless market outcome, creating a demand for liquidity. Following Hart and Moore (1994), we introduce market friction, a *hold-up problem* in the model as follows: entrepreneurs have the expertise, or, the necessary human capital, on operating projects—only they can ensure the success of the projects with full returns. If depositors operate the projects by themselves instead, they can only receive an inferior return of $\underline{\gamma} R_s$ ($0 \leq \underline{\gamma} < 1$). Assume that $\underline{\gamma} R_s > 1$, $s = 1, 2$. As a result, in the matching market in $t = 0$, if depositors ask for a return in $t = 1$ higher than $\underline{\gamma} R_s$, entrepreneurs would simply threaten to refuse operating any project. So entrepreneurs can only commit to pay a fraction $\underline{\gamma}$ of their return to depositors; as a result, if depositors were to make direct lending to entrepreneurs under the hold-up problem, they would still lend only to safe projects, but their consumption would be worse off at $\underline{\gamma} R_1$, compared with the outcome of the frictionless matching market in the benchmark scenario.

Contracting with banks subject to hold-up problem Banks, as financial intermediaries, have better collection skills than depositors: they have better expertise in asset management so that even if entrepreneurs threaten to walk away from their projects, banks can still recover γR_s, with $\gamma > \underline{\gamma}$ from the projects. Thus, if banks make lending contracts with entrepreneurs, they can make a higher return of γR_s from the loans; therefore, depositors would be better off if they could deposit funds in banks and delegate banks to contract with entrepreneurs, i.e., making banks as financial intermediaries channeling funds from depositors to entrepreneurs.

However, such arrangement creates further hold-up problem for banks, as banks have the incentive to abuse their collecting expertise. In $t = 1$, after collecting returns from entrepreneurs whose projects return early, banks would then have the incentive to force depositors into renegotiation: instead of paying out the entire collected returns to depositors, banks—with the monopolistic power on collecting projects' returns—would only want to pay 1 to depositors, and depositors would be forced to accept. This would make depositors worse off, even compared with the outcome in the frictional matching market with hold-up problem. This leads to market breakdown: knowing that banks would always abuse their collecting expertise, depositors would never deposit in banks in $t = 0$ so that banking would not be feasible at all.

Contracting with banks subject to bank runs Diamond and Rajan (2001) show that, standard *demand deposit contract* that promises a fixed payment d_0, with $d_0 \geq 1$, that is payable at any time after $t=0$, noncontingent on the state of the world is able to eliminate the hold-up problem of banks and makes banking feasible. Under such demand deposit contract, depositors are entitled to run on a bank, demanding d_0, once they perceive that the bank cannot honor the contracts—for example, if the bank attempts to renegotiate in $t=1$. Should a bank run happen, the bank would be forced to liquidate all assets with inferior return $c<1$; knowing this, it will not abuse its collecting expertise, and depositors are hence willing to deposit in $t=0$. In this model, if banks are competing to pay out all collected return γR_s, $s=1,2$ to depositors in $t=1$, depositors are better off than the outcome of frictional matching market with hold-up problem.

Such demand deposit contract is thus an efficient commitment device to cope with that hold-up problem; it provides banks with a credible disciplinary mechanism to gain the trust from depositors not to abuse their superior collection skills, making financial intermediation feasible and improving depositors' welfare. In this sense, banks' liquidity creation is built upon fragility in banking: the more liquidity a bank creates, i.e., the higher d_0 it promises depositors in $t=0$, the higher is the likelihood that it cannot meet depositors' withdrawal demand in $t=1$ when its interim return is subject to exogenous shocks and a bank run occurs. The optimal solution for banks is thus determined by the trade-off between liquidity creation and fragility.

TIMING OF THE MODEL

The timing of events goes as follows:

- In $t=0$, banks compete for depositors by offering them fixed demand deposit contracts that promise a return d_0 in $t=1$.

At the same time, banks decide the proportion α of deposits to be invested in the safe projects, or, *liquid assets*, and proportion $1-\alpha$ of deposits to be invested in the risky projects, or, *illiquid assets*. Depositors have rational expectations: they deposit in banks that offer them the highest expected return, after they get to know banks' plans on the investment portfolios;

- In an intermediate period $t=\frac{1}{2}$ the value of p is revealed, and this is public information. Given the value of p, if one bank will not be able to meet its depositors' claims in $t=1$, the depositors will run on the bank in $t=\frac{1}{2}$ because of the first-come-first-served rule in banking. If a bank experiences a run in this intermediate period, it has to liquidate all unmatured assets, i.e., both safe and risky projects. Each unit of liquidated asset (project) yields a poor return c, with $0 \leq c < 1$;

- If there is no bank run in $t=\frac{1}{2}$, in $t=1$ banks collect a proportion γ, $0 < \gamma < 1$, from the return of early projects (safe projects plus those risky projects that return early). The projects' owners, call them early entrepreneurs, retain the rest. To maximize depositors' return, banks can raise additional resources from early entrepreneurs in a liquidity market: banks borrow from early entrepreneurs, promising a gross borrowing rate r and using their delayed projects as collateral. Since entrepreneurs are indifferent between consuming in $t=1$ and $t=2$, they will be willing to lend to banks as long as $r \geq 1$. Banks make payouts to depositors using both the return collected from early projects and the liquidity borrowed from the liquidity market;

- In $t=2$, banks collect return from late projects and pay back early entrepreneurs.

When the economy is under normal state in $t=1$, the timing of the model is summarized in Figure 2.5. When the economy is under crisis state in $t=1$, the timing of the model is summarized in Figure 2.6.

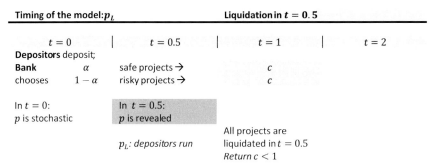

Figure 2.5 *The timing of events, normal state*

Figure 2.6 *The timing of events, crisis state*

2.4.2 CONSTRAINED EFFICIENCY

SOCIAL PLANNER'S SOLUTION

Before solving for the banks' problem, to see the best possible outcome from the model, we first analyze the outcome if resources are allocated by a social planner who maximizes the depositors' payoff. This provides the reference point for the market equilibrium in which banks serve as financial intermediaries. With depositors being impatient, the social planner will choose the share α invested in liquid, safe projects so as to maximize the resources available to pay out depositors in $t=1$. Given $p_s R_2 < R_1$, in the absence of hold-up problems, the planner will invest only in liquid assets or safe projects, as this maximizes resources available in $t=1$. But due to the hold-up problem caused by entrepreneurs, the social planner can implement only a *constrained efficient solution*: if the planner had unlimited taxation authority, she could eliminate the hold-up problem completely by taxing the entrepreneurs' rent and redistributing the resources to the depositors. Again, all resources would be invested only in liquid, safe, projects, and the entrepreneurs' rents would be transferred to the depositors in $t=1$. However, allowing for non-distortionary taxation biases the comparison between the market and the planner's solution, giving the planner an unfair advantage. Effectively, redistribution via lump-sum taxation would make both hold-up and liquidity constraints non-binding, assuming the relevant liquidity problem away. To make the planner's constrained optimization problem interesting, let us assume that non-distortionary taxation is not feasible in $t=1$. In order not to distort the comparison in favor of banks, furthermore assume that the planner has the same collection skills (the same γ) as financial intermediaries.

To find the optimal solution for the planner, first assume that there is no uncertainty on p_s, $s = H, L$, that p is fixed at either p_H or p_L in $t=0$; then the social planner maximizes depositors' return by choosing its investment portfolio at $t=0$ such that

$$\alpha_s = \arg\max_{\alpha_s} \gamma \left\{ \alpha_s R_1 + (1-\alpha_s) \left[p_s R_2 + \frac{(1-p_s)R_2}{r_s} \right] \right\}, \text{ s.t. } r_s \geq 1.$$

It says that the social planner invests a share α_s of its assets in safe projects, and $1-\alpha_s$ on risky projects. Then in $t=1$, she collects $\gamma \alpha_s R_1$ return from the safe projects, as well as $\gamma(1-\alpha_s)R_2$ from the risky projects that return early. She also borrows

$$(1-\gamma)\alpha_s R_1 + (1-\gamma)(1-\alpha_s)R_2$$

at gross interest rate r_s from the entrepreneurs who obtain returns at $t=1$, using her claims on the delayed projects

$$\gamma(1-\alpha_s)(1-p_s)R_2$$

as collateral. Therefore, to maximize the total return for depositors, the social planner shall choose an α_s that minimize her cost in $t=1$ on borrowing from all the early entrepreneurs, that is to make

$$r_s = \frac{\gamma(1-\alpha_s)(1-p_s)R_2}{(1-\gamma)\alpha_s R_1 + (1-\gamma)(1-\alpha_s)R_2} = 1 \qquad (2.34)$$

which corresponds to

$$\alpha_s = \frac{\gamma - p_s}{\gamma - p_s + (1-\gamma)\dfrac{R_1}{R_2}}.$$

One can immediately see that

$$\frac{\partial \alpha_s}{\partial p_s} < 0,$$

or, $\alpha_H < \alpha_L$ with $p_H > p_L$. Because when p is higher, intermediate liquidity supply in $t=1$ is higher so that there is less need to invest in liquid, safe assets with low yield in $t=0$.

Depositors' expected return, call it d^*_{0s}, is thus the collected return from all early-returned projects, plus funds borrowed from early entrepreneurs,

$$d^*_{0s} = \alpha_s R_1 + p_s(1-\alpha_s)R_2.$$

Using the equilibrium borrowing rate (2.34), d^*_{0s} can also be expressed as

$$d^*_{0s} = \gamma[\alpha_s R_1 + (1-\alpha_s)R_2]. \qquad (2.35)$$

Obviously, without liquidity constraint or hold-up problem, the social planner would invest all resources in risky projects to maximize aggregate output; however, under liquidity constraint and hold-up problem, the social planner has to invest in a combination of safe and risky projects to meet depositors' liquidity demand. However, the hold-up problem also creates an opportunity to "roll over" the investments in delayed projects, by borrowing from early entrepreneurs in $t=1$; this increases liquidity creation in $t=1$: as equation (2.35) shows, $d^*_{0s} > \gamma R_1$, so that depositors are better off than the outcome in frictional matching market subject hold-up problem.

What is the solution to social planner's problem, if there is uncertainty on p_s, $s = H, L$, in $t = 0$? Given that the likelihood of crisis state in $t = 1$, $1 - \pi$, is close to zero, or, p_H will be most likely realized, the optimal solution for the planner is to choose α_H as if it were always in normal state in $t = 1$. Because α_H ensures that depositors' return is maximized with a probability that is almost 1, choosing any α other than α_H to increase depositors' return in crisis state would miss the maximized return for depositors almost for sure. As a result, α_H is still optimal for the planner, as long as the likelihood of crisis in $t = 1$ is sufficiently low.

Overall, with uncertainty on p_s, depositors' expected return, $E[R(\alpha_H, \pi)]$, in the planner's solution is

$$E[R(\alpha_H, \pi)] = \pi d^*_{0H} + (1-\pi) d^*_{0H|L} \qquad (2.36)$$

in which d^*_{0H} is defined by (2.35) and $d^*_{0H|L} = \alpha_H R_1 + (1-\alpha_H) p_L R_2$.

BANKING SOLUTION

What is the market equilibrium, if perfectly competitive banks are providing financial intermediation between depositors and entrepreneurs? As is shown, to convince depositors that banks will not abuse their collecting expertise, banks shall offer a fixed demand deposit contract to depositors that allows them to withdraw d_0 at any time after $t = 0$. Banks compete with each other in $t = 0$, by choosing investment portfolios that maximize depositors' expected return; that is, a bank chooses to invest a share α of its deposits in safe assets, and a share $1 - \alpha$ of its deposits in risky assets. Figure 2.7 shows a bank's balance sheet in $t = 0$.

In $t = 1$, the bank collects a share of γ returns from early entrepreneurs, it will also borrow the rest, a share of $1 - \gamma$ returns from early entrepreneurs, against the delayed risky projects as collateral. In this way, the bank is able to maximize depositors' return, which is paid out from the collected return and borrowed resources from early entrepreneurs. Figure 2.8 shows the bank's balance sheet after paying out depositors (in normal state) in $t = 1$.

Assets	Liabilities
Safe assets α_H	Deposits 1
Risky assets $1 - \alpha_H$	

Figure 2.7 A bank's balance sheet in $t = 0$

Assets	Liabilities
Delayed risky assets:	Claims from early entrepreneurs:
$(1 - p_H)(1 - \alpha_H)R_2$	$(1-\gamma)[\,_H R_1 + (1 - \alpha_H)R_2]$

Figure 2.8 A bank's balance sheet in $t = 1$, after withdraw

Similar to the planner's solution, the bank's problem is to maximize depositors' expected return by choosing α in $t = 0$. In the same vein, the optimal solution to the bank's problem is the same α_H: as long as the likelihood of crisis in $t = 1$ is sufficiently low, the bank shall maximize depositors' return in normal state and neglect crisis state.

However, once the bank chooses α_H in $t = 0$, the deposit contract is fixed at d^*_{0H}. This is fine only if normal state is revealed in $t = \frac{1}{2}$ so that depositors will wait until $t = 1$ and withdraw d^*_{0H}. However, if crisis state is revealed in $t = \frac{1}{2}$, depositors will find that the bank will only be able to provide liquidity as much as

$$\alpha_H R_1 + p_L(1-\alpha_H)R_2 < \alpha_H R_1 + p_H(1-\alpha_H)R_2 = d^*_{0H},$$

so that the bank will not be able to meet depositors' demand in $t = 1$. Knowing this, depositors will all run on the bank in $t = \frac{1}{2}$ and demand d^*_{0H}, forcing the bank to liquidate all assets with return c; however, given $0 \leq c < 1$ the bank's liquidation value is lower than depositors' total claims, the bank is bankrupted.

Overall, depositors' expected return, $E[R(\alpha_H, \pi, c)]$, in the banking solution is

$$E[R(\alpha_H, \pi, c)] = \pi d^*_{0H} + (1-\pi)c \qquad (2.37)$$

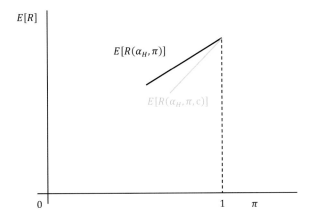

Figure 2.9 Depositors' expected return

Notes: the black line denotes depositors' expected return in the social planner's solution, as a function of α_H and π. The gray line denotes depositors expected return in the banking solution, as a function of α_H, π, and c.

in which d^*_{0H} is defined by (2.35). Comparing (2.36) and (2.37), it is easy to see that

$$E[R(\alpha_H, \pi, c)] < E[R(\alpha_H, \pi)]$$

for any $\pi < 1$, given that $c < 1 < d^*_{0H|L}$. Figure 2.9 compares depositors' expected returns as functions of π in both solutions: because of the costly liquidation in crisis state under the banking equilibrium, depositors' expected return is almost always lower in banking solution. However, as long as the likelihood of crisis in $t = 1$ is sufficiently low, depositors are still better off in banking solution than in frictional matching market subject hold-up problem, given that $d^*_{0H} > \gamma R_1$.

2.4.3 MARKET LIQUIDITY AND FUNDING LIQUIDITY

This simple model shows that when depositors demand liquidity in $t=1$, banks can create liquidity in two ways: one way is to convert assets to cash, in this model, it is by collecting returns from early assets in normal state or liquidating assets in crisis state. In principle, a bank can always convert its assets to cash, although such conversion is often subject to a discount on assets' face value; this implies—as we see in the model—a bank always needs to maintain a certain level of liquidity and hold liquid assets, in order to avoid the high discount on liquidating illiquid assets. Such capability for a bank to create liquidity by converting assets to cash is called the bank's *market liquidity*.

The other way is to create liquidity by rolling over liabilities, in this model, it is by having the early entrepreneurs as new creditors, to replace the out-going depositors and keep funding the high-yield, illiquid assets. Banks, that "borrow short and lend long", are featured by maturity mismatch in their balance sheets: assets are often illiquid and take a long time to mature—such as mortgage and government bonds, while liabilities are often of short maturities—an extreme is on-demand deposit that can be withdrawn at any time; however, when some creditors leave—for example, when depositors withdraw, as long as a bank is able to find new creditors to replace the outgoing creditors, the bank can still stay liquid and keep the illiquid assets going. This implies that a bank needs to maintain reliable, stable funding resources to ensure debt rollovers whenever necessary. Such capability for a bank to roll over its liabilities—by taking in new deposits, borrowing from other banks in interbank market, etc.—is called the bank's *funding liquidity*.

A bank's liquidity creation or *liquidity management* is thus to meet liquidity demand by actively managing its market liquidity and funding liquidity. Mismanagement, or varying market conditions that affect banks' market liquidity and funding liquidity may expose banks to liquidity risks. Furthermore, market liquidity and funding liquidity also interact with each other, and such interaction may amplify a bank's liquidity stress and lead to a *liquidity spiral*. Next, we briefly discuss what factors may affect banks' market liquidity and funding liquidity, and how liquidity spiral arises.

MARKET LIQUIDITY

A bank faces risks in the market's valuation on its assets. The market value of bank assets is usually below the face value: when bank assets are sold in the market, the price is subject to a discount. If these discounts are too high, banks will not be able to raise sufficient resources in interbank lending or asset market sales, causing further problems in liquidity management.

Market liquidity is an indicator of the ease of converting assets to cash when needed without incurring a large discount on such assets; it is asset-specific. The market liquidity of assets affects the extent to which banks can raise funding through asset sales or liquidation. Highly liquid assets can be sold quickly without any discount, whereas illiquid assets may take a long time to sell and/or have to be sold at a discount.

The market liquidity of assets also affects the banks' ability for borrowing on the interbank market when these assets are used for collateral. The value of collateral is also subject to a discount, called *haircut*. The haircut incurred on assets used as collateral will be larger, the larger the discount when sold on the market.

Market liquidity of bank assets varies from time to time because of many frictions in the financial market, including:

1. Moral hazard problems. Bank assets are often backed by ongoing projects. Since project managers cannot be perfectly monitored, they may act in a manner that promotes their private benefit instead the creditors' best interests, so that returns from projects may be lower than promised. Hence when these assets are sold in the market, investors may be willing to buy such assets only at a discount on their face value;
2. Adverse selection problems. As buyers have less knowledge than sellers about asset quality, buyers cannot tell whether they are being sold bad assets; because of this, sellers can always promote bad assets ("lemons") as good ones. Fearing of buying lemons, investors will only agree to buy assets with substantial discounts. Both moral hazard problems and adverse selection problems are caused by asymmetric information, which will be extensively discussed in Chapter 3;
3. Complexity in financial product design can also reduce market liquidity, especially during the crises. When a market is under stress,

some financial products are too complicated and/or customized to be priced in short time; for example, it can be extremely challenging to identify the risks and reprice an entire asset pool that backs a structured product. Although only a few assets may be under water, price can still crash for all assets in the same asset class. The implication of banking complexity will be extensively discussed in Chapter 6.

FUNDING LIQUIDITY

A bank also faces the risk in the feasibility of funding liabilities, i.e., it may not be able to access funding sources at reasonable cost when it needs. We use the term funding liquidity to refer to the ease with which banks can raise funds by rolling over or taking on more debt. While the concept of market liquidity is asset-specific, the concept of funding liquidity reflects several institution-specific factors. A bank's funding liquidity depends on many factors, including:

1. The availability of liquidity suppliers in the market, which may change over the business cycles. For example, in normal times there are many active participants in interbank markets so that one bank can easily borrow from others for a short term at fairly low costs; in contrast, when markets are under stress there may be few lenders in the market and borrowing costs become very high;
2. Funding liquidity is affected by corporate governance: investors are more willing to lend to better managed banks;
3. Raising new debt implies that claims of existing creditors are diluted, so that the resistance of existing creditors against issuing new debt may impede banks' funding capability. Such conflict among investors, called *debt overhang*, reduces banks' funding liquidity;
4. The bank's funding structure. On the asset side, it usually takes a considerably long time for bank loans to mature, while on the liability side, the bank often needs to fund itself via debt claims that repay creditors in a short time. Such maturity mismatch implies that the bank needs to replace old creditors with new ones, or, to roll over the debt, to keep the long-term loans going. The higher degree of

maturity mismatch there is between the bank's assets and liabilities, the more frequently the bank needs to roll over the debts, hence the more uncertainty on the availability of new funding creditors, or, the lower the bank's funding liquidity is.

LIQUIDITY SPIRAL

Market liquidity and funding liquidity are not isolated from each other, instead, they are closely interconnected. Given that assets are often used as collateral when banks borrow, market liquidity and funding liquidity can reinforce each other, destabilizing banking systems under market stress and leading to liquidity spirals: in normal times, banks, by participating in asset markets, provide market liquidity to the system. Once some asset is mispriced at excessive discount, creating arbitrage opportunities, banks and other investors—acting as highly specialized arbitrageurs—buy the undervalued asset and so help to bring prices in line with fundamentals. So in normal times, arbitrageurs make illiquid markets more liquid, reducing market volatility.

But investors' capability to do so depends on their ability to obtain funding. Leveraged investors rely on market liquidity being available to perform arbitrage. Professional arbitrageurs may clearly spot an arbitrage opportunity to buy the undervalued assets, but they need outside funds from non-informed investors, i.e., they face funding constraint. Under extreme conditions, when prices diverge far from fundamental values, non-informed investors, judging investment skills from past performance and fearing a further decline, may not be willing to provide the funds needed to make arbitrage effective. When markets dry up, assets have to be sold at large discounts. For instance, in a financial crisis, many financial institutions need to raise cash by selling assets, but at the same time, they are all under stress so that buyers can hardly be found. This can create a *limit of arbitrage*, as Shleifer and Vishny (1997) demonstrate. Outside investors are likely to withdraw their funds at precisely the time as prices move further away from fundamental values and arbitrage opportunities improve. Thus, arbitrage becomes ineffective exactly at those times when most urgently needed, triggering *fire sales*. When a bank needs to sell assets in a fire sale during a crisis, the market price of assets can be depressed persistently due to a lack of buyers.

When things go wrong, liquidity dries up completely, making things much worse. If there is stress in markets for liquidity, banks cannot get enough funding via borrowing and they will need to sell illiquid assets instead. With many banks attempting to sell illiquid assets, a situation can arise where there are far fewer buyers relative to sellers of such assets. This generates downward pressure on asset prices, worsens market liquidity in the system, and increases haircut levels. This situation further reduces the value of bank assets as collateral, aggravating banks' funding liquidity, forcing banks to liquidate more assets which makes asset prices plummet even further… the entire banking system falls into a downward liquidity spiral, as Brunnermeier and Pedersen (2009) show.

2.4.4 SUMMARY

The Cao-Illing model provides a simple analytical framework on motivating the role of fragility in financial intermediation. Given the conflict of interests between banks and depositors may destroy financial intermediation, banks avoid market breakdown by making the intermediation structure fragile. The fixed, demandable deposit contract allows depositors to punish banks by initiating bank runs and destroying all values in banks, whenever they suspect that banks act against their interests. Such mechanism ensures necessary market discipline from depositors, and aligns banks' decisions with depositors' interests.

The model also presents two important concepts in banks' liquidity management, market liquidity and funding liquidity, and shows how they jointly affect banks' liquidity creation. Market liquidity and funding liquidity are not only asset-/liability-dependent, they are also time-varying and sensitive to market conditions. Market liquidity and funding liquidity reinforce each other through banks' balance sheets, and this feature leads to drastic and fast changes in banks' liquidity creation, causing abrupt market movements such as crashes and crises. Understanding sources of market liquidity and funding liquidity as well as their interactions is thus crucial for both banks' daily business and regulators' supervisory practice (see Chapter 12 for more details).

2.5 EMPIRICAL EVIDENCE: DRIVERS OF BANK RUNS AND POLICY RESPONSES

ARE BANK RUNS DRIVEN BY PANICS OR FUNDAMENTALS?

Are bank runs panic-driven or fundamental-driven? What are the roles of market sentiments and bank fundamentals in driving depositors to run on banks? These questions are highly important not only for economic research, but also for policy makers to better understand the sources of bank fragility and take proper responses in time.

Identifying the driving forces of bank runs is challenging, although bank runs are not unusual in history. Bank runs often happen during crises or market stresses, when bank fundamentals are deteriorating and rumors about the health of the banking system are spreading; at the same time, expectations on public intervention may also be built. With all factors being intertwined, it is usually difficult to find a clean identification that disentangles everything.

A few bank run episodes have been recently explored, shedding much light on motives behind bank runs. In March, 2001, a few days after the unexpected failure of the largest cooperative bank due to fraud in the state of Gujarat, India, Iyer and Puri (2012) document several runs on other cooperative banks in the same state were triggered. These bank runs took place when the state economy was performing well, and among the victim banks, some of them even had almost no exposure to the failed bank. Furthermore, a depositor was more likely to run if someone in his or her social network ran. All these episodes seem to suggest that the runs were driven by panics instead of deteriorating fundamentals in the victim banks. However, they also find that a depositor is less likely to run when her relationship with the bank is strong—if she has been with the bank for long and/or takes a loan from the bank; this implies that fundamentals affect depositors' incentive to run, too, because depositors having strong relationships with the bank also know its fundamentals better. Digging deeper into the evolution of a bank failure in 2009, India, Iyer et al. (2016) find that those depositors having strong relationships with the bank become more likely to run on the bank, when the bank is fundamentally insolvent, and substantial deposit outflows from those depositors even start long before the bank's insolvency becomes publicly known. This underlines the importance of inside information in triggering bank runs, as those depositors tend to be more informed than the others.

In May 1931, the failure of the largest Austrian bank triggered a systemic banking crisis in Germany. Strikingly, before the first major German bank, "Danatbank", declared bankruptcy in July, Blickle et al. (2020) find that there was no substantial deposit outflows from retail depositors. This stage was rather featured by silent bank runs in Germany with a sharp fall in interbank lending, reflecting banks' private information on their peers' fundamentals. Furthermore, during the systemic bank run—mainly by retail depositors—after July 1931, fundamentally sound banks even gained inflows of retail deposits, suggesting depositors' incentive to run is indeed affected by fundamentals. Investigating banking crises during the National Banking Era, 1863–1914, when the Federal Reserve System was absent, Gorton and Tallman (2016) argue that panic-driven bank runs mostly arise when depositors believe that the banking *system* is insolvent; correspondingly, such runs disappear when depositors' belief is reversed.

DOES DEPOSIT INSURANCE REDUCE THE LIKELIHOOD OF BANK RUNS?

According to the Diamond-Dybvig model in Section 2.2, bank run is completely eliminated by deposit insurance that provides full guarantee on deposits. Knowing that the promised returns for their deposits will be met, depositors will have no incentive to run on banks.

However, a serious concern in reality on deposit insurance is the potential moral hazard problem: with guarantee on deposits, banks will have the incentive to take excess risks, as potential losses will be taken over by deposit insurance scheme; therefore, banks have the incentive to take more risks and shift the risks to insured depositors, making the banking system more fragile. As a result, deposit insurance may deter depositors' incentive to run on banks, but it may make banks riskier and bank failure more likely.

Evidence shows that deposit insurance does reduce the incentive for insured depositors to run on banks. For example, in an event study, tracking the deposit outflows of a victim bank during the panic-driven bank runs in Gujarat, India, Iyer and Puri (2012) find that a depositor is less likely to run, if her balance is below the threshold for full insurance coverage; while a depositor is more likely to run not only if her balance exceeds the threshold, but also if her balance is not much below the threshold.

In contrast, more and more country-level evidence seems to show that deposit insurance may have the unintended consequence of encouraging banks' excess risk-taking, increasing the likelihood of bank failure. Using a dataset that covers 61 countries over 1980–1997—among which explicit deposit insurance scheme was only available in less than 20% of the countries in 1980, but the ratio increased to more than 50% in 1997— Demirgüç-Kunt and Detragiache (2002) test whether having a deposit insurance scheme in place reduces the likelihood of systemic banking crisis in a country, using a multivariate logit model. Besides using a dummy variable to indicate the availability of deposit insurance scheme, they also include important features in deposit insurance, such as coverage (limit in total coverage, coverage for foreign currency deposits, interbank deposits), designs (implicit or explicit insurance, compulsory or voluntary, etc.), and operators (public scheme or private scheme, etc.), with controlling for country-level characteristics. They find that explicit deposit insurance tends to increase the likelihood of systemic banking crisis, and the effect is stronger for countries with deregulation in banking and weak institutional environment where accumulating banking risks arising from the moral hazard problem are less likely to be contained. The negative effect of deposit insurance on bank stability is increasing in the coverage of insured deposits, or, the risk-shifting incentive of banks. Overall, Demirgüç-Kunt et al. (2008b) argue that deposit insurance alone is insufficient to guarantee stability of the banking system; other stability policies, such as strict regulation on capital adequacy, are indispensable complements.

2.6 EXERCISES

1. Show that for the social planner's problem that is defined as (2.1) with budget constraints (2.2) and (2.3), the optimal solution (c_1^*, c_2^*) fulfills $1 < c_1^* < c_2^* < R$.

2. **Risk sharing and financial intermediation**
   Consider a one-good, three-date economy: there are infinitely many *ex ante* identical consumers, each endowed with one unit of resource at $t = 0$. Consumption takes place either at $t = 1$ or $t = 2$, while the timing preference only gets revealed at $t = 1$. With probability π a consumer is an impatient one (type 1 consumer), who only values consumption at $t = 1$, while with probability $1 - \pi$ a consumer (type 2 consumer) is a patient one, who only values consumption at $t = 2$. A consumer's type is private information.

   Let c_i denote the consumption of a type $i = 1, 2$ consumer, and *ex post*, the utility from consumption is $u(c_i) = \frac{1}{1-\gamma} c_i^{1-\gamma}$ with $\gamma > 1$.

   The economy has two technologies of transferring resources between periods: storage technology with gross return equal to 1, and a long-term investment technology with a constant gross return $R > 1$ at $t = 2$ for every per unit invested at $t = 0$. If necessary, an ongoing long-term project can be liquidated, or, stopped prematurely at $t = 1$, with a return $0 < \delta < 1$.

   (a) Specify the social planner's problem, who wants to maximize a consumer's expected utility at $t = 0$ by allocating her endowments between two technologies.

       i. Compute the optimal allocation, and consumption for each type's consumer—denote the solution as (c_1^*, c_2^*). Show that $1 < c_1^* < c_2^* < R$;

       ii. Why aren't consumption levels for two types of consumers identical? Will there be liquidation at $t = 1$?

iii. What will happen to the consumers' optimal consumption when $\gamma \to +\infty$?
iv. If the utility function takes the form $u(c_i) = \sqrt{c_i}$, redo exercise (a) i. Do you still see $1 < c_1^* < c_2^* < R$? Why or why not?

(b) Suppose that the economy is in autarky such that every consumer has to allocate her endowments between two technologies by herself at $t = 0$. Show that the consumer's *ex post* consumption is inferior to the solution in (a) i.

(c) Suppose there is a bond market available at $t = 1$. At $t = 1$ competitive bond issuers purchase illiquid assets from impatient consumers, issue bonds against these illiquid assets, and sell bonds to the patient consumers (who can pay with the proceeds from their liquid assets). Each unit of bond bought at $t = 1$ will deliver one unit of consumption good to the bond holder at $t = 2$.

i. Compute the equilibrium bond price;
ii. Show that the consumer's *ex post* consumption is inferior to the solution in (a) i.

(d) Suppose there is a competitive banking sector in the economy, in which banks take consumers' endowments as deposits at $t = 0$ and allocate between the two technologies. Consumers withdraw c_i at $t = i$ according to their type i.

i. Show that banks can replicate the optimal solution achieved in (a) i.
ii. Compared with the result in (b), how can banks improve social welfare in the economy?

3 **Complete market and constrained efficiency, based on Allen and Gale (2007)**

The reason why a market for exchange in $t = 1$, as described in Section 2.2.3 Exchange Market, where patient and impatient consumers can exchange their assets does not achieve constrained efficient allocation is that the market is still incomplete, as there is no market in $t = 0$ where consumers can trade claims on their consumption in $t=1$ contingent on their types. Now we introduce such market in $t=0$, where a consumer can purchase t_1 consumption at a price q_1 if she is impatient and q_2 if she is patient, and the price of consumption in $t=1$ is normalized to be 1. There is still a market for goods in $t=1$, where the $t=2$ consumption can be purchased at a price s. Except these two markets, we follow the same setups as in Section 2.2.3 Exchange Market.

(a) Specify the budget constraint for a consumer in $t=0$;
(b) Using the budget constraint, derive the optimality condition for the consumer's choice on (c_1, c_2);
(c) The consumer can get 1 unit t_1 consumption in two ways: (i) purchase a claim of 1 unit t_1 consumption in $t=0$ at the price q_1; (ii) invest in 1 unit liquid asset in $t=0$. What condition is required for q_1, given that there is no arbitrage opportunity in equilibrium? Following the same reasoning, what condition is required for q_2 and p?
(d) Is the consumer's choice on (c_1, c_2) the same as (c_1^*, c_2^*) in Section 2.2.2? Why or why not?

4 Bank run and financial fragility

Consider the equilibrium with intermediation, as in Exercise 2 (d) in which banks offer consumers the deposit contracts (c_1^*, c_2^*) at $t=0$.

(a) Explain why there exist two (Nash) equilibria which are consistent with rational behavior for all agents: one in which only the early consumers withdraw at $t=1$, and another one—a sunspot equilibrium—in which everyone withdraws at $t=1$, no matter what type he or she is. What is the individual consumption level in the latter equilibrium? Does the latter equilibrium depend on late consumers' belief? Does the existence of multiple equilibria depend on the value of δ?
(b) Propose a mechanism that can eliminate the bank run equilibrium. Explain how it works.
(c) During the 2007–2009 crisis, several central banks purchased huge volume of securities, hoping to prevent price of illiquid

assets from falling too much. Explain why such unconventional policy helps eliminate panics in the banking sector.

Now, in the economy with financial intermediation (banks), as is specified in Exercise 2 (d), suppose that in $t=0$ it is a public knowledge that a bank run happens in $t=1$ with probability σ, $0<\sigma<1$. Assume that banks are perfectly competitive so that only those whose deposit contracts maximize consumers' expected utility will get deposits. Show that a bank's investment in liquid assets in $t=0$ is higher than that in Exercise 2 (d), and it increases with σ. Interpret.

5 **Pandemic and bank run**

Following Exercise 4: now we exclude the possibility of the sunspot bank run equilibrium that is characterized in Exercise 4 (a) and assume that patient consumers only withdraw at $t=1$ if their expected return at $t=2$ is too low.

Suppose, at the beginning of $t=1$, an unexpected pandemic hits the economy and many consumers—including some of the patient consumers—are infected and hospitalized so that they need to consume in $t=1$. It is known to the public that a population f (with $0<f<1-p$) of patient consumers are infected. Show that there will only be a bank run, that all consumers demand repayments at $t=1$, if f is above a certain threshold. Compute the threshold.

6 **Nominal deposits that eliminate bank runs, based on Skeie (2008)**

Consider the equilibrium with intermediation, as described in Exercise 2 (d). Now we make several modifications in the setups:

- In the beginning of $t=0$, a central bank creates fiat money and buys all endowments from the consumers at a price of 1. The consumers then deposit the money in banks in exchange for a *nominal* deposit contract (c_1^*, c_2^*) that promises that an impatient consumer can withdraw c_1^* amount of money in

$t=1$ and a patient consumer can withdraw c_2^* amount of money in $t=2$;
- Instead of conducting investment themselves, banks then lend all the collected deposits to entrepreneurs who have access to the two technologies. The *nominal* loan contract between banks and entrepreneurs requires that entrepreneurs have to allocate $\alpha^* = \pi c_1^*$ resources in the storage technology and $1-\alpha^*$ resources in the long-term investment technology, and the nominal gross loan rate is c_1^*/c_2^* if a loan is repaid in $t=1/t=2$. In $t=1$, banks can ask entrepreneurs to liquidate some of the long-term investments with a return $0 < \delta < 1$;
- Using the loans, entrepreneurs exchange money for endowments from the central bank. Afterwards the central bank extinguishes the money, and does not hold any goods any more. The central bank plays no role after $t=0$;
- In $t=1$, impatient consumers withdraw. To meet the cash demand of impatient consumers, banks recall some of the loans from the entrepreneurs and issue the equal amount of credit to impatient consumers. Impatient consumers use the credit to buy the products from the entrepreneurs, and entrepreneurs use the proceeds to repay the recalled loans;
- In $t=2$, patient consumers withdraw. To meet the cash demand of patient consumers, banks ask the entrepreneurs to repay the rest of the loans and issue the equal amount of credit to patient consumers. Patient consumers use the credit to buy the products from the entrepreneurs, and entrepreneurs use the proceeds to repay the remaining loans;
- In the goods market between consumers and entrepreneurs in $t=1/t=2$, price of the goods is determined by the *cash-in-the-market* principle, or, the ratio of total cash (consumer credit) to total output of goods in that period;
- In $t=0$, banks compete to maximize consumers' expected utility, and consumers gain utility from consuming *real* goods.

(a) Show that in equilibrium there is no liquidation of long-term investments.
(b) Show that the banks can replicate the optimal solution of the social planner's problem.
(c) Show that bank run that is characterized in Exercise 4 is no longer an equilibrium.

7 **Optimal risk-sharing under stochastic long-run return, based on Allen and Gale (1998)**

Continue with the social planner's problem in the Allen-Gale model, Section 2.3. Given the planner's optimal choice on c_1/c_2 after R is revealed $t=1$, solve problem (2.11) for the planner's optimal choice of α with

- Logarithm-form utility function, i.e., $u(\cdot) = \ln(\cdot)$;
- Distribution of R following

$$f(R) = \begin{cases} \dfrac{1}{3} & \text{for } 0 \leq R \leq 3, \\ 0 & \text{otherwise.} \end{cases}$$

Compute $\hat{R}$ under the optimal α, and delineate c_1 and c_2 as functions of R in a $c - R$ space.

NOTE

1 However, a constrained efficient solution can be achieved, if the market is made to be more *complete*, see Exercise 3.

CHAPTER 3

Information frictions in banking

3.1 INTRODUCTION

Both the economics of banking and banking in practice are heavily shaped by various information frictions. Participants in banking are not able to observe many things of interest, for example, depositors cannot observe the quality of their banks' assets, so that they cannot tell whether the banks will default on them or not; banks cannot perfectly observe what borrowers do with their loans so that they cannot tell whether these loans will be fully repaid; when one bank lends to another bank, the lender bank cannot precisely tell the borrow bank's risk... such *information asymmetry* often leads to *credit risks* that borrowers may default on lenders, and controlling credit risks is one of the most important tasks for banks' risk management.

In economics, when one agent (*agent*) makes decisions on behalf of, or affecting, another agent (*principal*), the conflict of interest between them leads to *principal-agent problem*. When information is asymmetric between principal and agent, several types of principal-agent problems may emerge. One is *adverse selection* problem, that emerges when an agent's own type is unknown to the principal. For example, when multiple banks sell assets in the market, some assets are good and worth more, but some are bad ("lemons", as is called by Akerlof (1970) and worth less, with the true types of assets on sale being unknown to buyers. Given that lemon sellers are willing to accept lower prices, competition among asset sellers drives down market price and drives good sellers out of market; such adverse selection leaves asset markets full of lemon sellers, and no buyer is willing to pay high prices in the market.

Another one is a *moral hazard* problem, that emerges when an agent's own action is not observed by the principle. For example, after a borrower is granted a loan from a bank, if the borrower's action is not observable to the bank, she will have the incentive to act for her own interest at the cost of the bank, say, pocketing the money and shirking in her project; such a moral hazard problem either leaves the bank a poor return on the loan, or forces the bank to "bribe" the borrower to act in the bank's interest.

As information frictions and associated principal-agent problems create credit risks and prevent financial resources from being allocated to people who make better use of them, a key role of banks in a financial system is exploring information from borrowers and lenders, and banks are expert in information production. For example, banks conduct monitoring on borrowers' projects to make sure that borrowers deliver desired returns on loans; banks screen through borrowers' loan applications to make sure that they do not lend to anyone with low credit quality. Banks' investments in information discovery and information production thus help improve the efficiency in allocating financial resources and improve social welfare.

However, banks cannot perfectly overcome all information frictions. Remaining financial frictions prevent banks from properly pricing risks, which further leads to distortions in banking outcomes, such as banks' risk management and lending supply. Furthermore, banks themselves are also subject to those principal-agent problems arising from information frictions; this may prevent banks from properly conducting intermediation services, or encourage banks to misbehave for their own benefit but at the cost of customers and other financial institutions. In this sense, banks may also contribute to systemic instabilities and risks under information frictions.

As information frictions may affect all participants and outcomes in banking activities, in this chapter, we will by no means provide a complete overview on information frictions in banking. Instead, we will examine a few scenarios in which banks may help alleviate information frictions or become subject to distortions induced by information frictions, and show how various information frictions can be integrated in banking analyses. These analytical frameworks will help us better understand the role of information frictions, when related issues arise in other chapters later in this book.

We will start with a simple moral hazard scenario in Section 3.2, in which borrowers may misreport their income and default on lenders, if their income is not observable to lenders. Lenders may overcome such problem by investing in monitoring borrowers' income, but this leads to a substantial social cost, as all individual lenders must pay for monitoring. Banking has the potential to improve monitoring efficiency and reduce the social cost, as the standard demand deposit contract provided by banks makes banks monitor on behalf of lenders; as a result, banks can delegate for lenders to monitor borrowers, instead of letting all individual lenders monitor borrowers. Banking thus increases monitoring efficiency and improves social welfare.

Section 3.3 focuses on another source of moral hazard, that borrowers' actions are not observed by lenders so that they have the incentive to act for their private benefit at the cost of lenders. In order to induce borrowers to act as desired, lenders have to give away some rent to borrowers, and this restricts lenders' lending capacity so that only borrowers with enough internal funding and relying less on external funding are able to borrow directly from lenders. Banks, as experts of monitoring and intermediaries between lenders and borrowers, can discipline borrowers and help extend funding to those borrowers with less internal funding, improving social welfare. However, banks themselves are subject to moral hazard problems, too, as they may not properly monitor on behalf of lenders; as a result, lenders have to give away rent to banks in exchange for proper monitoring. This sets a limit on banks' funding from lenders, hence lending to borrowers, and requires banks to hold internal funding, or, capital.

Section 3.4 and Section 3.5 focus on the consequences when borrowers' types are not observable to banks. Without being able to price individual borrowers' risk profiles in loan rates, banks have to offer a uniform lending rate to all borrowers. In Section 3.4, all borrowers are identical in expected return of their projects, while some are more likely to fail and default on their loans. Under such a setting, when banks set a higher loan rate, safe, prudent borrowers will be driven out of the credit market as they cannot afford the higher loan rate, such adverse selection thus leaves remaining potential borrowers on average riskier. For this reason, banks may keep the loan rate low to reduce potential borrowers' average default risk, with limited loan supply that is rationed among borrowers to reduce loan defaults. Adverse selection results in credit rationing and inefficiently low lending supply.

In contrast, in Section 3.5, borrowers' types differ from each other in expected return of their projects. Under such setting, when banks set a higher loan rate, "lemon" borrowers are driven out of market, such positive selection thus increases average credit quality of the remaining borrowers. For this reason, banks will lend at market clearing loan rate without credit rationing. However, market competition forces banks to lend too much and support some projects that are not socially desirable. Positive selection results in inefficient, excess bank lending.

3.2 BANK AS DELEGATED MONITOR

We start this section with a very simple question: in a relationship between a lender and a borrower, what will happen if the realized return of the borrower's project is her private information and not observable to the lender?

The answer is very simple, too: the borrower will have the incentive to under-report and default on the lender. Knowing this, the lender will never lend to the borrower.

One way to overcome such problem and make lending feasible is that the lender can monitor the borrower and get to know the true return at a cost, in this way, the lender can ensure herself to be repaid whenever the true return is high enough. However, when a big project has to be financed by a large number of lenders, letting all individual lenders monitor is socially costly.

Diamond (1984) demonstrates that having banks as financial intermediaries between lenders and borrowers can reduce the social cost of monitoring and improve welfare. Banks offer demand deposit contracts to lenders, and this ensures that banks monitor the borrowers in lenders' interest. Banks as delegated monitors thus reduce the social cost of debt enforcement. In this section, we examine such mechanism using a model based on Diamond (1984).

3.2.1 ASYMMETRIC INFORMATION AND MONITORING

Consider an economy in which there are n borrowers. Each borrower needs one unit of fund to start a project. All borrowers' projects are the same, such that for each project i, with one unit input, it generates a return of R_i

$$R_i = \begin{cases} R & \text{with probability } p, \\ 0 & \text{otherwise,} \end{cases}$$

with $R > 0$. The return of each borrower's project is independent and identically distributed (i.i.d.). Assume that $pR > 1$ so that all projects are socially desirable.

Assume that borrowers do not have initial wealth so that they need to borrow from lenders in order to start projects. As our bench mark, or the first-best scenario, if each project's realized return is observable, perfect competition will require all borrowers to promise a gross return of R to lenders. Lenders will collect R from every project that is successful, and lenders' expected return is pR. Therefore, in the first-best solution, all borrowers are supported, and lenders' total expected return is

$$n(pR-1). \tag{3.1}$$

However, things will change, if the true realized return of every borrower's project is the borrower's private information and not observable to others. In this case, one borrower always has the incentive to engage in *moral hazard*: no matter what the true realized return of her project is, the borrower will always report a return of 0 and repay 0 to her lender. As a lender, knowing that she will be always reported and repaid with 0 return, she will refuse to lend in the first place. As a result, the information friction makes the market break down and no borrower is supported.

CHAPTER THREE: INFORMATION FRICTIONS IN BANKING

To fix the market breakdown problem, suppose that a monitoring technology enables lenders to see borrowers' true realized returns, after paying a fixed monitoring cost of C, $C > 0$. The monitoring technology allows lenders to claim a positive repayment, if the realized return of a project is R. Assume that $pR > 1 + C$, so that it is still profitable for lenders to lend to borrowers, even after paying the monitoring cost. Therefore, if every lender has one unit to lend, under the monitoring technology, all borrowers will be supported, and lenders' total expected return is

$$n(pR - 1 - C), \qquad (3.2)$$

which is lower than in the first-best solution, (3.1). Information friction incurs a social cost of nC.

3.2.2 COSTLY MONITORING UNDER DIRECT LENDING

Now, suppose that lenders are small, in that each of them only has $\frac{1}{m}$ to lend; therefore, each borrower needs to borrow from m lenders to start her project, as Figure 3.1 shows. Such setup captures a more realistic scenario that large projects are often funded by numerous small investors.

Under asymmetric information that lenders cannot observe the true return of a project, the same moral hazard problem in Section 3.2.1 still prevails. Lenders can overcome the moral hazard problem by using the monitoring technology, however, given that lenders are atomistic and unorganized, each of them has to incur the monitoring cost to avoid receiving misreport from borrowers. The market outcome of direct

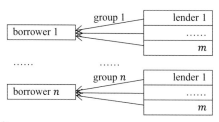

Figure 3.1 Direct lending

lending from lenders to borrowers depends on how costly the monitoring technology is:

- If monitoring technology is too costly that

$$C > \frac{pR-1}{m},$$

or monitoring cost exceeds a project's net return for each lender, lenders will not invest in monitoring, and will not lend. No borrower will be supported;

- If monitoring technology is not too costly that

$$C \leq \frac{pR-1}{m},$$

each lender will invest in monitoring and lend so that all borrowers will be supported. Assume that perfect competition among borrowers forces them to give all rents to lenders, lenders' total expected return is then

$$n(pR-1-mC), \qquad (3.3)$$

which is lower than in the first-best solution, (3.1). Information friction incurs a social cost of mnC, or mC per borrower.

3.2.3 BANK AND DELEGATED MONITORING

Will having a bank as financial intermediary help reduce the social cost of information friction? Suppose a bank is introduced into the economy, as Figure 3.2 shows: the bank collects funds, i.e., deposits, from lenders and lends to the borrowers.

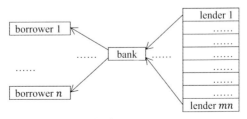

Figure 3.2 *Delegated monitoring with bank*

Under asymmetric information that the bank cannot observe the true return of a project, moral hazard problem still prevails so that the bank has to monitor borrowers and incurs a total monitoring cost of nC. However, the same moral hazard problem also exists between the bank and the lenders: after collecting returns from its loans to borrowers, the bank has the incentive to misreport, too, claiming the return from every project is zero and repaying nothing to lenders. By the same argument as before, in order to avoid the bank's misreport, each lender has to incur a monitoring cost of C to monitor the bank, if they want to deposit in the bank. Total monitoring cost in the economy is thus

$$nC + mnC, \qquad (3.4)$$

or $C + mC$ per borrower, which is even higher than that under direct lending, in which total social cost of monitoring is mnC, as (3.3) shows.

However, the fixed demand deposit contract which is usually provided by banks as is argued in Chapter 2, helps reduce monitoring cost. Under demand deposit contract, the bank collects deposits from lenders by offering them a deposit contract that promises a fixed deposit rate r_D. After the bank collects returns from its loans, if the bank's reported returns from all projects, $(\tilde{R}_1, \ldots, \tilde{R}_n)$ are not high enough to fulfill its deposit contracts, the lenders are entitled to liquidate the bank. An auditor from the banking supervisory authority will then audit the bank to find the bank's true collected return from its n borrowers, i.e., the bank's liquidation value, and lenders will share the bank's liquidation value less the auditing cost—denoted by $c(n)$, leaving the bank with nothing. Under such threat of forced liquidation, the bank will be honest on reporting, i.e., bank's reported returns should be the same as the true returns, $(\tilde{R}_1, \ldots, \tilde{R}_n) = (R_1, \ldots, R_n)$, in equilibrium. As a result, the demand deposit contract implies that individual lenders do not need to monitor the bank, and the bank is thus a *delegated monitor* for all lenders. Total social cost (from monitoring and auditing) incurred by information friction in this economy is thus

$$nC + c(n), \qquad (3.5)$$

or $C + \dfrac{c(n)}{n}$ per borrower.

Assume that if auditing occurs, auditor incurs a fixed cost of κ to figure out the true return from a project. Given that auditing cost only occurs if the bank's reported returns from all projects are not high enough to fulfill its deposit contracts, auditing cost $c(n)$ can be written as

$$\begin{aligned} c(n) &= n\kappa \mathrm{Prob}\left(\sum_{i=1}^{n} R_i < (1+r_D)n\right) \\ &= n\kappa \mathrm{Prob}\left(\frac{1}{n}\sum_{i=1}^{n} R_i < 1+r_D\right) \end{aligned} \qquad (3.6)$$

using the fact that the bank reports true returns $(R_1,\ldots,R_n)$.

On the other hand, to induce lenders to deposit in the bank, participation constraint for lenders must hold, that they must break even with their deposits. Given the demand deposit contract with the bank, lenders either share liquidation value of the bank, or receive a gross return of $1+r_D$ on their deposits, lenders' participation constraint implies

$$E\left[\min\left\{\frac{1}{n}\sum_{i=1}^{n} R_i, 1+r_D\right\}\right] \geq 1. \qquad (3.7)$$

And with a profit maximizing bank, condition (3.7) should hold with equality.

When n is large, $n \to +\infty$, by the Law of Large Numbers,

$$\lim_{n \to +\infty} \frac{1}{n}\sum_{i=1}^{n} R_i = pR.$$

As it is assumed that $pR > 1+C > 1$, condition (3.7) implies that in equilibrium, $r_D = 0$. Therefore, by equation (3.6), auditing cost per borrower, when $n \to +\infty$, becomes

$$\begin{aligned} \lim_{n \to +\infty} \frac{c(n)}{n} &= \kappa \mathrm{Prob}\left(\frac{1}{n}\sum_{i=1}^{n} R_i \leq 1\right) \\ &= \kappa \mathrm{Prob}(pR < 1) \\ &= 0 \end{aligned} \qquad (3.8)$$

given that that $pR>1+C>1$. That is, when the number of borrowers is infinitely large, the bank's credit risk is fully diversified and the probability of liquidation falls to 0. Interestingly, the bank will still be honest with reporting, even if liquidation probability is 0: should the bank misreport high return as low, liquidation that follows would leave it with nothing. Demand deposit contract is thus a credible threat that disciplines the bank's behavior.

Given the result in (3.8), from (3.5), information friction induced social cost (from monitoring and auditing) per borrower is thus C when the number of borrowers is large, which is strictly lower than the social cost under direct lending (when it is feasible) as in (3.3), whenever $m>1$.

Overall, when the borrower's return is private information, the moral hazard problem induces misreporting so that lending is only feasible if the costly monitoring technology is used. A bank that provides demand deposit contract and serves as a delegated monitor reduces social cost incurred by information friction, thus improves social welfare.

3.2.4 SUMMARY

The Diamond model provides important insights on how a bank reduces the enforcement cost of debt and improves social welfare, as a delegated monitor for lenders. When projects' payoff is private information, borrowers engage in moral hazard and misreport their cash flow, causing the lending market to break down. In order to make lending feasible, individual lenders have to invest in costly monitoring technology as an enforcement device for debt. A bank, collecting funds from a large number of lenders and lending to borrowers, is able to improve social welfare by reducing debt enforcement cost for two reasons: first, demand deposit contract provided by the bank implies that a bank is liquidated if the deposit contract is not fulfilled by its reported asset return, and lenders to the bank share the liquidation value after auditing, leaving nothing for the bank. Demand deposit contract is thus a credible threat to the bank, a discipline device that forces the bank to be honest with reporting its asset return to lenders; as a result, lenders do not need to invest in costly monitoring on the bank any more, reducing debt enforcement cost. Furthermore, with a sufficiently large number of borrowers to serve, the bank's liquidation probability is low so that per-borrower auditing cost is almost zero. Second, with the bank disciplined by a demand deposit contract, the debt enforcement cost only incurs when the bank delegates for lenders to monitor the borrowers; this reduces total monitoring cost in the economy, compared with direct lending from lenders to borrowers in which all individual lenders have to pay for costly monitoring. Banking, as a mechanism of delegated monitoring, thus increases efficiency in debt enforcement and improves social welfare.

3.3 MONITORING AND CAPITAL

The Diamond model demonstrates that bank lending is superior to direct lending, in that banks as delegated monitors are more efficient in enforcing debt contracts. However, in reality, bank lending co-exists with, rather than replaces, direct lending; for example, although many firms borrow from banks, some firms do raise funding from the bond market or stock market. Therefore, direct lending may be appealing for reasons that are not captured by the Diamond model.

Instead of assuming that borrowers do not have their own wealth as in the Diamond model, Holmström and Tirole (1997) show that, under asymmetric information, borrowers' own wealth, or, capitalization, matters for the sources of their funding. This is because borrowers' choices on their projects are their private information and unobservable to lenders: the moral hazard problem arises such that a borrower prefers choosing a bad project that benefits herself at the cost of lenders to a good project that benefits lenders. In order to induce borrowers to choose the good project, lenders have to give up some rent to borrowers, which limits the amount of funds that lenders are willing to provide. For this reason, borrowers that are well capitalized and require less external funding are able to directly borrow from lenders.

Banks, which are expert at monitoring and serve as intermediaries between lenders and borrowers, can extend lending to less capitalized borrowers who cannot borrow directly from lenders. However, the same moral hazard problem prevails in bank lending, too, as banks may not properly monitor for the interest of lenders. This limits banks' funding/lending capacity and requires banks to hold capital, too. In this section, we present such a mechanism through a model based on Holmström and Tirole (1997).

3.3.1 MODEL SETUP

Consider an economy in which a continuum of entrepreneurs has exclusive access to two types of projects, $\{G, B\}$, each project requires I initial investment to start with and yields a verifiable net return y if it is successful, or 0 otherwise.

- A good project G has a probability of success $0 < p_G < 1$;
- A bad project B has a probability of success p_B with $p_B < p_G$. However, an entrepreneur receives B private benefit if she operates a bad project.

Figure 3.3 summarizes the payoff structure of the two types of projects.

Each of the entrepreneurs owns wealth A which is publicly observable. The distribution of A follows a probability density function $f(A)$. Entrepreneurs' choices on projects are private information and not observable.

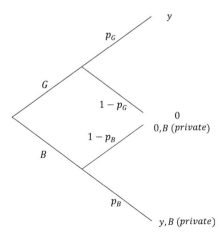

Figure 3.3 *Projects' payoff structure*

There are also a continuum of consumers in the economy who are endowed with cash and have the opportunity to invest in risk-free assets that yield a risk-free net return R. Assume that

$$p_G y > RI > p_B y + B,$$

that is, good projects increase social welfare, but bad projects do not. Assume that $A < I$ for all entrepreneurs, so that they compete for funding provided by consumers.

3.3.2 DIRECT LENDING

First of all, we let consumers and entrepreneurs meet in a matching market and allow consumers to lend directly. If the economy is frictionless without information asymmetries, consumers would only lend to entrepreneurs if they choose good projects, and capture all the rents, i.e., consumers capture the projects' entire return in the first-best solution, $r^{C,FB} = y$, whenever the projects are successful. In addition, all entrepreneurs should be supported with funding, given that good projects are socially desirable.

However, once entrepreneurs' choices on projects are not observable to consumers, there is a moral hazard that entrepreneurs tend to choose the bad projects for their private benefit, at the cost of consumers. Therefore, in order to induce entrepreneurs to choose good projects, the consumers' share r_D^C in the projects' shall not be too high so that entrepreneurs self-select the good projects that give them higher profit than the bad projects, i.e.

$$p_G \left(y - r_D^C \right) \geq p_B \left(y - r_D^C \right) + B \qquad (3.9)$$

which implies that

$$r_D^C \leq y - \frac{B}{p_G - p_B} = y - \frac{B}{\Delta p} < r_D^{C,FB}, \qquad (3.10)$$

in which $\Delta p \equiv p_G - p_B$. Inequality (3.9) is the incentive compatibility (IC) constraint that consumers are able to induce entrepreneurs to choose the desirable projects under asymmetric information. The highest share r_D^C that consumers can claim from the projects' return, as characterized by (3.10), is lower than the first-best solution by $\frac{B}{\Delta p}$: this is exactly the *information rent* that consumers need to pay for the desired choice made by the entrepreneurs.

Consumers' claim r_D^C shall also ensure that consumers are willing to participate, i.e., they prefer lending L_D^C to entrepreneurs to investing in risk-free assets. This leads to consumers' participation constraint (PC), as in (3.11):

$$p_G r_D^C \geq R L_D^C, \text{ or, } L_D^C \leq \frac{p_G r_D^C}{R}, \qquad (3.11)$$

which also sets an upper bound for L_D^C. Combining with (IC) in (3.9) leads to

$$L_D^C \leq \frac{p_G}{R}\left(y - \frac{B}{\Delta p}\right). \qquad (3.12)$$

On the other hand, for any entrepreneur, she can only start her project if her total funding—partially from her own wealth A, partially from borrowing from consumers—exceeds I, as (3.13) states:

$$\begin{aligned} A + L_D^C &\geq I, \\ A &\geq I - \frac{p_G}{R}\left(y - \frac{B}{\Delta p}\right) \\ &= \bar{A}(R). \end{aligned} \qquad (3.13)$$

Combining with the restriction on L_D^C in (3.12), (3.13) states that only those entrepreneurs whose wealth exceeds the threshold $\bar{A}(R)$ can directly borrow from consumers and start their projects.

3.3.3 BANKING SOLUTION

Now suppose a bank is established in this economy, that can raise funding from various sources and lend to entrepreneurs. The bank issues shares L_B^B to shareholders and collects deposits L_B^C from consumers, this allows

Assets	Liabilities
Loan to entrepreneur L_B	Bank capital L_B^B
	Deposits L_B^C

Figure 3.4 A bank's balance sheet

it to issue L_B loans to entrepreneurs. In addition, to capture the reality, shareholders require a return on equity (ROE) β that is higher than the risk-free rate R. Figure 3.4 summarizes the bank's balance sheet.

Here, the bank is special that it has a *monitoring* technology: after spending a non-observable cost $C > 0$ on monitoring the entrepreneurs, entrepreneurs' private benefit falls to $b < B$ if they operate bad projects.

Now the return from the loans will be split among entrepreneurs (r_B^E), bank's shareholders (r_B^B), and consumers (r_B^C),

$$y = r_B^E + r_B^B + r_B^C.$$

Again, the moral hazard problem of the entrepreneurs implies that, in order to induce them to choose the good projects, entrepreneurs shall keep a share r_B^E that fulfills their incentive compatibility constraint, (IC-E) as specified in (3.14)

$$p_G r_B^E \geq p_B r_B^E + b, \text{ i.e., } r_B^B + r_B^C \leq y - \frac{b}{\Delta p} \quad \text{(IC-E)} \qquad (3.14)$$

that is, under the bank's monitoring, r_B^E shall make entrepreneurs better off for choosing good projects.

However, given that the bank's monitoring cost C is non-observable, the bank is subject to a moral hazard problem, too: it can shirk in monitoring and save the monitoring cost, at the cost of consumers. Therefore, to induce the bank to properly monitor, bank's share r_B^B shall fulfill its incentive compatibility constraint, (IC-B), and make the bank better off on monitoring, as (3.15) states:

$$p_G r_B^B - C \geq p_B r_B^B \text{ i.e., } r_B^B \geq \frac{C}{\Delta p}. \quad \text{(IC-B)} \qquad (3.15)$$

Furthermore, the bank shareholders' participation constraint (PC-B), as in (3.16), states that their expected return cannot be lower than their required ROE, i.e.

$$p_G r_B^B \geq \beta L_B^B \text{ i.e., } L_B^B(\beta) \leq \frac{p_G r_B^B}{\beta} = \frac{p_G C}{\beta \Delta p} \quad \text{(PC-B)} \qquad (3.16)$$

which defines the upper bound for the shareholders' total investments in the bank, L_B^B. Similarly, consumers' participation constraint (PC-C), as in (3.17), states that their expected return from bank deposits L_B^C cannot be lower than investing in risk-free assets,

$$p_G r_B^C \geq R L_B^C \text{ i.e., } L_B^C \leq \frac{p_G r_B^C}{R} \quad \text{(PC-C)} \qquad (3.17)$$

which defines the upper bound for the consumers' total deposits in the bank, L_B^C. Combining (3.14) and (3.15) yields

$$L_B^C \leq \frac{p_G}{R}\left(y - \frac{b+C}{\Delta p}\right) \qquad (3.18)$$

Given the upper bounds L_B^B defined by (3.16) and L_B^C defined by (3.18), for any entrepreneur, she can only start her project if her total funding—partially from her own wealth A, partially from borrowing from consumers and bank shareholders—exceeds I, as (3.19) states:

$$\begin{aligned} A + L_B^C + L_B^B &\geq I, \\ A &\geq I - \frac{p_G C}{\beta \Delta p} - \frac{p_G}{R}\left(y - \frac{b+C}{\Delta p}\right) \\ &= \underline{A}(\beta, R), \end{aligned} \qquad (3.19)$$

that is, those entrepreneurs whose wealth exceeds the threshold $\underline{A}(\beta, R)$ can raise funding from the bank and start their projects. Compared with $\overline{A}(R)$ that is defined by (3.13), it is easy to see that $\underline{A}(\beta, R) < \overline{A}(R)$, as long as C is small enough.

The two thresholds, $\overline{A}(R)$ and $\underline{A}(\beta, R)$, separate the entrepreneurs into three groups over the distribution in their wealth, $f(A)$, as Figure 3.5 shows. The areas below $f(A)$ thus characterize the population of these

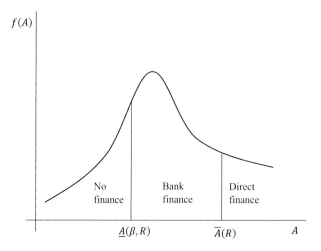

Figure 3.5 *Entrepreneurs' access to funding*

three groups. Because of entrepreneurs' moral hazard, the consumers can only directly lend to entrepreneurs who have sufficient stakes in the projects, i.e., those with higher own wealth A above $\overline{A}(R)$ can access to direct finance. Using its expertise in monitoring, a bank can extend lending to less well capitalized entrepreneurs, those with own wealth A between $\overline{A}(R)$ and $\underline{A}(\beta, R)$, improving social welfare. However, the bank itself is subject to moral hazard, too; this requires the bank to have its own stake in monitoring, and limits the total feasible funding in the banking solution. As a result, the least well capitalized entrepreneurs with own wealth A below $\underline{A}(\beta, R)$ will never get funding—a loss in social welfare due to asymmetric information, compared with the first-best solution.

Overall, having banks as experts of monitoring in the economy improves social welfare by extending more credits to entrepreneurs who cannot borrow directly from consumers; however, the least well capitalized entrepreneurs will never be supported, even with bank lending. This reflects the social welfare loss that is incurred by information friction.

3.3.4 SUMMARY

The Holmström-Tirole model illustrates the role of capital funding when a moral hazard problem arises from borrowers' unobservable choices on their projects, and how banks as experts on monitoring are able to extend lending to less capitalized borrowers, improving social welfare.

One appealing feature in Holmström-Tirole model is the co-existence of direct lending and bank lending. In the presence of moral hazard problems, lenders have to give away some rents to borrowers, in order to induce borrowers to act in lenders' interest. This sets a limit on how much lenders are willing to lend; therefore, well capitalized borrowers that do not need too much external funding can borrow directly from lenders. Borrowers with intermediate capitalization can borrow from banks, given that banks have the expertise of monitoring so that they can ensure borrowers to act in lenders' interest. However, banks themselves are subject to moral hazard problems, too, so that lenders must give away some rents to banks and induce banks to act in their interest. This also sets a limit on the capacity of banks' funding from lenders—hence lending to borrowers, and requires banks to hold capital. Such a "double-decker" moral hazard problem motivates the role of capital in both firms and banks, and predicts that better capitalized firms choose to borrow directly from the market, while less capitalized firms may borrow from banks.

Another appealing feature in the Holmström-Tirole model is that it captures the linkages between banking and macroeconomy. Note that the thresholds, $\overline{A}(R)$ as in (3.13) and $\underline{A}(\beta, R)$ as in (3.19) are functions of R and y: therefore, $\overline{A}(R)$ and $\underline{A}(\beta, R)$ will shift if monetary policy affects the risk-free rate R or if business cycles affect asset return y, and total credit supply to the real economy—the sum of direct finance and bank finance, as Figure 3.5 shows—will be affected as well. Such change in total credit supply may further affect macroeconomy. Such a mechanism is analyzed in Exercise 1, and further discussions on banking-macro linkages will be presented in Chapter 8.

3.4 CREDIT RATIONING

Information friction does not only affect eligibility of borrowers, as is shown in the Holmström-Tirole model, but also affects banks' lending decisions. People have observed since a long time ago that banks' lending supply to borrowers is not easily explained by competitive market: *credit rationing* persists that there are always some borrowers whose credit demand is not satisfied, even though they are willing to pay banks higher loan rates, as is observed by Keynes (1930):

> The relaxation or contraction of credit by the Banking System does not operate merely through a change in the rate charged to borrowers; it also functions through a change in the abundance of credit. If the supply of credit were distributed in an absolutely free competitive market, these two conditions, quantity and price, would be uniquely correlated with one another and we should not need to consider them separately. But in practice, the conditions of a free competitive market for bank-loans are imperfectly fulfilled. There is an habitual system of rationing in the attitude of banks to borrowers—the amount lent to any individual being governed not solely by the security and rate of interest offered, but also by reference to the borrower's purposes and his standing with the bank as a valuable or influential client. Thus, there is normally a fringe of unsatisfied borrowers who are not considered to have the first claims on a bank's favors, but to whom the bank would be quite ready to lend if it were to find itself in a position to lend more. The existence of this unsatisfied fringe allows the Banking System a means of influencing the rate of investment supplementary to the mere changes in the short-term rate of interest.

Of course, in reality, credit rationing may arise *temporarily*: for example, when a bank's lending capacity is constrained by its balance sheet liquidity, it may turn down some borrowers and ration its credit supply. However, such friction shall be easily eliminated by markets, as the bank can raise more liquidity from interbank market and expand lending, or those turned-down borrowers can switch to other banks and obtain funding; therefore, it is particularly puzzling when credit rationing is a persistent phenomenon: if there is an excess demand from borrowers, why does loan rate not increase to clear the market, as standard economic theory predicts?

Stiglitz and Weiss (1981) propose that credit rationing can persist in the credit market, as a result of information friction. The reason is that borrowers are of different types: some are prudent ones operating projects with low returns and high probability of success, while some are gamblers operating projects with high returns and low probability of success; the type of borrower is private information. Although banks make an effort to screen borrowers, they cannot perfectly tell the type of each borrower. As a result, raising loan rate leads to two diverting effects for a bank: it increases the bank's profit, but it also drives prudent borrowers out of the bank's customer pool, as these borrowers cannot afford high loan rate; such *adverse selection* makes the bank's loans more likely to fail, and decreases the bank's profit. As a result, the bank may choose a relatively low loan rate to keep sufficient prudent borrowers in its customer pool and ration lending among borrowers, instead of choosing a higher loan rate that clears the market—as too high loan rate may lead to too high concentration of gamblers in the customer pool with too high loan default rate.

In this section, we illustrate the mechanism of credit rationing, based on a model from Stiglitz and Weiss (1981).

3.4.1 MODEL SETUP

Consider an economy that is populated by many risk-neutral entrepreneurs (whose population is normalized to be 1) and many risk-neutral banks:

- Each entrepreneur has a project which needs initial investment k, but she only has her own wealth $W < k$ so that she needs to borrow $L = k - W$ to start the project. She also has an outside option to deposit her wealth in banks with safe return δ;
- All entrepreneurs' projects are identical in expected return, but different in the probability of return. For entrepreneur i's project:
    - It returns R_i if it is successful, with probability p_i that is independent and identically distributed (i.i.d.) and follows

the same probability density function (pdf) $f(p_i)$ for all entrepreneurs; otherwise it returns zero;
- The project's expected return $R_i p_i$ is identical at R_0 for all entrepreneurs;
- The likelihood of success p_i, or, the "type" of the entrepreneur, is her private information and not observable by banks.

- Banks may issue loan L to each entrepreneur who wants to start her project, without knowing the entrepreneur's type p_i. Banks compete in the deposit market, therefore, each of them wants to set a loan rate r in order to maximize the revenue from loans and the gross return to depositors. Assume that $R_i > (1+r)L$ for all entrepreneurs, i.e., an entrepreneur's loan is fully repaid when her project is successful; otherwise, nothing is paid back. Banks do not hold any equity; they raise funding entirely from depositors. Depositors' aggregate supply of deposit, call it $d(\delta)$, is a strictly increasing function of deposit rate δ.

3.4.2 CREDIT RATIONING IN MARKET EQUILIBRIUM

We start from analyzing entrepreneur's decision problem. The expected return to an individual entrepreneur i, $E[\pi_i]$, is

$$E[\pi_i] = p_i[R_i - (1+r)L] = R_0 - p_i(1+r)L, \qquad (3.20)$$
$$E[\pi_i] \geq (1+\delta)W \qquad (3.21)$$

given $R_0 = R_i p_i$, and (3.21) is the entrepreneur's participation constraint that $E[\pi_i]$ must be high enough so that the entrepreneur prefers to initiate her project instead of saving her wealth in a bank and earning a gross return $(1+\delta)W$. Combing (3.20) and (3.21), one can see that, with given loan rate r, only riskier entrepreneurs—entrepreneurs with sufficiently risky projects, i.e., entrepreneurs whose type p_i is lower than the threshold value $\bar{p}(r)$, are willing to initiate their projects

$$p_i \leq \frac{R_0 - (1+\delta)W}{(1+r)L} = \bar{p}(r), \qquad (3.22)$$

and all entrepreneurs' total demand for loans $D(r)$ is

$$D(r) = L \int_{\underline{p}(r)}^{\overline{p}(r)} f(p_i) dp_i$$

in which $\int_0^{\overline{p}(r)} f(p_i) dp_i$ characterizes the population of banks' customer pool, or, entrepreneurs who are willing to borrow from the banks.

Note that the threshold, $\overline{p}$, in (3.22) decreases with loan rate r, $\frac{d\overline{p}(r)}{dr} < 0$: when the loan rate is set to be higher, only the riskier entrepreneurs are willing to borrow from banks because only entrepreneurs with higher R_i can afford a higher loan rate. In other words, "prudent" entrepreneurs are driven out of banks' customer pool as a result of *adverse selection*. As the left part of Figure 3.6 shows, given the distribution of entrepreneurs' types $f(p_i)$, the shaded area is the banks' customer pool whose size shrinks with an increasing r (decreasing $\overline{p}(r)$). This implies that the entrepreneurs' demand for loans, $D(r)$, is a downward sloping function of r, as the right part of Figure 3.6 shows.

Next, we explore the banks' loan supply by investigating banks' decision problem. A representative bank maximizes its expected revenue $E[\pi_b]$ from its loans, by setting the loan rate r—being unable to observe entrepreneurs' types, the bank can only offer a uniform r for all borrowers:

$$\max_r E[\pi_b] = (1+r) L \int_0^{\overline{p}(r)} p_i f(p_i) dp_i \qquad (3.23)$$

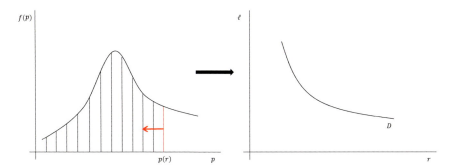

Figure 3.6 *Entrepreneurs' demand for loans*

in which $\int_0^{\bar{p}(r)} p_i f(p_i) dp_i$ is the mean likelihood of success for each entrepreneur in the customer pool.

How does the bank's choice on r affect its revenue? Taking derivative of $E[\pi_b]$ in (3.23) with respect to r yields

$$\frac{dE[\pi_b]}{dr} = L \underbrace{\int_0^{\bar{p}(r)} p_i f(p_i) dp_i}_{(A)} + \underbrace{\frac{d\bar{p}(r)}{dr}(1+r) L \bar{p}(r) f(\bar{p}(r))}_{(B)}$$

which suggests that there are two diverting effects:

- Part (A) in the derivative is positive, reflecting the positive effect of loan rate on the bank's revenue;
- However, part (B) in the derivative is negative, because $\frac{d\bar{p}(r)}{dr} < 0$, reflecting the adverse selection effect: higher r reduces the threshold $\bar{p}$, making the pool smaller and making the average remaining entrepreneurs in the customer pool riskier so that loans are more likely to be defaulted.

Under such trade-off, the bank's optimal choice on loan rate, call it r^*, is determined by the first order condition of the bank's decision problem (3.23)

$$\frac{dE[\pi_b]}{dr^*} = 0.$$

Note that banks hold no equity, so that a bank's loan supply, call it $S(r)$, is equal to how many deposits it can raise from the depositors, $d(\delta)$. To see how $d(\delta)$ responds to the bank's choice on loan rate r, remember that perfect competition in the deposit market forces banks to give away all revenue to depositors,

$$E[\pi_b] = \underbrace{(1+r) L \int_0^{\bar{p}(r)} p_i f(p_i) dp_i}_{\text{total revenue}} = \underbrace{(1+\delta) L \int_0^{\bar{p}(r)} f(p_i) dp_i}_{\text{funding cost}}. \qquad (3.24)$$

Solving for δ from (3.24) yields

$$1+\delta = \frac{(1+r)\int_0^{\bar{p}(r)} p_i f(p_i)dp_i}{\int_0^{\bar{p}(r)} f(p_i)dp_i}.$$

Taking derivative of δ with respect to r using the Leibniz's rule (see Exercise 3),

$$\frac{d\delta}{dr} = \underbrace{\frac{\int_0^{\bar{p}(r)} p_i f(p_i)dp_i}{\int_0^{\bar{p}(r)} f(p_i)dp_i} - \frac{(1+r)\int_0^{\bar{p}(r)} p_i f(p_i)dp_i \bar{p}'(r)f(\bar{p})}{\left[\int_0^{\bar{p}(r)} f(p_i)dp_i\right]^2}}_{(A)}$$

$$+ \underbrace{\frac{(1+r)\bar{p}'(r)\bar{p}f(\bar{p})}{\int_0^{\bar{p}(r)} f(p_i)dp_i}}_{(B)} \quad (3.25)$$

The loan rate r has two diverting effects on deposit rate δ:

- Part (A) in the derivative is positive, since $\bar{p}'(r)<0$, the positive effect of loan rate on the bank's revenue allows the bank to offer a higher deposit rate;
- However, part (B) in the derivative is negative, since $\bar{p}'(r)<0$, reflecting the adverse selection effect: higher r reduces the threshold $\bar{p}$, making the customer pool shrink and making the average remaining entrepreneurs in the customer pool riskier so that loans are more likely to be defaulted, reducing the bank's revenue; this reduces the deposit rate that the bank can offer the depositors.

When loan rate r is very small, $r \to 0$, the profit channel dominates, so that higher r leads to higher bank profit to be distributed among depositors, increasing the deposit rate δ. However, after r reaches a certain level, the adverse selection channel is severe enough and starts to dominate, this leads to more defaults of the entrepreneurs, reducing bank profit, hence reducing the deposit rate δ.

Given that $S(r)=d(\delta)$ and $d(\delta)$ increases with δ, the relationship between $S(r)$ and r should exhibit the same pattern as the relationship between δ and r. As Figure 3.7 shows, banks' supply function should be a hump-shaped curve, due to the two diverting effects of loan rate r.

Put the supply (Figure 3.7) and demand (Figure 3.6) curves together. If the adverse selection effect is not too severe, the demand curve may cross the supply curve before the supply curve bends, as Figure 3.8. In this case, the equilibrium outcome for loan rate and loan supply, (r^*, l^*), is just the same as in a standard competitive equilibrium.

However, if the adverse selection effect is severe enough that the banks' supply curve starts to bend before it is crossed by the demand curve, as shown in Figure 3.9. The cross of supply and demand curves, $(\hat{r}, \hat{l})$, reflects the market clearing interest rate and the corresponding credit supply.

Is the market-clearing loan rate, $\hat{r}$, the optimal choice of banks in equilibrium? No, because $\hat{r}$ is inferior to $r^* < \hat{r}$ under which banks achieve maximized profit for depositors. That is, the equilibrium choice of banks is not the market clearing outcome $(\hat{r}, \hat{l})$, but rather, loan rate r^* with corresponding loan supply l^*. However, a lower loan rate r^* in equilibrium implies a higher credit demand $\tilde{l}$ from the entrepreneurs' demand curve,

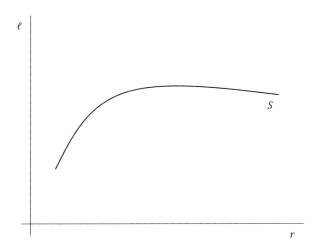

Figure 3.7 *Depositors' supply of deposits*

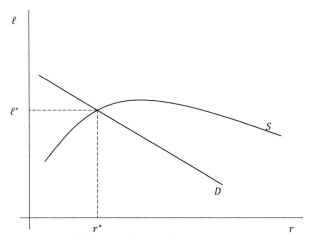

Figure 3.8 *Competitive equilibrium without credit rationing*

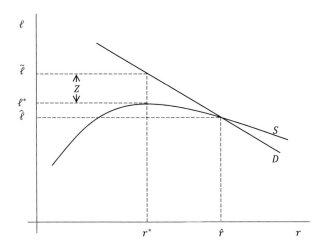

Figure 3.9 *Credit rationing*

which means an "unsatisfied fringe of borrowers" (Keynes 1930) that is characterized by the gap $Z = \tilde{l} - l^*$—a credit rationing!

3.4.3 ADVERSE SELECTION AND LENDING EFFICIENCY

Now let us stick to the credit rationing equilibrium, as Figure 3.9 illustrates. Given that credit has to be rationed in the market equilibrium with information friction, the natural question is, is such credit rationing equilibrium socially optimal?

BENCHMARK: SOCIALLY OPTIMAL SOLUTION WITHOUT INFORMATION FRICTION

The benchmark, socially optimal solution or the first-best solution, is achieved when there is no information friction. Being able to observe each entrepreneur's type, banks are able to charge an entrepreneur-specific loan rate r_i, which should fulfill entrepreneurs' participation constraints, i.e., entrepreneur i's expected return, $E[\pi_i]$, must be high enough so that the entrepreneur prefers to initiate her project instead of saving her wealth in a bank,

$$\begin{aligned} E[\pi_i] &= p_i[R_i - (1+r_i)L] = R_0 - p_i(1+r_i)L, \\ &\geq (1+\delta)W. \end{aligned} \quad (3.26)$$

At the same time, perfect competition implies that banks have to maximize depositors' return and earn zero profit,

$$\max_{r_i} \int_0^1 p_i(1+r_i)L\,di = (1+\delta)L, \quad (3.27)$$

that is, banks forward all revenue made from loans to depositors.

Solve banks' maximization problem (3.27) with constraint (3.26), and it is easy to see that in equilibrium,

$$\begin{aligned} R_0 - \int_0^1 p_i(1+r_i)L\,di &= R_0 - (1+\delta)L \\ &= (1+\delta)W, \\ R_0 &= (1+\delta)k, \end{aligned}$$

using the fact that $L = k - W$. This characterizes the equilibrium deposit rate, $\hat{\delta}$, in socially optimal solution

$$1+\hat{\delta}=\frac{R_0}{k}. \tag{3.28}$$

BANK LENDING UNDER ADVERSE SELECTION

Now, with credit rationing under information friction, the equilibrium condition (3.24) implies

$$(1+r)L\frac{\int_0^{\bar{p}(r)} p_i f(p_i)dp_i}{\int_0^{\bar{p}(r)} f(p_i)dp_i}=(1+\delta)L. \tag{3.29}$$

It is also known from entrepreneurs' participation constraint (3.21) that the marginal entrepreneur is characterized by the threshold $\bar{p}$

$$R_0-\bar{p}(1+r)L=(1+\delta)W. \tag{3.30}$$

Adding (3.29) and (3.30) yields

$$R_0-(1+r)L\frac{\int_0^{\bar{p}(r)}(\bar{p}-p_i)f(p_i)dp_i}{\int_0^{\bar{p}(r)} f(p_i)dp_i}=(1+\delta)k$$

using the fact that $L=k-W$. The equilibrium deposit rate is thus

$$1+\delta=\frac{R_0-(1+r)L\dfrac{\int_0^{\bar{p}(r)}(\bar{p}-p_i)f(p_i)dp_i}{\int_0^{\bar{p}(r)} f(p_i)dp_i}}{k}. \tag{3.31}$$

Furthermore, it is easy to see that

$$\int_0^{\bar{p}(r)}(\bar{p}-p_i)f(p_i)dp_i>0$$

as long as $\bar{p}(r) > 0$. Comparing with equilibrium deposit rate in social optimal solution (3.28), equation (3.31) thus implies

$$\delta < \hat{\delta}. \qquad (3.32)$$

Given that lending supply equals total deposit $d(\delta)$ and depositors' deposit supply $d(\delta)$ is assumed to increase with deposit rate δ, inequality (3.32) implies that deposit supply under credit rationing is lower than socially optimal deposit supply, hence lending under credit rationing is lower than lending in socially optimal solution.

3.4.4 SUMMARY

The Stiglitz-Weiss model demonstrates why there is a persistent excess demand in credit market, that some borrowers' demand for credit is turned down even if they are willing to pay higher loan rates, and market loan rate does not rise to clear the market. When borrowers' types are not precisely observable, banks can only offer them a uniform loan rate so that borrowers' credit risks are not well priced in the loan rate. As a result, a bank's expected return on lending is not always an increasing function of loan rate. Setting a higher loan rate may increase bank's return from loans, but it also increases the bank's credit risk because adverse selection drives prudent borrowers out of the bank's customer pool; therefore, a higher default risk of loans may decrease the bank's return from loans. These two diverting effects lead to a hump-shaped supply curve for bank lending, as a result, banks may rather choose the loan rate that maximizes their expected return under certain circumstances, instead of the market-clearing loan rate that may be so high as to make candidate borrowers too risky. In equilibrium, such credit rationing leads to inefficiently low level of bank lending, incurring a loss in social welfare due to information friction. The model implies that, once credit rationing arises in equilibrium from the underlying adverse selection problem, it is not socially desirable if policy makers attempt to restore market clearing by inducing a higher loan rate in the credit market, which will only increase loan default risk at a cost of social welfare.

3.5 POSITIVE SELECTION AND EXCESS LENDING

The Stiglitz-Weiss model assumes that all entrepreneurs' projects yield the same expected return, and all projects would be socially desirable, should there be no information friction. Some entrepreneurs are riskier from the banks' perspective than others just because they are less likely to be successful; given that entrepreneurs have limited liability, banks are more likely to bear the default risk from these entrepreneurs if such default risk cannot be priced in the loan rate due to information friction. For this reason, adverse selection makes borrowers in a bank's customer pool riskier, when the bank attempts to charge a higher loan rate.

However, in reality, many borrowers have higher credit risks because the expected returns from their projects are inferior, i.e., these projects may not even be socially desirable, or, they are just "lemons" (Akerlof 1970). In reality, banks invest in costly screening technology in order to avoid lending to lemons, but what will happen if banks cannot perfectly distinguish between lemons and good borrowers?

De Meza and Webb (1987) argue that when borrower types are not observable, banks' setting a higher loan rate drives lemons out of potential borrowers, as a higher loan rate is not affordable for bad borrowers, leading to a *positive selection*; as a result, the quality of remaining potential borrowers is improved. Under positive selection, banks' expected return from loans strictly increases with loan rate, and the credit market is cleared in equilibrium without credit rationing. However, positive selection also encourages banks to lend too much, with a social cost of lending to projects that are not socially desirable. In this section, we discuss the mechanism of positive selection by a model based on De Meza and Webb (1987).

3.5.1 MARKET EQUILIBRIUM UNDER POSITIVE SELECTION

Keep most of the settings the same as in Section 3.4.1, except the payoff structure of the project. Suppose now that for an arbitrary entrepreneur i, her project returns R_i such that

$$R_i = \begin{cases} R_0 & \text{with probability } p_i, \\ 0 & \text{otherwise,} \end{cases}$$

with R_0 being a positive constant. That is, entrepreneurs differ from each other in the probability of success, p_i, with $0 \leq p_i \leq 1$. Assume that p_i is independent and identically distributed (i.i.d.) and follows the same probability density function (pdf) $f(p_i)$.

Similarly as in the Stiglitz-Weiss model, we start from analyzing the decision problem of entrepreneur i. The expected return to her project, $E[\pi_i]$, is

$$E[\pi_i] = p_i[R_0 - (1+r)L], \qquad (3.33)$$
$$E[\pi_i] \geq (1+\delta)W \qquad (3.34)$$

and (3.34) is the entrepreneur's participation constraint that $E[\pi_i]$ must be high enough so that the entrepreneur prefers to initiate her project instead of saving her wealth in a bank and earning a gross return $(1+\delta)W$. Combing (3.33) and (3.34), this means that with given loan rate r and deposit rate δ, only an entrepreneur whose p_i exceeds the threshold value $\bar{p}$ will choose to borrow from bank, i.e.,

$$p_i \geq \frac{(1+\delta)W}{R_0 - (1+r)L} \equiv \bar{p}. \qquad (3.35)$$

The entrepreneurs' total demand for loans $D(r)$ is thus

$$D(r) = L \int_{\bar{p}(r)}^{1} f(p_i) dp_i \qquad (3.36)$$

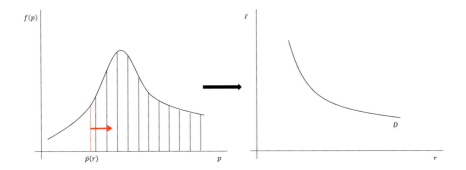

Figure 3.10 Entrepreneurs' demand for loans

in which $\int_{\bar{p}(r)}^{1} f(p_i) dp_i$ characterizes the population of banks' customer pool, or, entrepreneurs who are willing to borrow from the banks.

Note that from (3.35), the threshold $\bar{p}$ increases with loan rate r, $\frac{d\bar{p}(r)}{dr} > 0$. That is, when the loan rate is set to be higher, only the safer entrepreneurs are able to afford a higher loan rate and willing to borrow from banks; in other words, safer entrepreneurs are concentrated in banks' customer pool as a result of *positive selection*. As the left part of Figure 3.10 shows, given the distribution of entrepreneurs' types $f(p_i)$, the shaded area is the banks' customer pool whose size shrinks with an increasing r (increasing $\bar{p}(r)$). This implies that the entrepreneurs' demand for loans $D(r)$ is a downward sloping function of r, as the right part of Figure 3.10 shows. Compared with Figure 3.6, although increasing loan rate r also leads to falling loan demand, under positive selection, the quality of banks' customer pool is improved.

Given entrepreneurs' loan demand, a bank maximizes its expected revenue $E[\pi_b]$ from its loans, by setting a uniform loan rate r for all borrowers:

$$\max_r E[\pi_b] = (1+r)L \int_{\bar{p}(r)}^{1} p_i f(p_i) dp_i \qquad (3.37)$$

in which $\int_{\bar{p}(r)} p_i f(p_i) dp_i$ is the mean likelihood of success for each entrepreneur in the customer pool. Taking first-order derivative of $E[\pi_b]$ with respect to r on (3.37) yields

$$\frac{dE[\pi_b]}{dr} = \underbrace{\int_{\bar{p}(r)} p_i f(p_i) dp_i}_{(A)} - \underbrace{\frac{d\bar{p}(r)}{dr}(1+r)L\bar{p}(r)f(\bar{p}(r))}_{(B)}. \qquad (3.38)$$

Again, as (3.38) shows, a higher lending rate leads to two diverting effects:

- Part (A) is positive, reflecting the positive effect of loan rate on the bank's revenue;
- Part (B) is negative, given that $\frac{d\bar{p}(r)}{dr} > 0$, reflecting the fact that a higher loan rate reduces loan demand.

Under perfect competition, the bank earns zero profit, so that its total revenue equals total funding cost of deposits, i.e.,

$$E[\pi_b] = \underbrace{(1+r)L\int_{\bar{p}(r)}^{1} p_i f(p_i) dp_i}_{\text{total revenue}} = \underbrace{(1+\delta)L\int_{\bar{p}(r)}^{1} f(p_i) dp_i}_{\text{funding cost}}. \qquad (3.39)$$

Solving for δ yields

$$1+\delta = \frac{(1+r)\int_{\bar{p}(r)}^{1} p_i f(p_i) dp_i}{\int_{\bar{p}(r)}^{1} f(p_i) dp_i}. \qquad (3.40)$$

Taking first-order derivative of δ with respect to r on (3.40) yields

$$\frac{d\delta}{dr} = \frac{(1+r)\bar{p}'(r)f(\bar{p})\int_{\bar{p}(r)}^{1} p_i f(p_i) dp_i}{\left[\int_{\bar{p}(r)}^{1} f(p_i) dp_i\right]^2} + \frac{\int_{\bar{p}(r)}^{1} p_i f(p_i) dp_i - (1+r)\bar{p}'(r)f(\bar{p})}{\int_{\bar{p}(r)}^{1} f(p_i) dp_i}$$

Given that

$$\int_{\bar{p}(r)}^{1} p_i f(p_i) dp_i > \int_{\bar{p}(r)}^{1} \bar{p} f(p_i) dp_i$$

as long as $\bar{p}<1$, obviously,

$$(1+r)\bar{p}'(r)f(\bar{p})\int_{\bar{p}(r)}^{1} p_i f(p_i)dp_i > (1+r)\bar{p}'(r)f(\bar{p})\int_{\bar{p}(r)}^{1} \bar{p}f(p_i)dp_i,$$

which makes

$$\frac{d\delta}{dr}>0.$$

Compared with the bending supply curve as in (3.25), here, the bank's loan supply $S(r)$ is strictly upward sloping, increasing with r. Together with the strictly downward sloping demand curve in (3.36), the equilibrium is characterized by a market-clearing loan rate r without credit rationing.

3.5.2 POSITIVE SELECTION AND EXCESS LENDING

Now we further compare the outcome of bank lending under positive selection with the outcome in socially optimal solution.

BENCHMARK: SOCIALLY OPTIMAL SOLUTION WITHOUT INFORMATION FRICTION

With entrepreneurs' likelihood of success being distributed over $0 \le p_i \le 1$, entrepreneurs differ from each other in their projects' expected return, $p_i R_0$. Therefore, following the same argument in Section 3.4.3 on the benchmark socially optimal solution without information friction, it is only socially optimal to lend to entrepreneur i if

$$p_i R_0 \ge (1+\delta)k$$

which defines the threshold value $\hat{p}$

$$\hat{p}=\frac{(1+\delta)k}{R_0}. \tag{3.41}$$

In socially optimal solution, banks only lend to entrepreneur i if $p_i \ge \hat{p}$.

BANK LENDING UNDER POSITIVE SELECTION

Unlike in the Stiglitz-Weiss model with adverse selection where information friction leads to inefficiently low lending, with positive selection, the De Meza-Webb model yields too much lending in excess of a socially desirable level. To see this, rewrite the equilibrium condition (3.39)

$$(1+r)L\frac{\int_{\bar{p}(r)}^{1} p_i f(p_i)dp_i}{\int_{\bar{p}(r)}^{1} f(p_i)dp_i} = (1+\delta)L. \tag{3.42}$$

It is also known from entrepreneurs' participation constraint (3.35) that the marginal entrepreneur is characterized by the threshold $\bar{p}$

$$\bar{p}[R_0 - (1+r)L] = (1+\delta)W. \tag{3.43}$$

Adding (3.42) with (3.43) yields

$$\bar{p}R_0 + (1+r)L\frac{\int_{\bar{p}(r)}^{1}(p_i - \bar{p})f(p_i)dp_i}{\int_{\bar{p}(r)}^{1} f(p_i)dp_i} = (1+\delta)k, \tag{3.44}$$

using the fact that $L = k - W$. Given that

$$\int_{\bar{p}(r)}^{1}(p_i - \bar{p})f(p_i)dp_i > 0$$

as long as $\bar{p}(r) < 1$, (3.44) implies that

$$\bar{p}R_0 < (1+\delta)k. \tag{3.45}$$

Comparing (3.45) with (3.41) implies that

$$\bar{p} < \hat{p}$$

under a given deposit rate δ. This means that under positive selection, the credit quality of the threshold entrepreneur is inferior to the one in the socially optimal solution. That is, under positive selection, bank lending is in excess of socially optimal level, in that banks are lending to some entrepreneurs whose projects are actually not socially desirable.

3.5.3 SUMMARY

The De Meza-Webb model shows that when borrowers' types are not perfectly observable, banking outcome depends on borrowers' risk profiles. Similar to the Stiglitz-Weiss model, banks can only offer a uniform loan rate when borrowers' types are not observable; differently, when borrowers differ from each other in the expected returns of their projects as in the De Meza-Webb model, raising loan rate drives risky borrowers out of banks' customer pools, as bad borrowers cannot afford a higher loan rate. As a result, a higher loan rate leads to positive selection and cleanses customer pools, therefore, banks' expected return from loans increases with loan rate, and competitive equilibrium will be achieved without credit rationing.

However, information friction still leads to too much inefficient bank lending, under positive selection, in that banks lend to some of the entrepreneurs whose projects are not socially desirable. The reason is that, under perfect competition, banks compete to maximize depositors' return, and this makes banks' loan rate inefficiently low so that some of the socially undesirable projects are supported. This suggests that policy makers may restore efficiency by inducing a higher loan rate in the credit market, or imposing a tax on banks' interest income.

3.6 EMPIRICAL EVIDENCE

3.6.1 RELATIONSHIP BANKING

One important way for banks to overcome information frictions in reality is to explore *relationship banking*, through which banks explore customer-specific information to facilitate their lending decisions by building close and durable relationships with their customers. According to Boot (2000) and Gorton and Winton (2003), relationship banking is defined as the provision of financial services by a financial intermediary that

- Invests in obtaining customer-specific information, often proprietary in nature; and
- Evaluates the profitability of these investments through multiple interactions with the same customer over time and/or across products.

The contrast of relationship banking is *transaction-oriented banking*, or transactional banking that "focuses on a single transaction with a customer, or multiple identical transactions with various customers, often based on non-proprietary information and standardized contracts."

Obviously, relationship banking helps eliminate information asymmetries between banks and borrowers and benefits both sides. For example, if one customer has a checking account and savings account in a bank for a while, when she applies for a mortgage loan from the same bank, the bank may be able to better judge her credit worthiness through her transaction records and banking activities from the past; such relationship banking thus enables banks to collect information on customers' credit worthiness and helps banks better evaluate customers to make better financial contracts in the future. Particularly, relationship banking helps banks collect the *soft information* of their customers which is crucial for discovering customers' true credit quality but is not covered by standardized measures, such as credit scores. With the confidential and proprietary information collected through relationship banking, banks can improve their risk management by properly pricing customers' risks, and customers may benefit, too, in that truly credit-worthy customers are more likely offered more favorable rates—this is particularly important under market stress, as the fear of lending to lemons prevents banks from lending to borrowers whom they do not know well, as Bolton et al. (2016) show. Banks gain a competitive advantage over their competitors, as they are able to offer better rates for their high-quality customers with long-term relationships. A long-term relationship itself may also be a discipline between banks and borrowers, the reputation effect and long-term benefit discourage moral hazard such as misreporting and strategic default, and this in turn further reduces debt enforcement costs such as monitoring cost, improving welfare for both banks and borrowers.

However, relationship banking also has its dark side. With collected proprietary information of its customers, a bank becomes a monopoly of such information and thus has the incentive to extract more rents from its customers, as is shown by Sharpe (1990) and Rajan (1992); this may distort credit allocation. Borrowers are also "locked in" the relationship, as migrating to another bank with no existing relationship implies a high initial borrowing cost because of information asymmetry; knowing this, their relationship bank may have the incentive to extort more rents from them.

From the borrowers' perspective, Bharath et al. (2011) find that relationship lending has limited effect on loan rates for the largest firms, possibly due to the reason that these firms rely more on market funding, so that these firms' financial information is much disseminated in the market and relationship banking does not produce more information for the lending banks. However, for the other firms, relationship lending matters, in that repeated borrowing from the same bank reduces loan rate by 10–17 basis points. Agarwal et al. (2018b) examine how relationship banking affects performance of credit cards, when some of the card holders have savings and investment accounts in the same bank. Following 100,000 credit card accounts for 24 months with these accounts being linked to other relationships that account holders have in the same bank, they define a wide variety of relationship measures for each account holder, including a simple dummy variable that equals 1 if the account holder has at least one other relationship with the bank, number of relationships (breadth of relationship), types of relationships (such as deposit, investment, or loan relationships), duration of the relationships, etc. Agarwal et al. (2018b) found that a banking relationship reduces default risk, lowers attrition (closing an account without default), and increases card utilization. This suggests that relationship banking provides additional benefit to the bank, beyond the standardized hard information on credit quality such as credit score, with better monitoring customers and predicting customers' behavior.

Similar results have been found in Puri et al. (2017) from the lenders' perspective, who scrutinize loan applications and performance records for the universe of consumer loans issued by savings banks in Germany, from late 2004 to mid-2008. They find that relationship banking, even just by having a customer owning a simple transaction account in a bank for a period, helps the bank better assess the customer's credit worthiness through her transaction records and significantly reduces the default probability of the loan granted to the customer. From the borrowers' perspective, Beck et al. (2018) find that the benefit of relationship banking is the most pronounced during economic downturns. Using survey data covering 14,100 firms across 21 countries in emerging Europe combined with location information of lending banks, they classify lending banks as either relying on relationship lending or transactional lending. They find that during the 2007–2009 financial crisis, with greater presence of relationship-lending banks, fewer nearby firms face binding credit constraints, while such an effect did not appear in the normal year of 2005, implying that relationship banking is particularly effective in providing a funding guarantee for borrowers during the downturn, when information frictions become prevalent, just as Bolton et al. (2016) predict. Furthermore, they also find the positive effect of relationship banking is stronger for small firms and opaque firms lacking tangible assets that tend to be more sensitive to information frictions. Relationship banking thus has a non-negligible real effect.

On the other hand, evidence also shows that strategic banks do exploit their monopoly on the proprietary information collected in relationship banking to extract rents from borrowers. Schenone (2010) focuses on comparing the loan rates that borrowing firms incur before and after their initial public offerings (IPO). As firms must comply with disclosure requirements after IPOs, a lot of information that used to be exclusively held by their relationship banks becomes public, so that those banks lose their monopoly on the information. Schenone finds that before IPO, firms with the most intensive relationships with banks pay the highest loan rates, while after IPO, loan rates drop significantly and become inversely correlated with relationship intensity. A clear evidence that relationship banks exploit their information monopoly for rents. Agarwal and Hauswald (2010) find that banks use the proprietary, soft information collected from relationship banking strategically under competition pressure from their competitors. Examining loan applications by small firms in a major U.S. bank, they identify the bank's proprietary, soft information from the difference between bank's internal credit score and publicly available credit rating. They find that a borrower with higher proprietary credit score is offered with a lower loan rate, but the reduction in loan rate is less when the borrower is located closer to the bank's branch, i.e., when the bank has higher market power in the local credit market so that it is more likely to extract rents from the borrower.

3.6.2 CREDIT RATIONING

How relevant is credit rationing, as is predicted by Stiglitz and Weiss (1981), in reality? Identifying credit rationing in data remains an empirical challenge, since credit rationing is a supply side phenomenon, while data available are mostly based on loan contracts which are results of equilibrium in supply and demand. One way to solve this issue is to test whether the responses of credit market to exogenous shocks, such as monetary policy shocks, can be explained by the theory. Analyzing the Federal Reserve's Survey of Terms of Bank Lending dataset that contains contract information on over one million commercial loans made from 1977 to 1988, Berger and Udell (1992) observe that loan rates are sticky such that the premium of loan rate over risk-free rate *drops* significantly when real risk-free rate doubles, which is in line with the prediction of credit rationing. However, they also observe that under a monetary policy tightening, the share of new loans that are issued under commitment does not necessarily increase, which is in contrast to the prediction of credit rationing: when the credit market is tighter, borrowers without commitment should be subject to tighter rationing, while borrowers with commitment should be free from rationing as they are protected by contracts; as a result, the share of new loans that are issued under commitment should rise in theory.

New evidence from the supply side of credit markets emerges recently. Berg (2018) looks through 16,855 loan application records from 13,484 small and medium sized non-financial firms during 2009–2012 from a major German bank. The bank processes the loan applications by the following procedure: first, based on the hard information collected from the applicant, a continuous internal rating ranging from 0.5 (best) to 11.5 (worst) is assigned to the borrower. For any borrower with rating below 7, the loan officer can grant the loan without consent from the risk management department; a borrower with rating of 8 or 9 is subject to further review by the risk management department; a borrower with rating of 10 or 11 is subject to a special and even stricter reviewing procedure.

Figure 3.11 depicts the acceptance probability of loan applications as a function of the borrowers' ratings. There are clear jumps across the

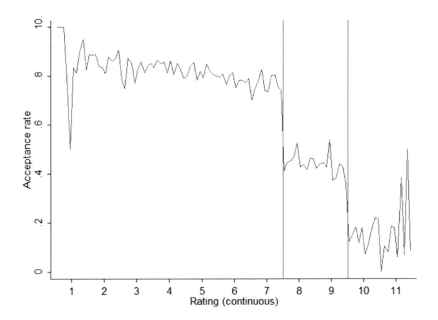

Figure 3.11 Loan acceptance rates by rating
Source: Berg (2018).

cutoffs, i.e., 7.5 and 9.5, in the ratings that divert loan applications to different reviewing procedures—Berg (2018) estimates that the acceptance rate drops by 28% across the cutoffs,—while such jumps are not observed for the loan rates. However, borrowers just below and just above a cutoff are very similar in terms of credit quality so that their probabilities to get loans shall be similar in theory, too; therefore, the discontinuity in acceptance rate across the thresholds is clear evidence of credit rationing: with a tiny increase in borrowers' credit rating, the bank chooses to reject substantially more applications instead of charging higher interest rate.

3.7 EXERCISES

1 **Market segmentation, loanable funds, and real effects, based on Holmström and Tirole (1997)**

   Continue with the Holmström-Tirole model from Section 3.3. Keeping all the settings unchanged and assuming that the credit market is segmented as Figure 3.5 shows, with $\underline{A}(\beta,R) < \overline{A}(R)$.

   (a) Suppose, at this stage, the risk-free rate R is exogenously set by the central bank, but shareholders' required ROE, β, is endogenized by the demand and supply of bank capital. Define the cumulative distribution function (cdf) of entrepreneurs' initial wealth A as $F(A)$.

   i. Characterize the aggregate demand for bank capital.
   ii. Assume that bank shareholders' aggregate supply of bank capital is a fixed volume $\overline{L_B}$. Characterize how equilibrium β is affected by the value of $\overline{L_B}$.
   iii. Discuss the market outcomes after an exogenous "capital flight", i.e., a fall in $\overline{L_B}$.

(b) Now suppose that the risk-free rate R is also endogenized, by the supply from and demand for the funding provided by the consumers. Assume that consumers' aggregate funding supply to the credit market, $S(R)$, is a strictly increasing function of R.

    i. Characterize the aggregate demand for consumers' funding.

    ii. Combining the result from question (a) ii, characterize how equilibrium β and R are jointly determined.

    iii. Discuss the market outcomes after an exogenous "saving glut", i.e., an increase in S.

2 Asymmetric information, monitoring, and market segmentation

Consider a risk-neutral firm, protected by limited liability, that wants to finance a project at a cost $I = 1$. The project takes one period to complete. The firm has no initial wealth; hence to undertake the project the firm has to borrow from somewhere. There are many households with enough resources ("deep pockets") to finance the project. If the firm and a household sign a contract (claiming that the household lends x, and R is to be repaid per unit lent if the project succeeds), the household grants a loan and the firm takes an action that affects the riskiness of the project. The firm has two options. The first option is to take a safer project, as given by the lottery $\{(p, G); (1-p, 0)\}$. This project returns G with probability p, and returns 0 with probability $1-p$. The other option is a riskier project, as given by the lottery $\{(pq, B); (1-pq, 0)\}$. The household cannot observe the action taken. The risk-free rate of return available to the household is normalized to 1.

We assume that $pG > 1 > pqB$, and $B > G$. The two inequalities can be satisfied at the same time only if $1 > q > 0$. Hence, the risky project has a higher gross return in case of success than the safe project ($B > G$), but succeeds less often ($q < 1$). Suppose that the household observes whether the project succeeds or fails (but in case of success the household does not observe whether the return is G or B).

(a) Provide a graphical illustration of how the payoffs of the two projects to the firm vary with R, and derive a critical value of R, denoted by $\hat{R}$, below which the firm chooses the safe project and above which the firm chooses the risky project.

(b) Which conditions have to be satisfied in a (competitive) credit market equilibrium?

Now let's introduce banks in the economy. Banks have a monitoring technology. By incurring a monitoring cost, c, a bank is able to prevent the firm from undertaking the risky project, and to induce the firm to choose the safe project. A bank monitors whenever it finances a project. Suppose that the banking sector is competitive.

(c) Derive the conditions for a competitive equilibrium if banks are the only lenders available.

(d) For which values of p will we have only direct finance, only bank lending, and no lending, respectively?

3   In the Stiglitz and Weiss (1981) model (Section 3.4), when perfect competition in the deposit market forces banks to return all revenue to depositors as is defined in (3.24), *ceteris paribus*, show how deposit rate δ reacts to the loan rate r.

4 **Adverse selection and credit market**

In an economy there is a large number of risk-neutral entrepreneurs who are protected by limited liability, and have no initial wealth. The entrepreneurs undertake projects at a cost $I = 1$. The financing of each project is done by a monopolistic and risk-neutral bank. Projects can be of two types: good and safe (undertaken by good entrepreneurs), or bad and risky (undertaken by bad entrepreneurs). The type of an entrepreneur is known only to the entrepreneur himself. The fraction of good entrepreneurs in the economy is a with $0 < a < 1$. The good project has a gross return equal to G with probability p, and a gross return equal to 0 with probability $1-p$. The bad project has a gross return equal to B with probability q, and a gross return equal to 0 with probability $1-q$. Assume that

$1 > p > q > 0$, $B > G$ and $pG > qB > 1$. All agents know the probability distributions. To focus on the adverse selection problem, we further assume that the bank does not have deposit insurance so that her behavior is not distorted by the limited liability.

(a) First, assume complete information. Show that the bank can extract all profits by extending loans at terms that depend on the type of the entrepreneur.

(b) Suppose next that only the entrepreneurs know their own type. Illustrate how the mixture of loan applicants will change as the gross rate of return demanded by the bank changes. Explain how the bank's *expected* return will vary with the gross rate of return demanded. Is there a gross rate of return for which only good entrepreneurs demand a loan?

(c) Which gross rate of return will a profit-maximizing monopolistic bank choose? What is critical to your answer?

(d) Assume now that all entrepreneurs have wealth W such that $0 < W < 1$ and $W < \frac{B-G}{\frac{1}{q}-\frac{1}{p}}$. Which gross rate of return will a profit-maximizing monopolistic bank choose?

5 Costly state verification and banking equilibrium

Consider an economy that is populated by many risk-neutral entrepreneurs (whose population is normalized to be 1) and many risk-neutral banks.

Each entrepreneur has a project which needs initial investment k, but she only has her own wealth $W < k$ so she needs to borrow $L = k - W$ to start the project. Each project yields a random gross return R, such that

$$R = \begin{cases} R_H, & \text{with probability } p, \\ R_L, & \text{with probability } 1-p. \end{cases}$$

Assume that $0 < R_L < L < R_H$. Banks charge lending rate r on loans for entrepreneurs; banks' funding rate δ is exogenously given.

CHAPTER THREE: INFORMATION FRICTIONS IN BANKING

Assume that entrepreneurs' expected return from the project, $E[R]$, is higher than $(1+\delta)k$.

The loan contract between a bank and an entrepreneur requires the entrepreneur to repay the bank if $R-(1+r)D>0$: otherwise, the entrepreneur defaults, incurs bankruptcy, and loses the entire project's return to the bank, and the bank has to pay an additional bankruptcy cost C. Assume that $R_L > C$.

(a) Compute the entrepreneur's expected profit and the bank's expected profit.

(b) Assume that banks are engaged in perfect competition in the deposit market and earn zero profit. How is banks' lending rate r affected by entrepreneurs' initial wealth W?

(c) Suppose entrepreneurs also have the option to deposit their own wealth in the banks, instead of working on projects. Show that entrepreneurs only initiate projects, if the expected return from the projects is high enough, so that $E[R]-(1+\delta)k-(1-p)C \geq 0$.

(d) Now assume that the true return, R, is only observable for the entrepreneurs. Whether an entrepreneur repays her loan or defaults depends on her reported R to the bank. What R will entrepreneurs choose to report to banks? Expecting entrepreneurs' reported R, will banks grant loans to entrepreneurs?

(e) Keeping the assumption in question (d), now assume that the economy extends to two periods. In each period, entrepreneurs can borrow from banks and work on projects. Assume that one entrepreneur's project return is independently and identically distributed (i.i.d.) in the two periods. If an entrepreneur fails to repay the bank in the first period, she will be denied for receiving a loan in the second period; otherwise she will receive a loan again in the second period and repeat the project. How should the loan contract be designed so as to provide incentives for entrepreneurs to report true R in period 1? To simplify computation, assume banks' bankruptcy cost $C=0$.

CHAPTER 4
Industrial organization of banking

4.1 INTRODUCTION

Industrial organization is a field in economics that focuses on the behavior of firms and evolution of markets. The key questions that have been intensively studied in industrial organization are also very important for banking, including

1. Competition and market structure: banking, as many other industries, is usually far from being perfectly competitive. In many countries, the banking sector is often characterized by substantial *market concentration*, i.e., a few big banks account for large shares in deposit and credit markets. Figure 4.1 shows the evolution in market share for the five largest banks in China, Germany, Japan, the UK, and the US, over two decades. In countries such as Germany,

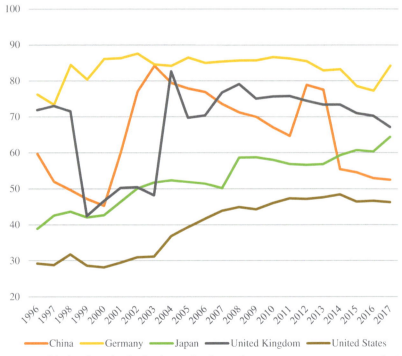

Figure 4.1 *Market share for the five largest banks in China, Germany, Japan, UK, and US, 1996–2017*
Data source: World Bank Global Financial Development Database.

Japan, and the UK, the top five banks account for more than half of credit market. In countries such as Japan and the US, the market concentration has been increasing over the past two decades, and such a trend was not interrupted by the 2007–2009 global financial crisis. The key question is: what does such high market concentration imply for market outcomes?

2 Market power and bank behavior. High market concentration tends to be associated with concentration of *market power*, so that banks may choose to set prices—for example, loan rates and deposit rates—that maximize their profit at the cost of consumers' welfare, or set barriers that prevent competition;

3 Regulation against market power. The possibility that banks may abuse their market power, such as monopolistic pricing, deterring entries of potential competitors, etc., leads to questions on how regulatory rules shall be designed to improve market efficiency and social welfare.

However, banks are special firms with several distinguishing features. First, banks are financial intermediaries, meaning that they are competing in a two-sided market both for depositors and borrowers; this substantially complicates banks' behavior so that conventional wisdom in industrial organization, which is often based on a one-sided market, cannot be easily extended to such two-sided setting.

Second, and more importantly, besides price setting, banks' behavior is heavily shaped by the risks they take. In general, risk-taking is an essential feature of banking: by creating liquidity services for depositors through balance sheets with maturity mismatch, banks also expose themselves to liquidity risks; banks are exposed to credit risks, too: the asymmetric information between banks and borrowers means that banks must screen loan applicants carefully to avoid lending to less credit-worthy borrowers, and during loan maturity, banks must properly monitor borrowers to prevent default. However, banks do have the incentive to take more risks than they should: banks are highly leveraged so that they are operating mostly with other people's money; as banks are firms with limited liability, when they fail, the bankruptcy cost is mostly borne by someone else.

As a result, since banks are not fully punished on the downside, they have the incentive to increase risk-taking and bet for the higher yield on the upside. Such *excess* risk-taking increases the likelihood of bank failure, as well as bankruptcy cost for bank creditors.

Banks' risk-taking behavior thus raises a crucial question on the relationship between banking competition and stability of banks. As bank failure often creates adverse shocks to macroeconomy and incurs enormous cost not only for creditors but also for taxpayers, such question is particularly pivotal for policy makers. Should competition unconditionally increase stability of the banking system, standard regulatory policies that facilitate competition would be unquestionably desirable. However, should competition erode banks' incentive to take due diligence or encourage them to engage in excess risk-taking, regulators would face a trade-off between promoting competition and maintaining financial stability, or even have to sacrifice competition to some extent if certain market power would contain banks' desire on excess risk-taking.

Since conventional questions in industrial organization, such as price setting and barriers to entry, are extensively covered by various textbooks (for example, Tirole 1988, Martin 2002) and mostly applicable to banks, in this chapter, we will rather skip them and focus more on the banking-specific question, i.e., how banking competition may affect stability of banks. In Section 4.2, we present a simple Klein-Monti model that captures the standard industrial organization view on banks' price setting behavior, in response to competition. We then move on to see how banks' behavior changes, if they incorporate risks in their decision-making.

In Section 4.3, the Boyd-De Nicolò model suggests that the relationship between competition and stability depends on the market in which banks compete and who are taking the risks. If banks compete in the deposit market and take risks themselves, then more competition bids up deposit rate, i.e., banks' funding cost, and encourages banks to take higher risks in their own investments—competition reduces stability, as *franchise value hypothesis* claims. In contrast, if banks compete in the credit market and borrowers are taking risks, then more competition reduces loan rate and lowers borrowers' incentive to choose riskier projects—competition increases stability, as *moral hazard hypothesis* claims.

However, the Hellmann-Murdock-Stiglitz model in Section 4.4 demonstrates that banks' risk-taking incentive may change in dynamic decision-making: banks' incentive to "gamble" for higher short-run yield with higher likelihood to fail and exit the market may be offset by the higher likelihood to survive and enjoy the lower yields for longer run with choosing to be "prudent", so that the relationship between competition and stability depends on the balance between short-run and long-run returns.

Section 4.5 further shows that the relationship between competition and stability is further complicated by asymmetric information: when banks cannot perfectly identify the truly credit-worthy borrowers by screening loan applications, a new entrant bank to the credit market faces *winner's curse*—a pool of loan applicants that is riskier than those who are granted loans by incumbent banks. Increasing bank competition with market entry thus increases the likelihood of loan default, or, competition reduces stability.

4.2 PRICE SETTING OF COMPETITIVE BANKS

First, by applying standard industrial organization approach to banks, in this section, we analyze how banks set their prices—deposit rates and loan rates—and see how competition affects market prices.

Consider a generic bank's problem à la Klein (1971) and Monti (1972). The bank is operating a balance sheet, as Figure 4.2 shows. The bank is funded by deposits D, with a share of α being required to be held as reserves for each unit of deposit, and issues loans L. The bank also has

Assets	Liabilities
Loans L	Interbank borrowing $-B$
Reserves αD	Deposits D

Figure 4.2 A generic bank's balance sheet

access to interbank market with a constant interbank lending rate r, and B denotes its *net* position on the interbank market. As a convention, $B<0$ means that the bank is a net borrower in the interbank market, and $B>0$ means that the bank is a net lender. It is easy to see that $B=D-(L+\alpha D)$.

The bank is engaged in monopolistic competition in both credit and deposit markets. It faces borrowers' downward-sloping demand curve for loans, $L(r_L)$, for the loan rate r_L it charges on the borrowers, and depositors' upward-sloping supply curve for deposits, $D(r_D)$, for the deposit rate r_D it offers to the depositors. Denote the loan rate and deposit rate by the inverse functions $r_L(L)$, and $r_D(D)$, then

- Depositors' upward-sloping supply curve for deposits implies that $r_D(0) \geq 0, r'_D(D)>0$, and $r''_D(D) \geq 0$;
- Borrowers' downward-sloping demand curve for loans implies that $r_L(0)>0, r'_L(L)<0, r''_D(L) \leq 0$.

Suppose the bank also has to incur a convex operating cost, $C(L,D)$, on collecting deposits and issuing loans, that is,

$$\frac{\partial C}{\partial L}>0, \frac{\partial C}{\partial D}>0, \frac{\partial^2 C}{\partial L^2} \geq 0, \frac{\partial^2 C}{\partial D^2} \geq 0.$$

Now the bank's decision problem is thus to set optimal rates r_L and r_D to maximize its profit, i.e.,

$$\begin{aligned}\max_{\{r_L,r_D\}} \Pi &= r_L(L)L - r_D(D)D + rB - C(L,D) \\ &= r_L(L)L - r_D(D)D + r[D-(L+\alpha D)] - C(L,D) \quad (4.1)\end{aligned}$$

using $B=D-(L+\alpha D)$. First-order conditions of problem (4.1) lead to

$$\frac{\partial \Pi}{\partial L} = r'_L(L)L + r_L(L) - r - \frac{\partial C(L,D)}{\partial L} = 0, \quad (4.2)$$

$$\frac{\partial \Pi}{\partial D} = -r'_D(D)D - r_D(D) + r - \alpha r - \frac{\partial C(L,D)}{\partial D} = 0. \quad (4.3)$$

Note that the elasticity of loan demand ϵ_L can be expressed as

$$\epsilon_L = -\frac{r_L}{L}\frac{\partial L}{\partial r_L}$$

and the elasticity of deposit supply ϵ_D can be expressed as

$$\epsilon_D = \frac{r_D}{D}\frac{\partial D}{\partial r_D},$$

the first-order conditions (4.2) and (4.3) can be rewritten as

$$\frac{r_L - r - C_L(L,D)}{r_L} = \frac{1}{\epsilon_L}, \quad (4.4)$$

$$\frac{r(1-\alpha) - r_D - C_D(L,D)}{r_D} = \frac{1}{\epsilon_D} \quad (4.5)$$

in which we use $C_L(L,D) = \frac{\partial C(L,D)}{\partial L}, C_D(L,D) = \frac{\partial C(L,D)}{\partial D}$ to economize notations.

Equations (4.4) and (4.5) contain the Klein-Monti model's key insights on the relationship between market competition and banks' pricing behavior. Note that elasticity of loan demand ϵ_L/elasticity of deposit supply ϵ_D indirectly reflects the intensity of competition in loan/deposit market: the more intensive the competition is, the higher is the elasticity, as a bank's borrowers/depositors are easier to be "stolen" by its rivalries offering more attractive loan/deposit rate. As in equation (4.4), the equilibrium loan rate r_L falls when ϵ_L rises; in equation (4.5), the equilibrium deposit rate r_L rises when ϵ_D increases. Furthermore,

$$\lim_{\epsilon_L \to +\infty} r_L = r + C_L(L,D), \quad (4.6)$$

$$\lim_{\epsilon_D \to +\infty} r_D = r(1-\alpha) - C_L(L,D), \quad (4.7)$$

implying that banks earn zero profit under perfect market competition: in a perfectly competitive loan market with $\epsilon_L \to +\infty$, (4.6) means that banks' marginal return from loan is totally offset by marginal cost of funding; in a perfectly competitive deposit market with $\epsilon_D \to +\infty$, (4.7) means that banks pay depositors all returns from interest-bearing loans $r(1-\alpha)$, deducted by the operating cost $C_L(L,D)$. Overall, the results are in line with standard theories in industrial organization, that banks' rent falls with increasing competition, and more competition increases consumers' (i.e., depositors' and borrowers') welfare.

4.3 COMPETITION AND STABILITY: A STATIC CHOICE

Next, we address the question on the relationship between banking competition and bank risk. Incorporating banks' risk-taking behavior in banking competition is complicated by the fact that banks as financial intermediaries compete both in the deposit market and credit market, and risks may be taken by banks, borrowers, or both. Therefore, we take the model in Boyd and De Nicolò (2005) which allows analyzing competition in both deposit and credit markets, as well as integrating risk-taking decisions from both banks and borrowers. The model thus addresses two hypotheses on the relationship between banking competition and stability of banks:

1 *Franchise value hypothesis*: if banks compete in the deposit market and take risks themselves, then more competition bids up the deposit rate, i.e., banks' funding cost, and encourages banks who aim to maximize their *franchise value* to take higher risks in their own investments. Competition thus reduces stability;
2 *Moral hazard hypothesis*: if banks compete in the credit market and borrowers are making decisions on risk-taking, then more competition reduces loan rate and lowers borrowers' incentive to choose riskier projects. Competition thus increases stability.

4.3.1 FRANCHISE VALUE HYPOTHESIS

Consider an economy over two periods, with augmented settings from the Klein-Monti model. In period $t=0$, there are N risk neutral banks engaged in Cournot competition in the deposit market, or, competition on the quantity of deposits they attempt to raise: each bank i wants to collect D_i deposits from depositors, and the market deposit rate will be determined by the market-clearing rate $r_D\left(\sum_i^N D_i\right)$, which is determined by depositors' total deposit supply to all banks, $\sum_i^N D_i$, and reflects an upward-sloping supply function for depositors such that depositors' total deposit supply is increasing and convex in market deposit rate r_D,

$r_D(0) \geq 0$, $r'_D(\cdot) > 0$, and $r''_D(\cdot) \geq 0$.

Banks have no initial resources so that they completely rely on raising funding from depositors. Banks have access to a constant return-to-scale technology with a varying net return R which may take any value from a uniform distribution over $[0, \overline{R}]$. After collecting deposits, a bank can choose a project with certain return level R, and the project's probability of success is determined by a function $p(R)$, i.e., the project will return R with probability $p(R)$ and 0 otherwise. Assume that

$$p(0) = 1, \ p(\overline{R}) = 0, \ p'(\cdot) < 0, \text{ and } p''(\cdot) \leq 0.$$

That is, the higher a project's R is, the lower is the probability that the project succeeds, hence the riskier is the project.

In period $t = 1$, banks repay depositors if their projects return, or default if their projects fail. Depositors are fully insured; they are repaid in any case so that their deposit supply only depends on the market deposit rate r_D, not on bank risk. Banks pay a flat insurance premium rate $\alpha > 0$ per unit of deposit from their profit.

A representative bank i's problem is to maximize its profit by choosing a project R_i and quantity of deposit D_i, taking other banks' decisions as given, i.e.,

$$\max_{\{R_i, D_i\}} \Pi_i = p(R_i) \left[R_i D_i - r_D \left(\sum_{j \neq i} D_j + D_i \right) D_i - \alpha D_i \right]. \qquad (4.8)$$

The bank only makes a positive profit when its project succeeds with probability $p(R_i)$, otherwise it defaults and makes zero profit because of limited liability. Given that banks are symmetric, the optimal solution $\{R^*, D^*\}$ applies to all banks and can be derived from the first order conditions for (4.8)

$$\begin{cases} p'(R^*) \left[R^* D^* - r_D(ND^*) D^* - \alpha D^* \right] + p(R^*) D^* = 0, \\ R^* - r'_D(ND^*) D^* - r_D(ND^*) - \alpha = 0. \end{cases} \qquad (4.9)$$

To understand the result more easily, let us apply certain functional forms for $p(\cdot)$ and $r_D(\cdot)$: assume $p(R) = 1 - AR$ with $A > 0$ and $R \in [0, \frac{1}{A}]$, as well as $r_D(D) = B_0 + B_1 D$ with B_0 and $B_1 > 0$, solving for R^* from equilibrium condition (4.9):

$$R^* = \frac{\frac{1}{A} + \alpha + B_0 - \frac{N}{N+1}(\alpha + B_0)}{2 - \frac{N}{N+1}}.$$

One can see that $\frac{\partial R^*}{\partial N} > 0$, i.e., when the number of banks, or, competition in the deposit market increases, banks choose riskier projects with higher return. Under perfect competition, $\lim_{N \to +\infty} R^* = \bar{R} = \frac{1}{A}$ so that banks take the highest risk. Overall, competition reduces stability of banks.

The key mechanism behind such result is that competition in the deposit market bids up deposit rate and increases banks' funding cost. With limited liability, when a bank's project fails, the bankruptcy cost is fully borne by the insured depositors, so that the bank can neglect the cost of bank failure; with increasing funding cost driven by more competition in deposit market, a bank who aims to maximize profit (franchise value) will choose riskier projects to gamble for the higher return on the upside because all downside risk will be shifted to insured depositors.

4.3.2 MORAL HAZARD HYPOTHESIS

Now assume that, instead of banks' operating risky projects themselves, risk-neutral entrepreneurs borrow from banks and choose risky projects in period $t = 0$. Each entrepreneur needs one unit of funding from banks. Banks are engaged in Cournot competition in the credit market to compete for borrowing entrepreneurs, or competition on the quantity of loans they attempt to issue: each bank i wants to lend D_i to entrepreneurs by collecting D_i deposits from depositors; the market loan rate will be determined by the market-clearing rate $r_L\left(\sum_i^N D_i\right)$, which is determined by entrepreneurs' total loan demand to all banks, $\sum_i^N D_i$, and

CHAPTER FOUR: INDUSTRIAL ORGANIZATION OF BANKING

reflects a downward-sloping demand function for borrowers such that entrepreneurs' total loan demand is decreasing and concave in market deposit rate r_D,

$$r_L(0) > 0,\ r'_L(\cdot) < 0,\ r''_D(\cdot) \leq 0,\ \text{and}\ r_L(0) > r_D(0)$$

for a positive net interest margin. Other setups stay the same.

We solve for the equilibrium by backward induction. Given an equilibrium loan rate in the credit market, r_L, an entrepreneur's choice on her project is determined by profit maximization, i.e.,

$$\max_{R \in [0, \bar{R}]} \Pi_e = p(R)(R - r_L). \tag{4.10}$$

The entrepreneur only makes a positive profit when its project succeeds with probability $p(R)$, otherwise it defaults and makes zero profit because of limited liability.

The entrepreneur's optimal choice on the project's risk profile, denoted by R^*, is characterized by the first order condition of (4.10)

$$\frac{\partial \Pi_e}{\partial R} = p'(R)(R - r_L) + p(R) = 0 \Rightarrow R^* + \frac{p(R^*)}{p'(R^*)} = r_L. \tag{4.11}$$

Knowing the response of entrepreneurs to market loan rate, a bank's optimal choice on loan issuance D_i is to maximize its profit, taking entrepreneurs' optimal choice (4.11) as given:

$$\max_{D_i} \Pi_i = p(R)\left[r_L\left(\sum_{j \neq i} D_j + D_i\right) D_i - r_D\left(\sum_{j \neq i} D_j + D_i\right) D_i - \alpha D_i \right],$$

$$\text{s.t.} \quad R + \frac{p(R)}{p'(R)} = r_L \text{ with } 0 \leq R \leq \bar{R}. \tag{4.12}$$

In order to understand the result more easily, let us apply certain functional forms for $p(\cdot)$, $r_L(\cdot)$, and $r_D(\cdot)$: assume $p(R) = 1 - AR$ with $A > 0$ and $R \in \left[0, \frac{1}{A}\right]$, $r_L(L) = \frac{1}{A} - CL$ with $C > 0$, as well as $r_D(D) = B_0 + B_1 D$ with B_0 and $B_1 > 0$, and solve for the equilibrium condition from the first-order condition of (4.12),

$$D^* = \frac{\frac{1}{A} - (\alpha + B_0)(N+1)}{N(C+B_1)(N+2)}$$

as well as

$$R^* = \frac{1}{A} - \frac{\frac{1}{A} - (\alpha + B_0)(N+1)}{(C+B_1)(N+2)} \frac{C}{2}.$$

One can see that $\frac{\partial R^*}{\partial N} < 0$, i.e., when the number of banks, or, competition in the credit market increases, entrepreneurs choose less risky projects with lower return. Under perfect competition, $\lim_{N \to +\infty} r_L - r_D - \alpha = 0$, or, banks' marginal revenue r_L equals marginal cost $r_D + \alpha$, leaving themselves zero profit.

The key mechanism behind such results is moral hazard in excess risk-taking caused by limited liability lies on the side of entrepreneurs: the higher loan rate they face, the higher incentive they have to choose riskier projects. With banks' competition driving down market loan rate, the moral hazard problem for entrepreneurs is eased so that they are able to achieve maximized profit by choosing safer projects. This reduces banks' credit risks and increases stability of the banking system.

4.3.3 SUMMARY

The Boyd-De Nicolò model clearly shows how the relationship between banking competition and stability of banks is complicated by sources of financial risks and markets, which has crucial implications for policy makers: in the design of competition policies in banking, regulators must be careful with markets affected as well as risk-taking incentives for all market participants that are involved, and understand the trade-off between competition efficiency and financial stability.

The competition-stability relationship may be further complicated by the trade-off between banks' market power and risk buffer, as Martínez-Miera and Repullo (2010) argue. For example, in the moral hazard hypothesis, although competition in the credit market reduces borrowers' credit risks, it also reduces banks' net interest margin which may be used as a buffer against losses. As a result, when banks are also facing idiosyncratic risk in loan losses which is not captured by the Boyd-De Nicolò model, banks may be more likely to fail because banks' profit margin is too thin to absorb such losses.

The competition-stability relationship may also be complicated by economic dynamics, which are not captured by the static Boyd-De Nicolò model. Although under the franchise value hypothesis, banks tend to take higher risks, Hellmann et al. (2000) argue that this may not be optimal in the long run, as the likelihood of bank failure from excess risk taking is also higher so that banks have to exit the market and miss all the returns in the future. This may restrict banks' risk-taking incentives to gamble for short-run profit.

4.4 COMPETITION AND STABILITY: A DYNAMIC CHOICE

Next, we examine how banks' risk-taking incentive may be changed by the trade-off between short-run and long-run benefit. Using a simple model based on Hellmann et al. (2000), we show that if the long run benefit from staying in business outweighs the short-run profit from "gamble and exit" strategy, banks may choose to be prudent even if they are franchise value maximizers.

4.4.1 RISK-TAKING AS DYNAMIC DECISION-MAKING

Consider an economy with infinite horizon $t = 0,1,\ldots,+\infty$. There are N risk neutral profit-maximizing banks in the deposit market, and banks' common discount factor is $0 < \delta < 1$. There are two stages in each period t:

Stage 1 A representative bank i offers a deposit rate r_i to depositors, given that its rivalries offer $\mathbf{r}_{-i} = [r_1,\ldots,r_{i-1},r_{i+1},\ldots,r_N]$. The volume of deposits it can collect is determined by depositors' upward-sloping deposit supply curve $D(r_i, \mathbf{r}_{-i})$ that is increasing in r_i and decreasing in $\mathbf{r}_{-i}$. That is, bank i can collect more deposits by offering a higher deposit rate, while its rivals can steal business from it by raising their deposit rate offers;

Stage 2 Bank i can choose to be either a prudent bank investing in an asset with safe return α by the end of the stage, or a gambling bank investing in an asset that returns γ with probability θ or 0 otherwise by the end of the stage. Assume $\gamma > \alpha > \theta\gamma$. If a gambling bank fails, it loses its banking license forever and must exit the market. Depositors are repaid by returns from bank assets; assume that depositors are fully insured so that they are fully repaid even under bank failure.

Bank i's one-period payoff is $\pi_P(r_i, \mathbf{r}_{-i}) = (\alpha - r_i) D(r_i, \mathbf{r}_{-i})$ if it chooses to be prudent, or $\pi_G(r_i, \mathbf{r}_{-i}) = \theta(\gamma - r_i) D(r_i, \mathbf{r}_{-i})$ if it chooses to gamble. The franchise value for a prudent bank is thus denoted by

$$V_P(r_i, \mathbf{r}_{-i}) = \sum_{t=0}^{+\infty} \delta^t \pi_P(r_i, \mathbf{r}_{-i}) = \frac{\pi_P(r_i, \mathbf{r}_{-i})}{1-\delta},$$

if its payoff is symmetric in every period.

4.4.2 RISK-TAKING: SHORT-RUN GAIN VERSUS LONG-RUN LOSS

The sufficient *no-gambling condition* that a bank chooses to be always prudent is that it makes it worse off even to gamble once. That is, in any period t

- If a bank chooses to be prudent in t, and to be prudent in the future, its franchise value is

$$\pi_P(r_i, \mathbf{r}_{-i}) + \delta V_P(r_i, \mathbf{r}_{-i});$$

- If a bank chooses to gamble in t, and to be prudent in the future, its franchise value is

CHAPTER FOUR: INDUSTRIAL ORGANIZATION OF BANKING

$$\pi_G(r_i, \mathbf{r}_{-i}) + \theta \delta V_P(r_i, \mathbf{r}_{-i}) + (1-\theta) \cdot 0,$$

as the probability that it survives gambling is θ. In other words, gambling is a *trigger strategy* that leads to the punishment that a gambling bank is barred from banking business forever with probability $1-\theta$.

A bank chooses to be prudent in any t only if

$$\pi_P(r_i, \mathbf{r}_{-i}) + \delta V_P(r_i, \mathbf{r}_{-i}) \geq \pi_G(r_i, \mathbf{r}_{-i}) + \theta \delta V_P(r_i, \mathbf{r}_{-i}),$$

which is equivalent to

$$r_i \leq (1-\delta)\frac{\alpha - \theta \gamma}{1-\theta} + \delta \alpha \equiv \hat{r}$$

—banks choose to coordinate to be prudent only if the equilibrium deposit rate is not higher than the threshold value $\hat{r}$. Furthermore, we can see that

$$\begin{aligned} \hat{r} &= (1-\delta)\frac{\alpha - \theta \gamma}{1-\theta} + \delta \alpha \\ &< (1-\delta)\frac{\alpha - \theta \alpha}{1-\theta} + \delta \alpha \\ &= \alpha, \\ \hat{r} &< \alpha. \end{aligned} \quad (4.13)$$

Given banks' investment choice in Stage 2—say, they choose to be prudent—the optimal choice on deposit rate is determined by profit maximization

$$r_P = \arg\max_{r_i}\{V_P(r_i, \mathbf{r}_{-i})\}. \quad (4.14)$$

By asymmetry, all banks choose r_P, that is derived from the first-order condition of (4.14)

$$-D(r_P, \mathbf{r}_P) + (\alpha - r_P)\frac{\partial D(r_P, \mathbf{r}_P)}{\partial r_P} = 0. \quad (4.15)$$

Denote the elasticity of deposit supply as

$$\epsilon = \frac{\partial D(r_p, \mathbf{r}_p)}{\partial r_p} \frac{r_p}{D(r_p, \mathbf{r}_p)},$$

equation (4.15) can be written as

$$r_p = \alpha \frac{\epsilon}{\epsilon + 1}.$$

The optimal deposit rate, r_p, increases monotonically with ϵ on $0 \leq \epsilon < +\infty$, which reflects the degree of deposit market competition:

1. When $\epsilon \to 0$, or, when a bank is a monopoly, $\lim_{\epsilon \to 0} r_p = 0$ so that the bank keeps all the rent and leaves nothing to depositors; in contrast,
2. When $\epsilon \to +\infty$, or, when banks are in a perfect competition, $\lim_{\epsilon \to +\infty} r_p = \alpha$ so that banks give all the rents to depositors.

However, condition (4.13) suggests that banks are able to coordinate to be prudent in the long run, but only if $r_p \leq \hat{r} < \alpha$, or, when deposit market competition is not too fierce, as is shown in Figure 4.3. That is, only if banks retain some market power so that they can extract some rent from depositors, the gain from staying in the business is attractive enough for them to be prudent; otherwise they will rather gamble for the upside and shift all bankruptcy risk to insured depositors, even if the chance to fail and get out of business is high.

4.4.3 POLICY IMPLICATION

The Hellmann-Murdock-Stiglitz model suggests that regulators shall be cautious when they deregulate the banks to promote competition in the deposit market, as increasing competition may erode banks' profit in the long run, destroy their coordination to be prudent, and make gambling

Figure 4.3 *Deposit market competition and banks' risk-taking*

more appealing so that deregulation may shift banks from prudent equilibrium to gambling equilibrium and destabilize banks.

On the other hand, deregulation may still be appealing for regulators, with the gains in social welfare, such as reducing inequality through improving access to credit (see more in Section 4.6), etc., which is not covered in the model. To maintain banks' incentive to be prudent during deregulation, two types of policies may be considered:

1. One type of policy works through the profit side of the coordination game, for example, to set a cap on deposit rate $\bar{r} \leq \hat{r}$ and ensure that banks still earn enough profit after deregulation;
2. The other type of policy works through the cost side of the trigger strategy in the coordination game, for example, to increase capital requirement so that banks are punished harder when they fail in gambling (see Exercise 3).

4.5 MARKET ENTRY UNDER ASYMMETRIC INFORMATION

The relationship between banking competition and stability of banks is also affected by information asymmetry, as under asymmetric information, competition itself may influence credit risks. For example, when borrowers' credit worthiness is private information, low quality borrowers always have the incentive to mimic high quality ones, leading to adverse selection problem; in response, banks actively screen loan applications to avoid lending to lemons and reduce credit risk, although banks' screening technology is imperfect and banks make errors on approving loan applications. Given that an applicant can always apply at another bank, if she is rejected by one bank, before she is granted a loan by any bank. Therefore, after all rejected applicants have tried all banks in the market, remaining applicants in the pool of potential borrowers are more likely to be lemons—as long as banks' screening technology is precise enough. In this case, any new entrant bank to the credit market—which effectively increases market competition—will face a pool of potential borrowers whose quality is worse than average borrowers who have been granted loans by incumbent banks, and loans extended by the entrant are more likely to default. Such *winner's curse* on new entrants implies that increasing banking competition from market entry reduces stability of the banking sector. In this section, we examine such a scenario through a model based on Broecker (1990) and Shaffer (1998).

4.5.1 CREDIT MARKET WITH IMPERFECT SCREENING

Consider a credit market in which N potential borrowers are applying for loans from n banks, with $N > n$. Each borrower needs to borrow 1 dollar from a bank. There are two types of borrowers:

- A fraction a of borrowers are good borrowers. With probability π_H, a good borrower will repay her bank; otherwise she defaults;
- A fraction $1-a$ of borrowers are bad borrowers. With probability π_L, a bad borrower will repay her bank; otherwise she defaults.

The true type of a borrower is private information and cannot be observed directly by banks in the lending stage; the information is only revealed to banks when it is time for the borrower to repay. Assume that $0 < \pi_L < \pi_H < 1$.

Suppose that the lending rate r is constant for all banks, so a bank will earn $R_H = (1+r)\pi_H - 1$ if it lends to a good borrower, and $R_L = (1+r)\pi_L - 1$ if it lends to a bad borrower. Assume that $R_H > 0 > R_L$, i.e., the bank earns a profit if it lends to a good borrower, and suffers from a loss if it lends to a bad borrower. Therefore, if the types of borrowers are publicly known in the lending stage, a bank will never lend to a bad borrower.

In the lending stage, the true type of a potential borrower is not observed by the bank, so the likelihood for a bank to meet a good or bad borrower is $p(\mathcal{H}) = a$ or $p(\mathcal{L}) = 1-a$. However, by reviewing every potential borrower's application, a lending bank receives a noisy signal about the applicant's type, such that

- If the applicant is a truly good borrower, the probability that the signal indicates that she is good is $p(H|\mathcal{H})$; however, with a probability $1-p(H|\mathcal{H})$, the signal indicates that she is bad;
- If the applicant is a truly bad borrower, the probability that the signal indicates that she is bad is $p(L|\mathcal{L})$; however, with a probability $1-p(L|\mathcal{L})$, the signal indicates that she is good.

Assume that the signal is informative enough so that $p(H|\mathcal{H}) > \frac{1}{2}$, and $p(L|\mathcal{L}) > \frac{1}{2}$; for this reason, the bank will lend if the signal indicates the applicant is good.

4.5.2 COMPETITION AND MARKET OUTCOME

MONOPOLY

Let us start with the simplest case that there is only one bank in the market, $n=1$. The bank will receive N applications, but it will only lend to

$$\underbrace{p(H|\mathcal{H})aN}_{(A)} + \underbrace{(1-p(L|\mathcal{L}))(1-a)N}_{(B)}$$

borrowers, including (A) those truly good borrowers with good signals received by the bank, and (B) those truly bad borrowers with good signals mistakenly received by the bank (so-called *type-I error* in statistics). The bank's expected profit is therefore

$$\Pi(N=1) = p(H|\mathcal{H})aNR_H + (1-p(L|\mathcal{L}))(1-a)NR_L,$$

so that its expected loan loss rate is

$$\frac{p(H|\mathcal{H})a(1-\pi_H) + (1-p(L|\mathcal{L}))(1-a)(1-\pi_L)}{p(H|\mathcal{H})a + (1-p(L|\mathcal{L}))(1-a)}.$$

DUOPOLY

Now assume that there are two banks in the market, and each of them receives $\frac{N}{2}$, half of the loan applications. Following similar calculation as in the previous case, after making lending decisions, each bank's expected profit from the borrowers is $\dfrac{\Pi(N=1)}{2}$.

However, assume that rejected applicants can apply again in the other bank, and banks cannot distinguish between initial applicants who apply for the first time and subsequent applicants who have been rejected by the other bank. Therefore, besides the loans issued to initial applicants, each bank additionally issues

$$p(H|\mathcal{H})(1-p(H|\mathcal{H}))a\frac{N}{2}+(1-p(L|\mathcal{L}))p(L|\mathcal{L})(1-a)\frac{N}{2}$$

loans to subsequent applicants, i.e., total credit supply in the market increases when the number of banks increases from one to two.

For each bank, the total expected profit is therefore

$$\frac{\Pi(N=1)+p(H|\mathcal{H})(1-p(H|\mathcal{H}))aNR_H+(1-p(L|\mathcal{L}))p(L|\mathcal{L})(1-a)NR_L}{2}$$

$$=\frac{p(H|\mathcal{H})(2-p(H|\mathcal{H}))aNR_H+(1-p(L|\mathcal{L}))(1+p(L|\mathcal{L}))p(L|\mathcal{L})(1-a)NR_L}{2}$$

and its expected loan loss rate is

$$\frac{p(H|\mathcal{H})(2-p(H|\mathcal{H}))a(1-\pi_H)+(1-p(L|\mathcal{L}))(1+p(L|\mathcal{L}))(1-a)(1-\pi_L)}{p(H|\mathcal{H})(2-p(H|\mathcal{H}))a+(1-p(L|\mathcal{L}))(1+p(L|\mathcal{L}))(1-a)}.$$

MONOPOLISTIC COMPETITION

Now assume that there are n banks ($n > 2$) in the market, and keep the assumption that rejected applicants can apply again in another bank. Repeating the same procedure, one can see that a bank's expected loan loss rate is

$$\frac{a\left[1-(1-p(H|\mathcal{H}))^n\right](1-\pi_H)+(1-a)\left[1-(p(L|\mathcal{L}))^n\right](1-\pi_L)}{a\left[1-(1-p(H|\mathcal{H}))^n\right]+(1-a)\left[1-(p(L|\mathcal{L}))^n\right]}.$$

We can further see that the expected loan loss rate is increasing with n. In the extreme case that the number of banks is infinite, $n \to +\infty$, the expected loan loss rate becomes

$$a(1-\pi_H)+(1-a)(1-\pi_L),$$

which is the maximal loss from all defaulted borrowers in the whole population!

The reason is that, as long as banks' signals are informative, a truly good applicant is more likely to be approved by the first bank she approaches. If banks do not know an applicant has been rejected by other banks, a truly bad applicant is able to shop around until a bank makes a mistake and grants her a loan. When the number of banks is infinite, any applicant has infinite opportunities to apply so that any one will in the end obtain a loan from a bank, and the default risks from all potential failed borrowers will be materialized.

4.5.3 WINNER'S CURSE ON MARKET ENTRY

So far, we have established that an increasing number of banks is associated with higher default risk in the banking system, however, an even worse implication is that the default risk is higher for a new entrant, compared with the incumbents. This is because after the applicants have been screened by all incumbent banks, the pool of "leftover" applicants has a higher concentration of truly bad borrowers. If the new entrant bank has just the same screening technology as the incumbents, it will only select a higher ratio of bad borrowers from the remaining pool. A "winner's curse".

To see this clearly, assume that there are n banks competing in the credit market. In the end of the lending stage, after potential borrowers finish the application round, those rejected by all banks include

- Truly bad borrowers who always get bad signals on their applications, and

- Truly good borrowers who always mistakenly get bad signals on their applications (so-called *type-II* error of screening banks),

and their population is

$$a(1-p(H|\mathcal{H}))^n + (1-a)(p(L|\mathcal{L}))^n.$$

Suppose now, after the lending stage, a new bank enters the market so that those "leftover" potential borrowers can borrow from the new entrant. Among the "leftover" potential borrowers, the ratio of truly good borrowers to truly bad borrowers is

$$\frac{a(1-p(H|\mathcal{H}))^n}{(1-a)(p(L|\mathcal{L}))^n}.$$

Compared with the case with $n-1$ banks in the market, this ratio grows at a rate of

$$\frac{1-p(H|\mathcal{H})}{p(L|\mathcal{L})} < 1$$

because $p(H|\mathcal{H}) > \frac{1}{2}$, $p(L|\mathcal{L}) > \frac{1}{2}$. That is, the quality of the remaining borrower pool is lower for the entrant than incumbents, implying a higher loan loss rate for new loans extended by the entrant.

To conclude, the average credit quality of remaining potential borrowers falls, after all potential borrowers have been screened by all banks. This leads to winner's curse on new entrants, so that their loans granted for the remaining borrowers are more likely to fail. Increasing banking competition from market entry thus reduces the stability of the banking sector.

4.6 EMPIRICAL EVIDENCE

The industrial organization approach to banking has spurred huge effort on empirical research. A large strand of literature focuses on classical industrial organization questions regarding the impacts of market competition on bank efficiency and banks' pricing strategies. Berger et al. (2004) provide an excellent review on related research.

It is by no means possible to thoroughly review the wide spectrum of empirical questions on industrial organization of banks. In this section, we would rather focus on the empirical tests for the theories that we have covered, as well as strategies for the design of empirical research:

1. First of all, we discuss how to measure market structure and market competition, as well as pros and cons of using these measures in empirical exercises;
2. We further discuss how to identify the effects of competition on banks' (risk-taking) behavior, to isolate the competition effects from other confounding socioeconomic factors such as banking regulation and market evolution;
3. The competition effects on allocation efficiency and consequences for the real economy. Although bank competition tends to improve banks' *operational* efficiency, it is not clear whether the allocation of financial resources is consequently improved, i.e., whether resources are allocated to borrowers who can make better use of them. A related crucial question for policy makers is whether/how more bank competition improves social welfare.

4.6.1 MEASURING THE INTENSITY OF COMPETITION

The first challenge to quantify the effect of bank competition is to properly measure the degree of competition. In practice, there is no single perfect indicator that characterizes competition in a market; rather, various indicators are designed to capture certain features of bank competition through

- Market share, such as N-bank concentration ratio (CRn) and Herfindahl–Hirschman Index (HHI), based on the assumption that a bank with bigger market share is more likely to exercise higher market power, implying a lower degree of market competition;

- Bank performance, in response to exogenous shocks, compared with the theoretical prediction from certain competition setup. One example is H-statistic, which is constructed by exploring the difference in the elasticity of a bank's revenue to input prices, under different market competition structure;
- Profit-cost margin (PCM), such as Lerner Index (LI) and Boone Indicator (BI), based on the assumption that a bank with higher market power/facing lower market competition is more likely to charge a higher mark-up over its marginal cost.

The construction of these measures is explained in details as follows, as well as pros and cons in using these measures to characterize market competition. In practice, one often needs to deploy multiple measures to better capture the status of market competition.

N-bank concentration ratio (CRn) CRn is the simple sum of the market shares of *n* largest banks in the market.

Herfindahl–Hirschman Index (HHI) HHI is a widely used measure of market concentration, named after economists Orris Herfindahl and Albert Hirschman. It is defined as the sum of squared market shares of banks competing in the same market, i.e., for a market in which *N* banks are competing, with any bank *i*'s market share being s_i, the market concentration index

$$HHI = \sum_{i}^{N} s_i^2.$$

When the market is approaching being fully concentrated, $s_i \to 1$ so that $HHI \to 1$; on the other hand, when the market is approaching being highly decentralized, $s_i \to 0$ so that $HHI \to 0$.

It is worth noting that higher CRn/HHI, or higher market concentration, does not necessarily mean banks have higher market power or the market competition is lower. For example, suppose a market is equally shared by two banks with $HHI = 0.5$ which looks highly concentrated; however, if the banks are engaged in Bertrand competition and make zero profit, the market can still be highly competitive. Even for an extremely concentrated market with only one bank ($HHI = 1$), as long as the market is contestable (Baumol et al. 1982) by the potential new entrants, the incumbent bank is not able to fully exercise its market power.

Furthermore, the simple measures of market concentration such as CRn or HHI are not necessarily *exogenous* indicators of market power or the inverse of competition intensity, instead, these measures are often *endogenous* results of more efficient banks' winning market share over their less efficient competitors; as a consequence, using these measures as independent variables in empirical exercises may be subject to endogeneity critiques.

H-statistic To reflect the contestability of the market competition, Panzar and Rosse (1977) and Panzar and Rosse (1987) propose the measure as the sum of the elasticities of a bank's revenue to the input prices. For example, in a two-factor production function in which the bank's revenue $R(w,r)$ is a function of labor and capital inputs, and w/r is wage rate/rental price for capital. H-statistic is thus

$$H = \frac{\partial R(w,r)}{\partial w}\frac{w}{R(w,r)} + \frac{\partial R(w,r)}{\partial r}\frac{r}{R(w,r)}.$$

Standard market competition theories (see, for example, Tirole 1988 or Martin 2002) suggest that, under perfect competition, an increase in input price leads to a rise of the same amount, in marginal cost as well as in revenue, making H-statistic approach 1; in contrast, under monopoly, an increase in input price leads to a rise in marginal cost and thus a fall in output, hence a fall in revenue, making H-statistic negative. H-statistic is thus related to the market competition structure such that

- H-statistic equals 1: perfect competition;
- H-statistic between 0 and 1: monopolistic competition;
- H-statistic below 0: collusive competition or monopoly.

Lerner Index (LI) Higher market power may be related to higher profit-cost margin (PCM). Developed by Lerner (1934), the index measures a bank's market power by its capability to charge a mark-up in price P above marginal cost (MC),

$$LI = \frac{P-MC}{P}.$$

For a bank that maximizes its profit $\Pi(Q) = P(Q)Q - C(Q)$ with a downward sloping demand curve $Q(P)$ and a convex cost function $C(Q)$, the optimality is achieved under the first-order condition

$$\frac{\partial \Pi}{\partial Q} = \frac{\partial P}{\partial Q}Q + P - \frac{\partial C}{\partial Q} = 0 \Rightarrow \frac{P-MC}{P} = \frac{1}{\epsilon}$$

with marginal cost $MC = \frac{\partial C}{\partial Q}$ and demand elasticity $\epsilon = -\frac{\partial Q}{\partial P}\frac{P}{Q}$. That is, the higher is a bank's market power, the higher mark-up it can charge, and the lower demand elasticity it faces.

Boone Indicator (BI) Traditional PCM measure may fail to capture the heterogeneity in individual bank's efficiency and lead to bias interpretation on competition structure. Boone (2008) thus proposes a measure based on relative profit differences (RPD) which assumes that market competition increases profit share of the most efficient banks, and less efficient banks are punished by losing profit share. For example, consider three banks of different efficiency level (say, in terms of cost efficiency) $n_1 > n_2 > n_3$—efficiency ranked in decreasing order. Denote RPD as the profit difference between two banks, $\pi(n_i) - \pi(n_j)$, then the ratio $\frac{\pi(n_1) - \pi(n_2)}{\pi(n_2) - \pi(n_3)}$ increases with stronger market competition, i.e., the relative profit rises for the most efficient bank; whereas the traditional PCM measures will falsely interpret it as increasing market power.

Based on such argument, Boone Indicator (BI), β, can be estimated through the following regression equation

$$\ln s_i = \alpha + \beta MC_i$$

in which s_i is the market share for bank i and MC_i is its marginal cost, thus β is the elasticity of a bank's market share to marginal cost. $\beta = 0$ implies that the bank is a monopoly, while a negative sign in β reflects the punishment of competition on inefficient banks. The more negative β is, the more competitive is the market.

4.6.2 IDENTIFYING THE COMPETITION EFFECTS ON BANK BEHAVIOR

One main concern about identification is the impact of banking regulation. Banking is one of the most heavily regulated industries, therefore, the structure of banking competition and banks' behavior are both largely shaped by the underlying regulation, leading to severe endogeneity problems in model specification. In literature, three approaches have been deployed for clean identification:

- The first one is to explore the pre-regulation era, the period when regulatory agencies and policies were largely absent;
- The second one is to explore the wave of deregulation in 1980s and 1990s across the world, when many restrictions on banking competition were relaxed;
- The third one is to explore the correlation between cross-country variation in banking regulation and the outcome variables, controlling for bank-level and country-level characteristics.

EXPLORING THE PRE-REGULATION ERA

One way to isolate the confounding effects of banking regulation is to focus on the early age of banking when banks were mostly free from regulation. Braggion et al. (2017) study a data set of over 30,000 loans granted by 43 English and Welsh banks between 1885 and 1925, when banking regulation was almost non-existing and invariant—this removes the confounding effects that regulation may generate. All loans are matched with county-level banking concentration (measured by HHI). It is found that when local banking concentration is high and the implied competition is low, banks choose to be safer: they lend less per granted loan, and require more collateral from borrowers; as a result, the ratio of non-performing loans also falls. The evidence seems to be consistent with the *franchise value hypothesis*.

Carlson et al. (2019) explore the capital requirement in a similar lightly-regulated period—the National Banking Era (1863–1913) in the US banking history—for identification. Instead of a restriction on leverage, capital requirement was merely the minimum *size* of equity to found a bank, or a fixed cost for entry, and it varies with the population of a bank's location. Therefore, a change in local official population statistics, as a result of decennial census, may affect the entry barrier of new entrants, hence the contestability of local market for banking. Increasing local population may result in a higher entry cost, reducing the number of new entrants, hence reducing local market competition: in this case, they find that incumbent banks' credit supply falls, as well as their likelihood of failure, implying that weaker competition reduces banks' risk-taking.

EXPLORING THE WAVE OF DEREGULATION

The waves of regulation and deregulation on entry and expansion of banks in US history make the US an ideal laboratory to study the impacts of changes in competition. Kroszner and Strahan (2014) provide a vivid recount of causes, consequences, and implications of regulation and deregulation in the US banking industry. Throughout the past century, the degree of banking competition was largely shaped by state-level restrictions on entry and expansion of banks. The key events include

- The 1927 McFadden Act authorized the states over limiting banks' *intrastate* branching activities. Since then, states only allowed banks to own subsidiaries within states, and some states only allowed banks to operate no more than one office (so-called "unit banking") to prevent banks from having any branches;
- To circumvent intrastate branching restrictions by the McFadden Act, banks built multibank holding companies (MBHCs) that operated across states. The loophole was filled by the Douglas Amendment to the 1956 Bank Holding Company (BHC) Act, which effectively barred *interstate* branching, making it impossible for bank holding companies to operate outside the states where their headquarters were located;
- State-level restrictions on intrastate branching had been gradually lifted since 1930s, and by 1970 intrastate branching was permitted in twelve states. The big wave of deregulating intrastate branching

came in 1970s and 1980s, and by 1994, almost all states removed the restrictions. The deregulation often took a two-step approach: first, MBHCs were allowed to acquire banks, and convert acquired banks and subsidiaries into branches; second, MBHCs were permitted to open new branches;
- States started to deregulate interstate branching from the late 1970s. The Reigle-Neal Interstate Banking and Branching Efficiency Act (IBBEA) of 1994 formally removed all restrictions on interstate banking across the US. Figure 4.4 from Célerier and Matray (2019) shows that, after IBBEA of 1994, the share of interstate branches has been steadily rising in the US.

Keeley (1990) is among the first to exploit the deregulation wave regarding intrastate and interstate banking in the 1970s and 1980s, using state-level relaxation on branching, establishing MHBCs, and interstate entry as key variables to proxy the degree of bank competition on the state level. It is found that removing states' protection from competition leads to a fall in banks' market value, implying a fall in banks' mark-up

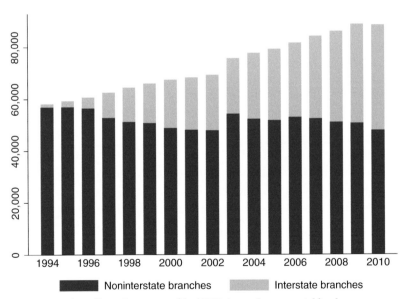

Figure 4.4 Number of branches operated by FDIC-insured commercial banks
Source: Célerier and Matray (2019).

as a result of lower market power. However, this is also associated with a fall in banks' asset value, as well as a higher risk premium on uninsured deposits, implying higher bank risk. Zooming in to market competition structure on the metropolitan level during a 5-year sample period following the passage of IBBEA 1994, Dick (2006) finds that although the oligopolistic competition structure remains largely intact, loan rates decrease and deposit rates increase, implying a fall in banks' net interest margin. Deregulation on interstate banking seems to make the market more contestable and consumers benefit from larger banking networks, while the net effect on the riskiness of banks is unclear: as Hughes et al. (1996) suggest, the geographical diversification enables banks to better hedge against regional shocks, while improved cost efficiency may induce banks to take more risks in their portfolios. As for bank performance, Jayaratne and Strahan (1998) document improved profitability and loan quality after removing restrictions on intrastate branching and—to a lesser extent—interstate branching. One possible reason is that less efficient and malfunctioning banks which were previously protected by state regulation are now replaced by more efficient competitors, leading to improvements in bank performance—at least in the short run.

EXPLORING THE CROSS-COUNTRY VARIATIONS

Using bank-level data from BANKSCOPE, including 35,834 bank-year observations covering banks from 50 countries during 1994–2001, Claessens and Laeven (2004) measure bank competition using H-statistic. The H-statistic estimates are mostly between 0.60 and 0.80, suggesting that banking competition is featured by monopolistic competition. Regressing estimated H-statistic H_i on country characteristics C_i of country i,

$$H_i = \alpha + \beta C_i + \epsilon_i,$$

they find that banks are more competitive in countries with better economic development (for instance, higher GDP per capita), *more* concentrated banking sector, higher foreign bank ownership, and lower restriction for new entrants—underlining the importance of contestability on determining the effective competition.

Fungáčová et al. (2017) compute the cost of bank credit, using firm-level data from Amadeus, including over 13 million firm-year observations for more than 4.5 million firms from EU 20 countries during 2001–2011, Fungáčová et al. (2017) employ a wide range of competition indicators such as CR5, HHI, LI, and H-statistic. Overall, their results consistently show that firms' cost of funding increases with the degree of competition, and such effect is more pronounced for SMEs, suggesting that the information channel of competition dominates.

4.6.3 REAL EFFECTS OF BANKING COMPETITION

Banking competition may affect real economy in many ways. The most direct effect may be borrowers' funding cost. For example, Rice and Strahan (2010) explore the cross-state variations in barriers to entry during the phasing-in period of IBBEA after 1994, when states can maintain certain barriers to interstate banking, such as minimum age requirement on acquired banks, restrictions on opening new branches, etc. Using the outcomes of three waves from the Survey of Small Business Finance, 1993–2003, in which the pre-IBBEA survey of 1993 serves as a control group, they find that after 1994 small firms' borrowing cost is, on average, 80–100 basis points lower in states with fewer barriers to interstate banking, while there is no significant difference in the volume of firms' debt funding, implying that increasing post-deregulation banking competition improves small firms' access to credit through reducing funding cost.

Several studies explore the deregulation wave in the US from 1970s to 2000s, to identify the competition effects on social welfare. Beck et al. (2010) focus on the impact of removing *intrastate* branching restrictions on income distribution. As deregulation took place at different times across states, this allows them to explore a difference-in-differences strategy for identification, as long as the cross-state timing of bank branch deregulation was unaffected by the distribution of income. Specifically, they estimate an equation

$$Y_{st} = \alpha + \beta D_{st} + \delta X_{st} + A_s + B_t + \epsilon_{st} \qquad (4.16)$$

in which Y_{st} is the outcome variable in state s and year t, X_{st} contains state-level controls, A_s/B_t captures state/year fixed effects. The variable that captures deregulation is D_{st}, which is a dummy variable that equals 1 for state s that was after deregulation in year t, and 0 otherwise. Applying this methodology using distribution of income computed from Current Population Survey (CPS), an annual survey of about 60,000 households across the United States, they find that removing intrastate branching restrictions leads to a fall of 60% standard deviation of Gini coefficient, suggesting a falling inequality in income, and this mainly comes from the lower part of the income distribution.

They further show the dynamics of the relationship between deregulation and inequality (log Gini coefficient, $\ln(Gini)$) from 10 years before to 15 years after deregulation in state s by estimating

$$\ln(Gini)_{st} = \alpha + \beta_1 D_{st}^{-10} + \beta_2 D_{st}^{-9} + \ldots + \beta_{25} D_{st}^{+15} + A_s + B_t + \epsilon_{st} \quad (4.17)$$

in which D_{st}^{-i}/D_{st}^{+i} is a dummy variable that equals 1 if year t is i year(s) before/after the deregulation in state s, 0 otherwise, and A_s/B_t captures state/year fixed effects; β s then reflect the dynamics in the impact of deregulation on income inequality over time. Figure 4.5 shows the results of estimates, $\beta_1, \beta_2, \ldots, \beta_{25}$ from (4.17): although the impact was not significant from zero before deregulation starts in year 0—suggesting the estimate from (4.16) is not biased by the pre-deregulation trends, income inequality falls significantly after deregulation and the effect persists even 15 years afterwards.

Deregulation that removes *interstate* branching restrictions increases financial inclusion for low-income households, as Célerier and Matray (2019) document. As Figure 4.4 shows, after interstate branching restrictions started to be removed in 1994, the share of interstate branches (gray bars) in total number of bank branches in the US increased substantially. Using a similar difference-in-differences structure as (4.16), they find that totally removing the restrictions increases the density of bank branches by 20%, implying a stronger post-deregulation bank competition. Applying the information about income and demographics for 107,386 low-income households from Survey of Income and Program Participation (SIPP) during 1993–2005, they find that full deregulation in

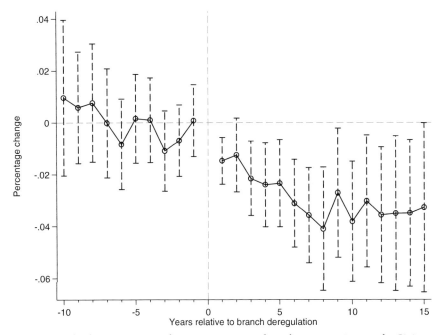

Figure 4.5 *The dynamic impact of removing intrastate branching restrictions on the Gini coefficient in the US, 1976–1994*

Source: Beck et al. (2010), over a 25-year window from 10 years before deregulation to 15 years after deregulation. The dashed lines represent 95% confidence intervals, adjusted for state-level clustering.

a state increases the probability for a household to hold a bank account by about 4%, and as a result, these households accumulate more wealth, consume more durable goods, and are less likely to face financial stresses.

4.7 EXERCISES

1. **Understanding bank competition in your country/region through data**

    Exploring the data resources listed in Exercise 1, Chapter 1, depending on data availability, try to answer the following questions regarding bank competition in your country/region:

    (a) Plot the time trends in the measurements of bank competition, such as CRn, HHI, H-statistic, Lerner Index, etc., for your country/region.

i. What are the general trends in bank competition in your country/region?
ii. What may explain the trends?
iii. Can you design empirical tests on your hypotheses?

(b) Entry and exit:

i. Are there major mergers and acquisitions (M&As) in your sample period?
ii. Are there any new major entrants, especially those from the multinational global banks? Are there any major exits?
iii. Are there any regulation or deregulation on entry or branching restrictions, both on the national level and regional level?
iv. What are the consequences on bank competition after these episodes?

2 **Transaction cost, monopolistic competition, and bank entry, based on Salop (1979)**

Consider an economy with N banks, indexed by $i=1,2,\ldots,N$, and a continuum of depositors whose population is normalized to D. The depositors are evenly distributed along a circular street, as Figure 4.6 shows. The circumference of the street is normalized to 1.

Each depositor has one unit of endowment. Banks collect endowments from depositors and invest the deposits in a production technology with a constant rate of return r. To reach a bank and deposit, a depositor must incur a transaction cost of c for

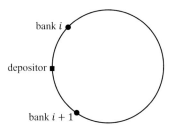

Figure 4.6 Banks and depositors in the circular world

each unit of distance between her location and the bank's office. For each bank i, a fixed cost f must be paid to open its office.

(a) Assume that, in the beginning of the world, a social planner creates the banking system by locating the banks symmetrically along the street. Compute the total social cost of the banking system, i.e., the sum of banks' total fixed costs and depositors' total transaction costs.

(b) What is the optimal number of banks, if the planner aims to minimize the social cost of the banking system? From now on, assume that, without any social planner, the entry to the banking system is free in the beginning of the world, i.e., N banks simultaneously locate themselves and open their offices along the street. Banks attract depositors in their neighborhood by offering deposit rates r_D^i, $i=1,2,\ldots,N$.

(c) Consider two neighboring banks, i and $i+1$, as Figure 4.6 shows. Define the marginal depositor living between the two banks as a depositor who is indifferent between going to bank i or bank $i+1$, under their offered deposit rates, r_D^i and r_D^{i+1}. Compute the distance between the marginal depositor and bank i, and total deposit supply to this bank.

(d) What is the optimal deposit rate r_D^i that maximizes bank i's profit, taking its neighbors' deposit rates as given? Assume that all banks are symmetric, compute the equilibrium market deposit rate and each bank's profit.

(e) Free-entry implies that a bank is willing to enter the banking system as long as its profit fully covers the fixed cost f. What is the number of banks in equilibrium under free-entry? Is it different from the result in question (b)?

3 **Financial liberalization and dynamic moral hazard, based on Hellmann et al. (2000)**

Consider a banking sector with a finite number N limited liability banks that may operate over an infinite discrete time horizon, $T \to +\infty$. In each period, a representative bank i offers an interest rate on deposits of r_i in competition with other banks which offer depositors interest rates $\mathbf{r}_{-i}$. The total volume of deposits mobilized by the bank is $D(r_i, \mathbf{r}_{-i})$, with the volume of deposits increasing in the bank's own interest rate and decreasing in the competitors' rate, i.e., $\dfrac{\partial D}{\partial r_i} > 0$ and $\dfrac{\partial D}{\partial r_j} < 0$, $\forall j \neq i$. Depositors have full deposit insurance, so the volume of deposits depends only on the interest rates offered.

After liabilities have been raised in the beginning of each period, the bank allocates its assets on either of two assets available: the prudent asset, with a return α, and the gambling asset, with a return of γ with probability θ and 0 with probability $1-\theta$. The prudent asset has higher expected return, $\alpha > \theta\gamma$, but if the gamble succeeds, the bank earns higher private return, $\gamma > \alpha$. When the gamble fails, the bank will lose its license of banking from the next period onward. Banks' discount factor is $0 < \delta < 1$.

The bank's liabilities include both the deposits it collects and its own capital k, which is expressed as a percentage of the deposits mobilized so that the total assets invested equal $(1+k)D(r_i, \mathbf{r}_{-i})$. The bank's owners have also an alternative use of their capital that ensures a return equal to ρ. This implies that the opportunity cost of capital is ρ.

The prudent asset ensures per-period profit

$$\pi_P(r_i, \mathbf{r}_{-i}, k) \equiv m_P(r_i, k) D(r_i, \mathbf{r}_{-i}).$$

When the bank gambles, the per-period profit is

$$\pi_G(r_i, \mathbf{r}_{-i}, k) \equiv m_G(r_i, k) D(r_i, \mathbf{r}_{-i}).$$

$m_P(r_i, k)$ is the effective profit margin earned on each unit of deposit if the bank chooses the prudent asset, while $m_G(r_i, k)$ is the effective profit margin earned on each unit of deposit if the bank chooses the gambling asset.

(a) Compute $m_P(r_i, k)$ and $m_G(r_i, k)$ in an unregulated market in which banks are free to choose any level of k. Each period can be divided into 3 stages:

Stage 1 Banks decide simultaneously their interest rates;

Stage 2 Each bank decides its own capital level;
Stage 3 Each bank decides whether to invest in the prudent asset or in the gambling asset.

The *no-gambling condition* under which only prudent assets are preferred under such settings has the form $r \leq \hat{r}(k)$ (i.e., the threshold interest rate $\hat{r}$ is a function of k).

(b) Compute $\hat{r}(k)$ under symmetric equilibrium in which all the banks choose the prudent asset and set the same interest rate r_P. Show that the first order condition requires
$$m_P(r_P, k) = \frac{D(r_P, \mathbf{r}_P)}{\frac{\partial D(r_P, \mathbf{r}_P)}{\partial r_i}},$$
and the equilibrium interest rate can be written as $r_P = f(\alpha, \rho, k, \epsilon)$, in which ϵ is the elasticity of deposit demand $D(r_P, \mathbf{r}_P)$ with respect to interest rate r_P.

(c) Compute $f(\alpha, \rho, k, \epsilon)$.

(d) If $\rho > \alpha$, what is the optimal k for the bank?
Keep $\rho > \alpha$. Suppose now a regulation is introduced, requiring a bank to invest an amount of own capital equal no less than a share k^R of its total deposits mobilized.

(e) What is the effect of an increase in k^R on r_P and on $\hat{r}$? Are there values of δ for which $\frac{\delta \hat{r}}{\delta k} < 0$?

(f) Assume now that $\hat{r}(k)$ is increasing in k. Draw r_P and $\hat{r}$ as a function of k.
Let $\underline{k}$ be defined by the equation $r_P(\underline{k}) = \hat{r}(\underline{k})$. Consider two alternative policies, both sufficient to ensure that banks choose the prudent investment:

Policy 1 Impose $k^R > \underline{k}$;

Policy 2 A cap on the interest rate that requires banks to offer no higher than $r_P(k^R)$, together with a capital requirement of k_0, which satisfies $\hat{r}(k_0) = r_P(k^R)$.

(g) If policy 1 is chosen, show where k_0 lies in the graph drawn for question (f). Which of the two policies is optimal for the regulator?

4 **Imperfect screening and credit rating, based on Shaffer (1998)**
   Following all the settings in Section 4.5, assume that there are n banks competing in the credit market. Instead of having each bank observe a private signal from each applicant, now assume that there is a credit rating agency providing credit scores of all potential borrowers for all banks; that is, when an applicant approaches multiple banks, these banks will see the same credit score of her. Precisely, a credit score is a noisy signal about the applicant's type, such that

   - If the applicant is a truly good borrower, the probability that the signal indicates that she is good is $\zeta(H|\mathcal{H})$;
   - If the applicant is a truly bad borrower, the probability that the signal indicates that she is bad is $\zeta(L|\mathcal{L})$.

   (a) What is the average loan loss rate, if all banks rely on the common credit scores? Suppose $p(H|\mathcal{H})=p(L|\mathcal{L})=0.9$, $n=20$, and $\zeta(H|\mathcal{H})=\zeta(L|\mathcal{L})$, what is the minimum $\zeta(H|\mathcal{H})/\zeta(L|\mathcal{L})$ that achieves the same loan loss rate, compared with the case in Section 4.5 where each bank observes a private signal $p(H|\mathcal{H})/p(L|\mathcal{L})$ from each applicant?
   (b) Suppose $p(H|\mathcal{H})=p(L|\mathcal{L})=0.9$, $n=20$, $\zeta(H|\mathcal{H})=\zeta(L|\mathcal{L})$, $\pi_H=1$, $\pi_L=0.5$, $a=0.8$, and $r=0.1$. What is the minimum $\zeta(H|\mathcal{H})/\zeta(L|\mathcal{L})$ that achieves the same expected profit for each bank, compared with the case in Section 4.5 where each bank observes a private signal $p(H|\mathcal{H})/p(L|\mathcal{L})$ from each applicant?
   (c) Continue with question (b), keep all parameters the same, except $\pi_L=0.8$ and $a=0.9$, compute the minimum $\zeta(H|\mathcal{H})/\zeta(L|\mathcal{L})$. Comparing the results in questions (b) and (c), when are banks more likely to prefer using common credit scores instead of individual signals?

CHAPTER 5
Securitized banking

5.1 INTRODUCTION

In many people's mind, banking, or financial intermediation, may be best characterized as in Figure 5.1: a bank takes deposits from households and firms who have funds to save, and issues loans to households and firms who need funding; just as the figure shows, a bank may raise deposits from some households to issue mortgage loans to other households. The bank then collects mortgage payments from the borrowers and returns some of the proceeds to the depositors, earning a profit from the difference between lending rate and deposit rate—the so-called net interest margin.

However, modern banking has gone far beyond such "traditional" intermediation chain, as Shin (2010) shows; instead, the same intermediation service between depositing households and borrowing households may be carried out through a very long intermediation chain, as is shown in Figure 5.2. First, mortgage loans are pooled and financed by mortgage-backed securities (MBS), then these securities

Figure 5.1 *Traditional intermediation chain*
Source: Shin (2010).

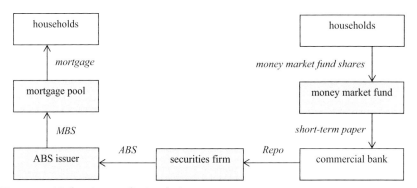

Figure 5.2 *Modern intermediation chain*
Source: Shin (2010). MBS: mortgage-backed security, ABS: asset-backed security.

are transferred to asset-backed security (ABS) issuers and may be further packed into new products such as collateralized debt obligation (CDO). Institutional investors, as well as commercial banks hold those securities that are produced in the intermediation chain, and they use these securities as collateral for funding in the so-called repo market. Commercial banks may raise funding by issuing short-term commercial papers that are sold to money market funds, and the "depositor" households may hold the shares of money market funds. Of course, such a complicated intermediation procedure is not restricted to mortgage loans; it also applies to almost every type of bank credit, such as credit cards, students' loans, or corporate lending.

Two key features stand out from this long, modern intermediation chain. The first is *securitization*, that loan issuing banks do not hold loans on their balance sheets any more, instead, loans are sold and transferred to other financial institutions to produce various securities that are backed by these loans. Second, banks rely less on retail deposits collected from depositors, but rather, they raise a large quantity of funding from other financial institutions, via repurchase agreement (*repo*) using those produced securities as collateral. As much of modern intermediation chain is based on securitization, such intermediation chain is often called *securitized banking*.

5.1.1 RISK APPETITE AND SECURITIZATION

Why do banks bother to abandon the simple, straightforward traditional intermediation chain and go for much more complex securitized banking? One reason is that securitization provides much desired risk allocation and risk sharing for the financial market, when market participants have different *risk appetites*, or, the willingness to bear risks. For example, a pensioner may need steady and risk-free cash flow from her investments, while a hedge fund is much more willing to take risks. In the presence of substantial differences in people's risk appetites, standard debt contracts such as deposit contract provided in traditional banking, obviously cannot fit all.

We can see how securitization improves risk sharing among people with different risk appetites through a simple example. Suppose that there are investment opportunities on three different assets, $\{A,B,C\}$. As Table 5.1 shows, each of the assets needs an initial investments to start with.

There are four states of the world, $\{1,2,3,4\}$, with equal probabilities. Return on each asset varies across states, and Table 5.2 shows each asset's state-contingent returns, as well as each asset's expected return and the state-contingent total returns of all assets. Note that the expected return of each asset exceeds its initial investment, implying that all of them are socially desirable.

Suppose that there are three investors who seek investment opportunities. They are different in wealth and state-contingent required returns, or, "risk appetite":

- Investor 1 has 400 unit wealth, and she needs a safe, risk-free payoff—resembling a pensioner;
- Investor 2 has 200 unit wealth, and she does not have any requirement on payoff—resembling a hedge fund;
- Investor 3 has 350 unit wealth, and she needs a return of at least 100 in state 1—resembling a bank that needs to meet liquidity demand in a certain state.

Investors' wealth and return requirements are summarized in Table 5.3.

Table 5.1 Initial investments required by the assets

	Asset A	Asset B	Asset C
Required initial investments	400	250	300

Table 5.2 Payoff structure of the assets

	Asset A	Asset B	Asset C	Total
State 1	1000	800	0	1800
State 2	800	200	400	1400
State 3	200	200	600	1000
State 4	0	0	400	400
Mean	500	300	350	1150

Table 5.3 Initial investments required by the assets

	Investor 1	Investor 2	Investor 3
Wealth	400	200	350
Requirement	risk-free	nothing	return $\geq$ 100 in state 1

BENCHMARK: FRICTIONLESS ECONOMY

What will be the realized resource allocation in this economy? Our benchmark is the first-best solution for the hypothetical, frictionless economy in which investors have no requirements on payoffs. In this case, given that assets have positive net present values, a social planner will pool the wealth, 950, from all investors, invest in all three assets that require 950 total initial investment, and distribute the proceeds from the assets in each state among investors with their gross expected return rates being no lower than 1. As a result, social welfare is maximized, as all assets are supported.

MATCHING MARKET

Now, given investors' different risk appetites, what will be the realized resource allocation in this economy, should there be no such social planner? Assume that we allow investors to match and pick up desired assets by themselves. It is easy to see that

- Investor 1 will not invest, as all assets are risky;
- Investor 2 will not invest, as one needs at least 250 to acquire an asset;
- Investor 3 will invest in asset B, given that the initial investment is feasible and her payoff requirement is met.

In the outcome, only one asset B is supported, which is obviously inferior to the first-best solution.

TRADITIONAL BANKING SOLUTION

Would the traditional banking solution improve the allocation? Suppose now there is a bank that can pool funds, or, "deposits" from investors and invest on behalf of them. Assume that investors have equal seniority over claiming the bank's assets, i.e., when the bank fails, they share bank assets in proportion to their deposits. It is easy to see that

- It is impossible to collect funds from all three investors and invest in all three assets: the total payoff in state 4 is only 400, by equal seniority, investor 1's claim is worth less than 400 and she has to incur a loss, so that it is impossible to provide her a risk-free return;
- It is only possible to collect funds from investors 2 and 3, then invest in either assets B and C, or A only.

The outcome from the banking solution is thus inferior to the first-best solution, too.

SECURITIZATION SOLUTION

Now we allow the bank to "securitize" the assets: the bank pools all three assets, and issues three securities whose returns are backed by the assets to the investors. The bank promises a state-contingent payoff for each of the securities, which is summarized in Table 5.4.

It is easy to see that in each state the total return from the assets is entirely paid off to the security holders, and the investors are willing to buy these securities: investor 1 is willing to buy security 1 because it yields a risk-free return across states; investors 2 and 3 are willing to buy securities 2 and 3, respectively, as their risk preferences are fulfilled. As a result, all three assets are supported by the securitization solution, and the first-best solution is achieved. That is, securitization achieves optimal risk-sharing, by creating asset-backed securities that fit investors' risk appetites.

Table 5.4 State-contingent payoff structure of the structured securities

	Security 1	Security 2	Security 3	Total
State 1	400	600	800	1800
State 2	400	400	600	1400
State 3	400	200	400	1000
State 4	400	0	0	400
Mean	400	300	450	1150

5.1.2 PROCEDURE OF SECURITIZATION

In reality, securitization is conducted in very much the same way. Figure 5.3 explains how securitization is worked out in a highly simplified chart. A stylized financial intermediary, call it a bank, issues loans to the borrowers. The loans are illiquid to the bank as long as they stay on the bank's balance sheet. The bank can then "liquidize" the illiquid loans to raise funding for the other investment opportunities and remove the loans from its balance sheet. To do so, the bank *originates to distribute*: a special purpose vehicle (SPV) is established to buy the loans originated from the bank and package them into securities. A characteristic feature in this process is tranching, that the asset pool is sliced into various layers, or tranches. And each of the tranches is sold to investors with a different appetite for risks.

The securitization process can go further. As Figure 5.3 shows, some of the securitization tranches may be purchased by collateralized debt obligation (CDO) issuers, and CDO issuers may refine the securities and slice them again into CDO tranches, then sell them to finance the purchase. In each stage of securitization, the tranches differ in their seniorities. A higher layer in the tranches enjoys higher seniority in the debt claim, and hence the priority in repayment. The most senior

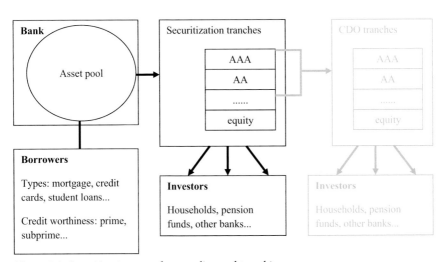

Figure 5.3 *Securitization procedure: pooling and tranching*

tranche is paid out first, followed by the subordinated ones such as the "mezzanine" tranche, junior tranche, and equity tranche—just like a cascade of cash. When it comes to a loss, the loss is first borne by the most junior tranche, and then the mezzanine tranche, and so on. As the most senior tranche is supposed to bear the least risk, typically it receives the highest credit rating. The rating becomes lower when moving down the tranches.

The most senior tranche with the highest credit rating is regarded as "bankruptcy remote" and least risky, with default probability being next to zero. In normal times, it is generally seen as safe as government bonds and widely accepted as eligible collateral by banks and financial institutions. For the less senior tranches, CDO issuers may repack them with fresh assets from elsewhere and go on with the securitization procedure, producing new CDO tranches, i.e., CDO of CDO, or CDO^2. The same procedure may continue with producing CDO^3, and so on.

5.1.3 REPO AND SECURITIZED BANKING

Out of securitization, high quality tranches are often held by banks and other financial institutions as eligible collateral in short-term borrowing using the so-called *repurchase agreements* (repo). Figure 5.4 how securitization and repo lending transform traditional banking into *securitized banking*: after issuing mortgage loans, the lending bank sells loans to securitizers and the loans are moved out of its balance sheet. As a reward, the bank receives cash and securities from loan sales and securitization. Using the securities as collateral, the bank raises funding from creditors in the money market through repo.

Figure 5.5 shows how repo works. In a repo agreement, the lender lends cash—say the amount of X—to the borrower today, against eligible collateral—say, AAA-rated securitization tranches with face value of Z, with a promise to repurchase the securities tomorrow at the price of Y. In this way, the lender provides the amount X of cash to the borrower over the agreement period. The interest rate the lender charges on the agreement, which is basically the lending rate,

$$\frac{Y-X}{X}\times 100\%,$$

is called *repo rate*. The discount on collateral value,

$$\frac{Z-X}{Z}\times 100\%,$$

is called *haircut* to reflect the risk in the return of security in collateral: should the borrower default, the lender would seize the collateral and recover its lending X by selling the collateral in the market. Therefore, the riskier the security is, the higher the haircut is required by the lender.

Repo that only involves lender and borrower, as is shown in Figure 5.5, is called *bi-party repo*. Due to high *counterparty risk* that the borrower or lender may default, bi-party repo is mostly used between large financial institutions with low counterparty risks. A more common repo

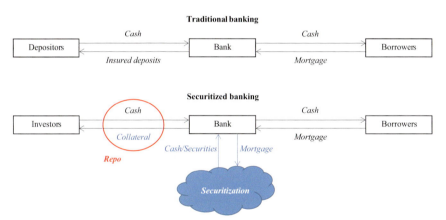

Figure 5.4 *Traditional banking versus securitized banking*

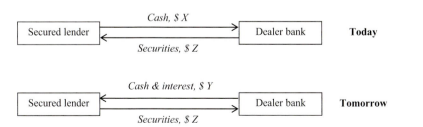

Figure 5.5 *Bi-party repo*

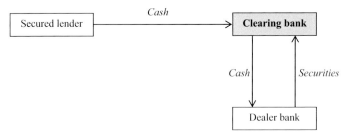

Figure 5.6 Tri-party repo

relationship is the so-called *tri-party repo*, as Figure 5.6 shows, in which a *clearing bank* serves as the intermediary between lender and borrower to reduce counterparty risks. The clearing bank takes the custody of the securities, or, repo collateral, settles the agreements, and supervises the delivery of cash and collateral.

Securitization and repo have greatly reshaped the banking industry. The most prominent feature in securitized banking is that many non-bank financial institutions are involved in the intermediation chain, such as securitizers, ABS/CDO issuers, money market funds, etc., as Figure 5.2 shows. These financial institutions are not traditional banks that are defined in banking legislation; they are often not subject to banking regulation, and not eligible for central bank facilities. For this reason, they are often called *shadow banks*. Due to limit of space, we will not show more details on shadow banking, as it is nowadays a highly complex system. Interested readers may refer to extensive surveys such as Pozsar et al. (2012), Adrian and Ashcraft (2012), and International Monetary Fund (2014).

Although securitized banking is very much different in many ways, compared with traditional banking, their business models are also quite comparable, as is shown in Table 5.5, summarized in Gorton and Metrick (2012). Traditional banking is based on fractional reserve banking against liquidity risks, and central bank liquidity facilities provide public liquidity insurance for banks; securitized banking relies on haircuts in repo, that provide private insurance for lenders. In traditional banking, depositors are guaranteed by (public) deposit insurance, while in securitized banking, creditors are protected by high-quality collateral when borrowers default; banks' funding cost

Table 5.5 Traditional banking versus securitized banking

Traditional banking	Securitized banking

(1) Cushion: reserves
    Minimum ratio set by regulator
    Can be borrowed from central bank
(2) Backstop: deposit insurance
    Public guarantee
(3) Funding cost: deposit rates
    Can be raised to attract depositors
(4) Products: loans on balance sheet
	(1) Cushion: haircuts
	    Minimum level set by counterparties
	    No access to central bank
	(2) Backstop: collateral
	    Cash or high quality assets
	(3) Funding cost: repo rates
	    Can be raised to attract counterparties
	(4) Products: securitized loans
	    Some may be kept on balance sheet and used as collateral in repo

Source: Gorton and Metrick (2012).

in traditional banking is deposit rate paid for depositors, while banks' funding cost in securitized banking is repo rate paid for creditors; the main products in traditional banking are loans that stay in banks' balance sheet, while the main products in securitized banking are securitized loans that are sold to securitizers.

In securitized banking, banks are heavily intertwined with non-bank financial institutions: banks are providing assets as input for securitization, and bank funding heavily relies on the repo market that is much based on securities produced in securitization. There are good reasons why banks move towards securitization-based banking. On the positive side, expertise of financial institutions involved in securitization allows them to produce financial products that better fit investors' different risk appetites for better risk allocation and risk sharing; the repo market allows banks to borrow from a wide variety of financial institutions—banks and non-banks—at lower cost. On the negative side, securitized banking allows banks to move activities along the intermediation chain into non-regulated shadow banks, which reduces banks regulatory cost but also shifts risks to the shadow; if anything goes wrong in shadow banks, it will backfire and destabilize banks. This is particularly of a concern when banks originate to distribute: the fact that risky loans will be sold to securitizers and moved off banks' balance sheets may reduce banks' incentive to properly screen the loan applications; as a result of lax screening, too many risky loans, or, *subprime loans*, will be securitized. This increases the probability of default to securities produced in securitization; once such default happens, haircuts on related securities will rise in the repo market, which may create trouble for banks that raise funding from the repo market.

Bank intermediation also becomes more fragile under securitized banking. The main reason is that repo, the key mechanism that banks rely on, is built on securities as collateral that are highly sensitive to information and market stress. In normal times, securities in repo are usually of high quality and are believed to be insensitive to adverse private information; as a result, haircuts on these securities are low in the repo market. However, under market stress with rising uncertainties on the quality of underlying assets in these securities, those information-insensitive securities may suddenly become information-sensitive that repo lenders will ask for higher haircuts on these securities, creating troubles for borrowers in the repo market. With rising haircuts, banks may not be able to refinance and this may force them to deleverage, for example, by asset fire sale, which may further aggravate the market.

The experience in the repo market during the 2007–2009 financial crisis provides a vivid episode on the fragility in securitized banking. Before the crisis, banks in the US issued a large quantity of substandard, or, subprime mortgage loans during housing boom, by securitization, and these subprime assets were transformed into a wide variety of securities that were used as collateral in the repo market. In mid-2007, when more and more subprime loans defaulted, haircuts on subprime-related securities started to rise. However, structure of these securities is highly complex, and after many rounds of mixing with other assets and repacking, it is difficult to locate the affected assets and reprice the securities in a short time; as a response, without being able to know the true quality of affected securities, market participants have to ask for a higher haircut, for fear of buying "lemons". As Figure 5.7 shows, haircuts on subprime-related securities rose sharply in response to market stresses in 2008, and went up to 100% after the collapse of Lehman Brothers in September 2008. More

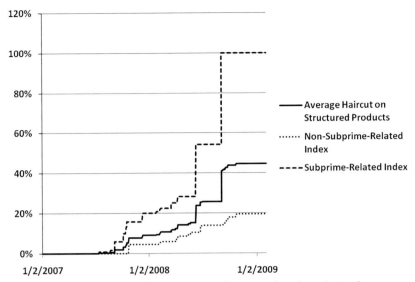

Figure 5.7 Repo haircuts on different categories of structured products during the 2007–2009 financial crisis

Source: Gorton and Metrick (2009). Notes: the solid lines denote the average haircut on structured products, the dashed lines denote the average haircut on subprime-related products, and the dotted lines denote the average haircut on non-subprime related products.

strikingly, even securities that were not related to subprime assets suffered from substantially rising haircuts, because complex structure in these securities prevents market participants from properly inferring how much they are related to subprime assets. Such large haircuts led to a freeze in the repo market so that banks could not roll over their debts, forcing them into costly deleveraging and liquidation—resembling bank runs in traditional banking, although instead of having depositors explicitly queue in front of banks, "bank run" here rather arises from banks' incapability to refinance from the repo market due to prohibitively high haircuts, or, a quiet *run on the repos*.

In the rest of this chapter, we will focus on the implication of securitized banking on financial stability. In Section 5.2, we examine how banks' incentive in screening loan applications is affected by securitization, i.e., when banks know that the loans will be sold to securitizers. We show that if banks' screening effort improves the quality of loans, the benefit will be shared by banks and securitizers while the cost is fully borne by banks. In this sense, loan screening exhibits a property of positive externality. As a result, banks' screening effort is inefficiently low in equilibrium, reducing the quality of granted loans and increasing instability in the financial system.

In Section 5.3, we show how securitization and haircut reinforce each other and make securitized banking more fragile. Banks originate to distribute, so that they can expand lending through securitizing loans; later, the repo market allows them to increase leverage. However, in the downturn, rising haircut forces banks into costly liquidation, and the falling asset price caused by asset fire sale leads to more liquidation and puts banks into a downward deleveraging spiral. Securitized banking thus implies more volatility in bank lending.

In Section 5.4, we discuss how repo runs—repo market frictions that prevent banks from rolling over their debts—arise in securitized banking. Similar to the static Diamond-Dybvig model in Chapter 2, Section 2.2, banks face liquidity shocks from investors' withdrawal demand, while in dynamics, they create liquidity by rolling over long-term debts via refinancing themselves with repo. Fragility in banking dynamics arises in repo runs, so that investors refuse to refinance with banks, making banks fail. Banks are more vulnerable to repo runs, if they are more leveraged, rely more on short-term repo funding, or hold fewer liquidity buffers.

5.2 LOAN SALE AND SCREENING

In securitized banking, a key feature in bank lending is that banks no longer keep all loans on their balance sheets, but rather, they move loans off balance sheets and sell to market investors such as securitizers. However, will banks still conduct proper risk management and risk analysis, if they know that loans they issue will not be held by themselves in the future? In this section, we answer this question with a simple model based on Gorton and Pennacchi (1995).

5.2.1 MODELLING LOAN SALE AND SCREENING EFFORT

Consider a bank's profit maximization problem, given that it may sell part of a loan to market investors—for example, securitizers who produce structured securities out of the loan. Assume that the loan requires one unit of initial funding, and yields a stochastic return x, $0 \leq x \leq R$ at the end of T periods. The return x follows a joint cumulative distribution function of $F(x,e)$, in which e denotes the bank's effort of screening. The market participants only know the cumulative distribution function $F(x,e)$, but they cannot observe the bank's screening effort e, that is, e is the bank's private information. Assume that

$$F(x, \lambda e + (1-\lambda)e') \leq \lambda F(x,e) + (1-\lambda) F(x,e') \quad (5.1)$$
$$\text{for any} \quad 0 < \lambda < 1, \quad (5.2)$$

with arbitrary e and e'. The assumption (5.1) implies that screening is desirable; it improves loan quality so that higher screening effort increases mean return of the loan, while the marginal return in loan quality is diminishing in e.

The bank's screening technology is featured by constant return to scale (CRS), which can be captured by a cost function $c(e) = ce$, with c being a positive constant.

The bank can sell a share s ($0 < s < 1$) of the loan to market investors who are risk-neutral and retain the rest of the loan, $1-s$, on its balance sheet. That is, the loan is partially funded by market investors who require an expected return—call it r_s—on the purchased loan; besides that, the rest of the loan is funded by depositors who require a deposit rate of r_d.

The bank's demand for deposit, D, is thus given by

$$D = 1 - \exp(-r_s T) \int_0^R sx \, dF(x,e),$$

in which

$$\exp(-r_s T) \int_0^R sx \, dF(x,e)$$

is the present value of market investors' total claim on bank asset.

The bank's profit is maximized by its choice on the screening effort, e, as well as the size of the loan to be sold, s, i.e.,

$$\max_{(e,s)} \Pi = \int_0^R (1-s)x dF(x,e) - c(e) - \exp(r_d T) D, \quad (5.3)$$

$$\text{s.t.} \quad 0 \leq s \leq 1$$

in which $-\exp(r_d T)D$ is the bank's funding cost on deposits.

5.2.2 INEFFICIENT SCREENING WITH LOAN SALES

Notice that at any effort level e, the bank's revenue is

$$\int_0^R (1-s)x dF(x,e),$$

the incentive compatibility (IC) constraint thus requires that for every effort that is made, the marginal revenue cannot be below marginal cost, i.e.

$$\int_0^R (1-s)x dF_e(x,e) \geq c'(e), \text{ (IC)} \quad (5.4)$$

in which $F_e(x,e)$ is the marginal cumulative distribution with respect to effort level e, reflecting the marginal contribution of screening effort to loan quality. Using the fact that the expected return of the loan, denoted by $\bar{x}$, is

$$\bar{x} = E[x] = \int_0^R x dF(x,e),$$

the marginal contribution of screening effort to $\bar{x}$, denoted by $\bar{x}_e$, is given by

$$\bar{x}_e = \frac{\partial \bar{x}}{\partial e} = \int_0^R x dF_e(x,e).$$

Condition (5.4) (IC) can be written as

$$\bar{x}_e = \frac{c}{1-s}$$

which must be binding in the optimal solution.

Compared with the case in which the bank keeps the entire loan on its balance sheet ($s=0$), profit maximization implies that

$$\bar{x}_e\big|_{s=0} = c'(e) = c,$$

therefore, any positive sale of the loan $s>0$ implies the equilibrium effort in screening is inefficient, as

$$\bar{x}_e\big|_{0<s<1} > c,$$

given that the marginal return of $\bar{x}$ is diminishing in e, by assumption (5.2).

The bank's optimization problem (5.3) under (IC) (5.4) can be solved from joint first-order conditions

$$\frac{\partial \Pi}{\partial e} = 0,$$

$$\frac{\partial \Pi}{\partial s} = 0.$$

Readers are asked to solve for optimal e and s in equilibrium in Exercise 2.

5.2.3 SUMMARY

The Gorton-Pennacchi model provides a simple framework on banks' screening incentive affected by loan sales, with sharp insights: when some of the loans are sold to market investors, for example, securitizers, any improvement in loan quality will not only benefit the issuing bank, but also benefit the investors; on the other hand, the cost on improving loan quality by screening is completely borne by the bank. That is, screening generates a positive externality on market investors. As a response, the bank will exert less effort, when part of its loans will be sold in the market. Furthermore, beyond the externality associated with loan screening, in reality, loan sales also create moral hazard for banks: as risky loans will not stay on banks' balance sheets in the future, banks have the incentive to lower lending standard in order to issue more loans for sale, as the credit risks in these loans will be shifted to investors. For these reasons, allowing banks to sell loans may lead to lower bank lending standards and higher credit risks in the loans, threatening the stability of the financial system.

5.3 SECURITIZED BANKING AND FINANCIAL INSTABILITY

Securitized banking is based on two key mechanisms: securitization and repo, and they reinforce each other. Securitization produces liquid, high quality securities out of illiquid, risky loans; this allows banks to access cheaper funding in the repo market, using these securities as collateral, which in turn enables banks to issue more loans for securitization. In this section, using a model by Shleifer and Vishny (2010) that characterizes both securitization and repo, we investigate how interaction between securitization and repo adds more fragility in the banking system.

5.3.1 ORIGINATE-TO-DISTRIBUTE AND REPO

Consider an economy that lives for three periods, $t=1,2,3$. There are identical projects, each requiring one unit of initial investment to start with, and the projects are operated by entrepreneurs. The projects can be initiated in either $t=1$ or $t=2$, and each of these projects returns $R>1$ in $t=3$. Entrepreneurs receive loans from the banks, and the banks raise funds through leveraging.

Suppose each bank starts with equity E_0, and the equity level becomes E_t for period t. And the banks claim a share γ, $0 \leq \gamma \leq 1$ out of the entrepreneurs' profit, $R-1$.

For simplicity, assume that the entrepreneurs pay zero interest rate for their loans from banks. Banks *originate to distribute*: after lending to the entrepreneurs, banks securitize the loans and sell the securities in the market. To make it simple, there is no pooling or tranching in securitization, and the only requirement is that one bank has to keep a share d, $0 \leq d \leq 1$ of the loans on its balance sheet. In this case, each security means one unit of loan which pays out one unit in $t=3$. The price of the security in period t is denoted by P_t. To focus on the interesting cases, assume

$$P_2 < 1 \leq P_1 \tag{5.5}$$

and the banks have perfect information about P_2 in $t=1$, so that the banks are willing to securitize the loans in $t=1$ and keep the securities in $t=2$. To finance its activities, one bank can turn to the repo market, raising L_t short-term debt, using its entire security holdings as collateral with a constant haircut h. Therefore, the maximum short-term borrowing that one bank can initiate from the repo market in period t is $1-h$ of collateral value.

5.3.2 MARKET EQUILIBRIUM
SECURITIZATION EQUILIBRIUM WITHOUT REPO

As a reference case, suppose $h=1$ so that no repo lending is available. But a bank can still finance its loans to entrepreneurs via securitization, because the security price is high, $P_1 \geq 1$ as assumed in (5.5). Since only a share d of the loans has to be financed directly out of a bank's own capital, in $t=1$ it is able to finance

$$N = \frac{E_0}{d}$$

projects and make a profit of

$$\gamma(R-1)\frac{E_0}{d}$$

from the loans.

By assumption $P_2 < 1$, the bank only engages in securitization in $t=1$ but not in $t=2$ because the security price is too low, $P_2 < 1$—assumption (5.5) thus ensures that banks have incentive to securitize in $t=1$, but they are deterred to do so in $t=2$. Instead, the bank may have the incentive to sell its security holdings in $t=2$ to issue new loans, but whether it is willing to do so or not depends on the benefit and cost: if the bank sells one security in $t=2$ instead of receiving one unit payoff from the security in $t=3$, the opportunity cost is

$$\frac{1-P_2}{P_2},$$

while the profit from issuing a new loan is $\gamma(R-1)$. Assume from now on that the bank prefers to keep the security, i.e.

$$\frac{1-P_2}{P_2} > \gamma(R-1). \tag{5.6}$$

In addition, the bank may have the incentive to keep some cash in $t=1$ to invest in the undervalued security in $t=2$. Suppose that the bank takes some cash C out of its endowment E_0 for this purpose, then its total profit from loans and security investment is

$$\gamma(R-1)\frac{E_0-C}{d} + \frac{C}{P_2}(1-P_2).$$

Assume further that the bank has no incentive to keep cash in $t=1$, i.e., the profit with no security investment in $t=2$ is strictly higher, such that

$$\begin{aligned}\gamma(R-1)\frac{E_0}{d} &> \gamma(R-1)\frac{E_0-C}{d} + \frac{C}{P_2}(1-P_1), \text{ for any } C>0, \\ \frac{\gamma(R-1)}{d} &> \frac{1-P_2}{P_2}.\end{aligned} \tag{5.7}$$

If both conditions (5.6) and (5.7) hold, banks will fully engage in securitization in $t=1$ and keep the security until maturity. In this case, securitization improves social welfare: banks are able to finance more projects than if there is no securitization available so that the bank can only finance with its equity, given that

$$N = \frac{E_0}{d} > E_0,$$

and banks make higher profit with securitization, as

$$\gamma(R-1)\frac{E_0}{d} > \gamma(R-1)E_0.$$

In the next step, we focus only on such full securitization case, under conditions (5.6) and (5.7).

SECURITIZATION EQUILIBRIUM WITH REPO

Now we extend the model to allow for repo, with $0 < h < 1$. Note that in any period t, one bank posts all its assets, $E_t + L_t$, in order to raise short-term debt L_t in repo market, which implies a haircut of

$$h_t = \frac{E_t}{E_t + L_t}.$$

For simplicity, assume that $P_1 = 1$ and the bank maximizes its loans in $t = 1$. The bank is able to finance the projects up to

$$N = \frac{E_0 + L_1}{d}.$$

Given that haircut h_t must be maintained, the maximum short-term repo borrowing the bank can raise is

$$L_1 = (1 - h_1) N d \qquad (5.8)$$

using all the projects as collateral. The number of financed projects is therefore

$$N = \frac{E_0}{d h_1}.$$

With $h_1 < 1$, one bank can further expand its balance sheet and finance more projects via leveraging up through repo. The lower h_1 is, the larger is the bank's initial balance sheet. Notice that the haircut $h_1 = \dfrac{E_1}{E_1 + L_1}$ implies that

$$L_1 = (1 - h_1) \dfrac{E_1}{h_1}.$$

Compared with (5.8), one can see that $Nd = \dfrac{E_1}{h_1}$.

Now, when it comes to $t = 2$, with price P_2 falling to a sufficiently low level, the bank is not able to issue new loans by securitization. Furthermore, the bank even has to liquidate some of its assets, denoted by S, to maintain the haircut requirement. By selling S assets at price P_2, the bank still holds $Nd - S$ assets, and $L_2 = L_1 - P_2 S$ liabilities to investors. Computing from the balance sheet, the bank's equity value is now

$$E_2 = (Nd - S) P_2 - (L_1 - P_2 S) = Nd P_2 - L_1,$$

implying a haircut of

$$h_2 = \dfrac{E_2}{E_2 + L_2} = \dfrac{Nd P_2 - L_1}{(Nd - S) P_2}. \qquad (5.9)$$

It is known that $L_1 = (1 - h_1) \dfrac{E_1}{h_1}$ and $Nd = \dfrac{E_1}{h_1}$; insert them into (5.9) to endogenize S,

$$S = \dfrac{E_1}{h_1} \dfrac{h_2 P_2 + 1 - P_2 - h_1}{h_2 P_2} = Nd \dfrac{h_2 P_2 + 1 - P_2 - h_1}{h_2 P_2}. \qquad (5.10)$$

In order to focus on the key mechanism, without much loss of generality we assume that the haircut h is fixed for both $t = 1$ and $t = 2$, $h_1 = h_2 = h$. Equation (5.10) is therefore simplified as

$$S = \dfrac{E_1}{h_1} \dfrac{1 - P_2}{P_2} \dfrac{1 - h}{h} = Nd \dfrac{1 - P_2}{P_2} \dfrac{1 - h}{h}. \qquad (5.11)$$

Equation (5.11) implies that, with a given h, $\frac{\partial S}{\partial P_2}<0$ so that the required liquidation increases with a larger asset price shock. The bank even has to liquidate all its assets and exit the market with $S=Nd$, when P_2 falls below $1-h$. For simplicity, we only focus on the partial liquidation case, i.e., $P_2>1-h$ always holds, for the rest of this section. Furthermore, equation (5.11) also implies that

$$\frac{\partial S}{\partial h}=-E_1\frac{1-P_2}{P_2h^2}-2E_1\left(\frac{1-P_2}{P_2}\frac{1-h}{h^3}\right)<0.$$

That is, when the haircut is smaller, or, when the bank is more leveraged by repo, the bank needs to liquidate more assets. One can also see that

$$\frac{\partial^2 S}{\partial h^2}=4E_1\frac{1-P_2}{P_2h^3}+6E_1\left(\frac{1-P_2}{P_2}\frac{1-h}{h^4}\right)>0$$

from equation (5.11), S is strictly decreasing and convex in h under any given P_2. The bank must liquidate part of its asset holdings as long as $h<1$, and the lower h is, the more elastic S becomes. This implies that, under certain price shock in P_2, financial institutions with higher leverage are forced to make more early liquidation, thus they are more vulnerable to economic downturns.

Equation (5.11) further implies that

$$\frac{\partial^2 S}{\partial h \partial P_2}=2E_1\frac{1-h}{P_2^2 h^3}>0, \qquad (5.12)$$

or, asset price and haircut are complementary to each other. The more the bank is initially leveraged, the more sensitive is S to the asset price shock. Note that the relationship (5.12) does not fully reflect what may happen in financial crises, because the haircut h and asset price P_2 in the model are both exogenously given and not correlated, while this may not be true during crises. If we do endogenize h and P_2 in the model to capture the reality that they may reinforce each other during crises, we may expect even higher asset price volatility and even more forced liquidation. Readers are asked to explore this in Exercise 4.

So far we assume that the haircut h remains the same for both periods. However, what has been often observed in reality is that when the negative asset price shock on P_2 is revealed, the value of the financial institutions' assets deteriorates so that they have to face a higher haircut that is required by investors. This will put escalating pressure on one bank's balance sheet and the bank has to deleverage, leading to further liquidation. Given that all the banks are homogeneous in this model, the entire banking sector will run into a collective fire sale.

To see this, suppose that the haircut increases when P_2 is revealed, i.e., $h_1 < h_2$. The quantity of liquidated assets S is given by equation (5.10). Again, in order to focus on the partial liquidation case, we assume that $1 > P_2 > 1 - h_1$. To see the impact of haircut on S, differentiate (5.10) with respect to h_1, one can find that

$$\frac{\partial S}{\partial h_1} = -E_1 \frac{(1-h_1) - P_2(1-h_2)}{h_1^2 h_2 P_2} - E_1 \frac{1}{h_1 h_2 P_2} < 0. \tag{5.13}$$

With low haircut in $t=1$, the bank is highly leveraged and thus has to liquidate more assets when time goes bad. To make it worse, as in reality, haircut increases during the downturn, $h_1 < h_2$, which forces banks to put more assets on sale, as

$$\frac{\partial S}{\partial h_2} = \frac{E_1}{h_1^2 h_2} \frac{P_2 - (1-h_1)}{h_2 P_2} < 0. \tag{5.14}$$

Overall, the model thus shows how repo lending allows banks to increase leverage, and key contribution of the increased bank leverage to financial instability through premature liquidation and fire sale is well unveiled by inequalities (5.13) and (5.14): on one hand, more leverage allows the banks to expand their balance sheets for higher profit, and the expansion in balance sheets is larger when the economy is booming and the haircut is low. On the other hand, high initial leverage also leads to more forced liquidation in the downturn, just as (5.13) implies. To make things worse, haircut is often counniercyclical such that banks have to face a higher haircut when the market is under stress, and this leads to further inefficient liquidation of long assets, as $\frac{\partial S}{\partial h_2} > 0$ suggests. On aggregate, such leverage cycle amplifies price shocks in the market and contributes to higher volatility over business cycles, as a consequence of the originate-to-distribute model.

5.3.3 SUMMARY

The compact Shleifer-Vishny model presents the mechanism of how financial instability arises endogenously within modern banking, by incorporating two key ingredients of securitized banking: securitization and repo. Via "originate-to-distribute" model, banks expand their lending through securitizing the loans. Using the securities as collateral, banks are able to leverage up and finance more investments through short-term lending in the repo market. The securitized banking system exhibits a strong feature of procyclicality: banks' balance sheets are further expanded when time is good and haircut is low, but they suffer from a bigger blow when time is bad and they are forced into liquidation. The rising haircut during downturn forces banks to deleverage and conduct more costly liquidation. To make it worse, such forced liquidation takes place in a falling asset market, i.e., exactly at the time when asset buyers have plummeting willingness to pay—as Exercise 4 demonstrates. Asset buyers' limit of arbitrage pushes the asset price to drop further, and forced liquidation of individual banks may finally evolve to a system-wide fire sale, leading to a systemic meltdown.

5.4 REPO RUNS

What made the 2007–2009 financial crisis different, as Gorton (2010) notes, is the silent and rather invisible run on banks by other financial institutions instead of a run by the depositors (although episodes of bank runs by depositors were still observed). The reason is that, in modern securitized banking, banks rely much on the repo market for funding, in which lending is over-collateralized with a haircut on collateral's face value. Haircut is sensitive to market stress, and may be prohibitively high in crises so that banks find it extremely difficult to refinance in the repo market and are forced to deleverage—such refusal for refinancing much resembles a run on the repo.

To better understand banks' vulnerability to repo runs, in this section, we look for the conditions under which repo runs break out in a dynamic banking model, following Martin et al. (2014).

5.4.1 MODELLING DYNAMIC COLLATERALIZED LENDING

Consider an economy with infinite time horizon, $t = 0,1,\ldots,+\infty$, and in each period t, a population N of investors—call them generation t—is born. Investors that are born in any period t live for three periods $\{y,m,o\}$: they are "young" (denoted by y) in period t, "middle-aged" (denoted by m) in period $t+1$, and "old" (denoted by o) in period $t+2$.

Similar to the Diamond-Dybvig model in Section 2.2, each investor is endowed with one unit of goods when they are born, then when they are in their middle age, the liquidity shock arrives so that a share $p/1-p$ of investors turns out to be impatient/patient and want to consume in their middle/old age; the time preference of consumption is private information for individual investors, and whether one investor is impatient or patient is unknown when she is young. Therefore, the utility function of a generation t investor is

$$U_t\left(c_{t+1}^m, c_{t+2}^o\right) = \begin{cases} u\left(c_{t+1}^m\right) & \text{with probability } p, \\ u\left(c_{t+2}^o\right) & \text{with probability } 1-p \end{cases}$$

in which c_{t+1}^m/c_{t+2}^o denotes her consumption in period $t+1/t+2$ when she is middle-aged/old, and the utility function $u(\cdot)$ is neoclassical such that $u'(\cdot) > 0$, $u''(\cdot) < 0$; in addition, the coefficient of relative risk aversion $-\frac{cu''(c)}{u'(c)} > 1$.

The economy is also populated by M infinitely-lived, risk-neutral banks who have access to profitable investment technologies but no endowments so that they have to borrow from investors for funding. There are two technologies in the economy: one is a storage technology, accessible to both investors and banks, that returns 1 in period $t+1$ for each unit invested (or, short assets) in period t; the other one is an investment technology which is only accessible to banks. For I_{it} invested by bank i in the investment technology in period t (or, long assets), the return is

$$\begin{cases} R_i I_{it} & \text{if } I_{it} < \overline{I}_i, \\ R_i \overline{I}_i & \text{if } I_{it} \geq \overline{I}_i \end{cases}$$

in period $t+2$, with $R_i > 1$, and $\overline{I}_i$ denotes the bank's investment capacity. To make the model simpler, assume that prematurely liquidated long assets in period $t+1$ yield 0 return. Furthermore, different from the Diamond-Dybvig model, we now assume that R_i is not verifiable for investors so that banks can always default; knowing this, investors will always require collateral when they lend to banks: suppose that bank i posts k_{it} collateral for each unit borrowed.

The role of banks in investment is motivated by banks' inalienable human capital (Hart and Moore 1994): if bank i's long assets are taken over by investors before they mature, the assets' realized return is only $\gamma_{it} R_i$, with $0 < \gamma_{it} < 1$. Assume that banks' total demand for funding always exceeds the total funding supply from the investors—even after some of the banks are bankrupt—so that banks are engaged in a perfect competition for investors' funding.

Figure 5.8 summarizes the timing of events over three adjacent periods, without any repo run. For any representative bank i in period t, it starts with the cash holding $C_{i,t-1}$ from the previous period, collects the return from the long assets invested two periods ago, invests I_{it}, holds cash C_{it}, borrows b_{it} from generation t investors, repays $r^m_{i,t-1}$ for generation $t-1$ impatient middle-aged investors, repays $r^o_{i,t-2}$ for generation $t-2$ patient old investors, then the bank's profit in period t is denoted by

$$\pi_{it} = R_i I_{i,t-2} + C_{i,t-1} + b_{it} - p r^m_{i,t-1} b_{i,t-1} - (1-p) r^o_{i,t-2} b_{i,t-2} - I_{it} - C_{it}. \quad (5.15)$$

THE MICROECONOMICS OF BANKING

$t-2$	$t-1$	t
• Generation $t-2$, young, deposit $b_{i,t-2}$	• Generation $t-1$, young, deposit $b_{i,t-1}$	• Generation t, young, deposit b_{it}
• Generation $t-4$, old, patient, withdraw $r^o_{i,t-4} b_{i,t-4}$	• Generation $t-3$, old, patient, withdraw $r^o_{i,t-3} b_{i,t-3}$	• Generation $t-2$, old, patient, withdraw $r^o_{i,t-2} b_{i,t-2}$
• Generation $t-3$, middle-aged, impatient, withdraw $r^m_{i,t-3} b_{i,t-3}$	• Generation $t-2$, middle-aged, impatient, withdraw $r^m_{i,t-2} b_{i,t-2}$	• Generation $t-1$, middle-aged, impatient, withdraw $r^m_{i,t-1} b_{i,t-1}$
• Generation $t-3$, middle-aged, patient, refinance	• Generation $t-2$, middle-aged, patient, refinance	• Generation $t-1$, middle-aged, patient, refinance
• Bank i: collects $R_i I_{i,t-4}$, invests $I_{i,t-2}$, adjusts cash balance $\Delta C_{i,t-2}$	• Bank i: collects $R_i I_{i,t-3}$, invests $I_{i,t-1}$, adjusts cash balance $\Delta C_{i,t-1}$	• Bank i: collects $R_i I_{i,t-2}$, invests I_{it}, adjusts cash balance $\Delta C_{i,t}$

Figure 5.8 *Timing of events without repo runs*

Then, in any period τ, with a constant discount factor β, the bank's decision problem is to maximize its franchise value, i.e.

$$\max_{\{r^m_{i,t-1}, r^o_{i,t-2}, b_{it}, k_{it}\}} \sum_{t=\tau}^{+\infty} \beta^{t-\tau} \pi_{it}. \quad (5.16)$$

The bank's constraint is that it needs to convince patient, generation $t-1$ middle-aged investors to roll over their funding, $(1-p)r^m_{i,t-1} b_{i,t-1}$, as well as to raise fresh funding b_{it} from the young generation t investors, using repo contracts. That is, funding provided by generation $t-1$ middle-aged investors and young generation t investors must be collateralized by bank's pledgeable assets. Note that the bank's pledgeable assets that can be used as collateral include

- Investment $I_{i,t-1}$ that will mature in $t+1$;
- Investment $I_{i,t}$ that will mature in $t+2$.

Assume the bank can pledge k_{it} units of collateral to raise one unit of funds from investors in the repo market, i.e., with a haircut of $\frac{k_{it}-1}{k_{it}}$. To make it simple, assume that each of these two pledgeable assets accounts for half of the bank's collateral, that is, every one unit of raised funding is backed by $\frac{1}{2}k_{it}$ units of each of the two pledgeable assets. To convince generation $t-1$ middle-aged investors to stay and the young generation t investors to deposit, the expected return of the collateral for one unit funding must be at least as high as the expected return from one unit of funding, i.e.

$$\frac{1}{2}k_{it}R_i + \frac{1}{2}k_{it}\beta R_i \geq E_t[r]. \tag{5.17}$$

The bank's problem in each period t is thus defined by maximizing the object function (5.16) subject to the collateral constraint (5.17).

5.4.2 NON-RUN EQUILIBRIUM

To focus on the key questions, suppose that the economy has been in the non-run equilibrium, i.e., the steady state $\{r_i^m, r_i^o, k_i, b_i, I_i, C_i\}$ that is invariant with t and not subject to any repo run. Then it is straightforward to see that

$$r_i^o = r_i^{m2} = r^2 \tag{5.18}$$

—in which r denotes one-period deposit rate—in equilibrium to rule out arbitrage opportunities, because

- If $r_i^o < r_i^{m2}$, patient middle-age investors would mimic impatient investors and withdraw, then mimic young investors and re-deposit;
- If $r_i^o > r_i^{m2}$, impatient middle-age investors would make themselves better off by (1) mimicking patient investors to withdraw $r_i^o b_i$ in the next period; (2) borrowing weakly higher than $r_i^m b_i$ from someone in the young generation and consuming, then repaying in the next period using $r_i^o b_i$ from the withdrawal. The lender from the young generation would agree because in the next period, (1) if she turned out to be an impatient middle-aged, her consumption would be $\frac{r_i^o}{r_i^m}b_i > r_i^m b_i$ —better off than if she saved in the bank; (2) if she turned out to be a patient middle-aged, she could mimic the young investors and save in the bank for one period—her consumption would be $r_i^o b_i$ which would be as good as if she saved in the bank.

As a result, the patient middle-age investors always roll over their funds, should there be no repo run.

Assume that, for the investment technology, the net present value of investment is always positive, or,

$$\beta^2 R_i - 1 > 0; \tag{5.19}$$

as a result, the bank will not invest above its full capacity, i.e.,

$$I_i \leq \overline{I}_i \tag{5.20}$$

in the steady state and will hold zero cash,

$$C_i = 0. \tag{5.21}$$

For each unit of investment on behalf of the investors, the present value of profit is

$$\beta^2 \left[R_i - (1-p)r^2 \right] - \beta p r$$

while the present value of profit from each unit of investment funded by the bank's own money is

$$\beta^2 R_i - 1.$$

Market competition ensures that banks are indifferent between funding resources, i.e.

$$\beta^2 \left[R_i - (1-p)r^2 \right] - \beta p r = \beta^2 R_i - 1, \text{ or, } r = \overline{r} \equiv \frac{1}{\beta} > 1. \tag{5.22}$$

Given that $\beta^2 R_i - 1 > 0$ so that banks always make positive profit from their own investments, in equilibrium, banks should also make positive profit from providing intermediation services for investors.

Now we characterize the steady state for the non-run equilibrium $\{r_i^m, r_i^o, k_i, b_i, I_i, C_i\}$. First of all, in the steady state, variables are invariant with t, and the bank shall make non-negative profit

$$\pi_i = R_i I_i + b_i - p\frac{1}{\beta}b_i - (1-p)\frac{1}{\beta^2}b_i - I_i \geq 0, \tag{5.23}$$

using the facts that there is zero cash holding in equilibrium as equation (5.21) states, and deposit rates are given by (5.18) and (5.22). Condition (5.23) thus defines the bank's deposits

$$b_i \leq \frac{(R_i - 1)\beta^2}{(1-\beta)(1+\beta-p)} I_i$$

which is equivalent to

$$b_i \leq \frac{1+\beta}{1+\beta-p} \bar{I}_i \tag{5.24}$$

using the assumption (5.19), and $I_i = \bar{I}_i$ to maximize the bank's profit (5.23), given that I_i is bounded above at $\bar{I}_i$ according to (5.20).

As for the collateral constraint, first, collateralization ratio k_i needs to fulfill (5.17), that is,

$$\frac{1}{2}k_i R_i + \frac{1}{2}k_i \beta R_i \geq \bar{r} = \frac{1}{\beta}, \tag{5.25}$$

and second, in steady state, borrowers' total claims in the bank shall be totally collateralized in every period, that is,

$$k_i \left[b_i + (1-p)b_i \bar{r} \right] \leq 2\bar{I}_i. \tag{5.26}$$

Borrowers' total claims include the newly collected deposits from the young generation, b_i, and the patient middle-aged investors, $(1-p)b_i\bar{r}$; by (5.20), as the highest investments in long assets in each period is $\bar{I}_i$, the maximal collateralizeable long assets is thus $2\bar{I}_i$, including the long assets invested in the current period and in the last period.

Combining conditions (5.25) and (5.26), in the non-run steady state, any collateralization ratio k_i is feasible as long as

$$\frac{2}{\beta(1+\beta)R_i} \leq k_i \leq \frac{2\beta\overline{I}_i}{(1+\beta-p)b_i}. \tag{5.27}$$

To summarize, the non-run equilibrium is characterized by

- Full investment capacity on long assets, $I_i = \overline{I}_i$;
- Zero cash holding, $C_i = 0$;
- Incentive compatible deposit rates, $r^o = r^{m2} = \overline{r}^2$, with $\overline{r} = \frac{1}{\beta}$;
- Non-negative bank profit $\Pi_i \geq 0$;
- Bank deposits b_i and collateralization ratio k_i fulfill (5.24) and (5.27), respectively.

5.4.3 RUN ON THE REPOS

Section 5.4.2 characterizes the non-run equilibrium, which resembles a dynamic version of the Diamond-Dybvig model (Chapter 2, Section 2.2) with collateral constraint. Compared with the standard Diamond-Dybvig model, the natural question is: is there also an equilibrium with repo run, along with the non-run equilibrium?

Before we answer this question, we need to characterize repo run in such dynamic setup. Remember, in the standard Diamond-Dybvig model, a bank run is basically a funding liquidity dry-up: patient consumers want to withdraw early, as a result, the bank is not able to roll over its debt. In the similar vein, under the current dynamic setup, a repo run as the result of funding liquidity dry-up means

1. Patient middle-aged investors refuse to roll over their debts, which resembles patient consumers' early withdrawal in the one-round Diamond-Dybvig model, *and*
2. Young generation refuses to deposit in the bank—which only arises in the dynamic setting.

Suppose a bank is under the non-run equilibrium that is characterized in Section 5.4.2 throughout the history before period t. Then, should a repo run break out in the beginning of an arbitrary period t, the cash demand from all withdrawing investors would be

$$b_i \bar{r} + (1-p)\bar{r}^2 b_i \tag{5.28}$$

which includes repayment obligations for impatient middle-aged investors, $pb_i\bar{r}$, early withdrawing patient middle-aged investors, $(1-p)b_i\bar{r}$, and patient old-aged investors, $(1-p)\bar{r}^2 b_i$. Out of the bank's assets, $\overline{I}_i$ of long assets invested in $t-2$ mature and generate $R_i \overline{I}_i$ of cash supply, $\overline{I}_i$ of long assets invested in $t-1$ are immature and cannot be converted to cash—as we assumed. Therefore, whether a repo run will happen or not depends on the comparison between cash demand and supply, which leads to three cases:

CASE 1: NO REPO RUN

First, if the bank can meet the cash demand (5.28) out of its profit from the matured long assets,

$$(R_i - 1)\overline{I}_i \geq b_i\bar{r} + (1-p)\bar{r}^2 b_i, \tag{5.29}$$

then after repaying all investors the bank, even without being able to collect deposits from young investors of generation t, is still able to keep investing $\overline{I}_i$ in period t without deviating from the non-run equilibrium solution—as if nothing happens. Knowing this, investors would have no incentive to run on the bank, as patient middle-aged generation $t-1$ investors would be better off with withdrawing in $t+1$, and young investors of generation t would be better off with depositing in the bank than being in autarky. Condition (5.29) thus describes the case in which non-run equilibrium is the unique equilibrium.

CASE 2: REPO RUN WITH BANKRUPTCY

The opposite case to Case 1 is that the bank cannot meet the cash demand (5.28) out of its total cash supply from the matured long assets,

$$R_i \bar{I}_i < b_i \bar{r} + (1-p)\bar{r}^2 b_i. \tag{5.30}$$

If this is the case, a repo run will be self-fulfilling: the bank will be bankrupted after period t so that none of the patient middle-aged investors will wait till $t+1$, and none of the young investors will deposit in the bank, either. Condition (5.30) thus describes the case in which repo run equilibrium is another equilibrium, and a bank suffering from repo run will be bankrupted.

CASE 3: INTERMEDIATE CASE

There is a tricky case, that both conditions (5.29) and (5.30) are violated. On one hand, violation of condition (5.30) means that, should a repo run happen, the bank would be able to meet the cash demand (5.28) out of its total cash supply from the matured long assets, so that it would not be bankrupted. On the other hand, violation of condition (5.29) means that the bank could only invest

$$R_i \bar{I}_i - \left[b_i \bar{r} + (1-p)\bar{r}^2 b_i \right] < \bar{I}_i$$

in period t, given that young investors of generation t would not deposit in the repo run. Therefore, should a repo run happen in period t, the bank would receive $R\bar{I}_i$ from the matured long assets in $t+1$ but would not need to pay out anything; this would allow the bank to recover its equilibrium investment $\bar{I}_i$ in $t+1$. However, this just implies that repo run is not an equilibrium: should one patient middle-aged investor not join the run and wait until $t+1$, she would be better off with higher return $\bar{r}^2$, given that the bank would survive the run and receive $R\bar{I}_i$ from the matured long assets in $t+1$. The same reasoning also applies for young investors of generation t. Therefore, in this case where both conditions (5.29) and (5.30) are violated, non-run equilibrium is still the unique equilibrium.

To summarize, non-run equilibrium is the unique equilibrium in both Case 1 and 3; that means, a bank is free from repo runs if Case 2 does not exist, or

$$R_i \overline{I}_i \geq b_i \overline{r} + (1-p)\overline{r}^2 b_i. \tag{5.31}$$

by condition (5.30). Applying $\overline{r} = \frac{1}{\beta}$ in equilibrium, condition (5.31) leads to

$$\beta^2 R_i \overline{I}_i \geq (1-p+\beta)\overline{r}^2 b_i. \tag{5.32}$$

Therefore, when condition (5.32) holds, a bank that relies on repo funding is immune to repo runs. Condition (5.32) is more likely to hold, when

1. Maturity mismatch is lower in the bank's balance sheet, or, $\frac{b_i}{\overline{I}_i}$ is lower so that the bank is less exposed to funding liquidity risk, or, rollover risk that arises from short-term funding;
2. Return from long-term investment, R_i, is higher so that the bank has sufficient buffer to cushion potential repo runs.

5.4.4 SUMMARY

The Martin-Skeie-von Thadden model provides rich insights on banking fragility arising from repo funding. In a dynamic setting, with maturity mismatch in balance sheet, a bank has to rely on short-term funding from the repo market to refinance its long-term investment; this exposes the bank to funding liquidity risk arising from repo runs, that creditors' refusal to refinance may lead to bankruptcy. The model suggests that, to improve resilience and avoid destructive repo runs, banks must reduce their funding liquidity risk, i.e. reliance on short-term funding. The model also demonstrates that banks are vulnerable to negative shock on asset returns, for example, falling asset returns induced by business cycles, as the Allen-Gale model in Chapter 2, Section 2.3 predicts in a static setting. The model thus sheds much lights on understanding sources of fragility in securitized banking and necessary policies to improve stability of banks.

5.5 EMPIRICAL EVIDENCE

5.5.1 DOES SECURITIZATION ENCOURAGE BANKS' RISK-TAKING?

One of the most controversial issues on securitized banking is whether securitization increases banks' risk-taking, as is predicted by Gorton and Pennacchi (1995). We first present evidence from various studies, then continue with identification strategy to test the causal link between securitization and risk-taking.

QUALITY OF SECURITIZED LOANS: GENERAL EVIDENCE

Banks may have lower incentive to screen their loans, if these loans are originated to distribute (OTD), as is documented by Purnanandam (2011). Using detailed loan-level data from the Home Mortgage Disclosure Act (HMDA), Purnanandam (2011) finds that default rate of loans is higher for high-OTD banks, compared with low-OTD banks, controlling for various bank characteristics, which suggests that the quality of OTD loans is likely to be inferior. Furthermore, if a bank exerts sufficient effort on screening its borrowers through collecting more soft information, then the bank is more likely to charge different interest rates for seemingly (in terms of hard information) similar borrowers. By comparing the interest rate distribution over similar pools of borrowers, Purnanandam (2011) finds tighter distribution of interest rates in high-OTD banks, implying that their screening criteria are more lax. Dell'Ariccia et al. (2012) find that, controlling for mortgage securitization, the denial rates are lower in the areas of the US that experience faster credit growth, implying a lower bank lending standard.

Jiang et al. (2014a) document similar reduced screening effort of banks—as shown in Purnanandam (2011)—on those loans with a perceived higher *ex ante* probability of sale in the future, during loan origination. However, Jiang et al. (2014b) find that such moral hazard in loan origination backfires, too, when banks try to sell the loans to investors in the securitization market: anticipating banks' lax screening on their originated loans, investors attempt to collect more information on the loans for sale and manage to cream-skim the loans of higher quality for purchase. As a result, loans remaining on the banks' balance sheets *ex post* incur higher delinquency rates than sold loans. A similar pattern is also observed by Agarwal et al. (2012), that in the prime market (loans intended for the government sponsored enterprises (GSEs)), originators choose to sell low-default-risk loans to the secondary market in the pre-2007 period. However, they also find that those loans have higher prepayment risks, reflecting the fact that GSEs only impose controls on default risks of the prime mortgage loans, since GSEs only guarantee against default risk to investors. As for the mortgage loans that are not sold in the securitization market and remain on banks' balance sheets, Agarwal et al. (2011) suggest that these loans are more likely to be renegotiated when they are distressed, compared with the loans that are sold, and renegotiation tends to be more efficient than simply letting the distressed loans default. Similar evidence is observed in Piskorski et al. (2010) that the likelihood of foreclosure when a loan is seriously delinquent is lower if the loan is held by banks than if it is securitized, as renegotiation is often restricted by securitization.

Direct evidence on lower quality of securitized loans is documented by Griffin and Maturana (2016), caused by originating banks' moral hazard of misreporting the loans. Investigating several millions of mortgage loans that were issued during 2002–2011 in the US—some of which were backed by non-agency MBS,—they identify three indicators of potential misreporting: unreported second lien (or, "silent seconds") that allows a borrower to take additional debt and makes initial debt more likely to default, owner occupancy misreporting that allows a borrower to reduce down payment, and appraisal overstatement on the value for the property that allows the borrowers to borrow more. They find that around 48% of loans are misreported at least in one way, and the likelihood is similar in both low and full documentation loans. Overall, misreporting increases the likelihood of delinquency by 51%, implying that the securitization market to some extent resembles a market for lemons. Indeed, using zip-code-level data, Mian and Sufi (2017) find that the discrepancy between borrowers' mean income in the mortgage applications (recorded in HMDA data) and mean income from the American Community Survey (ACS) became widened during 2000–2005, especially for those marginal borrowers who used to be more likely to be rejected in mortgage loan application before 2000, which suggests that the borrowers' income—especially subprime borrowers' income—was systematically overstated during the pre-2007 real estate boom.

Similarly, evidence on certain characteristics of the lemon market is found by Downing et al. (2009) in another segment of the securitization procedure, where mortgage-backed securities from GSEs are sold to SPVs during 1991–2002: securities that were sold ("lemons") performed worse than the securities that were not sold.

Although the evidence on banks' excess risk-taking in the mortgage-related securitization market is abundant, the findings in the other securitization markets are relatively less clear-cut. Shivdasani and Wang (2011) show that during 2004–2007, the leveraged buyout (LBO) boom was fueled by aggressive bank loans that were securitized for collateralized loan obligations (CLOs), but there is no evidence that CLO-funded LBOs underperform. Examining the corporate loans that were originated and securitized for CLOs, Benmelech et al. (2012) find no consistent evidence that securitized loans perform worse than non-securitized loans originated by the same bank—measured by market-based measures such as secondary market loan prices and borrowers' credit quality measured by changes in credit default swap (CDS) spreads. However, market-based measures for loans and borrowers of different credit quality may co-move during financial crises, blurring the real differences; using a more comprehensive dataset and using default as a direct measure of loan quality, Bord and Santos (2015) find that securitized loans are more likely to fail, compared with non-securitized loans originated by the same bank. Wang and Xia (2014) document that when corporate loans are more likely to be securitized through CLOs, banks exert less effort on monitoring these loans, so that banks are more tolerant with covenant violations and tend to grant waivers without changing loan terms. In turn, banks' lack of monitoring incentives may encourage borrowers' moral hazard, increasing credit risks in the securitized loans.

SECURITIZATION AND RISK MANAGEMENT: IDENTIFICATION

Although the correlation between securitization and banks' risk-taking has been well documented in the literature, identifying a causal link between these two can still be challenging, mainly because it is difficult to isolate differences in loan outcomes independent of contract and borrower characteristics. Keys et al. (2010) explore a rule of thumb in securitization for identification purpose: underwriting guidelines from GSEs, i.e., Fannie Mae and Freddie Mac, require that no lending should be provided to risky borrowers whose FICO scores (a widely-used credit score created by the Fair Isaac Corporation) are below 620. As a result, loans issued to borrowers with FICO scores just above 620 have a significantly higher unconditional probability of being securitized and hence are more liquid in the market, than loans issued to borrowers with scores just below 620. Such "securitization rule-of-thumb" does not only affect loans securitized by GSEs, but also loans securitized in the non-agency market, as investors believe that loans with FICO scores above 620 are of higher quality. This jump in the ease of securitization implies that securitization lenders have much lower incentive to collect information, especially the soft information that is less accessible for investors, on borrowers with scores just above 620, compared with borrowers with scores just below 620, although these two groups of borrowers have almost identical risk profiles. Such feature makes it suitable to apply *regression discontinuity design* (RDD, see Imbens and Lemieux 2008 and Imbens and Kalyanaraman 2012 for more technical details), to identify the causal effects of a jump for securitization rate of loans (so-called *intervention*) on banks' risk-taking, by assigning a threshold above which the likelihood of a loan's being securitized is higher.

In general, RDD estimates a regression equation (5.33)

$$Y_i = \alpha + \beta T_i + \theta f\left(i - i^*\right) + \delta T_i \times f\left(i - i^*\right) + \epsilon_i \quad (5.33)$$

in which Y_i is the dependent variable that is subject to intervention, i is the variable with a threshold i^*, T_i is a dummy variable that equals 1 if $i \geq i^*$ and 0 otherwise, and function $f\left(i - i^*\right)$ is a high-order polynomial to fit the smoothed curves above and below i^*. Then when $i^- \to i^*$—making $f(i - i^*) \to 0, -\beta$ becomes the magnitude of the discontinuity in Y at the threshold, i^*.

Applying this method on one million or more securitized subprime loans in the non-agency market, Keys et al. (2010) find that, among the low-documentation loans—whose borrowers provide little or no information (especially, soft information) regarding their employment, income, or assets,—there is almost a 100% jump for the securitization rate at the threshold, implying that the jump for securitization rate at the FICO=620 threshold is accompanied by a fall in information collection from the borrowers, or, a reduced screening effort. Keys et al. (2012) extend the same analysis to prime mortgage loans and find similar patterns in reduced screening.

Bubb and Kaufman (2014) suggest that looking only at securitized loans may not be sufficient for RDD strategy, as there may be other reasons than a jump for the ease of securitization that contribute to the discontinuity in default rate across the threshold. They analyze a dataset that covers over half of outstanding mortgages originated between January 2003 and June 2009 in the United States, containing more than 32 million active loans—including those securitized and those not securitized, and find "origination rule-of-thumb", i.e., originators of the loans follow GSEs' underwriting guidelines and exert most of their effort in screening loan applications above FICO cutoffs, even in the absence of changes in the probability of securitization. Affected by originators' rule of thumb, the causal effect of securitization on banks' risk-taking, estimated by RDD strategy, may thus be biased.

5.5.2 SECURITIZATION AND BANK PERFORMANCE

Securitization may improve banks' performance in many ways. By allocating risks to investors with different risk appetites, banks incur lower funding costs and improve credit risk management; by moving away from the traditional interest income out of on-balance sheet loans towards the non-interest income or fee income out of the securitized assets, banks can better diversify their income and expense; by moving illiquid, risky loans out of balance sheet, banks can improve liquidity and increase risk-weighted capital ratio, and so on. However, securitization procedure is also subject to adverse selection and moral hazard problems, as many studies in Section 5.5.1 have shown, in the originate-to-distribute model, banks have the incentive to lower lending standard and screening effort, for the loans to be securitized; such phenomenon is especially severe for sub-standard borrowers. This deteriorates banks' asset quality and increases banks' on-balance sheet risks, as banks often provide guarantees for securitized loans and retain tranches from securitized assets, undermining banks' performance. As a result, the overall impact of securitization on bank performance is not clear-cut.

To identify the impact of securitization on bank performance, it is natural to think of comparing performance of securitizing banks (treatment group) with non-securitizing banks (control group). However, such an estimate may be biased, as banks' choice on securitization is not randomly assigned, but rather endogenously selected; that is, only banks with certain characteristics choose to securitize, and these banks may *ex ante* perform differently compared with those non-securitizing banks. If we do not consider the endogenous securitization choice, we would wrongly attribute the securitizing banks' intrinsic performance difference to the impact if securitization.

One way to address this endogeneity issue, as suggested by Casu et al. (2013), is to "construct" a control group by matching non-securitizing banks to securitizing banks, via *propensity score matching* (PSM) using observable bank characteristics. Precisely, suppose that in a sample over a certain time horizon, some banks choose to securitize at some points. Define treatment—which is whether a bank i chooses to securitize in period t or not in this case—as a binary variable $s_{i,t}$, such that

$$s_{i,t} = \begin{cases} 1 & \text{if the bank chooses to securitize,} \\ 0 & \text{otherwise,} \end{cases}$$

and suppose that a set of banks' pre-securitization characteristics $X_{i,t-1}$ determine the likelihood that bank i chooses to securitize, i.e.,

$p(X_{i,t-1}) = \text{Prob}(s_i = 1 | X_{i,t-1})$, with $0 < p(X_{i,t-1}) < 1$. The likelihood $p(X_{i,t-1})$ can be used as a *propensity score* to measure a bank's probabilistic choice on securitization.

Next, match banks that never securitize ("non-securitizers") with banks who choose to securitize and have a similar propensity score $p(X_{i,t-1})$ ("securitizers"). Out of the matched pairs, take those non-securitizers as control group and securitizers as treatment group. Suppose the change in bank i's performance measure y one period after t is $\Delta y_{i,t+1}^{s_{i,t}}$, then the *average treatment effect* (ATE) is defined as

$$ATE = E\left[\Delta y_{i,t+1}^1 | s_{i,t} = 1, X_{i,t-1}\right] - E\left[\Delta y_{i,t+1}^0 | s_{i,t} = 0, X_{i,t-1}\right]$$

in which $E\left[\Delta y_{i,t+1}^1 | s_{i,t} = 1, X_{i,t-1}\right]$ is the average change in performance for the securitizers and $E\left[\Delta y_{i,t+1}^0 | s_{i,t} = 0, X_{i,t-1}\right]$ is the average change in performance for the non-securitizers. As matched banks in the control group have the same propensities to securitize as treated banks, the treatment is thus rather "randomly" assigned among those banks; therefore, *ATE* is the causal effect of securitization on bank performance.

Using Federal Reserve's quarterly Call Reports that are filed by insured commercial banks in 2001–2008, Casu et al. (2013) match banks by propensity scores based on their balance sheet characteristics. The left chart of Figure 5.9 shows the distribution of propensity scores before matching, suggesting that securitizers are indeed very much different from the non-securitizers and banks' securitization choices are endogenous. After matching, as the right chart shows, treated banks are indeed "similar" to the controls, suggesting that the endogenous selection is controlled by PSM.

In the unmatched sample, securitizers tend to be more profitable, but with higher funding costs, less liquidity, lower capital ratio, and credit risk exposure. However, these differences disappear in the matched sample, implying that differences in bank performance are not caused by securitization; in other words, for treated banks, the benefits and costs of securitization are likely to cancel each other out.

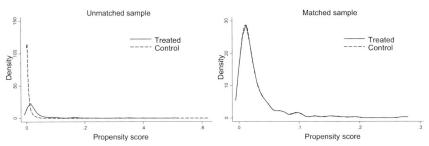

Figure 5.9 *Distribution of propensity scores before and after matching*
Source: Casu et al. (2013). Notes: the treated banks are first-time securitizers during the sample time horizon, and the controls are non-securitizers throughout the entire time horizon.

5.5.3 INTERNATIONAL EVIDENCE

The securitization market in the US, especially the mortgage-based securitization, is heavily driven by the GSEs, such institutional feature leads to market segmentation and affects market participants' behavior across market segments, making the US market a special case compared with many of the other economies. Therefore, to what extent the other countries can learn from the US experience is an interesting question for policy makers. In addition, history of securitization-based banking in most of the other economies are much shorter than the US; as a result, in the earlier stage of market development, market participants in these economies may have different concerns and take different strategies, compared with their peers in the US.

Affinito and Tagliaferri (2010) examine the take-off of securitization in Italy before 2007. They find that less capitalized, less profitable, less liquid and riskier banks are more likely to securitize their loans and start securitization practice earlier. Once a bank starts securitization, it tends to operate with lower capital ratio afterwards—implying that securitization may reduce the cost of capital. Using a dataset containing over one million prime mortgages, both securitized and not securitized, originated by 50 Italian banks during 1995–2006, Albertazzi et al. (2015) investigate whether those loans that are securitized are also those characterized by a higher probability of default. This involves jointly estimating an equation for the probability of securitization and an equation for the probability of default. They find that securitized loans are not associated with higher default probability, and banks retain a higher share of risk in securitizing high-quality loans. This suggests that for a nascent securitization market, such as in Italy, banks' incentive to build up their reputation prevents them from selling lemons to the market.

Similar results are also observed in other "emerging" securitization markets such as Spain: Cardone-Riportella et al. (2010) analyze the driving force behind Spanish banks' securitization boom during 2000–2007. Estimating the probability that a bank chooses to securitize, they find that the likelihood is higher for banks with tighter liquidity constraints and higher cost-to-income ratio, implying that improving liquidity and profitability motivates banks to securitize. Given that Spanish banks retain a large share of risk in securitization, banks' credit risks are not observed to rise, suggesting that the transfer of credit risk may not be the first-order concern.

Investigating the euro-denominated syndicated corporate loan market, Kara et al. (2016) do not observe that in the run-up to the 2007–2009 global financial crisis, the distribution of loan rates over comparable loans is tighter for banks that are more active in originating asset-backed securities, compared with the less active banks—no evidence for lax screening and lower lending standard (Purnanandam 2011), so that banks' lending standard tends to be more driven by the credit cycles rather than securitization itself. This is in line with findings in the US that the evidence on banks' excess risk-taking in the non-mortgage securitization market is less obvious.

5.6 EXERCISES

1 **Mortgage-backed securities**
Suppose, in $t=0$, an investment bank is issuing mortgage-backed security (MBS), against an asset pool with two *ex ante* identical mortgage loans. Each loan will yield a gross return R, $R>1$ in $t=1$, with an unconditional probability p ("repay"), or 0 otherwise

("default"). Assume that the returns of the two mortgage loans are independent and identically distributed (i.i.d.).

In $t=0$, two mortgage-backed securities of identical size are issued:

- A senior tranche that will yield a gross return R in $t=1$ if at least one mortgage loan is repaid;
- A junior tranche that will yield a gross return R in $t=1$ only if both mortgage loans are repaid.

(a) Compute the expected return of each security.
From now on, assume that the returns of the two mortgage loans are correlated in a way that the probability that both loans are repaid is $(1+\epsilon)p^2$, $\epsilon>0$, and the probability that both loans default is $(1+\epsilon)(1-p)^2$.

(b) Compute the expected return of each security. How does the correlation in return change your result, compared with that in question (a)?

2 **Pricing structured products, based on Gorton (2008)**
Consider a stylized economy with three financial instruments available:

- A single piece of (subprime) mortgage;
- Mortgage-backed security (MBS) of this single mortgage. The MBS tranching only contains a junior tranche and a senior one;
- A collateralized debt obligation (CDO) with the simplest junior-senior tranches, which is based on purchasing the senior tranche of the MBS.

The economy lives for two dates, $t=0,1$:

- In $t=0$ the lender has to finance the mortgage which has a face value of W. The mortgage is financed by securitization, and the senior tranche of the MBS is purchased by the CDO. The details are explained below;
- In $t=1$ the mortgage needs to be refinanced—perhaps due to an unexpected increase in interest rate. If it is not refinanced,

it will default and the lender will be able to recover a value of R. In this case, the lender incurs a loss $L_M = W - R$. If it is refinanced, the renewed mortgage has a new value of M. Obviously, the mortgage will not be refinanced if $M < R$.

During the securitization in $t = 0$, the lender sells the mortgage to the security holders at its face value, W, and the aggregate return to the security holders in $t = 1$ will be either W if the mortgage is refinanced or R if it defaults. The junior tranche in the securitization has a face value of N, and the senior tranche has a face value of $W - N$. This means that the first loss worth N will be borne by the junior tranche, and the senior tranche starts to incur the cost only if the loss exceeds N. Thus, if the loss to the securities is below N, the senior tranche will stay intact; otherwise the senior tranche should take the remaining loss once the entire junior tranche is wiped out.

(a) Show that, for the senior tranche of MBS, the loss in $t = 1$ can be characterized by $L_S = [L_M - N, 0]$ and the payoff in $t = 1$ is $V_S = \min[W - N, W - L_S]$.

Note that the senior tranche of MBS is sold to a CDO, which also has two tranches, one junior and one senior. Suppose that the junior tranche in the CDO has a face value of N_C and the senior tranche has a face value of $W - N - N_C$. The senior tranche stays intact if the loss to the CDO, or the senior tranche of MBS, is fully absorbed by the junior tranche of the CDO; otherwise the senior tranche has to take the remaining loss.

(b) Show that, for the senior tranche of CDO, the payoff in $t = 1$ is $V_C = W - N - N_C - \max\left[\max(L_M - N, 0) - N_C, 0\right]$.

3 **Loan sales and originator's guarantee, based on Gorton and Pennacchi (1995)**

Consider the bank's problem that is characterized in Section 5.2. Keeping all the settings unchanged, with one additional assumption: the bank provides a guarantee for a share γ of the loan that is sold to the market investors, against the realized losses in the loan's return—precisely, the bank covers $L-x$ for investors, for any realized $x<L$. In addition, with an exogenous probability $0<p<1$, the bank becomes insolvent and is forced to default on the guarantee.

(a) Specify the bank's profit maximization problem and the bank's incentive compatibility constraint.
(b) Rewrite the bank's incentive compatibility constraint in terms of the loan's mean return. With positive loan sale $s>0$, how is the bank's implied screening effort level, compared with the bank's screening effort level without the loan sale?
(c) Using the definition of compounded promised yield on the loan sale $r_{ls} = \frac{1}{T}\ln\left(\frac{Ls}{1-D}\right)$ in which D denotes the total deposits, assuming that the mean return of the loan $\bar{x}(e)$ varies with the level of screening effort e as $\bar{x}(e) = L[1-\alpha\exp(-\beta e)]$, solve for the bank's optimal volume on loan sale, s.

  i. How does the spread in the bank's funding sources, $r_d - r_s$, affect the equilibrium s?
  ii. How does the premium in the loan sale, $r_{ls} - r_s$, affect the equilibrium s?
  iii. How does the probability of the bank's insolvency affect the equilibrium s?

4 Originate-to-distribute and the limit of arbitrage, based on Shleifer and Vishny (2010)

When analyzing the securitization equilibrium with repo lending $(0<h<1)$ in Shleifer-Vishny model, as in Section 5.3, security price P_2 is taken as exogenously given. However, when banks suffering from a negative asset price shock have to liquidate the long assets, such fire sale may lead to further decline in asset prices that force banks to liquidate more long assets. To capture such a feedback mechanism between fire sale and plummeting asset price, in this exercise, we endogenize the security price P_2. To focus on the feedback mechanism, we assume that the haircut h remains constant, $h_1 = h_2 = h$, and keep all other settings the same as in the model.

Assume that a group of "noise traders" also participate in the asset market in $t = 2$. The noise traders have deep pockets so that they are able to purchase all the assets on sale in the market.

The demand for long assets D_n from these noise traders follows a simple demand function which is the inverse of asset price and subject to a demand shock, σ,

$$D_n(P_2) = N\left(\frac{1-\sigma}{P_2}\right).$$

The demand for long assets D_b from the banks after liquidation equals banks' total asset holdings,

$$D_b(P_2) = Nd - S.$$

The aggregate supply of the long assets is just the number of projects. Therefore, by market clearing condition,

$$D_n(P_2) + D_b(P_2) = N.$$

(a) Compute the equilibrium asset price P_2.
(b) Assume that the parameter values ensure that P_2 is always positive, $P_2 > 0$. How does the demand shock from noise traders, σ, affect P_2?
(c) Show that P_2 is more sensitive to σ, when h is small.

CHAPTER 6
Complexity in banking

6.1 INTRODUCTION

Banks and financial institutions have been becoming more and more complex over the past few decades. Complexity in banking brought attention to regulators and researchers during the 2007–2009 global financial crisis, when complex structured financial products suffered from huge losses and almost brought down the entire financial system. Since then, more questions have been raised on why banks choose to be so complex and what complexity in banking means for the stability of the financial system.

Banks are complex in many dimensions. They are complex in their organizational structure, they are complex in the products that they design to offer customers, they are complex in how they interconnect with each other through financial claims, and they are overall opaque to outsiders so that information on their investment portfolios as well as their gains and losses is limited. Let us have a quick look through these dimensions.

6.1.1 ORGANIZATIONAL COMPLEXITY

Banks, especially big banks, are complex financial firms. They often open branches in different geographical locations, they sometimes choose to be "universal banks" that provide a wide spectrum of services covering investment banking, insurance, real estate, etc., and many of them are organized as bank holding companies with a complex organizational structure inside. In many ways, banks' complex organizational structure is beneficial for both banks and society, for example, branching over different geographical locations helps banks better diversify and reduce their exposure to regional risks, as well as improve local customers' access to finance; banks' coverage on varieties of businesses provides economies of scope to customers and helps them "lock in" customers who look for multiple financial services; complex organizational structure inside banking companies helps improve operational efficiency. On the other hand, there is also a dark side with banks' organizational complexity:

a bank branch's loan losses from regional shock may force the banking company to adjust investment in other regions, so that an adverse regional shock may spread to the entire economy; banks may abuse their proprietary data collected in one business and exploit rents from the same customers in another business; banks' complex organizational structure is also subject to suspects of arbitrage against regulation.

6.1.2 COMPLEXITY IN PRODUCTS

Banks also create complex financial products, the most notable ones include those highly complex structured products in securitized banking, as in Chapter 5. Complex financial products may be better customized to match customers' different risk appetites and improve efficiency, as Section 5.1, Chapter 5 demonstrates, but they may also be exploited by banks to obfuscate customers and extract more rents.

Another potential problem associated with complex products is the computational complexity that grows exponentially when financial products become more complex. Pricing a financial product becomes highly challenging, when it combines a large number of financial assets, so that certain assumptions are often needed and certain risks are neglected. When the product is further tranched and repacked with other products by other financial intermediaries, more information on risks may be lost along the intermediation chain. Such lost information may become a trigger for crises in the future, once any neglected risk is revealed. Computational complexity also prevents complex products from being properly re-priced in a reasonable time, when fundamentals of underlying assets change. This creates a pressure on asset prices when the market is under stress: for example, when certain assets suffer from losses, it is almost impossible to re-price all complex structured products in the market that are associated with these assets and determine the precise impacts on their prices in a short time, as a result, prices of all related products will collapse. Just as in the episodes in the onset of 2007–2009 global financial crisis, troubles in subprime mortgages led to price collapse of all structured products.

6.1.3 NETWORK COMPLEXITY

Another distinguishing feature in banking is that banks form complex networks. Banks borrow from and lend to each other, so that these borrowing and lending connect them through a web of claims. Interbank network provides a risk-sharing mechanism for banks, for example, the well-functioning of a banking system often relies on a well-functioning interbank market, in which banks with temporary liquidity shortage are able to fulfill customers' liquidity demand by borrowing from banks with liquidity surplus. However, such interconnection also means that one bank's failure can become its creditor banks' trouble and create losses for creditor banks; the *contagion* can go on if losses in these banks make them fail to honor their liabilities to other banks... small problems in part of a banking network can thus quickly spread to other banks and across borders; a small ripple can evolve into a tsunami that sweeps the world.

6.1.4 OPACITY

Typically, an average bank is more opaque than a non-financial firm, as it is more difficult for outsiders to acquire information on a bank's portfolio or decipher the bank's health by disclosed information. On one hand, the nature of banks' intermediation service implies that opacity is appealing to certain degrees: banks are providing money-like liquidity service to depositors which shall not be sensitive to asset returns, therefore, keeping portfolios opaque reduces volatility in depositors' valuation of their deposits. On the other hand, opacity may increase the likelihood of bank runs, when there is any negative signal on banks' health. Furthermore, opacity may also be a strategic choice of banks, who want to hide their risk-taking behavior away from creditors and regulators.

The questions on implications of complexity in finance inspired a lot of research in recent years (Brunnermeier and Oehmke 2009 provide an extensive review on the issues). In this chapter, we focus on three analytical frameworks that address implications of banking complexity from different angles. In Section 6.2, we examine banks' incentive to create complex products, as a strategy in winning market competition; in Section 6.3, we analyze how a banking network provides risk-sharing and how the network is vulnerable to contagion of risks; in Section 6.4, we explain to what degree opacity is desirable for banks' intermediation services.

6.2 STRATEGIC COMPLEXITY IN PRODUCT

In this section, we explore reasons why banks are so keen on making their products more complicated. In the past few decades, together with other financial institutions, banks have been creating numerous new products and services—particularly those under the name of "financial innovation"—many of which are highly complex. Very often, customers and buyers have to read through pages of small print to better understand payoff structures and risks. Although complex financial products may improve risk allocation, as we have learned from the example in Chapter 5, Section 5.1, more and more questions have been raised after the 2007–2009 financial crisis on these products and services, especially on whether their complexity generates more value added than risks introduced. Just as the former Federal Reserve chairman, Paul Volcker, stated:

> How many other [financial] innovations can you tell me that have been as important to the individual as the automatic teller machine, which in fact is more of a mechanical than a financial one? (*The Wall Street Journal*, December 14, 2009)

Insights from recent research in industrial organization on firms' incentive to obfuscate consumers may help us explain banks' excess interests in producing complex products and services. Inspired by the sophisticated pricing schemes of internet retailers, Ellison and Ellison (2009) argue that retailers can reduce the price sensitivity and capture some rent via obfuscation—practices that "frustrate investor search or make it less damaging to firms". Applying this idea in finance, Carlin and Manso (2010) show that banks and financial firms indeed have similar incentive to increase wasteful obfuscation design, misguiding the investors who attempt to learn about the products.

Increasing product complexity through obfuscation also relates to a well-established concept in industrial organization, *price dispersion*, which provides a reason behind banks' practice in actively producing complex products. The idea is that complexity opens a second dimension of market competition, making it more difficult for the uninformed investors to discover the true cost of the products. Therefore, in a prevailing mixed strategy equilibrium, banks can deviate from competitive pricing by designing more sophisticated products, and the prices become dispersed together with product complexity, generating higher profit for banks from the uninformed investors who are disoriented and purchase those products, which is in line with theories in industrial organization on price dispersion, such as d'Aspremont et al. (1979), Varian (1980), and Stahl (1989). Following the literature on obfuscation and price dispersion, in this section, we present a mechanism for how banks exercise their market power through creating complexity in their products using a model based on Carlin (2009).

6.2.1 MODEL SETUP: AGENTS, PREFERENCES, AND TECHNOLOGIES

Consider an economy in which there are N banks producing a homogeneous product for retail customers, or, small investors. The product is universal in the sense that it can be used by the investors to buy consumption goods, or to be used as an investment fund. There are a continuum of risk neutral investors whose population is normalized to be 1, who want to invest in a unit of financial product. A representative investor i's problem is to maximize her utility

$$u_i = v - P_i,$$

in which v is the fundamental value of the financial product and P_i is the price paid by investor i. The value v is public information among all the investors. The investors are divided into two groups according to the information they obtain about the prices charged by the banks, denoted by P_j, $j=1,\ldots,N$,

1. A fraction μ of the investors are financial experts or, informed investors, who are perfectly informed about all the P_j in the market and only buy the financial product at the lowest price $\underline{P} = \min\{P_j\}_{j=1}^{N}$. The population of the financial experts, measured by μ, is endogenously determined by the overall "complexity" of the financial products, which we will explain later;
2. A fraction $1-\mu$ of the investors are uninformed investors, who are completely uninformed about the P_j in the market and simply buy the financial product from a randomly chosen bank that asks for a price P_j. As all the banks have identical probability to be met by an uninformed investor, the expected price the representative uninformed investor pays is therefore $\overline{P} = \frac{1}{N}\sum_{j=1}^{N} P_j$. Uninformed investors are willing to buy the financial product only if $0 \leq P_j \leq v$.

Besides setting the price of financial product, a bank j can also choose the complexity of its product, denoted by $\underline{k} \leq k_j \leq \overline{k}$. Assume that the banks can choose any k between $\underline{k}$ and $\overline{k}$ with zero cost, i.e., the cost for bank j on setting k_j is

$$C_j(k_j) = \begin{cases} 0, & \text{if } \underline{k} \leq k_j \leq \overline{k}, \\ +\infty, & \text{otherwise} \end{cases}$$

so that any k outside the range of $[\underline{k}, \overline{k}]$ is not feasible.

The more the average complexity of financial products in the market is, the more difficult it becomes to be informed about all the P_j, i.e., the less investors are able to be financial experts. Therefore, the population of the financial experts, μ, shrinks if the banks successfully coordinate to increase the financial complexity. Precisely, given any k_j with $\underline{k} \leq k_j \leq \overline{k}$, $j=1,\ldots,N$, μ is a function that maps overall financial complexity to a value between 0 and 1

$$\mu : [\underline{k}, \overline{k}]^N \to (0,1)$$

with $\frac{\partial \mu}{\partial k_j} < 0$ for any individual bank j. Assume zero complementarity between the choices on complexity by any two arbitrary banks m and n, $\frac{\partial^2 \mu}{\partial k_m \partial k_n} = 0$, for any $m = 1, \ldots, N$, $n = 1, \ldots, N$, and $m \neq n$.

6.2.2 MARKET POWER AND PRODUCT COMPLEXITY

The investors and banks engage in a two-period game. In the first period, $t = 0$, each bank simultaneously chooses the complexity of its product, k_j, and posts the price P_j of the product. Then, in the second period, $t = 1$, the investors purchase the products from the banks at the posted prices.

The market equilibrium is solved by backward induction. Starting from $t = 1$, given the strategic profile of the banks, (P_j, k_j), $j = 1, \ldots, N$, chosen in $t = 0$, and without loss of generality the prices being ranked in the ascending order, $P_1 \leq P_2 \leq \ldots \leq P_N$, the bank(s) with the lowest price(s) will serve all the financial experts plus part of the uninformed investors, and the other banks will only serve the rest of the uninformed investors. Suppose that M banks choose the lowest price P_1, i.e., $P_1 = \ldots = P_M$ and they share the demand of the financial experts. Then the strategic profile for each of these banks, (P_1, k_l^*), $l = 1, \ldots, M$ is the equilibrium outcome only if it maximizes banks' expected profit when the banks set their strategies at $t = 0$

$$(P_1, k_l^*) = \arg\max_{(P_1, k_l)} \Pi_1(P_1, k_l) = \arg\max_{(P_1, k_l)} P_1 \left(\frac{\mu}{M} + \frac{1-\mu}{N} \right).$$

And for the banks with higher prices, the strategic profile for each of these banks, (P_h^*, k_h^*), $h = M+1, \ldots, N$, is the equilibrium outcome only if it is profit maximizing in $t = 0$ as well,

$$(P_h^*, k_h^*) = \arg\max_{(P_h, k_h)} \Pi_h(P_h, k_h) = \arg\max_{(P_h, k_h)} P_h \left(\frac{1-\mu}{N} \right).$$

What does the market equilibrium look like? First of all, it is not difficult to find out that there does not exist any pure strategy equilibrium in which all banks set a symmetric price P. To see this, assume that all banks choose a uniform price P^*, although they may differ from each other in k. We distinguish several cases:

1. If P^* is equal to the marginal cost, i.e., $P^* = 0$, so that all banks earn zero profit, one deviating bank j will profit from setting $P_j > 0$ because it makes strictly positive profit from serving $\frac{1}{N}$ of the uninformed investors, although it loses all the financial experts;
2. If P^* is strictly positive, i.e., $0 < P^* \leq v$, all banks share both financial experts and uninformed customers, with each one earning a profit $\frac{P^*}{N}$
   (a) If banks do not choose the same k so that there is at least one bank z who sets $k_z > \underline{k}$, one deviating bank j will profit from setting $P_j = P^* - \epsilon$, in which ϵ is arbitrarily small, and $k_j = \underline{k}$. By undercutting its competitors with a lower price, it attracts all the financial experts while still maintaining $\frac{1}{N}$ of the uninformed investors; by setting $k_j = \underline{k}$ it may lower (if bank j coincides with bank z) the average financial complexity and increase the population of the experts, further increasing its profit;
   (b) Even if all banks choose $\underline{k}$, the deviator can secure the increase in profit by simply undercutting its competitors with a lower price.

Therefore, the market equilibrium must be a mixed strategy equilibrium characterized by price dispersion, i.e., the equilibrium price P_j^*, $j=1,\ldots,N$, is randomly drawn from a cumulative distribution function $F^*(P)$. Furthermore, it can also be seen that there is no mass point P^m on $F^*(P)$ in which many banks choose the same P^m, because one deviator from these banks can profit from assigning a bit higher probability on the price level $P^m - \epsilon$ and a bit lower probability on P^m, with ϵ being arbitrarily small.

Second, one can also see that banks are dispersed in product complexity as well. Since the conditional probability of a bank being the one offering the lowest price is high when a low price is drawn from $F^*(P)$, it will be better for the bank to set the lowest possible k, i.e., $\underline{k}$, to maximize the population of the financial experts, hence its expected profit. Similarly, it will be better for the bank to set the highest possible k, i.e., $\overline{k}$, to maximize the population of the uninformed investors, when a high price is drawn from $F^*(P)$. Therefore, the equilibrium is characterized by a mixed strategy equilibrium in which a representative bank j chooses a strategic profile $\left(P_j^*, k_j^*\left(P_j^*\right)\right)$ in which P_j^* is randomly drawn from a cumulative distribution function $F^*(P)$ and the complementary complexity of the financial product is set to be

$$k_j^*\left(P_j^*\right) = \begin{cases} \underline{k} & \text{if } P_j^* < \hat{P}, \\ \overline{k} & \text{if } P_j^* > \hat{P}, \\ \underline{k} \leq k_j \leq \overline{k} & \text{if } P_j^* = \hat{P} \end{cases}$$

in which $\hat{P}$ denotes the cutoff value between the high price and low price drawn from $F^*(P)$.

To get some knowledge about the cutoff value, $\hat{P}$, suppose that in a materialized equilibrium outcome bank j makes a random draw for price P_j and sets a corresponding complexity $k_j(P_j)$. The bank can certainly sell its product to some of the uninformed investors and get a profit $P_j \dfrac{1-\mu}{N}$, whereas whether it is able to attract the financial experts depends on whether P_j is the lowest price among all the banks, i.e., $P_j = P_1$ in our notation. The probability that P_j is the lowest price is equal to the probability that each of the other banks' prices are higher than P_j, i.e.,

$$\text{Prob}\left(P_n > P_j, n=1,\ldots,N \text{ and } n \neq j\right) = \prod_{n \neq j} \text{Prob}\left(P_n > P_j\right)$$
$$= \left[1 - F\left(P_j\right)\right]^{N-1}.$$

Therefore, the expected profit of bank j is

$$\Pi_j\left(P_j, k_j\right) = P_j \left\{ \left[1 - F\left(P_j\right)\right]^{N-1} E\left[\mu \mid P_j = P_1\right] + \frac{1-\mu}{N} \right\}.$$

Note that bank j only attracts all of the financial experts when its price is the lowest, therefore, the corresponding population of the experts is the conditional expectation on μ. Taking derivative of $\Pi_j(P_j, k_j)$ with respect to k_j, one can get

$$\frac{\partial \Pi_j}{\partial k_j} = P_j \left\{ \left[1 - F(P_j)\right]^{N-1} \frac{\partial E[\mu | P_j = P_1]}{\partial k_j} - \frac{1}{N} \frac{\partial \mu}{\partial k_j} \right\}$$

$$= P_j \frac{\partial \mu}{\partial k_j} \left\{ \left[1 - F(P_j)\right]^{N-1} - \frac{1}{N} \right\}$$

in which the second step is the result of the assumption on zero complementarity that $\frac{\partial^2 \mu}{\partial k_j \partial k_n} = 0$, $n = 1, \ldots, N$, and $n \neq j$, i.e., the choices of the other banks on k does not change bank j's marginal contribution to μ so that

$$\frac{\partial E[\mu | P_j = P_1]}{\partial k_j} = \frac{\partial \mu}{\partial k_j}.$$

Define the cutoff value $\hat{P}$ as the P_j that makes $\frac{\partial \Pi_j}{\partial k_j} = 0$, or

$$\left[1 - F(\hat{P})\right]^{N-1} - \frac{1}{N} = 0,$$

and solve for $\hat{P}$

$$\hat{P} = F^{-1}\left(1 - \left[\frac{1}{N}\right]^{\frac{1}{N-1}}\right).$$

Therefore, given that $\frac{\partial \mu}{\partial k_j} < 0$,

- If $P_j^* < \hat{P}$, $\frac{\partial \Pi_j}{\partial k_j} < 0$ so that $k_j^* = \underline{k}$;

- If $P_j^* > \hat{P}$, $\frac{\partial \Pi_j}{\partial k_j} > 0$ so that $k_j^* = \overline{k}$;

- If $P_j^* = \hat{P}$, $\frac{\partial \Pi_j}{\partial k_j} = 0$ so that k_j^* can take any value.

In this model the banks compete in two dimensions, financial complexity and price, and the two dimensions interact with each other: one bank may either undercut its competitors to win all the financial experts—in this case a lower level of average complexity is desired to make a larger expert group, or raise its price to maximize the profit from the uninformed investors—in this case a higher level of average complexity is desired to make a larger group of the uninformed. As a result, the equilibrium is featured by the banks dispersed in the prices and heterogeneous in their product complexity.

6.2.3 SUMMARY

One can learn two lessons from the Carlin model. First, in the mixed strategy equilibrium, banks set prices higher than zero, the marginal cost. Although one bank can undercut the rivalries and attract all the financial experts, there is a reversed incentive by the other banks to raise their prices, hence the profit, because they are guaranteed to attract a fixed share of the uninformed investors, anyway; second, the price dispersion along with a substantial average financial complexity cannot be solved by raising competition in the banking sector. To see this, notice that $\hat{P}$ is declining with N, or, $\frac{\partial \hat{P}}{\partial N}<0$, increasing the likelihood of banks' drawing a price higher than $\hat{P}$ and choosing the highest complexity, i.e., increasing market competition by having more banks will increase the probability of banks' setting a higher product complexity $\bar{k}$, therefore, the overall complexity in the market increases. This is because increasing competition with having more banks erodes each bank's profit by reducing the share of uninformed investors for everyone, therefore, banks will coordinate to complicate their products and enlarge the population of the uninformed investors, since each bank's decision on k changes μ in the margin, $\frac{\partial \mu}{\partial k_j}<0$, for any bank j.

6.3 NETWORK COMPLEXITY

The banking industry is characterized by its complex interbank network. Banks actively borrow from and lend to each other; the borrowing and lending between banks thus create a complex web of claims. Such interbank network provides a risk-sharing mechanism between banks, for example, when banks are subject to idiosyncratic liquidity shocks from their depositors, a bank who faces liquidity shortage can borrow from those who have liquidity surplus, without the need to liquidate high-yield long assets; this makes banks better off and improves efficiency. However, interbank networks also open a channel of risk contagion, for example, when some banks in the network are hit by losses in their assets, these banks may have to default on the debts of their creditor banks. This leads to losses in the assets of creditor banks, and may force these banks to default on their creditor banks, too, like dominoes. As a result, local stress may spread to the entire banking network, just as what has been observed in many banking crises in the past.

6.3.1 BANKING NETWORK AS A WEB OF CLAIMS

To see how banks affect each other through interbank linkages, consider a generic banking network that is created by interbank claims, following Eisenberg and Noe (2001). In an economy that lives for two periods, $t = 0,1$, there is a banking sector with n risk-neutral, leveraged banks, which finance their loans by equity and debts. Banks' debts are raised from interbank lending.

Initially, in $t = 0$ the face value of the total debts issued by representative bank i, $i = 1,\ldots,n$, is denoted by $\bar{x}_i$; among all bank i's debts, the proportion held by bank j, $j = 1,\ldots,n$, is denoted by π_{ij}, i.e., bank i borrows $\bar{x}_i \pi_{ij}$ from bank j. The book value of bank i's equity is denoted by $\bar{e}_i$, and $\bar{y}_i$ is the face value of bank i's loans. As Figure 6.1 shows, the balance sheet of bank i implies that

Assets	Liabilities
Loans $\bar{y}_i$	Equity $\bar{e}_i$
Interbank lending $\sum_{j=1}^{n} \bar{x}_j \pi_{ji}$	Debts $\bar{x}_i$

Figure 6.1 Bank i's balance sheet in $t = 0$

$$\bar{y}_i + \sum_{j=1}^{n} \bar{x}_j \pi_{ji} = \bar{e}_i + \bar{x}_i$$

in which $\sum_{j=1}^{n} \bar{x}_j \pi_{ji}$ denotes total lending of bank i to all other banks in the network.

There is an aggregate credit risk for all banks in the banking sector, such that in $t=1$ the total realized return from any bank i's loans is $\tilde{y}_i = \gamma \bar{y}_i$, in which γ is randomly drawn from a distribution function over $0 \leq \gamma \leq 1$.

Because of the credit risk, bank i may not be able to fully honor its debt, $\bar{x}_i$. Suppose that in $t=1$ the total realized repayment from bank i's debts is $\tilde{x}_i$. If $\tilde{x}_i < \bar{x}_i$, the bank has to default and the creditors share $\tilde{x}_i$ with equal seniority, for example, bank j receives $\tilde{x}_i \pi_{ij}$ from bank i. The realized value of bank i's assets is denoted by

$$\tilde{a}_i = \tilde{y}_i + \sum_{j=1}^{n} \tilde{x}_j \pi_{ji}, \qquad (6.1)$$

which is the maximum value that bank i's creditors can claim, given that the bank's equity can be partially or even fully wiped out. Therefore, the total realized repayment from bank i's debts $\tilde{x}_i$ is

$$\tilde{x}_i = \min\{\tilde{a}_i, \bar{x}_i\}. \qquad (6.2)$$

Note that $\tilde{a}_i$ depends on the realized repayment from the debts of all banks, as (6.1) shows. Denote the realized debt repayment from all banks by a vector $x = (\tilde{x}_1, \ldots, \tilde{x}_n)$, equation (6.2) can thus be generalized as the realized repayments for all banks in the entire banking network, which is a mapping $F(\cdot)$ that translates the realized value of all the banks' debts into the value that the banks realize from their debt holdings,

$$x = F(x, \bar{x}) \qquad (6.3)$$

in which $\bar{x} = (\bar{x}_1, \ldots, \bar{x}_n)$ is a vector capturing the face value of all the banks' debts. Equation (6.3) also means that vector x is a fixed point in the mapping; as Eisenberg and Noe (2001) prove, there is a unique solution for x, i.e., one can solve (6.3) for each bank's realized debt payment $\tilde{x}_i$, $i = 1, \ldots, n$ after an aggregate shock γ is realized.

Bank i's market value of equity in $t = 1$ is therefore

$$\tilde{e}_i = \max\left\{\tilde{y}_i + \sum_{j=1}^n \tilde{x}_j \pi_{ji} - \tilde{x}_i, 0\right\} = \max\{\tilde{a}_i - \tilde{x}_i, 0\}.$$

The unique solution for fixed point x also implies an algorithm of solving for x, i.e., each bank's realized debt payment under aggregate shock γ: starting with an arbitrary guessing on x, the mapping $F(\cdot)$ ensures a convergence to the fixed point solution, after iterations. To see how it works, suppose that we start with a guessing $x^0 = (0, \ldots, 0)$ such that all banks repay nothing on their debts. However, as long as $\gamma > 0$, every bank has a positive return from its loans, $\tilde{y}_i > 0$, implying a positive value for its debts, i.e., if we feed x^0 into the mapping $F(\cdot)$, the realized value should be positive at least for some banks,

$$x^1 = F(x^0, \bar{x}) \geq x^0,$$

implying that $x^0 = (0, \ldots, 0)$ cannot be an equilibrium solution. We can continue feeding x^1 into the mapping $F(\cdot)$, and if the outcome x^2 gives

$$x^2 = F(x^1, \bar{x}) \geq x^1,$$

x^2 is still off equilibrium. Then we continue with the same procedure, until the t-th round when

$$x^{t+1} = F(x^t, \bar{x}) = x^t,$$

then x^t is the fixed point, or, the equilibrium solution for x in (6.3).

This simple generic framework clearly shows, under aggregate credit risk, how every bank is affected by all other banks in a banking network, which is connected by interbank claims. The same analysis can also be applied for idiosyncratic credit risk, for example, when only some banks suffer from loan losses. As we can expect, such generic network structure means that other connected banks may also be affected, given that banks with loan losses may have to default on their creditor banks, which results in a contagion over the network.

As we can see, how much is a bank affected by other banks in contagion depends on its "connectedness", or how many banks it connects with, and the "strength" of connections with stressed banks, for example, bank i's claim on a stressed bank j, π_{ji}. That is, network structure is crucial for analyzing banks' vulnerability to contagion. Furthermore, network effects on banks may be both positive and negative, depending on types of risks: for example, if banks are dealing with idiosyncratic liquidity risks so that at a certain point some banks face higher than expected withdrawal demand from depositors while other banks face lower than expected withdrawal demand, banks with liquidity shortage can borrow from banks with liquidity surplus through interbank lending network; network in this case actually improves banks' risk-sharing. To see how implications of network on risks in the banking system depend on network structure and risks, next we build banking systems on specific network structures, following Allen and Gale (2000), and see how risk-sharing and contagion arise in banking networks.

6.3.2 RISK SHARING THROUGH FINANCIAL NETWORKS

Consider an economy with two groups of agents: depositors and banks. The economy extends over three periods, $t = 0, 1, 2$. It is assumed that

1. The banking industry spreads over four *ex ante* identical regions, $i = A, B, C, D$, each with one representative bank as regional financial intermediary;
2. In each region, there is a continuum of *ex ante* identical depositors, each of which is endowed with one unit of consumption good in $t = 0$. *Ex post*, the true preference of each depositor is revealed in $t = 1$, such that

(a) With probability $p, 0 < p < 1$, one depositor is an impatient depositor so that she only values consumption in $t = 1$, i.e., $u_e = u(c_1)$;

(b) With probability $1 - p$, one depositor is a patient depositor so that she only values consumption in $t = 2$, i.e., $u_l = u(c_2)$.

It is worth noting that in each region the banking industry is assumed to be perfectly competitive in the deposit market. Banks are symmetric, so that we regard each of the regions, A, B, C, or D, as being represented by one bank. We call each representative bank A, B, C, or D, for simplicity.

Similar to the settings in Diamond and Dybvig (1983), the banks offer demand deposit contracts. The difference here is that one bank can have both depositors and the other bank has its customers, i.e., the banks can hold deposits of each other as interbank deposits. Assume that all the depositors are equal, so one bank has the same kind of claim as the depositors' for its deposits in the other banks. More details about interbank deposits will be explained later.

The regions are heterogeneous in p, so the probability for a depositor in region i being an impatient depositor is denoted by p_i. For each region there are two states with equal probability, i.e., $p_i = p_H, p_L$ with $p_H > p_L$, and $\text{Prob}(p_i = p_H) = 0.5$. There are two states of the world S_j—characterized by p s in the regions (p_A, p_B, p_C, p_D)—with equal probability: either $S_1 = (p_H, p_L, p_H, p_L)$ or $S_2 = (p_L, p_H, p_L, p_H)$. One depositor's preference is her private information; therefore, a patient depositor can imitate the impatient depositor by withdrawing early and consuming late.

As in Diamond and Dybvig (1983), there are two technologies available: one is the storage technology, transforming one unit input in t into one unit output in $t+1$, the other one is the production technology that transforms one unit input in t into $R > 1$ unit output in $t+2$. If the production is interrupted in $t+1$, only value c, $0 < c < 1$ can be recovered.

Similar to Diamond and Dybvig (1983), one bank invests in both short and long assets in $t = 0$. In $t = 1$ the bank uses the proceeds from the short assets plus, if necessary, the liquidated value of some long assets, to repay the impatient consumers. In $t = 2$, the proceeds from all remaining long assets are paid out to the patient consumers.

BENCHMARK: THE SOCIAL PLANNER'S SOLUTION

As a benchmark, the constrained efficient allocation in this economy is characterized by the social planner's problem in $t = 0$ to maximize a representative consumer's expected utility

$$\max_{\{\alpha, c_1, c_2\}} E[p]u(c_1) + (1 - E[p])u(c_2), \quad (6.4)$$

$$s.t. \quad E[p]c_1 = \alpha, \quad (6.5)$$

$$(1 - E[p])c_2 = R(1 - \alpha) \quad (6.6)$$

in which $E[p] = \frac{p_H + p_L}{2}$. It is easy to see that, except that p is replaced by $E[p]$, the social planner's solution here is almost identical to that in Section 2.2, $u'(c_1^*) = Ru'(c_2^*)$, $\alpha^* = E[p]c_1^*$, with $1 < c_1^* < c_2^* < R$. That is, with regional shocks being idiosyncratic, in $t = 1$, the planner just needs to reallocate the liquidity from the regions with excess liquidity supply (regions with p_L) to the regions with excess liquidity demand (regions with p_H).

BANKING SOLUTION

With segmented market structure and regional liquidity shocks, whether the constrained efficient allocation can be replicated by a decentralized, market equilibrium crucially depends on the structure of the banking sector, i.e., how the banks are interconnected with each other. In an interconnected banking network, the banks are able to exchange deposits before the liquidity shock is revealed in $t = 1$ and insure against the uncertainty of regional consumers' time preferences. On the contrary, the first best allocation is never achieved by the regional banks isolated from the other regions. To see this, suppose that one bank in an isolated region

i chooses $\{\alpha^*, c_1^*, c_2^*\}$ in $t=0$, with $\alpha^* = E[p]c_1^*$. However, when it turns out that $p_i = p_H$, the bank cannot meet the demand of impatient consumers by only using the yield of the liquid assets, given that $p_H c_1^* > \alpha^*$; therefore, part of the illiquid assets have to be liquidated. As a result, the realized consumption for the patient depositors, $\tilde{c}_2$, must be smaller than c_2^*. To make it worse, if the liquidation return c is small enough such that $\tilde{c}_2 < c_1^*$, the patient consumers will prefer to mimic the impatient ones and withdraw in $t=1$, leading to a bank run.

To see the impact of the structure of the banking sector on the market equilibrium, we start from the case of a complete banking network. As Figure 6.2 shows, each region is connected with all the other three, two being negatively correlated in p and one positively correlated. The interbank deposit market allows the bank in region i to hold $d^i = \dfrac{p_H - E[p]}{2}$ deposits in each of the other regions before $t=1$. It is assumed that the interbank deposit contract is the same as the deposit contract of the consumers, i.e., the return of one unit of interbank deposit is c_1/c_2 if it is withdrawn in $t=1/t=2$.

To find the optimal solution $\{\alpha, c_1, c_2\}$ of bank i, suppose that in $t=1$, p_i turns out to be p_H. The total deposit claims of the bank include the liquidity demand from the impatient consumers and the other bank under p_H, and the total liquidity available includes its own investment on liquid assets plus the deposits in the other regional banks. The budget constraint of such bank is therefore

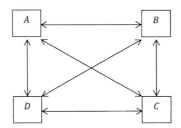

Figure 6.2 *Complete network*

Notes: the arrows describe the direction of deposit flows, for instance, bank A holds deposits from bank B, and bank B also holds deposits from bank A.

$$\left(p_H + \frac{p_H - E[p]}{2}\right)c_1 = \alpha + \frac{3(p_H - E[p])}{2}c_1$$

which is identical to (6.5). Correspondingly, the bank from a region with low liquidity demand p_L has to meet the demand of both its impatient consumers and the other regional banks under p_H out of the yields of its liquid assets

$$\left[p_L + \frac{2(p_H - E[p])}{2}\right]c_1 = \alpha$$

which is identical to (6.5), too. In $t = 2$, all the patient consumers and banks holding interbank deposits are repaid.

The budget constraint of bank i is

$$\left[(1 - p_H) + \frac{2(p_H - E[p])}{2}\right]c_2 = R(1 - \alpha)$$

which is identical to (6.6), and the budget constraint of a regional bank under p_L is

$$\left[(1 - p_L) + \frac{p_H - E[p]}{2}\right]c_2 = R(1 - \alpha) + \frac{3(p_H - E[p])}{2}c_2$$

which is identical to (6.6), too.

Since each bank maximizes the regional representative consumer's expected utility, $E[p]u(c_1) + (1 - E[p])(c_2)$, in $t = 0$—which is the same

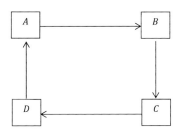

Figure 6.3 Incomplete network (I)

Notes: the arrows describe the direction of deposit flows, for instance, bank A holds deposits from bank D, and bank B holds deposits from bank A, etc.

as (6.4)—and the budget constraints for the following periods are no different from (6.5) and (6.6), the market equilibrium outcome should be the same as the constrained efficient allocation defined by the planner's problem. Therefore, the constrained efficient allocation is achieved in the complete network where the banks can hedge against the liquidity shocks by holding deposits between each other.

Furthermore, as long as banks are not perfectly correlated in p_i so that they are able to hedge against idiosyncratic liquidity shocks by holding deposits between each other, the constrained efficient allocation can be replicated by a decentralized banking equilibrium even in incomplete networks where a bank does not necessarily hold deposit positions from all the other banks, such as the banking networks shown in Figures 6.3 and 6.4 (see Exercises 1).

6.3.3 CONTAGION OVER BANKING NETWORK

Next, we will see whether the banking network is able to sustain liquidity shocks and bank runs. In the rest of this section, we assume that the banking network structure is specified as in Figure 6.3—readers can verify that the same methodology can be applied for other network structures, such as those in Figures 6.2 and 6.4.

Keep the same setting as before, that two states of the world may be materialized in $t=1$ with equal probability. In addition, assume that there is a "crisis state", $\bar{S}$, that may be materialized in $t=1$ with zero probability: in crisis state, the demand for liquidity is $E[p] = \frac{p_H + p_L}{2}$ in regions B, C, and D, while the demand for liquidity is $E[p] + \epsilon, \epsilon > 0$ in regions A, as Figure 6.5 shows.

The additional crisis state resembles a banking crisis in the real world, which is a rare event. As the likelihood of the crisis state is close to zero, banks do not need to take it into account in $t=0$ so that they still choose the same $\{\alpha^*, c_1^*, c_2^*\}$ as in the social planner's solution, and deposit $d^* = p_H - E[p]$ in their neighboring banks, as Figure 6.3 shows (readers

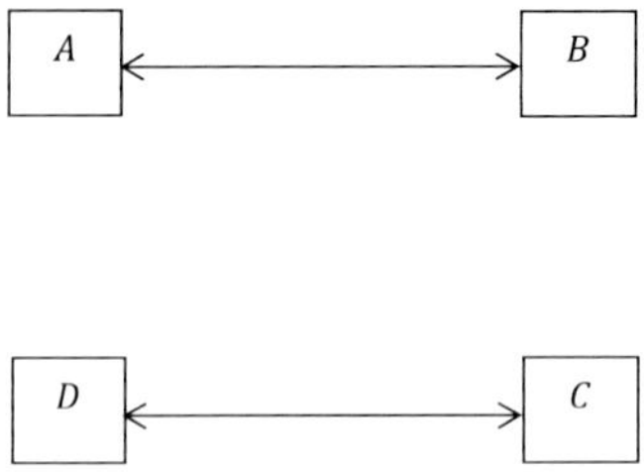

THE MICROECONOMICS OF BANKING

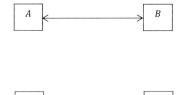

Figure 6.4 *Incomplete network (II)*

Notes: the arrows describe the direction of deposit flows, for instance, bank A holds deposits from bank B, and bank B also holds deposits from bank A, etc.

	A	B	C	D
S_1	p_H	p_L	p_H	p_L
S_2	p_L	p_H	p_L	p_H
$\bar{S}$	$E[p] + \epsilon$	$E[p]$	$E[p]$	$E[p]$

Figure 6.5 *Regional liquidity shock*

are asked to verify this in Exercise 1). Then we can focus on what happens in $t = 1$, when the crisis state is revealed as a shock to the optimal solution.

ILLIQUIDITY, INSOLVENCY, AND LIQUIDATION PECKING ORDER

The new, crisis state raises the question on what may happen to banks during a crisis. In the same vein as the Diamond-Dybvig model in Chapter 2, Section 2.2, in such crisis state, a bank can face one of the following three situations:

1. The bank may still be *liquid*, if it can meet entire withdrawal demand by using only the proceeds from its liquid assets which include its holdings of short assets and deposits in other banks;
2. The bank may be *illiquid* but still *solvent*, if it can meet entire withdrawal demand by using the proceeds from its liquid assets and liquidating part of its long assets;
3. The bank may be *insolvent* and *bankrupted*, if it cannot meet withdrawal demand even after liquidating all of its long assets.

What choices does a bank have to sustain a crisis? Resembling reality, the easiest way to raise liquidity is to collect proceeds from its own liquid assets; a slightly more costly way is to withdraw its deposits in other banks which may be subject to certain transaction cost in reality; the most costly way is to liquidate its long assets, as the liquidation value c of long assets is very low ($0 < c < 1$). Therefore, there is a "pecking order" when a bank tries to raise liquidity during a crisis: it will start with collecting proceeds from its own liquid assets, then continue with withdrawing interbank deposits, and take liquidating long assets as the last option.

If a bank has to liquidate long assets, the benefit from doing so is to increase c_1 with sacrificing c_2, while the cost is to forgo higher long run return R by collecting the liquidation value c. Therefore, liquidating long assets as the last option in the pecking order requires that the cost outweighs the benefit in equilibrium,

$$\frac{R}{c} > \frac{c_2^*}{c_1^*}. \tag{6.7}$$

LIQUIDITY BUFFER AND SOLVENCY

After defining the liquidation pecking order, now we can see what may happen to bank A under liquidity shock. In order to see what situation bank A will face, we define a shadow value for bank A's deposits in $t=1$, c^A, should bank A suffer a bank run and have to go down through the entire pecking order, as

$$c^A = \frac{\alpha^* + (1-\alpha^*)c + d^* c^B}{1+d^*}, \tag{6.8}$$

which is the ratio of total liquidity supply to total deposits, i.e.,

- Total liquidity supply in the numerator includes collected proceeds from short assets, α^*, liquidation value of long assets, $(1-\alpha^*)c$, and withdrawn interbank deposits from bank B. Note that how much bank A can withdraw from bank B depends on the status of bank B: if bank B is not insolvent, bank A's claims can be fully met so that

$c^B = c_1^*$; otherwise $c^B < c_1^*$ if bank B is bankrupted, and c^B needs to be computed in the same way as equation (6.8);
- Total deposits in the denominator include those withdrawing depositors from region A who consist of the entire population of 1, and bank D's withdrawing deposits of volume d^*.

It is then straightforward to see that bank A is *insolvent* and *bankrupted* from (6.8), once there is a bank run on bank A, because

$$c^A < c_1^*,$$

given that $c^B \leq c_1^*$ and $0 < 1 < c$.

Next, we characterize the condition under which a bank is just *illiquid*, but not *insolvent* or *bankrupted*. Remember that if a bank is illiquid, it has to liquidate some of its long assets to stay solvent, and the pecking order implies that the bank also needs to withdraw its interbank deposits. However, withdrawing interbank deposits will lead to liquidity shortage in its neighboring bank, forcing the neighboring bank to withdraw its interbank deposits... as a result, all interbank deposits of all banks will be withdrawn. For any bank in the network of Figure 6.3, the cross-region inflow of deposits is just canceled out by the outflow so that the bank's *net* liquidity position will not be changed by the interbank withdrawal.

For any bank facing a population of p impatient depositors, if it is illiquid so that it has to liquidate some of its long assets, l, to fulfill the withdrawal demand in $t = 1$, it can still avoid a bank run as long as the incentive compatibility constraint is fulfilled, that patient depositors are better off with waiting until $t = 2$ and withdrawing $\tilde{c}_2$, with $\tilde{c}_2 \geq c_1^*$. In other words, the remaining long assets in $t = 2$ must ensure that each patient depositor can withdraw at least c_1^*

$$\frac{(1-\alpha^*-l)R}{1-p} \geq c_1^*,$$

which defines the limit of liquidation,

$$l \leq 1-\alpha^* - \frac{(1-p)c_1^*}{R} = \bar{l}$$

so that the maximal long assets that can be liquidated without triggering bankruptcy is $\bar{l}$, and we define the corresponding liquidation value as *liquidity buffer*, $b(p)$

$$b(p) \equiv c\bar{l} = c\left[1-\alpha^* - \frac{(1-p)c_1^*}{R}\right].$$

That is, $b(p)$ characterizes the bank's buffer that can be used to absorb liquidity shocks and keep the bank solvent. Applying this concept on bank A in the crisis state, the liquidity shock will be fully absorbed by its liquidity buffer as long as

$$\epsilon c_1^* \leq b(p^A), \tag{6.9}$$

in which $p^A = E[p] + \epsilon$.

Condition (6.9) thus characterizes the requirement that bank A is not bankrupted in the crisis. If (6.9) is fulfilled, bank A survives the crisis and is able to honor its deposit contracts with all of its depositors.

INSOLVENCY AND CONTAGION

From the analysis above, we can infer that the other banks are not affected by the crisis, if bank A is just illiquid (of course, the other banks are not affected, either, if bank A is liquid). Then what will happen, if bank A is *insolvent* and *bankrupted*, i.e., when condition (6.9) is violated?

Obviously, bank D will be immediately affected, as its deposits in bank A will not be fully redeemed, which implies a liquidity shock to bank D in $t=1$, as

$$c^A \leq \bar{c}^A = \frac{\alpha^* + (1-\alpha^*)c + d^*c_1^*}{1+d^*} < c_1^*,$$

by (6.8), conditional on bank B is able to honor its deposit contract.

Following the same argument above, bank D could survive the liquidity shock, only if

$$d_0^*\left(c_1^* - \overline{c}^A\right) \leq b(E[p]), \qquad (6.10)$$

that is, bank D's loss in interbank deposits—it still has to meet c_1^* with bank C while it can only redeem at most $\overline{c}^A$ from bank A—can be fully absorbed by its liquidity buffer. If condition (6.10) holds, bank D suffers from the crisis, too, from the forced early liquidation as a result of contagion through interbank deposits, but bank C and bank B will still stay intact.

However, what will happen if condition (6.10) is violated? Then bank D is bankrupted so that its neighboring bank, bank C is under liquidity shock, as bank C can only redeem

$$c^D \leq \overline{c}^D = \frac{\alpha^* + (1-\alpha^*)c + d^*\overline{c}^A}{1+d^*} < c_1^*.$$

However, whether bank C survives the liquidity shock or not depends on whether

$$d_0^*\left(c_1^* - \overline{c}^D\right) \leq b(E[p]), \qquad (6.11)$$

which is the same as condition (6.10). Therefore, violation of condition (6.10) implies violation of condition (6.11), or, bankruptcy of bank D leads to bankruptcy of bank C.

Using the same reasoning, it is easy to see that, after bank C is bankrupted, bank B will be bankrupted, too—a crisis that initially only hits bank A brings down all banks in the network, as a result of contagion through interbank claims!

6.3.4 SUMMARY

The seminal work of the Allen-Gale network model has inspired numerous studies on contagion through banking networks. The model is very simple, but the implications are rich and striking: on one hand, banking networks provide a risk sharing mechanism for its members. By holding deposits of each other, one bank facing idiosyncratic liquidity shock can easily raise funding from the other part of the network where cheaper liquidity supply is available, and the first best allocation can be achieved by the interbank market within the banking network. However, the banking network also creates banks' exposure to each other, making the entire financial system vulnerable to contagions. One bank's failure may increase the other banks' exposure to risks, even lead to a systemic meltdown.

One key question on the Allen-Gale network model is how risk-sharing over an interbank network and banks' vulnerability to contagion depend on the network structure, i.e., comparing different network structures such as Figures 6.2, 6.3, and 6.4, does more *completeness* in network structure lead to better interbank risk-sharing or make contagion more likely to happen? The answer is addressed by Acemoglu et al. (2015), based on a more general setup in terms of number of connecting banks and network structures. Intuitively, as long as negative liquidity shocks on one part of a network are small, a more complete network exhibits higher stability because small shocks can be easily absorbed by buffers provided by a larger number of connected banks. However, such result is reversed if negative shocks are large enough, more complete network makes contagion and systemic collapse more likely to happen; in this case, incomplete network may be more resilient because the adverse shocks may be contained within a small neighborhood, instead of spreading over the entire interbank network.

6.4 OPACITY AND BANKING

In this section, we explain why banks are opaque to outsiders, based on the analytical framework in Dang et al. (2017). The reason is that the main product that banks offer depositors is a money-like liquidity service so that depositors are always able to withdraw from their deposit accounts at any time, while such service is backed by banks' risky assets with highly volatile returns; to make liquidity service insensitive to asset returns, banks have to prevent depositors from accessing information on their balance sheets and avoid depositors to reevaluate their deposits. In this way, banks attract depositors who are subject to liquidity preference shocks and need liquidity insurance; this is in contrast to more transparent financial institutions, such as bond market, in which liquidity supply is volatile and sensitive to revealed information on asset returns.

6.4.1 MODEL SETUP: AGENTS, PREFERENCES, AND TECHNOLOGIES

Consider an economy with one good that extends over three periods, $t=0,1,2$. There are three types of agents in the economy:

- An entrepreneur living through all three periods. She can choose between two projects, each of which needs an initial investment I in $t=0$ and will return in $t=2$. One project is a bad project that will return 0 in $t=2$; the other project is a good project that will return $R>I$ in $t=2$ with probability p, or 0, otherwise. The good project is socially desirable with $pR>I$. In addition, a project in progress cannot be liquidated prematurely;
- One early consumer that is born in $t=0$ with endowment e, and dies after $t=2$;
- N identical late consumers ($N>1$) that are born in $t=1$ with endowment e each, and die after $t=2$.

The entrepreneur derives utility, u_F, from its total consumption over time, c_{Ft}

$$u_F = c_{F0} + c_{F1} + c_{F2},$$

so that she has no preference on the timing of consumption.

In contrast, consumers have special liquidity preferences, or, preferences on the timing of consumption: they prefer to consume in the period after their birth up to $\bar{k}$, that is, for the early consumer, her utility u_E from her consumption c_{Et}, $t=0,1,2$, is characterized by

$$u_E = c_{E0} + c_{E1} + \alpha \min\{c_{E1}, \bar{k}\} + c_{E2} \text{ with } \alpha > 0$$

so that she gains extra utility from her consumption c_{E1} in $t=1$, $\alpha \min\{c_{E1}, \bar{k}\}$, up to a level of $\bar{k}$. This also implies that, should there be no resource constraint, the early consumer shall consume at least $\bar{k}$ in $t=1$.

Similarly, for a representative late consumer, her utility u_L from her consumption $c_{Lt}, t = 1, 2$, is characterized by

$$u_L = c_{L1} + c_{L2} + \alpha \min\{c_{L2}, \overline{k}\}.$$

To focus on the interesting scenario, assume that the early consumer is able to fully finance the entrepreneur, $e > I$, or fulfill her liquidity preference in $t = 1$, $e > \overline{k}$, however, she is not able to do both, i.e.,

$$e < I + \overline{k}.$$

That is, if the early consumer lends I to the entrepreneur in $t = 0$, she will not fulfill her liquidity demand in $t = 1$, because the entrepreneur's project is not mature yet so that the lending cannot be called back. However, if one of the late consumers can join the lending scheme with her endowment e in $t = 1$ in certain way—which will be discussed later, the entrepreneur's debt is able to be rolled over, and both the early and the late consumers can fulfill their liquidity demand in $t = 1$ and $t = 2$, respectively, i.e.

$$2e > I + 2\overline{k}. \tag{6.12}$$

6.4.2 MARKET FUNDING, BANK FUNDING, AND THE ROLE OF OPACITY

Now we establish institutions in this economy where opacity plays a role. We focus on two institutions that can possibly channel funds from consumers to the entrepreneur:

- *Bond market*, in which the entrepreneur can issue bond in $t = 0$ through a bond issuer, then the early consumer invests in the bond in $t = 0$ and sells the bond to late consumers in $t = 1$. In this way, the early consumer can consume the proceeds from the bond sale in $t = 1$, and late consumers can redeem the bond for their consumption in $t = 2$;
- *Banking*, that a bank can provide a deposit contract for the early consumer in $t = 0$, promising a non-contingent, fixed return d_{E1} in $t = 1$. The bank then provides funding for the entrepreneur through

$t=0$ to $t=2$, and rolls over the debt by collecting deposits from a late consumer in $t=1$. The late consumer withdraws $d_{L,2}$ from the bank in $t=2$ for consumption.

Bond market and banks are different in *opacity*, i.e., how much information is disclosed. If the entrepreneur chooses bond funding, in $t=0$, the bond issuer receives a credit report for the entrepreneur, and the report will be disclosed to all market participants; if the entrepreneur chooses borrowing from the bank instead, in $t=0$, the bank receives the same credit report, but the report will be kept secret.

We further assume that, with the credit report, in $t=0$ an agent can infer whether the entrepreneur chooses a good or bad project. However, when the project is in progress, in $t=1$, an agent who has access to the report can perfectly forecast the project's return in $t=2$. With this assumption, the bond market is *transparent*, so that late consumers know the project's return in the future when they enter the market in $t=1$. In contrast, the bank is *opaque* so that a late consumer does not know the project's return in the future when she deposits in the bank in $t=1$.

BENCHMARK: THE SOCIAL PLANNER'S PROBLEM

We start our analysis from the benchmark, or, the first-best solution to the social planner's problem. It is straightforward to see that the first-best solution is characterized by:

1. In $t=0$, the social planner transfers I from the early consumer to the entrepreneur and lets the entrepreneur choose the good project;
2. In $t=1$, the social planner transfers I from late consumers to the early consumer. Assume that the transfer I is evenly borne by all N late consumers and N is large enough, so that

$$\frac{I}{N} \leq e - \bar{k}. \tag{6.13}$$

That is, even after the transfer, each late consumer still has at least $\bar{k}$ for consumption in $t=2$;

3. In $t=2$, the social planner pays $\frac{I}{P}$ out of the project's return (which is feasible because $pR > I$) to all N late consumers—and the transfer is evenly distributed among late consumers—if the project succeeds with return R, and 0 if the project fails. Condition (6.13) then ensures that late consumers are able to meet their liquidity demand in $t=2$ by themselves even if the project fails, and social planner's repaying late consumers by $\frac{I}{P}$ when the project succeeds compensates their consumption beyond the "essential" liquidity demand $\overline{k}$.

Under the first-best solution, the early consumer's utility is thus $u_E^{FB} = e + \alpha \overline{k}$, each late consumer's expected utility is $E\left[u_L^{FB}\right] = e + \alpha \overline{k}$, and the entrepreneur's expected utility is $E\left[u_F^{FB}\right] = pR - I$.

AUTARKY SOLUTION

The other extreme case is autarky, under which the entrepreneur, the early consumer, and the late consumers can do nothing except directly match their needs. Under autarky, the early consumer cannot lend to the entrepreneur, because she needs to consume at least $\overline{k}, \overline{k} > e - I$ in $t=1$ while the entrepreneur can only repay in $t=2$; such lending is not feasible even if late consumers are born in $t=1$ with extra resources: it is not feasible for late consumers to lend to the early consumer and roll over the entrepreneur's debt, because late consumers cannot make such contract with the early consumer and the entrepreneur in $t=0$. Therefore, there is no lending in autarky and consumers just consume their own endowments. Each consumer can only optimize their own utility by choosing the timing of consumption, so that the early consumer's utility is $u_E^A = e + \alpha \overline{k}$, each late consumer's utility is $u_L^A = e + \alpha \overline{k}$, and the entrepreneur's utility is $u_F^A = 0 < E\left[u_F^{FB}\right]$.

Compare the autarky solution with the first-best solution, the loss in social welfare arises from the failure of direct lending: early and late consumers have different liquidity preferences so that no contract is feasible between them and the socially desirable long-term project cannot be carried out. Therefore, certain intermediation technology, such as bond market or banking, may help match the demands of consumers and the entrepreneur, and achieve better resource allocation than autarky.

SOLUTION UNDER TRANSPARENT BOND MARKET

One institution that can provide such intermediation technology is the bond market: to finance her project, in $t=0$ the entrepreneur approaches a bond issuer with a credit report, to issue bond with face value b^j in $t=1$ that is contingent on the project's return in $t=2$—j denotes whether the entrepreneur's project succeeds (call it state G) or fails (call it state B), $j=G,B$. Obviously, $b^B \leq 0$, and $b^G \leq R$. The bond market is *transparent* so that the entrepreneur's credit report is disclosed to the public.

The bond is sold to the early consumer in $t=0$ for price I, and the early consumer stores $e-I$, denote $s \equiv e-I$—note that $s<\bar{k}$ because $e<I+\bar{k}$. Then in $t=1$, the early consumer can sell the bond to meet her liquidity demand. Now the late consumers with access to entrepreneur's credit report are able to forecast the project's return, depending on their forecast, they compete to buy the bond at a certain price—assume that after the sale, the bond is evenly held by late consumers. The timing of events is summarized in Figure 6.6.

$t = 0$	$t = 1$	$t = 2$
• Entrepreneur issues bond via an issuer, with face value b^j, $j = G, B$, in $t = 1$	• Late consumers enter, observe $j = G, B$	• Project returns
• Credit report of entrepreneur is disclosed to public	• Early consumer sells bond to late consumers for b^j	• Late consumers redeem bond and consume
• Early consumer purchases bond with I	• Early consumer consumes	
• Entrepreneur starts project	• Project in progress	

Figure 6.6 *Bond market with the early consumer*

Obviously, the entrepreneur certainly chooses the good project in $t=0$, if she wants to raise funding through the bond market where her credit report is disclosed to the public; therefore, we now only focus on the market outcome with the good project being funded. The bond market equilibrium can be solved by backward induction. Starting with $t=1$, given that late consumers perfectly forecast the project's return

- If the project will fail, the market price for the bond is $b^B = 0$;
- If the project will succeed, the market price for the bond is $0 \leq b^G \leq R$. And the early consumer has to sell the bond to fulfill her liquidity demand, i.e., $b^G \geq \bar{k} - s$.

Therefore, the early consumer consumes her saving s in $t=1$, when consumption yields higher utility, and whether her consumption in $t=1$ reaches $\bar{k}$ or not depends on the project's future return.

Expecting such outcomes of b^j in $t=1$, in $t=0$, the early consumer's expected utility in the bond market solution, $E[u_E^M]$ is

$$E[u_E^M] = s + \alpha s + p[b^G + \alpha(\bar{k} - s)]. \tag{6.14}$$

However, the early consumer is only willing to enter the bond market in $t=0$ if she is better off than staying in autarky,

$$E[u_E^M] \geq u_E^A. \tag{6.15}$$

And condition (6.15) implies that the equilibrium bond price b^G is bounded from below. Insert (6.14) into (6.15) and solve for b^G,

$$b^G \geq \frac{I}{p} + \frac{\alpha(1-p)(\bar{k}-s)}{p} = \underline{b}^G. \tag{6.16}$$

Bond price b^G cannot exceed the project's return, $b^G \leq R$. Together with (6.16), two cases arise:

1. If $\underline{b}^G \leq R$, any b^G with $\underline{b}^G \leq b^G \leq R$ ensures that the early consumer participates in the bond market in $t=0$, according to (6.15). Knowing that late consumers will compete to buy the bond in $t=1$, the profit maximizing entrepreneur shall set b^G as low as possible in the first place in $t=0$. In equilibrium, $b^G = \underline{b}^G$;

2. If $\underline{b}^G > R$, then no feasible b^G will attract the early consumer to participate in the bond market in $t=0$, according to (6.15), and all consumers will stay in autarky. In this case, the bond issuer has to buy the bond in $t=0$, however, the monopolistic bond issuer will request to take all of the project's return in the future, i.e., $b^G = R$.

Combine these two cases, we can express the equilibrium bond price b^G as

$$b^G = \min\{\underline{b}^G, R\}. \tag{6.17}$$

Furthermore, as we show in the first case, if the early consumer enters the bond market in $t=0$ and sells the bond at $\underline{b}^G$ in $t=1$ under the good state, the competition among late consumers implies that they earn zero profit from the entrepreneur; that is, the entrepreneur repays the bond holders $\underline{b}^G$ in $t=2$. Entrepreneur's total cost of bond market funding, I^B, is

$$I^B = p\underline{b}^G + (1-p)b^B = I + \alpha(1-p)(\overline{k}-s) > I, \tag{6.18}$$

given that $b^B = 0$.

How about social welfare in the bond market solution? First of all, if the early consumer participates the bond market, the entrepreneur is better off than in autarky, as her expected utility under bond market funding, $E\left[u_F^M\right]$ is given by

$$E\left[u_F^M\right] = pR - I^B > 0 = u_F^A.$$

On the other hand, $E\left[u_F^M\right]$ is below her utility in the first-best solution,

$$\begin{aligned} E\left[u_F^{FB}\right] - E\left[u_F^M\right] &= pR - I - \left(pR - I^B\right) \\ &= \alpha(1-p)(\overline{k}-s) \\ &> 0, \end{aligned} \tag{6.19}$$

if the early consumer participates the bond market. If not, the bond issuer will keep the bond and get the entire rent of R in $t=2$, so that

$$\begin{aligned} E\left[u_F^{FB}\right] - E\left[u_F^M\right] &= pR - I - (pR - pR) \\ &= pR - I \\ &> 0. \end{aligned} \tag{6.20}$$

Combining (6.19) and (6.20), the social welfare loss under the bond market solution—relative to the first-best solution—can be written as

$$E\left[u_F^{FB}\right] - E\left[u_F^M\right] = \min\left\{\alpha(1-p)(\bar{k}-s), pR-I\right\} \quad (6.21)$$

Notice that the social welfare loss only comes from the entrepreneur, as readers can verify that the expected utility, $E\left[u_E^M\right]/E\left[u_L^M\right]$, for the early consumer/a representative late consumer is the same as the one in the first-best,

$$E\left[u_E^M\right] = E\left[u_L^M\right] = e + \alpha\bar{k}.$$

Why is there a loss in social welfare associated with the bond market solution, in which liquidity demands of consumers and entrepreneur are matched? It is because consumers' liquidity preferences make their utility functions *globally concave* or *globally risk-averse*, although the utility functions are *locally risk-neutral*. To see this, Figure 6.7 illustrates the early consumer's utility function: because of liquidity preference, consumption up to $\bar{k}$ in $t=1$ gains higher utility so that from point O to point A, the slope of utility curve is higher at $1+\alpha$, and the slope becomes 1 for the consumption above $\bar{k}$.

The kink at point A leads to risk aversion: in $t=1$, early consumer's consumption is $s + b^G > e$ under good state with point H on the utility curve, or $s < e$ under bad state with point L on the curve. To induce the early consumer to participate in the bond market, the expected utility—as point C denotes—should be at least as high as the utility in autarky, as point B denotes. The global concavity of the utility curve implies a risk premium from B to C: the early consumer requires a higher expected consumption,

$$s + b^G - e = \alpha(1-p)(\bar{k}-s)$$

to participate in the bond market, and this increases the entrepreneur's funding cost by the same amount, as (6.18) shows. Such risk premium leads to the loss in social welfare, as in (6.21).

The very fundamental reason why such risk premium arises is that the transparency of the bond market implies excess volatility in bond price in

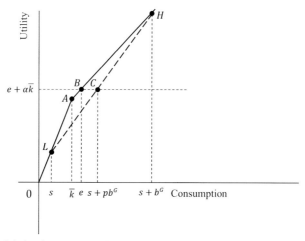

Figure 6.7 Global risk aversion and local risk neutrality

$t = 1$, as a response to the new information on the project's future return. This is the source of inefficiency in the bond market solution.

SOLUTION WITH OPAQUE BANK

Now we continue to see whether an opaque bank as financial intermediary makes any difference. With a bank in presence, in $t = 0$, the early consumer deposits her endowment e in the bank, and the deposit contract promises non-contingent repayment d_{E1} in $t = 1$, as well as repayment d_{E2}^j, $j = G, B$, in $t = 2$ that is contingent on the state j. Based on her credit report, the entrepreneur borrows I from the bank, and the loan contract requires her repayment r^j, $j = G, B$, in $t = 2$ that is contingent on the state j. The bank is *opaque* that the entrepreneur's credit report is not disclosed to public. With investment I, entrepreneur starts her project.

In $t = 1$, the bank collects deposit of e from one late consumer, and the deposit contract promises repayment d_{L2}^j, $j = G, B$, in $t = 2$ that is contingent on the state j. Early consumer withdraws d_{E1} for consumption.

In $t = 2$, the state j is revealed. The entrepreneur repays r^j to the bank, and early/late consumer withdraws d_{E2}^j / d_{L2}^j for consumption.

$t = 0$	$t = 1$	$t = 2$
• Early consumer deposits e in bank with $\{d_{E1}, d_{E2}^G, d_{E2}^B\}$	• A late consumer deposits e in bank with $\{d_{L2}^G, d_{L2}^B\}$	• Project returns under state G/B
• Entrepreneur borrows I from bank with $\{r^G, r^B\}$ for $t = 2$	• Early consumer withdraws d_{E1} and consumes	• Entrepreneur repays r^G/r^B to bank
• Credit report of entrepreneur is kept secret	• Project in progress	• Early consumer withdraws d_{E2}^G/d_{E2}^B and consumes
• Entrepreneur starts project		• Late consumer withdraws d_{L2}^G/d_{L2}^B and consumes

Figure 6.8 Banking solution

The timing of the banking solution is summarized in Figure 6.8.

Again, with the entrepreneur's credit report, the bank will only lend to her if she chooses the good project. Therefore, we will only focus on the banking solution with the good project being chosen. Before solving for banking solution, notice that the early consumer needs to fulfill her liquidity demand $\bar{k}$ by d_{E1} in $t=1$. Once this is guaranteed, there is an infinite number of $\{d_{E1}, d_{E2}^G, d_{E2}^B\}$ that makes her indifferent. In further analysis, assume that the bank sets $d_{E1} = \bar{k}$ and $d_{E2}^B = 0$. In addition, the entrepreneur is not able to repay the bank if her project fails, thus $r^B = 0$.

The banking solution can be solved by backward induction: after $t=1$, bank's total cash holding c_{B1} is

$$c_{B1} = e - I + e - d_{E1} = 2e - I - \bar{k} > \bar{k}$$

by assumption (6.12); then after the state is revealed in $t=2$, bank's total cash holding becomes $c_{B2}^B = c_{B1} + r^B = c_{B1}$ under state B, or $c_{B2}^G = c_{B1} + r^G$ under state G.

With $d_{E1} = \bar{k}$ and $d_{E2}^B = 0$, the early consumer only deposits in the bank in $t=0$ if she is better off than in autarky, i.e.,

$$\bar{k} + \alpha\bar{k} + pd_{E2}^G + (1-p)d_{E2}^B \geq e + \alpha\bar{k}.$$

In equilibrium, the bank shall set d_{E2}^G which just makes this constraint binding, solve to get

$$d_{E2}^G = \frac{e - \bar{k}}{p}.$$

Under state B in $t = 2$, bank's cash holdings are claimed by consumers, $c_{B2}^B = d_{E2}^B + d_{L2}^B$. With d_{E2}^B being fixed at 0, $d_{L2}^B = c_{B2}^B = 2e - I - \bar{k} > \bar{k}$. The late consumer only deposits in the bank in $t = 1$ if she is better off than in autarky, i.e.,

$$\bar{k} + \alpha\bar{k} + p(d_{L2}^G - \bar{k}) + (1-p)(d_{L2}^B - \bar{k}) \geq e + \alpha\bar{k},$$

and the equilibrium d_{L2}^G shall just make this constraint binding, solve to get

$$d_{L2}^G = e + \frac{1-p}{p}(I + \bar{k} - e) > e > \bar{k}.$$

Note that both d_{L2}^G and d_{L2}^B are larger than $\bar{k}$, implying that the late consumer is able to fulfill her liquidity demand in $t = 2$.

Finally, assume that the entrepreneur has higher bargaining power in $t = 0$ and extracts all the rents through $\{r^G, r^B\}$. With $r^B = 0$, entrepreneur sets r^G so that the bank is just able to meet d_{E2}^G and d_{L2}^G by its cash holdings c_{B2}^G, i.e.

$$c_{B2}^G = 2e - I - \bar{k} + r^G = d_{E2}^G + d_{L2}^G,$$

solve to get

$$r^G = \frac{I}{p}.$$

The entrepreneur's expected utility under banking solution, $E[u_F^B]$, is thus given by

$$E[u_F^B] = pR - pr^G - (1-p)r^B = pR - I = u_F^{FB}$$

which is the same as in the first-best solution. Readers can further verify that, with deposit contract $\{d_{E1}, d_{E2}^G, d_{E2}^B\}/\{d_{L2}^G, d_{L2}^B\}$, the expected utility, $E[u_E^B]/E[u_L^B]$, for the early/late consumer is the same as the one in the first-best,

$$E[u_E^B] = E[u_L^B] = e + \alpha \overline{k}.$$

The banking solution thus replicates the first-best solution.

6.4.3 SUMMARY

The Dang-Gorton-Holmström-Ordoñez model unveils a crucial element in banking that banks are intrinsically opaque, and opacity in banks' balance sheets allows them to provide safe, demandable liquidity service that is insensitive to banks' volatile asset returns. This is particularly important for depositors who are subject to liquidity preference shocks and hence need liquidity insurance.

What is not covered in this model is how opacity may affect banks' fragility. Given that banks are opaque, any leaked negative information on a bank's asset return—even if it is imprecise—may become a coordination device for depositors to initiate a bank run, as Morris and Shin (2002) demonstrate; under certain circumstances, such a coordinated bank run is more likely to happen if such information is provided by the public, for instance, by a regulator who publishes stress test results for banks. More opaque banks are thus more vulnerable to adverse information shocks. Furthermore, opacity may also be banks' strategic choice, that within opaque balance sheets, banks can hide their risk-taking away from depositors and regulators; such excess risk-taking in the disguise of opacity may increase fragility of banks.

What is also not covered in the Dang-Gorton-Holmström-Ordoñez model is that less opacity, or more transparency in banks' balance sheets allows creditors to better monitor and discipline banks: with more transparency, if a bank attempts to take excess risk, creditors will discover and punish it by asking for higher risk premium, and the increased funding cost will deter the bank from taking more risks. Such market discipline mechanism is well reflected in the current global standard for banking regulation, the so-called Basel III, with new emphases on improving information disclosure and enhancing market participants' capability to monitor and discipline banks.

6.5 EMPIRICAL EVIDENCE

6.5.1 INTERBANK NETWORK AND CONTAGION

Modelling and forecasting financial contagion is challenging, due to the complex nature of financial networks as well as the complex driving forces behind contagion. One way is to explore statistical correlations between markets and market participants, such as Dungey et al. (2011) and Diebold and Yilmaz (2015). The groundbreaking work of Eisenberg and Noe (2001) opens the possibility to model a banking network as a web of claims, and the fixed point result of Eisenberg and Noe (2001) implies that a unique solution can be solved for after the banking network is perturbed, as is shown in Section 6.3.1. This allows policy makers to use such a banking network for policy analysis, for example, to stress-test banks and simulate the outcome of a banking network under certain hypothetical shocks. Since then, a variety of studies have focused on exploring banking network structures for policy analysis, such as Bech et al. (2010) and Gai et al. (2011).

Besides applying banking network for simulation, identifying contagion over an interbank network is challenging, not only due to the lack of data on interbank exposures that are necessary to construct the network structure, but also due to the fact that failure of a systemically influential bank is a rare event and is often intertwined with bailout effort from monetary and financial authorities. Iyer and Peydró (2011) tackle these challenges by an ideal natural experiment in India, where a large cooperative bank unexpectedly failed because of fraud and was not bailed out. Using a comprehensive dataset that covers interbank exposure, they find that after the event, deposit outflow is stronger in banks that are more exposed to the failed bank, and the effect is stronger for less well-capitalized banks, reflecting depositors' concerns on those banks' fundamentals. More importantly, among surviving banks, stronger deposit outflows are also observed in banks that have no direct exposure to the failed bank, but only indirect exposure through other banks in the interbank market; this clearly shows a contagion over the interbank network.

6.5.2 OPACITY MEASURES AND BANK RISK

Do more opaque banks take more risks? The very first challenge to answer this question is the measurement of bank opacity, as opacity itself means elements—such as banks' balance sheet components, investment portfolios, performance indicators, etc.—that are not easily observed by outsiders. In practice, one way to address this challenge is to dig deeper into the market data, finding the discrepancies and inconsistencies that are not explained by the publicly observable variables; the other way is to explore the supervisory data that contain more details on banks' balance sheets.

MARKET MEASURES ON BANK OPACITY

Bank opacity can be proxied by the discretionary, or abnormal part of certain market indicators. That is, if there are systematic discrepancies and inconsistencies in these indicators that cannot be explained by the publicly available information, these discrepancies and inconsistencies are then more likely to reflect those opaque elements in banks' balance sheets.

One such indicator is loan loss provision (LLP) that is disclosed by banks. As the most important way in which banks manage earnings and regulatory capital, LLP is typically an allowance that is set aside by a bank, as a provision to cover loan losses. To assess what is "hidden" there, Beatty and Liao (2014) propose a regression as follows:

$$LLP_{i,t} = \sum_{j=-m}^{n} \alpha_j NPL_{i,t+j} + \beta X_{i,t} + \gamma Z_t + \zeta Reg_t + \sum_{j=-m}^{n} \eta_j NPL_{i,t+j} \times Reg_t$$
$$+ \phi X_{i,t} \times Reg_t + \psi Z_t \times Reg_t + \delta + \epsilon_{i,t} \quad (6.22)$$

in which $NPL_{i,t}$ is bank i's non-performing loan ratio in quarter t, $X_{i,t}$ is a vector that contains bank-level controls (may be lagged), Z_t is a vector that contains macroeconomic controls, Reg_t measures regulatory requirements, and δ contains any necessary fixed effects to be considered. Specifically, *NPL* does not only include information on non-performing loans from the past *m* periods that requires the bank to set LLP, it also contains information on non-performing loans for the future *n* periods, to reflect the forward-looking expense set aside by the bank.

Regression equation (6.22) thus attempts to explain LLP by a wide spectrum of observable variables, and what is not explained—the error term $\epsilon_{i,t}$—is then used as a proxy for bank opacity.

Using LLP-based opacity proxy, Jiang et al. (2016) exploit the deregulation wave in the US through 1980s and 1990s as a natural experiment to investigate the impact of increasing banking competition on bank opacity. They find enhanced competition reduces bank opacity, and this potentially improves the market's capability to monitor banks and reduces fragility of banks.

Using opacity proxy constructed from LLP and related accounting variables, Chen et al. (2018b) find evidence that supports the Dang-Gorton-Holmström-Ordoñez model: examining uninsured deposit flows in US commercial banks from 1994 to 2013, they find that uninsured deposit flows are more sensitive to information about bank performance for banks that are less opaque, suggesting that opacity is a crucial element for banks to provide stable liquidity service. Kim et al. (2020) find that more transparent banks are associated with lower stock return volatility, implying that market perceives less opaque banks as being less subject to excess risk-taking—which is in line with Baumann and Nier (2004) who find that banks with more information disclosure face lower stock return volatility and such banks are less likely to fail (Nier 2005). Zheng (2020) finds that bank opacity, proxied by LLP discrepancies, has a negative effect on banks' lending growth, and this is because more opaque banks have more difficulties with wholesale funding. This suggests the effect from market discipline: as wholesale lenders are less insured or guaranteed compared with retail depositors, they are more sensitive to banks' potential risks, therefore, interpreting bank opacity as a disguise of risk-taking, they will demand higher risk premium from more opaque banks so that these banks are punished by higher funding cost. This is in line with Demirgüç-Kunt et al. (2008a) who find that banks complying with Basel requirements on information disclosure perform better.

Fosu et al. (2017) proxy bank opacity by market analysts' forecast error on banks' earnings, which reflects the elements on banks' balance sheets that were previously unknown to the public. Using financial statements of US bank holding companies in 1995–2013, they find that higher bank opacity is associated with higher bank risk, measured by banks' z-scores, and such positive link between opacity and bank risk-taking is weakened by increasing banking competition.

BALANCE SHEET MEASURES ON BANK OPACITY

Whereas market-based opacity measures are good at capturing market participants' perception of bank risk and as such better predict investors' reaction to banks' behavior, the sources of opacity—often arising from how banks allocate their investments among a wide spectrum of assets with various degrees of opacity—remain less well understood. In addition, market-based measures are only available for a small number of large, listed banks. However, for the rest of the banking sector, i.e., a large number of unlisted banks that often account for a substantial share of a banking system but are subject to much lower information disclosure requirements, the relationship between opacity and bank risk is less understood. For these reasons, several recent studies attempt to explore the supervisory data that reveal more details directly from banks' balance sheets, to extract measures of opacity out of balance sheet items from the perspective of outside investors and lenders.

One example is the balance sheet item "available-for-sale (AFS) securities". Generally speaking, security holdings on banks' balance sheets can be classified in either "AFS securities"—securities that are purchased with the intent of selling before they reach maturity, or "held-to-maturity (HTM) securities"—securities that are purchased with the intent of selling after they reach maturity. While HTM securities are accounted for at amortized cost so that their gains and losses are only reported after maturity, AFS securities are marked-to-market so that their (unrealized) gains and losses are reflected immediately in banks' equity value. As a result, AFS assets are easily valued, based on publicly available and verifiable information. Hence, for banks with more AFS securities, it is essentially easier for market participants to evaluate the health of the institution, and banks' balance sheet opacity is thus likely to be lower.

The other example is banks' off-balance sheet items. Although off-balance sheet items are not observable for investors and depositors, banks are often by law obliged to provide assessments of the value of these items to the financial supervisory authorities. As these items are off-balance sheet and not subject to disclosure requirements, there is significantly less information available to outsiders about factors which ultimately affect banks' payoffs on these assets. A bank is thus more opaque, if more of its asset holdings are off-balance sheet.

Fuster and Vickery (2018) exploit a reform in accounting rules in the US, 2013, to comply with Basel III capital accord, as a natural experiment, to study the reaction in banks' balance sheet opacity and the implication for bank risk. The reform removes "accumulated other comprehensive income (AOCI)" filter for investment securities, so that affected banks have to reshuffle assets under AOIC to AFS or HTM. They find that affected banks are 20% more likely to classify risky assets as HTM rather than AFS, implying their clear preference on increasing balance sheet opacity; these banks also tend to take more risks in asset reshuffling, suggesting a positive link between balance sheet opacity and bank risk.

Exploring quarterly balance sheet reports of all Norwegian banks over two decades, Cao and Juelsrud (2020) find that banks with more AFS securities have lower realized risk, while banks with more off-balance sheet items have higher realized risk. They also find that the positive correlation between balance sheet opacity and bank risk is weaker for better capitalized banks, probably because banks with more skin-in-the-game have less incentive to take excess risks, hence less incentive to exploit opacity as a disguise of risk-taking; such positive correlation is also weaker for banks that rely more on interbank market funding, probably because market participants interpret opacity as a sign of excess risk-taking and thus punish more opaque banks by higher funding costs.

6.6 EXERCISES

1 **Idiosyncratic liquidity shocks in incomplete banking networks, based on Allen and Gale (2000)**
   Show that the constrained efficient allocation, as defined in Section 6.3.2, can be replicated by decentralized banking equilibrium in incomplete networks described by Figures 6.3 and 6.4. Furthermore, show that the constrained efficient allocation can also be replicated by decentralized banking equilibrium in another incomplete network described by Figure 6.9.

2 **Private information acquisition in banking, based on Dang et al. (2017)**
   In this exercise, we explore the impact of private information acquisition on banking solution. Consider the banking solution in the Dang-Gorton-Holmström-Ordoñez model, as described in Section 6.4.2. Keep all settings unchanged, except that, although the

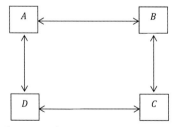

Figure 6.9 *Another incomplete network*

Notes: the arrows describe the direction of deposit flows, for instance, bank A holds deposits from bank B, and bank B also holds deposits from bank A, etc.

bank is opaque and keeps the entrepreneur's credit report a secret, a late consumer has the option to make an effort to access the credit report in $t=1$ and then perfectly forecast the project's future return. The late consumer has to incur a cost of σ in her consumption, for the effort in information acquisition.

(a) Suppose that in $t=1$ the bank offers the same deposit contract $\{d_{L2}^G, d_{L2}^B\}$ as in the model to a late consumer. Before depositing in the bank, the late consumer pays σ to access the credit report.

  i. Does the late consumer's decision to deposit depend on the future state?
  ii. Compute the late consumer's expected utility, with deposit contract $\{d_{L2}^G, d_{L2}^B\}$ and information acquisition.
  iii. Under what condition will the late consumer deposit in the bank in $t=1$ without making any effort in information acquisition?

(b) Show that the banking solution breaks down if the condition in question (a) iii. is violated.

(c) Given that the condition in question (a) iii. is violated:

  i. Show that the bank can prevent the late consumer's information acquisition and raise deposit from the late consumer, if the entrepreneur's project is divisible, i.e., the entrepreneur only carries out η unit of project, $0<\eta<1$, and the bank only lends ηI to the entrepreneur in $t=0$.
  ii. Compute η and the entrepreneur's expected utility.

3 **Strategic bank opacity, based on Wagner (2007)**

Consider an economy that is populated by a group of investors and a banker. They are all risk neutral and do not discount the future. The economy lasts for three periods:

- In $t=0$, the banker raises deposits from investors to finance one project; then she decides in which project to invest. There are two types of projects available: transparent and opaque ones—denoted by type $t=T, O$, respectively, and there is a finite number of projects for each type. Besides choosing the type of investment project, the banker can also choose the project's probability p, $0<p<1$, of delivering a high return in $t=2$—call it a high state H (correspondingly, a low return with probability $1-p$ in $t=2$—call it a low state L);

- In $t=1$, investors have the chance to set a required return on their deposits in the bank. If a transparent project is chosen by the bank in $t=0$, in $t=1$ investors can perfectly forecast its return in $t=2$; if an opaque project is chosen by the bank in $t=0$, in $t=1$ investors know nothing about the project's realized return in $t=2$ except the probability of the high state p.

- In $t=2$, the project matures, allowing the banker to extract a return of R_H/R_L ($R_H > R_L$) under H/L state, respectively. If investors take over the project before they are repaid, they are only able to generate $\beta R_H/\beta R_L$ ($0<\beta<1$) return, due to inalienable human capital characterized in Section 2.4, based on Hart and Moore (1994). To avoid the bank's incentive to renegotiate, after the state of the world is revealed, deposit contract gives investors the privilege to run on the bank, i.e., demand their deposits—with the promised return that is set in $t=1$—back any time before the deposit contracts are repaid (similar to the features in the Cao-Illing model, characterized in Section 2.4). If the banker cannot meet investors' demand, she has to declare bankruptcy and let investors take over the project.

(a) Consider the investors' problem in $t=1$, given that they have learned whether the banker has chosen a transparent or an opaque project in $t=0$.

   i. If the banker has chosen a transparent project in $t=0$, how much return will investors require for $t=2$? What are the payoffs for investors and the banker, respectively?

   ii. If the banker has chosen an opaque project in $t=0$, how much return will investors require for $t=2$? Will there be a bank run in $t=2$, after the state of the world is revealed?

What are the expected payoffs for investors and the banker, respectively, in $t=1$?
(b) Based on your results in the previous questions, show that the banker's optimal choice in $t=0$ is to choose an opaque project.
(c) Show how the banker's choice on p in $t=0$ affects the likelihood of a bank run in $t=2$. Is there any optimal choice for the banker on the value of p?

4 **Universal banking, asset allocation, and risk-taking**
In this exercise, we explore how universal banking—a system in which banks provide a wide variety of financial services to customers—affects banks' risk-taking behavior through their asset allocation, based on an augmented Dang-Gorton-Holmström-Ordoñez model.

Keeping the settings of the Dang-Gorton-Holmström-Ordoñez model in Section 6.4 mostly unchanged, except that

- The bank is the only financial firm in the economy, that provides a mixture of deposit contract and bond for consumers. In $t=0$, the bank collects early consumer's endowment e, and provides a "take-it-or-leave-it" contract with the early consumer, including I being invested in bond and $e-I$ invested in a safe asset that will return in $t=1$ with gross return rate r. Liquidity creation is costly, and the cost C is a strictly increasing and convex function of the face value of deposits, i.e.

$$C(e-I) = \frac{1}{2}c\left[(e-I)r\right]^2, \text{ with } c>0,$$

in which c is a positive constant;
- Instead of lending to the entrepreneur, the bank invests in the good project itself. The good project will return $f(I)$, with $f(I)>0$ in $t=2$ under good state (G) with probability p, or 0 under bad state (B). The state is not known in $t=0$, but it is revealed in $t=1$. The project cannot be liquidated in $t=1$, and assume that

$f'(I) > 0, f''(I) < 0$, and $\lim_{I \to 0} f'(I) = +\infty$.

The bond that is issued in $t=0$ is backed by the good project;
- In $t=1$, the state j, $j=G,B$, is revealed. The bank sells the bond through a "take-it-or-leave-it" offer with the price b^j to a late consumer, and repays the early consumer using the proceeds from both safe asset and bond sale. In $t=2$, the bank repays the bond holder—the late consumer—out of proceeds from the good project.

(a) Given the bank's investment portfolio in $t=0$, compute the bank's optimal price offer b^j, $j=G,B$, in $t=1$.

(b) Given the bank's optimal price offer b^j in $t=1$, compute the bank's optimal investment I in the good project in $t=0$. Compute the expected utility for the early and the late consumer, respectively, as well as the expected utility for the bank, then compare with the outcomes in the planner's solution.

(c) Suppose that, in $t=0$, before the bank meets the early consumer, a technological progress improves the return of safe asset, leading to a higher r.

  i. How will the bank adjust its optimal investment I in the good project?
  ii. How does such adjustment depend on consumer's risk aversion, credit risk of the good project, and cost of liquidity creation?

PART III
The macroeconomics and political economy of banking

CHAPTER 7
Central banking

7.1 INTRODUCTION

Since the first central bank, Sveriges Riksbank started operations in Sweden, 1668, central banks have been established in most economies and monetary unions, as domestic monetary authorities. Usually, a central bank is not only a monopolistic issuer of legal tender banknotes and coins, but also an institution that is designed to stabilize the economy through its monetary policy. In reality, a central bank is well characterized by its legal mandates: although those mandates differ across central banks, maintaining price stability is usually mandatory for most central banks; very often, central banks also endeavor to preserve the stability of a financial system. Although nowadays central banks are probably best known in mass media for their periodical adjustments in monetary policy rates and their forecasts on macro economy, in history, many central banks—notably the Federal Reserve System—were created as public institutions to provide desired credibility in the financial system and act as the lender of last resort during financial crises.

One of the most important activities in a central bank is to stabilize the economy by its monetary policy, which influences monetary conditions in the economy, further affecting real economic activities such as households' saving and consumption, firms' investment and employment, etc. In normal times, monetary policy is conducted through the central bank's role as the bank of banks: through buying and selling securities in the open market, the central bank affects liquidity in the banking system, so that banks with liquidity constraints have to respond with adjustments in funding and lending in their balance sheets; the central bank also provides liquidity facilities to absorb liquidity in the banking system or to inject liquidity into the system, so that the central bank provides liquidity insurance for banks. In abnormal times or crises, the central bank acts as the lender of last resort, easing market stresses and cleaning the clogged conduits in the banking system to restart a well-functioning banking system. In many ways, the strategic position of the central bank makes it a pivotal part in the banking system, with banks' behavior and banking outcomes often being shaped by central bank activities. Being an active participant in the banking system, the central bank conducts monetary policy through banks to make impacts on real economy; therefore, it is important to understand the interaction between the central bank and banks, as a first step to understand banks' role in the macro economy.

Central bank policy, especially monetary policy, may affect real economy in many ways. The channels through with monetary policy makes impacts on real economy, the so-called *transmission mechanisms of monetary policy*, are among the most important questions in macroeconomics; recent literature, such as Woodford (2004), Galí (2015), Walsh (2017), and Cao and Illing (2019), just to name a few, provides extensive survey for macroeconomic perspectives on monetary policy. In this chapter, we would rather focus on the banking perspective of monetary policy, i.e., how the central bank conducts its monetary policy through operations with banks, how banks react to monetary policy by adjusting their credit supply to the real economy (so-called *bank lending channel of monetary policy*), as well as how monetary policy affects banks' incentives to take risks (so-called *risk-taking channel of monetary policy*).

In Section 7.2, we discuss how the central bank exploits the bank lending channel and conducts monetary policy, i.e., how the central bank influences banks' credit supply to real economy through its policy instruments. To do so, the central bank may make use of *quantity tools* as well as *price tools*:

- Fractional reserve banking implies that banks' capability to lend out of their *loanable funds* is restricted by statutory reserve requirements; therefore, total lending from banks is bounded if the central bank keeps total bank reserves in the banking system under control, using its quantity tools that target quantities of items in banks' balance sheets;
- However, in reality, banks' marginal credit supply is not necessarily limited by its loanable funds in their liabilities, but rather, a bank issues more loans, or, *creates money*, as long as the its marginal gain from loan issuance exceeds marginal cost from its increasing exposure to credit risk and cost of liquidity management; therefore, the central bank is able to affect banks' lending supply by its price tools that change banks' cost of liquidity.

In this section, we will then see how bank lending may be affected by the central bank's quantity and price tools through highly stylized models, and briefly describe how they are conducted in practice—both in normal times and in crises.

Based on how monetary policy is conducted in practice, as Section 7.2 characterizes, in Section 7.3, we formally present the bank lending channel of monetary policy, i.e., the mechanism how banks internalize monetary policy in their liquidity management and adjust their lending decisions. On the margin, extra lending increases a bank's profit from new loans, but this also exposes the bank to higher liquidity risk that it may not have a sufficient liquidity buffer to meet depositors' withdrawal demand. The liquidity risk may be eased through the bank's liquidity management, by building up a liquidity buffer though the interbank market; therefore, the funding cost in the interbank market determines the bank's marginal cost in liquidity management. Monetary policy influences the lending rate in the interbank market, hence marginal cost of bank lending, so that it affects banks' lending decisions.

Monetary policy implementation also affects banks' risk-taking incentives; next, we examine the risk-taking channel of monetary policy. Through its liquidity facilities, the central bank is actively involved in banks' maturity transmission so that banks may be encouraged to take inefficiently high liquidity risks. In Section 7.4, we show how the central bank's liquidity tools affect banks' liquidity risks, by transforming a real economy model in which banks issue deposit contracts on real goods transactions into a monetary economy model in which banks issue nominal contracts settled by fiat money. Two key features of the central bank affect banks' liquidity management the most:

1 First, the central bank issues fiat money as a medium for transaction; for banks, fiat money, rather than real good, is used to meet the withdrawal demand of depositors;
2 Second, money is also the most liquid asset in the financial market, therefore, the central bank's liquidity facilities that provide liquidity

to banks against collateral imply that the central bank is an active participant of maturity transformation activities in the banking system.

Without restrictions on banks' liquidity creation, banks will have the incentive to create too much nominal liquidity, by producing too many illiquid assets as central bank collateral; this makes depositors worse off, as they receive lower *real* consumption produced from liquid assets, although their *nominal* return is high.

We then investigate how monetary policy affects banks' taking credit risks. In Section 7.5, we consider a bank's decision problem on its balance sheet risk, with moral hazard to shift credit risks to creditors, in reaction to the central bank's setting monetary policy rate. The bank's incentive to take credit risks is then a balance of several diverting effects: with increasing monetary policy rate, the rising funding cost forces the bank to increase risk-taking and shift bankruptcy cost to depositors (so-called *risk-shifting channel*); however, when higher monetary policy rate passes through to increase market lending rate, higher profit from performing loans implies that the bank also has incentive to reduce risk-taking (so-called *pass-through channel*); with higher funding cost, the bank also has to reduce its reliance on debts, hence leverage, which reduces the room to issue risky loans (so-called *leverage channel*). Overall, higher monetary policy rate reduces risks in banks' balance sheets.

7.2 CENTRAL BANKING IN PRACTICE

In this section, we briefly show how the central bank keeps bank lending under control, through its monetary policy tools. In principle, these tools include tools targeting quantities of items in banks' balance sheets, as well as tools targeting costs of banks' liquidity management. We first present simple frameworks that motivate these two types of tools, then we show how monetary policy tools are implemented in practice, both in normal times and crises.

7.2.1 QUANTITY TOOLS AND PRICE TOOLS

FRACTIONAL RESERVE BANKING AND MONEY MULTIPLIER

Fractional reserve banking provides the central bank a way to influence bank lending through quantitative control on bank reserves in the banking system. As we show in the Diamond-Dybvig model in Chapter 2, Section 2.2, given funds collected in bank liabilities (called *loanable funds*), a bank has to hold a certain amount of reserves to meet depositors' withdrawal demand; therefore, how much the bank can lend out of its loanable funds is restricted by bank reserves. This implies that if the central bank changes reserves in banking, it will affect total credit supply from banks.

We can formalize this idea by a simple thought experiment. Suppose a closed economy kick-starts its monetary and banking system in the following way:

- First, a central bank is established and it supplies M_0 cash for the economy. The cash is lent to the first bank created in the economy—call it First Bank—to start banking service for the economy. Every bank in this economy is required to keep a fraction k ($0 < k < 1$) of deposits as reserves, First Bank thus holds M_0 deposits and provides $(1-k)M_0$ loans;
- Suppose all borrowers of First Bank buy goods from producers who are depositors of the second bank created in the economy—call it Second Bank, then after the purchase the producers deposit all their income, this allows Second Bank to start its lending business. Following the same procedure, Second Bank lends to borrowers, and they buy goods from producers who are depositors of Third Bank;
- The chain of bank creation goes on until the n th Bank is created.

Figure 7.1 characterizes the chain of bank creation, as well as each bank's balance sheet.

First Bank			
Assets		**Liabilities**	
Loans $(1-k)M_0$		Deposits M_0	
Reserves kM_0			

Second Bank			
Assets		**Liabilities**	
Loans $(1-k)M_0$		Deposits $(1-k)M_0$	
Reserves $k(1-k)M_0$			

Figure 7.1 *Creation of banks and their balance sheets*

Total money supply in this economy is the sum of deposits in all banks, call it M_1, which is

$$M_1 = M_0 + (1-k)M_0 + \ldots + (1-k)^{n-1} M_0 = \frac{1-(1-k)^n}{k} M_0. \quad (7.1)$$

When the number of banks goes to infinity, total money supply (7.1) becomes

$$\lim_{n \to +\infty} M_1 = \frac{1}{k} M_0,$$

given that $0 < k < 1$. That is, the total money supply in this economy is $\frac{1}{k}$ times of *central bank money* M_0—call it *high-powered money*, and $\frac{1}{k}$ is thus called *money multiplier*.

Correspondingly, total credit supply from all banks is $(1-k)M_1$, and with a large number of banks,

$$\lim_{n \to +\infty} (1-k) M_1 = \frac{1-k}{k} M_0.$$

This implies that by targeting the supply of central bank money, M_0, the central bank is able to keep total credit supply from the banking system under control, under a fixed reserve requirement k. Alternatively, the central bank can also influence bank lending by changing k.

Although quantitative targets on money supply and adjustments in reserve requirements are extensively explored by many central banks (see, for example, Chen et al. 2018a for an in-depth analysis on quantity tools of the People's Bank of China), it is often challenging to conduct quantitative policies in reality. Many countries do not have statutory reserve requirements for banks (for example, Canada, Norway, and the UK), making it difficult to determine proper money multipliers. Even in countries with statutory reserve requirements, reserve constraints are often not binding in banks. For example, in the US and Euro area, banks are currently operating with a large amount of reserves in excess to required reserves, making quantity tools less effective in affecting bank lending.

MONEY CREATION AND INTEREST RATE TARGETS

The other approach is to explore the cost factors in banks' liquidity management. In reality, a bank's credit supply is not limited by its loanable funds; instead, whether a bank issues one more loan or not depends on the trade-off between marginal revenue from the loan and marginal cost in its liquidity management, i.e., the cost of raising extra funding from interbank market to reduce its liquidity risk exposure. If monetary policy makes such funding cost higher, the bank will be reluctant to increase lending. Usually the central bank uses price tools such as a short-term interest rate to influence banks' funding cost.

In reality, liquidity management is one key issue in the core of banks' daily business. It also plays a crucial role in the implementation of monetary policy. To see how the central bank's price tools affect bank lending through bank liquidity management, consider a stylized bank that is managing a balance sheet as shown in the left chart of Figure 7.2. The asset side contains loans to firms and households, holdings of liquid assets, as well as central bank reserves. On the liability side, the funding comes from the bank's own equity, and demand deposits from depositors. When the bank decides to issue a new loan, it does not necessarily need to raise loanable funds before the loan issuance, but rather, it just issues the loan that becomes part of the assets, and creates a credit line, or, a deposit account for the debtor, as shown in the right chart of Figure 7.2. The debtor can withdraw from the credit line, and in the future will repay the bank the loan with interest. The interest income will become the bank's

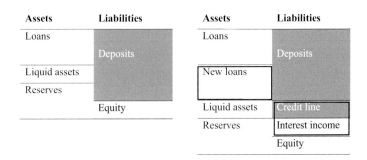

Figure 7.2 *Loan expansion and money creation*

profit, increasing its net worth, or, equity. In this way, banks can expand loan supply, or, *create money* at a stroke of a pen.

However, banks cannot create money without limit. Although banks earn profit from loan issuance, they also expose themselves to several risks. The most obvious risk from the loan issuance is credit risk, i.e., the likelihood that the debtor cannot repay when the loan is due. When the loan is non-performing and the value of the loan cannot be fully recovered, the bank will incur a loss in its equity. If total losses exceed equity, the bank will go bankrupt. The less obvious risk is liquidity risk, or, the likelihood that banks cannot meet their monetary obligations when they come due. We can see how liquidity risks emerge after a new loan has been issued as follows: the debtor receiving the loan may withdraw from her deposit account at any time; for example, after a household receives a mortgage loan, a deposit account is created simultaneously, and the household may need cash out of the account to pay the home developer. Such withdrawal leads to an equivalent fall in the bank's reserves, as the left chart of Figure 7.3 shows. If the decline in reserves is so large that the level of bank reserves falls below the required reserve ratio, new reserves need to be raised immediately to fulfill the reserve requirement. The bank may directly sell some of its assets to raise cash, but mostly, it borrows from the central bank's discount window or from other banks (as shown in the right chart of Figure 7.3), using eligible liquid assets, such as government securities, as collateral. However, the bank needs to pay interest on such loans, and this erodes some of its equity.

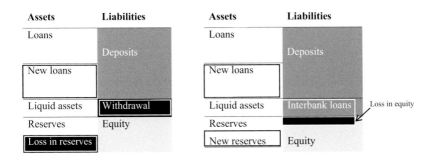

Figure 7.3 *Deposit withdraw and rebalancing*

From the bank's point of view, it will choose to issue new loans, if its revenue from loan issuance exceeds its loss from loan default plus its cost of rebalancing reserves through interbank market. Therefore, the central bank's price tools such as short-term policy rate that affect banks' funding cost influence banks' credit supply.

7.2.2 CONDUCTING MONETARY POLICY IN NORMAL TIMES

In the rest of this section, we briefly discuss how monetary policy is conducted in practice, through interactions between the central bank and banks. We first focus on how the central bank achieves its target, by using short-term policy rate as its main monetary policy instrument in normal times. It is worth noting that central banks around the world differ very much in their monetary policy instruments, implementation procedures, and policy targets, so that there is no single model that fits all central banks. Although the stylized central bank in this section resembles the Fed, it attempts to capture the most common features of central banks in advanced economies, so that readers are able to apply the framework on a number of central banks with minor modifications.

Figure 7.4 shows a stylized central bank's balance sheet. Its liabilities include cash in circulation—the legal tender as medium for transaction as well as for value storage—and bank reserves. Bank reserves are the deposit accounts where banks deposit electronic cash at the central bank. In many countries, banks are required to hold a certain amount of reserves to meet the cash demand from depositors; even in countries without such requirements, banks do have strong incentives to hold reserves as buffers. The central bank may pay interest on banks' reserves.

Assets	Liabilities (MB)
• Loan to banks, BR	• Cash in circulation
• Government securities, NBR	• Bank reserves
• Other securities, NBR	

Figure 7.4 A stylized central bank's balance sheet

A central bank can adjust its money supply through both cash in circulation and banks' reserve accounts. Thus, total liabilities constitute the money base (MB) of the economy.

As in Figure 7.4, the central bank assets include:

- Loans to banks. Banks can raise reserves by borrowing from the central bank via its discount window, paying a discount rate on these loans. Usually these loans are overnight loans, but the maturity can be longer under certain circumstances. A central bank has the commitment to lending to banks without limit, especially when banks are not able to borrow from elsewhere, i.e., the central bank is the *lender-of-last-resort* (LOLR) in a banking system. Bank reserves obtained from the discount window are called borrowed reserves (BR);
- Securities purchased by the central bank. These securities are mostly, but not restricted to, government securities. When the central bank buys securities in open market operation, no matter whether from banks or from non-bank institutions/individuals, the cash that the central bank pays eventually ends up either as cash held by individuals or as bank reserves, increasing the level of reserves in the banking sector. With the reverse operation, when the central bank sells securities, it drains reserves from banks. Bank reserves obtained from security purchases are called non-borrowed reserves (NBR).

Aggregating across the entire central bank's balance sheet, the money base is equal to the sum of two types of bank reserves, i.e., $MB = BR + NBR$.

It is worth noting here that institutional details differ slightly from country to country. Some central banks, such as the European Central Bank, do not directly purchase securities from the primary market; instead, they adjust bank reserves in market operations using reverse repurchase agreements (repo, see Chapter 5, Section 5.1.3). In a reverse repo agreement, the central bank increases bank reserves by lending cash to the banks, against eligible collateral. The private bank has to post securities (usually these are highly liquid securities such as government securities or corporate bonds, but other assets may also be accepted), with a promise to repurchase the securities after a certain period at agreed price.

Changes in the central bank's balance sheet affect banks' balance sheets through reserves. As we know, to meet the cash demand from depositors, banks need to hold reserves—usually deposited in the central bank's deposit accounts. When the central bank purchases securities (or accepts securities as repo) in open market operation, bank reserves will rise. This allows banks to take more checkable deposits. At the same time, it can issue more loans on the asset side; increasing bank reserves thus implies an expansionary monetary policy, leading to an increase in aggregate credit supply. The opposite happens when the central bank sells securities under a contractionary monetary policy.

Holding reserves is costly for banks. Although frequently the central bank pays interest on (part of) bank reserves, the interest return from reserves is much lower than other assets such as loans. Therefore, banks usually hold required reserves, but they try to minimize holdings of excess reserves. However, due to daily fluctuations in bank liabilities, at the end of the day there are always some banks short of reserves, as well as other banks with excess reserves. Therefore, banks can trade with each other in the interbank market for reserves (in the US, this is called federal funds market), so that banks can raise reserves via overnight interbank loans at the market interest rate (it is called federal funds rate in the US). As an alternative, banks can also borrow reserves from the central bank's discount window. Interbank loans and discount loans are usually collateralized; therefore, banks also hold safe assets such as government securities on their balance sheets. The interest rate in the market for reserves is usually the one that monetary policy targets. The central bank intervenes in the market to keep the rate close to its target.

Briefly speaking, monetary policy is conducted via the central bank's balance sheet management—namely, through open market operations, accounts for bank reserves, and discount window—which directly affects elements in the banks' balance sheets: bank reserves, securities, discount loans, etc., shifting the equilibrium in the market for reserves. This leads to a change in the interbank lending rate for reserves, and supply of bank lending.

Supply of and demand for bank reserves determine the equilibrium rate in the market for reserves. First, banks' demand for reserves is a decreasing function of the market rate for reserves: the lower the rate, the cheaper it is for banks to borrow, so the higher the demand for reserves. However, the rate cannot fall below the interest rate that the central bank pays on bank reserves, as banks can deposit in the central bank at this rate as much as they want. Therefore, as Figure 7.5 shows, the demand curve R_D for reserves is a decreasing function of the market rate for reserves, and bounded below by the interest rate paid on the central bank's reserve accounts, i_r.

The central bank's supply of bank reserves comes from two sources: open market operation (non-borrowed reserves, NBR) and discount loans (borrowed reserves, BR). During the period between two open market operations, the supply of NBR is fixed by the previous open market operation, therefore, its supply curve is a vertical line—R_S curve in Figure 7.5. Beyond NBR, banks can borrow as much as they want from the discount window at the discount rate i_d, therefore, the supply curve of bank reserves is bounded above by i_d.

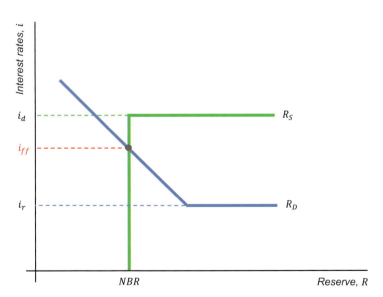

Figure 7.5 Supply and demand in the market for reserves

Notes: the kinked blue line R_D denotes banks' demand for reserves; the kinked green line R_S denotes the central bank's supply of bank reserves; i_d denotes the central bank's discount rate; i_r denotes the interest rate paid on the central bank's reserve accounts; i_{ff} denotes the market rate for reserves.

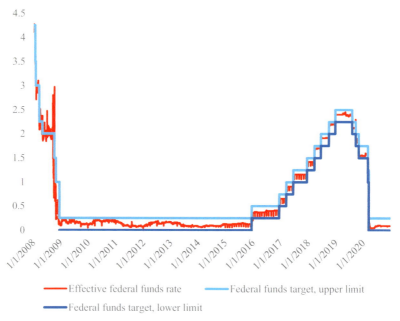

Figure 7.6 *Effective federal funds rate and the corridor system, 01/2005–10/2020*
Data source: Federal Reserve Economic Data (FRED) from Federal Reserve Bank of St. Louis.

In equilibrium, the market rate for reserves, i_{ff}, is determined by the intersection of supply and demand curves. The equilibrium rate can only move within the corridor that is bounded by the "floor" i_r and the "ceiling" i_d. In practice, by simply narrowing the corridor around its target policy rate via changing i_r and i_d, the central bank can reduce the volatility of i_{ff} and keep it close to the monetary policy rate.

Figure 7.6 shows how such a *corridor system* functions for the Fed. Except for the extreme times in 2008, the target monetary policy rate, or effective federal funds rate, is mostly bounded between the ceiling (upper limit) and the floor (lower limit, from October 2008 onward).

7.2.3 CONDUCTING MONETARY POLICY IN FINANCIAL CRISES

Conducting monetary policy during crises is challenging, when banks are failing, the financial market is under stress, and interbank lending is frozen. The priority for the central bank is thus to clean the mess in the banking system and restore the bank lending channel by restarting banks as well-functioning financial intermediaries. To do so, the central bank may need to resort to instruments and tools that are rather "unconventional". Next, we discuss desired monetary policies during crises, using experience in the 2007–2009 global financial crisis as an example.

The biggest barrier for banks to restart financial intermediation and function as main providers of financial resources to the real economy is that banks' funding costs during financial crises are prohibitively high. The central bank thus needs proper policy tools to address such a problem. To better understand the central bank's calculus during crises, we may decompose banks' funding cost, or, the interest rate r that one bank charges on the loan to another bank, into two parts:

$$r = i + \rho \qquad (7.2)$$

in which i is the risk-free rate that can be proxied by the monetary policy rate, and ρ is the risk premium for the loan. The risk premium comes from the lending bank's perception on the counterparty risk, that is, how likely the borrowing bank is going to fail during the maturity of the loan. During normal times, ρ is very small, especially for large banks; however, it can be extremely high during crises. Figure 7.7 shows the risk premium measured by the spread between 3-month LIBOR (London Interbank Offered Rate) and 3-month TED rate (US Treasury bill rate, a proxy for risk-free rate) during the 2007–2009 crisis. It spiked with each market turbulence, especially after the collapse of Lehman Brothers in September 2008. The interbank lending rate became so high that the market was nearly frozen.

The risk premium, or banks' counterparty risk, mainly comes from two sources:

1. Solvency risk, that the counterparty may become insolvent;
2. Liquidity risk, that the counterparty may not be able to meet its monetary obligations, including

    (a) Market liquidity risk, that the bank cannot convert its assets to cash to fulfill the demand. The banks hold too much illiquid assets whose conversion to cash incurs large discounts;

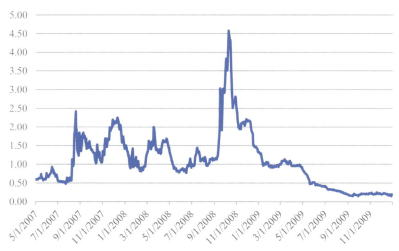

Figure 7.7 TED spread, 05/2007–12/2009
Data source: Federal Reserve Economic Data (FRED) from Federal Reserve Bank of St. Louis. TED spread is calculated as the spread between 3-month LIBOR based on US dollars and 3-month Treasury Bill.

(b) Funding liquidity risk, that the bank cannot raise funding in the market at a reasonable price.

As equation (7.2) suggests, to restart the banking system, desired monetary policy needs to reduce the interbank funding cost r by targeting i and ρ. The central bank has to choose among a variety of options. For those banks that are already insolvent, orderly closure is the solution to avoid further damage to the system. However, if the insolvent bank is systemically important and the closure generates costly spillovers to the other financial institutions, it may be better for the public to bail it out, take it over, and provide necessary guarantees to ensure that it still provides the desired services for the rest of the system. During a crisis, it is hard if not impossible to distinguish between those banks which are truly insolvent and those banks who are illiquid yet solvent, provided policy succeeds in combating the crisis.

CUTTING MONETARY POLICY RATE

Reducing the risk-free rate i in equation 7.2 is relatively simple. The central bank lowers the risk-free rate by drastically cutting its policy

CHAPTER SEVEN: CENTRAL BANKING

Figure 7.8 *Monetary policy rates in the US, Euro area, and UK, 01/2005–10/2020*
Data source: Federal Reserve Economic Data (FRED) from Federal Reserve Bank of St. Louis. The light-shaded area to the left denotes the period of 2007–2009 Global Financial Crisis, and the light-shaded area to the right denotes the period of the COVID-19 Pandemic, from March 2020 onwards.

rate in short time. As Figure 7.8 shows, the Fed, ECB, and the Bank of England, among other central banks, aggressively cut their monetary policy rates to almost zero in 2008, and the rates stayed low for a considerably long time before these economies started to recover. In several economies, including the Euro area, Japan, Switzerland, Denmark, and Sweden, key policy rates were even set below zero.

TARGETED LIQUIDITY PROVISION

To reduce the risk premium ρ in equation 7.2 is somewhat tricky, as such risk premium reflects banks' perception on the risks of their counterparties, that suffer from high insolvency and illiquidity risks.

THE MACROECONOMICS AND POLITICAL ECONOMY OF BANKING

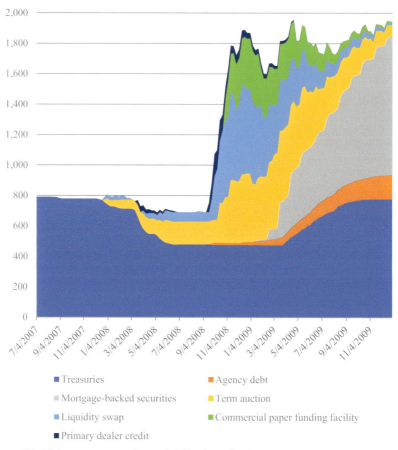

Figure 7.9 Main components of assets held by the Federal Reserve System, 07/2007–12/2009, in billion US dollars

Data source: Federal Reserve Economic Data (FRED) from Federal Reserve Bank of St. Louis. This chart only includes the main asset components, so that the sum of these components is slightly smaller than the total assets.

Insolvency risks may be reduced by orderly closing down insolvent banks and bailing out insolvent banks that are systemically important. Banks' liquidity risks can be addressed by improving banks' funding liquidity and market liquidity. To ease banks' funding liquidity problem, the central bank commits to be the lender-of-last-resort for the entire banking system, providing unlimited funding sources for the banks. The discount rate can be lowered to reduce banks' funding cost, and the maturity of discount loans can be extended from overnight to several months to reduce banks' funding liquidity risk in debt rollover. In the 2007–2009 crisis, the Fed

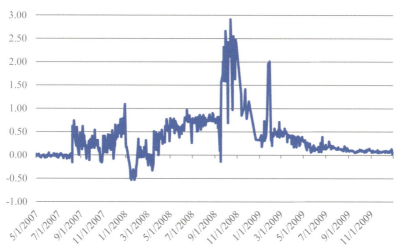

Figure 7.10 *Spread between 3-month commercial paper and federal funds rate, 05/2007–12/2009*

Data source: Federal Reserve Economic Data (FRED) from Federal Reserve Bank of St. Louis. The series is calculated as the spread between 3-month AA financial commercial paper and effective federal funds rate.

offered targeted liquidity aid to systemically important institutions in the US; it also made currency swap agreements with several central banks, such as the European Central Bank, Bank of England, Norges Bank, etc., to provide stable foreign currency funding for global banks.

QUALITATIVE EASING

To ease banks' market liquidity problem, the central bank needs to extract illiquid assets from banks' balance sheets and replace them with liquid assets. The central bank can thus use its balance sheet as an instrument, buying illiquid assets from and at the same time selling its holdings of government securities to the banks to improve the liquidity in bank assets. Such operation does not increase bank reserves in the system, but instead, only qualitatively changes the composition of bank non-reserve assets. The strategy is thus called *qualitative easing*.

The period before September 2009 in Figure 7.9 shows the qualitative easing period of the Fed during the crisis. Traditionally, the Fed held mainly safe short-term Treasury securities. In the first phase of the crisis, the Fed sold a large share of these liquid assets without expanding its overall balance sheet and instead bought risky assets from the financial sector. The stock of traditional Treasuries fell sharply in this period. However, with the collapse of Lehman Brothers, the Fed started to face another limit: the volume of government securities on its balance sheet was too low to conduct necessary market operations in the future. Therefore, the Fed could not improve banks' market liquidity further without affecting bank reserves or significantly expanding its own balance sheet.

Prompt monetary policy responses during the 2007–2009 financial crisis that aimed to cut risk-free rate i and reduce risk premium ρ through addressing banks' insolvency risks and liquidity risks effectively reduced banks' funding costs, and allowed banks to return to normal. Figure 7.7 shows that the risk-premium in interbank lending quickly fell in late 2008, and almost to zero after mid-2009. Figure 7.10 provides evidence from risk premium on commercial paper, which returned to the pre-crisis level after mid-2009.

QUANTITATIVE EASING

While calming down the financial market and restarting banks may be effectively quick, it takes much longer for the real economy that is impaired by the crisis and stuck in deep recession to recover so that stimulation from expansionary monetary policy is desirable for a longer run. However, at this stage—for example, by late 2009—central banks may have run out of ammunition from their conventional toolboxes. Short-term interest rates have reached zero lower bound (ZLB), although negative policy rates may be conducted, the room to cut policy rates further is limited. At this stage, a central bank needs unconventional tools to continue with monetary expansion.

Quantitative easing (QE) is thus conducted for this purpose. In QE, the central bank purchases financial assets, such as government securities, agency debts, mortgage-backed securities (MBS), covered bonds directly from banks and non-bank institutions. For example, in the US, the Fed

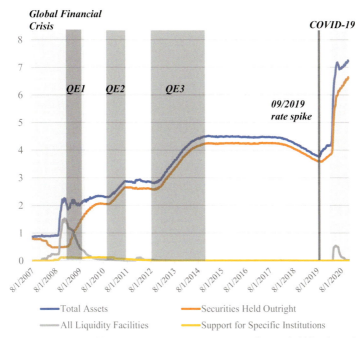

Figure 7.11 *The size (in trillion US dollars) and composition of assets held by the Federal Reserve System, 08/2007–12/2020*

Data source: Board of Governors of the Federal Reserve System, "Recent balance sheet trends", available on https://www.federalreserve.gov/monetarypolicy/bst.htm. The shaded area to the left denotes the period of 2007–2009 Global Financial Crisis, and the shaded area to the right denotes the period of the COVID-19 Pandemic, from March 2020 onwards. The three dark-shaded areas denote the periods of QE1, QE2, and QE3, from the left to the right, respectively. The vertical line to the right denotes the spike in the repo rate in mid-September, 2020.

conducted three stages of QE programs, namely QE1, QE2, and QE3. Quantitative easing leads to a substantial expansion of the central bank's balance sheet, as well as a large quantity of excess reserves in the banking sector which incentivizes banks to increase lending to the real economy.

Quantitative easing led to a substantial expansion of the monetary base. Figure 7.11 presents the increase in the monetary base in the US. The Fed's total assets grew from less than one trillion dollars before the crisis to about 4.5 trillion dollars after QE3. After the crisis, arguments on the *exit strategy* after QE began to emerge, so that the Fed started to scale down its balance sheet, but its normalization effort was interrupted in 2020 after the COVID-19 pandemic broke out and the Fed restarted its asset purchase programs.

7.3 MONETARY POLICY, LIQUIDITY MANAGEMENT, AND BANK LENDING

After illustrating how a central bank achieves its monetary policy target on banks' funding cost, now we continue to see how banks adjust their lending, in reaction to adjustments in monetary policy rates—the so-called bank lending channel. Just as is argued in Section 7.2.1, banks increase lending if marginal revenue from lending exceeds marginal cost of liquidity management, i.e., the cost of rebalancing reserves, abstract from credit risks. We describe the mechanism through a simple model based on Bianchi and Bigio (2020).

7.3.1 BANK LENDING AND LIQUIDITY RISK EXPOSURE

Consider a banking sector where banks maximize their dividends that are paid to the shareholders after three periods, $t = 0, 1, 2$. There is an infinite number of competitive banks, and the banks are indexed by $0 \leq i \leq 1$. Figure 7.12 shows a representative bank's balance sheet in period t, similar to Figure 7.2: on the liability side it funds itself by issuing equity E_t to shareholders, and raising demand deposits (deposits that can be withdrawn any time on demand) D_t from depositors at the gross deposit rate r_D; on the asset side it holds reserves R_t and issues loans L_t. Assume that reserves are denominated in nominal terms, while loans, equity, and deposits are in real terms. Deposits are a numeraire good.

A bank enters period $t = 0$ with its balance sheet $\{L_0, R_0, D_0, E_0\}$. We call the period between $t = 0$ and $t = 1$ "lending stage" in which the bank decides on new loan issuance. During the lending stage, the bank issues new loans I_0—denote the market price of the bank loans as q_0—and raises

Assets	Liabilities
Loans L_t	Deposits D_t
Reserves R_t	Equity E_t

Figure 7.12 *Bank's balance sheets*

new reserves φ_0 at price p_0. At the same time, the existing loans L_0 are repaid—note that bank deposits fall by L_0 after the repayment. The laws of motion, or, the intertemporal resource constraints, for the balance sheet during the lending stage is characterized by

$$\frac{D_1}{r^D} = D_0 + q_0 I_0 + p_0 \varphi_0 - L_0, \tag{7.3}$$

$$L_1 = I_0, \tag{7.4}$$

$$R_1 = R_0 + \varphi_0. \tag{7.5}$$

Banks are subject to capital requirement, i.e., the ratio of equity to total assets must be above a certain threshold. This is equivalent to require that

$$\frac{D_1}{r^D} \leq \kappa \underbrace{\left(q_1 L_1 + p_1 R_1 - \frac{D_1}{r^D} \right)}_{\text{equity value}} \tag{7.6}$$

in which κ is a constant number, and the bank's equity value can be computed through balance sheet identity.

Now, in period $t=1$, a random share ω_1 of bank deposits are withdrawn by the depositors. Assume that the cumulative distribution function of ω_1 follows $F(\omega_1)$, with $-\infty < \omega_1 < 1$. If $\omega_1 > 0$, there is an outflow of bank deposits; if $\omega_1 < 0$, the bank receives deposits.

There is a reserve requirement imposed by the central bank, i.e., the ratio of bank reserves to demand deposits shall not fall below a constant value ρ, $0 \leq \rho \leq 1$, at any time t

$$p_t R_t \geq \frac{\rho D_t (1 - \omega_t)}{r^D}. \tag{7.7}$$

After the withdrawal shock in $t=1$, the bank's reserves may fall below the required level. The shortfall is

$$x = \underbrace{\frac{\rho D_1 (1 - \omega_1)}{r^D}}_{(A)} - \underbrace{\left(p_1 R_1 - \frac{\omega_1 D_1}{r^D} \right)}_{(B)} \tag{7.8}$$

in which term (A) is the required reserve level, and term (B) is the actual reserve level after withdrawal—note that when deposits are withdrawn, there is an equal amount fall in bank reserves. To fulfill the reserve requirement, from now on the bank needs to close the gap x. We call the period between $t=1$ and $t=2$ "balancing stage". In this stage:

1. If $x>0$, the bank needs to borrow reserves from other banks at interest rate χ_b;
2. If $x<0$, it implies that the bank holds excess reserves. In such circumstance, the bank can lend its excess reserves x at the market interbank lending rate χ_l.

Whether the bank is a borrowing or a lending bank depends on the level of the withdrawal shock it experiences. Suppose there is a $\underline{\omega}_1$ that makes

$$x = 0 = \frac{\rho D_1(1-\omega_1)}{r^D} - \left(p_1 R_1 - \frac{\omega_1 D_1}{r^D}\right), \tag{7.9}$$

that is,

$$\underline{\omega}_1 = \frac{r^D p_1 R_1 - \rho D_1}{(1-\rho) D_1}, \tag{7.10}$$

then the bank is a lending bank if $\omega_1 < \underline{\omega}_1$, and it is a borrowing bank if $\underline{\omega}_1 < \omega_1 < 1$.

The laws of motion for the balance sheet during the balancing stage are characterized by

$$R_2 = R_1 - \frac{\omega_1 D_1}{p_1}, \tag{7.11}$$

$$L_2 = L_1, \tag{7.12}$$

$$D_2 = D_1(1-\omega_1) + \chi(x) \tag{7.13}$$

in which

$$\chi(x) = \begin{cases} \chi_l x & \text{if } x \leq 0, \\ \chi_b x & \text{if } x > 0. \end{cases}$$

After $t = 2$, the bank is dissolved. All bank loans are repaid, remaining depositors withdraw, and the rest is distributed to the shareholders as dividends, DIV

$$DIV = p_2 R_2 + q_2 L_2 - \frac{D_2}{r^D}. \tag{7.14}$$

7.3.2 LIQUIDITY MANAGEMENT AND BANK LENDING CHANNEL

Assume that the prices for loans and bank reserves are invariant over time, so that we can drop the time subscript for p and q as follows. Note that once the bank fixes its loan supply I_0 and new reserves φ_0 in the lending stage $t = 0$, it just reacts passively to meet all the constraints in the balancing stage after the withdrawal shock is materialized. Therefore, the bank's problem to maximize expected DIV is to choose its loan supply I_0 and new reserves φ_0 in the lending stage with the intertemporal resource constraints as well as regulatory requirements

$$\max_{\{I_0, \varphi_0\}} E_0[DIV], \tag{7.15}$$

$$\text{s.t.} \quad R_2 = R_1 - \frac{\omega_1 D_1}{p}, \tag{7.16}$$

$$L_2 = L_1, \tag{7.17}$$

$$D_2 = D_1(1 - \omega_1) + \chi(x), \tag{7.18}$$

$$\frac{D_1}{r^D} = D_0 + qI_0 + p\varphi_0 - L_0, \tag{7.19}$$

$$L_1 = I_0, \tag{7.20}$$

$$R_1 = R_0 + \varphi_0, \tag{7.21}$$

$$x = \frac{\rho D_1 (1 - \omega_1)}{r^D} - \left(pR_1 - \frac{\omega_1 D_1}{r^D} \right), \tag{7.22}$$

$$\frac{D_1}{r^D} \leq \kappa \left(qL_1 + pR_1 - \frac{D_1}{r^D} \right). \tag{7.23}$$

Using the intertemporal resource constraints, the bank's dividends can be rewritten as

$$DIV = pR_2 + qL_2 - \frac{D_2}{r^D} \tag{7.24}$$

$$= p\left(R_0 + \varphi_0 - \frac{\omega_1 D_1}{p}\right) + qI_0 - \frac{D_1(1-\omega_1) + \chi(x)}{r^D}, \tag{7.25}$$

$$\frac{D_1}{r^D} = D_0 + qI_0 + p\varphi_0 - L_0. \tag{7.26}$$

To simplify the analysis, assume that the capital requirement is not binding so that we have one less constraint to consider. Note that the expected rebalancing cost $\chi(x)$ can be computed as

$$E_0[\chi(x)] = \underbrace{\int_{-\infty}^{\underline{\omega}_1} \chi_l x \, dF(\omega_1)}_{(A)} + \underbrace{\int_{\underline{\omega}_1}^{1} \chi_b x \, dF(\omega_1)}_{(B)} \tag{7.27}$$

in which term (A) is the return on lending if the bank is a lending bank in the balancing stage, while term (B) is the cost of borrowing if the bank is a borrowing bank.

The bank's optimal decision is determined by the first-order conditions with respect to I_0 and φ_0. The first-order condition with respect to I_0 leads to

$$\frac{\partial E_0[DIV]}{\partial I_0} = 0$$

$$= (1-r^D)\bar{\omega}_1 q - \frac{1}{r^D} \times \left[\int_{-\infty}^{\underline{\omega}_1} \chi_l f(\omega_1) \frac{\partial x}{\partial I_0} d\omega_1 + \chi_l x f(\underline{\omega}_1) \frac{\partial \underline{\omega}_1}{\partial I_0} \right.$$

$$\left. + \int_{\underline{\omega}_1}^{1} \chi_b f(\omega_1) \frac{\partial x}{\partial I_0} d\omega_1 - \chi_b x f(\underline{\omega}_1) \frac{\partial \underline{\omega}_1}{\partial I_0} \right]$$

$$= (1-r^D)\bar{\omega}_1 q - \frac{1}{r^D} \times \left\{ (\chi_b - \chi_l) x f(\underline{\omega}_1) \frac{r^{D2} pR_1}{1-\rho} D_1^{-2} q \right.$$

$$+ \chi_l q E\left[\rho(1-\omega_1) + \omega_1 \mid \omega_1 < \underline{\omega}_1\right]$$

$$\left. + \chi_b q E\left[\rho(1-\omega_1) + \omega_1 \mid \underline{\omega}_1 < \omega_1 < 1\right] \right\},$$

in which $\bar{\omega}_1$ denotes the unconditional mean of ω_1,

$$\bar{\omega}_1 = \int_{-\infty}^{1} \omega_1 f(\omega_1) d\omega_1,$$

the term $E\left[\rho(1-\omega_1)+\omega_1\,|\,\omega_1<\underline{\omega}_1\right]$ is the conditional expectation of $\rho(1-\omega_1)+\omega_1$ for all $\omega_1<\underline{\omega}_1$, and the term $E\left[\rho(1-\omega_1)+\omega_1\,|\,\underline{\omega}_1<\omega_1<1\right]$ is the conditional expectation of $\rho(1-\omega_1)+\omega_1$ for all $\underline{\omega}_1<\omega_1<1$. Rearrange the first-order condition to get

$$\left(r^D-1\right)\bar{\omega}_1 = \frac{1}{r^D}\left\{\underbrace{(\chi_l-\chi_b)xf(\underline{\omega}_1)\frac{r^{D2}pR_1}{1-\rho}D_1^{-2}}_{(A)}\right.$$

$$\underbrace{-\chi_b E\left[\rho(1-\omega_1)+\omega_1\,|\,\underline{\omega}_1<\omega_1<1\right]}_{(B)}$$

$$\left.\underbrace{-\chi_l q E\left[\rho(1-\omega_1)+\omega_1\,|\,\omega_1<\underline{\omega}_1\right]}_{(C)}\right\}.$$

This equation shows clearly the trade-off on the liability side the bank faces when it decides to change its loan supply on the margin. Suppose that the bank increases its loan supply by one unit, the left hand side of the equation is the net contribution to DIV before balancing—note that $\left(r^D-1\right)\bar{\omega}_1$ comes from the derivative of $E_0[DIV]$, excluding $\chi(x)$ term, with respect to I_0. The right hand side of the equation comes from the marginal cost to DIV in rebalancing, as the result of marginal increase in loan supply:

1. Term (A) captures the marginal cost coming directly from shifting the threshold $\underline{\omega}_1$. Suppose a bank is with ω_1 slightly lower than $\underline{\omega}_1$, so it would have been a lending bank and could have lent to other banks for interest profit χ_l; however, by increasing one unit of loan supply, $\underline{\omega}_1$ falls, the bank becomes a borrowing bank and instead has to borrow at the interest cost χ_b. Term (A) thus shows the opportunity cost directly associated with the shifting threshold;
2. Higher loan supply corresponds to an equal rise in demand deposits. After the withdrawal shock, the bank becomes more likely to have

a shortfall in reserves and needs to borrow. Term (B) is thus the expected marginal increase in the borrowing cost for new reserves;

3 The bank also becomes less likely to have excess reserves before the balancing stage, therefore, Term (C) reflects the expected marginal fall in the profit in interbank lending.

The other first-order condition for the bank's problem determines the level of new reserves φ_0

$$\frac{\partial E_0[DIV]}{\partial \varphi_0} = 0$$

$$= (1-r^D)\bar{\omega}_1 p - \frac{1}{r^D} \times \left[\int_{-\infty}^{\underline{\omega}_1} \chi_l f(\omega_1) \frac{\partial x}{\partial \varphi_0} d\omega_1 + \chi_l x f(\underline{\omega}_1) \frac{\partial \underline{\omega}_1}{\partial \varphi_0} \right.$$

$$\left. + \int_{\underline{\omega}_1}^{1} \chi_b f(\omega_1) \frac{\partial x}{\partial \varphi_0} d\omega_1 - \chi_b x f(\underline{\omega}_1) \frac{\partial \underline{\omega}_1}{\partial \varphi_0} \right]$$

$$= (1-r^D)\bar{\omega}_1 p - \frac{1}{r^D} \times \left\{ (\chi_l - \chi_b) x f(\underline{\omega}_1) \frac{r^D p(1-\rho)D_1 - r^{D2} p^2 (R_0 + \varphi_0)(1-\rho)}{(1-\rho)^2 D_1^2} \right.$$

$$+ \chi_l E\left[\rho(1-\omega_1)q + \omega_1 q - p \,|\, \omega_1 < \underline{\omega}_1 \right]$$

$$\left. + \chi_b E\left[\rho(1-\omega_1)q + \omega_1 q - p \,|\, \underline{\omega}_1 < \omega_1 < 1 \right] \right\}$$

Rearrange the equation to get

$$(r^D - 1)\bar{\omega}_1 p = \frac{1}{r^D} \times \left\{ \underbrace{(\chi_l - \chi_b) x f(\underline{\omega}_1) \frac{r^{D2} p^2 (R_0 + \varphi_0)(1-\rho) - r^D p(1-\rho)D_1}{(1-\rho)^2 D_1^2}}_{(A)} \right.$$

$$\underbrace{- \chi_b E\left[\rho(1-\omega_1)q + \omega_1 q - p \,|\, \underline{\omega}_1 < \omega_1 < 1 \right]}_{(B)}$$

$$\left. \underbrace{- \chi_l E\left[\rho(1-\omega_1)q + \omega_1 q - p \,|\, \omega_1 < \underline{\omega}_1 \right]}_{(C)} \right\}.$$

This equation shows clearly the trade-off on the asset side the bank faces when it decides to change its reserves level on the margin during the lending stage. Suppose that the bank increases its reserves by one unit, the left hand side of the equation is the net contribution to DIV before balancing—note that $(r^D - 1)\bar{\omega}_1 p$ comes from the derivative of $E_0[DIV]$, excluding $\chi(x)$ term, with respect to φ_0. The right hand side of the equation comes from the marginal cost to DIV in rebalancing, as the result of marginal increase in reserves: term (A) reflects the shift in the cost on the threshold, while term (B) captures the marginal reduction in the borrowing cost due to reduced exposure to funding liquidity risk during the balance stage, and term (C) is the marginal benefit from interbank lending due to the increased likelihood of holding excess reserves after the withdrawal shock.

In brief, the model implies that bank lending is constrained by banks' liquidity management practice. When a new loan is issued, a demandable deposit account is simultaneously created for the borrower, and the bank has an increased exposure to funding liquidity risk, i.e., it becomes more likely that the bank needs to borrow from the market if reserves fall below the required level after withdrawals from the deposit accounts. The equilibrium bank lending is therefore determined by the marginal return from loan supply and the marginal cost from liquidity management.

In this framework, monetary policy affects bank lending, and further real economy activities, via shifting interbank market rates. In the model, χ_l and χ_b resemble the interest rate paid on reserves and the discount rate, respectively: assume that banks do not trade reserves with each other, but rather, the central bank serves as an intermediary between banks. Banks with excess reserves deposit in the central bank with interest rate χ_l, and the central bank lends to banks with deficits in reserves through the discount window at the rate χ_b. The banks react in their loan supply I_0 when the central bank conducts its monetary policy through χ_l and χ_b. For example, when the central bank implements an expansionary monetary policy by setting lower χ_b, it reduces the cost of financing reserve deficits in the future, the balancing stage. Knowing this, banks will choose higher I_0 in the lending stage.

7.3.3 SUMMARY

The Bianchi-Bigio model provides a clear illustration on banks' lending decisions in response to monetary policy rate adjustments, which affect banks' cost of rebalancing reserves. In this framework, bank lending is the optimal outcome of liquidity management, which vary with market conditions but does not rely on banks' loanable funds.

It is also worth noting that for simplicity in this model, we focused only on funding liquidity risk, i.e., banks only face uncertainties in their liabilities. However, in reality, market liquidity risk and credit risk are also major concerns in liquidity management, i.e., banks need to hold liquid assets as collateral for borrowing from other banks, and loans may be non-performing; they both affect bank lending, and a monetary transmission mechanism may have farther reaching impacts to other dimensions. For example, when the central bank relaxes monetary policy by setting lower χ_b, banks' funding liquidity risk is reduced. This does not only allow banks to issue more loans, but also provides more headroom for banks to provide more loans for high yield, but as riskier projects, increasing credit risk. In reality, lax monetary policies such as policy rate cuts or lending guarantees for banks are often introduced to stimulate the real economy; however, one has to keep in mind that credit risk may rise in the banking system, and such risk-taking channel—if not contained—can eventually result in excess risk taking leading to financial instabilities or even financial crises. We will explore such a risk-taking channel in the next two sections.

7.4 MONETARY POLICY, MATURITY TRANSFORMATION, AND LIQUIDITY RISKS

Monetary policy affects not only volume of bank lending, but also banks' incentive to take risks in their balance sheets, leading to a risk-taking channel of monetary policy. Such risk-taking channel has important implications for the central bank's monetary policy implication, as the by-products of bank risk-taking may even derail the financial system. In this section we focus on banks' liquidity risks, and then continue with banks' credit risks in the next section.

In reality, central bank is actively involved in banks' maturity transformation, through its role in issuing money and providing liquidity facilities to banks. Central bank issues fiat money as medium for transaction which is for banks to settle deposit contracts, too; on the other hand, money is the most liquid asset, and banks can obtain money from the central bank's discount loans against collateral. Without additional restrictions on banks' liquidity creation, banks have the incentive to take inefficiently high liquidity risks by producing more illiquid assets as central bank collateral. In this way, depositors receive higher *nominal* returns, but become worse off with lower *real* returns from liquid assets. We show the mechanism using a simple model based on Cao and Illing (2021).

7.4.1 MATURITY TRANSFORMATION IN A MONETARY ECONOMY

Our model is a monetary version of the Cao-Illing model, described in Chapter 2, Section 2.4. Given that we need to address the interaction between the central bank's monetary policy implementation and banks' maturity transformation, we have to go beyond the original model in which all contracts are settled by real goods and make all contracts denominated in fiat money.

We keep most of the settings in the Cao-Illing model unchanged except that from now on the economy is a monetary economy so that all contracts will be *nominal* and all goods transactions are paid by cash—a standard cash-in-advance constraint assumption à la Lucas and Stokey (1987). A central bank acts as the monetary authority, providing fiat money to the banks through banks' deposit accounts in the central bank, where banks' cash reserves are stored. The central bank issues money in two ways, reflecting dual roles of money:

1. Money as the medium of goods transaction. In this monetary economy, all the transactions of goods are committed via the exchanges of cash versus goods. Fiat money is issued by the central bank to facilitate the transactions, therefore, the quantity of money in circulation is equal to the transaction demand for money in each period. For simplicity, assume that the quantity of money issued for the purpose of goods transaction in each period is equal to the quantity of real goods in transaction, i.e., we normalize the price level—in the absence of additional liquidity provision—to be 1. After all transactions are settled in the end of each period, all cash supply for transactional purposes during the period returns to the central bank;
2. Money as liquidity. Banks can obtain additional fiat money from the central bank's discount window to meet their demand for liquidity subject to the central bank's policy rate, using their illiquid assets as collateral.

With these simple rules on money issuance and money provision, we can show that the constrained efficiency in the Cao-Illing model can be supported in this monetary economy. In each period, money is introduced to the economy in the following way:

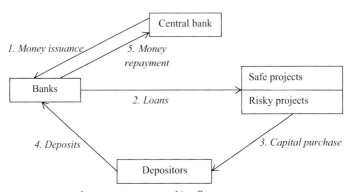

Figure 7.13 *Monetizing the economy in period $t = 0$*
Notes: the arrows show the direction of money flows, and the numbers indicate the sequence of money flows.

IN PERIOD t = 0

Figure 7.13 shows the flows of money and goods throughout the sequence:

1. Banks receive 1 unit of cash supply from the central bank to facilitate goods transaction in $t=0$, which is equal to the entrepreneurs' demand for buying the endowments of the depositors;
2. Banks issue loans to the entrepreneurs, a share of α_H, with

$$\alpha_H = \frac{\gamma - p_H}{\gamma - p_H + (1-\gamma)\frac{R_1}{R_2}}$$

   for the entrepreneurs operating safe projects (short term loans), $1-\alpha_H$ for those operating risky projects (long term loans);
3. Entrepreneurs use the loans to purchase the depositors' endowments, as the capital input to their projects;
4. Depositors deposit the money in the banks. Banks offer depositors the nominal demand deposit contracts that promise d_0, with

$$d_0 = \alpha_H R_1 + (1-\alpha_H) p_H R_2 = \gamma \left[\alpha_H R_1 + (1-\alpha_H) R_2 \right],$$

   nominal return in $t=1$ for each unit of deposit;
5. At the end of the period, banks hold one unit of deposit as liability and return one unit of cash to the central bank through their deposit accounts in the central bank.

IN PERIOD t = 1, GOOD STATE

Suppose in $t=\frac{1}{2}$ it is revealed that the economy will be in the good state with p_H, Figure 7.14 shows the flows of money throughout the period $t=1$:

1. Banks receive $\alpha_H R_1 + (1-\alpha_H) p_H R_2$ units of cash supply through their deposit accounts in the central bank, which is equal to the aggregate output from early entrepreneurs' project, or, the depositors' cash

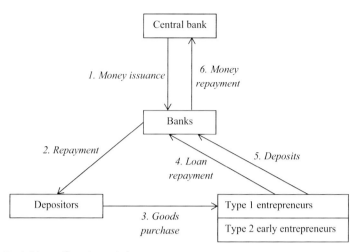

Figure 7.14 Money flows in period $t=1$

demand for buying the consumption goods from the entrepreneurs whose projects return early;

2. Banks repay $\alpha_H R_1 + (1-\alpha_H) p_H R_2 = d_0$ to the depositors;
3. The depositors purchase $d_0 = \alpha_H R_1 + (1-\alpha_H) p_H R_2$ consumption goods from the early entrepreneurs;
4. The early entrepreneurs repay their loans, $\gamma[\alpha_H R_1 + (1-\alpha_H) p_H R_2]$, to the banks, and
5. Deposit $(1-\gamma)[\alpha_H R_1 + (1-\alpha_H) p_H R_2]$ in the banks at gross deposit rate $r=1$;
6. At the end of the period, banks hold $(1-\gamma)[\alpha_H R_1 + (1-\alpha_H) p_H R_2]$ early entrepreneurs' deposits as liabilities, and return all the cash, d_0, to the central bank through their deposit accounts in the central bank.

IN PERIOD $t = 2$, AFTER THE GOOD STATE

After the good state in period $t=1$, Figure 7.15 shows the flows of money throughout the subsequent period $t=2$:

1. Banks receive $(1-\alpha_H)(1-p_H) R_2$ units of cash through their deposit accounts in the central bank, which is equal to the aggregate output from the late entrepreneurs' projects;

CHAPTER SEVEN: CENTRAL BANKING

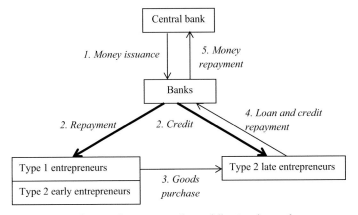

Figure 7.15 *Sequence of money flows in period* $t=2$ *following the good state*

2 Banks repay $(1-\gamma)\left[\alpha_H R_1 + (1-\alpha_H) p_H R_2\right]$, which is equal to
$$\gamma(1-\alpha_H)(1-p_H)R_2$$
to the early entrepreneurs. Late entrepreneurs receive
$$(1-\gamma)(1-\alpha_H)(1-p_H)R_2$$
credit from banks: because of the cash-in-advance constraint, even the producers (late entrepreneurs) themselves must pay cash to buy consumption goods from each other;

3 The early entrepreneurs purchase
$$(1-\gamma)\left[\alpha_H R_1 + (1-\alpha_H) p_H R_2\right] = \gamma(1-\alpha_H)(1-p_H)R_2$$
consumption goods from the late entrepreneurs, and late entrepreneurs purchase $(1-\gamma)(1-\alpha_H)(1-p_H)R_2$ consumption goods from each other of the late entrepreneurs;

4 The late entrepreneurs repay their loans $\gamma(1-\alpha_H)(1-p_H)R_2$ and credit $(1-\gamma)(1-\alpha_H)(1-p_H)R_2$, to the banks;

5 At the end of the period, banks return all the cash, $(1-\alpha_H)(1-p_H)R_2$, to the central bank through their deposit accounts in the central bank. All claims between the central bank, banks, and entrepreneurs are cleared.

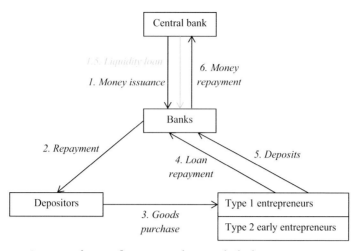

Figure 7.16 Sequence of money flows in period t = 1 in the bad state

IN PERIOD t = 1, BAD STATE

In good times, the banks are able to fulfill depositors' cash demand and there is no need for the central bank in liquidity provision. However, if it is revealed in $t = \frac{1}{2}$ that the economy will in the bad state with real output being $\alpha_H R_1 + (1-\alpha_H) p_L R_2$ which is lower than depositors' withdrawal demand d_0, the liquidity stress of the banks can be alleviated by the central bank's discount loans. The mechanism is shown as Figure 7.16:

1. Banks receive $S_1 = \alpha_H R_1 + (1-\alpha_H) p_L R_2$ units of cash supply through their deposit accounts in the central bank, which is equal to the aggregate output from early entrepreneurs' project. When it comes to the repayment to the depositors, as cash supply for goods transaction, S_1, is

$$S_1 < \alpha_H R_1 + (1-\alpha_H) p_H R_2 = d_0,$$

cash supply from the central bank, i.e., S_1, is insufficient to meet all deposit contracts. Therefore

1. Banks obtain $S_2 = (1-\alpha_H)(p_H - p_L) R_2$ liquidity through discount loans from the central bank using their holdings of $\gamma(1-\alpha_H)(1-p_L) R_2$ illiquid assets as collateral, given the policy rate

r^M being normalized to be 1. We provide more details about the discount loans after presenting the sequence of events in period $t = 2$ after the bad state;

2. Banks repay $S_1 + S_2 = d_0$ cash to the depositors;
3. The depositors pay d_0 to purchase $\alpha_H R_1 + (1-\alpha_H) p_L R_2$ consumption goods from the early entrepreneurs at the price
$$\frac{d_0}{\alpha_H R_1 + (1-\alpha_H) p_L R_2} > 1;$$
4. The early entrepreneurs repay their loans, $\gamma[\alpha_H R_1 + (1-\alpha_H) p_L R_2]$, to the banks, and
5. Deposit the rest of their nominal income, $d_0 - \gamma[\gamma_H R_1 + (1-\gamma_H) p_L R_2] = \gamma(1-\alpha_H)(1-p_L)R_2$, in the banks with gross deposit rate being 1;
6. Banks hold $\gamma(1-\alpha_H)(1-p_L)R_2$ early entrepreneurs' deposits as liabilities, and return all the cash, d_0, to the central bank through their deposit accounts in the central bank.

IN PERIOD t = 2, AFTER THE BAD STATE

In the subsequent period $t = 2$, the return of illiquid assets is realized. The flow of money is shown as in Figure 7.17.

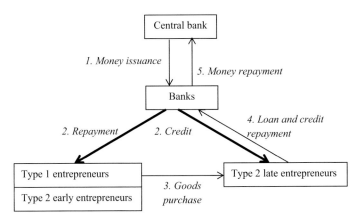

Figure 7.17 *Sequence of money flows in period $t = 2$ following the bad state*

1 Banks receive $(1-\alpha_H)(1-p_L)R_2$ units of cash through their deposit accounts in the central bank, which is equal to the aggregate output from the late entrepreneurs' projects;
2 Banks repay $\gamma(1-\alpha_H)(1-p_L)R_2$ to the early entrepreneurs. Late entrepreneurs receive $(1-\gamma)(1-\alpha_H)(1-p_L)R_2$ credit from banks;
3 The early entrepreneurs purchase $\gamma(1-\alpha_H)(1-p_L)R_2$ consumption goods from the late entrepreneurs, and the late entrepreneurs purchase $(1-\gamma)(1-\alpha_H)(1-p_L)R_2$ consumption goods from each other of the late entrepreneurs;
4 The late entrepreneurs repay their loans $\gamma(1-\alpha_H)(1-p_L)R_2$ and credit $(1-\gamma)(1-\alpha_H)(1-p_L)R_2$ to the banks;
5 At the end of the period, banks return all the cash, $(1-\alpha_H)(1-p_L)R_2$, to the central bank through their deposit accounts in the central bank. All claims between the central bank, banks, and entrepreneurs are cleared.

Note that the need for banks to apply for extra money through the central bank's discount window in period $t=1$ is the result of the "no-free-lunch" condition that the central bank's cash supply for goods transaction equals the real output of the period. In the bad state, the real output/cash supply for goods in transaction is lower, i.e.

$$S_1 = \alpha_H R_1 + (1-\alpha_H)p_L R_2 < \alpha_H R_1 + (1-\alpha_H)p_H R_2 = d_0$$

so that banks cannot fulfill the nominal deposit contracts by the transactional cash supply only. Banks can then obtain extra money through discount loans from the central bank, as long as these loans can be collateralized by banks' pledgeable long assets. To see that the discount loans are indeed collateralized, note that banks obtain

$$S_2 = (1-\alpha_H)(p_H - p_L)R_2$$

discount loans under the bad state in $t=1$, allowing them to repay depositors $d_0 = S_1 + S_2$. In the goods transaction that follows, early entrepreneurs are paid by d_0, and this increases their nominal income to $\gamma(1-\alpha_H)(1-p_L)R_2$ (compared with their nominal income

$\gamma(1-\alpha_H)(1-p_H)R_2$ that is lower than $\gamma(1-\alpha_H)(1-p_L)R_2$ under the good state). At the same time, banks' pledgeable assets in the subsequent period $t=2$ are $\gamma(1-\alpha_H)(1-p_L)R_2$—just enough to repay early entrepreneurs if they deposit in the banks in $t=1$. Therefore, early entrepreneurs are willing to deposit in $t=1$, in other words, the money injected into the banking system through discount loans (which becomes part of early entrepreneurs' deposits) is fully collateralized by banks' pledgeable long assets, or, backed by the economy's real output in the future.

In the presence of nominal contracts and the central bank as monetary authority, all the money that is issued in the beginning of each period will be returned to the central bank through banks' deposit accounts by the end of the same period, therefore, banks will not default on money. However, the collateral requirement for the discount loans is still necessary in this monetary economy to rule out the indeterminate explosive outcomes: as banks in the model are strategic, without the collateral requirement, deposit market competition would force them to bid up the nominal promise d_0 to infinity, given they can always obtain sufficient money through discount loans (if they are uncollateralized) to repay depositors, because they are able to return all the money to the central bank by the end of the period. Such need for determinacy also explains why, in the real world, uncollateralized cash in circulation for transactional purposes co-exists with collateralized discount loans.

It is then easy to see that, in such monetary economy, depositors' *real* consumption equals the real output in both states, i.e., $\alpha_H R_1+(1-\alpha_H)p_H R_2$ and $\alpha_H R_1+(1-\alpha_H)p_L R_2$ in good state and bad state, respectively, and depositors' expected consumption, $E[R(\alpha_H,\pi)]$ is given by

$$E[R(\alpha_H,\pi)]=\pi[\alpha_H R_1+(1-\alpha_H)p_H R_2]+(1-\pi)[\alpha_H R_1+(1-\alpha_H)p_L R_2]$$

which is exactly the same as in the constrained efficient solution, defined by (2.36).

7.4.2 CENTRAL BANKING AND EXCESS LIQUIDITY RISK

Although the constrained efficiency can be supported by the monetary economics, as Section 7.4.1 shows, unfortunately, it is not implementable without further restrictions on banks' liquidity creation. To see this, we only need to show that the allocation in Section 7.4.1 is not an equilibrium outcome, or, a bank will find it profitable to deviate from the constrained efficient solution.

Suppose that one bank i deviates from the constrained efficient solution by setting its investment in liquid assets, $\tilde{\alpha}$, with $\tilde{\alpha} < \alpha_H$, as well as offering a deposit contract promising $\tilde{d}_0 = \gamma\left[\tilde{\alpha}R_1 + (1-\tilde{\alpha})R_2\right]$ in $t=0$, then this bank will suffer from liquidity shortage in $t=\frac{1}{2}$ even in the good state, as its realized return from early projects cannot meet $\tilde{d}_0$,

$$\begin{aligned}
\tilde{\alpha}R_1 + (1-\tilde{\alpha})p_H R_2 &< \alpha_H R_1 + (1-\alpha_H)p_H R_2 \\
&= \gamma\left[\alpha_H R_1 + (1-\alpha_H)R_2\right] \\
&= d_0 \\
&< \gamma\left[\tilde{\alpha}R_1 + (1-\tilde{\alpha})R_2\right] \\
&= \tilde{d}_0
\end{aligned}$$

using the fact that α_H maximizes return from early projects. However, with lower $\tilde{\alpha}$, the bank invests more in illiquid assets, allowing it to borrow from the central bank's discount window in $t=1$ and meet the nominal withdrawal demand $\tilde{d}_0$. This allows the bank to offer higher nominal return to its depositors $\tilde{d}_0$, higher than d_0 that is offered by the other banks, and win all depositors from the other banks.

Knowing this, in equilibrium, no bank has incentive to invest in liquid assets, that is, all banks will choose $\alpha = 0$. With $\alpha = 0$, banks are able to offer the highest possible nominal return to depositors, γR_2. However, depositors only benefit from *real* consumption, which comes from realized return from early projects, i.e., $\gamma p_H R_2$ in the good state and $\gamma p_L R_2$ in the bad state under $\alpha = 0$. Depositors' expected consumption, $E[R(0,\pi)]$ is given by

$$E[R(0,\pi)] = \pi\gamma p_H R_2 + (1-\pi)\gamma p_L R_2$$
$$< E[R(\alpha_H,\pi)],$$

which is lower than expected consumption in the constrained efficient solution, $E[R(\alpha_H,\pi)]$.

7.4.3 SUMMARY

This simple model setup with a monetary economy demonstrates how monetary policy affects liquidity risks in the banking system. This is due to the dual role of money, which is used both as a medium for transaction and liquid assets which can be obtained from the central bank discount window, using illiquid assets as collateral. As banks compete to promise higher *nominal* return for depositors, they will engage in excess investment in illiquid assets. Although under pure liquidity risk and central bank liquidity facility there is no costly bank run in this model, inefficiency does arise from excess investment in illiquid assets that reduces depositors' *real* consumption which is produced from liquid assets.

This simple model thus shows that monetary policy regime itself cannot maintain optimal liquidity creation and contain excess liquidity risks in the banking system; the risk-taking channel of monetary policy thus needs to be accommodated by stability policy in association with monetary policy. For example, in this model, a candidate policy may be to impose a requirement in $t=0$ that banks must invest at least α_H in liquid assets—resembling the *liquidity coverage ratio* (LCR) requirement in Basel III. We leave further discussion on liquidity regulation to Chapter 12.

7.5 RISK-TAKING CHANNELS OF MONETARY POLICY

Monetary policy also affects banks' incentive in taking credit risks. For example, when monetary policy rate is low, so as banks' funding cost and liquidity risk, banks with limited liability will have the incentive to engage in riskier, high-yield activities; just as the long-lasting low interest rate environment in the US and Europe before 2007 encouraged banks to "search for yield" and sowed the seeds for the crisis. In this section, we illustrate banks' choice on credit risk in reaction to changes in monetary policy, based on the model from Dell'Ariccia et al. (2014).

7.5.1 MODELLING BANKS' RISK-SHIFTING INCENTIVES

Consider a representative bank's decision problem as follows: the bank faces a downward-sloping demand curve for loans, i.e., loan demand L falls with the bank's gross lending rate r_L, $L'(r_L) < 0$.

Loans are risky because of moral hazard problem, but the bank has a monitoring technology to affect loans' probability of success. By exerting monitoring effort $0 \leq p \leq 1$, the probability of loan's success will be p, but the bank has to incur a monitoring cost of $\frac{1}{2}cp^2$, with c being constant and $c > 0$ for every unit of loan. However, the bank's true effort level p is private information and only known to the bank.

Loans in the bank are funded by bank equity and deposits: a fraction k of bank liabilities comes from equity, and a fraction $1-k$ of bank liabilities comes from deposits. The bank's choice on capitalization k is publicly observable. Assume that the gross risk-free rate in this economy is r^* which is affected by central bank's monetary policy.

The bank's decisions are made in three stages:

Stage 1 The bank chooses its capital ratio k and offers depositors a deposit contract with gross deposit rate r_D. Depositors deposit in the bank;
Stage 2 The bank issues loans to borrowers with a gross loan rate r_L;
Stage 3 The bank chooses its monitoring effort p.

To capture the fact that a substantial part of bank liabilities is funded by uninsured creditors, assume that depositors are not insured so that they are only willing to lend to the bank if their expected gross return is no lower than the risk-free rate. Although the bank's monitoring effort p, or, the probability that depositors are repaid, is not observable, depositors are able to infer p through the bank's choice on k: because of limited liability, the lower k is, the less "skin-in-the-game" the bank has, the higher incentive the bank has to take higher risk, betting for the high return of the risky assets return and shifting most of the cost to creditors if the assets default, implying a lower p that the bank will choose. Therefore, after observing the bank's choice on k, depositors will infer the bank's choice on p, call it $E[p|k]$, and depositors' participation constraint, (PC-D), requires that they will only deposit in the bank if the expected gross return from deposits is no lower than the risk-free rate under the bank's deposit rate r_D, i.e.

$$r_D E[p|k] \geq r^*. \text{ (PC-D)} \quad (7.28)$$

Equity is more costly than deposits, as shareholders require a higher return on equity (ROE) β, and $\beta = r^* + \epsilon$ with $\epsilon > 0$. As the bank operates in the interest of shareholders, p is observable for them, shareholders' participation constraint, (PC-E), requires that they will only invest in the bank if their gross return r_E when the bank is successful makes their ROE no less than β, i.e.

$$r_E p \geq \beta = r^* + \epsilon. \text{ (PC-E)} \quad (7.29)$$

7.5.2 RISK-TAKING CHANNELS

The bank's optimal decision problem can be solved by backward induction.

STAGE 3: CHOICE ON MONITORING EFFORT, p

Starting from stage 3, given that k, r_D, and r_L are previously chosen, the bank chooses its effort level p to maximize its expected return Π, i.e.

$$\max_p \Pi = \left\{ p[r_L - r_D(1-k) - r_E k] - \frac{1}{2}cp^2 \right\} L(r_L)$$

$$= \left\{ p[r_L - r_D(1-k)] - (r^* + \epsilon)k - \frac{1}{2}cp^2 \right\} L(r_L) \quad (7.30)$$

using the fact that in equilibrium (PC-E), (7.29) is binding. First-order condition for (7.30) yields

$$\frac{\partial \Pi}{\partial p} = \left[r_L - r_D(1-k) - cp\right]L(r_L) = 0,$$

$$p = \frac{r_L - r_D(1-k)}{c}. \tag{7.31}$$

For regularity $0 \leq p \leq 1$, assume that the value of c always ensures $p \leq 1$.

As in equilibrium depositors' expectation on p, $E[p|k]$ must be correct

$$E[p|k] = p,$$

using the fact that in equilibrium (PC-D), (7.28) is binding, the equilibrium deposit rate is given by

$$r_D = \frac{r^*}{p}.$$

Combine with equation (7.31), the optimal p in equilibrium can be solved as

$$p = \frac{1}{2c}\left(r_L + \sqrt{r_L^2 - 4cr^*(1-k)}\right). \tag{7.32}$$

Equation (7.32) implies that

$$\frac{\partial p}{\partial r^*} < 0, \tag{7.33}$$

that is, higher monetary policy rate r^*, or, higher funding cost of deposits, leads to lower monitoring effort and higher credit risk, *all else equal*. This fits the franchise value hypothesis on bank risk-taking, as in Chapter 4, Section 4.3, that higher funding cost forces banks to take higher risk to maintain franchise value given that they can shift most of bankruptcy cost to depositors when loans are non-performing—we may call it *risk-shifting effect*. However, r_L and k in equation (7.31) are endogenous and also affected by r^*, the general equilibrium effect of r^* on bank risk-taking is not yet clear before we solve r_L and k.

STAGE 2: CHOICE ON LOAN RATE, r_L

Now given the bank's choice on p, we can take one step back and solve for optimal r_L in stage 2. That is, the bank solves the maximization problem

$$\max_{r_L} \quad \Pi = \left\{ p\left[r_L - r_D(1-k)\right] - (r^* + \epsilon)k - \frac{1}{2}cp^2 \right\} L(r_L),$$

$$\text{s.t.} \quad p = \frac{r_L - r_D(1-k)}{c}. \quad (7.34)$$

First-order condition for (7.34) yields

$$\frac{\partial \Pi}{\partial r_L} = \frac{\partial L(r_L)}{\partial r_L} \left\{ \frac{\left[r_L - r_D(1-k)\right]^2}{2c} - (r^* + \epsilon)k \right\} + L(r_L) \frac{r_L - r_D(1-k)}{c}$$

$$= 0. \quad (7.35)$$

Note that the first-order condition (7.35) is an implicit function of r_L and r^*, denote it by $\Phi(r_L, r^*)$, then apply implicit function theorem to get

$$\frac{\partial r_L}{\partial r^*} = -\frac{\frac{\partial \Phi}{\partial r^*}}{\frac{\partial \Phi}{\partial r_L}} > 0. \quad (7.36)$$

The derivation is left as your exercise. That is, (7.36) characterizes the monetary policy *pass-through*, that rising monetary policy rate r^* leads to a higher loan rate r_L. However, this also means that the bank will have an higher incentive to monitor, to increase the probability of collecting r_L, *all else equal*, so that higher monetary policy rate r^* reduces the bank's risk-taking—we may call it *pass-through effect*. This is exactly the opposite to the impact of r^* on bank risk-taking, directly through its choice on p, or, the risk-shifting effect that we have established in (7.33).

In addition, given that $L'(r_L) < 0$, (7.36) also implies that a rise in monetary policy rate r^* leads to a fall in bank lending L, which exactly reflects the *bank lending channel* of monetary policy.

STAGE 1: CHOICE ON CAPITAL RATIO, k

Now given the bank's choices in stages 2 and 3, we can solve for optimal k in stage 1. That is, the bank solves the maximization problem

$$\max_k \quad \Pi = \left\{ p\left[r_L - r_D(1-k)\right] - \left(r^* + \epsilon\right)k - \frac{1}{2}cp^2 \right\} L(r_L),$$

$$\text{s.t.} \quad p(k), r_L(k), r_D = \frac{r^*}{p}$$

(7.37)

using the fact that in equilibrium (PC-D), (7.28) is binding, $r_D = \frac{r^*}{p}$. Note that p and r_L are given by optimal solution in later stages and they are both functions of k.

The first-order condition of (7.37) yields

$$\frac{d\Pi}{dk} = \frac{\partial \Pi}{\partial k} + \frac{\partial \Pi}{\partial p}\frac{\partial p}{\partial k} + + \frac{\partial \Pi}{\partial r_L}\frac{\partial r_L}{\partial k} = 0.$$

(7.38)

From equation (7.38), Dell'Ariccia et al. (2014) show that, generically, around the optimal k

$$\frac{dk}{dr^*} > 0$$

(7.39)

if interior solution exists by applying the implicit function theorem on (7.38). (7.39) states that higher monetary policy leads to lower bank leverage, or more skin-in-the-game, implying a lower incentive for bank risk-taking, *all else equal*. We may call this *leverage effect* of monetary policy.

To see everything through in a clearer way, without much loss of generality, let us now assume that the loan demand function is given by

$$L(r_L) = 100 - 8r_L,$$

and solve k, r_L, and p numerically through the first-order conditions, (7.31), (7.35), and (7.38).

Figure 7.18 shows the simulation result for bank's optimal capital ratio, as a function of monetary policy rate r^*. Around the reasonable value of r^*, $r^* \to 1$, increasing r^* leads to a rise in k, or, a fall in bank leverage.

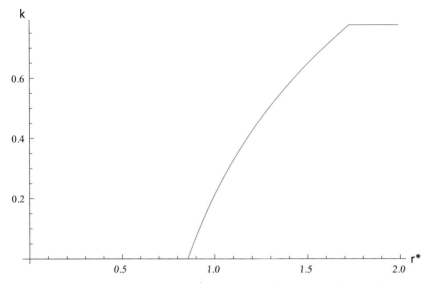

Figure 7.18 Bank's choice on capital ratio k as a function of monetary policy rate r^*
Source: Dell'Ariccia et al.

Notes: (2014) the loan demand function is given by $L(r_L)=100-8r_L$, $c=9$, and $\epsilon=0.06$. It is assumed that 35% of bank liabilities are insured deposits which are paid with a risk-free rate, so that only the rest, uninsured deposits are paid with r_D.

As is shown through the first-order conditions, (7.31), (7.35), and (7.38), monetary policy rate r^* can affect bank's risk-taking incentive through three channels:

Risk-shifting channel Higher r^* increases the bank's funding cost and incentivizes it to shift bankruptcy cost towards depositors. Higher r^* thus reduces p and increases risk-taking;

Pass-through channel Higher r^* increases the bank's profit through higher loan rate r_L; this incentivizes the bank to reduce the probability of default. Higher r^* thus increases p and reduces risk-taking;

Leverage channel Higher r^* increases the bank's capital ratio k and results in more skin-in-the-game; this incentivizes the bank to reduce the probability of default, hence bankruptcy cost. Higher r^* thus increases p and reduces risk-taking.

Given the diverting effects through different channels, what is the *net* effect of monetary policy on bank risk-taking? Dell'Ariccia et al. (2014)

show that within the range in which k increases with r^*, p increases with r^*, too. That is, once higher r^* induces the bank to reduce its leverage, the net effect of r^* leads to higher monitoring effort p, hence lower risk-taking. On the contrary, when monetary policy rate r^* is lower, the bank has the incentive to leverage up by reducing k and its monitoring effort p which increases the probability of default—this is exactly the so-called *risk-taking channel of monetary policy*.

Figure 7.19 shows the result from numerical simulation, using the same model setups as in Figure 7.18. In the same region in which k increases with r^*, bank's monitoring effort p also increases with r^* which exhibits the property of risk-taking channel of monetary policy.

7.5.3 SUMMARY

Dell'Ariccia-Laeven-Marquez model characterizes the key channels through which monetary policy affects banks' credit risks. Monetary policy has diverting effects on banks' adjustments in balance sheet risks: tightening

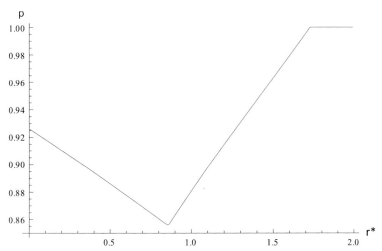

Figure 7.19 *Bank's choice on monitoring effort p as a function of monetary policy rate r^**
Source: Dell'Ariccia et al.
Notes: (2014) the loan demand function is given by $L(r_L) = 100 - 8r_L$, $c = 9$, and $\epsilon = 0.06$. It is assumed that 35% of bank liabilities are insured deposits which are paid with a risk-free rate, so that only the rest, uninsured deposits are paid with r_D.

monetary policy may induce banks with limited liability to take higher risks, hoping to shift bankruptcy cost to creditors, while increasing profit from a higher lending rate will encourage banks to reduce risk exposure, and contractionary monetary policy also forces banks to deleverage, reducing probability of default. Overall, tightening monetary policy restricts banks' risk-taking. Support on the Dell'Ariccia-Laeven-Marquez type of risk-taking channel of monetary policy is further provided by Adrian and Shin (2014), which demonstrate that banks' leverage adjustment induced by monetary policy is a dominating channel for banks' risk-taking. We leave more discussion on the leverage channel to Chapter 8, Section 8.5.

7.6 EMPIRICAL EVIDENCE

7.6.1 IDENTIFYING BANK LENDING CHANNEL

One important empirical question in central banking is how effective monetary policy is in influencing banks' credit supply to the real economy, or, the quantitative effect of bank lending channel of monetary policy transmission. Such a question is not only of great interest in normal times, for example, to quantify the change in banks' total credit supply to the real economy under one percentage rise in key policy rate, it is also crucial in abnormal times, for example, to better understand to what extent central bank's QE policy eases borrowers' access to bank credit.

However, identifying the bank lending channel, i.e., how monetary policy affects bank lending, is challenging. One main obstacle is to distinguish supply-side shocks, i.e., changes in bank lending are caused by shocks (for example, monetary policy shocks) to banks, from demand-side shocks, i.e., changes in bank lending are caused by shocks from credit demand of borrowers (for example, during recession, firms borrow less due to contraction in their activities). If we simply regress the volume of bank lending to monetary policy measures, we may wrongly attribute variations in lending that are caused by borrowers' demand to bank lending channel of monetary policy, leading to bias in estimates. Two widely used identification strategies are designed in practice to distinguish supply-side from demand-side shocks, regarding two different types of monetary policy shocks. One strategy is to study those borrowers who borrow from multiple banks that are affected by monetary policy differently, or, by *idiosyncratic* monetary policy shocks (for example, the central bank's targeted liquidity provision that varies across banks), proposed by Khwaja and Mian (2008); another strategy is to explore how the sensitivity of bank lending to banks' liquidity constraints—which mostly pertains to banks' credit supply decision—reacts to *aggregate* monetary shocks to banks' funding condition (for example, changes in monetary policy rate that affect interbank lending rate for all banks), proposed by Kashyap and Stein (2000).

IDENTIFICATION STRATEGY À LA KHWAJA AND MIAN (2008)

To identify how bank lending reacts to *idiosyncratic* monetary policy shocks, Khwaja and Mian (2008) explore credit register, that records loan contracts between individual banks and borrowers, to properly identify bank lending channels and isolate the supply-side shocks. The Khwaja-Mian approach focuses on those borrowers who borrow from multiple banks that are subject to bank-specific monetary policy shocks and are affected by monetary policy differently: briefly speaking, for each borrower, its credit demand at certain times is more or less fixed; therefore, if its loans with various banks react differently to a monetary policy shock, such differences are most likely due to banks' different exposures to the monetary policy shock. A simple, stylized model based on Khwaja and Mian (2008) as follows explains how the identification strategy works.

Consider an economy living over two periods, $t = 0,1$, with a number of banks and firms. Assume that one bank can only lend to one firm, but one firm can borrow from multiple banks, as Figure 7.20 illustrates.

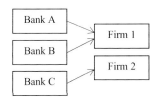

Figure 7.20 *Bank-firm relationships*

Assets	Liabilities
Loan L_{ij}	Deposits D_i
	Equity E_i

Figure 7.21 *A bank's balance sheet in each period*

In either period, a bank i lends L_{ij} to firm j, and it is funded by deposits D_i and equity E_i. Here we should interpret "deposits" and "equity" in a broader sense: deposits can include retail deposits as well as interbank deposits (or, "wholesale funding"), while equity refers to funding instruments that are more costly such as bonds and common equity. Bank's balance sheet in either period is illustrated in Figure 7.21, so that $L_{ij} \equiv D_i + E_i$.

The bank can raise deposits with zero deposit rate up to $\bar{D}_i$; beyond that, it has to rely on costly equity funding with a convex cost function $\alpha_E E_i^2$, $\alpha_E > 0$. Firm j's demand for loan, L_{ij}, is a downward sloping function with loan rate r_{ij}. Assume that r_{ij} is linear in L_{ij}, so that $r_{ij} = \bar{r}_j - \alpha_L L_{ij}$, with $\bar{r}_j$ being constant for firm j. Until now we neglect the time superscript of all variables as long as they are the same within either period.

Assume that in the end of period 0, the economy experiences two types of shocks:

- "Supply shocks", or shocks to the funding condition of credit suppliers—banks, such that supply of deposits for bank i in period 1 becomes

$$\bar{D}_i^1 = \bar{D}_i + \delta + \delta_i$$

in which δ is an aggregate shock to all banks, and δ_i is an idiosyncratic shock that only pertains to bank i;
- "Demand shocks", that the receiver of credit, firm j, experiences productivity shocks so that the loan rate it is willing to pay becomes

$$r_{ij}^1 = \bar{r}_j - \alpha_L L_{ij} + \eta + \eta_j$$

in which η is an aggregate shock to all firms, and η_j is an idiosyncratic shock that only pertains to firm j.

In the presence of the shocks, the bank has to rebalance its lending, L^1_{ij}, in $t=1$.

The bank's optimal decision problem in $t=0$ is solved by

$$\max_{L_{ij}} \left(\bar{r}_j - \alpha_L L_{ij}\right) L_{ij} - \alpha_E \left(L_{ij} - \bar{D}_i\right)^2,$$

and the first-order condition yields

$$L_{ij} = \frac{1}{2}\frac{1}{\alpha_L + \alpha_E}\bar{r}_j + \frac{\alpha_E}{\alpha_L + \alpha_E}\bar{D}_i. \tag{7.40}$$

Similarly, the bank's optimal decision problem in $t=1$ is

$$\max_{L^1_{ij}} \left(\bar{r}_j - \alpha_L L^1_{ij} + \eta + \eta_j\right) L^1_{ij} - \alpha_E \left(L^1_{ij} - \bar{D}_i - \delta - \delta_i\right)^2,$$

which yields

$$L^1_{ij} = \frac{1}{2}\frac{1}{\alpha_L + \alpha_E}\left(\bar{r}_j + \eta + \eta_j\right) + \frac{\alpha_E}{\alpha_L + \alpha_E}\left(\bar{D}_i + \delta + \delta_i\right). \tag{7.41}$$

Subtract (7.40) from (7.41) leads to

$$\begin{aligned}\Delta L_{ij} &= \frac{1}{2}\frac{1}{\alpha_L + \alpha_E}\left(\eta + \eta_j\right) + \frac{\alpha_E}{\alpha_L + \alpha_E}\left(\delta + \delta_i\right)\\ &= \underbrace{\frac{1}{\alpha_L + \alpha_E}\left(\frac{1}{2}\eta + \alpha_E \delta\right)}_{(A)} + \underbrace{\frac{\alpha_E}{\alpha_L + \alpha_E}\delta_i + \frac{1}{2}\frac{1}{\alpha_L + \alpha_E}\eta_j}_{(B)}\end{aligned} \tag{7.42}$$

in which part (A) captures aggregate shocks that are constant to all banks, while part (B) includes idiosyncratic bank- and firm-level shocks. Denote δ_i by ΔD_i as the measure of funding shock to bank i, equation (7.42) implies that, to identify how bank lending reacts to bank i's funding shock, we just need to estimate an OLS regression

$$\Delta L_{ij} = \beta_0 + \beta_1 \Delta D_i + \beta_2 \eta_j + \epsilon_{ij} \tag{7.43}$$

in which β_0 is the constant term, η_j is firm idiosyncratic shock, and ϵ_{ij} is the error term. The estimated coefficient β_1 thus captures how banks' funding condition affects bank lending. When ΔD_i proxies how bank i's funding condition is affected by monetary policy shock, for example, how bank i's funding is affected by the central bank's asset purchase in a QE program or the central bank's targeted liquid provision, (7.43) defines an equation estimating the bank lending channel of such monetary policy.

However, such estimate is not unbiased. One obvious reason is that ΔD_i and η_j may be correlated: suppose that the firm suffers a negative technological shock η_j—for example, if firm j is an oil-producing firm after oil price crashes—that increases its probability of default; knowing this, depositors in bank i will reduce their deposits, leading to a falling ΔD_i. Such correlation results in estimate bias. For this reason, if we want to estimate bank lending channel of monetary policy by simply regressing bank lending on funding condition variables, such as

$$\Delta L_{ij} = \beta_0 + \beta_1 \Delta D_i + \sigma_{ij}, \tag{7.44}$$

in which ΔD_i measures the change in bank i's funding condition after the monetary policy shock, the estimate β_1 is biased: comparing (7.44) with (7.43), firms' idiosyncratic demand shocks are now absorbed in the error term σ_{ij}, making it correlated with ΔD_i. Therefore, we will wrongly attribute part of ΔL_{ij} that is caused by the technological shock to bank lending channel of monetary policy.

One way to solve this issue, as Khwaja and Mian (2008) propose, is to focus only on firms borrowing from multiple banks, such as Firm 1 in Figure 7.20, and estimate

$$\Delta L_{ij} = \beta_j + \beta_1 \Delta D_i + \epsilon_{ij}, \tag{7.45}$$

with β_j being firm fixed effect, instead. As equation (7.45) is estimated under first difference, β_j absorbs all firm idiosyncratic demand shocks η_j.

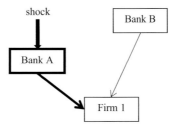

Figure 7.22 *Khwaja-Mian identification strategy*

Regression (7.45) is thus to test, within the same firm, how banks with different funding shock exposure ΔD_i —as a result of certain monetary policy shock—differ in lending. As Figure 7.22 illustrates, given that all lending banks are subject to the same firm's demand shock, a change in shock-affected bank's lending must be due to this bank's supply shock that is driven by the monetary policy.

Using such identification strategy, Khwaja and Mian (2008) examine banks' lending supply in response to a freeze on dollar deposit accounts in Pakistan, 1998, imposed by the government for fear of balance of payment problems. Depositors' reaction to empty their dollar deposit accounts led to funding liquidity shocks to banks, and each bank's exposure to the liquidity shock depends on its reliance on dollar funding; this allows them to use the identification strategy to isolate the impact on banks' lending supply, based on credit registry data. They find that credit supply falls more in banks with higher liquidity shock exposure. More examples using Khwaja-Mian identification will be presented in Section 7.6.3.

Khwaja-Mian identification relies on large scale, highly granular credit register data, which are currently only available in a few countries, and idiosyncratic monetary policy shocks that affect individual bank's funding condition differently. To focus only on firms borrowing from multiple banks, a large share—it is not unusual that 80% or more—of observations have to be dropped, raising the question whether the gain from identification outweighs the loss of information from discarded data. Furthermore, one potential threat to Khwaja-Mian identification strategy is that firms may receive different types of loans from banks, which may create trouble for identification. Using credit-registry data for Spain and Peru, Ivashina et al. (2020) find that commercial credit mainly includes asset-based loans, cash-flow loans, trade finance, and leasing, so that firms may choose certain loan types when they borrow from certain banks. Therefore, when conducting Khwaja-Mian identification with certain monetary policy shock, even if we only focus on firms that borrow from multiple banks, change in firm j's loan provided by bank i may not only reflect bank i's credit *supply*, but may also reflect firm j's *demand* for a certain *type* of loan. Khwaja-Mian identification may thus still result in estimation bias. Furthermore, based on data from Spain and Peru, Ivashina et al. (2020) find that the bank lending channel of monetary policy goes primarily through cash-flow loans, whereas asset-based loans are mostly insensitive to monetary policy. Given that market shares of different loan types vary greatly across countries, their results therefore suggest that the loan type dimension needs more scrutiny in identifying the bank lending channel of monetary policy.

SEMI-STRUCTURAL MODEL À LA KASHYAP AND STEIN (2000)

To identify how bank lending reacts to *aggregate* monetary policy shocks, for example, key monetary policy rate adjustments that change the market funding condition for all banks, Kashyap and Stein (2000) propose an identification strategy that is based on a theory-founded, "semi-structural" framework and bank-level data for estimation.

To see how the identification strategy works, consider a stylized bank which manages the balance sheet as Figure 7.23 shows. Out of total funding resources D, the bank issues a total amount of L illiquid, risky loans and holds an amount of B liquidity buffer.

As Bianchi-Bigio model in Section 7.3 predicts, the capability that the bank issues more loans depends on the marginal cost of liquidity management. For this stylized bank, when it issues new loans, the more liquidity buffer it holds on its balance sheet, the less funding it has to raise from the interbank market to rebalance its liquidity reserves after loan issuance, i.e., holding more liquidity buffer reduces the loan issuing bank's marginal cost of liquidity management. Under an aggregate monetary policy shock, say, when monetary policy is tightening with a higher key

Assets	Liabilities
Loans L	Deposits D
Liquidity buffer B	

Figure 7.23 *A generic bank's balance sheet*

policy rate r and hence higher interbank lending rate, the bank's new loan issuance will be more dependent on its liquidity buffer, i.e.,

$$\frac{\partial^2 L}{\partial B \partial r} > 0, \qquad (7.46)$$

and such relationship only matters for the bank's loan supply. This implies that, if we can find the relationship (7.46) in the data, it must come from the response in the bank's lending *supply* to changes in monetary policy rate, or, the bank lending channel.

In order to test the hypothesis in (7.46), Kashyap and Stein (2000) take a two-step regression approach. In step one, they run the following cross-sectional regression for banks grouped by their asset size

$$\Delta \ln L_{i,t} = \sum_{j=1}^{m} \alpha_{t,j} \Delta \ln L_{i,t-j} + \beta_t B_{i,t-1} + \psi_t CONTROLS_{i,t-1} + \epsilon_{i,t}, \qquad (7.47)$$

in which $\Delta \ln L_i$ is the growth rate in lending for bank i in quarter t, $B_{i,t-1}$ is liquidity buffer measured by the ratio of non-required holdings of liquid assets (excess reserves and government securities, required reserves are not included) to total assets, $CONTROLS_{i,t-1}$ contains lagged control variables reflecting features of the bank's balance sheet, such as capitalization ratio, asset size, and value of non-performing loans. The key variable here, liquidity buffer measure $B_{i,t}$, reflects the bank's capability in adjusting loan issuance by using its liquidity buffer.

Take the time series β_t generated from the first step for the second-step regression

$$\beta_t = \phi_0 + \sum_{k=1}^{n} \phi_k r_{t-k} + \delta_t controls_t + \mu_t \qquad (7.48)$$

in which r_t is the monetary policy rate in quarter t, $controls_t$ contains (lagged) macro variables such as GDP growth rate to capture the demand side effect from the business cycles.

Note that an endogeneity problem may still exist in the two-step regression: a bank's lending and its holdings of liquid assets $B_{i,t}$ may be both driven by business cycles; for example, during economic boom, a bank is willing to lend more for higher profit in the good time, and the bank's liquidity buffer also increases as a result of rising deposits during the boom. One way to address this issue, as Cetorelli and Goldberg (2012) suggest, is to regress $B_{i,t}$ on the share of commercial/industrial (C&I) lending in total lending, $\left(\dfrac{C\&I}{TotalLending}\right)_{i,t}$, and non-performing loan ratio, $NPL_{i,t}$

$$B_{i,t} = \gamma_0 + \gamma_1 \left(\dfrac{C\&I}{TotalLending}\right)_{i,t} + \gamma_2 NPL_{i,t} + v_{i,t}. \qquad (7.49)$$

The impacts of business cycles on bank liquidity are captured by these two regressors. Then we use the residual of the regression (7.49), $v_{i,t}$, which is orthogonal to business cycles, as an instrumental variable for $B_{i,t}$; the endogeneity problem arising from business cycles is thus corrected.

In the first regression (7.47), the coefficient β_t reflects the sensitivity of bank lending to balance sheet liquidity. When monetary policy is tightened and the policy rate rises, making interbank lending more costly, bank lending should be more sensitive to liquidity strength indicator β_t, as the bank is less likely to fully absorb the monetary shock by using its liquidity buffer and costly interbank funding without adjusting its loan supply, should the monetary transmission mechanism exist and work through the bank's liquidity management. Therefore, in the second-step regression (7.48), the sum of coefficients for lagged monetary policy rate r_t, $\sum_{k=1}^{n} \phi_k$, which reflects the accumulated impacts of monetary policy over n quarters on the sensitivity parameter β_t, should be positive.

Based on the quarterly balance sheet report of every insured US commercial bank from 1976 to 1993, Kashyap and Stein (2000) find it indeed significant and positive, i.e., the monetary transmission through banks' liquidity management is supported. Furthermore, they find that lending from small banks reacts more to monetary policy than lending from large banks, as the smaller ones' lending is more sensitive to liquidity buffers.

More supportive evidence emerges as more micro-level data become available. Campello (2002) shows that the small American banks that are members of big financial conglomerates react less to monetary policy in their lending supplies, compared with the stand-alone ones, as the former have the access to the internal liquidity market within the conglomerates, making them more easy to obtain funding and better able to shield themselves from the monetary shocks. Ashcraft (2006) finds that lending from small American banks that are affiliated with large banks is less affected by monetary shocks than the lending from standalone small banks, because the former have better access to federal funds market so that they are less liquidity constrained.

7.6.2 RISK-TAKING CHANNEL OF MONETARY POLICY

The risk-taking channel, as is coined by Borio and Zhu (2012), that banks adjust their risk-taking in reaction to monetary policy, has been a crucial element in the transmission of monetary policy, while it only started to gain much attention after the 2007–2009 global financial crisis. It has been argued, for example by Rajan (2006), that the period in early 2000s with too low monetary policy rate for too long has sowed the seeds for the crisis, as in low interest rate environment financial institutions are encouraged to "search for yield" and invest excessively in risky assets. Adrian and Shin (2014) demonstrate that a low interest rate increases the value of banks' balance sheets with falling liquidity risks and credit risks, increasing the capacity for taking more risks. This allows banks to leverage and expand their balance sheets, by investing in riskier assets (see Chapter 8, Section 8.5 for more details). Low interest rate does not only lead to the expansion in the *volume* of lending, but also in risk-taking. Such a risk-taking channel increases fragility in the banking system during normal times, as well as the likelihood of crises in the future.

Jiménez et al. (2014) present some strong evidence on how banks' risk taking varies in the monetary transmission mechanism. Using the credit register in Spain that contains bank-firm level data on both loan applications and outcomes in 2002–2009, they exploit a two-stage regression: the first one explains banks' decisions on granting loans to firms by the *ex ante* credit risk of the firms and monetary policy rate,

$$\begin{aligned}
Granted_{bit} = & \ \beta_1 FirmRisk_{it} \\
& + \beta_2 \Delta OvernightRate_{t-1} \times FirmRisk_{it} \\
& + \beta_3 \Delta OvernightRate_{t-1} \times \ln BankCapital_{b,t-1} \times FirmRisk_{it} \\
& + X_{bit} + \mu_b + \gamma_i + \delta_t + \epsilon_{bit}
\end{aligned}$$

in which $Granted_{bit}$ is a dummy variable which equals 1 if firm i's loan application is granted by bank b in month t, $FirmRisk_{it}$ is a dummy variable which equals 1 if firm i has outstanding non-performing loans in t, $\Delta OvernightRate_t$ denotes change in the Euro area overnight rate, $\ln BankCapital_{bt}$ denotes bank's capital ratio in logarithm form, X_{bit} includes bank- and firm-level controls, and $\mu_b/\gamma_i/\delta_t$ denotes bank/firm/time fixed effects.

The second one explains the performance of granted loans by the same explanatory variables,

$$\begin{aligned}
\ln Credit_{bit} = & \ \beta'_1 FirmRisk_{it} \\
& + \beta'_2 \Delta OvernightRate_{t-1} \times FirmRisk_{it} \\
& + \beta'_3 \Delta OvernightRate_{t-1} \times \ln BankCapital_{b,t-1} \times FirmRisk_{it} \\
& + X_{bit} + \mu_b + \gamma_i + \delta_t + \epsilon_{bit}
\end{aligned}$$

in which $\ln Credit_{bit}$ denotes the amount of granted credit from bank b to firm i in month t, in logarithm form.

They find that lax monetary policy encourages riskier (poorly capitalized) banks to issue loans to *ex ante* risky firms, with lower lending standard (more lenient requirements on collateral), and these loans are more likely to be non-performing in the future. A clear evidence for risk-taking channel, Delis and Kouretas (2011) document a similar negative relationship between monetary policy rate and bank risk-taking based on data from Euro area banks. Jiménez et al. (2012) investigate a mirror scenario when monetary policy rate increases. They find that the contraction in bank lending is particularly stronger for riskier banks, i.e., banks with weaker capitalization, suggesting an accommodating effect of high interest rate on banks' risk-taking.

7.6.3 BANK LENDING UNDER UNCONVENTIONAL MONETARY POLICY

The impact of unconventional monetary policy, particularly during and after the 2007–2009 financial crisis, on banking outcomes and bank activities has been intensively studied. We cannot provide a thorough view on this topic, instead, we will focus on two issues that currently draw much attention from both researchers and policy makers.

BANKING BELOW ZERO LOWER BOUND

It was conventionally assumed that zero was the lower bound of monetary policy rate; however, several central banks have set their policy rates below zero after the crisis. Currently, the list includes Sveriges Riksbank, the Danish National Bank, ECB, the Swiss National Bank, and the Bank of Japan. By imposing negative interest rate on banks' excess reserves in the central bank, policy makers intend to induce banks to switch from reserves into other assets, hence increasing bank lending and stimulating the real economy.

However, whether negative interest rate necessarily leads to monetary expansion through bank lending is not yet clear. In fact, how bank lending responds to negative interest rate largely depends on policy rate *pass-through*, i.e., how other rates, such as deposit rates, loan rates, etc. react to negative interest rate. It is sometime suspected that such pass-through may be incomplete: for instance, banks may find it hard to set negative rate on retail deposits (they may implicitly do so, though, through charging fees on deposit accounts), for fear that depositors will withdraw all cash out of deposit accounts (although it is also believed that depositors may tolerate small negative rate, in exchange for using banking services), while it may be easier to set negative rate on corporate deposits, as it is more difficult for firms to withdraw and hold a large amount of cash themselves. If pass-through is incomplete, negative interest rate may only reduce banks' net interest margin and their profits, making banks scale down their balance sheets and cut back lending instead; just as

Brunnermeier and Koby (2018) argue, there may even be a *reversal rate*, below which making policy rate more negative only leads to contraction in bank lending.

Evidence on policy rate pass-through under negative interest rate is documented by Eggertsson et al. (2019), based on the experience in Sweden. They find that the pass-through of policy rate to retail deposit rate stops when the policy rate falls below -0.25%, while the two rates usually go hand in hand otherwise. Given that half of bank liabilities are deposits, such collapse in pass-through may increase banks' funding cost and reduce banks' net worth. Once the pass-through of policy rate to retail deposit rate stops, lending rate stops responding to policy rate, too, and mortgage rate even slightly increases. Particularly, those banks relying more on deposit funding are less likely to cut lending rates, when deposit rate stops falling with policy rate. In addition, they find bank equity value falls with policy rate when policy rate is negative, while bank equity value increases after policy rate cut when policy rate is positive. All the evidence seems to support Brunnermeier and Koby (2018), that when policy rate becomes sufficiently negative, imperfect policy rate pass-through erodes banks' profits so that the effect of policy rate cuts on bank lending may be no more expansionary. A similar effect is found in Heider et al. (2019), based on syndicated loans issued by banks in the Euro area from 2013 to 2015. They find that those banks with higher reliance on deposit funding lend less and take more risks after policy rate falls below zero.

Bottero et al. (2019) focus on banks' rebalancing balance sheets in response to negative interest rate, using credit register data in Italy covering the universe of borrowers and lenders. Given that negative interest rate punishes banks with more balance sheet liquidity, they find that those more affected banks expand credit supply, especially to riskier and smaller firms, suggesting an expansionary effect. They do not find evidence that banks relying on more retail deposits reduce credit supply, as these banks seem to maintain their profits by charging fees on deposit accounts.

ZOMBIE LENDING

After a decade of accommodating monetary policy through aggressive and unconventional monetary policy practice in advanced economies since the Great Recession, fears arise among policy makers about banks' *zombie lending*, i.e., keeping rolling over the loans that would otherwise be non-performing. Such phenomenon gained much attention in Japan, during its decades-long economic stagnation after asset price bubble collapsed in early 1990s, as is documented by Caballero et al. (2008). During the downturn, when many firms go bust and their loans become non-performing, writing off those performing loans will lead to large cost of capital for banks. Given that banks themselves may be subject to binding constraints from regulatory capital adequacy ratio in the downturn, banks thus have the incentive to keep these bad loans afloat and "evergreen" by rolling over the loans instead of writing them off, just to keep these unprofitable borrowers, or, "zombies", alive. Such lending to zombies is thus particularly appealing, when low interest rate makes the rolling-over cost low, and when banks face tightening capital constraints.

However, keeping zombies alive is costly for the real economy. Zombies may distort market competition by subsidized funding, and zombie lending crowds out the financial resources that should otherwise be allocated to more productive firms. Caballero et al. (2008) detect zombies by firms that receive subsidized credit from banks, and find that job creation and productivity are lower in industries dominated by zombies.

Acharya et al. (2019) document evidence on zombie lending in Europe, using ECB's Outright Monetary Transactions (OMT) program that leads to banks' windfall gain in capitalization in 2012 as a natural experiment, and suggest that post-crisis weak economic recovery in Europe may be related to zombie lending. They find that banks that remain weakly capitalized after OMT are more likely to extend lending with subsidized interest rates, or, below-market loan rates—a clear feature of zombie lending. In total, roughly 8% of post-OMT loans are extended to zombies. Furthermore, they find that zombie lending does not make any real effect for zombie firms, and it crowds out lending to productive firms. Keeping zombies alive also creates excess production capacity and downward pressure on prices, so that zombie lending generates a deflationary effect on real economy, as Acharya et al.(2020) demonstrate.

7.7 EXERCISES

1. **Supply and demand in the market for reserves**
   Answer the following questions using the supply and demand analysis of the market for reserves in Section 7.2.2.

   (a) Why is it that a decrease in the discount rate does not normally lead to an increase in borrowed reserves?
   (b) Suppose that a central bank has just lowered the discount rate. Does this signal that the central bank is moving to a more expansionary monetary policy? Why or why not?
   (c) Using the supply and demand analysis of the market for reserves, indicate what happens to the equilibrium market rate, borrowed reserves, and non-borrowed reserves if

   i. The economy is unexpectedly strong, leading to an increase in the amount of bank deposits;
   ii. Banks expect an unusually large increase in withdrawals from deposit accounts in the future;
   iii. The central bank raises the target rate;
   iv. The central bank raises the interest rate on reserves above the current equilibrium market rate;
   v. The central bank reduces reserve requirements;
   vi. The central bank reduces reserve requirements, and then conducts an open market sale of securities.

CHAPTER 8
The banking-macro linkages

8.1 INTRODUCTION

Banks are playing a strategic role in the macroeconomy. The banking sector provides a large share of financial resources to the real economy so that financial frictions in banking have crucial implications for economic development and wealth distribution; banks are among the first part of the transmission chain of monetary policy so that banking outcomes under monetary expansion or contraction affect the banking effectiveness of monetary policy; and failure of banks yields severe consequences for the entire economy and enormous cost even for long-run growth. On the other hand, banks have little role in conventional macroeconomics, and financial frictions in banking are almost irrelevant in traditional macroeconomic analyses. That was why the Great Recession came as a surprise for many macroeconomists and policy makers, and conventional macroeconomics was criticized for failing to predict the Recession.

However, macroeconomists have long been trying to account for financial frictions and the role of banks in macroeconomic analytical frameworks, at least since as early as Bernanke and Gertler (1989) and Kiyotaki and Moore (1997). The early literature on banking-macro linkages captures one of the most important insights in financial frictions: the ubiquitous principal-agent problems in the financial market. As is discussed in Chapter 3, under asymmetric information between lenders and borrowers, borrowers have the incentive to misreport and default (such as in the Diamond model [Diamond 1984], Chapter 3, Section 3.2), and borrowers may have the incentive to pocket some private benefit at the cost of lenders (such as in the Holmström-Tirole model [Holmström and Tirole 1997], Chapter 3, Section 3.3); as a consequence, lenders' lending capacity is limited and borrowers face borrowing constraints from their own wealth. Business cycles affect borrowers, own wealth, or, *net worth*, hence their borrowing capacity from lenders. Expansion or contraction in borrowing and lending further affects borrowers' economic activities such as consumption, investment, and employment, the modified borrowing constraint thus has a feedback effect on the real economy and amplifies the initial business cycle shock. Financial friction thus plays a role as *financial accelerator*, in that credit availability varies with business cycles, and amplifies business cycles. We may call such mechanism as *business-driven credit cycles*.

The mechanism of financial accelerator has been intensively explored in macroeconomic research, especially after the Great Recession, and is now an important, integrated element of New Keynesian macroeconomics. The drawback of such mechanism is that it is founded on borrower-side frictions, while the lenders—very often, banks—are mostly passive and merely function as amplifiers in black boxes, or, as a veil (Gertler and Kiyotaki 2010). However, as we have seen from the previous chapters, banks are far more than passive accelerators, instead, they are often trouble makers themselves. Financial frictions do not only impose constraints on borrowers' borrowing capacity, but more importantly, such frictions distort banks' decision making as well as credit allocation. Distortions in banking outcomes obviously have important implications on real economic activities and resource distribution; fragilities and instabilities caused by banking activities destabilize the macroeconomy. In this sense, banking generated credit booms and busts also affect real economy. We may call such channel as *credit-driven business cycles*.

In this chapter, we focus on banking-macro linkages, i.e., the mechanisms of how financial frictions in banking may affect macroeconomic outcomes. We will cover the implications of both borrower-side frictions which have been more integrated in macroeconomic analytical frameworks, and bank-side frictions, which have been so far less incorporated in macroeconomic literature.

We start with principal-agent problems that lead to either borrowing constraints for borrowers or funding constraints for banks. In Section 8.2, financial friction arises from borrower side, when costly state verification problem limits borrowers' borrowing capacity and banks arise as delegated monitors. Business cycle shocks affect the borrowing constraints, and variations in total credit availability further affect the real economy, exhibiting a financial accelerator effect. In Section 8.3, we switch to the borrowing constraint on the bank side, in which bankers' moral hazard problem limits their funding from depositors, hence their lending supply to the economy, and requires banks to hold a stake in lending. A shock from the real economy influences banks' net worth and their funding capacity, making them adjust lending supply; such feedback thus amplifies the shock in the real economy.

Based on borrowers' borrowing constraints, Section 8.4 shows how occasionally binding constraints may lead to a switch in regimes, so that an economy may be trapped in deep recession and crisis even under a mild adverse shock in business cycles. When borrowing constraint becomes binding, deteriorating economic conditions generate a downward pressure on collateral value, further tightening borrowing constraints. This forces borrowers into deleveraging that aggravates economic condition. Borrowing constraints and worsening economic condition thus reinforce each other so that the economy is trapped in a downward cycle.

In Sections 8.5 and 8.6, we explore how banks' adjustments in their leverages, the so-called *leverage cycles*, increase economic volatility. Banks take leverage to increase their investment opportunities, while leverage that banks take is restricted by risk management: they need to hold sufficient equity to absorb losses. When the real economy booms, banks' profit becomes higher, raising the value of their equity and allowing them to borrow more, and vice versa, amplifying the initial shocks and increasing the volatilities in the economy. We present two mechanisms that generate leverage cycles: one is through asset prices (Section 8.5), and the other one is through funding supply of lenders in general equilibrium (Section 8.6).

8.2 COSTLY STATE VERIFICATION AND THE FINANCIAL ACCELERATOR

The financial accelerator, first explored by Bernanke and Gertler (1989), is among the pioneer ideas that integrate the financial frictions in the standard dynamic macroeconomics models. The credit constraint arises from the problem that the borrowers have the incentive to seek for private rents, so the lenders have to implement a costly auditing technology to monitor the borrowers. If the return of borrower's projects is not publicly observable without incurring costs, it is not feasible to arrange state contingent contracts with repayments dependent on the actual outcome of the investment—contrary to what usually is taken as granted in many standard models. There is a costly state verification problem. As has been well known for a long time since Townsend (1979), under such conditions a standard debt contract may be optimal, minimizing the verification costs. It has the following simple structure: borrowers have to pay back a fixed amount prearranged for repayment, independent of the actual return. Only in case the borrower claims that the actual return is not sufficient to honor repayment the true state needs to be verified. So only if the borrower defaults, verification costs have to be incurred. Thus, no borrower has an incentive to falsely claim bankruptcy in order to renege on repayment, because that claim will be verified at least with some positive probability. Those who declare bankruptcy are monitored by their creditors and lose everything.

Bernanke and Gertler (1989) have been the first to apply this insight into a dynamic general equilibrium macro models. The costly state verification model has now become the most widely used model of financial frictions in macroeconomics. A key insight is that this friction causes a financial accelerator mechanism, so credit-market frictions may significantly amplify both real and nominal shocks. Endogenous feedback mechanisms in credit markets work to amplify and propagate shocks to the macro-economy: relatively small shocks (such as modest changes in real interest rates induced by monetary policy) can have large real effects, resulting in widespread economic boom or bust. The intuition behind is fairly straightforward: with financial frictions, the borrower's net worth determines the borrowing capacity. The larger their own stake, the less serious the incentive problem. In good times, a borrower has plenty of their own funds, and hence expected agency costs are rather low, reducing effective interest rates. In contrast, the lower the wealth, the more serious the agency problem and so the higher the effective borrowing costs. This accelerator is a general feature of many models with credit frictions.

In this section, we just present a two period structure in order to illustrate the key mechanism as simple as possible. Many nonstandard assumptions that we introduce in this setting are designed to achieve analytical solutions and to see clearly the working mechanism. We use an overlapping generation model of Samuelson-Diamond type (see Samuelson 1958, Diamond 1965) with endogenous capital formation, because capital formation is at the core of the investment problem. In each generation, the population consists of a fraction of depositors with standard intertemporal preferences and a fraction of entrepreneurs. Only entrepreneurs can build capital, by operating specific projects. But entrepreneurs differ in their cost of production. Only low cost types will be able to realize their project. High cost types will get no funding. Each project has a stochastic return. For tractability, the return of capital can take on just two values. It can be either high or low.[1] To simplify saving decisions, we assume that entrepreneurs want to consume only when they are old, so they invest all their current income as equity in their own projects provided they get sufficient funding. But projects are lumpy and need additional outside finance. With the return's being not verifiable without cost, agency costs and frictions distort the outcome relative to the first best, with capital investment being too low. Furthermore, shocks to equity lead to fluctuations in capital production.

8.2.1 LENDING UNDER COSTLY STATE VERIFICATION

Consider a Samuelson-Diamond type economy in discrete time $t = 0,1,...$ populated by overlapping generations. The population of each generation is constant with one unit mass. A new generation is born at each period t,—call it generation t,—who work to earn labor income at t when they are young using their labor endowment (normalized to be 1), and save for future consumption after they are retired at $t+1$. In each generation the population is exogenously divided into two groups of agents when they are born:

1. A fraction η are entrepreneurs who own their specific production technology, which will be explained later in more detail.

The entrepreneurs are heterogeneous in the cost of production ω, which is uniformly distributed with support $[0,1]$. In the rest of this section, the entrepreneurs are ranked by their ω. The entrepreneurs do not consume when they are young, but consume their lifetime income when old;

2. The remaining fraction $1-\eta$ are depositors. These depositors consume in both periods. The life-time utility function of one representative generation t depositor is

$$U_t = u(c_t^y) + \beta u(c_{t+1}^o)$$

in which c_t^y (c_{t+1}^o) is consumption at t ($t+1$) when being young (old), and β is the discount factor. $u(\cdot)$ is strictly concave and twice differentiable.

There are two goods in the economy:

1. A consumption good—the output from production using capital and labor. This good can either be consumed, or used as input by entrepreneurs for the production of capital. As explained below, entrepreneurs can convert the consumption good into capital in the next period. The consumption good can also be stored, with gross return rate $r \geq 1$ for one period;
2. A capital good, which is not consumable, but can be used as input for producing the consumption good. In each period the depreciation rate of capital is 100%.

TECHNOLOGIES

There are different technologies for producing the consumption good and the capital good, respectively:

1. The consumption good is produced via a neoclassical technology, with labor and capital as inputs, $Y_t = \tilde{\theta}_t F(K_t, L_t)$ in which Y_t is the aggregate output in period t, K_t the aggregate capital stock, and L_t the labor supply. $\tilde{\theta}_t$ represents the random exogenous technological

shock which is i.i.d. over time with mean θ. The production function is homogeneous of degree 1 so that it can be written in per capita form

$$y_t = \tilde{\theta}_t f(k_t);$$

2. The capital good is produced through the entrepreneurs' projects. Each entrepreneur has one unit of project, which transfers y units of consumption good into k units of capital, to be used as the next period's capital input for producing consumption good. For an entrepreneur with type ω, the technology is characterized by

$$k = \begin{cases} 0 & \text{if } y < x(\omega), \\ \kappa_i & \text{if } y \geq x(\omega). \end{cases}$$

That is, each project needs to incur a fixed cost $x(\omega)$, which is an increasing function of ω. The marginal product of the project is θ if the input exceeds the threshold $x(\omega)$. The output κ_i can take two values: with probability π the output is high κ_H, and with probability $1-\pi$ the output is low $\kappa_L < \kappa_H$. Denote the expected value of κ_i as $\pi \kappa_H + (1-\pi)\kappa_L$.

THE AGENCY PROBLEM

The exact output of each project is private information for the entrepreneur owning the project, it cannot be directly verified by the outsiders. Therefore, the entrepreneur can misreport κ_H as κ_L and pocket the difference $\kappa_H - \kappa_L$ as private benefit. The other agents can learn the true value only by employing auditing. Auditing costs γ units of capital goods; it gives the exact value of output as public information. This agency problem is a classic costly state verification problem. The micro foundation has been provided by Townsend (1979), as well as Gale and Hellwig (1985).

In any period t with i_t projects deployed and a share of h_t audited, the capital intensity expected for $t+1$ is

$$k_{t+1} = (\kappa - h_t \gamma) i_t.$$

8.2.2 MARKET EQUILIBRIUM WITH NO ASYMMETRIC INFORMATION

As a reference, we first analyze the market equilibrium with perfect information, i.e., the case that there is no auditing cost to learn the true output of one project, $\gamma=0$. For any period t, denote the next period price of capital as q_{t+1}. Thus the expected return of a project invested at t is $q_{t+1}\kappa$, and the opportunity cost of investing in a project instead of storage is $rx(\omega)$. An entrepreneur will invest in his project only if the expected return exceeds opportunity cost. The profitability constraint for entrepreneur ω—call it (PC-ω)—is

$$q_{t+1}\kappa \geq rx(\omega). \mid (\text{PC}-\omega) \quad (8.1)$$

There is the cut-off value $\bar{\omega} = x^{-1}\left(\dfrac{q_{t+1}\kappa}{r}\right)$ separating the entrepreneurs: for those with low cost $\omega \leq \bar{\omega}$ it is profitable to undertake the investment, while for those with high costs $\omega > \bar{\omega}$ storage is more profitable. To focus on the interesting case, assume that the aggregate saving in the economy is large enough to finance the entrepreneurs' projects, i.e.

$$\underbrace{\eta w_t}_{(A)} + \underbrace{(1-\eta)(w_t - c_t^y)}_{(B)} > \int_0^{\bar{\omega}} x(\omega) d\omega.$$

Part (A) in the left hand side is the aggregate wage income of the entrepreneurs, and part (B) is the depositors' net income after consumption.

Out of all the entrepreneurs—whose population is η—only a share of $\bar{\omega}$ carry out the projects. As long as $\gamma=0$, the total number of the projects undertaken at t is

$$i_t = \bar{\omega}\eta. \tag{8.2}$$

So the expected capital intensity for $t+1$ is

$$k_{t+1} = \kappa i_t = \kappa\bar{\omega}\eta. \tag{8.3}$$

Combining (8.3) with (8.1) gives the equilibrium capital price

$$q_{t+1} = \frac{r}{\kappa} x\left(\frac{k_{t+1}}{\kappa\eta}\right). \tag{8.4}$$

The larger q_{t+1}, the higher the cut-off value $\bar{\omega}$, so the more entrepreneurs are willing to invest in projects producing capital. Thus, Equation (8.4) defines the supply curve (S) of capital as shown in Figure 8.1. The supply curve is upward sloping since

$$\frac{\partial q_{t+1}}{\partial k_{t+1}} = \frac{r}{\kappa^2 \eta} x'\left(\frac{k_{t+1}}{\kappa\eta}\right) > 0.$$

On the other hand, in a competitive capital market, the capital price q_{t+1} is determined by productivity. The expected marginal product of capital is:

$$q_{t+1} = E_t\left[\tilde{\theta}_{t+1}\right] f'(k_{t+1}) = \theta f'(k_{t+1}). \tag{8.5}$$

This defines the demand of capital, curve (D) in Figure 8.1, which is downward sloping since

$$\frac{\partial q_{t+1}}{\partial k_{t+1}} = \theta f''(k_{t+1}) < 0.$$

The equilibrium capital price and intensity are jointly determined by (8.4) and (8.5). As long as all other parameters are constant, in equilibrium, q and k will be constant over time. The economy builds up its capital stock k^* independent of the initial capital intensity k_0, just as in standard overlapping generation models.

8.2.3 MARKET EQUILIBRIUM WITH ASYMMETRIC INFORMATION

Now suppose that because of a costly state verification problem, the outsiders have to incur an auditing cost to learn the true output value of

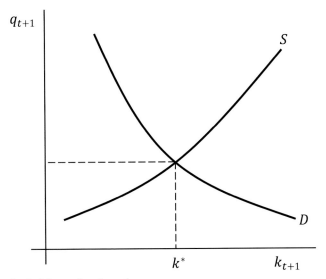

Figure 8.1 *Capital demand and supply*

the projects. This affects those entrepreneurs who need to borrow, i.e., those with small cost ω—the project's net present value is positive— provided the financing cost $x(\omega)$ exceeds the entrepreneur's savings: that is the wage income in the first period of life, or $x(\omega) > w_t$.

The optimal contract for the borrowers is determined by the revelation principle (the general theorem is explained in Mas-Colell et al. 1995, Chapter 23), which is characterized by

1. Participation constraint for depositors (PC-i): the expected return from lending must exceed the return from storage;
2. The incentive compatibility, or truth telling constraint (IC): entrepreneurs should not lie about the projects' outcomes;
3. Limited liability (LL): entrepreneurs only have limited liability.

To find the optimal contract, notice that the entrepreneur only gets private benefit if he announces the project's outcome as κ_L while the true one is κ_H. Therefore, there is no need to audit if the entrepreneur announces κ_H. Auditing is only necessary for the announcement κ_L.

Suppose a representative generation t entrepreneur's consumption is c_t^i if he announces κ_i, $i \in \{H, L\}$. When he announces κ_L, he will be audited with probability $p_t \in [0,1]$. After auditing, a contract specifies the consumption c_t^a if he tells the truth, and c_t^l if he lies. The optimal contract for the entrepreneur is to find

$$\{p_t, c_t^H, c_t^L, c_t^a, c_t^l\} = \arg\max (1-\pi)\left[p_t c_t^a + (1-p_t) c_t^L\right] + \pi c_t^H,$$

s.t.
$$(1-\pi)\left[q_{t+1}\kappa_L - p_t(c_t^a + q_{t+1}\gamma) - (1-p_t)c_t^L\right] + \pi\left(q_{t+1}\kappa_H - c_t^H\right)$$
$$\geq r\left[x(\omega) - w_t\right], \text{ (PC-}i\text{)}$$
$$c_t^H \geq (1-p_t)\left[q_{t+1}(\kappa_H - \kappa_L) + c_t^L\right] + p_t c_t^l, \text{ (IC)}$$
$$c_t^L \geq 0, \text{ (LL-1)}$$
$$c_t^a \geq 0. \text{ (LL-2)} \tag{8.6}$$

First of all, we see that in order to meet (IC) it is optimal to maximize the punishment for lying, i.e., to make sure that consumption will be minimized in that case: $c_t^l = 0$. Given that the entrepreneur always tells the truth, (PC-i) says that the expected return of the entrepreneur's project must be sufficient to repay the depositors, with the expected capital price being q_{t+1}. Further, expected consumption maximization as in object function (8.6) implies that (PC-i) is always binding. (IC) means that when κ_H is realized, the expected consumption from telling the truth must exceed that from telling a lie. (LL-1) and (LL-2) mean that there is limited liability for the entrepreneur in the bad state: even after being audited, consumption cannot be negative.

The optimal contract depends on the value of the entrepreneur's project. In the best case, the value always exceeds the entrepreneur's liability to depositors, even in the bad state. In this case, there is no need to audit, so $p_t = 0$:

$$p_t = 0 \text{ if } q_{t+1}\kappa_L \geq r\left[x(\omega) - w_t\right].$$

For given q_{t+1}, $x(\omega)$, define the minimum income level with which the entrepreneur is able to borrow without being audited as

$$w_t^*(\omega) = x(\omega) - \frac{q_{t+1}\kappa_L}{r}. \tag{8.7}$$

With $p_t = 0$, (PC-i) implies that under optimal contract

$$(1-\pi)\left(q_{t+1}\kappa_L - c_t^L\right) + \pi\left(q_{t+1}\kappa_H - c_t^H\right) = r\left[x(\omega) - w_t\right],$$

and the expected consumption of the entrepreneur is the profit from capital production

$$E[c_t] = q_{t+1}\kappa_L - r[x(\omega) - w_t]. \tag{8.8}$$

Obviously, the problem gets more interesting but also more complicated if $q_{t+1}\kappa_L < r[x(\omega) - w_t]$. Now, the value of the entrepreneur's project is not sufficient to meet the entrepreneur's liability to depositors in the bad state, so the entrepreneur would have to default. The incentive problem for entrepreneurs to misreport is the temptation to get a private benefit from $\kappa_H - \kappa_L$ by claiming κ_L. To make it least attractive to pretend a return κ_L in the good state (if κ_H is realized), the optimal contract will set $c_t^a = 0$ and $c_t^L = 0$, simplifying the (IC) condition to: $c_t^H \geq (1 - p_t)[q_{t+1}(\kappa_H - \kappa_L)]$. As long as κ_H is not too large compared to κ_L, misreporting would not be worthwhile even for $p_t = 0$. In the following, we concentrate on the interesting case that there is indeed a moral hazard problem, such that $c_t^H < [q_{t+1}(\kappa_H - \kappa_L)]$. Should there be no auditing, the entrepreneur would now always have the incentive to misreport κ_H as κ_L and pocket the difference $\kappa_H - \kappa_L$ as private benefit, making the loan contract break down. Therefore, in equilibrium, the probability of auditing, p_t, must be large enough to deter such moral hazard problem. The object function (8.6) implies that all its constraints are binding. So the equilibrium p_t can be solved as

$$p_t = \frac{r[x(\omega) - w_t] - q_{t+1}\kappa_L}{\pi q_{t+1}(\kappa_H - \kappa_L) - (1 - \pi)q_{t+1}\gamma}. \tag{8.9}$$

As long as the gain from deterring misreporting, $\pi q_{t+1}(\kappa_H - \kappa_L)$, exceeds the cost of auditing, $(1 - \pi)q_{t+1}\gamma$, the probability of auditing, p_t, is always positive. One can further infer from (8.9) that p_t decreases with the entrepreneur's own saving, w_t. The intuition behind is fairly straightforward: the higher the own stake the entrepreneur holds in the investment, the less he needs to borrow and hence, the less private benefit he would get from misreporting. So the higher the stake, the less severe the moral hazard problem is. Obviously, with increasing inside funds, there is less need for external finance, reducing the agency cost.

Applying (8.9) in (PC-i), the expected consumption of the entrepreneur is

$$E[c_t] = \frac{\pi q_{t+1}(\kappa_H - \kappa_L)}{\pi q_{t+1}(\kappa_H - \kappa_L) - (1-\pi)q_{t+1}\gamma}\{q_{t+1}\kappa - r[x(\omega) - w_t] - (1-\pi)q_{t+1}\gamma\}.$$
(8.10)

From (8.8), we see that $\frac{\partial E[c_t]}{\partial w_t} = r$ when there is no agency problem. In this case, any additional unit of saving will become an additional unit of investment on the project, returning the market rate of investment. In contrast, now we have $\frac{\partial E[c_t]}{\partial w_t} = \frac{\pi q_{t+1}(\kappa_H - \kappa_L)}{\pi q_{t+1}(\kappa_H - \kappa_L) - (1-\pi)q_{t+1}\gamma} r > r.$ With costly state verification, having one additional unit of internal funds has two effects: first, as before it returns r from the capital market; second, by having one unit more "inside" funding from own pocket, the entrepreneur needs one unit less "outside" funding from borrowing. Since agency costs are reduced, this allows him to create more resources for consumption. Agency costs create a wedge between internal and external funding: the effective cost of external finance exceeds r. For that reason, fewer entrepreneurs will carry out their projects compared to the solution without frictions.

For an arbitrary entrepreneur ω, whether he will be successful in getting sufficient funding to carry out his project depends on his expected profit: the difference between the expected return of the project and its opportunity cost including auditing cost, $E_t[R_{t+1}(\omega)] = q_{t+1}\kappa - rx(\omega) - p(1-\pi)q_{t+1}\gamma$. So expected profit depends on his type ω and the probability of being audited. There are several generic cases:

1. He is never able to start the project because the expected profit of the project is negative, even when in the absence of auditing cost with $p = 0$,

$$E_t[R_{t+1}(\omega)] = q_{t+1}\kappa - rx(\omega) < 0,$$

or,

$$\omega > \bar{\omega} = x^{-1}\left(\frac{q_{t+1}\kappa}{r}\right);$$

2. He is always able to start the project because the expected profit is always positive, even when there is the maximum auditing cost with $p=1$,

$$E_t\left[R_{t+1}(\omega)\right]=q_{t+1}\kappa-rx(\omega)-(1-\pi)q_{t+1}\gamma>0,$$

or,

$$0\leq\omega<\underline{\omega}=x^{-1}\left(\frac{q_{t+1}\kappa-(1-\pi)q_{t+1}\gamma}{r}\right);$$

3. For the intermediate range $\underline{\omega}<\omega<\bar{\omega}$, whether he is successful depends on the auditing probability p.

Those in case 1 will become depositors, lending their income to the successful entrepreneurs instead of operating the projects by themselves. Those in case 2 are certainly successful entrepreneurs, but whether their projects will be audited or not depends on their income—there is no auditing only if the wage income exceeds $w_t^*(\omega)$ so that the project is fully collateralized (compared with equation 8.7). There is auditing if the wage income is below $w_t^*(\omega)$, and the auditing probability is given by (8.9) as

$$p_t=\frac{r[x(\omega)-w_t]-q_{t+1}\kappa_L}{\pi q_{t+1}(\kappa_H-\kappa_L)-(1-\pi)q_{t+1}\gamma}.$$

Those in case 3 are ambiguous, call them "swinging entrepreneurs". As (8.9) shows, the auditing probability p is negatively correlated with w_t. Therefore, if these entrepreneurs contract directly with depositors, when an entrepreneur has efficiently low ω and his w_t is high enough to make $E_t\left[R_{t+1}(\omega)\right]>0$, the entrepreneur will carry out the project. In contrast, when an entrepreneur is not sufficiently efficient and his w_t is not high enough that the auditing probability p (and hence the auditing cost) is so high to make $E_t\left[R_{t+1}(\omega)\right]=q_{t+1}\kappa-rx(\omega)-(1-\pi)q_{t+1}\gamma<0$, the entrepreneur will be barred from running his project.

However, even for the least efficient swinging entrepreneur, i.e., the entrepreneur whose ω is close to $\bar{\omega}$, his project is still profitable, or, socially beneficial, should there be no auditing. Therefore, there is a need for financial intermediation that allows all swinging entrepreneurs to invest and improves social welfare. Such financial intermediation is introduced in the following way:

- Suppose that all swinging entrepreneurs delegate their projects to the most efficient person among them, i.e., the entrepreneur whose ω is the closest to $\underline{\omega}$ —call him a "banker" with efficiency level ω^*;
- The banker pools all wage income w_t from swinging entrepreneurs and invests only in fully collateralized projects that need $w_t^*(\omega^*)$ "inside" funding each. The banker borrows the rest ("outside" funding) from depositors to initiate these projects;
- To focus only on the borrowers' problem, assume that the banker is perfectly monitored by the other entrepreneurs and works only for the group's interest, i.e., there is no friction in the financial intermediation;
- The profit from the projects is distributed among all swinging entrepreneurs, proportional to the inverse of each one's efficiency level ω.

In the presence of financial intermediation, the entrepreneurs divide themselves into three groups, as Figure 8.2 shows:

- The most efficient entrepreneurs, or, successful entrepreneurs, contract directly with depositors—call it "direct finance", each of them is able to carry out his own project, even sometimes subject to a small fee of auditing;
- The less efficient entrepreneurs, or, swinging entrepreneurs, delegate their projects to the bank—call it "bank finance". The bank has the expertise in producing fully collateralized projects, or, safe assets, to the depositors. Although the bank can only fund fewer projects than the population of swinging entrepreneurs (note that the number of collateralized projects that can be funded by one entrepreneur's income, $\dfrac{w_t}{w_t^*(\omega^*)}$, is less than 1 for this group), it allows all of them—even the less efficient ones—to benefit from the supported projects and avoid the high auditing cost which these entrepreneurs would have to incur, should they contract directly with the depositors;

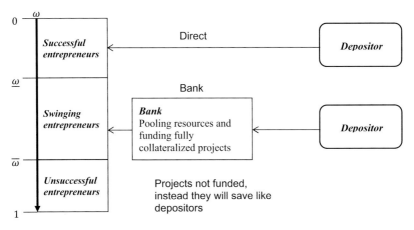

Figure 8.2 *Funding structure of the economy*

- The least efficient entrepreneurs, or, unsuccessful entrepreneurs, whose projects are too expensive to be profitable for funding. Those entrepreneurs will not get any funding and will instead invest their own funds in other projects just like the depositors.

The funding structure resembles the reality fairly well: well established, usually big firms, can easily fund themselves directly from investors, for example, on the bond market, subject to small fees charged by bookrunners, credit rating agencies, etc. Less well established, typically small and medium size firms, usually cannot access the bond market, but they can still apply for bank loans; it is often very hard for the start-up firms with few tangible assets to raise funding. Similar funding structure arises from other agency cost based models, such as Holmström and Tirole (1997) in Chapter 3, Section 3.3.

Now, under such funding structure in the economy, the production of capital will be carried out by the successful entrepreneurs (possibly with auditing) and the delegated swinging entrepreneurs (without auditing):

$$k_{t+1} = \left[\underbrace{\kappa \underline{\omega} - \pi \gamma \int_0^{\underline{\omega}} p_t(\omega) d\omega}_{(A)} + \underbrace{\kappa \int_{\underline{\omega}}^{\bar{\omega}} \frac{w_t}{w_t^*(\omega^*)} d\omega}_{(B)} \right] \eta, \qquad (8.11)$$

in which term (A) is the capital production from the (partially) audited directly financed projects deducting the auditing cost, term (B) from the non-audited bank financed projects, and in term (A)

$$p_t(\omega) = \begin{cases} \dfrac{r[x(\omega)-w_t]-q_{t+1}\kappa_L}{\pi q_{t+1}(\kappa_H-\kappa_L)-(1-\pi)q_{t+1}\gamma} & \text{if } w_t < w_t^*(\omega), \\ 0 & \text{otherwise.} \end{cases}$$

In contrast to the market equilibrium without financial friction where q and k are constant over time, here the agency problem generates both short-term (intra-period) and long-term fluctuations through the supply curve of capital, although the demand curve remains the same as before, as Figure 8.3 shows.

First of all, notice that the supply curve of capital with financial friction (such as the dark gray curve S') is always above the supply curve without financial friction (the black curve S) as Figure 8.3 shows, since the agency problem implies a dead weight loss in capital production (the triangle ΔABE in the figure, corresponding to a lower capital production $k' < k^*$). This can be easily seen from (8.11):

$$k_{t+1} = \left[\kappa\underline{\omega} - \pi\gamma \int_0^{\underline{\omega}} p_t(\omega)d\omega + \kappa \int_{\underline{\omega}}^{\bar{\omega}} \dfrac{w_t}{w_t^*(\omega^*)} d\omega \int_{\underline{\omega}}^{\bar{\omega}} \right] \eta$$

$$< \left[\kappa\underline{\omega} + \kappa(\bar{\omega}-\underline{\omega}) \right] \eta$$

$$= \kappa\bar{\omega}\eta,$$

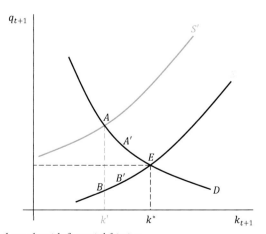

Figure 8.3 *Capital supply with financial friction*

given that $\pi\gamma \int_0^{\bar{\omega}} p_t(\omega)d\omega \geq 0$ and $\frac{w_t}{w_t^*(\omega^*)} < 1$, that the total capital output is always lower than that in the frictionless economy, $\kappa\bar{\omega}\eta$, as in (8.3).

In the short-run, notice that the supply of capital k_{t+1} depends on the number of the entrepreneurs who participate the capital production at t, and this depends on the entrepreneurs' income w_t. The neoclassical production function $y_t = \tilde{\theta}_t f(k_t)$ implies that $w_t = \tilde{\theta}_t[f(k_t) - k_t f'(k_t)]$, which depends on the technological shock $\tilde{\theta}_t$. When the realized $\tilde{\theta}_t$ is high, the entrepreneurs' wage income increases, too. This increases the net worth of the projects from the successful entrepreneurs, making them more likely to face lower probability of being audited, or even completely collateralized so that there is no need for auditing at all. As a result, the agency cost is lower and there will be more resources devoted to capital production. Further, the increase in the entrepreneurs' income makes the bank able to finance more fully collateralized projects, given the number of collateralized projects that can be funded by one entrepreneur's income, $\frac{w_t}{w_t^*(\omega^*)}$, is increasing in w_t. These two effects jointly shift the capital supply curve S'' closer to the frictionless equilibrium supply curve S, leading to a higher level of capital production k'' and reduced dead weight loss in capital production (the triangle $\Delta A'B'E$), as Figure 8.3 shows. Formally, from (8.11) one can see that

$$\frac{\partial k_{t+1}}{\partial w_t} = \left[-\pi\gamma \int_0^{\bar{\omega}} \frac{\partial p_t(\omega)}{\partial w_t} d\omega + \kappa \int_{\underline{\omega}}^{\bar{\omega}} \frac{\partial \frac{w_t}{w_t^*(\omega^*)}}{\partial w_t} d\omega \right] \eta$$

$$= \left[\underbrace{-\pi\gamma \int_0^{\bar{\omega}} \frac{\partial p_t(\omega)}{\partial w_t} d\omega}_{(A) \geq 0} + \underbrace{\kappa \int_{\underline{\omega}}^{\bar{\omega}} \frac{\partial \frac{1}{w_t^*(\omega^*)}}{\partial w_t} d\omega}_{(B) > 0} \right] \eta,$$

given that $\frac{\partial p_t(\omega)}{\partial w_t} \leq 0, \frac{\partial k_{t+1}}{\partial w_t} > 0$. Term (A) and (B) reflect the effects from reduced auditing cost in the directly financed projects and increased number of bank financed projects, respectively.

The interesting feature here is that the economic boom does not only increase the net worth of the projects which enables the entrepreneurs to expand their balance sheets, but also makes more entrepreneurs accessible to outside funding which further increases the capital output—exhibiting a financial accelerator effect.

On the contrary, when the realized $\tilde{\theta}_t$ is low, the entrepreneurs' wage income declines. The fall in the projects' net worth both increases the auditing costs for the successful entrepreneurs and drives down the number of bank financed projects. These two effects jointly shift the capital supply curve away from the frictionless equilibrium supply curve S, leading to a lower level of capital production and increased dead weight loss in capital production.

Such short-run fluctuations also ripple into the long-run future. Since the impact of fluctuations in the level of capital will persist for some time, the impact on economic activity is likely to be more persistent than the initial shock. A positive technological shock $\tilde{\theta}_t$ leads to higher capital output from period t projects, or, higher capital input k_{t+1} for period $t+1$ production. This makes the economy more resilient in the next period, i.e., when there is a negative technological shock $\tilde{\theta}_{t+1}$ the wage income w_{t+1} won't decline as long as the shock is small, so that there is even a persistent economic growth in the mid-term.[2]

8.2.4 SUMMARY

The financial accelerator is a powerful modelling device for introducing the financial frictions in the standard macroeconomic model in a tractable way. The idea is heavily explored to uncover the impact of credit constraints on macro economy, following Bernanke et al. (1999) that integrate the financial accelerator in a full-fledged dynamic stochastic general equilibrium (DSGE) model.

The Bernanke-Gertler model focuses only on the borrower side frictions, assuming perfectly functioning financial intermediaries. Nevertheless, the role of the bank in the model is non-trivial: it provides an insurance for the depositors, by producing safe assets (fully collateralized projects); therefore, depositors are free from bankruptcy cost in the bad state. On the other hand, all less efficient entrepreneurs are able to access external funding and exempted from costly auditing, improving social welfare—these are exactly what financial intermediaries are doing in the real world, making them socially desirable institutions.

However, as we have seen from previous chapters, financial intermediaries are prone to incentive problems themselves, and banking outcomes under principal-agent problems often lead to a fragile banking structure; this also has profound implications for the macroeconomy. In the next sections, we will see how problems arise from the frictions inside financial intermediaries.

8.3 MORAL HAZARD AND BANK LENDING

The Bernanke-Gertler model provides important insight on how financial frictions affect borrowing constraints and amplify business cycles. However, the approach is largely based on borrower-side frictions, leaving financial intermediaries or banks largely in a black box. In fact, financial frictions also affect bank behavior and banking outcomes, which influence the real economy.

In this section, following a similar vein as in the Bernanke-Gertler model that borrowing constraints arise from principal-agent problems, in this section, we focus on bank-side borrowing constraints and show how bank side financial frictions affect bank lending using a simple model based on Gertler and Kiyotaki (2010) and Gertler and Karadi (2011).

8.3.1 AGGREGATE DEPOSIT SUPPLY WITHOUT FINANCIAL FRICTION

Consider an economy that is populated by many identical households who live for two periods, $t=1,2$. Each of the households has an initial wealth N to start with. In each household, some members are workers, while the others are bankers. To focus on the financial friction, we abstract from the production sector in this economy and assume that for a representative household

1. In $t=1$ the workers work and earn a fixed labor income y. They deposit d in competitive banks and leave the rest for the entire household's current consumption. The bankers establish banks, using the household's initial wealth N. Bankers offer deposits to workers from all households on a competitive market, taking the deposit rate r as given. Using these funds, banks issue loans L to firms (which we do not explicitly model);
2. In $t=2$ the loans yield a fixed gross return R. Workers withdraw deposits from banks with gross return r. Bankers then dissolve their bank, and pay out the banks' profit—call it π to their own household.

We assume that consumption is shared equally across all members within a household. Each household maximizes utility from consumption in both periods, i.e.,

$$\max_{\{c_1,c_2\}} u(c_1)+u(c_2).$$

Suppose the utility function takes the form of $u(c)=\dfrac{c^{1-\gamma}}{1-\gamma}, \gamma > 0$. The budget constraint of the household for $t=1$ is

$$c_1+d \leq y$$

and for $t=2$ the budget constraint is

$$c_2 \leq rd+\pi.$$

In addition $c_1>0$, $c_2>0$, and $d>0$. The solution to the household's problem is therefore

$$c_1 = \frac{yr+\pi}{r^{\frac{1}{\gamma}}+r}, d=y-c_1, c_2=rd+\pi.$$

Assets	Liabilities
Loans, L	Equity, N
	Deposits, d

Figure 8.4 *The banks' balance sheet*

Let us now endogenize the banks' profit, π, analyzing the bankers' decision problem. Note that bankers use their own household's wealth N as equity. They get deposits d from workers, and issue loans L to firms; this implies a bank's balance sheet as Figure 8.4 shows.

The banks' problem is thus to maximize profits with $L = N + d$:

$$\max_{d} \pi = RL - rd.$$

Without financial friction, the equilibrium is characterized by the conditions

1. Bankers and households solve their decision problems, and
2. The market for deposits is cleared.

In equilibrium, R must be equal to r; otherwise, banks would either accept no deposit if $R < r$, or demand infinite deposits if $R > r$.

Before we introduce financial friction, we compute the planner's problem as a benchmark. A social planner maximizes a representative household's welfare by

$$\max_{\{c_1, c_2\}} u(c_1) + u(c_2),$$

$$\text{s.t.} \quad c_1 + d \leq y,$$

$$c_2 \leq rd + \pi,$$

$$\pi = RL - rd = R(N + d) - rd,$$

$$c_1 > 0, c_2 > 0, d > 0, R = r.$$

The solution is almost the same as the solution to the household's problem:

$$c_1 = \frac{yr + \pi}{r^{\frac{1}{\gamma}} + r}, \quad d = y - \frac{yr + \pi}{r^{\frac{1}{\gamma}} + r}, \quad c_2 = R(N + d).$$

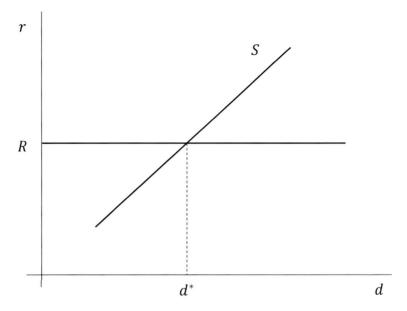

Figure 8.5 *Deposit market equilibrium in the absence of moral hazard*

In the absence of financial frictions, the household's supply of deposits, $S = d = y - \dfrac{yr + R(N+d) - rd}{r^{\frac{1}{\gamma}} + r}$, is upward sloping with respect to deposit rate r, and banks' demand for deposits is infinitely elastic at the constant deposit rate $r = R$. The equilibrium is characterized in Figure 8.5.

8.3.2 AGGREGATE DEPOSIT DEMAND UNDER FINANCIAL FRICTION

Now we introduce a financial friction arising from banker's moral hazard problem: instead of honoring all the claims and paying out the remaining profit, bankers have the opportunity to divert a share θ of banks' total assets for their private consumption and leave only the rest to the depositors. With insufficient funds to honor deposit contracts, they have to default in $t = 2$. The higher the amount of funds d deposited at some bank, the stronger the temptation to the banker to divert assets. Being aware of the moral hazard problem, in $t = 1$, depositors can infer the likelihood of default of a bank. They will only deposit in those banks which will not default. So there is an incentive compatibility constraint: a banker's profit from the no-default option must exceed the private benefit from diverting assets:

$$\pi = R(N+d) - rd \geq \theta R(N+d).$$

Obviously, this gives an upper bound to the amount of deposits d that a bank can collect. It will be limited by the own equity N and meets the following condition:

$$0 \leq d \leq \frac{(1-\theta)RN}{r-(1-\theta)R}. \quad \text{(IC)}$$

The banks' problem is thus characterized by maximizing profits subject to the incentive constraint (IC). To find the solution, first note that banks will not take any deposit if $R < r$. They are indifferent if $R = r$ as long as (IC) holds, or, $d \leq \frac{(1-\theta)N}{\theta}$. For $R > r$, banks are willing to accept deposits, but the actual amount savers are willing to deposit is bounded by (IC). In addition, since $0 \leq d$ the deposit rate is bounded below, $r > (1-\theta)R$. To summarize, banks' demand for deposits, as a function of r, is

$$D = \begin{cases} \left[0, \dfrac{(1-\theta)N}{\theta}\right], & \text{if } r = R, \\ \dfrac{(1-\theta)RN}{r-(1-\theta)R}, & \text{if } (1-\theta)R < r < R. \end{cases}$$

The equilibrium is presented in Figure 8.6. The supply curve is still upward sloping, while the demand curve for deposits is kinked: it stays horizontal at $r = R$ as long as $d \leq \frac{(1-\theta)N}{\theta}$. Then, it becomes downward sloping with r. To see the implication of moral hazard, suppose banks start with high initial wealth N so that in equilibrium, the supply curve crosses the demand curve on the horizontal part, with no interest rate spread, or, $r = R$. In that case, bankers' stake in their bank is high: they can earn higher profit as stake holders than by diverting some private benefits. When banks' net worth is high enough, there will be no strategic default.

However, things change if the bankers' stake value is low. Suppose households' initial wealth N is falling, possibly as a result of recession

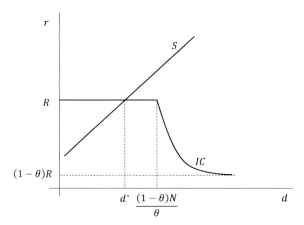

Figure 8.6 Deposit market equilibrium in the presence of moral hazard with high equity

in the real economy. This has an immediate impact on the demand for deposits: falling N shifts the IC curve to the left. If N is low enough, the supply curve will cross the demand curve on its downward sloping part in equilibrium. The intuition is clear: with low banks' net worth, bankers have less stake in the banks, so strategic default becomes attractive. The gain from private benefit in the default is high, while the loss in losing the stakes is low. With temptation for default being so prominent, in order to maintain the financial intermediation service, bankers need to get paid some information rent in order to stay in business instead of defaulting. So the rate for depositors is now lower than the return R, dampening incentives to save.

As is shown in Figure 8.7, the new equilibrium in the deposit market is thus characterized by an interest rate spread $R-r>0$ and lower bank deposits; as a result, bank lending, $L = N+d$, will be inefficiently low.

8.3.3 SUMMARY

The Gertler-Karadi-Kiyotaki model is among the pioneers that examine the implication of bank-side financial frictions on macroeconomic outcomes. Banks have the incentive to engage in moral hazard and pocket private benefit at the cost of depositors. Such moral hazard limits the deposits banks can raise, and makes banks' funding sensitive to banks' net worth. Therefore, when adverse business cycles' shocks reduce banks' net worth,

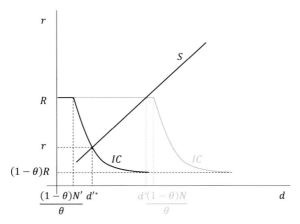

Figure 8.7 Drop in deposits when moral hazard problem dominates. Black IC is the new demand curve under falling households' initial wealth N

binding borrowing constraints result in a sharp fall in bank funding, hence bank lending to the real economy, exacerbating the recession.

Ideally, in the Gertler-Karadi-Kiyotaki model, banks will be better off if they hold more capital and avoid binding borrowing constraints in the recession. However, individual banks hardly have the incentive to build up capital buffers, when the same financial frictions prevail, as Dávila and Korinek (2018) show: given the feedback between bank lending and real economic activities, one bank's investment in costly capital buffer stabilizes credit supply to the real economy and benefits other banks, too—a positive externality, so that individual banks tend to undervalue social benefit of having stronger buffers when their borrowing constraints are binding. A required capital adequacy ratio set by the regulator to internalize such externality is thus desirable to improve social welfare.

8.4 OVERBORROWING AND EXCESS VOLATILITY

Financial friction induced borrowing constraints do not only amplify business cycles, but also have the potential to generate extra volatility, especially when borrowing constraints are *occasionally* binding. That is, when the macroeconomy is in a boom, borrowers' net worth is high so that their borrowing is not constrained. However, when the economy is in recession and borrowers' net worth deteriorates, their borrowing constraints become binding. To make it worse, as borrowers' net worth is affected by macroeconomic performance, the net worth deteriorates in recession, too; this makes borrowing constraints even tighter and forces borrowers to deleverage. However, the costly deleverage makes the recession even worse and borrowers' net worth even lower… the feedback interaction between net worth and macroeconomy will trap the economy in a deep recession. In this section, we explain how occasionally binding borrowing constraints add extra volatility to macroeconomy, using a simplified model from Bianchi (2011).

8.4.1 COLLATERALIZED LENDING AND BORROWING CONSTRAINT

The analytical framework is based on a standard real business cycle (RBC) model with borrowing constraint. Consider, in an economy, a representative household maximizes its expected life time utility from consumption c_t in each period t, $t = 0,1,\ldots,+\infty$

$$\max_{\{c_t, b_{t+1}\}} E_0 \left[\sum_{t=0}^{+\infty} \beta^t u(c_t) \right] \tag{8.12}$$

with a discount factor of β, $0 < \beta < 1$. The utility function is standard and neoclassical, such that utility is strictly increasing and concave in consumption,

$$u'(c_t) > 0, u''(c_t) < 0, \text{and } -\frac{c_t u'''(c_t)}{u''(c_t)} > 0.$$

The last assumption states that the household's *relative prudence* is positive so that it has the incentive to conduct precautionary saving—saving more when the future income becomes riskier (see Kimball 1990 for more details).

Consumption is the aggregate of tradable good c^T and nontradable good c^N, with

$$c_t = \left[\left(c^T\right)^{-\eta} + \left(c^N\right)^{-\eta}\right]^{\frac{1}{\eta}}$$

in which η captures the elasticity of substitution between these two goods. The difference between these two goods is that non-tradable goods cannot be traded so that they must be consumed within each period, while tradable goods can be traded as a way to adjust total debt and consumption in each period.

In each period t, the household receives an endowment of tradable good y_t^T and an endowment of nontradable good y_t^N. It can borrow to increase consumption, so that the budget constraint is

$$b_{t+1} + c_t^T + p_t^N c_t^N = b_t(1+r) + y_t^T + p_t^N y_t^N \qquad (8.13)$$

in which b_t is the initial debt at the beginning of t, with price of tradables being numeraire $p_t^T = 1$ and price of nontradables being p_t^N. We follow the convention that $b_t < 0$ if it is debt. In addition, borrowing is collateralized by period t income

$$b_{t+1} \geq -\kappa\left(y_t^T + p_t^N y_t^N\right). \qquad (8.14)$$

Obviously, borrowing constraint (8.14) is a device to solve a moral hazard problem in debt finance: as the borrower can always get the money from the lender and run away, the borrower cannot borrow without providing collateral. If the borrower does run away, the lender can seize the collateral and recover her lending.

8.4.2 BINDING BORROWING CONSTRAINT AND EXCESS VOLATILITY

The household's optimization problem is thus defined by its object function (8.12), budget constraint (8.13), and borrowing constraint (8.14). The problem is solved by using Lagrangian

$$\mathcal{L} = E_0\left[\sum_{t=0}^{+\infty}\beta^t u(c_t)\right] + \sum_{i=0}^{+\infty}\lambda_{t+i}\left[b_{t+i}(1+r) + y_{t+i}^T + p_{t+i}^N y_{t+i}^N - b_{t+1+i} - c_{t+i}^T - p_{t+i}^N c_{t+i}^N\right]$$

$$+ \sum_{i=0}^{+\infty}\nu_{t+i}\left[b_{t+1+i} + \kappa\left(y_{t+i}^T + p_{t+i}^N y_{t+i}^N\right)\right]. \qquad (8.15)$$

The household's problem is solved by the first-order conditions of (8.15),

$$\frac{\partial \mathcal{L}}{\partial c_t^T} = 0, \qquad (8.16)$$

$$\frac{\partial \mathcal{L}}{\partial c_t^N} = 0, \qquad (8.17)$$

$$\frac{\partial \mathcal{L}}{\partial b_{t+1}} = 0. \qquad (8.18)$$

From equations (8.16) and (8.17), it's easily seen that

$$\frac{\partial c_t / \partial c_t^N}{\partial c_t / \partial c_t^T} = p_t^N$$

Applying the definition of c_t, it leads to

$$\left(\frac{c_t^T}{c_t^N}\right)^{1+\eta} = p_t^N. \qquad (8.19)$$

Note that condition (8.19) only involves the budget constraint, and is not related to the borrowing constraint.

Solving equation (8.18) to get

$$(1+r)\lambda_{t+1} - \lambda_t + v_t = 0. \qquad (8.20)$$

Note that the Kuhn-Tucker condition for the borrowing constraint with inequality implies that

$$v_t \begin{cases} = 0 & \text{if } b_{t+1} > -\kappa\left(y_t^T + p_t^N y_t^N\right), \\ \geq 0 & \text{if } b_{t+1} = -\kappa\left(y_t^T + p_t^N y_t^N\right). \end{cases}$$

This implies that the first-order condition (8.20) can be written as

$$\begin{cases} \dfrac{\partial u}{\partial c_t^T} = \beta(1+r)\dfrac{\partial u}{\partial c_{t+1}^T} & \text{if } b_{t+1} > -\kappa\left(y_t^T + p_t^N y_t^N\right), \\ \dfrac{\partial u}{\partial c_t^T} \geq \beta(1+r)\dfrac{\partial u}{\partial c_{t+1}^T} & \text{if } b_{t+1} = -\kappa\left(y_t^T + p_t^N y_t^N\right). \end{cases}$$

Note that when borrowing constraint is not binding, the first-order condition on the household's intertemporal consumption,

$$\frac{\partial u}{\partial c_t^T} = \beta(1+r)\frac{\partial u}{\partial c_{t+1}^T} \qquad (8.21)$$

is simply the Euler equation as in the standard RBC model. However, when borrowing constraint is binding, the first-order condition on the household's intertemporal consumption,

$$\frac{\partial u}{\partial c_t^T} \geq \beta(1+r)\frac{\partial u}{\partial c_{t+1}^T}$$

implies that marginal utility of consumption in period t is higher than the long-run trend, or, the consumption in period t is lower. That is, the household would like to borrow and consume more, but binding borrowing constraint prevents it from doing so, leading to a distortion in consumption.

Suppose an unexpected negative shock, say, a recession, arrives in period t, leading to a lower income from tradable good y_t^T. What will be the impact on the household's consumption?

Case 1: if borrowing constraint is not binding, or

$$b_{t+1} > -\kappa\left(y_t^T + p_t^N y_t^N\right),$$

the model collapses to a standard RBC model: as a nontradable good must be consumed, $y_t^N = c_t^N$; from budget constraint (8.13) for period t, a fall in y_t^T thus leads to falls in both c_t^T and b_{t+1}. With lower b_{t+1}, by the Euler equation (8.21) consumption in the next period, c_{t+1}^T, will fall, too. The income shock y_t^T is alleviated by smoothing in household consumption;

Case 2: if borrowing constraint is binding, or,

$$b_{t+1} = -\kappa\left(y_t^T + p_t^N y_t^N\right),$$

things will be totally different. Same as before, a nontradable good must be consumed, $y_t^N = c_t^N$, and a fall in y_t^T leads to a fall in c_t^T. However, by the equilibrium condition (8.19), a fall in consumption demand c_t^T leads to a fall in the price of nontradable good, p_t^N. Given that the household' borrowing constraint (8.14) is binding, a fall in p_t^N reduces collateral value and tightens borrowing constraint, thus results in a rise in b_{t+1} and a lower borrowing capacity. Now with higher b_{t+1}, the budget constraint (8.13) implies that consumption c_t^T must be cut further, to accommodate the falling borrowing capacity, while falling c_t^T imposes further downward pressure on p_t^N by condition (8.19), further aggravating the borrowing constraint (8.14)… this leads to a downward spiral which traps the economy in a deep recession with much lower equilibrium consumption, c_t^T.

A more interesting scenario arises when the borrowing constraint (8.14) is *occasionally* binding. Remember that when the borrowing constraint is not binding, the economy works well in that the household is able to borrow and smooth its consumption, should a recession be materialized in t in the economy, with only a moderate fall in c_t^T. However, if the household's borrowing constraint is almost binding before the recession, when the recession is materialized, even a moderate fall in c_t^T and subsequent fall in p_t^N may make the borrowing constraint binding. Once the borrowing constraint is binding, the household suddenly finds itself in the Case 2 scenario: it would like to borrow to smooth consumption, but its binding borrowing constraint prevents it from doing so; on the contrary, its falling collateral value and shrinking borrow capacity even force it to cut consumption, which further exacerbates its borrowing constraint… such "sudden-stop" of financing in the recession is just as Mark Twain (1835–1910) states:

> A banker is a fellow who lends you his umbrella when the sun is shining, but wants it back the minute it begins to rain.

8.4.3 SUMMARY

The Bianchi model illustrates how borrowing constraints may interact with economic conditions and reinforce each other. Such reinforcement is particularly destructive, when borrowing constraints are occasionally binding, which most likely occur in the recessions when credit is needed the most. Suddenly binding borrowing constraints may trap the economy in a deep recession.

One appealing feature of the Bianchi model is the nonlinear effects generated by the occasionally binding borrowing constraints, which addresses the sudden-stop feature of crises in reality. It is often challenging for macroeconomic models with financial frictions to capture the drastic and abrupt systemic failure during financial crises, and the technical difficulties in modelling nonlinearities limit the capability of macroeconomic models to predict the severity of crises. Occasionally binding borrowing constraints with regime switching, such as in the Bianchi model, thus provide a powerful tool in modelling crises. Recently, more achievements have been made in modelling off-equilibrium, nonlinear behavior of macroeconomic systems with financial frictions, such as Brunnermeier and Sannikov (2014) based on modelling financial accelerator effects using continuous-time approach, He and Krishnamurthy (2013) focusing on occasionally binding constraints on financial intermediation, Gertler and Kiyotaki (2015) incorporating the Diamond-Dybvig type of bank runs (see Chapter 2, Section 2.4.4) in macroeconomic modelling, Boissay et al. (2016) modelling crises through switching between multiple equilibria... while these approaches usually rely on highly technical global solution method which is beyond the scope of this book.

8.5 RISK MANAGEMENT AND THE LEVERAGE CYCLE

In this and next section, we focus on how financial frictions within banks amplify business cycles and add volatility to the macroeconomy, particularly on the leverage cycles coming from banks' active management on their balance sheets. As is shown in Adrian and Shin (2014) and Bruno and Shin (2015b), the size of the balance sheets of investment banks and the amount they borrow are procyclical. In particular, during normal times, these intermediaries borrow aggressively, build up leverage and load up on risk. This behavior raises the demand for risky assets during the boom. When risk and volatility increase, these institutions reverse this process. They shrink their balance sheets and deleverage. This reduces the supply of credit and the demand for risky assets, creating very powerful procyclicality that may threaten macroeconomic stability: if the process of deleveraging is sharp enough, failures and financial instability can follow. Risky borrowers who received credit in the boom period cannot finance themselves any longer. The highly leveraged positions put on in good times become a downward accelerator. In this section, we show how a leverage cycle that amplifies real and monetary policy shocks emerges as a result of banks' risk management practice, using the model from Cao (2012) which is based on Shin (2010).

8.5.1 MARKET EQUILIBRIUM AND ASSET PRICE

The risk management practice in financial institutions is widely based on the Value-at-Risk (VaR) assessments. The VaR of a portfolio of a bank's assets defines the worst loss over a certain time horizon such that with a pre-specified probability the realized loss is larger. Quantitatively, the VaR of a portfolio of assets at confidence level α means that the event that the realized loss L exceeds VaR happens at a probability no higher than $1-\alpha$, i.e., $\text{Prob}(L > VaR) \leq 1-\alpha$, or equivalently $\text{Prob}(L < VaR) \geq \alpha$.

For example, the VaR of a portfolio over one month at confidence level 99% means that the probability of having a loss larger than VaR does not exceed 1%, or with 99% probability the realized loss is below VaR within the next month. Since VaR gives a clear assessment on a financial firm's potential loss during a certain period and a reference about the buffer the firm needs to hold to avoid bankruptcy, it is widely adopted as a key indicator in risk management.

Banks' active management of their balance sheets using VaR brings extra volatility to asset prices and amplifies the market turbulence in the crises. The mechanism can be seen from the following model. Consider an economy that extends to two periods, $t = 0, 1$. There are two types of assets in this economy:

1. The risky assets. They are securities issued by a fix number of entrepreneurs, traded in the initial period, $t = 0$, at the price level P, and the holders of the assets get the return from the assets at $t = 1$. The stochastic return from one unit of risky asset holding, R, follows a uniform distribution over the interval $\left[\bar{R} - z, \bar{R} + z\right]$, with $z > 0$. The

expected value of R, $E[R]$ is $\bar{R}$, and the variance of R is therefore $\text{var}[R] = \dfrac{z^2}{3}$;

2. The riskless assets in the form of bank deposits, which pay a fixed gross return $r \geq 1$ for the holders.

There are also two groups of agents, with a unit of population for each group, in the economy:

1. The risk-neutral leveraged ("active") investors, call them banks, who manage their portfolios using VaR;
2. The risk-averse non-leveraged ("passive") depositors, or, consumers, who do not actively adjust their balance sheets. To capture the risk aversion, assume that the non-leveraged depositors have a mean-variance preference with utility function of consumption c being

$$E[u] = E[c] - \frac{1}{2\tau}\text{var}[c], \qquad (8.22)$$

in which $E[u]$ denotes the expected utility at $t=0$, and τ indicates the degree of consumers' tolerance on risks: the higher τ is, *ceteris paribus*, the more the consumers are tolerant on taking risks.

Both types of agents own an endowment e at the start of $t=0$.

For a representative consumer, as she does not like volatility in consumption, to reduce such volatility, she keeps some of her endowment as safe deposits in the banks in $t=0$, and invests the rest in risky assets, i.e., by purchasing q_p of risky assets at market price P. Her balance sheet in $t=0$ is characterized in Figure 8.8. Her realized return at $t=1$ is therefore

$$c = Rq_p - r(Pq_p - e).$$

Therefore, her investment decision at $t=0$ is defined by maximizing her expected utility

$$\begin{aligned}\max_{q_p} E[u] &= E\big[Rq_p - r(Pq_p - e)\big] - \frac{1}{2\tau}\text{var}\big[Rq_p - r(Pq_p - e)\big] \\ &= \bar{R}q_p - r(Pq_p - e) - \frac{1}{2\tau}\frac{z^2}{3}q_p^2.\end{aligned}$$

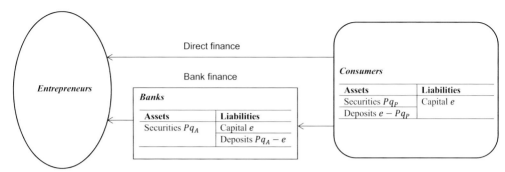

Figure 8.8 The balance sheets of banks and consumers in $t=0$

The first order condition $\dfrac{\partial E[u]}{\partial q_P}=0$ gives the unleveraged depositor's optimal level of holding risky assets, $q_P(P)$, characterized by

$$q_P(P)=\begin{cases}\dfrac{3\tau}{z^2}(\bar{R}-rp), & \bar{R}>P,\\ 0, & \text{otherwise.}\end{cases}$$

A representative bank, being risk-neutral, always wants to maximize profits by investing in risky assets as much as possible. Therefore, it takes debts (or, it leverages) by borrowing from consumers to expand the balance sheet, which is characterized in Figure 8.8. The investment decision at $t=0$ is to maximize expected return in $t=1$ by purchasing q_A of risky assets at market price P, borrowing Pq_A-e from consumers, given the VaR constraint in risk management

$$\max_{q_A} \quad E\left[Rq_A-r(Pq_A-e)\right]=(\bar{R}-rP)q_A+re,$$
$$\text{s.t.} \quad e\geq VaR.$$

Since the expected return is linear in q_A and e, the bank will maximize q_A as long as $\bar{R}>rP$, until the VaR constraint becomes binding.

For simplicity, assume that the VaR constraint requires that the bank should be able to stay solvent even in the worst state, i.e., be able to repay the depositors even when the payoff from the risky asset is the lowest, $\bar{R}-z$. This implies $(\bar{R}-z)q_A \geq r(Pq_A-e)$. When the VaR constraint is binding, $e=\left(P-\dfrac{\bar{R}}{r}+\dfrac{z}{r}\right)q_A$. Rewrite it as

$$q_A(P) = \frac{re}{rP - \overline{R} + z} \tag{8.23}$$

for the demand of risky assets from the leveraged banks.

To focus on the key mechanism, assume that in the short run the aggregate supply of risky assets is fixed at S —because the number of entrepreneurs is fixed, or equivalently, assume that the asset price adjusts much faster than asset quantity. Therefore, we have $q_A + q_P = S$. Depict $q_A(P)$ and $q_P(P)$ in the same space, as Figure 8.9 shows, the equilibrium asset price P and the demand of risky assets from both types of agents can be determined simultaneously.

8.5.2 VAR, ASSET PRICE, AND THE LEVERAGE CYCLE

To produce leverage cycles by the feedback between asset price and leverage in boom-bust cycles, suppose there is an unexpected shock to the risky assets' return at an intermediate period, call it $t = 0.5$, so that both banks and consumers have the chance to adjust their balance sheets. Assume that at $t = 0.5$, it turns out that the true distribution of the risky assets' return is $[\overline{R}' - z, \overline{R}' + z]$, $\overline{R}' > \overline{R}$, i.e., the economy is in a boom.

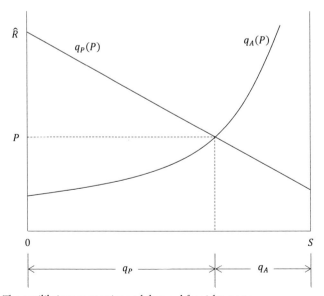

Figure 8.9 *The equilibrium asset price and demand for risky assets*

The impact of such positive shock to asset return, or economic fundamentals, on asset price is visualized in Figure 8.10. Both demand curves are shifted upwards, leading to a higher price level. This fits perfectly the observed fact that the asset price increases in the economic boom.

Although the equilibrium price P is simultaneously determined by the demand curves of banks and consumers once the shock to the fundamental value of the risky assets gets realized, we may break the entire process down in several steps to see how the shock to $\bar{R}$ propagates through the leverage channel:

1. The rising $\bar{R}$ increases the banks' demand of the risky assets, which is characterized by $q_A(P) = \dfrac{re}{rP - \bar{R} + z}$. With all other things equal, an upward shifted $q_A(P)$ line has a positive impact on the price level P;

2. With a higher price level, call it $\tilde{P}$, the value of banks' risky assets, $\tilde{P}q_A$, increases. From its balance sheet, this implies a higher level of equity value

$$\tilde{e} = \tilde{P}q_A - \left(\dfrac{\bar{R}-z}{r}\right)q_A, \qquad (8.24)$$

given its starting debt level $\left(\dfrac{\bar{R}-z}{r}\right)q_A$;

3. With a higher equity value, a bank's VaR constraint becomes relaxed as $\tilde{e} > e = VaR$. This allows the bank to expand its balance sheet, take in more debts and purchase more risky assets to $\tilde{q}_A > q_A$ in order to catch up with the improved fundamental value $\bar{R}'$. The expanded balance sheet is then featured by

$$\tilde{e} = \tilde{P}\tilde{q}_A - \left(\dfrac{\bar{R}'-z}{r}\right). \qquad (8.25)$$

Comparing equation (8.24) with (8.25), we can express the new demand of risky assets from the banks, using the old demand level

$$\tilde{q}_A = \dfrac{r\tilde{P}+z-\bar{R}}{r\tilde{P}+z-\bar{R}'}q_A = \left(1 + \dfrac{\bar{R}'-\bar{R}}{r\tilde{P}+z-\bar{R}'}\right); \qquad (8.26)$$

CHAPTER EIGHT: THE BANKING-MACRO LINKAGES

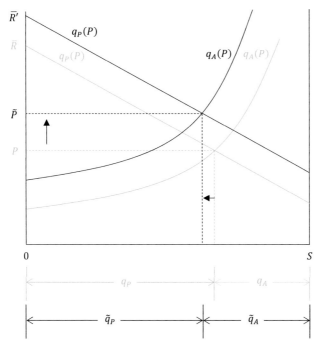

Figure 8.10 *Asset price rises in the boom phase*

4 Under the new circumstance, the demand level of risky assets from the consumers is

$$\tilde{q}_P = \frac{3\tau}{z^2}(\overline{R}' - r\tilde{P}) = S - \tilde{q}_A. \qquad (8.27)$$

Both equations, (8.26) and (8.27), determine the equilibrium demand for both types of agents,

$$\tilde{q}_A = \left[1 + \frac{\overline{R}' - \overline{R}}{z + (\tilde{q}_A - S)\frac{z^2}{3\tau}}\right] q_A. \qquad (8.28)$$

Denote the right hand side of (8.28) by $f(\tilde{q}_A)$. Note that its denominator part, $z + (\tilde{q}_A - S)\frac{z^2}{3\tau}$, comes from $r\tilde{P} + z - \overline{R}'$ of (8.23) which is positive. Therefore $f(\tilde{q}_A)$ is a downward sloping curve of $\tilde{q}_A$ and the solution to (8.28) is the intersection between $f(\tilde{q}_A)$ and $\tilde{q}_A$, as Figure 8.11 shows. As in the figure, with a higher $\overline{R}'$ the $f(\tilde{q}_A)$

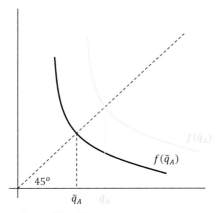

Figure 8.11 *Equilibrium demand for risky assets*

curve is shifted upwards, leading to a higher demand $\tilde{q}_A$ for risky assets. As a mirror case, $\tilde{q}_A$ falls if $\overline{R'} - \overline{R} < 0$.

Figure 8.12 summarizes the working mechanism of leverage channel in the boom. An initial positive shock to the bank's asset value leads to the increased value of bank capital; as a result of risk management through VaR, this allows the bank to expand its balance sheet by taking more debts to issue credits for purchasing risky securities, pushing up the asset price in the market. This further strengthens the bank's balance sheet, further increases the value of bank capital, and incentivizes the bank to take more debts. Through such virtuous cycle (as is summarized by the left chart of Figure 8.13), the initial small shock to bank assets ends up in a much more expanded supply of credits and higher asset price, as the right chart of Figure 8.12 shows.

Furthermore, note from (8.28) that $\tilde{q}_A$ becomes more sensitive to the fundamental shock $\overline{R'} - \overline{R}$ when z is smaller, as in this case, the banks get more leveraged, and the asset price becomes more volatile. The leverage in banks' balance sheets generates a higher flying asset price in the boom phase, while more devastating collapse when the economy comes to the downturn (the vicious cycle, as the right chart in Figure 8.13 shows).

The leverage channel increases the volatility in banks' credit supply, hence the volatility in the real economy; this is often not desirable. Even worse, beyond the excess volatility, it is worth noting that banks' risk taking combined with the leverage cycle may bring damaging consequences,

CHAPTER EIGHT: THE BANKING-MACRO LINKAGES

Assets	Liabilities
Securities $\tilde{P}q_A$	Capital $\tilde{e}$
	Deposits $\left(\frac{\bar{R}-z}{r}\right)q_A$

→

Assets	Liabilities
Securities $\tilde{P}\tilde{q}_A$	Capital $\tilde{e}$
	Deposits $\left(\frac{\bar{R}\prime-z}{r}\right)\tilde{q}_A$

Figure 8.12 Balance sheet expansion through bank leverage

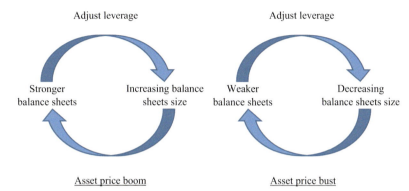

Figure 8.13 The virtuous and vicious cycles through bank leverage

even though this mechanism is not modelled here. Rising asset prices in the boom phase of leverage cycles often build up bubbles, while in the bust phase, plummeting asset prices are often accompanied by panics and fire sales that further destroy values in the financial market. A rising number of recent studies on the long human history of bubbles and bursts, such as Reinhart and Rogoff (2009) and Schularick and Taylor (2012), almost unanimously show that fast credit growth together with asset price boom is the single best leading indicator for financial crises.

8.5.3 SUMMARY

In the Shin model, the supply of assets as well as the population of investors (both active and passive) are assumed to be fixed. Leverage cycle arises out of active investors' risk management through VaR. Adrian and Shin (2014) argue that—given this mechanism—monetary policy is likely to trigger shifts in risk taking, contributing to global financial cycles. Changes in short-term policy rates will have an impact on the feedback loop between leverage and measures of risk. Easy credit conditions, inducing lower volatility, increase the risk appetite, resulting in higher leverage and rapid expansion of credit. When policy eventually tightens, the process is suddenly reversed, possibly violently. This mechanism reflects long-run buildups of financial risk rather than short-run swings in risk appetite.

Such procyclicality in leverage and risk-taking is often due to myopia of both risk managers and suppliers of funds to intermediaries. Using Value-at-Risk risk management methodologies, investment banks, their creditors, and their regulators judge the riskiness of assets mainly by past experience. So they tend to underestimate underlying risks during normal times and over-estimate them in periods of high volatility. This myopic behavior leads to excessive swings in lending and risk-seeking. A natural way to address this problem is to strengthen financial regulation such as to limit excessive cyclicality in lending standards, and to focus stress tests on the ability of institutions to bear tail risks, as Chapter 12, Section 12.3.2 shows.

8.6 GENERAL EQUILIBRIUM EFFECT AND THE LEVERAGE CYCLE

The leverage cycle can arise even without the explicit VaR constraint, as Geanakoplos (2010a) demonstrates. He develops a general equilibrium model of asset pricing in which collateral, leverage, and default play a central role. In this model, the price of an asset at any point in time is not simply determined by the expected future stream of revenues but also by access to leverage for different agents with varying beliefs about the probability of high returns. For many assets there is a class of buyer for whom the asset is more valuable than it is for the rest of the public. These buyers are willing to pay more, either because they know better how to hedge their exposure to the assets, or because they are more risk tolerant. Geanakoplos (2010a) shows that endogenous variations in leverage can have a huge impact on the price of assets, contributing to economic booms and busts. If the collateral requirement for a loan gets looser, buyers can get more outside funds through higher leveraged borrowing. They will spend it on the assets and drive those prices up. If they lose wealth, or lose the ability to borrow, they will buy less, so the asset will fall into more pessimistic hands and be valued less.

A fairly small decline in expectations about future revenues can result in a crash of asset prices because of two amplifying mechanisms: changes in the degree of equilibrium leverage, and the default of those who hold the most optimistic beliefs. So leverage gets too high in boom times, and too low in bad times. As a result, in boom times asset prices are too high, and in crisis times they are too low: the leverage cycle.

To illustrate the key idea, we consider a simple model with a single asset, two periods, and two future states in which the asset value will be either high or low. Beliefs about the relative likelihood of the two states vary across individuals. Borrowers and lenders can choose to enter or exit market when their expected returns on assets shift. Suppose initially that there is no borrowing. Then the price of the asset will be such that those who wish to sell their holdings at that price collectively own precisely the amount that those who wish to buy can collectively afford. Specifically, the price will partition the public into two groups: those who are more pessimistic about the future price sell to those who are more optimistic.

In a next step, we allow for borrowing, with the asset itself as collateral (as in mortgage contracts). Suppose that the amount of lending is constrained by the lowest possible future value of the collateral, so lenders are fully protected against loss. Even in this case, the asset price will be higher than it would be without borrowing: the most optimistic individuals will buy the asset on margin, while the others sell their holdings and lend money to the buyers. So the price is higher when margin purchases are possible even if there is no change in beliefs about the future value of the asset. The looser the collateral requirement, the higher are the prices of assets. The extent of leverage is determined jointly with the interest rate in the market for loans. Aggregate demand for and supply of credit nail down the equilibrium asset price. The leverage cycle is thus endogenously determined through the general equilibrium effect. Finally, we extend the baseline model to explain the impact of new information on leverage and asset prices. We show how leverage is built up after good news and how bad news can cause an asset price crash after excessive deleveraging. Endogenous leverage is an important part for understanding the financial crisis.

8.6.1 AGENTS, TIME PREFERENCES, AND TECHNOLOGY

Geanakoplos (2003), Geanakoplos (2010a), and Geanakoplos (2010b) consider an economy that extends to two periods, $t=0,1$. The only commodity in the economy is a consumption good C, which can be consumed at any time, stored, or used for investment. There are two states of the world, $S \in \{U, D\}$, as in Figure 8.14, namely "up" or "down", for $t=1$. The only asset in this economy is a risky asset Y, at $t=1$ each unit of Y returns R_U (R_D) units of consumption good in the state U (D). As a regularity condition, it is assumed that $R_U \geq 1 > R_D > 0$.

There is a continuum of investors, each of which is endowed with one unit of the asset Y and one unit of consumption good C at $t=0$. The investors are indifferent in the timing of consumption. The investors are heterogeneous in their belief at $t=0$ of the probability π that the economy goes up at $t=1$. For simplicity, suppose π is uniformly distributed and $\pi_i = i$ for an investor indexed by $i \in [0,1]$. The more the index gets close to 1 (0), the more optimistic (pessimistic) the investor becomes.

Assume that the short selling is not allowed in this economy. When the price of the asset Y is P at $t=0$, the investor i is (weakly) willing to buy the asset as long as she believes that P is (weakly) below the asset's expected value, i.e., $iR_U + (1-i)R_D \geq P$, otherwise she wants to sell the asset.

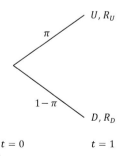

Figure 8.14 *The payoff of the risky assets*

Therefore the more optimistic investors tend to buy the assets and hence are natural buyers of the risky assets, and the more pessimistic ones tend to be natural sellers. Here we have the first novelty of this model: the types of investors are endogenously determined by their subjective expectation on the risky asset's return.

8.6.2 MARKET EQUILIBRIUM WITHOUT BORROWING

To get some flavor about the market equilibrium, we start from the reference case in which no borrowing is allowed, i.e., the buyers can only buy with their own endowments. For a representative investor i, let c_0^i denote her consumption at $t=0$, and c_U^i (c_D^i) denote her consumption at $t=1$ if the state of the world is U (D). Then at $t=0$ her *subjective* expected utility is

$$u^i = c_0^i + ic_U^i + (1-i)c_D^i. \tag{8.29}$$

Besides consuming c_0^i at $t=0$, the investor can also invest w_0^i as storage which can be consumed at $t=1$. Let y_0^i denote the investor's holding of risky assets for $t=1$. Given some risky assets are traded between the two types of the investors at price P, the investor's budget constraint at $t=0$ is therefore

$$c_0^i + w_0^i + P(y_0^i - 1) = 1. \tag{8.30}$$

With the payoff structure of the risky assets, the expected consumption at $t=1$ for each state is

$$c_U^i = w_0^i + R_U y_0^i, \tag{8.31}$$
$$c_D^i = w_0^i + R_D y_0^i. \tag{8.32}$$

The market clearing conditions must hold:

1. The aggregate $t=0$ consumption and storage is equal to the aggregate endowment of consumption good,

$$\int_0^1 (c_0^i + w_0^i) di = 1; \tag{8.33}$$

2. The aggregate $t=0$ holdings of risky assets should be equal to the aggregate endowment of risky assets,

$$\int_0^1 y_0^i di = 1; \tag{8.34}$$

3. The expected aggregate $t=1$ consumption in each state is equal to the expected return from all the risky assets plus the aggregate storage made at $t=0$,

$$\int_0^1 c_U^i di = R_U + \int_0^1 w_0^i di, \tag{8.35}$$

$$\int_0^1 c_D^i di = R_D + \int_0^1 w_0^i di. \tag{8.36}$$

The investor's problem is to choose the optimal $\left(c_0^i, w_0^i, y_0^i, c_U^i, c_D^i\right)$ to maximize the object function (8.29) with the budget constraints (8.30)-(8.32) and market clearing conditions (8.33)-(8.36).

Remember that the equilibrium price P divides the investors into two groups: with the boundary i^*, buyers are those with indices $i \in (i^*, 1]$, and seller are those with $i \in [0, i^*)$. Therefore, the equilibrium price P can be solved from the boundary buyer who is indifferent between buying and selling:

$$i^* R_U + (1-i^*) R_D = P. \tag{8.37}$$

Further, note that without borrowing, the buyers, whose measure is $1-i^*$, spend all their endowment of consumption good, to purchase the endowment of risky assets from the sellers, whose measure is i^*. The equilibrium price of the risky asset is therefore denoted by the ratio between the total expenditure and the purchased quantity, i.e.,

$$P = \frac{1-i^*}{i^*}. \tag{8.38}$$

The equilibrium price and the boundary buyer are jointly determined by (8.37) and (8.38), as Figure 8.15 shows.

8.6.3 MARKET EQUILIBRIUM WITH BORROWING

In our reference case, the buyers' demand of risky assets is limited by their endowments of consumption goods, given that borrowing is not allowed.

What will happen if borrowing is allowed in this economy? Obviously buyers tend to become borrowers to purchase more of the risky assets,— so long as their subjective expected return is higher than the asset price (resembling the active leveraged investors, or banks, in the Shin model). Sellers tend to become lenders (resembling the passive non-leveraged investors, or depositors, in the Shin model) so long as the market interest rate is weakly higher than 1. The extreme case is the buyer $i=1$: since the subjective expected return is $R_U > P$, the buyer is willing to borrow an infinite amount with interest rate R_U. However, the lenders, those $0 \leq i < i^*$, won't offer the lending because they believe that the probability of the state D at $t=1$ is strictly positive in which the borrower will have to default. Therefore, in order to avoid default, the lenders must require collateral from the borrowers as a commitment device.

Assume now that buyers can borrow from the sellers at $t=0$ and the loan contract between the borrowers and lenders is featured by

1. The contract is non-contingent, i.e., the lenders get the same return in both states, U and D;
2. In order to guarantee the safe return in both states, the lenders take the borrowers' risky assets as collateral.

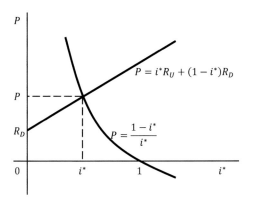

Figure 8.15 *The equilibrium price and the boundary buyer*

To find the market equilibrium, suppose that borrower i borrows $\dfrac{\phi_0^i}{1+r}$ at $t=0$ with interest rate r and promises to repay ϕ_0^i at $t=1$. The collateral requirement guarantees that the collateral value is sufficient to repay the loan even when the borrower has to default in the D state, i.e.,

$$R_D y_0^i \geq \phi_0^i. \tag{8.39}$$

This gives the limit of the buyer's borrowing capacity. Now the buyer's budget constraint at $t=0$ becomes

$$c_0^i + w_0^i + P(y_0^i - 1) = 1 + \frac{\phi_0^i}{1+r}. \tag{8.40}$$

The expected consumption at $t=1$ for each state is now

$$c_U^i = w_0^i + R_U y_0^i - \phi_0^i, \tag{8.41}$$
$$c_D^i = w_0^i + R_D y_0^i - \phi_0^i. \tag{8.42}$$

The market clearing conditions must hold:

1. For the aggregate $t=0$ consumption and storage,

$$\int_0^1 (c_0^i + w_0^i)\,di = 1; \tag{8.43}$$

2. For the aggregate $t=0$ holdings of risky assets,

$$\int_0^1 y_0^i\,di = 1; \tag{8.44}$$

3. For the expected aggregate $t=1$ consumption in each state,

$$\int_0^1 c_U^i\,di = R_U + \int_0^1 w_0^i\,di; \tag{8.45}$$

$$\int_0^1 c_D^i\,di = R_D + \int_0^1 w_0^i\,di; \tag{8.46}$$

4. Any investor i, is a borrower if $\phi_0^i > 0$ and a lender if $\phi_0^i < 0$. The lending and borrowing cancel out in aggregate, which makes

$$\int_0^1 \phi_0^i\,di = 0. \tag{8.47}$$

Now the investor's problem is to choose the optimal $\left(c_0^i, w_0^i, \phi_0^i, y_0^i, c_U^i, c_D^i\right)$ to maximize the object function (8.29) with the borrowing constraint (8.39), budget constraints (8.40)–(8.42), and market clearing conditions (8.43)–(8.47).

Similar to the reference case, the market equilibrium price P can be solved by the boundary buyer i^* with

$$i^* R_U + \left(1 - i^*\right) R_D = P. \tag{8.48}$$

In equilibrium, the buyers will hold the risky asset of the entire economy, which means a collateral value R_D. This allows all the buyers to borrow up to $\dfrac{R_D}{1+r}$ in total from the sellers to finance their purchase of risky asset, i^*, besides their endowment of consumption good, $1 - i^*$. Suppose that R_D is so low that the total collateral value of the economy is below the lenders' aggregate endowment of consumption good, $R_D \leq i^*$. The competition among the lenders will drive the equilibrium interest rate r down to 0. The equilibrium price of the risky asset is therefore

$$P = \frac{1 - i^* + R_D}{i^*}. \tag{8.49}$$

The equilibrium price and the boundary buyer are jointly determined by (8.48) and (8.49), as Figure 8.16 shows.

Compared with the reference market equilibrium without borrowing (depicted in gray), as Figure 8.16 shows, the access to tapping the credit from the lenders enables the borrowers to increase their expenditure on risky assets. This shifts the asset price to a higher level, given the aggregate supply of risky assets is inelastic. Facing a higher asset price, only those investors who are more optimistic are still willing to purchase, and this crowds out those who are less optimistic and raises the bar for one investor becoming a natural buyer.

One may suspect that the market equilibrium derived here is due to the assumption imposed that the loan contract is non-contingent, i.e., we have assumed that lenders must get the same return in both states, so that one buyer's borrowing is upper bounded by $R_D y_0^i$ and the aggregate borrowing is limited to R_D. One might conjecture that optimistic investors

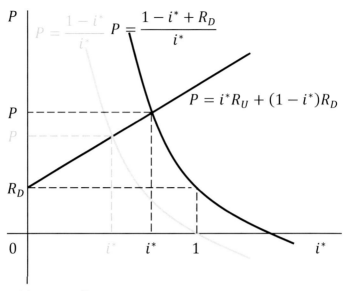

Figure 8.16 The impact of borrowing

would be able to borrow more if we relax this non-contingency restriction on the loan contract. For example, the most optimistic investor $i=1$ may promise a higher payoff $\tilde{R}y_0^1$, $R_D < \tilde{R} < R_U$, as $t=1$ return, to attract more loans from the lenders. However, this will not happen in equilibrium because of the heterogeneous beliefs of the investors. A natural seller, or a lender, believes that the collateral is worth $\tilde{R}y_0^1$ only with a low probability $i < i^*$ being convinced that it is worth just $R_D y_0^1$ with a fairly high probability $1-i$. Therefore, if the lender agrees to lend, she must take into account that with probability $1-i$ her loan is not fully pledgeable. Therefore, the lender will ask for a higher interest rate to insure against the high probability of default. However, the borrower $i=1$ believes that she will come up with state U with certainty so that she always has to pay the high interest rate to the lender. This is obviously dominated by just promising $R_D y_0^1$ and paying zero interest rate.

Note that in the market equilibrium with borrowing, the total value of risky assets is P, which is financed by the borrowers' endowment and the debt R_D raised from the lenders. The leverage ratio of the economy is therefore

$$L = \frac{P}{P - R_D}. \tag{8.50}$$

Now we have the second novelty of this model: in the market equilibrium, not only the asset price, but also the leverage of the economy is endogenized.

Using the simplest framework constructed by (8.48), (8.49), and (8.50), we are able to analyze the impact of economic fundamentals on the equilibrium leverage. For example, suppose that the investors become more optimistic such that at $t=0$ investor i believes that the economy goes down at $t=1$ with a lower probability $\pi = (1-i)^2 < 1-i$, and the chance that the economy goes up gets higher since $1-\pi = 1-(1-i)^2 > i$. As a result, the boundary investor becomes the one with $\left[1-\left(1-i^*\right)^2\right]R_U + \left(1-i^*\right)^2 R_D = P$. Given that the borrowing constraint $P = \frac{1-i^* + R_D}{i^*}$ remains the same as before, it is easily seen that the equilibrium price P goes up and the boundary i^* goes down. Intuitively, when the investors get more optimistic, those who were previously marginally below the boundary i^* now realize the expected payoff gets higher so that they will switch to be buyers. This increases the total expenditure on risky assets and imposes a positive pressure on asset price, as (8.49) shows. But when asset price gets higher, it makes the risky asset less appealing for the marginal buyers which prevents more sellers from joining the buyers. The equilibrium P and i^* thus reflect the balance between these two diverting effects.

Instead of a shock on π, now suppose the expected return of the risky asset in the upside, R_U, gets improved. As Figure 8.17 shows, this means a higher slope for $P = i^* R_U + (1-i^*) R_D$, leading unambiguously to a higher asset price P and lower equilibrium boundary i^*. That is, a higher R_U means a higher fundamental value of risky assets, implying a higher asset price. On the other hand, with higher R_U even previously less optimistic investors will find it worthwhile to hold risky assets since the expected return gets higher. Therefore, some of the natural sellers will be converted to buyers. The leverage $L = \frac{P}{P - R_D}$ becomes lower because of the higher

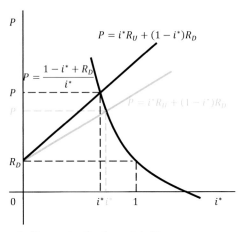

Figure 8.17 The impact of improving fundamentals (I)

asset price. The equilibrium price would have been even higher, should there be no shift in boundary i^*. In other words, the impact of higher R_U on asset price has been dampened by the fall in leverage.

Now suppose the expected return of the risky asset in the downside, R_D, gets improved. This means that both $P = \dfrac{1 - i^* + R_D}{i^*}$ and $P = i^* R_U + (1 - i^*) R_D$ are shifted upwards in Figure 8.18, and $P = i^* R_U + (1 - i^*) R_D$ gets flatter, implying a higher asset price P. To see impact on the equilibrium boundary i^*, combine (8.48) and (8.49) to get the implicit function $i^*(R_D)$

$$\frac{1 - i^* + R_D}{i^*} = i^* R_U + (1 - i^*) R_D.$$

Differentiating with respect to R_D yields

$$\frac{\partial i^*}{\partial R_D} = \frac{1 - i^* + i^{*2}}{1 + R_D + 2i^*(R_U - R_D)} > 0. \tag{8.51}$$

This means the equilibrium boundary i^* gets higher, too.

Here the rising boundary i^* comes as a result of the general equilibrium effect, which amplifies the impact of R_D through the feedback mechanism between the asset price and the leveraged investors' balance sheet. The improvement of the expected return on the downside relaxes the buyers' borrowing constraint through the improved collateral value, and this is

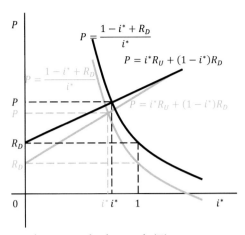

Figure 8.18 *The impact of improving fundamentals (II)*

immediately translated to a higher asset price through the multiplier,— $P = \frac{1-i^* + R_D}{i^*}$ implies that the shock to R_D is amplified by $\frac{1}{i^*} > 1$. However, the sharp rise in asset price also makes the buyers' feasibility constraint, $iR_U + (1-i)R_D \geq P$, less likely to hold. In the end, the marginal buyers who were previously just above the boundary i^*, are now crowded out, and only the more optimistic investors will stay as buyers. But when i^* rises, the total endowment of consumption good from the buyers falls, which brakes the rising trend in asset price through $P = \frac{1-i^* + R_D}{i^*}$ as a feedback. Finally, equation (8.50) suggests that in equilibrium the amplification effect outweighs the dampening effect.

8.6.4 THE BUSINESS CYCLE AND THE LEVERAGE CYCLE

As the simple general equilibrium model shows, by comparative analysis one can see the impact of fundamental value on asset prices through the lenders' balance sheet. One interesting extension to this baseline model is to analyze the impact of new information affecting investors' expectation on the fundamental value. We will show how leverage cycles may be amplified: leverage will be built up after good news; bad news can cause an asset price crash after excessive deleveraging.

To capture such leverage cycle, the model needs to be extended to introduce additional periods with new information arriving. Keeping the settings almost the same as in the baseline model, there is one additional intermediate date, $t=0.5$, in which investors can observe a signal regarding the risky asset's payoff in the future. For investor i with subjective probability π $(1-\pi)$, the signal is U (D). At $t=1$ the investors observe another signal, which is independent on, but of the same distribution of, the previous one, as Figure 8.19 shows. The $t=1$ payoff of the risky asset is R_D only if both signals are D. Again, suppose π is uniformly distributed and $\pi_i = i$ for an investor indexed by $i \in [0,1]$.

With an additional intermediate date, the investors will have a chance to reconsider their investments. Therefore, assume that all the loans only last for one period. At $t=0$, based on their expected payoff, the investors will be endogenously separated into buyers (or, borrowers) and sellers (or, lenders), and the equilibrium is characterized by the asset price P_0 and the boundary investor i_0^*. The borrowers get their loans from the lenders, using their assets as collateral. When it comes to $t=0.5$, conditional on the signal they receive, the investors have to adjust their expectation on $t=1$ payoff and reconsider their holdings of risky asset, i.e., the borrowers may want to increase or have to deplete their asset stocks, the lenders may want to liquidate the collateral or roll over their loans into the next

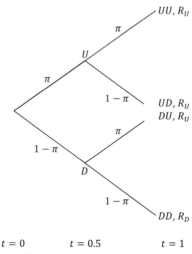

Figure 8.19 The 3-date extension

period (we will explain the details later). The equilibrium depends on the observed signal: asset price $P_{0.5,S}$ and the boundary investor $i^*_{0.5,S}$ under signal $S \in \{U,D\}$.

In the current 3-date model, the investors are more optimistic at $t=0$ than in the baseline model, since the investor i's subjective probability of having a low return R_D now is $(1-i)^2 < 1-i$. Therefore, similar to the comparative analysis of the last section, the equilibrium price P_0 and the boundary investor i^*_0 are connected by $\left[1-(1-i^*_0)^2\right]R_U + (1-i^*_0)^2 R_D = P_0$. As argued before, the equilibrium price P_0 tends to be higher than the baseline model, given that the investors are more optimistic.

The difference here is the buyer's borrowing capacity. Note that all the loans are short-term so that for the loans made at $t=0$, the collateral value is the value from liquidating the risky asset at $t=0.5$, i.e., the asset price $P_{0.5,S}$ which further depends on the signal observed at $t=0.5$. When $S=U$, it is easily seen that $P_{0.5,U} = R_U$ because R_U will be realized at $t=1$ with certainty; when $S=D$, $P_{0.5,D}$ is yet to be determined, but should be above R_D because there is still a positive probability of ending up with DU at $t=1$. In the end, the buyers' total borrowing capacity at $t=0$ should be larger than that in the baseline model. As is argued before, the equilibrium price P_0 tends to be higher, along with the buyers' higher borrowing capacity.

Suppose that with equilibrium P_0 and i^*_0 the time goes on from $t=0$ to $t=0.5$, when the first signal gets revealed. If $S=U$, the high return R_U is guaranteed with certainty, and the asset price will be bid up to R_U. The economy booms before the high return is materialized.

In contrast, if $S=D$, the economy incurs a crash. To make it worse, the downward spiral will be fueled by the general equilibrium effect. To see this, note that when signal D is observed,

1 For investor i the probability of having a low return becomes $1-i > (1-i)^2$, i.e., the investors become more pessimistic, implying a lower asset price $P_{0.5,D}$;
2 Therefore, the initial buyers at $t=0$ go bankrupted as Figure 8.20 shows, and all their asset holdings as collateral are seized by the initial sellers;

3. Now only the less optimistic investors $i \in [0, i_0^*)$ are still in the market. Given that all the investors are more pessimistic, the equilibrium price of the risky assets $P_{0.5,D}$ has to fall even further;
4. With a sufficiently low $P_{0.5,D}$, the investors on the top of $[0, i_0^*)$ are willing to buy the asset. However, the collateral value is only R_D in this case, implying that the borrowing capacity has been also contracted. Such deleveraging imposes more downside pressure on $P_{0.5,D}$.

In the end, the equilibrium ends up with a low $P_{0.5,D}$, and a lower boundary investor $i_{0.5,D}^*$ for the surviving investors.

Such a vicious spiral makes a perfectly analogy to a fire sale, and the key mechanism in the model explains how economic downturn triggers the disastrous fire sale. In contrast to the standard models with representative investors, i.e., all the investors are (at least *ex ante*) homogeneous in all dimensions, here from the beginning investors are heterogeneous in their subjective expectation of the future payoff from holding risky asset. Thus, by the simple "buy low, sell high" principle, all investors are endogenously separated into natural buyers and sellers: those more optimistic investors hold the asset, which they buy from the pessimistic ones using the funds borrowed from the sellers. Since borrowers need to post their asset as collateral, their leverage ratio is endogenously determined in equilibrium, too.

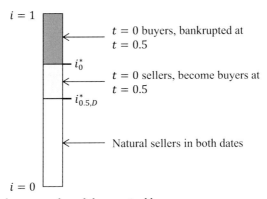

Figure 8.20 *The leverage cycle and the marginal buyer*

Certainly the asset price in equilibrium is determined by the law of demand and supply, however, what becomes more important here is who serves as a buyer or a seller when the shock is revealed. When the market becomes more optimistic about the fundamentals, the asset price is bid up, and the trend is then dampened by the leverage of the economy. But when a negative shock hits and the market becomes more pessimistic, after the first wave of asset price decline caused by the deteriorating fundamentals, the initial natural buyers, or the optimistic investors, get bankrupted and driven out of the market. This further aggravates the market outcome: now the buyers are less optimistic and their willingness to pay is low, and their borrowing capacity gets contracted because of the deterioration in the fundamentals. These two factors jointly depress the asset price even further into a full collapse, and the effect is amplified by deleveraging. Finally, it is not surprising that asset has to be sold at the fire sale price—simply because the optimistic buyers are all gone.

8.6.5 SUMMARY

The endogenous leverage cycle through general equilibrium in the Geanakoplos model sheds much light on many asset price puzzles both in the economic boom and in the financial crisis. One such puzzle is why during financial crises financial assets have to be sold at fire sale prices—quite often such prices are much lower than the assets' fundamental values—as this is obviously an arbitrage opportunity such that investors should buy assets at depressed prices and profit from selling them in the future once asset prices recover. But here such "limits to arbitrage" (as coined by Shleifer and Vishny 1997) arise quite naturally from the Geanakoplos model: there is a lack of demand for assets even at depressed prices, because the potential, most optimistic buyers are all bankrupted after the financial shock, and this allows fire sale prices to persist.

The leverage cycle framework, such as the Shin model and Geanakoplos model, exhibits a distinct contrast to the standard dynamic stochastic general equilibrium models, even those models with financial accelerator type of financial frictions. In the standard models, exogenous shock triggered price fluctuations cause (amplify) real volatilities, generating a distributional effect; while in the leverage cycle framework, price fluctuations are both cause and consequence of real volatilities—the feedback between asset prices and real volatilities leads to far larger and devastating boom-bust cycles.

8.7 EXERCISES

1 **Overborrowing and systemic risk, based on Bianchi (2011)**

   Consider a small open economy with a tradable goods sector and a nontradable goods sector. Only tradable goods can be traded internationally; nontradable goods have to be consumed domestically. The economy is populated by a continuum of identical households of measure one, living for two periods $t = 0, 1$, with preferences given by $u(c) = \ln c_0^T + \ln c_0^N + \ln c_1^T$, in which c_0^T, c_0^N, c_1^T are consumption of tradable goods at $t = 0$, consumption of nontradable goods at $t = 0$, consumption of tradable goods at $t = 1$, respectively.

   A representative household starts with initial asset b_0 at $t = 0$, and ends after $t = 1$ with zero asset, i.e., $b_2 = 0$. Note that b_0 can be positive or negative: when $b_0 < 0$, the household starts with initial debt. The timeline of events is as follows:

   - At $t = 0$, the representative household receives both an endowment of tradable goods y_0^T and an endowment of nontradable goods y_0^N for consumption. y_0^T is a random variable that is drawn from a distribution with cumulative distribution function $F(y)$, while y_0^N is constant. After (y_0^T, y_0^N) is revealed, the household can also borrow from abroad by purchasing a one-period, non-state contingent foreign bond denominated in units of tradables that demands a fixed interest rate r —normalized to be 0, determined exogenously in the world market. Normalize the price of tradables to 1 and denote the price of nontradable goods by p_0^N. In addition, the household's debt is securitized such that its total debt cannot exceed a fraction $0 < \kappa < 1$ of its total income from tradables and nontradables;

- At $t=1$, starting with total asset b_1 the representative household only receives an endowment of tradable goods y_1^T for consumption. y_1^T is constant.

(a) Specify the representative household's budget constraints, borrowing constraint, and life-time optimization problem.

(b) Compute the first order conditions for the household's optimization problem:

   i. Derive the first order conditions with respect to c_0^T and c_0^N, then determine p_0^N;
   ii. Derive the first order conditions with respect to c_1^T and b_1, then determine the Euler equation. Why is the borrowing constraint *occasionally* binding?

(c) Determine c_0^T:

   i. Under what condition(s) is the borrowing constraint not binding? In this case, use the results from question (b) to determine c_0^T;
   ii. When the borrowing constraint is binding, compute c_0^T.

(d) Consider two situations at $t=0$: the economy can be either in normal state $y_0^T = \bar{y}$, i.e., the household receives a mean value $\bar{y}$, or crisis state $y_0^T = \bar{y} - 1$, i.e., y_0^T is below the mean. Suppose the household knows the true state before it borrows.

   i. If borrowing constraint is not binding in both states how does c_0^T react to the crisis, compared with c_0^T in the normal state?
   ii. If borrowing constraint is binding in both states, how does c_0^T react to the crisis, compared with c_0^T in the normal state?

2 Value-at-Risk and leverage cycle, based on Shin (2010)

Consider the reverse case of the Shin model in Section 8.5. Keeping all settings unchanged, except the shock in $t=0.5$: suppose there is a shock to security return at the intermediate date, call it $t=0.5$, so that both types of investors have the chance to exchange in the security market and adjust their balance sheets; it turns out that the distribution of security return is $\left[\overline{R}'-z,\overline{R}'+z\right]$ with $\overline{R}'<\overline{R}$.

(a) Using $P-y$ curves, show the impact on both types' investors demand for securities and the new equilibrium security price;

(b) How does the shock to security return affect active investors' balance sheet? How do they adjust the balance sheet to meet VaR constraint? What's the consequence to the equilibrium asset price? Why is the leverage cycle "procyclical"?

NOTES

1 This is without loss of generality; it would be straightforward but mathematically complex to generalize for continuous stochastic return.

2 The long-run implication for such financial accelerator effect is not straightforward. Suppose that an economy starts with very low initial capital intensity k, or high marginal product of capital $\tilde{\theta}_0 f'(k_0)$. The high productivity of capital may outweigh the possible negative technological shock, and the economy starts accumulating capital although the growth path is stochastic due to the random shocks $\tilde{\theta}_t$ coming in each period. However, with time going on, the marginal product of capital diminishes when k becomes higher, a negative shock $\tilde{\theta}_t$ now may sharply decrease the labor income. With the presence of the financial accelerator, this suffocates many bank financed projects and highly raises the auditing cost; the economic growth may be completely reversed. And, to make it worse, such economic downturn will persist for some periods. Without further restrictions on the parameter values, the economic growth is hardly determinate. See Matsuyama (2008) for more discussion.

CHAPTER 9
International banking

9.1 INTRODUCTION

Banking has gone far beyond the physical borders between countries, and economies have become heavily intertwined with each other through the international banking network, as one of the most prominent outcomes after decades of financial globalization. As of the second quarter of 2020, outstanding claims through cross-border banking amount to above 16 trillion US dollars, according to the Bank for International Settlements (BIS) international banking statistics—down from its historical peak of over 22 trillion US dollars in early 2008, and cross-border claims through banks nowadays account for about half of total global financial claims. On the other hand, recent episodes such as the 2007–2009 global financial crisis and the subsequent European debt crisis, as well as current advocates for disintegration along with Brexit, China-United States trade war, as well as the COVID-19 pandemic, cast doubt on global financial integration and make people rethink the future of international banking.

What is special about international banking, compared with banking within borders as in the setups of almost all previous chapters? Overall, just as general banking facilitates risk-sharing among economic agents, international banking improves global risk-sharing and allocation of resources across countries. Different economies may be subject to different income shocks, different investors across the globe may have different risk appetites, and investment opportunities may arise in economies that are constrained by financial resources—with international banking, natural lenders and borrowers thus emerge from these scenarios and financial resources are allocated to places where they are better utilized.

However, alongside the "bright side" of international banking, there is also a "dark side" of it. Not surprisingly, international banking is subject to the same financial frictions and market failures that are discussed in the previous chapters, so that the same inefficiencies and anomalies are most likely to exist at an international level. But beyond this, what is really special about international banking is it creates channels through which shocks in one economy can spill over to other parts of the world. This is because banks are subject to regulatory and monetary policies in their "home countries" where they are headquartered, regulatory, monetary policy, or market shocks may make it appealing for banks to adjust their balance sheets, increasing or decreasing lending to the other countries, which constitutes a credit shock to borrowers in these countries so that banks "export" home shocks abroad. Such spillover may also happen in a reverse way, for example, monetary policy shock in a core economy such as the United States may affect the cost of money market funding for a foreign bank who relies on funding from a money market in the core economy, and encourage this bank to increase or decrease its funding; as a consequence, the bank then will have to adjust the lending supply in its home country so that it "imports"[1] the impact of foreign monetary policy. In extreme cases, when a financial crisis occurs in one country and causes a bank in this country to fail, the failed bank may further bring down its foreign counterparts through an international banking network, as Chapter 6, Section 6.3 demonstrates; this results in a contagion and spreads the crisis to other countries, just as we have observed from time to time in financial crises. Overall, through the international banking channel, cross-border spillovers of regulatory, monetary, market, and real economy shocks in one country affect lenders and borrowers in another country so that business cycles and monetary policies across the countries may be more "synchronized"; furthermore, such spillovers may also affect the effectiveness of policies in the recipient country: for example, if the central bank in a small open economy wants to accommodate domestic bank lending through tightening monetary policy and at the same time quantitative easing in a core economy creates an inflow of cross-border lending into this economy, the effectiveness of the desired monetary policy may be impaired. International banking thus also imposes increasing challenges to policy makers who attempt to stabilize an economy in a world connected by the banking network.

International banking is related to many fields of research: for example, there is a long list of literature on international capital flows to emerging market economies, as well as sovereign default, sovereign debt crises and currency crises; international banking is founded on the international monetary system whose formation and mechanisms at work have inspired fruitful studies and debates for many decades. Due to limited space, in this chapter we will only focus on several banking related questions: first, we look at the "bright side" and discuss how international banking facilitates global risk-sharing and improves cross-border resource allocation; second, we turn to the "dark side": from a global bank's view, we examine how local monetary policy shocks induce adjustments in the bank's global balance sheet and generate a spillover to the rest of the world.

International banking is an extremely complex system, as economies may be connected through banking in many ways. In the rest of this introductory section, we present some stylized facts of today's international banking and decipher the complex system in three dimensions, which are mutually related but reflect different perspectives of banking across borders:

1. The ownership dimension of international banking. Global banks are key players in international banking and they operate in multiple countries. When they experience shocks in one country, the adjustments in their global balance sheets will necessarily lead to shocks in the other countries;
2. The location dimension of international banking, which captures the origins and destinations of cross-border lending. International borrowing and lending may be conducted by global banks, but not necessarily so, for example, they may happen between two purely domestic banks—banks without subsidiaries or branches in countries other than the countries where they are headquartered—located in two different countries;
3. The currency dimension of international banking. Despite the large number of currencies in circulation around the world, around 90% of cross-border claims through the banking sector are denominated in just five "global currencies". Conversions between domestic currencies and global currencies expose lenders and borrowers to exchange rate risks, and the "core economies" that are issuing these global currencies also gain disproportionate influence on the other countries.

CHAPTER NINE: INTERNATIONAL BANKING

9.1.1 THE OWNERSHIP DIMENSION OF INTERNATIONAL BANKING

Banks may expand beyond their home countries and operate in other countries. To do so, banks may establish subsidiaries or branches in other countries, and the choices between branches and subsidiaries are largely driven by tax and regulation considerations. Banks are likely to prefer branches in countries with higher corporate taxes and lower regulatory restrictions on bank entry and on foreign branches, and to prefer subsidiaries when they seek to establish large retail operations in host countries (see Cerutti et al. 2007 for details).

Figure 9.1 shows the distribution of percentage ratio of foreign-controlled banks' assets in total bank assets for 138 jurisdictions around the world in 2016, in which a bank is defined as a *foreign-controlled bank* if foreigners own more than 50% of its equity. The horizontal axis contains the bins of percentage ratio, and the vertical axis shows the occurrence frequency

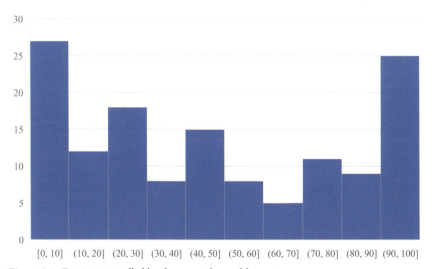

Figure 9.1 *Foreign-controlled banks across the world, 2016*

Notes: this histogram shows the distribution of percentage ratio of foreign-controlled banks' assets in total bank assets; the horizontal axis contains the bins of percentage ratio, and the vertical axis shows the occurrence frequency in each bin. A bank is defined as a foreign-controlled bank if foreigners own more than 50% of its equity. Data source: World Bank, Bank Regulation and Supervision Survey (available on https://www.worldbank.org/en/research/brief/BRSS, see details in Barth et al. 2013) for 138 reporting jurisdictions.

in each bin. It can be seen that, although in 27 jurisdictions foreign-controlled banks account for less than 10% of total bank assets, in 25 jurisdictions foreign-controlled banks account for more than 90% of total bank assets. Across the world, in an "average" country, foreign-controlled banks account for 46.76% of total bank assets, as of 2016.

Figure 9.2 shows the "ownership dimension" of international banking, in terms of foreign-controlled banks' share in total bank assets/credit in 19 EU countries. Although foreign banks only account for a minor share in total bank assets/credit in "core" countries such as Germany and France, foreign banks' presence is much more substantial in financial centers such as United Kingdom/Luxembourg, "peripheral" countries such as Ireland, or in Eastern European countries. It is not surprising that a peripheral country is often served by banks from its neighboring financial center, such as Ireland versus United Kingdom; while in Eastern European countries, foreign banks have won a lion's share of the market from incompetent domestic banks during the transition towards a market economy in these countries since 1990s.

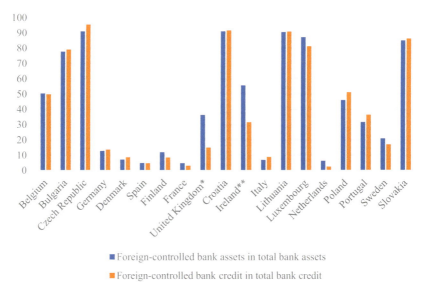

Figure 9.2 Foreign-controlled banks in selected EU countries, 2019

Notes: this chart shows the percentage ratio of foreign-controlled banks' assets/credit in total bank assets/credit in 19 EU countries. Vertical axis is in percentage points. * 2017 data, ** 2016 data. Data source: European Central Bank Statistical Data Warehouse.

9.1.2 THE LOCATION DIMENSION OF INTERNATIONAL BANKING

Who are borrowing through international banking? Figure 9.3 shows the destinations of international lending by locations of borrowing economies, in terms of outstanding cross-border claims through the banking sector. Developed countries, including European and non-European developed countries, seem to be the main borrowers; their share in cross-border claims peaked during the run-up to the 2007–2009 global financial crisis, and declined during the 2010s. The cross-border lending to the emerging market and developing countries rose substantially after the 2007–2009 financial crisis, and the offshore financial centers—such as Cayman Islands, Hong Kong, and Singapore, etc.—have been playing a non-negligible role in international banking.

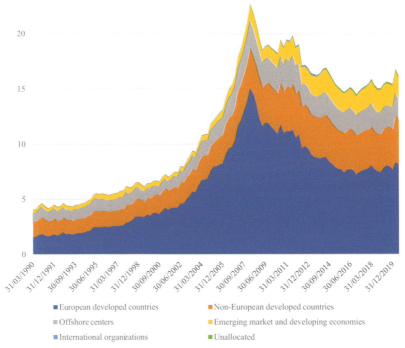

Figure 9.3 *Outstanding cross-border claims through banking sector in trillions of US dollars, by locations of borrowing economies, 1990Q1–2020Q2*
Data source: BIS international banking statistics, available on https://stats.bis.org/statx/toc/LBS.html.

Who are among the biggest borrowers through international banking? Figure 9.4 shows the outstanding cross-border claims through banking sector for some of the world's biggest borrowers as destinations of cross-border lending. These nine economies in the figure nowadays account for more than 60% of global cross-border claims. Unites States and United Kingdom are the two biggest destination economies, thanks to their large financial sectors and their status as global financial centers. Core countries in developed European countries, such as France, Germany, the Netherlands, and Switzerland, are also among the major borrowers. China used to be almost invisible before 2007, but has been become one of the main destination economies since then. The figure also includes three financial centers, Hong Kong, Luxembourg, and Singapore. As regional financial hubs, their claims through international banking exceed those much larger economies in the same regions. For example, the volume of cross-border lending to Luxembourg is

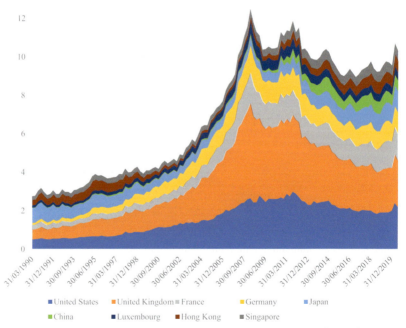

Figure 9.4 Outstanding cross-border claims through banking sector in trillions of US dollars, by borrowing economies, 1990Q1–2020Q2

Data source: BIS international banking statistics.

comparable to the Netherlands whose GDP is more than ten times larger than the former.

9.1.3 THE CURRENCY DIMENSION OF INTERNATIONAL BANKING

Figure 9.5 describes the "currency dimension" of international banking, in terms of percentage share of foreign currency denominated assets/liabilities in total bank assets/liabilities, for 18 European countries. We can see that such currency dimension can be very much different from the ownership dimension, characterized by Figure 9.2. In some countries, such as Czech Republic, although the majority of the banking sector is owned by foreigners, bank assets and liabilities are still largely denominated in domestic currencies; on the contrary, in some other countries such as Sweden, although the presence of

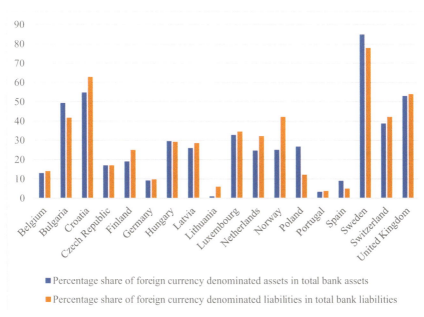

Figure 9.5 *Percentage share of foreign currency denominated assets/liabilities in total bank assets/liabilities for selected European countries, 2016*
Data source: World Bank, Bank Regulation and Supervision Survey.

foreign banks is low, bank assets and liabilities are largely denominated in foreign currencies.

Why do banks hold assets/liabilities in those currencies other than "domestic" currencies of countries in which they are operating? In reality, foreign currencies enter banks' balance sheets in many ways. On the liability side, banks, especially banks in small open economies, may often find it attractive to raise funding in the international money market—typically in popular international funding currencies such as US dollar, euro, pound sterling, Japanese yen, etc.—as international money market is more liquid than domestic one and it is easier to borrow in large volumes, too. Banks may also access to international capital market, issuing foreign currency denominated bonds or stocks to foreign investors in international financial centers. Foreign currencies can also end up in banks' liabilities in "passive" ways, for example, depositors may deposit foreign currencies in their domestic bank accounts.

On asset side, banks may directly invest in foreign currency denominated assets, and they may also issue foreign currency denominated loans to domestic borrowers—for example, a car maker in Sweden may borrow in US dollars from a Swedish bank, in order to pay its bill in the US. In emerging market economies, sometimes it is popular for domestic borrowers to borrow in foreign currencies for various reasons, such as the lack of trust for domestic currency, or taking advantage of lower interest rates on foreign currency denominated loans.

Which currencies are mostly used in international banking? Despite the large number of currencies in circulation in the world, most of cross-border banking claims are denominated in just a few "global currencies". Figure 9.6 shows the decomposition of outstanding cross-border claims through the banking sector by currencies. The shares of the most popular five currencies—US dollar, euro, Japanese yen, pound sterling, and Swiss franc—are relatively stable over the last two decades, and altogether they account for around 90% of total outstanding cross-border claims, as of 2020Q2. US dollar and euro, representing the two largest economies in the world today, together account for more than 77% of total outstanding cross-border claims.

CHAPTER NINE: INTERNATIONAL BANKING

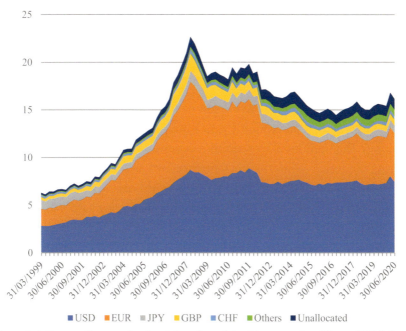

Figure 9.6 *Outstanding cross-border claims through banking sector in trillions of US dollars, by currencies, 1999Q1–2020Q2*

Notes: USD—US dollar, EUR—euro, JPY—Japanese yen, GBP—pound sterling, CHF—Swiss franc.
Data source: BIS international banking statistics.

The currency dimension adds an extra layer of complexity in international banking. A bank's assets and liabilities are not necessarily denominated in the same currencies, such *currency mismatch* exposes the bank to currency risk that arises from dynamics in exchange rates. For example, consider a bank that borrows in US dollars and invests in assets denominated in local currency. If local currency depreciates during the maturity of the assets, the bank will have to repay more in local currency. It is therefore important for banks to hedge against FX exposures. In addition, as cross-border claims are mostly denominated in one of the few global currencies, those core economies behind global currencies thus have higher potential to export monetary policy and real shocks through currency channel, as changes in money market interest rates and exchange rates of global currencies affect all financial claims denominated in these currencies.

9.2 INTERNATIONAL FINANCIAL MARKET AND GLOBAL RISK-SHARING: TRADITIONAL VIEW

Why do people bother to borrow or lend internationally? What benefit does an economy gain from participating in international banking? The traditional view on these questions focuses on global risk-sharing via access to international finance: by having the opportunity to borrow from and lend to the rest of the world, an economy is able to better allocate its resources over time, such risk-sharing across borders makes all economies better off. In this section, we take a standard two-period approach, as summarized in Obstfeld and Rogoff (1996), to see how international banking improves global risk-sharing and resource allocation, not only in an endowment economy where the income flow is exogenously given, but also in a production economy where agents do have the capability to shift resources across time periods.

9.2.1 GLOBAL RISK-SHARING IN AN ENDOWMENT ECONOMY

We first start with the simplest setup, with an endowment economy whose income flow is exogenously given. Consider a small open economy that extends to two periods, $t = 1, 2$. There are many homogeneous households living in this economy whose population is normalized to be 1; for a representative household, it receives an endowment of y_1/y_2 in $t = 1/t = 2$. The household's lifetime utility U depends on its consumption c_t in period t,

$$u(c_1, c_2) = u(c_1) + \beta u(c_2)$$

in which β is a discount factor with $0 < \beta < 1$, and the utility function $u(\cdot)$ is neoclassical, strictly increasing and concave, with $u'(\cdot) > 0, u''(\cdot) < 0$.

Households in this economy can participate in the international financial market—say, via global banking system—by saving b in a global bank with world interest rate r. By convention, the household makes a saving if $b>0$, or it borrows if $b<0$. The household's optimal decision problem is then to choose its consumption (c_1,c_2) and saving b to maximize its lifetime utility,

$$\max_{\{c_1,c_2,b\}} u(c_1,c_2)=u(c_1)+\beta u(c_2), \tag{9.1}$$
$$\text{s.t.} \quad c_1 = y_1 - b, \tag{9.2}$$
$$c_2 = y_2 + (1+r)b. \tag{9.3}$$

That is, the household makes a saving b in $t=1$, then in $t=2$ it consumes y_2 and the proceeds from saving, $(1+r)b$.

The first-order condition of the household's problem (9.1) leads to the Euler equation

$$u'(c_1^*)=\beta(1+r)u'(c_2^*) \tag{9.4}$$

in which (c_1^*,c_2^*) denotes the optimal solution.

Figure 9.7 illustrates the solution to the household's problem. First, combine the two periods' budget constraints (9.2) and (9.3), we get the household's lifetime budget constraint

$$c_2 = y_2 - (1+r)(c_1 - y_1)b, \tag{9.5}$$

which is the blue line in the figure. All consumption bundles (c_1,c_2) along this line are feasible, with the household's endowments (y_1,y_2) being given.

Along the lifetime budget constraint line (9.5), each point is crossed by an iso-utility curve, or, an indifference curve. As utility increases when an indifference curve moves towards the northeast direction, the point that gives the highest utility is point E that is just tangent to an indifference curve. The corresponding consumption bundle (c_1^*,c_2^*) is thus the optimal solution.

How does access to the international financial market improve households' welfare in this economy? Suppose the economy is in autarky,

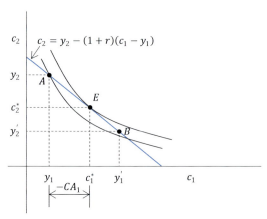

Figure 9.7 International financial market and global risk-sharing in an endowment economy

Notes: the blue line is the household's intertemporal budget constraint, and the downward sloping curves are iso-utility curves or indifference curves.

without any access to the international financial market. With each household's endowments (y_1, y_2) being the same, they have the same demand for consumption smoothing but there are no savers or borrowers to help them bring resources across periods, households thus have to consume their entire endowments in each period, i.e., $(c_1, c_2) = (y_1, y_2)$ as point A in Figure 9.7 shows. However, the indifference curve crossing point A is lower than the one crossing point E, implying that households' utility in autarky is lower.

In general, unless households' endowments are exactly $(y_1, y_2) = (c_1^*, c_2^*)$, households are strictly worse off in autarky. Access to the international financial market improves households' welfare: there are savers/borrowers somewhere else in the world who are willing to lend to/take deposits from this economy, allowing households to shift resources and smooth their consumption across periods. In the example of Figure 9.7, a household can borrow $b = c_1^* - y_1$ from abroad in $t = 1$ and consume c_1^* in $t = 1$; then in $t = 2$ it repays its debt $(1+r)b = (1+r)(c_1^* - y_1)$ out of y_2, and consumes the rest, c_2^*. In international finance, the economy's *current account balance* in period t, CA_t, is defined as the change in debt, i.e., $CA_t = b_{t+1} - b_t$; using this definition, households' debt financing in $t = 1$, b, thus equals $-CA_1$, as is shown in Figure 9.7.

Through this simple model, we can see how international banking—one of the institutions that provides access to international financial market—improves resource allocation. International banking intermediating lenders and borrowers shifts resources both across border and time periods, which helps smooth consumption and improve social welfare across countries. This also enables risk-sharing among countries: in each period, countries may receive different realized incomes, for instance, country A may receive (y_1, y_2) as point A in Figure 9.7, and country B may receive (y'_1, y'_2) as point B in Figure 9.7. In the presence of international banking, households in country A can be natural borrowers and households in country B can be natural savers; the possibility that households in country B lend to households in country A in $t=1$ through international banking helps households in both countries achieve the optimal consumption (c_1^*, c_2^*) at point E, making both countries better off.

9.2.2 GLOBAL RISK-SHARING IN A PRODUCTION ECONOMY

The welfare improving results arising from international banking hold in more general setups, for example, if we allow economies to produce their own value-added and households are able to shift resources across periods through investments. In a production economy, accessing the global financial market through international banking helps achieve optimal investment; by allocating credit to most productive places, international banking thus improves market efficiency and global risk-sharing.

To see this, continue with the model in Section 9.2.1. Keeping most settings unchanged, except that instead of receiving endowments in each period, the economy has access to production technology that transforms capital stock k_t into output y_t that can be used for consumption. The production function

$$y = f(k_t)$$

is neoclassical, strictly increasing and concave so that $f'(\cdot) > 0$, $f''(\cdot) < 0$.

Assume there is no depreciation on capital stock, and in each period t, an investment i_t can be added to increase next period's capital stock, i.e., the *law of motion* for capital stock is

$$k_{t+1} = k_t + i_t.$$

Given the production technology and the access to international finance, the household's problem is to choose a plan for consumption, investment, and saving/borrowing that maximizes its lifetime utility:

$$\max_{\{c_1, c_2, b, i_1, i_2\}} u(c_1, c_2) = u(c_1) + \beta u(c_2), \tag{9.6}$$

$$\text{s.t.} \quad c_1 = y_1 - b - i_1 = f(k_1) - b - i_1, \tag{9.7}$$

$$c_2 = y_2 + (1+r)b - i_2 = f(k_2) + (1+r)b - i_2, \tag{9.8}$$

$$k_2 = k_1 + i_1, \tag{9.9}$$

$$k_3 = k_2 + i_2. \tag{9.10}$$

Budget constraint in $t=1$, (9.7), states that consumption c_1 comes from output $y_1 = f(k_1)$, after making a saving b and investment i_1; constraint in $t=2$, (9.8), states that consumption c_2 comes from the proceeds from saving, $(1+r)b$, as well output $y_2 = f(k_2)$, after making an investment i_2, and (9.9)/(9.10) is the law of motion for capital stock across periods.

Before solving the household's problem, note that the household only lives over two periods so that there is no need to keep any capital stock after $t=2$, therefore, $k_3 = 0$ and $i_2 = -k_2$. First-order conditions with respect to c_1 and c_2 for problem (9.6) lead to the Euler equation for the household:

$$u'(c_1^*) = \beta(1+r)u'(c_2^*) \tag{9.11}$$

in which (c_1^*, c_2^*) denotes the optimal solution. This is exactly the same as the Euler equation (9.4) in the endowment economy. Furthermore, the first-order condition with respect to i_1 leads to

$$u'(c_1) = \beta u'(c_2)\left[f'(k_2) - 1\right].$$

Combine with the Euler equation (9.11) and get

$$f'(k_2^*) = r \tag{9.12}$$

in which k_2^* denotes the second period capital stock under the optimal solution. The market equilibrium is thus characterized by (9.11) and (9.12).

How can we see if international banking improves the efficiency of resource allocation and global risk-sharing? Again, we assume that the economy is in autarky, without access to the international financial market so that $b=0$ in problem (9.6). However, households can still shift resources across periods through investments, and the budget constraints (9.7) and (9.8) imply a household's lifetime budget constraint

$$\begin{aligned} c_2 &= f(k_2) + (1+r)b - i_2 \\ &= f\left[k_1 + f(k_1) - c_1\right] + k_1 + f(k_1) - c_1, \end{aligned} \tag{9.13}$$

using the fact that $i_2 = -k_2$ and $k_2 = k_1 + i_1 = k_1 + f(k_1) - c_1$. Then equation (9.13) characterizes all possible consumption bundles (c_1, c_2) using the production technology, with initial capital stock k_1 being given, therefore, equation (9.13) is called the *intertemporal production possibilities frontier*. We can further see from (9.13) that

$$\frac{dc_2}{dc_1} = -f'(k_2) - 1 < 0 \tag{9.14}$$

as well as

$$\frac{d^2 c_2}{dc_1^2} = f''(k_2) < 0. \tag{9.15}$$

Both (9.14) and (9.15) imply that the intertemporal production possibilities frontier is strictly decreasing and concave in c_1, as the red curve in Figure 9.8 shows.

In a $c_2 - c_1$ space, as Figure 9.8 shows, in autarky the optimal solution to the household's problem is to choose a consumption bundle along the intertemporal production possibilities frontier that maximizes its lifetime utility. The optimal solution is achieved at point A with (c_1^A, c_2^A) which

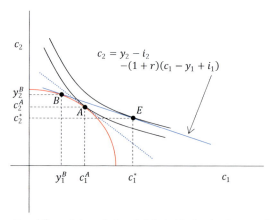

Figure 9.8 *International financial market and global risk-sharing in a production economy*
Notes: the red curve is the intertemporal production possibilities frontier, the solid blue line is the household's intertemporal budget constraint, the dotted blue line reflects the shadow interest rate in autarky, and the downward sloping curves are iso-utility curves or indifference curves.

is a tangent point between the indifference curve and the intertemporal production possibilities frontier.

Let us define the *shadow interest rate* in autarky, r^A as

$$r^A = f'(k_2^A)$$

in which k_2^A is the $t=2$ capital stock associated with point A. Shadow interest rate r^A thus measures the economy's marginal product in $t=2$ in autarky. From (9.14), we can also see that the slope of the tangent line through point A, as the dotted blue line in Figure 9.8 shows, is $-f'(k_2^A)-1=-r^A-1$.

Now let us open the border and allow the economy to access international banking. Assume that the world interest rate r is lower, $r < r^A$, then this immediately implies that, under autarky, the economy's marginal output in $t=2$ is higher than the borrowing cost r in the international financial market, $f'(k_2^A) > r$. This gives the chance for the economy to improve its intertemporal resource allocation: if a household borrows one dollar in $t=1$, and invests in its capital stock, then the marginal return from the increased capital stock k_2 in $t=2$, which is $f'(k_2^A)$, will be higher than the interest rate r to repay the debt.

Figure 9.8 visualizes how international banking improves resources allocation in autarky. In the presence of international banking, the household will choose a production plan so that the marginal output in $t=2$, $f'(k_2^B)$, equals world interest rate r, as point B shows. Given the opportunity to save or borrow, the household's lifetime budget constraint becomes

$$c_2 = y_2 - i_2 - (1+r)(c_1 - y_1 + i_1), \qquad (9.16)$$

as the solid blue line in Figure 9.8. Note that it is less steep than the tangent line through A, given $r^A > r$. Now with the output plan (y_1^B, y_2^B) at point B, the household's lifetime budget constraint allows it to choose any consumption bundle (c_1, c_2) along the solid blue line to maximize its lifetime utility. The optimal solution to the household's problem is given by point E with (c_1^*, c_2^*) which is tangent to a higher indifference curve. This implies that, with the production plan (y_1^B, y_2^B), the economy will incur a current account deficit $c_1^* - y_1^B$ in order to achieve a higher consumption in $t=1$, and use the increased output in $t=2$ to repay the debt.

9.2.3 SUMMARY

The traditional view of international banking, that is captured in this simple intertemporal optimization problem, shows much of the "bright side" of international banking, which provides economies frictionless access to international financial market that helps improve cross-border and intertemporal allocation of resources through debt instruments. This is even true for production economies, in which investment allows agents to shift resources over time.

However, in reality, international banking is never frictionless. As we have seen in the previous chapters, banking has the potential to improve resource allocation, but it also introduces an additional layer of problems as long as banks are subject to frictions and failures. The same financial frictions and market failures that we have seen before surely persist in the international setting. To make it worse, the lack of legal enforcement at the international level implies imperfect enforcement; this, as Broner and Ventura (2016) show, adds extra volatility in cross-border financial flows. Additionally, international banking is also heavily shaped by the international elements that are involved, such as exchange rate, international trade, sovereign risk, etc. All of these concerns call for a framework that explicitly integrates banks' incentives and behavior in a cross-border setup, as well as the features and frictions in international finance to better understand the pros and cons of international banking.

9.3 GLOBAL BANKS AND INTERNATIONAL TRANSMISSION OF MONETARY POLICY

To go beyond the "traditional view", Bräuning and Ivashina (2020) provide an analytical framework that explicitly considers the cross-border credit supply of a global bank that is subject to capital constraint, exchange rate dynamics, and monetary policies in both home and foreign countries. It reveals how global banks balance their investment opportunities at home and abroad, as a reaction to monetary policy shocks, and how monetary policy shock in one country spills over across borders. Such "bank perspective" thus offers more insights on how banking frictions affect international financial flows and synchronize business cycles around the globe.

9.3.1 MODEL SETUP: GLOBAL BANK AND GLOBAL BALANCE SHEET

Consider a world with two countries—"home" (call it country h) and "foreign" (call it country f)—over a time horizon of two periods, $t=0,1$. All investment decisions are made in $t=0$, and returns are realized in $t=1$. A global bank headquartered in country h provides financial intermediation services through its subsidiaries in both countries.

The bank has access to a lending technology: in the home country, it earns revenue $h(L^h)$ on total home lending L^h; in the foreign country, it earns revenue $f(L^f)$ on total foreign lending L^f. Both $h(\cdot)$ and $f(\cdot)$ are strictly concave functions, such that $h'(\cdot)>0$, $h''(\cdot)<0$, $f'(\cdot)>0$, and $f''(\cdot)<0$.

To abstract from the complex corridor system, as characterized in Chapter 7, Section 7.2.2, in this section we assume that central banks in home and foreign countries use a "floor" system, using interest rate paid on reserves as the main monetary policy tool.[2] The bank's home/foreign subsidiary holds reserves in a home/foreign central bank. Assume that R^h /R^f reserves are held in a home/foreign central bank, with interest rate r^h/ r^f paid on reserves. To focus on the key mechanism, assume that marginal return of the lending technology, $h'(\cdot)/f'(\cdot)$, does not depend on r^h/r^f.

Note that currencies are different in two countries. Denote S_t as period t spot exchange rate, and S_t means units of home currency per foreign currency. From now on, we express everything in terms of home currency.

In $t=0$, the bank as a whole has a fixed amount of equity, E, and faces a binding capital requirement, a capital adequacy ratio k on its total lending:

$$k\left(L^h + S_0 L^f\right) \leq E.$$

Except for equity financing, the bank can also collect deposits, D^h, in the home country for funding, incurring a gross funding cost d. Funding cost $d(D^h)$ is a convex function for deposit supply D^h, i.e., $d'(\cdot) > 0$, $d''(\cdot) > 0$. Figure 9.9 shows the consolidated balance sheet of the bank in $t=0$.

To fund its foreign subsidiary in $t=0$, the bank has to convert funds that are collected in home currency into foreign currency in the spot market. This generates a currency mismatch between assets and liabilities, which exposes the bank to exchange rate risk in the future: after foreign lending L^f returns in $t=1$, the bank needs to convert the foreign return to home currency; if home currency appreciates in $t=1$, i.e., the spot exchange rate $S_1 < S_0$, the bank will suffer a loss. To hedge against the currency risk,

Assets	Liabilities
Home lending L^h	
Foreign lending $S_0 L^f$	Total deposits D^h
Home reserves R^h	
Foreign reserves $S_0 R^f$	Equity E

Figure 9.9 Bank's consolidated balance sheets in $t = 0$

assume the bank has access to foreign exchange (FX) swaps such that the bank can purchase foreign currency at spot exchange rate S_0 in $t=0$ with agreement to sell at the forward exchange rate F_0 in $t=1$. Suppose the bank hedges H of its FX positions, leaving a volume of U unhedged. In addition, to take reality into account, that unhedged FX positions are subject to extra regulatory capital requirement, assume that a capital ratio k' is required for unhedged FX positions.

9.3.2 INTERNATIONAL TRANSMISSION OF MONETARY POLICY THROUGH GLOBAL BANKS

The bank's problem in $t=0$ is to maximize its expected profit in domestic currency,

$$\max_{\{D^h, R^h, R^f, L^h, L^f, H, U\}} (1+r^h)R^h + h(L^h) + F_0 H + UE[S_1] - d(D^h), \quad (9.17)$$

$$\text{s.t.} \quad k(L^h + S_0 L^f) + k' S_0 U \leq E, \quad (9.18)$$

$$H + U = (1+r^f)R^f + f(L^f), \quad (9.19)$$

$$D^h + E = R^h + L^h + S_0 R^f + S_0 L^f, \quad (9.20)$$

$$D^h \geq 0, \quad (9.21)$$

$$L^h \geq 0, \quad (9.22)$$

$$L^f \geq 0, \quad (9.23)$$

$$R^h \geq 0, \quad (9.24)$$

$$R^f \geq 0, \quad (9.25)$$

$$H \geq 0, \quad (9.26)$$

$$U \geq 0. \quad (9.27)$$

Object function (9.17) consists of the bank's gross return from holding reserves in home central bank $(1+r^h)R^h$, its return from home lending $h(L^h)$, the value of hedged foreign assets $F_0 H$, the value of unhedged foreign assets $UE[S_1]$ under expected spot exchange rate S_1 in $t=1$, and funding cost on deposits $d(D^h)$. Resource constraint (9.18) reflects the capital requirements on lending and unhedged FX positions; constraint (9.19) means the sum of hedged and unhedged FX assets (denominated in foreign currency) equals the value of FX assets, including the gross return from holding reserves in foreign central bank $(1+r^f)R^f$ and return from foreign lending $f(L^f)$; constraint (9.20) means total assets equal total liabilities in the bank's consolidated balance sheet, as Figure 9.9 shows. Constraints (9.21) to (9.27) require that all decision variables are non-negative.

The optimization problem is solved by Lagrangian. To ease computation, temporarily leave constraints (9.21) to (9.27) aside. Set up Lagrangian as

$$\begin{aligned}\mathcal{L} =\ & (1+r^h)R^h + h(L^h) + F_0 H + UE[S_1] - d(D^h) \\ & + \lambda\left[D^h + E - R^h - L^h - S_0 R^f - S_0 L^f\right] \\ & + \mu\left[E - k(L^h + S_0 L^f) - k' S_0 U\right] \\ & + v\left[(1+r^f)R^f + f(L^f) - H - U\right],\end{aligned}$$

and first-order conditions yield

$$\frac{\partial \mathcal{L}}{\partial R^h} = 1 + r^h - \lambda = 0, \tag{9.28}$$

$$\frac{\partial \mathcal{L}}{\partial R^f} = -\lambda S_0 + v(1+r^f) = 0, \tag{9.29}$$

$$\frac{\partial \mathcal{L}}{\partial L^h} = h'(L^h) - \lambda - \mu k = 0, \tag{9.30}$$

$$\frac{\partial \mathcal{L}}{\partial L^f} = -\lambda S_0 - \mu k S_0 + v f'(L^f) = 0, \tag{9.31}$$

$$\frac{\partial \mathcal{L}}{\partial D^h} = -d'(D^h) + \lambda = 0, \tag{9.32}$$

$$\frac{\partial \mathcal{L}}{\partial H} = F_0 - v = 0, \tag{9.33}$$

$$\frac{\partial \mathcal{L}}{\partial U} = E[S_1] - k' S_0 \mu - v = 0. \tag{9.34}$$

What can we see from the first-order conditions? First, combining (9.28) and (9.32) yields

$$d'(D^h) = 1 + r^h. \tag{9.35}$$

This means that, in equilibrium, the bank's marginal funding cost on raising deposits in home country equals the return on holding reserves in the home central bank.

Second, combining (9.28) and (9.30) yields

$$h'(L^h) = d'(D^h) + \mu k. \tag{9.36}$$

This means that, in equilibrium, the bank's marginal return from home lending equals the marginal cost of raising deposits, plus μk which reflects the shadow price of bank capital. That is, if there were no constraint from capital requirements or the capital constraint (9.18) is not binding ($\mu = 0$), the bank would lend until its marginal return from lending equals marginal cost on funding. However, if the capital constraint (9.18) is binding so that $\mu > 0$, the constraint will prevent the bank from lending as much as it wants, leading to a lower level of home lending L^h, given $h'(\cdot) > 0, h''(\cdot) < 0$. From now on, we assume that the capital constraint (9.18) is indeed binding.

Third, combining (9.28), (9.31), and (9.33) yields

$$\frac{F_0}{S_0} f'(L^f) = 1 + r^h + \mu k. \tag{9.37}$$

Note that $f'(L^f)$ is the bank's marginal return from foreign lending (in foreign currency) and $\frac{F_0}{S_0}$ is the premium on currency exchange, the left-hand side of (9.37) is thus the marginal return from foreign lending in home currency. Therefore, (9.37) implies that the bank's marginal return from foreign lending equals marginal cost of funding, plus the shadow price of bank capital under the binding capital constraint (9.18).

In addition, we can express $\frac{F_0}{S_0}$ by combining (9.28), (9.29), and (9.33)

$$1 + r^h = \frac{F_0}{S_0}(1 + r^f) \tag{9.38}$$

which is exactly *covered interest rate parity* (CIP) in standard international finance theory: non-arbitrage condition in international money market requires that the interest rate differential between two currencies should equal the differential between the forward and spot exchange rates.

Combining (9.37) and (9.38), we get

$$f'(L^f) = 1 + r^f + \frac{1+r^f}{1+r^h}\mu k. \qquad (9.39)$$

Again, if there were no constraint from capital requirements or the capital constraint (9.18) is not binding ($\mu = 0$), (9.39) becomes $f'(L^f) = 1 + r^f$ so that the bank's foreign lending only depends on foreign monetary policy rate r^f. In contrast, financial friction makes monetary policy spill over across the border: when the capital constraint (9.18) is binding ($\mu > 0$), (9.39) implies that foreign lending does not only depend on foreign monetary policy, but also depends on home monetary policy. To see such *spillover* effect, differentiating (9.39) with respect to r^h leads to

$$\frac{dL^f}{dr^h} = -\frac{(1+r^f)\mu k}{(1+r^f)^2 f''(L^f)} > 0, \qquad (9.40)$$

given that $f''(\cdot) < 0$. That is, expansionary monetary policy in the home country with a falling r^h leads to a contraction in foreign lending L^f.

Finally, combining (9.35), (9.36), (9.37), and (9.38) yields

$$h'(L^h) = \frac{1+r^h}{1+r^f} f'(L^f). \qquad (9.41)$$

To see the implication more clearly, we can assign certain functional forms for $h'(\cdot)$ and $f'(\cdot)$: assume that $h'(L^h) = \ln L^h$ and $f'(L^f) = \ln L^f$. Take logarithm on both sides of (9.41) to get

$$\ln L^f - \ln L^h = r^h - r^f = \Delta r. \qquad (9.42)$$

This means that the bank's home and foreign lending decisions are interconnected by the interest rate differential between the two countries, Δr. Suppose the interest rate differential rises, —either because of tightening home monetary policy (higher r^h) or because of loosening foreign monetary policy (lower r^f),—the bank will increase foreign lending *relative* to home lending.

9.3.3 SUMMARY

Bräuning-Ivashina model provides a simple analytical framework that integrates banking frictions and banks' optimal investment decisions, allowing us to better understand the role of global banks in cross-border monetary policy spillovers as well as international financial flows, which are results from global banks' portfolio adjustments. The model is analytically tractable, and also flexible enough to include more market frictions.

In the Bräuning-Ivashina model, what is not explicitly addressed, but relevant for reality, is the currency dimension of international banking. Without frictions in the FX market, the model naturally leads to a non-arbitrage, CIP condition as equation (9.38) states. However, one of the most distinguishing features in the international FX market during the last decade is the persistent break-down of CIP condition which is widely documented in recent literature (see, for example, Du et al. 2018b). Many reasons may cause the break-down: for example, demand for safe assets that leads to a premium for safe-haven government bonds (Du et al. 2018a and Jiang et al. 2020), market segmentation that prevents arbitrageur from eliminating CIP deviations (Rime et al. 2017), etc. The persistent breakdown of CIP condition implies that banks may favor borrowing/lending in certain currencies, this may create another layer of complexity in cross-border monetary policy spillover beyond the Bräuning-Ivashina model, as monetary policy—especially monetary policy in the core economies—certainly affects deviations from CIP condition.

9.4 EMPIRICAL EVIDENCE

9.4.1 INTERNATIONAL BANKING AND TRANSMISSION OF MONETARY POLICY

MONETARY POLICY SPILLOVER

International banking plays an important role in providing financial resources—particularly in emerging market economies, in which foreign banks often account for more than half of domestic lending. As foreign banks are subject to monetary policy in their home countries, their lending activities in the host countries may thus be affected by monetary policy at home. That is, monetary policy effectively spills over across borders by international banks, as the Bräuning-Ivashina model predicts.

Using the credit register that covers all business loans in Mexico over 2001–2015, Morais et al. (2019) identify how monetary policies—both conventional and unconventional—from core countries affect the credit supply to domestic firms through foreign banks, through the following regression:

$$y_{bit} = \sum_c \left(\alpha_1^c InterestRate_{t-1}^c + \alpha_2^c InterestRate_{t-1}^c \times c_b \right)$$
$$+ \sum_c \left(\beta_1^c QE_{t-1}^c + \beta_2^c QE_{t-1}^c \times c_b \right) + X_{ct} + \epsilon_{bit}$$

in which y_{bit} denotes lending from bank b to firm i in quarter t, $InterestRate_t^c$ denotes monetary policy rate of economy c, with c = US, UK, Euro area, Mexico, c_b denotes bank b's nationality, QE_t^c measures intensity of quantitative easing (QE) program in country c by annual change of the central bank's balance sheet size relative to GDP, and X_{ct} contains macro-level controls of all countries. They also focus on borrowers that borrow from both domestic and foreign banks, and distinguish between effects from domestic and foreign banks using Khwaja-Mian identification (see Chapter 7, Section 7.6.1).

Morais et al. (2019) find that monetary policy shocks from core economies affect domestic credit supply mainly through foreign banks that headquarter in these economies; in particular, foreign QE programs also have expansionary effects on domestic credit supply. As a mirror, Temesvary et al. (2018) demonstrate how international banks in the US transmit US monetary policy to foreign countries. They find that monetary tightening in the US leads to contraction in US banks' cross-border lending, and the contractionary effect is stronger for banks with tighter capital constraints. A similar effect is also found for unconventional monetary policy such as QE.

When market share of foreign banks is not high, such as in Turkey in which foreign banks only account for 12% of the domestic credit market, Baskaya et al. (2017) show that the spillover of core economies' monetary policy mainly takes place through domestic banks' cross-border funding—the currency dimension of international banking (see Section 9.1.3) prevails. Expansionary monetary policy in core countries increases capital inflow into Turkey, larger, better capitalized domestic banks increase their cross-border funding and lend more in the domestic credit market. Furthermore, domestic banks are found to be stabilizers during crises, in that foreign banks flee from emerging market economies and the gap in the domestic credit market is largely filled by domestic banks.

INTERNATIONAL BANKING AND DOMESTIC MONETARY POLICY TRANSMISSION

International banking may also affect domestic monetary policy transmission, both for core economies and for "recipient" economies. Using Kashyap-Stein identification strategy (see Section 7.6.1), Cetorelli and Goldberg (2012) find that US banks with branches in foreign countries are less affected by US monetary policy shocks. When US monetary policy is tightening, these banks are able to raise funding through their foreign branches to reduce their liquidity management cost, so that they are less responsive in cutting domestic lending, compared with banks without foreign branches. For those international banks, the bank lending channel of domestic monetary policy is thus weakened.

The bank lending channel of domestic monetary policy may be impaired in recipient countries, particularly when a substantial share of bank lending is denominated in foreign currencies. The reason is, in a small open economy, when banks fund themselves in foreign currencies and lend in foreign currencies, their activities are largely influenced by foreign monetary policy, not domestic monetary policy that mostly affects domestic money market in which transactions are largely denominated in domestic currency. Using supervisory data from Hungary, Ongena et al. (2021) find that expansionary domestic monetary policy has an expansionary effect on lending for banks with lower capital ratios in the domestic currency but not in the foreign currency, while expansionary foreign monetary policy leads to more expansion in foreign currency lending than domestic currency lending.

It is less clear, whether bank lending channel of domestic monetary policy is affected in recipient countries, when domestic lending is denominated in domestic currencies, even if banks raise funding in foreign currencies. Implementing domestic monetary policy in a recipient country (call it "home" country) may lead to a gap between the interest rate in home country, r^h, and the interest rate in the country where foreign currency (FX) funding comes from (call it "foreign" country), r^f. To make things simple, let us assume that r^h/r^f is the interest rate that a bank pays on funding through the home/foreign money market. However, once the gap between r^h and r^f emerges, the exchange rate between home and foreign currencies will close the gap: without friction in the FX market, given the spot exchange rate S_t in period $t=0,1$, this means

$$1+r^h = \frac{S_1}{S_0}(1+r^f).$$

That is, no matter if a bank raises one unit funding in domestic currency in $t=0$ and repays in $t=1$ at home interest rate r^h, or raises one unit funding in foreign currency in $t=0$ at spot exchange rate S_0, then in $t=1$ repays in foreign currency at spot exchange rate S_1 with foreign interest rate r^f, the funding cost shall be the same. Such *uncovered interest rate parity* (UIP) implies a non-arbitrage condition, so that with any change in domestic monetary policy rate, there will be an equal change in banks' funding cost, *independent* on banks' funding currencies; in other words, if UIP holds, FX funding does not affect domestic monetary policy transmission through the bank lending channel, as long as domestic lending is denominated in domestic currency.

The same argument applies if banks use a swap agreement to hedge against currency risk, i.e., borrowing in foreign currency in $t=0$ and converting to home currency at spot exchange rate S_0, at the same time making an agreement with a counterparty to convert from home currency back to foreign currency in $t=1$ at a pre-agreed forward exchange rate F_0. Non-arbitrage condition requires that

$$1+r^h = \frac{F_0}{S_0}(1+r^f),$$

which is exactly the same *covered interest rate parity* (CIP) as (9.38). This again implies that banks' funding currencies do not affect bank lending channel of domestic monetary policy.

However, UIP and CIP often do not hold in reality. Based on Norwegian banks' quarterly balance sheet reports over two decades, Cao and Dinger (2021) show that once UIP and CIP do not hold, banks are able to explore the arbitrage opportunity and choose the funding source—domestic or international money market—that gives them a cost advantage. Using UIP/CIP deviation—deviation of domestic currency's exchange rate from what is predicted by UIP/CIP as an indicator of FX funding supply, they find that domestic banks increase lending under expansionary monetary policy at home, while they do not cut lending when domestic monetary policy is tightening, as banks can switch to cheaper FX funding and maintain their lending. This implies that domestic monetary policy may be less effective, particularly when central banks attempt to "lean against the wind". On the macro level, using cross-border financial flow data, Avdjiev et al. (2019) also find that CIP deviation is strongly correlated with cross-border banking flows.

9.4.2 INTERNATIONAL RISK-TAKING CHANNEL

International banking may also affect banks' risk-taking behavior. Bruno and Shin (2015b) show that when domestic borrowers are exposed to currency mismatch, i.e., funding in foreign currencies but receiving cash flows in domestic currency, appreciation in domestic currency increases borrowers' profits, so as their net worth. For those global banks that lend to these borrowers, this means a falling credit risk of the borrowers and makes the banks' balance sheets stronger. This allows banks to take leverage, expand lending, and take more risks. Exchange rate dynamics and FX funding inflows thus create an international risk-taking channel. Using cross-border banking flow data, Bruno and Shin (2015a) and Bruno and Shin (2015b) find that domestic currency appreciation leads to increasing leverage of global banks and higher balance sheet risks.

Ioannidou et al. (2015) investigate the international risk-taking channel through the credit register of Bolivia, whose banking system was almost fully dollarized over the period of 1999–2003. Under an exchange rate regime of crawling peg with the US dollar, changes in the US federal funds rate are transmitted in Bolivian money market. They find that under expansionary monetary policy in the US, Bolivian banks issue new loans to *ex ante* less credit-worthy borrowers, which leads to a higher *ex post* default rate, implying banks' increasing risk-taking incentives.

9.5 EXERCISES

1 **International banking in numbers**
   Explore BIS international banking statistics, the World Bank's Bank Regulation and Supervision Survey, as well as other national/international data resources to better understand the implication of international banking for your country through the following questions:

   (a) Market structure and performance

   i. How many foreign banks, including foreign bank subsidiaries and branches, are there in your country?
   ii. What is their share in total bank assets? What is their share in lending market? Are they particularly targeting borrowers in certain sectors, such as real estate, shipping, etc.?
   iii. How do foreign banks perform, compared with domestic banks? You may measure their performance by return on assets (ROA), return on equity (ROE), z-score, non-performing loan (NPL) ratio, etc.

(a) Cross-border banking

    i. How important is cross-border banking in your country, compared with the other forms of cross-border financial inflows and outflows?

    ii. Which countries are major borrowers of your country? Which countries are major lenders to your country?

    iii. What are the main currencies for your country's cross-border claims?

2 Intertemporal approach to international banking: Endowment economy

Consider a small open economy which lasts for two periods, $t=1,2$. There is only one commodity that is tradable but it cannot be stored, and in each period the representative household is endowed with $y_1 = 100$ and $y_2 = 200$ of such good. The representative household has a perfect foresight and is able to borrow or save at a constant real interest rate in the first period. The exogenous world financial market interest rate is given as $r^* = 0.1$. The utility function of the representative household is

$$u(c_1, c_2) = \sqrt{c_1} + \beta \sqrt{c_2}$$

in which c_1/c_2 denotes the consumption in $t=1/t=2$, and β is the discount factor with $\beta = \dfrac{1}{1.1}$.

(a) Derive the Euler equation for the representative household and compute its optimal consumption in each period, call it (c_1^*, c_2^*). Is there any current account surplus or deficit in period 1?

(b) Now suppose that the economy does not have access to the international financial market, i.e., people in the economy have to live in autarky. Compare the residents' welfare in this case with that in question (a), and explain your findings.

(c) Now go back to question (a). Suppose the world market interest rate r^* can take other values. Then how much r^* should there be to make the residents indifferent between participating international financial market and living in autarky?

3 **Intertemporal approach to international banking: Production economy**

Follow the model of international banking with production economy, as in Section 9.2.2, and keep all settings unchanged. Now assume that the shadow interest rate in autarky, r^A, is lower than the world interest rate r, $r^A < r$.

Using the graphical approach, as Figure 9.8, show how international banking improves households' intertemporal resource allocation.

4 **Swap agreement and demand for reserves, based on Bräuning and Ivashina (2020)**

In this exercise, we continue with the Bräuning-Ivashina model in Section 9.3 and determine the bank's demand for global reserves through explicitly modelling of the bank's swap agreement.

Keep all the settings the same as in Section 9.3. Assume that the bank makes a swap agreement with a "counterparty"—a global, non-financial firm that is headquartered in a foreign country and operates in both countries. In $t=0$, the firm invests in projects in both countries, and in $t=1$ all projects return. The firm hence has the demand to convert foreign currency to home currency in $t=0$ before it can invest in home country, and to convert home currency to foreign currency in $t=1$ after home projects return. The firm's demand for currency exchange in both periods is exactly complementary to the bank's demand, so that it is feasible to serve as the bank's counterparty in the swap agreement: in $t=0$, the firm and the bank exchange currencies at the spot exchange rate S_0, and at the same time, agree to exchange currencies again in $t=1$ at the forward exchange rate F_0.

The firm is totally funded by its own wealth, W (in foreign currency), and as a non-financial firm, it does not hold any reserves. In $t=0$, the profit-maximizing firm chooses to invest $\hat{H}$ in home country, and $W - \hat{H}$ in foreign country; it thus swaps $\hat{H}$ with the bank. In $t=1$, the firm's investment in home/foreign country returns, with the return function being the logarithm of investment, i.e., $\mathcal{H}(\cdot) = \ln(\cdot) / \mathcal{F}(\cdot) = \ln(\cdot)$.

(a) Swap market equilibrium
   i. Specify the firm's optimization problem. Using the first-order condition, derive the firm's swap supply $\hat{H}$.
   ii. In equilibrium, the firm's swap supply is entirely taken by the bank. Express the equilibrium volume of swap as a function of r^h, r^f, W, and S_0.

(b) Comparative statics
   i. As in equation (9.42), define Δr as the interest rate differential between home and foreign countries. How does the equilibrium volume of swap vary with Δr?
   ii. Using your result, combining with the bank's budget constraint on swap (9.19), show how a bank's foreign reserves vary with Δr. Interpret your result.
   iii. Furthermore, show how a bank's home reserves vary with Δr. Interpret your result.

NOTES

1 Such an import/export view on international banking is analogous to "pull"/"push" factors in Calvo et al. (1993) and Calvo et al. (1996), on the discussion of capital flows to emerging market economies.
2 This is, however, not an oversimplification, as the floor system is also used by some central banks in reality. Bernhardsen and Kloster (2010) provide an insightful comparison between floor and corridor system.

CHAPTER 10
Political economy in banking

10.1 INTRODUCTION

In reality, banking is much affected by politics; governments and politicians are deeply involved in banking. As in many of modern economies, central banks are created to provide banking services for all banks in the economy—as we have seen in Chapter 7, and regulatory agencies are established to discipline banks—as we will see in Chapter 12. Aside from central banking and banking regulation, governments and politicians interact with the banking sector in many other dimensions.

One crucial channel through which politics and banking interact is government ownership of banks. Across the world, non-negligible bank ownership is held by government. Defining a bank as a *government-owned bank* if government share in the bank exceeds 20% of equity, La Porta et al. (2002) find that across the world government-owned banks' share in the number of total banks is 41.6% in 1995, compared with 58.9% in 1970. The world's share of banking assets controlled by government-owned banks is 48% as of 1995. In the World Bank's Bank Regulation and Supervision Survey, a *government-controlled bank* is defined as a bank whose government share exceeds 50%[1]; by this more stringent standard, government-controlled banks hold about 15% of total bank assets in an average jurisdiction in 2016. Figure 10.1 presents the histogram for percentage ratio of government-controlled banks' assets in total bank assets across the world as of 2016. Substantial government ownership and control worldwide in the banking sector imply an ample scope that government may influence banks' decisions and divert financial resources from the banking sector for its own interest.

Another crucial channel between politics and banking is personal connections among bankers and politicians. Managers of big banks are sometimes employed as government officials; retired politicians—many of them are former bank regulators—are sometimes hired as senior managers in big banks, not to mention that government officials are often appointed directly as managers in government-owned banks; bankers and politicians are often connected through social networks such as executive education programs, alumni clubs, and elite networks. Such personal

CHAPTER TEN: POLITICAL ECONOMY IN BANKING

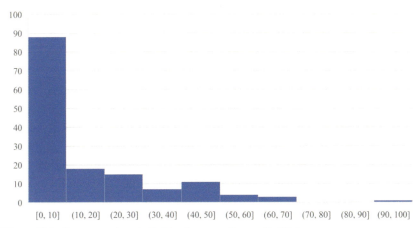

Figure 10.1 Government-controlled banks across the world, 2016

Notes: this histogram shows the distribution of percentage ratio of government-controlled banks' assets in total bank assets; the horizontal axis contains the bins of percentage ratio, and the vertical axis shows the occurrence frequency in each bin. A government-controlled bank is defined as a bank whose government share exceeds 50% of equity. Data sources: World Bank's Bank Regulation and Supervision Survey (Barth et al. 2013) for 143 reporting jurisdictions, together with the author's own update for China.

connections may help bankers and politicians to benefit from each other's expertise, but also create potentials that bankers and politicians may collude and act for their private interests, at the cost of the rest of society.

Both government ownership and banker-politician personal connections imply that banking and politics are inextricable intertwined in the real world, so that banking outcomes are often shaped by politics. For example, as banks are among the main providers of credit in an economy, politicians may find it extremely attractive to exploit banks' power in credit allocation and wide reach to voters. A politician who strives for reelections may direct her connected bankers to allocate more credit to electorates, increasing the likelihood of being reelected, although this may increase banks' credit risks. Politicians under higher fiscal pressure may tap local banks for cheaper funding sources, although increasing likelihood of government default may destabilize the banking system. On the other hand, bankers do not serve politicians for free, instead, they expect reciprocal reward from politicians. For example, banks that lend to heavily indebted governments may expect that they will be among the first to be bailed out by the governments during crises in the future; banks that conduct "political lending" for politicians may anticipate that their favor will be returned with less restrictions on them in the legislation of regulatory rules.

The *political economy in banking*, which is characterized by interactions between banking and politics in many dimensions, affects outcomes of banking, which may lead to a wide spectrum of consequences in the real economy. For example, politics may bias banks' credit allocation among borrowers, which may not only have further implications on inequality and economic growth, but also affect banks' credit risks and financial stability. Therefore, political economy in banking helps us better understand the banking channel of many issues in the political economy of the real world, as well as the political origins of various frictions in the banking sector.

This chapter will be mostly centered around banking, i.e., we will only focus on those banking outcomes that are affected by politics, instead of political outcomes that are affected by banking. Given that political economy involves numerous questions and methodologies, in this chapter, we mainly focus on two analytical frameworks that help us better understand the political influences on banking:

The first is the implication of government ownership for banking. In Section 10.2, we distinguish two channels of political influence through government ownership: the *ownership* channel that allows government to claim a share of banks' income, as well as the *control rights* channel that allows government to directly take part in banks' decision-making. These two channels are related to each other, but they are not the same. We then examine how banks' decision making is affected by government's ownership and control rights. Using a simple model based on Shleifer and Vishny (1994), we show that banking outcome is only efficient if the bank manager has full control over decision-making and does not cooperate with politicians who are only concerned with their political careers. Once such politicians gain control, and/or the bank manager cooperates with politicians, banking outcomes will be inefficient and contain too much wasteful investment.

The second is how credit cycles are shaped by political cycles. As one of the most important goals in a politician's political career—at least in democracies—is to be reelected, politicians may have the incentive to exploit their connections with bankers and divert credit allocation to electorates through the banks, in order to win more voters and increase the chances of being reelected. In Section 10.3, based on Nordhaus (1975) and MacRae (1977), we characterize a politician's optimal credit allocation problem over one election cycle, and show the politician's incentive to please voters by diverting credit from connected banks is the highest in an election year and the lowest in the year right after winning election. Election cycles thus create credit cycles.

In Section 10.4, we will go through a wide range of empirical evidence on political economy in banking, including how government ownership influences banking outcomes and bank performance, how legal system and legal rules shape bank lending, how election cycles generate credit cycles, how political economy affects efficiency in credit allocation, and so on.

10.2 GOVERNMENT OWNERSHIP AND BANKING OUTCOMES

One of the most crucial channels between politics and banking is government ownership of banks. In general, government may own—partially or entirely—a bank for a variety of reasons, including but not restricted to:

1 Government may set up banks to directly fund public goods that are either not profitable or too risky for private banks, such as infrastructure projects and strategic industries. Many of such banks are created as development banks, such as KfW (Kreditanstalt für Wiederaufbau) in Germany and China Development Bank (CDB) in China;

2 In developing economies with poorly protected property rights and less developed legal system, government may provide banking services by itself through state-owned banks that are backed by government's own credibility;

3 Government may hold shares in previous state-owned, policy-oriented banks, during their transition towards market-based banks by introducing private shares, examples include many banks in transition economies, such as Eastern European countries and China;
4 In the beginning of banking liberalization or a transition towards a market economy, when the barrier to entry is high and private capital is weak, government sometimes "kick-starts" creating new entrant banks through public-private partnership; in return, as an initial capital provider, government becomes banks' shareholder. One example is the creation of city commercial banks (CCBs) in China;
5 As a consequence of bank bailout and nationalization after bank failure. In this case, government replaces previous shareholders. For example, several Norwegian banks were taken over by the national government during the Nordic banking crisis in late 1980s and early 1990s.[2]

What does government ownership imply for banks? How does government influence banks through its ownership to achieve its goals? In this section, we discuss the role of government ownership in banking, and how government ownership affects banking outcomes.

10.2.1 GOVERNMENT OWNERSHIP AND BANKING: MAIN HYPOTHESES

Although in the real world there are many reasons why government owns banks, how bank's government ownership affects banking outcomes is not always clear, and sometimes complex. In general, the role of government ownership in banking can be motivated and interpreted by three theoretical frameworks in economics:

1 Market failure prevents private banks from achieving efficient allocation, and public goods in banking—such as development of rural banking infrastructure and maintaining the stability of the banking system—are hardly efficiently provided by the market; less well-functioning institutions, such as weak legal system, also prevent financial market from efficiently allocating financial resources. For

these reasons, government ownership of banks may help align banks' decision-making with public interests, or, implement the solution of a "benevolent social planner"—a *social view* as best summarized in Atkinson and Stiglitz (2015);

2. However, such a benevolent social planner does not exist in reality, rather, governments—as banks' shareholders—are delegated by politicians that are subject to the same market failure as private bank owners and bank managers. Because of asymmetric information, the *principal-agent view* implies that the "principal"—politicians delegating the government ownership may not have sufficient incentive to make an effort for the interests of the "agent"—the general public, leading to inferior bank management;

3. Furthermore, politicians have their own private interests, the *political economy view* argues that politicians have the incentive to exploit government ownership in banks to achieve their own agenda and benefit their own political careers.

As the need for public intervention to correct market failure and anomalies caused by asymmetric information has been intensively discussed in the previous chapters, and the analytical frameworks that are covered in these chapters are also suitable to motivate the social view and the principal-agent view, in this chapter, we will mostly focus on the third one, the political economy view of banks' government ownership. We explicitly model government ownership in banks as well as interactions between banker and politician, using the framework that is developed in Shleifer and Vishny (1994).

10.2.2 MODELLING GOVERNMENT OWNERSHIP AND CONTROL RIGHTS

AGENTS, TECHNOLOGIES, AND PREFERENCES

Consider an economy with a government (that is delegated by a politician) and a bank. To win support from voters and improve the chance of being reelected, the politician can require the bank to increase credit supply to the economy by L to please the voters. Assume that the extra bank credit is allocated to unproductive sectors so that the return from L is zero. To supply L, the bank needs to pay depositors a deposit rate $1+r$ which is subsidized by the government. By doing so, the politician pleases the depositors, too.

The total benefit that the politician derives from her policy on excess lending L is characterized by a function $B(L)$. Assume that prior to the credit policy, the bank earns a profit of π. The *ownership* of the bank is defined by how the bank's cash flow is split: assume that the bank manager claims a share α, $0 \leq \alpha \leq 1$ of the bank's cash flow, and the government claims $1-\alpha$. Therefore, the bank is completely private if $\alpha = 1$, and it is completely government-owned if $\alpha = 0$.

To induce the bank to carry out her credit policy, the politician subsidizes the bank via a transfer t from the government to the bank. As the government also claims a share of the bank's cash flow, the government's net cost of implementing the policy is

$$T = t - (1-\alpha)\left[t - (1+r)L\right] = \alpha t + (1-\alpha)(1+r)L.$$

Furthermore, to capture some elements in the modern political system, assume that the politician cannot mobilize the transfer without resistance, for example, the scrutiny from the Ministry of Finance; as a consequence, a political cost $C(T)$ has to be incurred by the politician for the net transfer T.

The equilibrium excess credit L and net transfer T are outcomes of bargaining between the politician and the bank manager. Assume that the politician and banker can bribe each other, denote a bribe from the bank manager to the politician by b, $b > 0$; if $b < 0$, the bribe is then made from the politician to the bank manager.

The utility function of the politician, u_P, is characterized by

$$u_P = B(L) - C(T) + b,$$

i.e., the politician gains from the political benefit of the credit policy, deducted by the political cost of the policy, plus the bribe. The utility function of the bank manager, u_B, is characterized by

$$u_B = \alpha[\pi+t-(1+r)L]-b$$
$$= \alpha\pi+T-(1+r)L-b.$$

Note that the benefits that the politician and bank manager receive are their private benefits, which do not mean any gain in social welfare. Quite on the contrary, such credit policy in this model is a pure social cost: first, excess bank credit L is provided for unproductive borrowers, implying an opportunity cost μL, $\mu>0$ for not lending to productive borrowers; second, government must fund the net transfer T through resources such as distortionary tax, implying a social cost τT, $\tau >0$. The social welfare for this credit policy is thus

$$w=-\mu L-\tau T.$$

OWNERSHIP VERSUS CONTROL RIGHTS

We also distinguish *control rights* from *ownership*: in contrast to ownership that defines how to "split the cake" and share the cash flow among the owners, control rights defines who makes decisions on certain variables. In the context of this model, obviously the politician has the control over the net public transfer T, while the choice on excess lending L may either be controlled by the politician or by the banker, under the government ownership. In market economies, ownership and control rights often go hand in hand, and an owner's control rights are in proportion to her equity share in a bank—the so-called "one-share-one-vote" principle. However, in reality, government as a bank owner may deliberately increase or decrease its control rights, unproportional to its share in bank ownership. The separation between ownership and control rights is thus important for understanding the political economy in banking, as such separation captures the complex setup of banks with government ownership in reality. Here are some examples:

1 If a bank is completely government owned, or, $\alpha \rightarrow 0$ such as a "Development Bank" in reality, L may be controlled by government; however, L may be controlled by the bank manager, too, if the bank is

"commercialized" and the control right is handed over to professional managers—this may happen in market economies, when government wants to improve the bank's efficiency by removing the political clout over the bank's daily business, and such phenomenon may also exist in a transitional economy, when government wants to make its banks market-oriented without being privatized;

2. If a bank is completely privately owned, or, $\alpha \rightarrow 1$, L may be controlled by the bank manager out of the one-share-one-vote principle; however, L may be controlled by government under certain circumstances: one example is when a bank is heavily regulated on certain business that it is allowed to be involved in; as a result, what the bank can do is rather shaped by government. Another example is when a bank is induced by government to lend to certain borrowers or industries, via subsidies, guarantees, or tax deduction.

Given the separations between ownership and control rights, for the rest of this section, we will distinguish between different setups for the control over excess lending L under a given private ownership α.

10.2.3 POLITICAL ECONOMY EQUILIBRIUM BENCHMARK: FIRST-BEST SOLUTION

We start solving the model from the benchmark, first-best solution, i.e., the outcome of the economy without political economy friction arising from a politician's seeking her own political benefit.

Should there be no political economy friction, the problem of a totally benevolent social planner is to maximize social welfare, i.e.,

$$\max_{\{L,T\}} w = -\mu L - \tau T.$$

Not surprisingly, the planner's solution, or, the first-best outcome of the economy is

$$L = 0 \text{ and } T = 0,$$

just because the excess credit supply for unproductive sector is a pure waste, so that the policy shall not be carried out in the first place.

POLITICAL ECONOMY SOLUTION WITHOUT BRIBE

Now we move on to see the banking outcome under political economy friction that the politician attempts to gain political benefit, using her leverage on the net transfer T. We first consider the scenario where there is no bribe between politician and bank manager.

Following our assumption on the separation between ownership and control rights, we distinguish two possibilities: excess credit supply L is controlled by government (i.e., by politician), or by the bank manager.

1 If L is controlled by the politician, her decision problem is then

$$\max_{\{L,T\}} \quad u_p = B(L) - C(T), \qquad (10.1)$$

$$\text{s.t.} \quad \alpha\pi + T - (1+r)L \geq 0. \qquad (10.2)$$

The politician chooses L and T to maximize her political benefit, as in the object function (10.1), while fulfilling the participation constraint (10.2) for the bank manager, i.e., the bank manager is only willing to carry out the credit policy if her profit is non-negative.

First-order conditions of the politician's problem lead to

$$T = (1+r)L - \alpha\pi, \qquad (10.3)$$
$$B'(L) = (1+r)C'(T). \qquad (10.4)$$

Equation (10.3) implies that, in equilibrium, the politician chooses a net transfer T that makes the bank earn zero profit, and the costly excess credit supply is partially funded by the bank's own cash flow $\alpha\pi$. The intuition is straightforward: because net transfer T is politically costly for the politician, she will try to keep T low and shift the cost for the credit policy to the bank as much as possible, until the marginal benefit for the politician equals the marginal cost from making the transfer, as equation (10.4) characterizes.

2. If L is controlled by the bank manager while T is controlled by the politician, the equilibrium outcome depends on how much they cooperate.

   (a) If they do not cooperate, in equilibrium the politician's choice on T must be the best response for the bank manager's choice on L, and vice versa. For any T that is chosen by the politician, to maximize her utility

   $$\max_{L} u_B = \alpha\pi + T - (1+r)L - b,$$

   the bank manager's best response is obviously to set $L=0$. Similarly, it is easy to see that for any L that is chosen by the bank manager, the utility-maximizing politician's best response is to choose $T=0$. Therefore, the non-cooperative equilibrium is characterized by $L=0$ and $T=0$.

   (b) In contrast, equilibrium outcomes may change if the politician and bank manager cooperate. Then the problem for them is to maximize their joint utility

   $$\max_{\{L,T\}} u_{P,B} = B(L) - C(T) + \alpha\pi + T - (1+r)L, \quad (10.5)$$

   and first-order conditions lead to

   $$\frac{\partial u_{P,B}}{\partial L} = B'(L) - (1+r) = 0, \quad (10.6)$$

   $$\frac{\partial u_{P,B}}{\partial T} = -C'(T) + 1 = 0. \quad (10.7)$$

   This means that, in cooperative equilibrium, optimal L and T are separable and do not depend on each other. The joint utility for the politician and bank manager is maximized when the marginal political benefit from excess lending equals the bank's marginal cost of funding, and they cooperate to maximize the transfer until the marginal cost of raising one unit of transfer is exactly one unit.

Overall, the first-best solution is only achieved if L is controlled by the bank manager, and the bank manager does not cooperate with the politician—this is fairly intuitive, as the bank manager controlling over L

CHAPTER TEN: POLITICAL ECONOMY IN BANKING

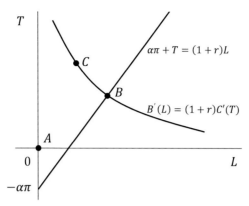

Figure 10.2 Control rights and political economy equilibria

Notes: the straight upward-sloping line delineates the bank manager's participation constraint so that the bank manager is only willing to carry out the credit policy if (T,L) is not below this line. The downward-sloping curve delineates the politician's optimization frontier $B'(L)=(1+r)C'(T)$. Point A is the bank manager's threat point, point B is the politician's threat point, and point C is the cooperative solution with $B'(L)=1+r$ and $C'(T)=1$.

will try to reduce wasteful lending, and the politician controlling over T will try to reduce political cost, as a result, the non-cooperating politician and bank manager will set both L and T to zero. Figure 10.2 summarizes the outcomes of political economy equilibria, when there is no bribe, under various settings on control rights and cooperation in the $T-L$ space. With politician's controlling over L, equilibrium outcome is denoted by point B; with bank manager's controlling over L, the non-cooperative solution is denoted by point A, while the cooperative solution that maximizes both parties' joint utility is denoted by point C, or the second-best solution.

POLITICAL ECONOMY SOLUTION WITH BARGAINING

As we can see so far, the first-best solution is only achieved in the non-cooperative equilibrium, with L being controlled by the bank manager. However, this is not quite realistic in the real world, as the politician and bank manager could benefit more if they cooperate or "collude".

Now we introduce a mechanism for the politician and bank manager to move out of non-cooperative equilibria and endogenously cooperate through a bribe: suppose the economy is initially in the non-cooperative equilibrium with L being controlled by the bank manager, i.e., point A (formally called as bank manager's *threat point*) in Figure 10.2 with utility of politician/bank manager being u_P^A/u_B^A, such that

$$u_P^A = 0,$$
$$u_B^A = \alpha\pi.$$

Now assume that the politician has an opportunity to convince the bank manager to cooperate on different (T,L) by bribing the bank manager with b, and the utility gain $\Delta u_P/\Delta u_B$ for the politician/bank manager is

$$\Delta u_P = u_P(T,L) - u_P^A = B(L) - C(T) + b,$$
$$\Delta u_B = u_B(T,L) - u_B^A = T - (1+r)L - b.$$

The outcome of a cooperative solution with bribe is defined by *Nash bargaining solution*, i.e., T, L, and b that maximize the product of utility gains:

$$\max_{\{T,L,b\}} \Delta u_P \Delta u_B = [B(L) - C(T) + b][T - (1+r)L - b].$$

First-order conditions lead to the optimal solution

$$b = \frac{1}{2}\{T - (1+r)L - [B(L) - C(T)]\},$$
$$B'(L) = 1+r,$$
$$C'(T) = 1$$

which is exactly the same as a cooperative solution that is characterized by (10.6) and (10.7). That is, bargaining through bribe achieves exactly the same outcome as in cooperative solution: point C in Figure 10.2.

What happens if the economy is initially in another non-cooperative equilibrium with L being controlled by a politician,[3] i.e., point B (politician's threat point) in Figure 10.2? Utility of politician/bank manager is u_P^B/u_B^B, such that

$$u_P^B = B(L^B) - C(T^B),$$
$$u_B^B = 0.$$

Then by bribing the politician with b, the bank manager wants to implement (T, L) with utility gains

$$\Delta u_P = u_P(T, L) - u_P^B = B(L) - C(T) + b - \left[B(L^B) - C(T^B) \right],$$
$$\Delta u_B = u_B(T, L) - u_B^B = \alpha\pi + T - (1+r)L - b,$$

and the Nash bargaining solution is

$$b = \frac{1}{2}\left\{ \alpha\pi + T - (1+r)L - \left[B(L) - C(T) - B(L^B) + C(T^B) \right] \right\},$$
$$B'(L) = 1+r,$$
$$C'(T) = 1.$$

Again, this is exactly the same as a cooperative solution that is characterized by (10.6) and (10.7). That is, when the politician and bank manager are allowed to bargain, the outcome is always the same as the one under full cooperation.

10.2.4 SUMMARY

The Shleifer-Vishny government ownership model on government ownership sheds much light on how government ownership affects banks' behavior. In the view of Shleifer and Vishny, the key driving force behind banking outcomes is the division of control rights, while government ownership is a veil. In the decision problem on a wasteful investment, the socially optimal outcome is only achieved when the bank manager controls lending and does not cooperate with politics—a solution under *laissez-faire*.

However, the role of government ownership is non-trivial: if a politician controls lending, she will exploit her ownership in the bank and shift the burden of costly funding to the bank. The politician and bank manager can make both of them better off by either engaging in full cooperation, or bargaining, to achieve the second-best solution. Therefore, in reality, if a *laissez-faire* solution is not possible, the politician and bank manager will collude in a certain way to be mutually beneficial.

10.3 POLITICAL CREDIT CYCLE

The underlying assumption in the Shleifer-Vishny model is that a politician wants to please voters. This is probably the exact motivation of politicians in reality, to win voters and to stay in office. In democracies, elections are conducted periodically so that before each election, politicians must mobilize resources—including financial resources—to gain votes. Therefore, accompanying political election cycles, credit cycles may be generated by politicians' efforts to win reelections.

In this section, we explore the mechanism of election-driven credit cycles, using an augmented model from Drazen (2000), based on Nordhaus (1975) and MacRae (1977).

10.3.1 REELECTION AND CREDIT SUPPLY TO VOTERS

Now we deviate from the issue of control rights and focus on how a politician maximizes the probability of getting reelected over an election cycle: suppose that the politician can influence banks' credit supply and stimulate the economy. If the economy performs better than what voters expect, the probability that the politician is reelected increases. Then what is the best way for the politician to conduct such credit policy, over the years preceding the election?

To formalize the question, consider an economy in which a politician strives to be reelected every four years. Suppose year t is an election year, and the politician is incumbent over year $\tau = t-3, t-2, t-1, t$. She has control over credit supply of banks, L_τ, in the economy; to make it simple, assume that an extra 1% increase in credit supply L_τ leads to 1% increase in GDP, Y_τ. To economize the notations, we use lower case alphabets to denote logarithm forms of L_τ and Y_τ, i.e.,

$$l_\tau = \ln L_\tau, \text{ and } y_\tau = \ln Y_\tau.$$

In each year τ, voters have an expectation on total output, or, GDP, denoted by y_τ^e. With realized GDP y_τ, the surprise to the voters is denoted by

$$\delta_\tau = y_\tau - y_\tau^e = l_\tau - l_\tau^e \qquad (10.8)$$

in which l_τ^e denotes the expectation on credit supply, given the one-for-one relationship between credit growth and GDP growth. Suppose the surprise is positive, $\delta_\tau > 0$, the politician's probability of getting reelected in the election year increases, the higher δ_τ is, the higher increase in the reelection probability is, and vice versa. Overall, as the reelection probability increases with δ_τ, the politician will obviously want to make δ_τ as high as possible. In addition, (10.8) also implies that the surprise in GDP equals the surprise in credit supply, so that we can focus on l_τ as the politician's decision variable for the rest of this section.

The politician, however, cannot choose l_τ freely. As we argue in Section 10.2.2, the politician has to incur a convex political cost for the credit policy that reduces her reelection probability, denoted by a cost function $c(l_\tau)$

$$c(l_\tau) = \frac{\theta}{2} l_\tau^2.$$

with θ being a constant and $\theta > 0$. We can then capture the politician's objective in a loss function

$$\mathcal{L}_\tau = -\delta_\tau + c(l_\tau) = -\delta_\tau + \frac{\theta}{2} l_\tau^2 \qquad (10.9)$$

in which $-\delta_\tau$ denotes the cost in her reelection probability from missing voters' expectation by $-\delta_\tau$, and $\frac{\theta}{2} l_\tau^2$ is the political cost of conducting the credit policy.

10.3.2 CREDIT SUPPLY OVER ELECTION CYCLES

Assume that the politician's performance is discounted by a factor of β, $0 < \beta < 1$, in the years preceding the election, the politician's loss function over her four years in the office is thus

$$\sum_{j=0}^{3} \beta^j \mathcal{L}_{t-j}. \qquad (10.10)$$

Voters form their expectation on credit supply, hence GDP, by *adaptive learning*. Precisely, voters' expectation in year τ is given by

$$l_\tau^e = l_{\tau-1} + \alpha\left(l_{\tau-1}^e - l_{\tau-1}\right) \tag{10.11}$$

in which α is a constant and $0 < \alpha < 1$. That is, in year τ, voters form the expectation l_τ^e based on combining what they learn from the last year's credit supply $l_{\tau-1}$ as well as last year's surprise $l_{\tau-1}^e - l_{\tau-1}$. Using this rule, (10.11) can be further written as

$$\begin{aligned} l_\tau^e &= l_{\tau-1} + \alpha\left[l_{\tau-2} + \alpha\left(l_{\tau-2}^e - l_{\tau-2}\right) - l_{\tau-1}\right] \\ &= (1-\alpha)l_{\tau-1} + \alpha\left[l_{\tau-2} + \alpha\left(l_{\tau-2}^e - l_{\tau-2}\right)\right] \\ &= \ldots\ldots \\ &= (1-\alpha)\sum_{i=1}^{+\infty} \alpha^{i-1} l_{\tau-i}. \end{aligned} \tag{10.12}$$

To simplify the computation, assume that α is small enough so that $\alpha^n \to 0$, n is integer and $n \geq 2$. Equation (10.12) can then be simplified as

$$l_\tau^e = (1-\alpha)l_{\tau-1} + \alpha l_{\tau-2}. \tag{10.13}$$

Knowing voters' expectation is formed as (10.13), the politician's loss function over the entire horizon (10.10) then becomes

$$\begin{aligned} \sum_{j=0}^{3} \beta^j \mathcal{L}_{t-j} &= \frac{\theta}{2}l_t^2 + (1-\alpha)l_{t-1} + \alpha l_{t-2} - l_t \\ &\quad + \beta\left[\frac{\theta}{2}l_{t-1}^2 + (1-\alpha)l_{t-2} + \alpha l_{t-3} - l_{t-1}\right] \\ &\quad + \beta^2\left[\frac{\theta}{2}l_{t-2}^2 + (1-\alpha)l_{t-3} + \alpha l_{t-4} - l_{t-2}\right] \\ &\quad + \beta^3\left[\frac{\theta}{2}l_{t-3}^2 + (1-\alpha)l_{t-4} + \alpha l_{t-5} - l_{t-3}\right]. \end{aligned} \tag{10.14}$$

The politician's optimization problem is then to choose a path of credit policy $\{l_{t-j}\}_{j=0}^{3}$ to minimize her loss function, i.e.

CHAPTER TEN: POLITICAL ECONOMY IN BANKING

$$\min_{\{l_{t-j}\}_{j=0}^{3}} \sum_{j=0}^{3} \beta^j \mathcal{L}_{t-j}$$

with $\sum_{j=0}^{3} \beta^j \mathcal{L}_{t-j}$ being defined by (10.14). First-order conditions yield the optimal solution, which is defined by

$$l_t = \frac{1}{\theta},$$

$$l_{t-1} = \frac{\alpha+\beta-1}{\beta}\frac{1}{\theta},$$

$$l_{t-2} = \frac{(\alpha+\beta)(\beta-1)}{\beta}\frac{1}{\theta},$$

$$l_{t-3} = \frac{(\alpha+\beta)(\beta-1)}{\beta}\frac{1}{\theta}.$$

Given that $\beta \to 1$, the optimal solution can be approximated as

$$l_t = \frac{1}{\theta},$$

$$l_{t-1} = \frac{\alpha}{\theta},$$

$$l_{t-2} = 0,$$

$$l_{t-3} = 0.$$

The result is striking, but fairly intuitive: as long as the politician stays in office, she will conduct most of the credit policy in the election year t, which stimulates the economy the most and wins her voters the most efficiently. However, once she is reelected, as there are still three years before the next election, she will start with zero stimulation ($l_{t-3}=0$), because in such an early stage she does not need to maintain a high expectation for voters at a high cost that does not benefit her reelection immediately; furthermore, she deliberately keeps credit supply low during the years preceding the election in order to keep voters' expectation low prior to the election year and maximize the effectiveness of credit policy in the election year: a clear political credit cycle that leads to lending expansion before elections and lending contraction after elections.

10.3.3 SUMMARY

The critiques of Nordhaus-MacRae model are mostly on how voters form their expectation, which is central to the results of the model. Expectation formed through adaptive learning implies that voters are irrational, i.e., they are naive, myopic, and backward-looking. Should voters be rational, after experiencing one entire election cycle, they should have learned that the good economic performance in the election year is merely created by the opportunistic politician, and a contraction in lending—hence economic activities—will follow right after the election. Knowing this, rational voters would never be fooled into electing a politician who attempts to attract voters by temporary credit expansion and economic stimulation, and in response, a rational politician would never conduct such short-run credit policy. Therefore, the Nordhaus-MacRae political credit cycle only arises if voters are irrational, who only learn about the economy through a short memory in the past and do not think about the future.

However, voters are not necessarily rational in the real world, and sometimes they do care more about short-run benefit and forget lessons they learn in the past. Recent empirical research has shown more and more evidence that voters are myopic and not necessarily forward-looking (see the empirical evidence in Section 10.4). As a result, political cycles are sometimes a non-negligible force in driving banks' lending decisions.

10.4 EMPIRICAL EVIDENCE

The width and depth of political economy in banking have inspired a large number of exciting studies. In this section, we briefly review empirical tests on the role of government ownership in banking, as well as political credit cycles. Beyond these, we also briefly review several related issues, such as the impact of institutional environment such as legal enforcement, banks' involvement in public finance, as well as credit misallocation induced by political economy.

10.4.1 GOVERNMENT OWNERSHIP AND BANKING OUTCOMES

IDENTIFYING POLITICAL ECONOMY ASSOCIATED WITH GOVERNMENT OWNERSHIP

To empirically identify the impacts of a bank's government ownership on banking is challenging. As Section 10.2 explains, government ownership may affect banking in at least three ways, and it is hardly possible to disentangle these effects from each other by using publicly observable variables such as bank performance indicators. For instance, when inferior performance of a government-owned bank is observed, it is hard to say whether it is a result that the bank is not a profit maximizer, and is more willing to invest in socially desirable but not necessarily profitable projects such as infrastructure (social view), or it is a result of mismanagement because of non-observable managerial effort (principal-agent view), or it is just a consequence of politicians' diverting bank credit towards their political patronage (political economy view).

Sapienza (2004) attempts to distinguish these effects by examining banks' pricing behavior, using information on the balance sheets and income statements of over 37,000 Italian firms. Banks in Italy have the access to a common pool of firms' credit scores; therefore, if a firm borrows from multiple banks, it shall expect to be granted the same loan rate. However, she finds that on average state-owned banks—that own 58% total bank assets in Italy, 1995—charge 44 basis points lower interest rates than non-state owned banks, such difference is larger in regions with more political patronage, and state-owned banks favor large enterprises. Altogether, these findings strongly support the political economy view, as is analyzed in Shleifer and Vishny (1994).

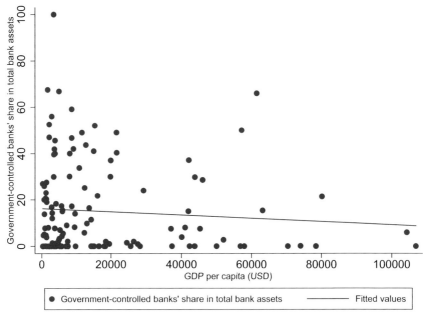

Figure 10.3 Government-controlled banks' share in total bank assets versus GDP per capita, 2016

Notes: the horizontal axis denotes government-controlled banks' share in total bank assets, in percentage points, and the vertical axis denotes GDP per capita in US dollars, 2016. The fitted value suggests a relationship of $y = 15.75 - 0.000038x$. A government-controlled bank is defined as a bank whose government share exceeds 50% of equity. Data sources: World Bank's Bank Regulation and Supervision Survey (Barth et al. 2013) for 140 reporting jurisdictions, together with the author's own update for China.

La Porta et al. (2002) attempt to disentangle different views on banks' government ownership through cross-country studies, by aggregating bank-level data from 1995. Defining a bank as government-owned if government share in the bank exceeds 20% of equity, they find that in an average country, government-owned banks account for almost 50% of total bank assets in 1995, and the share tends to be higher for poorer countries. More recent data still show a very similar stylized fact: for example, the World Bank defines a bank as government-controlled if government share exceeds 50% of equity, and Figure 10.3 plots government-controlled banks' share in total bank assets versus GDP per capita for 140 jurisdictions in 2016 survey. As we can see, existence of government-controlled banks is substantial for many countries, and the asset share of government-controlled banks is likely to be higher in low-income countries. Such observation seems to support the social view, as low-income countries often have less well-functioning institutions so that government ownership in banks is needed for better allocation of financial resources.

However, social review also implies that economies with higher government ownership in banks should perform better, in terms of economic growth, growth in firm investment and productivity, etc.—compared with economies with lower government ownership, controlled for GDP per capita,—because government ownership helps eliminate market and institutional failure; unfortunately, La Porta et al. (2002) observe only the opposite in the data that countries with higher government ownership perform *worse*, which still seems to hold in more recent data, as Figure 10.4 shows an inverse relationship between

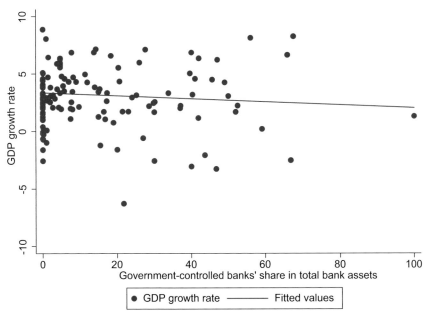

Figure 10.4 *Government-controlled banks' share in total bank assets and economic growth, 2016*

Notes: the horizontal axis denotes 2016 GDP growth rate, in percentage points, and the vertical axis denotes government-controlled banks' share in total bank assets, in percentage points. The fitted value suggests a relationship of $y = 2.98 - 0.0037x$. A government-controlled bank is defined as a bank whose government share exceeds 50% of equity. Data sources: World Bank's Bank Regulation and Supervision Survey (Barth et al. 2013) for 136 reporting jurisdictions, together with the author's own update for China.

government ownership in banks and economic growth. This suggests that the political economy effect may dominate, so that government ownership crowds out banks' credit supply to efficient borrowers and impedes economic growth.

Although numerous supportive facts are found for the political economy associated with government ownership, most evidence is indirect. Government ownership may affect the banking sector in many ways, many of which are implicit and unobservable such as implicit tax incentive, implicit coercion, etc. Shen and Lin (2012) test the political economy channel based on the political interference in the government-owned banks, measured by the turnover of executives in these banks. Focusing on 226 government-owned banks in 65 countries between 1993 and 2007, they proxy political interference in a bank if its executive is replaced within 12 months after a major election, as such replacement reflects the desire that newly elected politicians want to install their cronies in the banks for their own political benefit. Using return on assets (ROA), return on equity (ROE), net interest margin (NIM), and non-performing loan (NPL) as bank performance indicators, they find that given government-owned banks on average perform worse than private banks, government-owned banks suffering political interference perform even worse, which is direct evidence on the political economy effect of government ownership.

GOVERNMENT OWNERSHIP AND BANK PERFORMANCE

As government ownership is often associated with government's interference, government ownership has non-negligible implication for bank performance. Berger et al. (2009) investigate the impact of bank ownership on bank profit efficiency and cost efficiency, focusing on the dynamics of the banking system in China during the late 1990s and early 2000s. In the effort towards joining the World Trade Organization (WTO) in 2001, China started to liberalize its banking sector in mid-1990s, allowing private and foreign ownership in a banking system that was mostly government-owned which led to a retreat of government ownership in banks: branching of foreign banks was permitted, joint-stock commercial banks (JCBs) and city commercial banks (CCBs) with private and foreign ownership were created, and private and foreign investors were allowed to hold shares of big state-owned banks (so-called "Big Four"). They find that foreign banks are the most efficient ones, followed by private domestic banks, non-Big Four state-owned banks, and the Big Four who have the highest government ownership are the least efficient ones. Furthermore, they find that domestic banks with foreign ownership perform better than those without foreign ownership. Those findings suggest that reducing government ownership in banks helps overcome the inefficiencies arising from political economy related frictions, and such effect is stronger when government ownership is replaced by foreign ownership that is least subject to domestic frictions caused by political economy.

Bailey et al. (2011) relate the poor performance of government-owned banks to the distortion in banks' role as information producers. In principle, banks exert effort in screening borrowers and discover the true credit worthiness of potential borrowers; as a result, banks are producers of information and a bank loan is thus a certificate of credit quality for a borrower, especially when the borrower is new and has little credit history. Financial market shall also react to such certification positively, for example, after being granted a loan, a borrower would incur lower funding cost in the bond market, should the borrower further seek bond funding. However, examining bank loan announcements for all listed firms in China from 1999 to 2004, they find that the stock market reacts *negatively* to the announcements and stock prices of the borrowers fall; furthermore, based on firm-level characteristics, they find poorer firm profit, and cost performance predict *higher* likelihood of receiving a loan. Altogether, empirical evidence suggests failure in information production within government-owned banks.

10.4.2 LEGAL SYSTEMS AND BANKING

Development in banking is heavily shaped by institutions, especially by legal systems. A better legal system protects the legal rights of lenders and borrowers better, and thus more effectively reduces fraud and information manipulation. A well-developed legal system thus helps reduce transaction cost in banking and funding rate for borrowers, increase both credit demand and supply, and improve the efficiency in credit allocation.

Quantifying the effects of the legal system on banking may be challenging, as there are several major legal systems in the world, and within each legal system, legislation, legal rules, and law enforcement can be highly complex, too. For these reasons, related research usually focuses on laws that directly affect banking and finance—for example, commercial laws and banking acts, and legal procedures across different legal systems that directly affect banking legislation as well as law enforcement on lenders and borrowers.

LEGAL ORIGINS

National legal systems in the world mostly come from a few origins, and similar rules and procedures can be found in legal systems that follow the same origin. La Porta et al. (1998) follow the most accepted classification in comparative legal literature that identifies two main legal traditions: civil law and common law.

- The civil, or Romano-Germanic law, continental law, largely exists in continental Europe, East Asia, as well as current and former colonies of France, Spain, and Portugal. The civil law originated from Roman law; it is based on core statutes and codified legal text as a primary source of law, and mostly relies on legal scholars to formulate and interpret the legal rules;
- The common, or case law, exists in the UK, as well as current and former British colonies, such as the US, Canada, and Australia. It is "the body of law derived from judicial decisions, rather than from statutes or constitutions" (Black's Law Dictionary, 11th Edition, 2019). The law is largely based on court decisions, in contrast to the civil law which is based on written rules.

La Porta et al. (1997) find that legal rules protecting creditors and investors as well as the quality of law enforcement differ greatly and systematically across countries with different legal origins. For example, in terms of protection against expropriation by insiders, shareholders and creditors are better protected by the common law than the civil law, while among the sub-families of civil law, French civil law (which mostly exists in French/Spanish/Portuguese speaking countries) protects shareholders and creditors the least, but German civil law (which exists in German speaking and East Asian countries) and Scandinavian civil law (which exists in Scandinavia) provide relatively better protection. Quality of law enforcement is the lowest in French civil law countries. Djankov et al. (2003) find that courts in civil law countries are on average associated with higher duration, lower consistency, less fairness, and more corruption; consequently, legal origin also matters for debt enforcement (Djankov et al. 2008). La Porta et al. (1999) also relate legal origins with the quality of government—measured by efficiency, size, provision of public goods, political freedom, etc., and find that governments in French civil law or socialist law countries tend to perform worse; governments in these countries on average intervene more in economic life.

Differences in creditor protection and government quality associated with legal systems obviously have profound implications on the development of banking systems. La Porta et al. (2002) find that, although outside rich common law countries and Japan, government ownership of banks is non-negligible elsewhere, government share in the banking sector is the highest in French civil law countries, lower in German and Scandinavian ones, and the lowest in common law countries. Given that political economy in banking often emerges through government-bank connections such as government ownership in banks, such variations in government ownership imply that banks in countries from different legal origins may be affected by politics in quite different ways and to quite different degrees.

LEGAL RULES AND BANK LENDING

How much legal rules protect right holders in financial markets is obviously crucial in shaping banking relationships and bank lending, independent on the legal origins. In general, properly designed legal rules may enhance banking through two channels: first, through creditor protection; when repayments are easily enforced and collateral is effectively seized to recover lending when borrowers default, lenders will be more willing to provide funding. Second, through reducing informational frictions; if lenders have less to fear about financing lemons or fraud, they will be more willing to lend.

Following La Porta et al. (1997), Djankov et al. (2007) measure how much legal rules protect creditors by the power of secured lenders in bankruptcy, i.e., the capability of lenders to seize collateral, to be paid out first, and to protect their interests against competing claimants in debt restructuring or reorganization. Djankov et al. (2007) also measure the information enhancing channel by existence of credit registries. Using these measures for 129 countries in the world, they find that better creditor protection and information sharing lead to higher private credit supply to GDP ratio. Using a similar measure for creditor protection, Qian and Strahan (2007) provide more direct evidence on how legal rules affect bank lending through creditor protection, by examining bank loans made to large borrowers in 43 countries from late 1980s to 2003. They find that lenders are more willing to lend under better credit protection, with longer maturities and lower interest rates. For global banks, they are more willing to lend to countries with better creditor protection. Certain legal rules, such as credit protection, thus have profound implications for banking development, efficiency in credit allocation, as well as economic growth, as Demirgüç-Kunt and Maksimovic (1998) suggest in their cross-country studies.

Besides solely focusing on legal rules that protect creditors' claims on collateral in bankruptcy, as most law and banking literature does, Haselmann et al. (2010) argue that legal rules that protect creditors' claims outside bankruptcy are equally important. Such rules are mostly about eligible collateral, or what assets may be pledged as collateral. While the *bankruptcy rules* protect creditors' claims on collateral, such *collateral pledgeability rules* outside bankruptcy actually ensure banks' capability in securing lending by requiring collateral, which reduce banking frictions and enhance bank lending in the first place. Exploiting legal reforms in ten new Eastern European EU member countries as natural experiments, Haselmann et al. (2010) find that collateral pledgeability rules are more likely to increase bank lending than bankruptcy rules. Such effect is stronger for foreign banks, who benefit more from collateral pledgeability rules that reduce information frictions than domestic banks who enjoy informational advantages.

LAW ENFORCEMENT AND LEGAL ENVIRONMENT

Using a survey on loan supply and bank managers' perception on law enforcement covering 20 economies in transition from Eastern Europe and former Soviet Union, Haselmann and Wachtel (2010) find that when a country is perceived to provide better law enforcement by bank managers, banks there are more willing to accept collateral as a reliable way to secure lending. This helps overcome the frictions in bank lending: when lending is credibly secured by collateral, banks are more willing to lend to small, private firms without sufficient credit history, rather than to lend to governments that are less likely to default. Better law enforcement, or legal environment, thus has the potential to improve credit allocation and facilitate economic growth.

Besides cross-country studies, evidence on linkage between law enforcement and bank lending is also found within individual countries. Schiantarelli et al. (2020) document how Italian firms deliberately delay payments to those banks that suffer from non-performing loans, in areas where legal enforcement of recovering collateral is slow and ineffective. Such selective delay is explored by using the fact that some firms borrow from multiple banks: when one bank is weakened by loan losses, the expected value for a firm's continuing relationship is smaller, then if local legal enforcement is ineffective, the firm will choose to delay payment to this bank because the likelihood that the bank is able to recover the lending by seizing the collateral is low.

Focusing on the law-finance-growth nexus in China, Allen et al. (2005) argue that although poor law enforcement and legal environment do explain state-owned banks' inefficient credit allocation to ailing state-owned enterprises (SOEs), they do not explain the success story of the private sector that contributes to much of China's economic growth but always has been discriminated with access to bank finance. Alternative financing channels, that are more based on borrowers' reputation and relationships but less dependent on law enforcement, are fulfilling the credit demand of the private sector, instead.

10.4.3 POLITICAL TIES AND BANKING OUTCOMES
POLITICAL CONNECTION AND BANK LENDING

Political ties are often an important channel through which politicians and banks interact. Examining the firm credit register in Pakistan between 1996 and 2002, Khwaja and Mian (2005) find that firms with political connection receive more funding from government-owned banks. A firm is defined as *politically connected* if it has a politician on its board; then to see how political connection affects firms' bank funding, Khwaja and Mian (2005) focus on firms that borrow from both government-owned banks and non-government owned banks by estimating the following regression equation:

$$Y_{ij} = \alpha + \beta_1 Political_i \times Gov_j + \beta_2 Gov_j + \delta_i + \epsilon_{ij}, \qquad (10.15)$$

in which Gov_j is a dummy variable that equals 1 if the lending bank is a government-owned bank, and δ_i denotes firm fixed effects. The key coefficient is thus β_1, which measures whether a politically connected firm is favored by government-owned banks, compared with non-government owned banks, while term Gov_j controls for the possibility that government-owned banks' lending behavior may be systematically different, unconditional on the firm's type.

Khwaja and Mian (2005) discover that, on average, politically connected firms receive 45% more bank funding through government-owned banks. The favorable treatment for politically connected firms is stronger when politicians on the boards are in power. However, this is not because these firms are borrowers of better quality, in fact, these firms' default probability is 50% higher. Such credit misallocation costs up to 2% of GDP each year.

If political connection means preferential resource allocation, it must be desirable for firms. Indeed, Calomiris et al. (2010) find that the stock market reacts negatively on privatizing firms' government shares in China, for fearing losing the firms' political connections and associated economic privileges.

Political connection is not only important for borrowers to enjoy favorable funding conditions, it also matters for lending banks to gain implicit seniority of their debts when borrowers default. This is especially crucial when the borrowers are regional governments: politicians would choose not to default on a creditor bank, if the political power behind the bank is strong enough to affect the politicians' careers; this leads to selective default, that governments default first on creditor banks with the weakest political connections. Using loan-level data on bank lending to local governments in China, 2007–2013, Gao et al. (2020) characterize such selective default: given the overall default rate being 1.34%, the default rate is only 0.25% for China Development Bank (CDB) which ranks as a ministerial institution in Chinese political system, while the default rate is 1.42% for commercial banks. Gao et al. (2020) also find that the difference in the default rates is not explained by the credit quality of borrowers, as the *same* local governments pay off 99.5% of CDB loans but default on commercial banks within the same due time—a clear selective default which is inversely correlated with the strength of credit banks' political connections.

FORMATION OF POLITICAL CONNECTION

Political connection may be formed explicitly, through political networking and social clubbing (such as organized elite clubs à la Haselmann et al. 2018) Hung et al. (2017) screen curricula vitae of chief executive officers (CEOs) in Chinese commercial banks and measure banks' political connections by their CEOs' previous working experience as government officials. They find that politically connected banks perform better, with higher return on assets (ROA) and lower default risk. This is probably explained by the fact that, although these banks lend more to less efficient, state-owned enterprises (SOEs), the public guarantee on these borrowers reduces loan defaults. Hung et al. (2017) find the effect of political connection on bank performance is more pronounced, when a CEO used to work in the government of the city where the bank is headquartered, i.e., when the political connection is the strongest.

Political connection may be formed implicitly, when banks and politicians find common interests. For example, in the wave of delinquent mortgages after a housing bubble crash, politicians may want to delay foreclosure and ease the pressure of their voters, while banks may use the chance to gain favorable legislative outcomes from politicians in power; as a result, banks improve their political connections with those politicians by postponing foreclosure. Agarwal et al. (2018a) unveil how banks exploit the foreclosure policy as a key to connecting to financial regulators, as part of their lobbying effort. While the U.S. House of Representatives Financial Services Committee was designing new legislation on banking regulation after the 2007–2009 financial crisis, foreclosure on delinquent mortgages were delayed in the electoral districts of the Committee members, although the delinquency rates in these districts were the same as the others.

10.4.4 POLITICAL CREDIT CYCLES

POLITICAL CYCLES AND BANKING IN EMERGING MARKET ECONOMIES

The Nordhaus-MacRae model of political credit cycle is widely tested in various settings. Brown and Dinç (2005) investigate the implication of political cycles on banking through government's intervention on failing banks. Resolving troubled banks is not only financially expensive, but also politically costly, as politicians would be questioned by voters on their inability to avoid bank failure and cost for taxpayers. Therefore,

Nordhaus-MacRae type of theoretical models shall predict that the "political bank resolution cycle" would have exactly the opposite pattern to the political credit cycle, such that politicians shall avoid major bank failures before elections, as well as defer acknowledging and intervening failing banks until after the elections.

Focusing on episodes of major bank failures in 21 main emerging market economies, 1994–2000, Brown and Dinç (2005) identify the political bank resolution cycle by estimating an exponential hazard model for bank i in year t,

$$h(t) = \exp(\beta X_{i,t-1} + \gamma BeforeElection_{i,t} + \theta_t), \qquad (10.16)$$

in which vector $X_{i,t-1}$ contains lagged bank- and country-level control variables, $BeforeElection_{i,t}$ is a dummy variable that equals 1 if government intervention on the bank happens within one year before an election, and θ_t is the year dummy.

The key coefficient is thus γ: Brown and Dinç (2005) find that γ is negative and significant, implying that bank resolution is less likely to happen just before the election. Opposite to the political credit cycle that lending falls after election, Brown and Dinç (2005) show that most interventions take place within one year after election. Failed banks are mostly taken over by government, and after takeover, government cuts bank lending and employment, as the political cost of bank resolution is less of a concern in this stage.

Cole (2009) finds that, in election years, state governments in India deliberately divert bank credit towards agricultural lending through government-owned banks, which results in a 5–10% increase in agricultural credit. The effect is stronger in states where incumbents are more challenged in elections. However, such pre-election lending boom is inefficient: loan default rate rises after elections, and the lending spree does not increase agricultural output in the election years.

Agarwal et al. (2016) focus on the variations in borrowers' political relationships as a result of political cycles. In Mexico, senators are often chairmen of influential committees, therefore, turnover of senators implies changing controls of these important committees. Based on credit register from 2003 to 2012, Agarwal et al. (2016) find that during the political cycles, firms with political connections with the chairmen in power receive favorable funding terms from banks, although credit quality of these political loans is lower; as reciprocity, these banks extending more political loans receive more government borrowing with better credit quality.

POLITICAL CYCLES AND BANKING IN ADVANCED ECONOMIES

Political credit cycles do not only exist in countries with relatively weak institutions. Englmaier and Stowasser (2017) reveal the Nordhaus-MacRae type political credit cycle in Germany by investigating the county-level election cycles and the credit supply of local savings banks. Among the three pillars of the German banking system, commercial banks, savings banks (*Sparkassen*), and cooperative banks (*Genossenschaftsbanken*), savings banks and cooperative banks have very similar business models and customer bases, and are established as consortia of small regional banks that mostly focus on regional businesses. The key difference between savings banks and cooperative banks is that savings banks are owned and controlled by local governments, while cooperative banks are private-owned and free from political interference, which allows one to exploit cooperative banks as a control group for identifying the impacts of election cycles on savings banks' lending supply. Such an identification strategy leads to a regression equation such as

$$L_{ict} = \beta_0 + \beta_1 Elec_{ct} + \beta_2 Elec_{ct} \times Savings_i + \beta_3 Controls_t + \delta + \epsilon_{ict}$$

in which L_{ict} is lending from bank i in county c, year t, $Elec_{ct}$ is a dummy variable that equals 1 if year t is an election year of county c, and $Savings_i$ is a dummy variable that equals 1 if bank i is a savings bank. The vector of control variables, $Controls_t$, includes bank- and county-level characteristics, and δ captures various settings of fixed effects. β_2 is thus the key variable to understand the effect of election cycles on the lending of government-controlled savings banks.

Englmaier and Stowasser (2017) find that, as is predicted by the Nordhaus-MacRae model, in the election year of a county, local savings banks increase lending by 1.5%, or, 30 million euros per bank, and such stimulation vanishes after the election; furthermore, the stimulation effect is stronger when electoral competition is more fierce. They find that the political lending spree is also distortionary, as the lending decision is more political than commercial and recipients of loans are not necessarily credit-worthy; as a result, non-performing loans in a savings bank peak around three years after a local election. The political credit cycle thus does not only generate wasteful economic stimulus, but also destabilizes regional banking systems.

Digging deeper into the political credit cycle in Germany, Koetter and Popov (2020) find that, on the federal state level, the post-election contraction in credit supply to the real economy is aggravated by the post-election *expansion* in savings banks' lending to the new government, if the election leads to political party turnover. This implies that a new political party in power has the incentive to tap government-controlled banks to fund government expenditure, and this crowds out banks' lending to the real economy.

Examining the resolution of failing government-controlled savings banks in Germany, Behn et al. (2015) test the political bank resolution cycle hypothesis à la Brown and Dinç (2005). In principle, a failing local savings bank can be bailed out either by local government or by the federal state's savings bank association. Using a similar exponential hazard model, Behn et al. (2015) find local governments do not defer revealing bank failures until after elections, however, local governments do refrain from using taxpayers' money for bank bailout in the election years to avoid making themselves unpopular among voters. Overall, politicians' calculus on political benefit and cost is the driving force behind various cyclical patterns in banking that synchronize with political cycles.

10.4.5 MORAL SUASION AND HOME BIAS

Banks may also be exploited when government is in trouble with public finance. When government is heavily indebted, it may become difficult to roll over sovereign debts. New sovereign bonds need to be issued to replace the maturing debts, while the sovereign credit risk—especially in the downturn—will lead to lower demand from investors and higher bond yield. To avoid an undersubscribed auction for sovereign bonds that pushes up government's borrowing cost, government may engage in *moral suasion* to press domestic banks to hold domestic government bonds. Domestic banks may yield to the pressure, not necessarily because helping government under fiscal stress is a "moral" duty or banks are government-owned/-controlled, but also because banks hope that in exchange they will be bailed out in the future by the government. Such mutual interests may saturate domestic banks' balance sheets with domestic sovereign bonds, and sovereign default may potentially trigger a banking crisis.

Ongena et al. (2019) find strong evidence on moral suasion in the stressed countries, Greece, Ireland, Italy, Portugal, and Spain, during the European debt crisis starting from late 2009 through banks' monthly security holdings in these countries. The identification strategy benefits from the fact that most of new sovereign bonds are issued to roll over the existing sovereign debts that were raised many years ago, so that the supply of new sovereign bonds in the market is almost exogenously predetermined instead of being driven by the current economic situation, implying that new sovereign bond issuance is well justified to be used as exogenous supply shock to the market. Under such supply shocks, Ongena et al. (2019) discover that domestic banks—which are more subject to moral suasion—are more likely to buy domestic sovereign bonds during the months when their governments have larger sovereign debts to roll over, i.e., when new sovereign bond issuance is larger, compared with foreign banks in these countries. Especially, such effect only takes place during the sovereign debt crisis, when governments face much higher pressure from debt rollover and have the highest incentive to avoid hikes in sovereign bond yields that may arise from undersubscribed auctions;

moreover, such effect is particularly stronger for banks who were bailed out by the governments in history, reflecting those banks' expectation on receiving reciprocal favor from governments in the future.

Based on a wider selection of European countries, De Marco and Macchiavelli (2016) further find that such moral suasion effect is more pronounced for banks with political connections—measured not only by banks' government ownership, but also by their board members' affiliations with governments; this again confirms the political economy nature of moral suasion effect in banks' "home bias" towards holding domestic sovereign bonds. Moreover, by examining bank-level panel data on German banks' state bond portfolio, Ohls (2017) shows that such moral suasion also exists at a sub-national level: in Germany, state-owned banks hold more home state bonds than non-state owned home banks, especially when the home federal state faces tighter fiscal constraints, as the moral suasion hypothesis predicts.

10.4.6 POLITICAL ECONOMY AND ALLOCATION EFFICIENCY

GOVERNMENT OWNERSHIP AND BANK CREDIT ALLOCATION

Political economy in banking affects real economic performance mainly by its distortion in credit allocation. Carvalho (2014) presents the evidence on how credit misallocation takes place in a government-owned bank in Brazil, where the government-controlled national development bank provides around 30% funding for manufacturing firms' investments across the country. His identification strategy relies on the variation in the alliance between state and central governments after state and national elections. The hypothesis is that the central government may favor a state, if the state government is in the same ally. As the executives of the bank are appointed by the central government, the bank's lending decisions will well reflect the preferences of the central government, i.e., it will favor lending to the allied states. Indeed, firms eligible for lending from the allied states expand employment, compared with firms from the non-allied states, and the effect is more evident when incumbent governments face challenges in elections, suggesting that credit policy is exploited to strengthen incumbents' voter base and shifts employment towards the allied states.

PUBLIC GUARANTEE AND CREDIT ALLOCATION

Local banks are often explicitly or implicitly guaranteed by their stakeholder local governments, and such guarantees may reflect local officials' own interests and bias credit allocation. Exploring the European Court of Justice's decision to remove guarantees for a large number of German savings banks in 2001 as a natural experiment, Gropp et al. (2020) investigate the impact of public guarantee on credit allocation, using the Khwaja-Mian identification strategy (see Chapter 7, Section 7.6.1) and focusing on firms that borrow from both treated and non-treated banks to control for the demand-side effects from the borrowing firms. They find that under public guarantee, banks have lower incentive for screening and monitoring, and tend to keep lending relationships with less productive firms; such credit misallocation prevents more productive firms from entry and thus hinders economic growth. Removing public guarantees thus forces affected banks to improve risk management and reduce risk-taking, compared with unaffected banks, as documented by Gropp et al. (2014) through the same natural experiment in Germany.

Explicit or implicit public guarantee for certain *borrowers* also affects credit allocation, and misallocation of bank credit caused by public guarantee on borrowers may be more severe during recessions, as Cong et al. (2019) find: with increasing credit risks during recessions banks will prefer lending to borrowers that are secured by government, rather than non-guaranteed borrowers with better credit quality. Exploring the gigantic four trillion RMB stimulus plan in China, 2009–2010 in response to 2007–2009 global financial crisis as a natural experiment, they investigate the loan-level data from the 19 largest banks and exploit variations in banks' lending supply responses to the stimulation as well as pre-stimulus bank-firm relationships to control for demand-side effects. They find that the credit expansion during the stimulation disproportionately favors state-owned firms that enjoy implicit public guarantees, although their productivity is significantly inferior. In contrast, those non-blessed, i.e., private firms are less likely to obtain much needed credit and survive the recession, although they are more efficient.

PUBLIC FINANCE AND CREDIT ALLOCATION

Public finance may affect banks' credit allocation in several ways, and the consequences on social welfare are often ambiguous. Public finance includes direct government spending, for example, government may directly invest in projects such as infrastructure; public finance also includes provision of government credit, for example, providing government credit for strategically important firms in the name of "industrial policy", which can be arranged either through direct lending from government-owned policy banks or through subsidizing loans issued by commercial banks. On one hand, debt instruments to finance government spending or government credit reduce loanable funds and crowd out non-targeted, albeit more efficient borrowers, harmful for social welfare; on the other hand, positive externalities from supported projects and borrowers—such as infrastructure—may benefit and thus "crowd in" non-targeted borrowers, improving social welfare.

Using public debt data in China, Huang et al. (2020) find that public debt of local government crowds out local financial resources, leading to a fall in local private firms' investment. Such local crowding-out effect is especially stronger when local credit markets are more segmented so that it is more difficult for firms to borrow from alternative banks, i.e., when a borrowing firm located in a region with higher public debt is farther away from the closest bank in the neighboring municipality.

Ru (2018) examines the effect of government credit on private firm activities by investigating the lending of a policy bank, China Development Bank (CDB). In general, CDB provides funding for state-owned firms and municipal infrastructure projects. By identifying CDB credit shocks on municipality level, he finds that CDB funding for state-owned firms crowds out private firms in the same industry, but attracts (crowds in) private firms in downstream industries; and CDB-funded infrastructure projects crowd in private firms. The net effect on social welfare is not unambiguous.

CREDIT ALLOCATION IN BANKING LIBERALIZATION

Dinç and Gupta(2011) show that politicians' own interests have profound impact on privatizing government-owned firms and liberalizing government-controlled industries. The same concerns may well arise in the procedure of liberalizing banking industry. Kang et al. (2021) provide evidence on how officials exploit local banking liberalization to benefit their political careers. To promote banking competition and improve local access to credit, municipalities in China were allowed to set up their local banks, so-called city commercial banks (CCBs). Municipal governments are usually main shareholders of CCBs, and often directly appoint senior bank managers. Using CCB establishment as an experiment, combining with more than three million financial statements of firms over 16 years and municipality-level macroeconomic controls, they find that on average CCBs lead to *deteriorating* access to finance for average private firms, with falling debt finance and rising funding cost, which is in contrast to the conventional wisdom that local banking liberalization enhances local borrowers' access to finance (for example, Guiso et al. 2004). However, CCBs benefit private firms from infrastructure industry, with rising debt finance and falling funding cost, although these firms' credit quality is significantly lower, and worsens over time.

Why do CCBs prefer lending to inferior borrowers? Such puzzling fact may reflect the interest of main shareholders, municipal governments. Instead of striving for being reelected as in democracies, local officials in China have fixed terms in office and compete to be promoted afterwards. Under binding fiscal constraints for direct government spending, CCBs make it possible for local officials to divert financial resources towards projects that help them win the promotion tournament. To explore such conjecture, following Qian et al. (2011), Kang et al. (2021) construct a promotion pressure index (PPI) to capture three main promotion criteria for local officials: municipal GDP growth, fiscal surplus to fiscal income ratio, and employment rate, denoted by P_{ict}, $i=1,2,3$ as criteria i for municipality c in year t. Define pressure indicator ι_{ict} as

$$\iota_{ict} = \begin{cases} 1 & \text{if } P_{ict} \leq \bar{P}_{ict}, \\ 0 & \text{otherwise} \end{cases}$$

in which $\bar{P}_{ict}$ denotes the average of promotion criteria P_i for all municipalities in year t; that is, the pressure indicator ι_{ict} equals 1 if officials of municipality c perform worse than the average of their peers in year t on promotion criteria i. The PPI of municipality c in year t is computed as $PPI_{ct} = \sum_{i=1}^{3} \iota_{ict}$. Obviously, PPI_{ct} is an integer between 0 and 3.

Kang et al. (2021) find that credit misallocation towards infrastructure firms is more severe in municipalities under higher PPI. CCBs lead to higher local GDP growth in the first two years after establishment, which improves officials' promotion opportunity; however, such stimulating effect on economic growth diminishes afterwards. Further tests show that the increased investments in infrastructure do not generate desired positive externalities, with no evidence on improvements in local firms' performance; this suggests that such credit misallocation is wasteful for social welfare—not to mention that CCBs become warehouses of financial risks over time as a result of overlending to inferior borrowers, which is an increasing threat to financial stability.

10.5 EXERCISES

1 **Contestable election and credit cycles, based on Englmaier and Stowasser (2017)**
Consider an economy with politicians, voters, and a bank. Following the argument of the Nordhaus-MacRae model in Section 10.3.1 that politicians conduct credit policy through the bank under their control prior to elections, in order to stimulate the economy

and win votes from myopic voters whose support for the incumbent politician increases with the economic performance.

The bank is a standard intermediary that earns a revenue of $\Pi_t(L_t)$ from lending L_t in year t, and incurs a funding cost $C_t(L_t)$. $\Pi_t(L_t)$ is increasing in L_t and strictly concave; $C_t(L_t)$ is increasing in L_t and strictly convex:

$$\Pi_t'(L_t) > 0,\ \Pi_t''(L_t) < 0,\ C_t'(L_t) > 0,\ \text{and}\ C_t''(L_t) > 0.$$

Assume that a politician is a "semi" benevolent social planner such that she strives to maximize a social welfare function that includes her own political benefit; that is, her utility in year t is captured by

$$u_P = \psi(L_t) + \iota_t \phi\big(\xi(\psi(L_t))\big) + \Pi_t(L_t) - C_t(L_t)$$

in which ι_t is an indicator that

$$\iota_t = \begin{cases} 1 & \text{if } t \text{ is election year,} \\ 0 & \text{otherwise,} \end{cases}$$

$\psi(L_t)$ denotes GDP under credit supply L_t with $\psi'(L_t) > 0$, $\xi(\cdot)$ denotes the politician's expected vote share after implementing the credit policy with $\xi'(\cdot) > 0$, and $\phi(\cdot)$ denotes the politician's political benefit with $\phi'(\cdot) > 0$. $\psi(\cdot)$, $\phi(\cdot)$, and $\xi(\cdot)$ are all continuous functions.

(a) Show that a "totally" benevolent social planner, i.e., a politician that does not consider her political benefit, chooses higher credit supply, call it L_t^S, than the bank's efficient credit supply.
(b) Show that a politician as a "semi" benevolent social planner chooses her credit supply, call it L_t^P, with $L_t^P - L_t^S = \Delta L > 0$ in an election year.
(c) Suppose that the politician is only reelected if she wins a vote share ξ higher than a threshold $\bar{\xi}$; as a result, the marginal political benefit $\phi'(\cdot)$ is the highest around the neighborhood of $\bar{\xi}$. Show that a winning politician maximizes ΔL.

2. **Partisan credit cycles, based on Alesina (1987) and Alesina (1988)**
In this exercise, we modify the Nordhaus-MacRae model in Section 10.3.1 to allow two-party competition in the elections over infinite time horizon, $t = 0, 1, \ldots, +\infty$. Assume that there is an election every other period and two parties, $i = L, R$ ("left" and "right"), compete in the election period to get into power.

Assume that in each period t the party in power has the opportunity to conduct a credit policy, providing an extra credit supply of L_t to the economy through banks, and assume that an extra 1% increase in credit supply L_t leads to 1% increase in GDP, Y_t. We use lower case alphabets to denote logarithm forms of L_t and Y_t, i.e.,

$$l_t = \ln L_t, \text{ and } y_t = \ln Y_t.$$

In each period t, voters have an expectation on total output, or, GDP, denoted by y_t^e. With realized GDP y_t, the surprise to the voters is denoted by

$$\delta_t = y_t - y_t^e = l_t - l_t^e.$$

Voters are more likely to vote for the ruling party, if they are positively surprised. On the other hand, a convex political cost is incurred for the credit policy, denoted by a cost function $c(l_t)$

$$c(l_t) = \frac{\theta}{2} l_t^2$$

with θ being a constant and $\theta > 0$. To balance the gain and the cost, a ruling party i has targets on δ and l, call them $\overline{\delta}^i$ and $\overline{l}^i$, and the loss function for a ruling party in an election cycle is given by

$$\begin{aligned}\mathcal{L}_t^i &= \frac{1}{2}\left(\delta_t^i - \overline{\delta}^i\right)^2 + \frac{\theta^i}{2}\left(l_t^i - \overline{l}^i\right)^2 \\ &+ \beta\left[\frac{1}{2}\left(\delta_{t+1}^i - \overline{\delta}^i\right)^2 + \frac{\theta^i}{2}\left(l_{t+1}^i - \overline{l}^i\right)^2\right]\end{aligned}$$

with θ^i being a constant for party i and $\theta^i > 0$, β being a constant discount factor and $0 < \beta < 1$. The two parties are different in the parameter choices, reflecting their political goals, such that

$$\bar{\delta}^L \geq \bar{\delta}^R,$$
$$\bar{l}^L \geq \bar{l}^R,$$
$$\theta^L \leq \theta^R.$$

We further assume that voters are rational such that

$$l_t^e = E_{t-1}\left[l_t\right].$$

(a) Compute the optimal choice on l_t for each party, i.e., l_t^L and l_t^R, respectively.
(b) Assume that the probability that party L wins in period t is exogenously given as p^L. Then before the election, voters' expectation on credit supply can be also expressed as

$$l_t^e = p^L l_t^L + \left(1-p^L\right) l_t^R.$$

Compute l_t^L and l_t^R as functions of p^L.
(c) What is the difference in economic performance, between party L's and party R's first period in power? Does the difference persist in their second period?

NOTES

1 Throughout this chapter, we follow the same definitions of *government-owned bank* and *government-controlled bank* as of La Porta et al. (2002) and the World Bank, using the thresholds 20% and 50% government share in bank equity for these two types of banks, respectively.
2 Moe et al. (2004) provide a detailed recount. Note that government ownership is not necessarily equivalent to control rights, as government shares in such nationalized banks are often non-voting shares. See Section 10.2.2 for more discussions on ownership versus control rights.
3 Because the bank manager is totally passive in this case, it is also a non-cooperative setup.

PART IV
The economics of banking regulation

CHAPTER 11
Systemic risks and macroprudential regulation

11.1 INTRODUCTION

11.1.1 WHY IS BANKING REGULATION SPECIAL?

Banks, as firms in other industries, are subject to regulation. Compared with other industries, banks are rather heavily regulated, for reasons which are probably obvious. As we have shown in the previous chapters, banks eliminate financial frictions and improve social welfare, and banks also create failures that cannot be solved by themselves. Therefore, in principle, regulation is needed wherever banks fail to discipline themselves: regulators must create and enforce the rules of game for all banks, making sure that all banks comply with legal requirements on their businesses; regulators must prevent banks from abusing their market power to extort their competitors and customers, as well as maintain necessary market competition; regulators must correct market failures due to asymmetric information as well as punish fraud and deception, and so on.

However, compared with regulation in other heavily regulated industries such as telecommunications, banking regulation is also made different, by special characteristics in financial intermediation and the strategic status of banking industry in the economy. Banking regulation is particularly distinguished by several features:

- The main outcome of banking regulation is an extremely desirable public good: *financial stability*. As banks are among main providers of financial resources to the real economy, a well-functioning banking system is a foundation for a well-functioning economy. As is shown in Chapter 8, impacts of booms and busts in the banking sector may go well beyond financial system, as market failures and banking frictions amplify shocks and increase volatility in the real economy, generating not only prosperity and bubble, but also recession and crisis. Maintaining financial stability through banking regulation is thus the main goal for regulators to achieve;
- As maintaining financial stability is in the core of concerns, regulators sometimes need to assign more weight on "stability" than "price". For example, perfect competition that leaves firms zero profit and maximizes consumer welfare may be desirable for other

industries, it may not be desirable for regulators to leave banks no resource for building up buffers that enable banks to cushion against financial shocks and survive market stresses. When banking regulators face resource constraints, it may be marginally more rewarding to invest in regulatory policies that reduce fragility in banking and enhance resilience of banks;
- As regulation in other industries, protecting consumers against fraud, deception, and banks' abuse of market power, and so on is certainly a key issue in banking regulation, too. However, consumers are not the only group that need the most protection in banking regulation. Given the crucial role of banks in the economy, the cost of bank failure may go far beyond customers, creditors, and shareholders. Very often, associated with bank failure, costly public intervention needs to be swiftly staged, to resolve failing banks, mop up a malfunctioning financial system, and save the economy out of crisis; such cost is mostly borne by taxpayers. For this reason, in the design of regulatory rules in banking, taxpayer protection shall be at least as important as—if not more important than—consumer protection;
- The need for banking regulation does not only stem from market failure and misbehavior with respect to individual banks, it also stems from the *systemic risks*, the risks that are inherent in the system level and related to some common factors of financial institutions, the risks that are hardly identified merely on the bank level, and the risks whose materialization leads to comovement of financial markets and institutions, causing the disruption and dysfunction of the financial system. Implications of systemic risks have gained much attention among both researchers and regulators, particularly after the 2007–2009 global financial crisis. Next, we will see what systemic risk is, as well as causes and sources of systemic risks.

11.1.2 BANK-SPECIFIC VERSUS SYSTEMIC RISKS

Different from bank-specific risks that arise from individual banks' misbehavior and mismanagement, systemic risks arise from banks' collective failure in maintaining the resilience of the banking system.

Under systemic risks, banks are often excessively exposed to common risk factors and excessively interconnected with each other; under market stress, such common exposure and interbank connections result in comovements of banks and cascading bank failure, even cause the entire system to melt down.

There are many sources of systemic risks in a financial system. One large share of them arise from various externalities: one institution's behavior affects other institutions, however, this is not internalized in individual institution's decision-making, leading to excess risks in the system. One example is the impact of fire sale on asset price: when a troubled institution sells its risky assets, it generates a downward pressure on asset price, increasing the credit risks of other institutions who hold the same type of assets, i.e., one institution's asset fire sale has a *negative externality* on the rest of the system. However, *ex ante*, when a financial institution makes decisions on its investment portfolio, it does not take into account this externality; therefore, everyone tends to over invest in risky assets in order to benefit from all the high yields in the good time while the cost in asset fire sale is mostly shouldered by the others. In equilibrium, there is excess investment in risky assets across all financial institutions, increasing the fragility of the entire financial system.

Another example on externality is banks' holding liquid assets, say, reserves: the yields of liquid assets are typically very low compared with illiquid assets, therefore, holding liquid assets implies an opportunity cost for a bank; on the other hand, besides infrequently providing the holder liquidity buffer when being under stress, the liquid assets benefit other banks via being lent to those with liquidity shortages, i.e., one bank's holding liquid assets has a *positive externality* on the rest of the system, as it has to bear all the opportunity cost while others enjoy most of the benefit. Therefore, as Cao and Illing (2011) show, individual banks thus have a strong incentive to free ride on liquidity provision by others, holding low liquid assets individually. As shown in Figure 11.1, the share of liquid assets in banks' total assets fell almost to zero before the crisis in both the US and UK. Such systemic liquidity shortage increases the vulnerability of the financial system under market stress: liquidity buffer in the system can be easily exhausted, leading to a system wide liquidity crunch.

CHAPTER ELEVEN: SYSTEMIC RISKS AND MACROPRUDENTIAL REGULATION

Figure 11.1 Liquid assets as share of banks' balance sheets, US and UK
Data sources: Bank of England and FDIC Historical Bank Data.

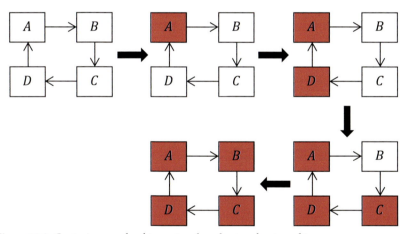

Figure 11.2 Contagion over banking network and network externality

Another important source of systemic risk arises from the network effect. Modern financial institutions are heavily connected to each other via lending and borrowing, forming a huge "web of claims"; therefore, the failure of one bank may bring down its immediate counterparts, and the bank failure can quickly spread over the entire network—in this sense, banks are "too connected to fail". Such mechanism can be easily seen from Figure 11.2, as proposed by Allen and Gale (2000) and presented

483

in Chapter 6, Section 6.3: the arrow means the flow of funding, i.e., bank A borrows from bank D, bank B borrows from bank A, etc. Now suppose that bank A fails, this incurs a loss to its immediate creditor, bank D, and bank D may fail if the loss is large enough... in the end, such domino effect may make all the connected banks in the network go bust. If a regulator only focuses on individual banks' operational risks, it will miss the systemic risk from the financial contagion over the banking network—the consequence of the *negative* externality such that banks benefit from interbank borrowing, while part of their bankruptcy costs are borne by the other banks in the network.

Bank-specific risks are relatively easy to identify, given that the underlying market failure and financial frictions are relatively well understood by theories in banking—many of which are reviewed in the previous chapters. In contrast, identifying systemic risks is far more challenging. As systemic risks often emerge from banks' coordination failure and the fact that individual banks' decision making does not take into account the externalities on the other banks, it is difficult to identify systemic risks from single bank's optimization problems, the approach that most of the analyses are based in the previous chapters; as a result, it is difficult for regulatory policies that only target bank-specific risks to prevent systemic risks from being built up. In fact, such *microprudential perspectives* that largely focus on limiting distress of individual financial institutions have been criticized for missing the signals on accumulating systemic risks globally before the 2007–2009 financial crisis and failing to respond before the crisis broke out.

After the crisis, systemic risk became one of the most important issues in banking research and regulatory practice. Exciting studies, both in banking theory and empirical research, have been addressing various sources of systemic risks and their contribution to systemic instability, *macroprudential perspectives* that emphasize identifying and containing systemic risks in both normal times and market stresses have been emphasized in the new global banking regulation standard—the so-called Basel III framework.

In this chapter, we present several mechanisms on how various systemic risks may arise. Section 11.2 focuses on the reason why banks prefer short-term to long-term debt contract and expose themselves to excess liquidity risks because of excess maturity mismatch in their balance sheets. In Section 11.3, we illustrate the reason why banks are reluctant to build a liquidity buffer, even if liquidity crunch is anticipated, so that the banking system is constantly suffering from systemic liquidity shortage and vulnerable to market liquidity stress. In Section 11.4, we focus on the comovement feature of the banking sector, and show how bank failure is contagious in the interbank market.

Based on the theoretical analyses on the sources of systemic risks, in Section 11.5, we discuss the features of macroprudential regulation that addresses systemic risks. In Section 11.6, we show how to measure systemic risks in the financial system, using market indicators.

11.2 MATURITY RAT RACE AND EXCESS MATURITY MISMATCH

We first revisit banks' role in maturity transformation. As is shown in Chapter 2, banks provide socially desirable liquidity service, by supporting long assets with short debts. Such maturity transformation improves social welfare, but it also exposes banks to liquidity risks, making the banking system fragile. Liquidity management is thus a key pillar in banks' daily business, mainly by holding liquid assets and relying on stable funding sources.

However, Brunnermeier and Oehmke (2013) argue that banks have the incentive to collectively engage in *excess* maturity mismatch, so that the entire banking system relies too much on short-term funding and banks are excessively exposed to rollover risks. The reason is that, given that information on the return of a bank's long assets evolves over time, debt contract with shorter maturity allows the bank to reprice its debts with updates on asset return, increasing the bank's profit. Although with shorter debt maturity, the bank needs more frequent refinancing from the interbank market that increases funding pressure—a negative externality—on other banks, an individual bank does not internalize such cost in its own decision on debt maturity. As a result, profit-maximizing banks will all have the incentive to shorten their debt maturities; consequently, the banking sector is characterized by excess maturity mismatch and reliance on short-term funding. This makes the banking system more fragile and more vulnerable to liquidity shocks, as even small liquidity stress in the market will create a funding problem for a large number of banks, or even a systemic liquidity crunch. In this section, we present the mechanism how a systemic liquidity risk from banks' excess maturity mismatch arises from a "maturity rat race", by a simple model based on Brunnermeier and Oehmke (2013).

11.2.1 MATURITY STRUCTURE OF DEBT CONTRACTS

Consider an economy that extends to three periods, $t = 0,1,2$. A risk-neutral bank in this economy wants to finance a long-term project that needs one unit input in $t = 0$ and returns in $t = 2$. In $t = 0$, the project is known to yield a gross return R_H with probability p_0, or R_L with probability $1 - p_0$. Assume that $R_H > 1 > R_L$.

The bank does not have any initial wealth, so that it totally relies on market funding provided by lenders. Two types of deposit contracts are available between the bank and lenders, as is shown in Figure 11.3:

- Short-term contract that only lasts two periods. The bank borrows from lenders in t, $t = 0,1$, and repays the lenders in $t+1$. Obviously, if some of the contracts are short-term, the bank has to roll over the short-term debts in the intermediate period $t = 1$, repaying the old

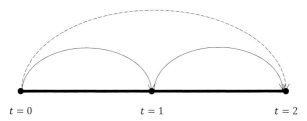

Figure 11.3 *Short-term contract versus long-term contract*

Notes: the solid curves denote the short-term contracts that require intermediate refinancing in $t = 1$, and the dash curve denotes the long-term contract.

lenders from $t=0$ and admitting new lenders. Denote the face value of a short-term contract as $d_{t,t+1}$, $t=0,1$, and assume that lenders make uncoordinated decisions in $t=1$ on whether they want to roll over the debts;
- Long-term contract that lasts three periods. The bank borrows from lenders in $t=0$, and repays the lenders in $t=2$. Denote the face value of a long-term contract as $d_{0,2}$

If the bank defaults, all debts have equal seniority that lenders share the value of the bank in proportion to the face values of their debts. Assume that lenders are competing with each other to provide funding for the bank, so that they are willing to take any deposit contract that yields an expected gross return no lower than 1.

In addition, assume that in $t=1$ a signal S, which may take two values $\{S_H, S_L\}$ ($S_H > S_L$), about the project's return is publicly observed. Precisely, the signal refers to an updated value of p_0, call it p_1, so that $S_H > S_L$ just means that p_1 is higher under the high signal, S_H. As we can see, for the expected return of the project after the signal is observed in $t=1$, $E_1[R]$,

$$E_1[R|S_H] > E_1[R|S_L],$$

or, formally, the good signal S_H *first-order stochastically dominates*[1] the bad signal S_L.

Since the project takes two periods to mature, prematurely liquidating the project incurs a liquidation cost; that is, liquidating the project in $t=1$ only yields $\delta E_1[R|S]$, $0 < \delta < 1$.

11.2.2 DEBT ROLLOVER AND MATURITY RAT RACE

Now given the payoff structure of the project and the information available in $t=0,1$, what is the bank's optimal choice on debt maturity? Shall it offer the lenders short-term contracts or long-term contracts?

We derive the answer to this question by guessing: first, we assume that the bank's optimal choice is offering all lenders long-term contracts. Then we allow one lender to deviate and get a short-term contract. If the bank can earn higher profit from this deviating lender, then long-term contract cannot be the bank's optimal choice.

If all lenders are offered long-term contracts in $t=0$, then they will receive $d_{0,2}$ if R_H is revealed in $t=2$, or R_L if R_L is revealed in $t=2$. They are willing to lend to the bank in $t=0$ as long as they break even,

$$(1-p_0)R_L + p_0 d_{0,2} = 1,$$

$$d_{0,2} = \frac{1-(1-p_0)R_L}{p_0}. \tag{11.1}$$

Now suppose that one lender deviates and is offered a short-term contract in $t=0$. This lender must be willing to lend at least in $t=0$, because no matter what signal is revealed in $t=1$, as long as $\delta E_1[R|S], 0<\delta<1$, the bank is always able to liquidate part of the project and repay the lender in $t=1$, i.e., $d_{0,1}=1$.

Then in $t=1$, when the signal S brings in more information about p_1, the deviating lender may decide whether to roll over her lending to the bank or not. If she decides to roll over, then

1. If R_H is revealed in $t=2$, she will receive $d_{1,2}$, while each of the other lenders will receive $d_{0,2}$;
2. If R_L is revealed in $t=2$, the bank defaults and she will share R_L together with other lenders, and her share is proportional to her claim in the bank, $\frac{d_{1,2}}{d_{0,2}}$.

She is only willing to roll over in $t=1$, if she is able to break even, i.e.,

$$(1-p_1)\frac{d_{1,2}}{d_{0,2}}R_L + p_1 d_{1,2} = 1,$$

$$d_{1,2} = \frac{1-(1-p_0)R_L}{p_0 R_L + p_1(1-R_L)}. \tag{11.2}$$

From the bank's point of view, in $t=0$, its revenue from the project is 0 when R_L is revealed in $t=2$ and it has to default, or R_H when R_H is revealed which is unconditional on the types of debt contracts.

The bank makes higher profit from one type of contracts only if the bank incurs a lower funding cost, i.e., the short-term contract is a better choice for the bank only if the funding cost for the rolling-over lender is lower. The difference in funding cost between long-term and short-term contracts is

$$E_0[p_1 d_{0,2}] - E_0[p_1 d_{1,2}]$$
$$= p_0 d_{0,2} - E_0[p_1 d_{1,2}] \tag{11.3}$$
$$= [1-(1-p_0)R_L]\left\{1 - E_0\left[\frac{p_1}{p_0 R_L + p_1(1-R_L)}\right]\right\}$$

using results in (11.1) and (11.2). Note that $\dfrac{p_1}{p_0 R_L + p_1(1-R_L)}$ is strictly concave in p_1, then for all $0 < R_L < 1$,

$$E\left[\frac{p_1}{p_0 R_L + p_1(1-R_L)}\right] < \frac{E_0[p_1]}{p_0 R_L + E_0[p_1](1-R_L)}$$
$$= \frac{p_0}{p_0 R_L + p_0(1-R_L)}$$
$$= 1$$

by Jensen's inequality.[2] Equation (11.3) thus implies that

$$E_0[p_1 d_{0,2}] - E_0[p_1 d_{1,2}] > 0,$$

or, the bank indeed makes a higher profit by offering a short-term contract in $t = 0$. As a result, the bank prefers to offer lenders short-term contracts in $t = 0$.

To see why a short-term contract reduces the bank's funding cost, note that by equation (11.3) the marginal funding cost of a debt contract depends on both the face value of the debt and the probability of repayment. Figure 11.4 compares the face values of short- and long-term contracts in $t = 1$: the face value of long-term contract, $d_{0,2}$, is predetermined in $t = 0$ by p_0, it is thus not affected by the new information S. However, the new information does affect the short-term debt: if the signal is S_L, implying

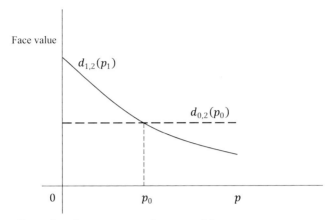

Figure 11.4 Face value, short-term versus long-term debt

Notes: the solid, downward-sloping curve denotes the face value of a short-term contract, $d_{1,2}(p_1)$, that varies with the realized probability of repayment p_1, and the horizontal dash line denotes the face value of a long-term contract, $d_{0,2}(p_0)$, that is invariant with p_1.

the probability of repayment in $t = 2$, p_1, is too low, the bank must offer the short-term lender a substantial risk premium in order to convince her to roll over the lending, making $d_{1,2}(p_1)$ higher than $d_{0,2}$. Conversely, if the signal implies that the probability of repayment p_1 is very high, then a low $d_{1,2}(p_1)$ is enough to induce short-term lenders to roll over.

The marginal funding cost of a debt contract, in correspondence to the realized probability of repayment p_1, is delineated in Figure 11.5. As for a long-term contract, its face value is predetermined by p_0 in $t = 0$, therefore, the bank's funding cost increases linearly with the realized probability of repayment p_1, as the dash line $p_1 d_{0,2}$ in the figure shows.

In contrast, as the marginal funding cost curve for a short-term contract $p_1 d_{1,2}$ shows, although when the realized p_1 is very low, the bank is forced to offer higher $d_{1,2}$ and this creates a cost disadvantage for the short-term contract—just as the area A between $p_1 d_{1,2}$ curve and $p_1 d_{0,2}$ line shows, when the realized p_1 is high enough, the bank has the flexibility to cut down its offer $d_{1,2}$ for short-term lenders, and this creates a cost advantage for the short-term contract—just as the area B between $p_1 d_{1,2}$ curve and $p_1 d_{0,2}$ line shows. It is thus optimal for the bank to choose the short-term contract, as area B is always larger than area A so that the cost advantage of the short-term contract dominates.

CHAPTER ELEVEN: SYSTEMIC RISKS AND MACROPRUDENTIAL REGULATION

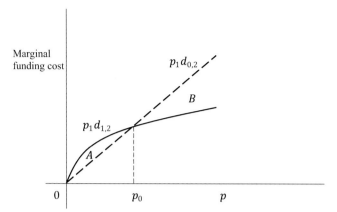

Figure 11.5 Marginal funding cost, short-term versus long-term debt

Notes: the solid, upward-sloping curve denotes the marginal funding cost of a short-term contract, $p_1 d_{1,2}$, as a strictly concave function of the realized probability of repayment p_1, and the dash line denotes the marginal funding cost of a long-term contract, $p_1 d_{0,2}$, that grows linearly in p_1.

The short-term contract leads to higher profit for the bank, but this also means that the bank has to refinance its debt more frequently. In this model, refinancing short-term contract means simply convincing incumbent creditors to stay, while in reality, banks often need to borrow through short-term interbank lending for debt refinancing. Obviously, for a bank choosing short-term debt and refinancing more frequently from the interbank market, it increases liquidity demand in the interbank market, generating an upward pressure on interbank lending rate and deteriorating other banks' funding condition—a negative externality. However, an individual bank does not take such externality into account in its choice on debt maturity; therefore, even if the bank in our model has to refinance from the interbank market, it will still choose the short-term debt contract in equilibrium. As a consequence, all banks will prefer a short-term contract to a long-term contract in their debt structure, and the entire banking system will be characterized by excess maturity mismatch and over reliance on short-term interbank lending.

Such "maturity rat race" leads to severe systemic liquidity risk. Nowadays a large share of banks' liabilities comes from short-term funding, mainly wholesale interbank lending with maturity as short as overnight. Having to roll over debt at high frequency significantly increases banks' exposure to rollover risks, and only a small liquidity shock in the interbank market may cause a large number of banks in trouble with funding and even lead to a liquidity crunch, as was observed in the summer of 2007. Such liquidity crunch may further force banks to bid up lending rate in the interbank market or liquidate illiquid assets in fire sales, but such responses only aggravate the liquidity shortage in the banking system, a small liquidity stress in the market may eventually develop into a systemic meltdown.[3]

11.2.3 SUMMARY

The Brunnermeier-Oehmke model unveils an important source of systemic liquidity risk, that banks may have the incentive to shorten debt maturity for higher profit, neglecting the fact that more funding from short-term interbank lending market increases funding pressure for all banks. As a consequence, a maturity rat race forces all banks to rely on extremely short-term funding, and the excess maturity mismatch in all banks' balance sheets leads to systemic liquidity risk.

The model also implies that policies reducing maturity mismatch and rollover risks in the banking system may be desirable. This is exactly addressed in the rules regarding Liquidity Coverage Ratio (LCR) and Net Stable Funding Ratio (NSFR) in Basel III (see more details in Chapter 12, Section 12.2.3) aiming to reduce banks' maturity mismatch. However, as banking is based on liquidity creation through maturity transformation, how to distinguish between desired and excess maturity mismatch, as well as how to curb systemic liquidity risks without damaging efficient maturity transformation, still remain challenges for policy makers in practice.

11.3 INEFFICIENT LIQUIDITY BUFFER AND SELLERS' STRIKE

Under systemic liquidity risk being built up, such as excess rollover risk as the Brunnermeier-Oehmke model shows, it is not surprising that a systemic event such as liquidity crunch breaks out when the banking system is exposed to an *unexpected* liquidity shock, for example, when BNP Paribas defaulted on its funds. What truly surprising is, that in the 13 months before the collapse of Lehman Brothers, banks did not build up a sufficient liquidity buffer even when a forthcoming liquidity crisis was in sight and anticipated.

For example, Figure 5.7 in Chapter 5, Section 5.1.3 shows how repo haircuts on all structured products, subprime-related products, and non-subprime related products, respectively, evolved over time. The striking feature in the figure is the steep hike in repo haircuts, after the Lehman Brothers collapse in September, 2008, leading to a freeze in the repo market; the subprime-related products were almost worthless, when their haircut reached almost 100%. Many people attribute such liquidity crunch to the "buyers' strike": given that it was known that subprime-related products were problematic, buyers would impose a heavy discount on these products, due to the concern of adverse selection, or, the fear of buying lemons.

However, at least two distinguishing features in Figure 5.7 are not well explained by the hypothesis of buyers' strike:

- First, if the adverse selection problem only pertains to the subprime-related products, why is there also a hike—albeit relatively smaller—in repo haircut on non-subprime related products?
- Second, even more strikingly, the crisis did not happen in one day, instead, the situation had been aggravating for one year before the Lehman Brothers collapse, and market participants had expected that the worst was yet to come. Then the question is, why didn't the banks prepare for the crisis, even when they saw the storm was accumulating?

This episode seems to suggests that certain market failure prevents banks from investing in a liquidity buffer, even if a liquidity crisis is anticipated, leaving banks with systemic liquidity shortage to survive the crisis. Diamond and Rajan (2011) explain such systemic liquidity shortage as a "sellers' strike", that prevents banks from increasing liquidity by selling assets before the crisis is materialized: with limited liabilities, preparing a liquidity buffer only benefits bank creditors, while banks have to bear the full cost.

Such positive externality makes banks reluctant to sell illiquid assets when asset price is still high, so that liquidity in the banking system is too low to avoid an anticipated liquidity crunch. In the following, we illustrate the mechanism through a simple model based on Diamond and Rajan (2011).

11.3.1 MODEL SETUP

Consider an economy that extends to 3 periods, $t = 0,1,2$. There are three types of risk-neutral agents:

- Depositors, who own deposit accounts in banks that have limited liabilities;
- Banks, who manage risky assets that are funded by the depositors, and meet depositors' withdrawal demand;
- Deep-pocket investors, who are potential buyers of bank assets.

The timing of events is as follows: in $t = 0$ each bank starts with an initial balance sheet from the past that consists of

- Illiquid, long assets that return Z in $t = 2$, and
- Deposits with face value D, and $D < Z$, i.e., a bank is able to cover depositors' withdrawal demand in $t = 2$ by the proceeds from long assets.

In $t = 0$, it is also known to the public that in $t = 1$, an aggregate liquidity shock is likely to take place for all banks: with probability q, $0 < q < 1$, the economy is in a crisis state and a fraction f, $0 < f < 1$ depositors will withdraw from banks. The only way for banks to meet depositors' early withdrawal is to sell the long assets in the asset market. With probability $1 - q$, the economy is in a normal state in $t = 1$, and nothing happens.

If the economy is in a normal state in $t = 1$, all depositors withdraw in $t = 2$. If the economy is in a crisis state and banks survive the crisis in $t = 1$, the remaining depositors withdraw in $t = 2$.

Banks can convert their long assets to cash in the asset market. Asset market opens in both $t = 0$ and $t = 1$, where banks can sell assets to investors at market price P_t, $t = 1,2$. We set the return of the long assets in $t = 2$ as numeraire.

11.3.2 MARKET EQUILIBRIUM

Given that banks already know in $t=0$ that a crisis may break out in $t=1$ so that they may need cash to meet early withdrawal demand from depositors, and they have the chance to sell assets for cash in the asset market that is open in both $t=0$ and $t=1$, the only question for banks is when is it optimal to sell assets.

In principle, a bank may have two alternative strategies, with regard to the timing of asset sales:

1. One is "wait-and-see", with the bank's balance sheet being tracked in Figure 11.6. It only enters the asset market when the crisis breaks out in $t=1$: by selling a share η_1 of long assets, the bank converts the future return $\eta_1 Z$ to cash at price P_1, fulfilling the early withdrawal demand fD. If the bank survives the crisis by doing so, in $t=2$, the remaining depositors are repaid by the proceeds from the remaining long assets. However, if the crisis is not materialized in $t=1$, the bank does nothing, and all claims are cleared in $t=2$;
2. The other one is "getting-ready-before-the-crisis", with the bank's balance sheet being tracked in Figure 11.6. In $t=0$, the bank participates in the asset market and builds up its cash buffer by converting a share η_0 of long assets to cash, which is just enough to meet the early withdrawal demand fD in $t=1$, if the crisis breaks out. In $t=1$, if the crisis is materialized, the early withdrawal demand is fulfilled by the bank's cash buffer; afterwards, the remaining

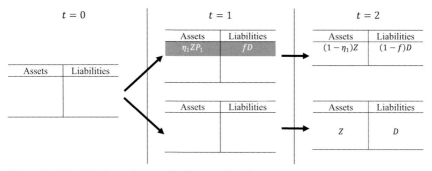

Figure 11.6 Bank balance sheet under "wait-and-see" strategy

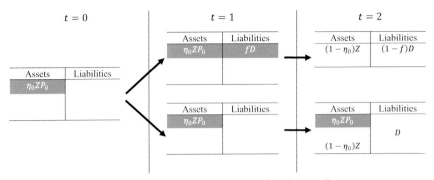

Figure 11.7 Bank balance sheet under "getting-ready-before-the-crisis" strategy

depositors are repaid by the proceeds from the remaining long assets in $t=2$. However, if the crisis is not materialized in $t=1$, the bank carries over the cash buffer to $t=2$, and repays all depositors by the cash buffer as well as return from the remaining long assets.

Obviously, whether the bank chooses "wait-and-see" or "getting-ready-before-the-crisis" depends on which strategy leads to higher profit.

To solve for the market equilibrium, we start with solving investors' decision problem:

- Suppose an investor participates in the asset market in $t=0$, paying P_0 for one unit asset return at $t=2$. The gross return is then $\frac{1}{P_0}$;
- Alternatively, the investor can hold cash until she participates in the asset market in $t=1$, paying P_1 for one unit asset return at $t=2$. However, she can only buy assets if banks are subject to the liquidity shock and forced to liquidate, the gross return is then $\frac{1}{P_1}$ in this case; otherwise she has to carry over the cash till $t=2$ with gross return 1. The expected return, if the investor chooses to participate in the asset market in $t=1$, is thus

$$q\frac{1}{P_1}+(1-q)\cdot 1.$$

To ensure that investors participate in both markets, in equilibrium, they must be indifferent to the timing of buying assets, i.e.,

$$\frac{1}{P_0} = q \cdot \frac{1}{P_1} + (1-q) \cdot 1,$$

$$P_0 = \frac{1}{\frac{q}{P_1} + 1 - q}. \tag{11.4}$$

Call P_0 as P_0^{bid}, i.e., the bid price of investors.

As for the bank's decision problem, we distinguish two cases. The first case is that banks are able to survive the crisis, by selling assets in the market, so that there is no insolvency in equilibrium. The second case is that banks are only able to survive the crisis if they "get ready before the crisis", while they cannot survive the crisis if they "wait and see": this is to capture the scenario that assets are often sold at substantial discounts during crises, therefore, if banks "wait and see" and only sell assets during the crisis in $t=1$, the market price P_1 will be too low so that banks cannot raise enough cash to meet early withdrawal demand and they are bankrupted. As a result, if "wait-and-see" is market equilibrium, the equilibrium is subject to insolvency in a crisis state.

MARKET EQUILIBRIUM WITHOUT INSOLVENCY RISK

Note that banks are solvent—or, they can raise enough cash via asset sales to meet depositors' early withdrawal demand,—as long as P_0 and P_1 are sufficiently large. Assume that P_0 and P_1 are sufficiently large so that banks are solvent under liquidity shocks, independent on the timing of asset sales, then in $t=0$ a bank must decide when to sell assets:

1. If it sells assets in $t=1$, it needs to sell a fraction of η_1 so that $\eta_1 Z P_1 = fD$, as Figure 11.6 shows. Expected profit of the bank is thus

$$q\underbrace{\left[(1-\eta_1)Z - (1-f)D\right]}_{(A)} + (1-q)\underbrace{(Z-D)}_{(B)} \tag{11.5}$$

$$= Z - D - qfD\left(\frac{1}{P_1} - 1\right).$$

Term (A)/term (B) denotes the bank's profit in $t=2$ under crisis/normal state in $t=1$.

2. If it sells assets in $t=0$, it needs to sell a fraction of η_0 so that $\eta_0 Z P_0 = fD$, as Figure 11.6 shows. Expected profit of the bank is thus

$$\underbrace{q\left[(1-\eta_0)Z-(1-f)D\right]}_{(A)}+\underbrace{(1-q)\left[(1-\eta_0)Z+\eta_0 Z P_0 - D\right]}_{(B)} \qquad (11.6)$$
$$= Z-D-fD\left(\frac{1}{P_0}-1\right).$$

Term (A)/term (B) denotes the bank's profit in $t=2$ under crisis/normal state in $t=1$.

To ensure banks participate both markets, in equilibrium, they must be indifferent to the timing of selling assets, i.e., expected returns in (11.5) and (11.6) shall be equal,

$$Z-D-qfD\left(\frac{1}{P_1}-1\right) = Z-D-fD\left(\frac{1}{P_0}-1\right),$$

$$P_0 = \frac{1}{\frac{q}{P_1}+1-q}.$$

Call P_0 as P_0^{ask} as the bank's ask price. It's easy to see that $P_0^{ask} = P_0^{bid}$, as in equation (11.4). That is, in equilibrium, under such $P_0^{ask} = P_0^{bid}$ and P_1 so that banks are always solvent, banks are indifferent between selling assets in $t=0$ and $t=1$. The reason is, without insolvency risk, banks bear the entire liquidation cost when they sell assets in the market; that investors' expected return is independent of the timing of buying assets implies that banks' liquidation cost is independent of the timing of selling assets so that their expected profit is independent of the timing of asset sales, either. Therefore, in equilibrium, there can be active asset sales in both $t=0$ and $t=1$.

MARKET EQUILIBRIUM WITH INSOLVENCY RISK

Now let us assume alternatively that P_1 is not sufficiently large: banks are only solvent if they sell assets in $t=0$, should liquidity shock occur in $t=1$. Banks are bankrupted if they choose to sell assets in $t=1$, as the liquidation value of long assets under P_1 is not enough to meet the early withdrawal demand, that is,

$$P_1\left[Z-(1-f)D\right] < fD. \tag{11.7}$$

Same as before, we characterize a representative bank's expected profit under different timing of asset sales:

1. If it sells assets in $t=0$ for a price P_0^{ask}, it needs to sell a fraction of η_0 so that $\eta_0 Z P_0 = fD$, as Figure 11.6 shows. The bank's profit is thus

   (a) Under crisis state in $t=1$ (with probability q),

   $$(1-\eta_0)Z-(1-f)D;$$

   (b) Under normal state in $t=1$ (with probability $1-q$),

   $$(1-\eta_0)Z+\eta_0 Z P_0 - D.$$

   Expected profit of the bank is thus

   $$q\left[(1-\eta_0)Z-(1-f)D\right]+(1-q)\left[(1-\eta_0)Z+\eta_0 Z P_0 - D\right]$$
   $$= Z-D-\left(\frac{1}{P_0^{ask}}-1\right)fD;$$

2. If the bank does not sell assets in $t=0$, it is bankrupted in a crisis state in $t=1$, and under limited liability the bank's profit is 0. Otherwise, if the crisis state is not materialized in $t=1$, the bank earns a profit of $Z-D$ in $t=2$. Overall, the bank's expected profit is

   $$(1-q)(Z-D)+q\cdot 0.$$

Comparing the bank's expected profits in both cases, a bank only participates in the asset market in $t=0$ if its expected profit is at least as high as when it chooses to participate in the asset market in $t=1$, i.e.,

$$Z-D-\left(\frac{1}{P_0^{ask}}-1\right)fD \geq (1-q)(Z-D),$$

$$P_0^{ask} \geq \frac{1}{1+q\left(\frac{Z-D}{fD}\right)}.$$

However, this implies that the bank's ask price is strictly higher than investors' bid price, as

$$\frac{1}{1+q\left(\frac{Z-D}{fD}\right)} > \frac{1}{\frac{q}{P_1}+1-q} = P_0^{bid},$$

because when the bank is insolvent in a crisis state by choosing "wait-and-see", (11.7) implies that

$$q\left(\frac{Z-D}{fD}\right) < \frac{q}{P_1}-q.$$

This suggests that in equilibrium, there is no trade in asset market in $t=0$, or, banks choose "wait-and-see" in $t=0$. As a result, in equilibrium, banks do not sell assets in $t=0$, and they are bankrupted in a crisis state in $t=1$ because the market price for assets, P_1, is too low for banks to raise enough cash and meet early withdrawal demand.

This result is, at first glance, surprising because even if banks clearly know that they will be bankrupted in a crisis state if they do not build a liquidity buffer by asset sales in $t=0$, they still choose to do nothing to prepare for the storm and hoard illiquid assets on their balance sheets. The reason is that banks' incentive to build a liquidity buffer is distorted by their limited liability under bankruptcy: if banks choose to build the buffer in $t=0$, the benefit mostly goes to depositors because they are guaranteed to be fully repaid in the crisis state, and the liquidation cost is fully borne by banks.

In contrast, if banks do not build a liquidity buffer in $t=0$, in a crisis state, their return is bounded below at zero by their limited liability, implying that much of the bankruptcy cost is borne by the depositors; however, if they are lucky and the crisis is not materialized in $t=1$, the intact illiquid assets generate maximum profit in $t=2$. In other words, limited liability means "Heads I win, tails I do not lose much" for banks who gamble for the good state in $t=1$, so that banks have no incentive to self-insure and increase liquidity holding in $t=0$; while banks will never be able to raise sufficient liquidity when a crisis state is materialized in $t=1$, as asset price in $t=1$ is too low for banks to survive by asset sales. The results confirm a well-known proverb in Wall Street:

> Liquidity is never there when you need it most.

11.3.3 SUMMARY

The Diamond-Rajan model on systemic liquidity shortage provides important insights on why liquidity buffer is systemically low, even when a liquidity crisis is anticipated. Holding liquidity benefits creditors, but a liquidity holding bank has to incur the opportunity cost of forgoing investing more in high-yield illiquid assets—a positive externality that leads to under investment in liquidity buffer. With limited liability, banks have the incentive to bet for good luck, so they would rather hold illiquid assets instead of selling them to build up a liquidity buffer. The positive externality and banks' limited liability lead to a sellers' strike, that banks never sell assets when they should, and they can never raise enough liquidity from asset market when they need it.

The model also suggests that policies that force banks to build up a liquidity buffer in normal times are desirable to address systemic liquidity shortage. For example, the rule regarding Liquidity Coverage Ratio (LCR) in Basel III requires one bank to hold enough liquidity that meets total liquidity outflow in the next 30 days under a stress scenario (see more details in Chapter 12, Section 12.2.3), that has the potential to build up a liquidity buffer before it becomes too late.

11.4 CONTAGION IN INTERBANK MARKET

Systemic risks do not only refer to those risks arising from banks' coordination failure in maintaining resilience of banking system *before* systemic events, they also refer to those structural factors in banking system that cause correlation, comovement, and contagion that lead to fast-evolving cascading failure and systemic meltdown *during* crises. Such comovement and contagion are often caused by correlation in banks' asset returns (for example, Acharya 2009), banks' common exposure to assets or investment portfolios (for example, Wagner 2011), and banks' interconnection through the network of interbank claims (for example, Allen and Gale 2000 that is presented in Chapter 6, Section 6.3).

In this section, we present the mechanism on how financial contagion takes place in the interbank market. Nowadays, banks often rely on the interbank market for funding; the interbank market does provide risk-sharing among banks; however, it also makes financial contagion possible: failing banks strive for survival so they will bid up the interbank lending rate, a negative externality that increases funding pressure for all other banks, making relatively fragile banks fail, which will further push up the interbank lending rate and put more banks in trouble. Such contagion through the interbank market will then amplify small bank failure into a systemic liquidity crunch. In a partial equilibrium model based on Diamond and Rajan (2005), we show how bank failure can spill over to the rest of the economy, through the rising cost of liquidity in the interbank market.

11.4.1 IDIOSYNCRATIC LIQUIDITY SHOCKS AND INTERBANK MARKET

Consider an economy that lives for three periods and four dates, $t=0,1,2$ with an intermediate date $t=\frac{1}{2}$. There are three groups of risk-neutral agents:

- Depositors, each of which is endowed with one unit of good in $t=0$. They are "impatient" and have a short time preference for consumption, i.e., they only value the consumption in $t=1$ for their investments made at $t=0$. Depositors only own an inferior storage technology so that they prefer to deposit their endowments in the banks as long as the expected gross return is no lower than 1;
- Entrepreneurs, each of which has no endowment, but, instead, a production project (*ex ante* identical across the production sector) that needs one unit of fixed cost in $t=0$. The entrepreneurs are indifferent in the timing of consumption. There are more projects than the investors' endowments so that the entrepreneurs have to compete for funding;
- A continuum of banks indexed by $0 \le i \le 1$, each of which has no endowment, but, instead, a special skill of collecting a share γ of the returns from the entrepreneurs' projects. This fact justifies the banks' role as intermediary, channeling the funds from the depositors to the entrepreneurs while handing over the returns from the entrepreneurs to the depositors.

There is an uncertainty concerning the timing of a project's return. After a project is initiated in $t=0$, there is a probability p that it returns $R>1$ in $t=1$—call it an early project, and a probability $1-p$ that it is delayed and returns R in $t=2$—call it a late project. The value of p is public information once it is revealed.

The banks, as lenders to the entrepreneurs, also have the authority to take over the projects and liquidate them before they mature. When a project, no matter being early or late, is liquidated before $t=1$, it returns c_1 immediately after liquidation, as well as remaining c_2 in $t=2$. This captures the fact that liquidation, or "restructuring" of an ongoing project usually takes time. Early liquidation is costly so that $c_1 + c_2 < 1 < \gamma R < R$.

The banks compete in the deposit market for the funds from the depositors, by offering them the non-contingent demand deposit contracts. As argued in Section 2.4, such demand deposit contract, which is subject to the bank run and creates the fragility in the banking sector, is necessary to avoid the banks from abusing their intermediation expertise.

The timing of the model is sketched in Figure 11.8.

1. In $t=0$ the banks receive deposits from the depositors, using the demand deposit contracts promising a return d_0 in $t=1$ for each unit of deposit. Then the entrepreneurs receive loans from the banks and start their projects;

2. In $t=\frac{1}{2}$, the state of the world s and the probability of a project being an early one, p, are revealed. The value p_i is heterogeneous for each bank i, which is randomly drawn from the same cumulative distribution function $F_s(p)$ in the state s. In $t=0$, the *ex ante* probability of getting into state s in $t=\frac{1}{2}$ is π_s. Without loss of generality, assume that p_i increases with a bank's index i. Further, by the Law of Large Numbers, the probability p_i is also the share of early projects for bank i.

Now the depositors are able to compute the bank i's expected return from all the projects. If the return is below the face value of the deposit claims, the depositors will run on the bank; the bank is then bankrupted and exits the market, as Figure 11.9 shows. Otherwise they wait and withdraw in $t=1$. Here any bank run caused purely by panic is excluded.

Notice that the banks have several resources of raising funds to repay the investors, including collecting the returns from the early

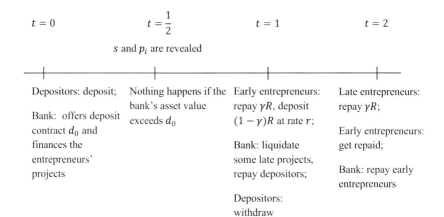

Figure 11.8 Timing of the model without bank run

CHAPTER ELEVEN: SYSTEMIC RISKS AND MACROPRUDENTIAL REGULATION

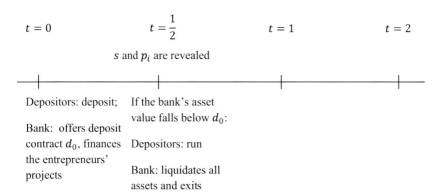

Figure 11.9 *Timing of the model with bank run*

projects, collecting new deposits from the early entrepreneurs, and liquidating the long assets;

3 In $t=1$, if the bank survives, it collects the returns from the early projects and competes with the other surviving banks for the early entrepreneurs' funds; the deposit market is cleared by the equilibrium deposit rate r. Then the depositors withdraw and consume;

4 In $t=2$, the surviving bank collects the returns from the late projects and repays deposits from the early entrepreneurs.

11.4.2 EQUILIBRIUM OUTCOMES IN THE INTERBANK MARKET

Since the banks engage in the perfect competition for the deposit in $t=0$, the representative bank i therefore simply aims to maximize the expected return for its depositors by liquidating a share μ_i of the late projects, i.e.,

$$\max_{\mu_i} \quad p_i\gamma R + \mu_i(1-p_i)\left(c_1 + \frac{c_2}{1+r}\right) + (1-\mu_i)(1-p_i)\frac{\gamma R}{1+r}, \quad (11.8)$$

$$\text{s.t.} \quad p_i\gamma R + \mu_i(1-p_i)\left(c_1 + \frac{c_2}{1+r}\right) + (1-\mu_i)(1-p_i)\frac{\gamma R}{1+r}$$

$$\geq d_0. \quad (11.9)$$

In the object function (11.8), $p_i \gamma R$ is the return directly collected from the early projects, $\mu_i(1-p_i)(c_1 + \frac{c_2}{1+r})$ is the return from liquidating the long assets, and $(1-\mu_i)(1-p_i)\frac{\gamma R}{1+r}$ is the present value of the late projects. The maximization problem only holds when the bank survives bank run, i.e., the bank is able to honor its liabilities to the depositors, as its budget constraint (11.9) states. If the bank experiences a run, the liquidated value of the bank's assets is constant at $c_1 + \frac{c_2}{1+r}$ and invariant to its strategy taken in $t=0$.

To solve the bank's problem, notice that the object function is linear in μ_i so that the optimal strategy on μ_i depends on the cost benefit comparison of asset liquidation. Therefore,

$$\mu_i = \begin{cases} 0 & \text{if } 0 \leq r \leq \frac{\gamma R - c_2}{c_1} - 1 \equiv \bar{r}, \\ 1 & \text{if } r > \bar{r}, \\ \tilde{\mu} \in [0,1] & \text{if } r = \bar{r}. \end{cases} \quad (11.10)$$

The result here suggests that the bank's liquidation decision depends on the equilibrium deposit rate r, which reflects the bank's cost on raising funds in the intermediate period, or, rolling over its debts, and is hence a measure of market liquidity. On the other hand, r is endogenously determined by the liquidity supply and demand, therefore, it will be interesting to see how r is formed and see its feedback on the market outcome.

Although the failing banks are dissolved in $t=\frac{1}{2}$ while the surviving ones repay their depositors in $t=1$, the depositors of the surviving banks just decide to wait in $t=\frac{1}{2}$ instead of to run once they conclude that the banks will be solvent under the expected deposit rate r in $t=1$. Regarding the depositors' decision of running on a bank, it is easily seen that

The bank's present value in $t=1$,

$$p_i \gamma R + \mu_i (1-p_i)\left(c_1 + \frac{c_2}{1+r}\right) + (1-\mu_i)(1-p_i)\frac{\gamma R}{1+r}$$

is negatively correlated with p_i since

$$\gamma R \geq (1-\mu_i)\frac{\gamma R}{1+r} \text{ and } \gamma R \geq \mu_i\left(c_1 + \frac{c_2}{1+r}\right).$$

Therefore, if there are bank runs in the economy, the banks within the lowest distribution of p_i, hence lowest indices of i, are the first ones who suffer from bank runs.

Since the bank runs caused by panic are excluded by design, one bank is immune to bank runs if

$$p_i \gamma R + (1-p_i)\left(c_1 + \frac{c_2}{1+r}\right) \geq d_0. \tag{11.11}$$

That is, even if the bank has to liquidate all its long assets ($\mu_i = 1$), the bank's present value in $t=1$ is still sufficient to repay the consumers. Therefore, if d_0 is not too high, the banks within the highest distribution of p_i will stay solvent.

The intermediate interest rate r can be calculated by the aggregate demand and supply of liquidity in $t=\frac{1}{2}$ and $t=1$. From the demand side, the liquidity demand is d_0 for a surviving bank i and $c_1 + \frac{c_2}{1+r}$ for a failing bank. From the supply side, the liquidity supply is $p_i R + \mu_i(1-p_i)c_1 + \frac{c_2}{1+r}$ for a surviving bank i and c_1 for a failing bank. Depending on the demand and supply of liquidity, the market rate r can be characterized by one of the following three generic cases:

1. $r=0$, as there is excess liquidity supply. Condition (11.10) implies that surviving banks do not need to liquidate any assets, or, $\mu_i = 0$. However, unlucky banks with too low realized p_i are not immune to bank runs, with condition (11.11) being violated. Define $p_i(1)$ as the threshold value of realized p_i that just enables a bank to survive under $r=0$, i.e.

$$p_i(1)\gamma R + (1-p_i(1))(c_1+c_2) = d_0$$

and $i^*(1)$ as the index of the corresponding bank, then all banks that rank between 0 and $i^*(1)$ will incur bank runs in $t=\frac{1}{2}$ and liquidate *all* projects, other banks will survive.

Excess liquidity supply in the interbank market in $t=1$ implies that

$$\underbrace{\int_0^{i^*(1)} c_1 dF(i)}_{(A)} + \underbrace{\int_{i^*(1)}^1 p_i R dF(i)}_{(B)} \geq \underbrace{\int_0^{i^*(1)} (c_1+c_2) dF(i)}_{(C)} + \underbrace{\int_{i^*(1)}^1 d_0 dF(i)}_{(D)}. \quad (11.12)$$

Term (A) is the liquidity supply from the insolvent banks—remember that they incur bank runs in $t=\frac{1}{2}$ so that they have to liquidate all assets; term (B) is the liquidity supply from the surviving banks' collecting proceeds from the early projects as well as deposits from the early entrepreneurs; term (C) is the liquidity demand from the insolvent banks which also need to convert future return c_2 to cash in $t=1$; and term (D) is the liquidity demand from the surviving banks' repaying depositors.

2. $0 < r < \bar{r}$, as condition (11.12) is violated, but according to condition (11.10), surviving banks still do not need to liquidate any assets, or, $\mu_i = 0$. Again, under such r, some unlucky banks with too low realized p_i are not immune to bank runs. Define $p_i(2)$ as the threshold value of realized p_i that just enables a bank to survive under r, i.e.

$$p_i(2) \gamma R + (1 - p_i(2)) \left(c_1 + \frac{c_2}{1+r} \right) = d_0 \quad (11.13)$$

and $i^*(2)$ as the index of the corresponding bank, then all banks that rank between 0 and $i^*(2)$ will incur bank runs in $t=\frac{1}{2}$ and other banks will survive. In this case, even under the worst possible scenario, $r = \bar{r}$, market liquidity supply should fulfill liquidity demand, i.e.,

$$\int_0^{i^*(2)} c_1 dF(i) + \int_{i^*(2)}^1 p_i R dF(i)$$
$$\geq \int_0^{i^*(2)} \left(c_1 + \frac{c_2}{1+\bar{r}} \right) dF(i) + \int_{i^*(2)}^1 d_0 dF(i). \quad (11.14)$$

CHAPTER ELEVEN: SYSTEMIC RISKS AND MACROPRUDENTIAL REGULATION

Then the market-clearing interest rate r is determined when liquidate supply equates demand,

$$\int_0^{i^*(2)} c_1 dF(i) + \int_{i^*(2)}^1 p_i R dF(i)$$

$$= \int_0^{i^*(2)} \left(c_1 + \frac{c_2}{1+\bar{r}} \right) dF(i) + \int_{i^*(2)}^1 d_0 dF(i). \quad (11.15)$$

The equilibrium interest rate r thus can be solved by equations (11.13) and (11.15).

3. $r = \bar{r}$, as condition (11.14) is violated, and according to condition (11.10), surviving banks have to liquidate part of their long assets, or, $0 < \mu_i < 1$. Equilibrium μ_i can be solved by market-clearing condition, i.e., market liquidity supply equates demand under μ_i

$$\int_0^{i^*(\bar{r})} c_1 dF(i) + \int_{i^*(\bar{r})}^1 \left[p_i R + \mu_i (1 - p_i) c_1 \right] dF(i)$$

$$= \int_0^{i^*(\bar{r})} \left(c_1 + \frac{c_2}{1+\bar{r}} \right) dF(i) + \int_{i^*(\bar{r})}^1 d_0 dF(i) \quad (11.16)$$

in which $i^*(\bar{r})$ is determined by corresponding $p_i(\bar{r})$ under

$$p_i(\bar{r}) \gamma R + (1 - p_i(\bar{r})) \left(c_1 + \frac{c_2}{1+r} \right) = d_0.$$

4. $r > \bar{r}$, and according to condition (11.10), surviving banks have to liquidate all of their long assets, or, $\mu_i = 1$. If there still exists a $p_i(3)$ that fulfills

$$p_i(3) \gamma R + (1 - p_i(3)) \left(c_1 + \frac{c_2}{1+r} \right) = d_0, \quad (11.17)$$

with a corresponding bank $i^*(3) < 1$, such that banks between $i^*(3)$ and 1 are still solvent, then equilibrium r is determined by equation (11.17) and the market-clearing condition that

$$\int_0^{i^*(3)} c_1 dF(i) + \int_{i^*(3)}^1 \left[p_i R + (1-p_i)c_1\right] dF(i)$$

$$= \int_0^{i^*(3)} \left(c_1 + \frac{c_2}{1+r}\right) dF(i) + \int_{i^*(3)}^1 d_0 dF(i). \quad (11.18)$$

However, if such $i^*(3)$ does not exist, all banks incur bank runs and become insolvent in $t=1$.

11.4.3 CONTAGION THROUGH THE INTERBANK MARKET

The direct question from the result is by what factors the market equilibria are separated into these three cases. The most straight observation is that the cut-off value i^* in each case depends on the realized p_i in $t=\frac{1}{2}$, given that d_0 has been already contracted in $t=0$ and taken as given in $t=1$. Remember that p_i is randomly drawn from a state-dependent distribution $F_s(p)$, which varies each time when a specific state s is materialized, and each $F_s(p)$ corresponds to a different level of aggregate liquidity demand and supply. Regarding the three generic cases, this implies:

1 When an $F_s(p)$ is revealed with a very high average p_i—call it $E_s(p)$—across all the banks, there will be more assets returning early, which leads to higher liquidity supply. In this case, only the banks in the tail, i.e., those with very low p_i, become bust from the bank run, and the abundant liquidity supply keeps the equilibrium interest rate at its lowest level, $r=0$;

2 When $E_s(p)$ is not very high for a revealed $F_s(p)$, there will be less long assets returning early. Then the surviving banks have to compete for the limited liquidity supply and the intermediate deposit rate, r, is bid up above one, but $E_s(p)$ is not low enough to force surviving banks to liquidate their long positions—as long as r is still below the threshold $\bar{r}$. The immediate effect of rising r is, by equation (11.13), the threshold $p_i(2)$ has to rise with r, so as the cut-off bank index $i^*(2)$—those who could just be able to survive case

1 will be insolvent, because $i^*(2) > i^*(1)$ when r rises above 0, and fewer banks will be solvent.

However, more bank failures furthers dry up market liquidity supply, as we can see from the left-hand side of equation (11.15): an insolvent bank only provides c_1 instead of p_iR; therefore, surviving banks will bid for higher r, which also depresses liquidity demand, $c_1 + \frac{c_2}{1+r}$, from the failing banks, as the right-hand side of equation (11.15) shows. However, this will further cause more bankruptcies by increasing $i^*(2)$... such contagion will continue until r is high enough to clear the market;

3. When $E_s(p)$ is very low for a revealed $F_s(p)$, there will be even fewer assets returning early. The intermediate deposit rate, r, is bid up to such a high level that the surviving banks even prefer liquidating their long assets to borrowing from the liquidity market, as condition (11.10) suggests. Since the early liquidation is very costly, making the banks with more illiquid assets more difficult to meet the demand deposit contract, more banks in the tail side will be insolvent.

With realized liquidity risks, the banks are interlinked through the liquidity market in the intermediate period, when the banks need to raise liquidity to repay the consumers. The ease of raising funds is indicated by the market interest rate r, which is determined by the aggregate liquidity supply. Once the realized distribution of the early projects implies a shortage in the aggregate liquidity supply, the interest rate r will be bid higher, eroding the present value of the assets for all the banks and making more illiquid banks fail.

11.4.4 SUMMARY

The Diamond-Rajan contagion model clearly shows the systemic contagion risk that arises from (one of) the most important banking infrastructure, the interbank market. In conventional wisdom, the interbank market provides risk-sharing against idiosyncratic liquidity risks, as banks with liquidity shortage can borrow from banks with liquidity surplus; however, the Diamond-Rajan contagion model shows that contagion of bank failure even occurs under idiosyncratic liquidity risks. The reason is that liquidation of failing banks drains liquidity from the interbank market and bids up equilibrium interest rate, increasing funding pressure and causing more banks to fail. This will further drain liquidity from the interbank market and raise the market lending rate... more banks will be brought down by the contagion.

The model implies that intervention in the interbank market during financial crises may effectively cut off financial contagion and avoid systemic meltdown. Such intervention may be swiftly cutting down monetary policy rate, or pumping liquidity into targeted institutions to increase liquidity supply in the market, as Chapter 7, Section 7.2.3 suggests, or closing down the insolvent banks to reduce financial contagion.

11.5 MACROPRUDENTIAL VERSUS MICROPRUDENTIAL PERSPECTIVES

Research on systemic risks in the past two decades has significantly deepened people's understanding on sources of instabilities in the financial system, and inspired regulators to rethink banking regulation. It is now widely agreed among both researchers and policy makers that merely maintaining stability of individual financial institutions does not necessarily mean that the entire financial system will stay healthy; as a result, traditional *microprudential* perspectives of banking regulation that mostly focus on limiting failure of single banks and supervising activities of atomistic banks may not succeed with keeping the entire banking system stable or reducing the likelihood of systemic breakdown. Therefore, during the post-crisis reform in global banking regulation standard, *macroprudential* perspectives that attempt to address sources of systemic risks and limit systemic distress have been much emphasized in the design of new regulatory rules.

Table 11.1 Macroprudential versus microprudential perspectives of banking regulation

	Macroprudential	Microprudential
Proximate objective	Limit financial system-wide distress	Limit distress of individual institutions
Ultimate objective	Avoid output (GDP) losses and costs for taxpayers	Consumer (investor and depositor) protection
Risk in modelling	(In part) endogenous	Exogenous
Correlations and common exposures across institutions	Important	Irrelevant
Calibration of prudential controls	In terms of system-wide distress; top-down	In terms of risks of individual institutions; bottom-up

Source: Borio (2003).

Key differences between macroprudential and microprudential perspectives of banking regulation, in objectives, risk modelling, assumptions and implementation, are briefly summarized in Table 11.1 by Borio (2003).

Proximate objective Macroprudential regulation aims to reduce distress in the banking system and the likelihood of systemic events such as systemic bank failures and crises; microprudential regulation aims to prevent failure of individual institutions, with the expectation that stability of each individual bank ensures stability of the banking system;

Ultimate objective Macroprudential regulation emphasizes the social cost of systemic failure so that its regulatory design aims to reduce such social cost, through rules and instruments preventing systemic events from happening, cutting off the spillover from bank failure to the real economy to avoid losses in real output, establishing buffers and allocating resources within the banking system for crisis resolution to reduce costs for taxpayers, etc.; microprudential regulation focuses on protecting the interests of individual bank customers, with more emphases on rules shielding customers against banks' anti-competition behavior such as exploitative pricing, ensuring bank customers are free from fraud and deception, protecting creditors' claims in bank resolution, etc.;

Risk in modelling From the macroprudential perspectives, risks in the banking system not only originate from outside, but also from outcomes of interactions among banks; therefore, when modelling risks in policy analyses and stress tests, it is crucial to take into account the risks that arise endogenously from within the banking system, such as *externalities* that individual bank's behavior may increase risk level of the entire banking system. From microprudential perspectives that focus on an individual bank's risk management practice, realized risks from bank balance sheets are triggered by factors outside of banks, so that they are simply taken as exogenously given;

Correlations and common exposures across institutions From macroprudential perspectives, substantial systemic risks lie in banks' interconnection, common exposure to certain risks, and correlation in asset returns, that lead to swift comovement, contagion, and cascading failure under market stress; therefore, taking into account such interconnection, common exposure, and correlation is extremely important in stabilizing policies and regulatory rules. From microprudential perspectives, although market comovement and contagion are crucial issues for public intervention *during* crises, they are rather irrelevant, *ex ante*, for assessing individual banks' risks or regulating individual banks' behavior;

Calibration of prudential controls Overall, macroprudential regulation emphasizes more on systemic implications of regulatory rules, following a top-down approach to regulatory design with a priority on maintaining systemic stability. Microprudential regulation attempts to stabilize the banking system by keeping individual banks in good health, following a bottom-up approach to regulatory design with a priority on disciplining each individual bank.

It is worth noting that macroprudential and microprudential regulation are complements, rather than substitutes to each other. The recent rise of macroprudential regulation and emphasis on systemic risks in the regulatory world are rather filling the gap that was long neglected, instead of replacing the conventional microprudential framework. Microprudential bank-level disciplines as well as microprudential supervision on individual banks, etc., are still indispensable elements in the twenty-first century's banking regulation practice.

Designing macroprudential rules and conducting macroprudential policies are also challenging, as development of macroprudential regulation goes hand in hand with research on systemic risks, which is not yet full-fledged. Therefore, the current macroprudential regulatory framework will surely evolve with market development and frontier economic research. In the next chapter, we will present a "big picture" of banking regulation, with an emphasis on how macroprudential perspectives are integrated in current regulatory practice.

11.6 EMPIRICAL EVIDENCE: MEASURING SYSTEMIC RISKS

Regulators cannot properly monitor and limit systemic risks without being able to identify and measure them, however, the complex and systemic nature of systemic risks makes it challenging to track and quantify systemic risks, partially because systemic events are so rare that statistical inferences based on a few observations are hardly feasible. In their groundbreaking work, Reinhart and Rogoff (2009) look through eight centuries of human history with financial crises around the world, and find that systemic crises most likely break out after abundant capital inflows, waves of financial innovation, housing booms, and financial liberalization. In their seminal work, Schularick and Taylor (2012) examine the history of financial crises in 14 developed countries over the years 1870–2008. They find lagged credit growth seems to be highly significant as a predictor of financial crises.

Recently, more and more systemic risk indicators are designed based on high-frequency market data. These indicators address the correlation, comovement, and contagion nature of systemic risks, and illustrate systemic instabilities through risk spillover among financial institutions, individual institutions' contribution to systemic fragility, as well as individual institutions' vulnerability contingent on the failure of other institutions. In this section, we present three market-based systemic risk measures that are widely used: CoVaR, systemic expected shortfall, and SRISK.

11.6.1 COVAR

Adrian and Brunnermeier (2016) propose a value-at-risk (VaR) based indicator of one bank's systemic importance, conditional on the events from the bank. Recall from Chapter 8, Section 8.5 that the VaR of a bank i at confidence level α, denoted by VaR_α^i, means that the event that the realized loss L^i exceeds VaR_α^i happens at a probability no higher than $1-\alpha$, i.e.,

$$\text{Prob}\left(L^i > VaR_\alpha^i\right) \leq 1-\alpha.$$

In similar vein, the *conditional, contingent, or contributing value-at-risk*, $CoVaR_\alpha^{j|C(L^i)}$, defines the VaR of bank j conditional on some event $C(L^i)$ of bank i, i.e.,

$$\text{Prob}\left(L^j \mid C(L^i) \geq CoVaR_\alpha^{j|C(L^i)}\right) \leq 1-\alpha. \qquad (11.19)$$

That is, given the event $C(L^i)$ that is associated with bank i's loss L^i, the event that bank j's realized loss L^j exceeds $CoVaR_\alpha^{j|C(L^i)}$ happens at a probability no higher than $1-\alpha$.

For example, suppose the event $C(L^i)$ is the failure of bank i, then $CoVaR_\alpha^{j|C(L^i)}$ in (11.19) measures bank j's VaR coming from this event with confidence level α. If we define j as the rest of the financial system, $CoVaR_\alpha^{j|C(L^i)}$ in (11.19) gives the measure on the stress of the financial system that arises from bank i's failure.

A more practical measure is the difference between $CoVaR_\alpha^{j|C(L^i)}$ under some extreme event—for example, bankruptcy—and $CoVaR_\alpha^{j|C(L^i)}$ in the orderly time. This gives the additional pressure that is caused by the event, or bank i's contribution to bank j:

$$\Delta CoVaR_\alpha^{j|i} = CoVaR_\alpha^{j|X^i=VaR_\alpha^i} - CoVaR_\alpha^{j|X^i=VaR_{median}^i}. \quad (11.20)$$

Again, if we define j as the rest of the financial system, $\Delta CoVaR_\alpha^{j|i}$ in (11.20) gives the additional stress on financial system in terms of VaR when bank i incurs a predefined loss, compared with VaR of the system under the "median" state of bank i. Obviously, in this case $\Delta CoVaR_\alpha^{j|i}$ captures the systemic risk bank i contributes to the rest of the system. To make $\Delta CoVaR_\alpha^{j|i}$ comparable across banks and reflect the differences in systemic risk contribution from banks of different sizes, one can take bank i's size into account, such as

$$\Delta^\$ CoVaR_\alpha^{j|i} = Size^i \cdot \Delta CoVaR_\alpha^{j|i}. \quad (11.21)$$

Bank i's size, $Size^i$, can be measured by its total assets or market capitalization.

Adrian and Brunnermeier (2016) estimate systemic $\Delta CoVaR_\alpha^{it}$—financial institutions' systemic risk contributions during crises—by quantile regressions, as by definition, VaR_α^i is just the α-quantile of bank i's losses. Based on a sample spanning over 1971–2013 and containing all publicly traded financial institutions in the US, Adrian and Brunnermeier (2016) find that $\Delta CoVaR_\alpha^{it}$ rises sharply with the onset of financial crises, implying stronger contagion between financial institutions. They also find that risk factors, such as bank leverage, maturity mismatch, etc., predict $\Delta CoVaR_\alpha^{it}$; these indicators thus provide important early warning prior to systemic events.

11.6.2 SYSTEMIC EXPECTED SHORTFALL

Acharya et al. (2017) propose that a bank's contribution to systemic risk can be measured by its systemic expected shortfall (SES). First, define expected shortfall (ES) of a bank at confidence level α, denoted by ES_α, as the conditional expected loss when the loss L exceeds VaR_α, i.e.,

$$ES_\alpha = E\left[L|L > VaR_\alpha\right]. \tag{11.22}$$

Further, one can examine the components of their contributions to ES_α. Suppose that there are J sources for the bank's loss, the loss from each source $j=1,\ldots,J$ with its weight in the bank's entire portfolio being y_j, is denoted by l_j. Then ES_α in (11.22) can be rewritten as

$$ES_\alpha = \sum_{j=1}^{J} y_j E\left[l_j | L > VaR_\alpha\right]. \tag{11.23}$$

The contribution of source j to the bank's overall loss, or the marginal expected shortfall of source j at confidence level α, MES_α^j, is defined as

$$MES_\alpha^j = \frac{\partial ES_\alpha}{\partial y_j} = E\left[l_j | L > VaR_\alpha\right]. \tag{11.24}$$

One can extend such idea and use the similar notion to analyze one bank's contribution to the aggregate risk in the financial system, or the systemic risk. As an analogy, the entire financial system can be viewed as one single bank, and when the financial system is in distress, the marginal expected shortfall of the system, as in (11.24), with respect to any individual bank i exactly captures the impact of the bank's failure on the systemic stability.

Note that there may be several concerns about generalizing the idea of MES for the financial system. First, a measure of one bank's contribution to the systemic risk should not only focus on the absolute value of loss, but rather, on its systemic impact, i.e., to what extent this bank's failure puts the other banks in trouble. Therefore, a proper measure is more likely an indicator of the externality of a bank's failure. Second, in practice, MES for a bank is usually estimated from the historical data, which is sufficiently informative for an institution's performance. But just as we learned from financial crises, historical data are hardly able to exhaust all the tail events, leaving the estimation inevitably biased. Third, as a practical issue, the indicator should be easy to compute and informative for both regulators and banking practitioners.

The systemic expected shortfall (SES^i) is defined as bank i's shortage in capital when the entire financial system is in distress and under-capitalized, i.e.,

$$SES^i = E\left[e^* - e^i \mid E < E^*\right] \quad (11.25)$$

in which $e^* - e^i$ is the difference between the bank's equity e^i and the required level e^*, conditional on the systemic under-capitalization such that the aggregate capital in all banks, E, is below the target E^*. If we measure bank i's contribution to systemic risk by its MES_α^i, following the idea of (11.24), Acharya et al. (2017) show that SES^i as in (11.25) can be expressed as a linear combination of MES_α^i and bank leverage.

The notion of VaR provides an anchor for the banks to actively adjust their balance sheets, via managing equity and/or assets holding, and SES^i presents the expected loss when such threshold is reached. SES^i captures the similar idea in another way. Here the threshold of the systemic event is defined by the adequate level of capitalization. During financial crises, an individual bank's capital ratio falls below the adequate level, along with the other banks in the financial system. The higher SES^i corresponds to the higher loss in the bank's asset holding, and the higher SES^i is, the more likely that the bank downsizes its balance sheet through costly deleveraging, imposing a downward pressure on asset prices and creating an externality on the other banks. Therefore, SES^i serves both as an indicator of individual bank's loss and as a proxy of the externalities the bank imposes on the financial system. As Acharya et al. (2017) demonstrate, SES predicts rising systemic risk during the 2007–2009 financial crisis.

11.6.3 SRISK

Exploring the idea that under-capitalization of individual banks generates negative externalities on systemic stability, Brownlees and Engle (2016) propose a measure, so-called SRISK, that is not dependent on observed systemic crisis to predict banks' capital shortfall in a systemic event.

Define bank i's capital shortfall in time t, CS_{it}, as the difference between the bank's required capitalization and actual capitalization, i.e.,

$$CS_{it} = k(D_{it} + E_{it}) - E_{it} \tag{11.26}$$

in which D_{it} denotes the book value of total debt, E_{it} denotes the market value of bank equity, and k denotes the regulatory capital ratio. Obviously, bank i is under-capitalized if $CS_{it} > 0$.

The main concern on a bank's capital short fall, is that under market stress such short fall generates negative externalities to other banks. Define market stress as a scenario when gross stock market return R_{t+1} falls below a threshold, C, then SRISK is defined as bank i's expected capital shortfall conditional on the market stress, i.e.

$$\begin{aligned} SRISK_{it} &= E_t[CS_{i,t+1} | R_{t+1} < C] \\ &= kE_t[D_{i,t+1} | R_{t+1} < C] - (1-k)E_t[E_{i,t+1} | R_{t+1} < C] \end{aligned} \tag{11.27}$$

using the definition of CS_{it} in (11.26). Using the fact that it is usually difficult to renegotiate debts under market stress, i.e.

$$E_t[D_{i,t+1} | R_{t+1} < C] = D_{it},$$

(11.27) can be rewritten as

$$SRISK_{it} = kD_{it} - (1-k)E_{it}\left(1 + E_t[R_{i,t+1} | R_{t+1} < C]\right) \tag{11.28}$$

in which $R_{i,t+1}$ denotes bank i's stock return. Given the bank's leverage ratio is

$$Leverage_{it} = \frac{D_{it} + E_{it}}{E_{it}},$$

define the bank's long-run marginal expected shortfall ($LRMES_{it}$) as

$$LRMES_{it} = -E_t[R_{i,t+1} | R_{t+1} < C],$$

definition (11.28) can be further rewritten as

$$SRISK_{it} = E_{it}\left(kLeverage_{it} + (1-k)LRMES_{it} - 1\right), \qquad (11.29)$$

in which E_{it} and $Leverage_{it}$ can be easily measured by bank balance sheet and market data, and $LRMES_{it}$ can be estimated by various techniques (for example, by the GARCH model that is constructed in Brownlees and Engle 2016). The total systemic risk across all financial institutions at certain point t can be constructed by summing up $SRISK_{it}$ in (11.29) for all financial institutions, $i = 1, \ldots, I$,

$$SRISK_t = \sum_{i=1}^{I} \max\{SRISK_{it}, 0\}.$$

That is, $SRISK_t$ reflects total capital shortage in the financial system under the market stress; in other words, it measures the total capital that is needed to bail out the entire system.

Overall, SRISK is a measure of shortage in bank capital during a systemic event that combines bank balance sheet characteristics and market expectations. Using a panel spanning over 2000–2012 and containing all US financial firms with market capitalization greater than five billion dollars as of the end of June 2007, Brownlees and Engle (2016) construct a SRISK series for institutions in the sample, and find that institutions with the highest expected capital shortfall before June 2007 played the most important roles in the financial crisis. Their constructed systemic risk measure $SRISK_t$ predicts the Fed's resolution effort during the crisis, and as an early warning indicator, forecasts the macroeconomic distress caused by the crisis.

11.7 EXERCISES

1 **Adverse selection, "buyers' strike", and market freeze**
 Consider a market in which there are N banks and N buyers of securities. Each bank owns a security that ensures a return R in the next period. Half of the securities ensure a return $R=1$, and half ensure a return $R=0$. If a bank does not sell the security, the

security is worth $\underline{R} = \tfrac{1}{2} R$ to the bank in the next period, while buyers get a utility from a security equal to its return. The time discount factor is normalized to 1. Banks know the return of their own security, while buyers only know the distribution of returns.

(a) Is there a price for which all securities are sold?
(b) Is there a price for which securities are sold only if $R = 0$?
(c) Will the result in question (a) change if $\underline{R} = R$ instead?

2 **Illiquid banks and private liquidity insurance, based on Diamond and Rajan (2011)**

Consider the market described in Section 11.3.1. Setups stay the same, except that there are multiple asset classes in banks' balance sheets. In particular, let's assume that P_1 is exogenous, and a fraction β of each bank's assets is composed of financial securities that can be sold in $t=0$ at P_0 or in $t=1$ at P_1. The rest of the assets can be liquidated. Each asset has liquidation value denoted by l, distributed uniformly between 0 and Z. Both the securities and the other assets have face value Z in period 2. The value of deposits is D, a shock hits in period 1 with probability q, and in case of shock depositors withdraw an amount fD of deposits in period 1. Assume that P_1 is sufficiently large that the bank expects to be solvent in period $t=1$ even if it does not sell any security in period $t=0$.

(a) What condition should P_0 and P_1 satisfy to ensure that investors are indifferent to buy securities in either $t=0$ or $t=1$?
(b) Let's say that the bank plans to sell a fraction η_1 of its securities at $t=1$ (if the shock hits), and not to sell any security in $t=0$. What fraction of the assets will be liquidated in case of shock? What is the average l of the liquidated assets? Can you find an expression for η_1?
(c) Let's say that the bank plans to sell a fraction η_0 of its security at date 0 *and not to sell any security in* $t=1$. Moreover, assume that P_0 and P_1 are such that the bank is indifferent to sell its securities in $t=0$ or in $t=1$. What fraction of the assets will be liquidated

in case of shock? What is the average l of the liquidated assets? Can you find an expression for η_0?

(d) Is it true that, under P_1 and P_0 that satisfy the condition you found in question (a), the bank is indifferent between selling securities in $t=0$ and in $t=1$?

3. **Free-riding and systemic liquidity shortages, based on Cao and Illing (2011)**

Consider the Cao-Illing model from Chapter 2, Section 2.4. Keeping all the setups unchanged, except the setting on uncertainty: instead of assuming crises are low probability events, from now on, assume that in $t=1$, the probability for the normal state π_H, can take any value between 0 and 1.

(a) Show that banks coordinate to choose α_H, as long as π_H is above a threshold. Compute the threshold, call it $\bar{\pi}_1$. Are there bankruptcies in either of the two states?

(b) Show that banks coordinate to choose α_L, as long as π_H is below a threshold. Compute the threshold, call it $\bar{\pi}_2$. Are there bankruptcies in either of the two states?

(c) Show that, for any π between $\bar{\pi}_1$ and $\bar{\pi}_2$, banks can coordinate neither on α_H nor on α_L, and there are always bankruptcies despite the state of the world.

4. **Excess maturity transformation and systemic liquidity risk, based on Kashyap and Stein (2012)**

Consider an economy that extends over three periods, $t=0,1,2$, with a continuum of banks whose population is normalized to be 1. The banks engage in maturity transformation that finance long-term assets with short-term debts.

In $t=0$, banks start business, each of them with one unit of capital. Bank capital yields an interim dividend in $t=1$, which is a stochastic variable that is uniformly distributed over an interval $[0,K]$.

A bank's problem is to choose investment I in illiquid assets in $t=0$. Illiquid assets only return in $t=2$, with expected payoff being RI. The bank finances a fraction α of the illiquid assets with short-term debt that is due in $t=1$, and a fraction $1-\alpha$ of the illiquid assets with long-term debt that is due in $t=2$. α is constant and exogenously given. The funding cost of short-term debt is lower than long-term debt: the gross two-period interest rate on long term debt is r, and the cost of rolling over short-term debt is $r-\Delta$, with $0<\Delta<r$.

With probability p, the economy is in a crisis state. A bank is distressed in the crisis state if its interim dividend is not large enough to service the short-term debts. Assume that stressed banks are not bankrupted, but rather, each of them has to incur a loss, $c\bar{I}$ with $c>0$, and $\bar{I}$ is the average of all banks' investment I. $\bar{I}$ thus reflects the illiquidity of the economy.

(a) Suppose a benevolent social planner makes the decision of I in $t=0$ for all banks to maximize banks' profit. Compute the social planner's choice on I.
(b) Suppose each bank makes a decision of I individually in $t=0$ to maximize its profit. Compute a bank's choice on I. Explain why it is different from the social planner's solution.
(c) In question (b), suppose a regulator is able to impose a tax rate τ on short-term debt. Compute the optimal τ that equalizes the bank's solution with the social planner's solution.

NOTES

1 A distribution $F(\cdot)$ first-order stochastically dominates a distribution $G(\cdot)$, if, for every non-decreasing function $u(x): \mathbb{R} \to \mathbb{R}$,
$$\int u(x)dF(x) \geq \int u(x)dG(x).$$

2 If x is a random variable and $f(x)$ is a concave function, then
$$E[f(x)] \leq f(E[x]).$$

3 How rollover risk causes freezes in the market is explicitly modelled by Acharya et al. (2011).

CHAPTER 12

Banking regulation in practice

> Now it is true that banks are very unpopular at the moment, but this [banking regulation] seems very much like a case of robbing Peter to pay Paul.
>
> "Taxing the banks? A vague idea that seems unlikely to work", *The Economist*, July 20th 2011

12.1 INTRODUCTION: BANKING REGULATION IN PRINCIPLES

It is probably not surprising that the banking industry is often one of the most heavily regulated industries across countries. One obvious reason is that banks are playing a crucial role in providing financial resources and desirable financial services to the real economy, so that bank failure and a banking crisis usually incur huge costs for the entire economy, as Chapter 1 shows. Enormous effort has been exerted by regulators around the world to discipline banks' behavior and enhance resilience of banks. Since 1980s, global standards for banking regulation have been crafted by the Basel Committee on Banking Supervision (BCBS), from the first version—so-called Basel I—released in 1988, to the current version—so-called Basel III—that is issued after the 2007–2009 financial crisis. Rules in Basel framework are widely adopted in major economies around the world.

What kind of banking regulation is desirable? In principle, or ideally, well-designed banking regulation shall be featured by the following characteristics:

1. Banking regulation shall be based on sound foundations. As banking regulation is mostly needed to fix market failures and externalities, banking regulation shall target well-defined problems that cannot be efficiently solved by the market. Regulatory policies shall be implemented through instruments whose mechanisms are well understood;

2   Banking regulation shall target *excess* risk-taking, but also maintain *necessary* risk-sharing. In many ways, banking services are based on risks: banks take liquidity risks that allow them to provide socially desirable liquidity insurance; banks take credit risks but this allows socially desirable activities such as research and development to be funded, facilitating economic growth. Therefore, desirable banking regulation shall not aim to eliminate risks, but rather, it shall be designed to curb excess risk-taking that benefits banks at the cost of the society;

3   Banking regulation shall combine both microprudential perspectives and macroprudential perspectives. Regulatory framework shall maintain resilience of each individual bank, but also shall improve resilience of systemically important banks whose instability may threaten the entire banking system and target frictions/externalities that contribute to systemic risks;

4   Regulatory policies shall be incentive compatible and waterproof against regulatory arbitrage. The regulator does conduct intensive assessments and analyses based on extensive data in its supervisory practice, but this does not mean that the regulator necessarily owns more information than market. Asymmetric information between regulator and regulated banks makes it possible for banks to arbitrage against regulatory policies; therefore, regulatory policies must be incentive compatible so that targeted banks self-select those policies that are designed for them. Regulator shall also ensure that there is no leak in the regulatory framework that allows banks to get around and undo the policies.

Although these principles are reasonable and clear, they are hardly met in reality. Regulators are not free from political influence that prevents them from properly addressing the true questions, for example, after a banking crisis, the regulator may be pressed by the public to tighten regulation in a short time, without well articulating the underlying problems. Banks are complex in their portfolios and products, so that it is not unusual that banks gradually "adapt" and eventually get around regulation—for example, by moving part of risky assets off balance sheets to unregulated shadow banks,—forcing the regulator to upgrade regulation, so that banking regulation becomes an endless cat-and-mouse game. As a result, banking regulation must evolve to keep up with the market.

Due to a limit of space, this chapter is not intended to cover all important issues in banking regulation (interested readers are very much encouraged to refer to Freixas et al. 2015 for a wide coverage of current issues in banking regulation). Instead, we will rather relate this chapter to the key mechanisms covered by previous chapters and focus on two main pillars in banking regulation: liquidity regulation and capital regulation, in Sections 12.2 and 12.3, respectively. In each section, we first start with a brief discussion on market failures and main financial frictions that prevent banks from building up sufficient buffers, then we review the main regulatory rules—especially those new rules in Basel III framework—that are designed to overcome such failures and frictions, followed by assessments on challenges and limits in implementing these rules in reality. Finally, we discuss a few recent issues in Section 12.4, such as how regulatory policies may interact with monetary policy, and whether they reinforce or counteract with each other.

12.2 LIQUIDITY REGULATION

Liquidity service is one of the most important services provided by banks. In this section, we first briefly discuss the sources of bank-level and systemic liquidity risks that justify liquidity regulation, and then provide a critical review on liquidity regulation.

12.2.1 IDIOSYNCRATIC AND SYSTEMIC LIQUIDITY RISKS

To provide liquidity service, banks engage in maturity transformation and expose themselves to liquidity risks, as we have extensively analyzed in Chapter 2. Except the typical market and funding liquidity risks that each individual bank faces in its daily business, various market failure, financial frictions, and externalities also prevent the banking system from building up sufficient liquidity buffers and sharing liquidity risks across banks, both in normal times and crises. In the following, we briefly discuss these idiosyncratic and systemic liquidity risks, as motivation for liquidity regulation.

MATURITY TRANSFORMATION AND IDIOSYNCRATIC LIQUIDITY RISKS

Banks face liquidity risks in their daily business, and this imposes instabilities in the banking system. A primary reason is the maturity mismatch between assets and liabilities: banks often issue risky, long-term loans with high yields and borrow from lenders by taking on short-term debt. Through maturity transformation, banks create liquidity and provide socially desirable liquidity insurance for depositors, but this also makes the banking systems fragile and exposes banks to market liquidity risks—that banks may not be able to convert assets to cash when needed without incurring a large discount on such assets, and funding liquidity risks—that banks may not be able to raise funding by rolling over existing debt or taking on more debt. For example, in the standard Diamond-Dybvig model (Diamond and Dybvig 1983) in Chapter 2, Section 2.2, under liquidity preference shock, proceeds from short-term assets cannot meet the cash demand of withdrawing depositors, so that banks need to raise cash from a portion of their long-term assets. As long-term assets can only be converted to cash at a discount before they actually mature, the remaining long-term assets may not be able to deliver sufficient returns to the long-term, patient depositors. Therefore, even patient depositors may wish to demand their cash early, forcing banks to liquidate all assets, leading to a bank run. Such fragility arising from banks' liquidity creation through maturity transformation has been extensively discussed in Chapter 2.

As individual banks are constantly exposed to liquidity risks, institutions that provide liquidity insurance for banks are thus desirable to reduce fragility of banks and maintain banks' desirable liquidity creation. Usually, the interbank market allows banks to fulfill their liquidity needs through borrowing from each other, and the central bank provides liquidity facilities to banks that are not able to raise sufficient funding from the market.

FINANCIAL FRICTIONS, EXTERNALITIES, AND SYSTEMIC LIQUIDITY RISKS

Although banks do have incentive to hold buffers to weather liquidity risks, however, there are frictions in the market for liquidity such that individual banks may not fully internalize the associated costs and benefits for the banking system in their liquidity management practices. As a result, banks' holding of liquidity buffers may not be socially optimal.

First, maturity transformation though bank balance sheet with maturity mismatch provides socially desirable liquidity insurance, however, *excess* maturity mismatch may lead to excess fragility in the banking system. As the Brunnermeier-Oehmke model (Brunnermeier and Oehmke 2013) in Chapter 11, Section 11.2 shows, compared with a long-term debt contract, a short-term contract allows banks to profit from adjusting their terms of funding once new information on asset return arrives, so that the cost advantage in short-term funding encourages banks to engage in the "maturity rat race" and shorten their debt maturity. As a result, banks rely more on short-term funding such as overnight repo lending, and the need to renew debt contracts more frequently exposes banks to higher funding liquidity risks, or, rollover risks: even a small stress in a money market may result in huge liquidity crunch of banks.

Second, limited liability prevents banks from building up sufficient liquidity buffers, as is argued by the Diamond-Rajan model (Diamond and Rajan 2011) in Chapter 11, Section 11.3, even if a credit crunch is expected. When a bank indeed builds up a sufficient liquidity buffer for a forthcoming crisis, if the crisis is materialized, the liquidity buffer mostly benefits creditors, but if the crisis is not materialized, the bank has to bear the full opportunity cost of forgoing investing more in high-yield, illiquid assets. In contrast, if the bank does not invest in the liquidity buffer and holds more illiquid assets instead, if the crisis is materialized and bankrupts the bank, under limited liability, most of the bankruptcy cost is borne by bank creditors, but if the crisis is not materialized, the bank can profit more from its illiquid assets. For this reason, a liquidity buffer in the banking system may be inefficiently low in normal times, making banks more vulnerable to liquidity risks.

Third, in normal times, holding highly liquid assets not only helps banks cover their own need for liquidity, but these assets can also be lent to other banks when they face liquidity shortages—a *positive externality*. However, banks have to incur the full opportunity cost of profiting less from holding liquid instead of high yield illiquid assets. As a result, there can be a systemic liquidity shortage among banks. During a market downturn, banks' liquidity holdings may not be sufficient to meet creditors' cash demand and raising additional market funding is challenging, resulting in a liquidity crunch.

Last, but not least, during the downturn, a liquidity crunch can be further worsened by banks' incentive for a precautionary hoarding of liquidity, as Gale and Yorulmazer (2013) argue—holding inefficiently large portfolios of highly liquid assets instead of lending to borrowers. This can drain the market supply of highly liquid assets in response to malfunctioning interbank markets during crises. For example, as is documented by Acharya and Merrouche (2013) using data from settlement banks in the UK, on average, banks' liquidity holdings increased by almost one-third immediately after the money market freeze in the period immediately following August 9, 2007, and the number was even higher for banks that expected greater volatility in liquidity demand and banks that had incurred larger losses during the crisis. The evidence suggests that such liquidity hoarding was mostly precautionary, but it exacerbated the freeze in interbank lending, thereby reducing lending to households and non-financial firms.

Liquidity hoarding arises from a *negative externality*: when banks face uncertainty of liquidity demand during a crunch, they start building a liquid buffer, hoarding liquidity by selling illiquid assets and raising liquidity from investors. This drains liquidity held by investors, making it costlier for other banks to raise liquidity; however, this cost is not taken into account by the hoarding banks, leading to a suboptimal, large liquidity stock in bank balance sheets and a freeze in the market for liquidity. Such liquidity hoarding is hardly eased even if the interbank lending rate rises, as the fear of adverse selection—fear of lending to bad borrowers—prevents banks with excess liquidity buffer from lending in the interbank market, as Heider et al. (2015) show.

Because banks' holding of liquidity buffers may not be socially optimal, public intervention is needed to correct the failure in market for reserves; especially during market stress when there is a systemic shortage of liquidity, central bank has to step in and inject liquidity into the banking system to avoid creditors' panic runs. In addition, regulatory policies are also desired to ensure banks to build up sufficient liquidity buffer in the first place during normal times, before the central bank is forced to fight the last war.

12.2.2 LENDER-OF-LAST-RESORT POLICY

Conventionally, regulating idiosyncratic and systemic liquidity risks often relies on the lender-of-last-resort (LOLR) policy, provided by the central bank. In principle, one of the main functions of a central bank is to act as the lender of last resort, i.e., to provide liquidity for banks that are unable to raise funding from the market during market stresses or crises, against eligible collateral. As Diamond-Dybvig model (Diamond and Dybvig 1983) in Chapter 2, Section 2.2 demonstrates, in theory, LOLR policy ensures that banks suffering from a pure illiquidity problem are able to pledge their illiquid assets and obtain funding from the central bank's LOLR facility, therefore, depositors' withdrawal demand is guaranteed to be fulfilled so that they will have no incentive to initiate bank runs. LOLR policy thus reduces fragility in the banking system.

In reality, how the central bank shall conduct LOLR policy is characterized by the classical doctrine, known as the *Bagehot Rules* proposed by Bagehot (1873). Briefly speaking, the rules include:

1. *Solvency rule*, that the central bank shall lend only against good collateral (valued at pre-stress or pre-crisis levels) to solvent banks;
2. *No-free-lunch rule*, that the central bank shall lend at a penalty rate to banks that are illiquid;
3. *Credibility rule*, that the policy needs to be credible such that the central bank shall announce its readiness to lend without limits.

Although these rules are straightforward and clear, it is very hard to strictly follow the rules in reality. Implementing the rules is often subject to various constraints that limit the effectiveness of the rules.

We examine these constraints and challenges in implementing each of the rules as follows.

DISTINGUISHING BETWEEN ILLIQUIDITY AND INSOLVENCY

It is certainly desirable that the central bank only lends to illiquid but solvent banks, mainly for two reasons: first, this ensures that the central bank will be fully repaid in the future when the illiquidity problem is eased, so that taxpayers do not need to suffer from losses in LOLR lending. Second, lending to insolvent banks will encourage the moral hazard problem, that banks will not exercise their due diligence in risk management, if the insolvency risk can be shifted to the central bank and losses can be covered by taxpayers; therefore, the solvency rule is needed to eliminate the moral hazard problem.

However, in reality, it is almost impossible to draw a line between illiquid and insolvent banks in emergency circumstances, so that it is almost a "myth" to believe that the central bank is able to distinguish between illiquidity and insolvency (Goodhart 1999, Goodhart and Illing 2002). When the market is under stress, it is usually hard to evaluate banks' assets in a short time, with rising uncertainties in the market preventing market participants from assessing the fundamentals and complexity in financial assets making it difficult to locate risks; as a result, it is almost impossible to tell whether a bank is still solvent. Furthermore, multiple equilibria may arise when the market is in the bust, as we have seen in the Diamond-Dybvig model (Diamond and Dybvig 1983) in Chapter 2, Section 2.2 that a fundamentally sound and solvent bank in the non-run equilibrium may become insolvent in the bank run equilibrium; a bank's solvency status may change quickly with market sentiment.

The implementation of solvency rule is further complicated by those *systemically important banks* (SIBs). Such banks are crucial for the stability of the banking system, because they are intensively connected with other banks through interbank claims and/or provide key financial services such as clearing or guarantee for many other banks; therefore, when an SIB becomes insolvent, it may become extremely costly to let it down, as its failure may blow up other banks and even lead to a systemic meltdown. For this reason, it is not unusual that LOLR policy is extended to bail out SIBs, even when they are clearly insolvent and taxpayers will certainly incur losses from LOLR lending, to prevent much more costly systemic failure. However, expecting to be bailed out by taxpayers' money in crises, the typical moral hazard problem may encourage SIBs to take more risks in normal times, so that a *too-big-to-fail* problem of SIBs may increase fragility of banking system.

TIME CONSISTENCY PROBLEM

The no-free-lunch rule attempts to ensure that, in normal times, banks shall raise liquidity from the interbank market instead of using central bank's liquidity facility as a cheap alternative; it also attempts to induce banks to build up necessary liquidity buffers in normal times by setting higher LOLR lending rate and making LOLR lending more costly.

However, such a rule may suffer from a severe *time consistency problem* and may be *dynamic inconsistent* in implementation: a LOLR lending rate may be set at a high, punishing level *ex ante* to deter banks from using LOLR lending as free lunch and encourage banks to self-insure with their own liquidity buffer, however, when a bank is indeed suffering from liquidity crunch, a high LOLR lending rate may make the bank more likely to fail. Considering the enormous social cost associated with bank failure, the central bank may reduce LOLR lending rate *ex post*, just to make the bank survive. However, such time inconsistency may make a high LOLR lending rate an incredible threat: knowing that they will be offered cheap LOLR lending under market stress, banks will not invest in sufficient liquidity buffer in the first place. Such a moral hazard problem may lead to too low liquidity buffer in the banking system in normal times and increase the fragility of banks.

Such a time consistency problem can be easily seen in the Cao-Illing model (Cao and Illing 2011) in Chapter 2, Section 2.4. As is shown in Figure 12.1, suppose that a central bank conducting LOLR policy is

CHAPTER TWELVE: BANKING REGULATION IN PRACTICE

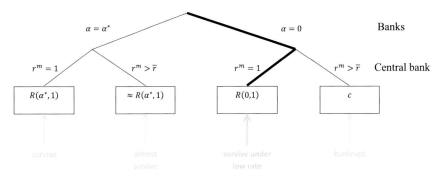

Figure 12.1 Time consistency problem in LOLR policy implementation

established in the economy. The central bank plays a sequential game with banks:

1. In $t=0$, banks choose their investment in liquid assets, α, and promise depositors a return of R when they raise deposits from depositors. To focus on the relevant cases, supposes banks can either choose $\alpha = \alpha^*$ in which α^* denotes the socially optimal liquidity holdings, α_H, or $\alpha = 0$. Promised return R depends on banks' choice on α;

2. In $t=1$, after the state of the world is revealed, the central bank offers LOLR lending at a gross lending rate r^m. Suppose the central bank can choose between low lending rate $r^m = 1$ and high lending rate $r^m > \bar{r}$, with the threshold rate $\bar{r}$ preventing banks from using LOLR lending under good state.

There are four possible outcomes from this sequential game:

1. If banks choose $\alpha = \alpha^*$, promise $d_{0H}^* = \gamma\left[\alpha_H R_1 + (1-\alpha_H)R_2\right]$ for depositors, and the central bank sets $r^m = 1$, under a crisis state, banks are able to repay depositors without incurring a bank run by borrowing $(1-\alpha_H)(p_H - p_L)R_2$ from the central bank, against the same face value of long assets as collateral. With setting α^* and surviving with probability 1, the depositor's expected return, denoted by $R(\alpha^*, 1)$, is given by

$$R(\alpha^*, 1) = d_{0H}^* = \gamma\left[\alpha_H R_1 + (1-\alpha_H)R_2\right];$$

2. If banks choose $\alpha=\alpha^*$, promise $d_{0H}^* = \gamma\left[\alpha_H R_1 + (1-\alpha_H) R_2\right]$ for depositors, and the central bank sets $r^m > \bar{r}$, under a crisis state, banks are not able to repay depositors, as high r^m prevents banks from raising sufficient liquidity through LOLR lending, so that they will suffer from a bank run. Given that the probability of a crisis state is low, the depositor's expected return is approximately $R(\alpha^*, 1)$;
3. If banks choose $\alpha=0$, promise γR_2 for depositors, and the central bank sets $r^m = 1$, banks can survive both states and offer $R(0,1) = \gamma R_2$ to depositors, as banks have enough illiquid assets to be used as collateral in LOLR lending;
4. If banks choose $\alpha=0$ and promise γR_2 for depositors, but the central bank sets $r^m > \bar{r}$, a bank run will occur under both states as high r^m prevents banks from raising sufficient liquidity, leaving depositors the liquidation value c.

Comparing among the outcomes, it is easy to see that the unique Nash equilibrium (as is shown by the thick lines) is that banks choose $\alpha=0$, promise γR_2 for depositors, and the central bank sets $r^m = 1$, given that $R(0,1) > R(\alpha^*, 1)$. The no-free-lunch rule $r^m > \bar{r}$, which aims to induce banks to choose $\alpha=\alpha^*$, is never credible.

When no-free-lunch rule is dynamic inconsistent and incredible, banks have the incentive to engage in moral hazard, take excess liquidity risks in normal times and rely on central bank intervention during crises—actually, banks' under-investment in liquid assets in normal times makes them more vulnerable to liquidity shocks, increasing the likelihood of systemic liquidity crunch.

Furthermore, such a time consistency problem is further exacerbated when banks are SIBs. Large social cost and contagion risk associated with SIB failure make it more likely that the central bank provides cheap LOLR lending to rescue failing SIBs *ex post*, violating the no-free-lunch rule. Knowing this, the moral hazard problem further encourages SIBs to take excess risks and makes them too-big-to-fail. As a result, providing free lunch to SIBs through LOLR policy in reality is rather a compromise on banks' moral hazard, to avoid bigger social cost, as is argued by Huang and Goodhart (1999). Examining 104 major bank failures around the world in 1980s and early 1990s, Goodhart and Schoenmaker (1995) do find that majority of failed banks were in fact not closed down.

REGULATORY CAPTURE

As is shown in the Diamond-Dybvig model (Diamond and Dybvig 1983) in Chapter 2, Section 2.2, a central bank's credible commitment on LOLR lending helps rule out bank run equilibrium, thus reducing financial fragility. However, in reality, public intervention such as LOLR policy during market stress is often subject to political pressure on rescuing certain institutions and *regulatory capture* that regulators may yield to the lobbying effort of special interest groups; outcomes from LOLR policy may be suboptimal. For example, as Kaufman (1991) argues, LOLR lending is often a disguised way to bail out insolvent banks.

For the reasons above, outcomes of LOLR policy are often limited by various compromises, and substantial credit risks may be shifted from banks' balance sheets to the central bank through LOLR lending and eventually become costs for taxpayers. More liquidity rules are thus needed to complement LOLR policy, to improve the efficiency of liquidity regulation.

12.2.3 REQUIREMENTS ON MARKET LIQUIDITY AND FUNDING LIQUIDITY

In Basel III framework, new liquidity rules are developed to address the limits in conducting LOLR policy, as well as sources of systemic liquidity risks. These rules include requirements on both banks' market liquidity (such as requirement on liquidity coverage ratio) and funding liquidity (such as requirement on net stable funding ratio), aiming to improve sharing of liquidity risks between the central bank and banks, and to ensure that banks build up liquidity buffers and reduce excess liquidity risk exposure before the central bank is forced to fight the last war.

REQUIREMENT ON LIQUIDITY COVERAGE RATIO

Liquidity Coverage Ratio (LCR) requirement targets banks' market liquidity risk. LCR is the ratio between a bank's holding of liquid assets—unencumbered, high-quality liquid assets (HQLA) that can be converted to cash to meet liquidity demand—and the assumed outflow of funding for the bank during a 30-day stressed funding scenario, i.e.,

$$\text{LCR} = \frac{\text{Stock of high-quality liquid assets}}{\text{Net cash outflows over 30-day stressed funding}} \times 100\%.$$

Usually LCR is required to be no lower than 100%.

For example, as for the stylized Cao-Illing model (Cao and Illing 2021) in Chapter 7, Section 7.4, LCR requirement is equivalent to requiring banks to hold a share of α^* liquid assets on their balance sheet in $t=0$, given that α^* maximizes depositors' expected real return in the presence of banks' access to central bank liquidity facilities. As for the Diamond-Rajan model (Diamond and Rajan 2011) in Chapter 11, Section 11.3, LCR requirement implies that banks are required to hold fD liquid assets in $t=0$, if the crisis state is expected to be materialized, in order to prevent banks from shifting bankruptcy risks to depositors.

REQUIREMENT ON NET STABLE FUNDING RATIO

Net Stable Funding Ratio (NSFR) requirement targets banks' funding liquidity risk. NSFR is the proportion of long-term assets which are funded by long-term, stable funding—such as customer long-term deposits, long-term wholesale funding, equity, etc., defined as

$$\text{NSFR} = \frac{\text{Amount of stable funding, available}}{\text{Amount of stable funding, required}} \times 100\%.$$

Usually NSFR is required to be no lower than 100%.

For example, as for the stylized Bianchi-Bigio model (Bianchi and Bigio 2020) in Chapter 7, Section 7.3, NSFR requirement is equivalent to requiring banks to fund its D_t with lower funding liquidity risks, or, liabilities with lower ω_1 so that the cost of banks' rebalancing reserves is lower—for instance, funding D_t with term deposits or bonds with longer maturities instead of overnight interbank lending.

EMPIRICAL EVIDENCE

In most countries, LCR and NSFR requirements were just phased in very recently, so that evidence from regulatory practice on effectiveness of these requirements and effects on banking outcomes is by far limited. Duijm and Wierts (2016) explore the Dutch experience of introducing the liquidity coverage requirement that resembles LCR in 2003. They find that the requirement induces banks to adjust their liabilities, shifting from short-term wholesale funding to more stable deposits during the aftermath of 2007–2009 crisis. They also find LCR requirement creates procyclicality in bank leverage and hence is not effective from a macroprudential perspective, in that banks exploit cheap liquidity, invest more in risky assets, and just maintain the minimum LCR before the crisis, leading to a systemic liquidity shortage when the crisis breaks out. Examining the banking outcomes under the same LCR policy experiment, Bonner and Eijffinger (2016) find that LCR requirement leads to higher demand for long-term interbank loans and higher loan rates. Furthermore, banks do not pass on the increased interbank funding cost to their borrowers, which decreases banks' net interest margins, suggesting limited impact on real economy.

In a similar study on LCR-type regulation introduced in the UK in 2010 by Banerjee and Mio (2018), it is observed that, since 2010, banks respond to this regulation by changing both asset-side composition (increasing cash, central bank reserves, government securities) and liability-side composition (reducing short-term wholesale funding). But banks neither downsize their balance sheets nor reduce lending to certain sectors, suggesting that the LCR requirement reduces systemic liquidity risk with little adverse impact on lending to the real economy.

12.2.4 LIQUIDITY REGULATION AND MONETARY POLICY IMPLEMENTATION: A CONCEPTUAL ASSESSMENT

As monetary policy is often implemented via adjusting liquidity in the banking system, liquidity regulation may influence the implementation of monetary policy, and vice versa. Under LCR and NSFR, in determining the composition of balance sheets, banks not only have to take into account reserve requirements (even in countries with no statutory reserve requirements, banks do have an implicit incentive of holding reserve buffers) but also comply with liquidity rules; this may lead to undesirable consequences and impose challenges to conducting monetary policy. For instance, when the central bank provides liquidity through market operation to the banking system, the outcome of the interbank lending rate now depends upon:

- Aggregate reserves in the banking sector;
- Effectiveness of liquidity requirements;
- Aggregate supply of high-quality liquid assets (HQLA) which are used as collateral for banks to borrow from the central bank.

Central bank operations are the most effective when liquidity requirements are close to binding for banks—as this is when banks have the highest incentive to adjust their balance sheets, and outcomes also depend on how liquidity operations are conducted. Two generic regimes may arise:

1. If only HQLA are taken as collateral, a central bank's liquidity injection does not change the LCR (because banks just swap HQLA for reserves) but only increases aggregate reserves and pushes the interbank overnight rate down; however, banks' LCR stress will not be eased by the operation;
2. If non-HQLA are taken as collateral, a central bank's liquidity injection increases aggregate HQLA (because banks swap non-HQLA for reserves), which both relaxes LCR requirements and increases reserves.

As is shown in Bech and Keister (2014, 2017), if the central bank follows the first regime (as most central banks do in reality) and only takes HQLA as collateral, the LCR rule may even force banks into liquidity hoarding—because a limited supply of HQLA restricts banks' accessibility to central bank liquidity facilities—and suboptimal, excess bank reserves in the system push the interbank lending rate too close to the floor; if the central bank follows the second regime and allows non-HQLA as collateral, banks would have the incentive to produce non-HQLA and shift the excessive risks to the central bank. The central bank may get stuck in such a dilemma.

Liquidity regulation may also change the nature of systemic liquidity risk and raise new problems for banking regulation. For example, absent of liquidity regulation, although banks face market liquidity risk if they want to raise funding by liquidating illiquid assets, the market asset price does reflect the cost of liquidity that can be internalized in banks' decisions for holding liquidity buffers on an *ex ante* basis. In contrast, by imposing the LCR, this mechanism no longer functions efficiently. The market will impose a large discount on asset prices for those banks that need to raise funding by selling assets, due to the adverse selection problem—asset buyers fear that banks are getting rid of bad assets because banks would have the incentive to retain high quality assets on their balance sheets to meet LCR. This may increase market liquidity risk for all banks especially during a market downturn, as Malherbe (2014) shows.

Another impact of liquidity requirements on systemic liquidity risk may arise from general equilibrium effects; specifically, changes in bank liquidity have an adverse impact on the funding sources that are available for banks. Remember, as is shown in Section 12.2.1, systemic liquidity risk may arise from two types of externalities:

1. Positive externalities that lead to systemic shortages of liquid assets in the banking sector; therefore, if banks need to raise liquidity, they would have insufficient liquid assets to pledge for external funding sources; and
2. Negative externalities that lead to hoarding of liquid assets in the banking sector, leaving too little external liquidity; therefore, when banks need to raise liquidity, there is insufficient liquidity supply from external funding sources.

Whether imposing liquidity requirements, such as the LCR, alleviates systemic liquidity risk depends on which type of externalities dominate. If positive externalities dominate, imposing the LCR reduces systemic liquidity risk, as it raises bank liquidity and increases banks' capability of borrowing in the market; on the contrary, if negative externalities dominate, imposing the LCR does not help reduce systemic liquidity risk due to the resulting shortage of banks' external funding sources. In this case, extending the central bank's liquidity facilities, such as enlarging the list of eligible assets used as collateral pledged for central bank liquidity, would be a better solution, as Kahn and Wagner (2020) demonstrate.

12.3 CAPITAL REGULATION

Capital regulation is another pillar in banking regulation. Holding more capital increases a bank's capacity to absorb losses, thus reducing the likelihood of bankruptcy. In this section, we briefly discuss how capital regulation improves resilience of banks, and then provide a critical review on capital regulation.

12.3.1 BANK CAPITAL AND RESILIENCE

Although the Modigliani-Miller theorem[1] states that funding structure is irrelevant to firm value, banks are nevertheless highly leveraged firms that usually only hold a small share of equity[2] in their liabilities, as the assumptions for the theorem are often violated in reality. Banks have good reason to choose high leverage, as higher leverage increases return to equity (ROE), and with limited liability, highly leveraged banks are able to shift most of the bankruptcy cost to creditors so that banks win in heads and do not lose much in tails. Imposing requirements on banks' capital ratio thus improves resilience of the banking system in two ways: first, it increases banks' capital buffer to absorb losses and reduces the likelihood of bank failure as well as subsequent contagion to other financial institutions and real economy; second, it increases banks' *skin-in-the-game* so that banks have to incur a higher bankruptcy cost on their own, discouraging banks from taking excess risks and hence also reducing the likelihood of bank failure.

Without capital regulation, banks tend to hold too little equity capital, as equity is usually more costly than other funding sources. Apparently, equity is costly from bank shareholders' perspective, as higher equity ratio reduces ROE. Besides this, various financial frictions make funding cost of equity higher than other bank liabilities. For example,

1. It has been for long documented (for example, Rajan and Zingales 1995) that debt instrument often enjoys tax advantage, compared with equity. Banks may thus prefer debt to equity because of such cost advantage;
2. Asymmetric information, that a bank manager knows more about the bank than investors, makes investors interpret new equity issuance as a bad signal on the bank's performance, as Myers and Majluf (1984) argue, making new equity issuance costly;
3. Conflict of interests may affect equity financing, as Jensen and Meckling (1976) argue. In highly leveraged banks, incumbent shareholders may also resist new equity issuance, for fear that the benefit will mainly accrue to debt holders—a classical *debt overhang* problem as is proposed by Myers (1977).

As capital is costly for banks so that they prefer to hold less, capital regulation is necessary to ensure sufficient capital buffer in banking system, as well as to curb banks' risk-taking incentives. Capital being costly also implies that the regulator is able to affect banks' credit supply by adjusting capital adequacy ratio; for example, when the regulator raises required capital ratio, if it is too costly for banks to meet the new requirement by issuing new equity, banks will have to deleverage and downsize balance sheets by cutting back lending.

Capital regulation has been playing a central role in global banking regulation framework since Basel I. Besides setting the required capital adequacy ratio for banks' entire balance sheets, the regulator may also assign *risk weights* for individual bank asset classes to address the different needs for loss absorption, or, cost of capital. For example, risk weight for safe government bonds may be 0, as their default probability is almost zero so that they do not need a capital buffer for loss absorption; in contrast, risk weight for risky loans may be 100%.

12.3.2 COUNTERCYCLICAL CAPITAL REQUIREMENT

However, capital regulation may not be as simple as just setting a capital adequacy ratio for banks that is deemed to be appropriate. It has been long argued that a rigid, time-invariant requirement on capital ratio, such as in Basel II, may lead to a procyclicality problem and amplified credit cycles (see, for example, Daníelsson et al. 2001), and even make the banking system more fragile. The mechanism can be demonstrated through Shin's leverage cycle model (Shin 2010) in Chapter 8, Section 8.5. Briefly speaking, as Figure 12.2 shows, for a stylized bank that is operating a balance sheet such as in chart (a), its asset value increases during a boom in the real economy, which makes its equity value increase to the shaded area in chart (b). Higher equity value relaxes the bank's value-at-risk (VaR) constraint, allowing the bank to borrow more debt and lend more, until the capital requirement becomes binding again, as chart (c) shows. The fixed, time-invariant requirement on capital ratio thus translates the initial boom in the real economy to a further credit boom. Such credit boom may fuel the boom in the real economy even further, leading to a virtuous cycle.

Conversely, the fixed, time-invariant requirement on capital may translate a bust in the real economy to a further credit crunch, as Figure 12.3

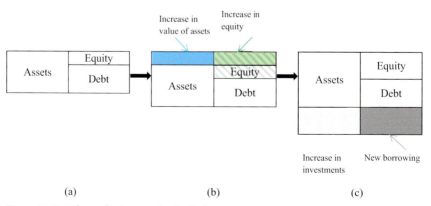

Figure 12.2 *Balance sheet expansion in the boom*

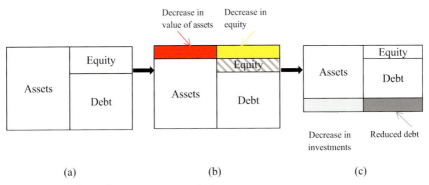

Figure 12.3 Balance sheet contraction in the bust

shows. When the real economy is in downturn, a bank that operates a balance sheet as in chart (a) suffers from a loss in its asset value, reducing its equity to the shaded area in chart (b). The binding VaR constraint forces the bank to cut back lending and deleverage, until the capital requirement becomes binding again, as chart (c) shows. Such credit crunch may aggravate the bust in the real economy, leading to a vicious circle. Overall, the time-invariant capital requirement has the potential to make the economy more volatile, due to its procyclical feature.

Countercyclical capital requirement is designed to fix the procyclicality problem, contain credit cycles, and reduce the volatility in real economy that is caused by leverage cycles. Under countercyclical capital requirement, banks are required to hold more capital during the boom, while during the bust, banks are allowed to hold less capital.

To see how such a requirement works, consider the bank with increased equity value in economic boom, as is shown in chart (b), Figure 12.2. If required capital holding is now increased by regulator to the shaded area, the bank's capital requirement will be binding so that it will not expand lending. Further credit boom is thus avoided. Conversely, when the bank suffers from equity loss in a downturn, as is shown in chart (b), Figure 12.3, if required capital holding is now decreased by the regulator to the shaded area, the bank's capital requirement will be met so that it will not cut back lending. Further credit crunch is thus avoided. Overall, credit cycles are contained under countercyclical capital requirement.

In Basel III framework, countercyclical capital requirement is implemented as countercyclical capital buffer (CCyB). Figure 12.4 shows implementation of CCyB in Norway, together with other Basel III capital rules. The phasing-in of Basel III capital rules began in 2012, when required capital ratio increased from 5.1% to 9%, which consists of minimum requirement, additional layer of capital conservation buffer as usable capital that can be drawn down when losses in individual banks are incurred, and systemic risk buffer that can be drawn down during systemic events, plus a further buffer for SIBs that aims to increase SIBs' resilience, and time-varying CCyB that is adjusted through credit cycles. Adjustments in CCyB are usually based on regulator's assessment on credit cycles; when CCyB is increased, banks are usually given a period of time to build up capital buffer through retained earnings, raising new equity from investors through seasoned equity offering (SEO), etc.

CCyB may be reduced during downturn and recession, to avoid a crunch in banks' credit supply to the real economy. Figure 12.5 presents an

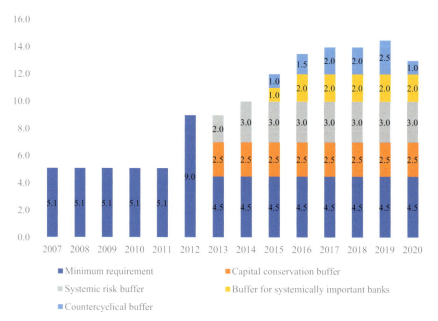

Figure 12.4 Composition of Pillar 1 Common Equity Tier 1 (CET1) requirements for Norwegian banks, 2007–2020

Source: Norges Bank's advice on the countercyclical capital buffer, available on https://www.norges-bank.no/en/.

example on how regulators adjust CCyB aggressively across 15 economies, during the COVID-19 pandemic. Economies fall into recession, after lockdown in the pandemic slows down economic activities; this may increase banks' loan losses and reduce banks' equity value, reducing CCyB thus prevents banks from deleveraging and encourages banks to maintain lending and continue supporting the real economy.

12.3.3 CAPITAL REQUIREMENT AND RISK-TAKING: A CONCEPTUAL ASSESSMENT

It is often believed that raising the requirement on bank's capital ratio helps increase resilience of banks, as a higher capital ratio, *ceteris paribus*, provides more cushion for banks to absorb losses and reduces bank failure. It is also often believed that increasing capital requirement reduces banks'

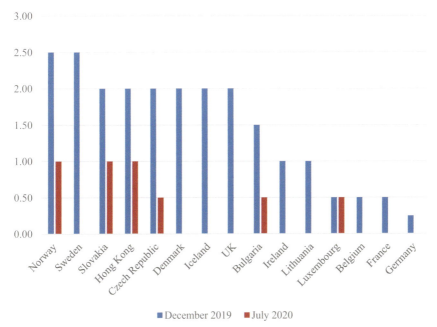

Figure 12.5 *Statutory countercyclical capital buffer adjustments in reaction to the COVID-19 pandemic, as of July 2020*

Source: Norges Bank (2020). The chart presents statutory countercyclical capital buffers in 15 economies before (December 2019) and during (July 2020) the COVID-19 pandemic. The vertical axis denotes countercyclical capital buffer requirements in percentage points.

risk-taking for mainly two reasons: first, higher capital ratio implies banks have more skin-in-the-game, so that they have to incur higher cost from losses if they take more risks; higher capital ratio thus discourages banks' excess risk-taking. Second, higher capital ratio also restricts banks' leverage, making it harder for banks to expand their balance sheets. This accommodates banks' credit supply and limits the volume of risky lending.

However, in reality, to what extent capital regulation reduces banks' risk-taking is not free from debate. First, it is not obvious that higher capital ratio reduces the volume of risky lending. One key assumption behind the accommodating effect of capital requirement on lending expansion is that capital is believed to be costly: raising new capital, for example, through SEO in the stock market, implies high cost on common equity issuance and required dividends for shareholders; therefore, when the regulator raises capital requirement, the high cost of capital prevents banks from increasing capital stock, forcing banks to downsize balance sheets by cutting back lending.

To see how costly capital limits bank lending, an example by Admati and Hellwig (2013) is shown in Figure 12.6. Suppose, initially, a bank is operating under a required capital ratio of 10%; with a stylized "Initial balance sheet", the bank's assets, i.e., 100 units of risky loans, are funded

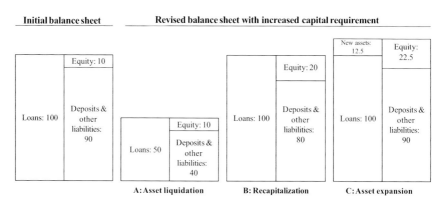

Figure 12.6 Alternative responses to increase in capital requirement
Source: *Admati and Hellwig (2013). The chart "Initial balance sheet" denotes a stylized bank's balance sheet under the initial required capital ratio of 10%, and the panel "Revised balance sheet with increased capital requirement" denotes three generic scenarios of the bank's possible responses to a new required capital ratio of 20%.*

by liabilities containing 10 units of common equity and 90 units of debt instruments.

Now suppose that regulatory requirement on capital ratio is increased to 20%: because it is too costly to issue 10 units of new equity and maintain the initial assets—as chart "B: Recapitalization" characterizes,—the bank has to cut back 50 units of risky lending to meet the new requirement with its initial equity, as chart "A: Asset liquidation" characterizes.

However, in reality, capital is not necessarily costly, or, whether capital is costly or not depends on how much banks benefit from holding more capital. For example, if the return from risky loans is sufficiently high, the stylized bank in Figure 12.6 may be willing to keep the loans and invest in costly capital instead, just as chart B suggests. If the return from risky loans is high enough, the bank may even find it attractive to invest more in capital stock so that it is able to expand lending even further, as chart "C: Asset expansion" characterizes! Therefore, stricter capital requirement *may* restrict risky lending, but it is not guaranteed to happen in reality. This also leads to a question on whether CCyB is able to accommodate credit cycles, as when CCyB is raised in the boom, it is also the time when banks are making higher profit from risky lending and willing to invest in new capital, and investors are more willing to invest in bank capital, too, so that bank capital may even be relatively cheaper; as a result, rising CCyB in the boom may not necessarily prevent banks from expanding balance sheets.

In practice, CCyB adjustments are based on regulator's assessments on credit cycles. One widely used indicator for such assessments is the credit-to-GDP gap, i.e., the deviation of credit-to-GDP ratio from its long-run trend, which has been shown as an important early warning indicator for banking crises in many countries (Borio and Drehmann 2009). However, the challenge to using credit-to-GDP gap as a credit cycle indicator is that credit cycles (that drive credit growth) do not necessarily coincide with business cycles (that drive GDP growth), as Brunnermeier et al. (2012) show; therefore, if credit growth does not fall with GDP growth in recession, making credit-to-GDP gap rise, the regulator may mistakenly interpret it as a credit boom and wrongly raise CCyB, as Repullo and Saurina (2012) argue. Furthermore, after CCyB is raised, banks must be given sufficient time to build up capital buffer before the new CCyB is effective, the regulator's decision on raising CCyB thus also depends on its forecast on credit cycles in the future which is by no means precise; therefore, it is difficult to ensure that the new CCyB addresses the right credit cycle, by the time when it becomes effective. Repullo and Suarez (2013) also show that frictions that prevent banks from raising capital in a downturn may encourage banks to build up extra capital buffer in normal times, in order to avoid costly forced deleveraging in the bust; such buffer stock may make banks less responsive to CCyB. Overall, these challenges in implementation limit the effectiveness of capital requirements on accommodating credit cycles.

It is not guaranteed, either, that a higher capital ratio necessarily curbs banks' risk-taking, even if higher capital ratio means more skin-in-the-game for banks. In response to more stringent capital requirement, in order to reduce assets' cost of capital, banks may engage in regulatory arbitrage and rebalance their portfolios with risk-weighted assets (RWA). In the outcomes, systemic risks may not be reduced (see more in Section 12.3.4). An increasing number of studies also show that the negative relationship between capital ratio and bank risk-taking may be impaired by more realistic setups and general equilibrium effects, for instance, De Nicolò et al. (2012) argue that capital requirement may interact with banks' liquidity risks; Challe et al. (2013) characterize a scenario that banks with opaque balance sheets may increase risk-taking, when higher capital ratio reduces equilibrium interest rate. All these concerns suggest that regulators have to carefully scrutinize banks' responses to adjustments in capital requirements, better understand the implications on banks' risk-taking, and complement capital requirement with other regulatory rules if necessary.

12.3.4 EMPIRICAL EVIDENCE
BENEFIT AND COST FOR THE REAL ECONOMY

For policy makers, one of the main concerns on capital regulation is its cost to the real economy. Imposing capital requirements may curb banks' risky lending, but it may also restrict lending to those risky but socially desirable activities such as research and development. Higher capital requirements may reduce banks' credit supply to the real economy, hence dampening economic growth. It is thus crucial for policy makers to understand the cost and benefit of capital regulation for the real economy.

Measuring real consequences of capital regulation is challenging. The real effects of capital regulation may not be properly identified, if we simply regress the outcome variables (such as bank lending, GDP growth) on banks' capital ratio, because of obvious endogeneity problem: for example, banks may have the incentive to adjust their capital stock in response to macroeconomic performance, leading to a reverse causality from GDP growth to capital ratio. Besides the endogeneity problem, results based on historical data have limited predictive power for capital requirements that are to be introduced, due to the classical *Lucas critique*, that banks under new capital requirements will behave differently from what they did in the past without such requirements; therefore, how bank lending/GDP growth varies with bank capitalization in the past will not remain the same way in the future, when new capital regulation is in place.

For these reasons, researchers usually use semi-structural or structural models to endogenize banks' choices on lending and capitalization, in order to capture the benefit and cost of banks' adjustments in their balance sheets. Regulatory capital adjustments in the past are also often explored as policy experiments, to better identify the causal effects of capital regulation on banking outcomes and real economy.

Table 12.1 summarizes results from various studies on real effects of capital regulation, using different methodologies and different data. The table lists the estimates of changes in banks' lending spread between loan rate and funding cost, lending volume, as well as GDP growth, over certain time horizons, in reaction to a one percentage point increase in capital ratio.

Across these studies, under higher capital requirement, banks' lending spread is often found to rise, possibly to compensate for the cost of raising new capital; lending volume also falls, more in the short run and less

Table 12.1 The impact of a one percentage point increase in capital ratios on lending spreads, lending volumes and GDP growth: Selected estimates in the literature

	Lending spread	Lending volume	GDP growth[1]	Methodology
MAG (2010)	+15–17bps	−1% to 2%	−4bps over 4 years	Loan pricing model to compute the lending rates needed to recoup the costs of rising capital cost, then feeding into macro models
BCBS (2010)	+13bps	n.a.	−9bps, permanent	Similar to MAG (2010), with additional estimates on reduced likelihood of financial crises
IIF (2011)[2]	+30–80bps	−0.8% to 1%	−6 to 12bps, over 5–10 years	Data from US, Eurozone, Japan, the UK and Switzerland. Computing the response in bank lending though a loan pricing model, then feeding them in a macro model
Slovik and Cournède (2011)	+8–20bps	n.a.	−4bps, over 9 years	Structural banking model to assess impacts on bank lending, then feeding them to OECD macro model
Elliott and Santos (2012)	+5–15bps	n.a.	n.a.	Data from US, Eurozone, and Japan. Computing the necessary response in lending rate to cover the rising cost of capital
Miles et al. (2013)	+5.5bps	n.a.	−4.5bps, permanent	Estimating the impact of equity beta on bank leverage in the UK, then feeding in a production function
Oxford Economics (2013)	+15bps	n.a.	−1.6bps, over 9 years	Based on loan pricing model and a structural macro model, with best/worst scenarios
De Nicolò (2015)	n.a.	−1.36%/−0.4%, short/long run	−50bps, cumulated	2SLS on a panel of about 1,400 banks in 43 advanced/emerging market economies during 1982–2013
Gavalas (2015)	+5/+2bps	−3.8%/−14.4%[3]	n.a.	GMM estimation, on banks in advanced European economies, during 2003Q1–2010Q4
Gambacorta and Shin (2018)	−4bps[4]	+0.6%	n.a.	Panel regression, data from 105 banks in 14 advanced economies, 1994–2012
Fidrmuc and Lind (2020)	n.a.	n.a.	−20bps, cumulated	Meta analysis based on 48 studies during 2009–2014, covering 25 major economies in the world

Source: Cohen and Scatigna (2016), together with author's own research. Notes: bps — basis points, one basis point is one hundredth of 1%, n.a. — not estimated in the paper.

[1] Impact on annual GDP growth rate, relative to baseline forecast, except "*cumulated*" which means cumulated loss over the long run relative to baseline forecast.
[2] Also includes impact of other regulatory measures.
[3] For economies that experienced/did not experience the 2007–2009 global financial crisis, respectively.
[4] Reduction in the cost of debt funding. However, the pass-through to lending spread may be less than one for one.

in the long run, which leads to a relatively small cost in GDP growth. However, opposite results also emerge in some of the studies, such as Gambacorta and Shin (2018), that rising capital requirement reduces lending spread and increases bank lending. This may be due to the fact that better capitalization makes banks more resilient, which may in turn reduce banks' funding cost as creditors may ask for lower risk premium. It may also be due to the fact, as Bahaj and Malherbe (2020) show, that capital regulation may be a substitute to government guarantees on banks; with higher capital requirement, banks become safer and value loans more, hence are willing to increase lending.

Overall, even if capital regulation may be costly for the real economy, it is still well justified as long as the cost is outweighed by its benefit for the economy in terms of reduced likelihood of banking crises which is often not explicitly modelled. Anyway, regulatory cost to avoid crises may be much smaller than the cost of saving the economy out of crises and mopping up after crashes, as Jeanne and Korinek (2020) demonstrate in their simulated model.

BANKS' REACTION TO ADJUSTMENTS IN CAPITAL REGULATION

As is shown in Section 12.3.3, in theory, how banks react to adjustments in capital requirement is not clear-cut, so that the outcomes in banking may not be necessarily what is desired by the regulator. For example, when the regulator intends to increase banks' resilience by increasing capital adequacy ratio, what may be the most desired is probably banks' "good deleveraging" through raising capital without sacrificing their credit supply to the real economy, as chart B in Figure 12.6 shows, while "bad deleveraging" such as drastically cutting back lending (as in chart A) or expanding risky lending (as in chart C) may be less desirable. Therefore, it is crucial for the regulator to understand banks' responses and properly evaluate the effectiveness of capital regulation.

Gropp et al. (2019) explore 2011 capital requirement conducted by the European Banking Authority (EBA) as a quasi-natural experiment, which requires some European banks to raise core tier 1 (CT1) capital ratio from 5% to 9% by mid-2012. The affected banks are selected within each member state using a country-specific selection rule, so that this alleviates the endogeneity concern arising from the selection criteria. Such exogenous variation in the bank selection across countries allows them to employ a difference-in-differences approach to identify how treated banks (those subject to increased capital requirements) adjust their balance sheets differently compared to the control banks (those not subject to the requirements). To distinguish between effects on credit supply and credit demand, they exploit Khwaja-Mian identification strategy as in Chapter 7, Section 7.6.1 that focuses on firms that borrow from multiple banks, and conduct the regression

$$\Delta \ln Lending_{bij} = \beta Capital\_req\_bank_{bi} + \gamma X_{bi} + \lambda_i + \delta_j + \epsilon_{bij},$$

in which $Lending_{bij}$ denotes lending from bank b in country i to firm j, $Capital\_req\_bank_{bi}$ is a dummy variable that equals 1 if bank b in country i is affected by the regulation, vector X_{bi} contains bank-level controls, and λ_i/δ_j denotes country/firm fixed effects.

Gropp et al. (2019) find that affected banks meet the new capital requirements mainly by reducing risk-weighted assets (RWA), that is, cutting back lending to firms as corporate loans carry higher risk weights, instead of raising fresh capital—consistent with the debt overhang theory. Adjusting capital requirement does make an impact on bank lending, which has further implication for the real economy.

Juelsrud and Wold (2020) document banks' portfolio rebalancing—towards reducing RWA—in banks' balance sheets, as a reaction to higher capital requirements. Exploiting 2013 reform in Norway that substantially raised banks' required capital adequacy ratio and examining the loan data that cover the *universe* of non-financial firms in Norway, they find that after the rise in required capital adequacy ratio, in short run, banks cut back lending to firms and increase mortgage lending, as the latter carries lower risk weight. In this way, they are able to effectively reduce RWA and meet the new capital requirement, without issuing new equity. As a result, banks' increasing common exposure to mortgage lending may increase systemic risk. Such portfolio rebalancing also makes an impact on real economy, as Juelsrud and Wold (2020) find that small firms borrowing from affected banks suffer from higher unemployment.

PROCYCLICALITY IN CAPITAL REQUIREMENTS AND CCYB

Capital adequacy requirement may lead to a procyclicality problem and amplify volatility in the economy; for example, in the downturn, binding capital requirement may force banks to deleverage and cut back lending, exacerbating the economic bust. Behn et al. (2016) document such procyclicality by exploiting the exogenous credit risk shock after the failure of Lehman Brothers in September 2008, using German credit register. Under Basel II, banks may choose between model-based or internal rating based (IRB) approach and standard approach (SA) to meet capital requirement: the former is based on banks' own risk modelling, while the latter is based on relatively fixed capital adequacy requirement; as a result, rising credit risk forces IRB banks to increase their statutory capital buffer, while it has no impact on SA banks in terms of capital requirement. Exploring such difference between IRB and SA banks, as well as Khwaja-Mian identification by examining the same firms borrowing from both IRB and SA banks, Behn et al. (2016) find that IRB banks cut back up to 4% of lending to accommodate a 0.5% average rise in statutory capital adequacy ratio, compared with SA banks that are not subject to the capital adequacy shock, exhibiting a strong procyclical effect in credit supply.

In Basel III, countercyclical capital requirement such as CCyB is designed to reduce the procyclicality problem. For most countries, CCyB is phased in very recently, so that evidence from regulatory practice on its effectiveness and effects on banking outcomes is relatively scant. Jiménez et al. (2017) explore the Spanish experience on CCyB-type of dynamic provisioning over credit cycles starting from 2000. Banks are required to build up provision funds in good times as a buffer to cushion against losses in bad times. The provision requirement is countercyclical in that it was increased before 2007, reduced during the 2007–2009 crisis, and increased again in 2012. Examining the credit register in Spain and exploring firms borrowing from multiple banks that are subject to different provision requirements, Jiménez et al. (2017) find that, before the crisis, banks that are subject to more provisioning lend less to firms, compared with banks that are subject to less provisioning; provisioning in good times does accommodate a credit boom. However, they also find limited contractionary effect on borrowing firms: although firms obtain less funding from banks that are more affected, those firms manage to maintain funding by switching to less affected banks. During the crisis, with reduced provision requirement, banks with more cut in provision requirement (i.e., banks that are subject to more provisioning before the crisis) are able to lend more to firms, while firms suffering from lending cut made by banks with less cut in provision requirement (i.e., banks that are subject to less provisioning before the crisis) cannot substitute with funding from the former banks. These findings suggest that CCyB has desirable features in smoothing credit cycles and reducing procyclicality in bank lending. Auer and Ongena (2019) examine the experience in Switzerland, in which CCyB was introduced in 2012 and is based on banks' engagement in domestic residential mortgage lending. They find that banks with more exposure to CCyB do reduce their residential mortgage loan issuance, however, such impact is fully offset by the increase in these banks' commercial lending; CCyB thus does not affect banks' total lending.

12.4 OTHER ISSUES

Banking regulation involves a large array of issues that can hardly be covered in this chapter. In this section, we focus on two other issues that are of increasing interests for both researchers and policy makers in recent years: one is how banking regulation, especially macroprudential regulation, interacts with monetary policy; the other is on new *bail-in* instruments designed to facilitate efficient bank resolution and reduce the cost for taxpayers.

12.4.1 INTERACTION BETWEEN BANKING REGULATION AND MONETARY POLICY

Banking regulation, such as regulation on liquidity and capital, affects banking outcomes such as bank lending. Particularly, in the recent years, the global regulatory framework has been reformed to address more macroprudential concerns, so that bank lending through credit cycles is explicitly targeted as one of the key systemic risk indicators and one of the triggers to tighten or loosen regulatory requirements. Therefore, banking regulation may potentially affect the bank lending channel of monetary policy, and the interaction between banking regulation and monetary policy may be more pronounced when regulators are becoming more macroprudential. Given that banking regulation and monetary policy may be conducted by different institutions with different policy mandates, banking regulation and monetary policy may reinforce each other or conflict with each other.

For example, Section 12.2.4 has shown how liquidity regulation may interact with monetary policy transmission; under different objectives of liquidity regulation and monetary policy, Cao and Chollete (2017) show that central bank conducting inflation-targeting monetary policy cannot achieve price stability and financial stability at the same time. Van den Heuvel (2002) argues that bank capitalization matters for monetary policy transmission, as a bank only increases lending under expansionary monetary policy if it has enough capital to buffer credit risks; because of such "bank capital channel", if the regulator increases the capital adequacy ratio under expansionary monetary policy, banks with tightening capital constraints will be reluctant to increase lending, which erodes the bank lending channel for monetary expansion. Quantitatively, Angelini et al. (2014) show how the lack of cooperation between capital regulation and monetary policy leads to excessive volatility under supply shocks; while these two policies may enhance each other under financial shocks. Such an issue is even more complicated, if regulatory/monetary policies spill over across borders through international banks and interact with regulatory/monetary policies in other countries, as is shown by Buch and Goldberg (2017) and Bussière et al. (2021).

Aiyar et al. (2016) investigate how the interaction between capital regulation and monetary policy affects bank lending, exploring a special feature in UK capital regulation, 1998–2007, that bank-specific, time-varying required capital adequacy ratios are set for regulated banks. Aiyar et al. (2016) find that a lending supply of large banks reacts to changes in capital requirements, but not to changes in monetary policy, while a lending supply of small banks reacts to both. In addition, they find little evidence on effects from interaction between capital regulation and monetary policy. Forbes et al. (2017) explore the same feature in UK capital regulation, while they focus on one unconventional monetary policy introduced in 2012—the Funding for Lending Scheme (FLS) that provides cheaper funding for banks to support lending to households and firms. Forbes et al. (2017) find tightening capital requirement leads to a fall in banks' cross-border lending, and the contractionary effect is stronger for banks specialized in FLS lending.

Based on Belgian credit register, De Jonghe et al. (2020) explore how adjustments in bank-specific, time-varying required capital adequacy ratios affect the transmission of ECB's QE program, in term of bank lending growth. They find that the stimulating effect of QE program on bank lending is weaker for those banks facing tighter capital requirement, implying that capital regulation reduces effectiveness of monetary policy transmission.

12.4.2 BAIL-IN

As is argued in Section 12.2.2, due to a time-consistency problem, the regulator bails out insolvent banks at the cost of taxpayers. In reality, the regulator is often forced to do so for the lack of alternative resolution solutions under the time pressure during crises. The idea of bail-in thus became more appealing after the 2007–2009 financial crisis, that certain mechanisms shall be established to swiftly downgrade failing banks' liability rights—for example, to convert debt to equity—and let creditors bear losses, hoping that bank resolution can be promptly triggered and carried out, cutting off contagion and reducing the need for costly public bailout.

One promising bail-in instrument, contingent convertible (CoCo) debt, has been introduced in Basel III and widely adopted. CoCo allows the conversion from debt to equity, once the conversion criterion is triggered; this increases banks' capital buffer during crises and reduces insolvency. The working mechanism as well as appealing features of CoCo can be seen from a simple stylized model as follows.

CONTINGENT CONVERTIBLE

The idea of using CoCo as a regulatory tool is suggested by Flannery (2005), that such convertible debts should have the following appealing features:

1. They are automatically converted into common equity if some trigger criterion is met—this usually means that the debt issuer's capital ratio falls below a predefined critical value, and "automatically" means that the debt contract does not contain any options for debt holders;
2. As long as the conversion does not happen, they have all the features of plain debts, i.e., the debt holders receive tax deductible interest payments;
3. In terms of seniority, they are subordinated to all the plain debt obligations;
4. The critical value of the capital ratio is measured by the outstanding equity's market value, and the conversion price is the current share price.

The following example, based on Flannery (2005), shows how such convertible debt works. Suppose that, as Figure 12.7, one bank's investments in $100 securities are backed by $80 from debts, $10 from

Assets	Liabilities
$100 securities	$80 debts
	$10 convertibles
	$10 equity

Figure 12.7 Balance sheet of a bank with CoCo

CoCo, and $10 from common equity. There are ten outstanding shares, therefore, the share price is $1. The adequate capital ratio defined by the banking regulation is 10%; the conversion thus automatically happens once the bank's capital ratio falls below 10%.

Suppose that the asset price fall, making the bank's security holding worth only $97. Then the value of equity falls to $7, as Figure 12.8 shows, and the share price becomes $0.7. The bank's capital ratio is now below the adequacy requirement, as $\frac{\$7}{\$97} \times 100\% \approx 7.22\% < 10\%$, and this triggers the conversion of the debts.

The convertibles are converted to common equity until the adequacy requirement is met again. This implies that $97 \times 10\% - \$7 = \$2.7$ is to be raised. As the conversion price is the current share price, this means that the convertibles worth $2.7 have been converted to $\frac{\$2.7}{\$0.7} \approx 3.86$ new outstanding shares for the convertible debt holders. Figure 12.9 provides the summary.

Compared with a bank without convertible debt financing, one can see how introducing the notion of convertible debt helps increase the resilience of banks in times of economic downturn. For such a bank, suppose the investment in securities worth $100 is financed by $90 from debts and $10 from equity, as in Figure 12.10.

Assets	Liabilities
	$80 debts
$97 securities	$10 convertibles
	$7 equity

Figure 12.8 Balance sheet of a bank with CoCo, after asset price shock

Assets	Liabilities
	$80 debts
$97 securities	$7.3 convertibles
	$9.7 equity

Figure 12.9 Recapitalization through debt conversion

CHAPTER TWELVE: BANKING REGULATION IN PRACTICE

Assets	Liabilities
$100 securities	$90 debts
	$10 equity

Figure 12.10 Balance sheet of a reference bank without CoCo

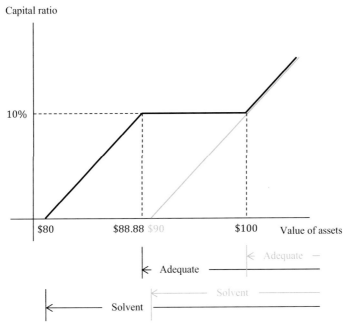

Figure 12.11 Bank recapitalization through CoCos versus common equity
Notes: the black/gray line shows how a bank's capital ratio varies with value of its assets with/without holding CoCos, starting with a balance sheet shown as in Figures 12.7/12.10.

Once there is a negative shock on the value of the reference bank's assets, the bank has to mop off its equity value, and the capital ratio is regarded as inadequate as long as the bank does not issue new equity. Without issuing new equity, as the gray line in Figure 12.11 shows, the capital ratio falls lower when the shock becomes larger, and the bank is insolvent once the value of assets falls below $90.

In contrast, the negative shock triggers debt conversion for the bank holding convertible debts, and the capital ratio can remain adequate without the need to issue new equity unless all the convertibles have been

561

converted, as the black line in Figure 12.11 shows. The bank's capital ratio is adequate as long as CoCos are available for conversion and the value of assets is above $88.88. Without issuing new equity, the bank has to shed off the value of equity once the value of assets goes below $88.88, but it still remains solvent whenever the value of assets is above $80. In contrast to the reference bank, the holding of convertible debts allows the bank to stay adequately capitalized when the value of risky assets falls between $100 and $88.88, and to stay solvent when the value of risky assets falls between $90 and $80.

To better understand how the convertible debts provide additional protection for the banks against shocks, Figure 12.12 depicts the value dynamics of the convertible debts. The black line tracks how much the debts are converted along with varying asset value: the conversion starts when asset value falls below $100 and ends up when the debts are completely converted. The gray line shows the value of the convertibles: although the conversion starts once the asset value falls below $100, the holders of convertibles will still be fully repaid with a mixture of cash and shares because the conversion price is the current share price. The payment to the convertibles shrinks at a time the asset value falls below

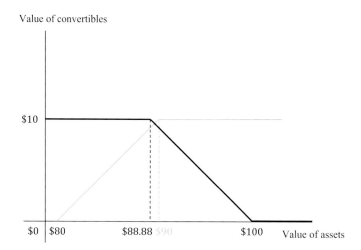

Figure 12.12 *The value of CoCos*

Notes: the black line shows how much of the debts is converted along with varying asset value, and the gray line shows the value of the convertibles.

$90, when the common equity holders are gone and part of the converted starts to be wiped out, too.

Another appealing feature under CoCos is the common equity holders' payoff. As Figure 12.13 shows, when the value of risky assets falls below $100, for both the bank with convertible debts and the reference bank, the common equity holders' share value has to decline to the same extent as the incurred loss. The only difference is the bank in our model can convert its debts into common equity and restore its capital ratio, but this does not make any difference in the common equity holders' payoff. Therefore, the dynamics of the common equity holders' payoffs for both banks (the solid black line for the bank with convertible debts in Figure 12.13, and the gray line for the reference bank) coincide. Such features imply that introducing convertible debts at least does not add extra incentive problems for the common equity holders. If the reference bank suffers from incentive problems coming from the common equity holders' payoff structure, such as debt overhang problem, adding convertible debts to the bank's balance sheet does not make the problems worse.

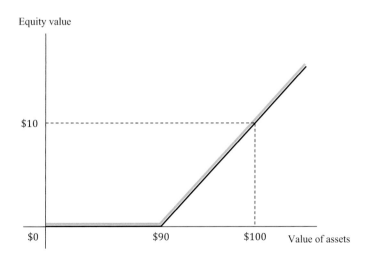

Figure 12.13 *The value of common equity in a bank with/without CoCos*
Notes: the black/gray line shows how value of common equity in a bank with/without CoCos varies with value of assets.

EMPIRICAL EVIDENCE

Although CoCo has many appealing features as a desirable bail-in instrument, how CoCo issuance affects banking outcomes such as risk-taking is not yet clear. Martynova and Perotti (2018) show that by reducing leverage upon conversion, CoCo reduces banks' *ex ante* risk-taking incentives. On the other hand, CoCo conversion also reduces the likelihood of bank runs and costly liquidation *ex post*, hence the market discipline effect on banks; this may encourage banks to take more risks, as Cao (2012) shows.

To examine the impact of CoCo issuance on issuer banks' balance sheets and risks, Avdjiev et al. (2020) establish an extensive dataset that covers all 731 CoCo issues across the world in 2009–2015. They find that CoCos are more likely issued by larger and better capitalized banks, and issuers' CDS spreads tend to fall after CoCo issuance, leading to lower market funding cost for the issuers; this implies reduced bank risk perceived by financial market. Avdjiev et al. (2020) also find terms of CoCo contracts matter, such that the positive effect on reducing perceived bank risk is stronger for those CoCos that credibly reduce solvency risk, such as CoCos that can be easily converted to loss-absorbing equity, CoCos with mechanical—instead of discretionary—triggers for conversion, etc. Analyzing all European banks' CoCo issues that took place before the end of 2017, Goncharenko et al. (2020) find that riskier banks with more volatile asset returns have difficulties in CoCo issuance and prefer issuing equity over CoCos. They interpret such results as evidence that riskier banks are more subject to future debt overhang.

Although CoCos are widely adopted worldwide and bail-in policies have been gradually integrated in many countries' regulatory frameworks after the 2007–2009 financial crisis, implementing bail-in policies is still rare. Based on an event study of the bail-in practice with the failed Banco Espírito Santo—the second-largest listed bank in Portugal— in 2014, Beck et al. (2020) provide one of the first analyses on the real effect of bail-in. After the collapse of the bank, shareholders and junior bond holders are required to bail-in the bank and hold its toxic assets. Exploring Portuguese credit register and using Khwaja-Mian identification by focusing the same firms borrowing from both bailed-in banks and other banks, Beck et al. (2020) find that firms with more exposure to the bailed-in bank suffer from more supply-driven contraction in credit supply; although these firms are able to maintain their credit supply by borrowing more from other banks, they tend to experience contraction in their credit lines. Increasing liquidity risks from tightening credit lines force affected small and medium-size firms to cut back investment and employment, bail-in practice thus generates adverse impacts on the real economy.

12.5 EXERCISES

1. **Moral hazard, risk-taking incentive of banks, and capital regulation**

    Consider a one-period economy with a monopoly profit-maximizing bank that can invest in either of the following two types of assets:

    - Good assets: one unit of safe asset yields a gross return G with probability p_G and 0 otherwise at the end of the period;
    - Bad assets: one unit of bad asset yields a gross return B with probability p_B and 0 otherwise at the end of the period.

    It is known that $G < B$, $p_G > p_B$ and $p_G G > p_B B > 1$. The bank has no capital and totally relies on deposits for its investment.

    There is no deposit insurance available in this economy. Depositors are risk neutral and they take deposit contracts from the bank at the beginning of the period. Depositors get repaid at the end of the period with a gross interest rate R if the bank's assets return, otherwise depositors get nothing. There is no asymmetric information. To ease the computation, we further assume that the bank's participation constraint is always fulfilled.

(a) Provide a graphical illustration of how the payoffs of the two types of assets vary with R, and compute the critical value of R, denoted by $\hat{R}$, below which the bank only invests in the good assets and above which the bank only invests in the bad assets. Compute $\hat{R}$.

(b) Recall that there is no deposit insurance available in this economy; this implies that depositors are happy to deposit as long as their expected gross return from deposits is no lower than 1. As the bank is a monopoly, depositors earn zero profit from deposits. For the values of p_G, G, p_B, B, find a condition under which depositors are willing to deposit and the bank invests only in the bad project.

(c) Now the bank has a choice to hold an amount of capital k for each unit of asset. Therefore, for each unit of the bank's asset, the bank has to raise k from the shareholders and $1-k$ from the depositors. The bank has to guarantee a return to equity (ROE) of ρ ($\rho>0$) for the shareholders, and we assume that the bank pays a gross return R for each $1-k$ unit of deposit.

  i. Suppose there is an R under which depositors are willing to deposit and the bank invests only in the bad assets. Compute R and the optimal level of capital for the profit-maximizing bank.

  ii. Suppose, instead, there is an R under which depositors are willing to deposit and the bank invests only in the good assets. Compute R and the optimal level of capital for the profit- maximizing bank.

  iii. Show there exists a threshold $\hat{\rho}$, such that for any $\rho<\hat{\rho}$, the profit-maximizing bank chooses an optimal capital level k^* and invests only in the good assets. Compute $\hat{\rho}$ and k^*.

2 Skin-in-the-game and capital requirement

Consider a profit-maximizing bank's one-shot decision problem as follows: it can invest 1 dollar in either of the two projects

- Project G, which yields a gross return R_G with probability p_G, or 0 otherwise;

- Project B, which yields a gross return R_B with probability p_B, or 0 otherwise.

Assume that although project B returns more if it is successful, $R_B > R_A$, the expected return of project G is higher, $p_G R_G > p_B R_B$.

The bank does not have any initial wealth, so that it raises funding from issuing k, $0 \le k \le 1$ equity capital and collecting $1 - k$ deposits from depositors. The capital ratio k is a constant that is set by the regulator. Assume that deposits are fully insured, and the premium that the bank has to pay the insurance scheme is normalized to 0. The gross deposit rate R_D is determined by a competitive deposit market so that the bank takes it as given. Equity holders require a gross return to equity (ROE) R_E that is no less than the deposit rate, $R_E \ge R_D$.

(a) Compute the bank's expected profit from investing in each type of the projects. Show that project G is always profitable, as long as $p_G R_G > R_E \ge R_D$.

(b) What is the condition for k and R_D, under which project B is more profitable than project G? Is it possible that the profit of project B is positive, while the profit of project G is negative?

(c) Now assume that $R_D < p_G R_G < R_E$.
What capital requirement k is needed for the regulator, in order to induce the bank to choose project G?

(d) Keep the assumption in question (c). Now assume that the representative bank in this economy is making dynamic decisions over an infinite time horizon, $t = 0, 1, \ldots, +\infty$. The capital requirement k is fixed by the regulator in the beginning of the world $t = 0$. In any period t,
- The bank receives funding from equity investors and depositors;
- Then the bank makes its choice on the project;
- In the end of the period, the chosen project returns. If the bank defaults, it is shut down by the regulator and will lose its banking license forever.

i. Assume that the bank's discount factor is β, $0 < \beta < 1$. What capital requirement k is needed for the regulator, in order to induce banks always to choose project G in every period?
ii. Explain why your result is different, compared with the result in question (c).

3 Efficient bank recapitalization, based on Homar and van Wijnbergen (2017)

Consider an economy that is populated by a bank, consumers whose population is normalized to be 1, and a regulator. Each consumer is born in $t=0$ with 1 unit of endowment, and they can invest in the bank via being either shareholders or depositors of the bank. Consumers are risk neutral: if they become depositors, they require a gross expected return equal to 1; if they become shareholders, they require a gross expected return strictly higher than 1.

The economy lasts for 3 periods, $t = 0, 1, 2$:

- In $t = 0$, the bank raises 1 unit of funding which consists of k equity that is collected from shareholders and $1-k$ deposits that are collected from depositors, then it issues 1 unit of loans to firms. The equity ratio k is a constant number that is required by the regulator. Each of the firms invests in *ex ante* the same projects that will return in $t = 2$. The projects' return is stochastic and unknown in this period. Firms have no initial wealth so that they totally rely on bank funding, and the bank is able to extract all yields from the projects;
- In $t = 1$, there is public information about each project's return in the future: (1) a share $1-q$ of the projects will be good and return $R > 1$ in $t = 2$ with certainty, and (2) a share q of the projects will be bad, so that they will only return R in $t = 2$ with probability p, or 0 otherwise. The bank has two options with bad projects:
  - Liquidating the bad projects, which generates a liquidation value $0 < \delta < 1$ for each liquidated project.

Then the bank can use the proceeds that are collected from liquidation to invest in good projects that return R each in $t=2$. Assume that, when choosing liquidation, the expected gross return of the bank is strictly higher than 1;
- Doing nothing and keeping the bad projects ("rollover"). In addition, assume that rollover is socially inferior such that the expected return from rolling over a bad project is lower than liquidating it, i.e., $p<\delta$.

- In $t=2$, the bank collects return from all projects and repays the depositors. The bank's shareholders claim the residual.

The regulator has a recapitalization technology: if needed in $t=1$, she can take over depositors with a guarantee on their repayment in $t=2$, and become shareholder of the bank herself. That is, using this technology, she can convert one unit of deposit to one unit of equity.

(a) Suppose that even if the bank chooses to roll over the bad projects in $t=1$, the bank is still solvent, but the expected gross return of the bank is strictly lower than 1. Assume that the bank is only insolvent if it chooses to roll over the bad projects in $t=1$, and the projects fail in $t=2$. Characterize the condition on which the bank, representing the interests of shareholders, chooses liquidation instead of rollover. What is the lowest capital ratio $\underline{k}$ that the regulator needs to fulfill this condition? How is $\underline{k}$ affected by q and δ?

(b) Suppose that the economy starts in $t=0$ with a k that just fulfills the condition characterized in question (a), or, k is higher but indefinitely close to $\underline{k}$, $k \to \underline{k}^+$. In $t=1$, assume that the economy is hit by an *unexpected* shock that the share of bad projects is $q+\epsilon$, $\epsilon>0$. Show that the bank only chooses liquidation instead of rollover if the regulator recapitalizes the bank and increases the bank's equity ratio. Compute the minimum amount of new equity that the regulator needs to inject.

4 Bank capital, deposit insurance, and bailout

In this exercise, we see how limited liability affects banks' risk-taking behavior as well as the need for central bank's bail-out.

Consider an economy that is populated by many identical risk-neutral banks so that we can pick up an arbitrary representative bank and investigate its behavior. The bank makes loans at time 0, and the loans mature at time 1. The bank has limited liability. Deposits are insured. The market for deposits is competitive. For simplicity we assume that the market interest rate on insured deposits is zero. Figure 12.14 shows the balance sheets of the bank in period 0 and period 1. The insurance premium is proportional to the level of deposits: $P = \phi D$ ($\phi > 0$). The premium has to be paid upfront, which means that equity must at least be sufficient to cover the insurance premium, $E \geq P$.

Period 0

Assets	Liabilities
Loans L	Deposits D
Insurance premium P	Equity E

Period 1

Assets	Liabilities
Loan repayment $\tilde{L}$	Deposits D
Insurance payment $\tilde{S}$	Net value $\tilde{E}$

Figure 12.14 Bank's balance sheets

(a) Assume that in period 0 the bank has a given level of equity, E. Use the balance sheet for period 0 to show that

　　i. If the bank lends L, it needs to collect deposits as much as
$$D = \frac{L-E}{1-\phi};$$

　　ii. The maximum amount that the bank can lend is $L^{max} = \frac{E}{\phi}$.

CHAPTER TWELVE: BANKING REGULATION IN PRACTICE

(b) The payout from the insurance fund is

$$\tilde{S} = \begin{cases} 0 & \text{if } \tilde{L} \geq D, \\ D - \tilde{L} & \text{if } \tilde{L} < D. \end{cases} \quad (12.1)$$

Show how you can express the net profits of the bank's owners, $\Pi = \tilde{E} - E$, in terms of L, $\tilde{L}$ and E for each of the two cases in (12.1).

(c) Suppose the gross repayment on the loans is $(R+\Delta)L$ with probability $\frac{1}{2}$ and $(R-\Delta)L$ with probability $\frac{1}{2}$. Assume $R > 1$ and $R - 1 < \Delta < 1$. Show that there is no risk that the bank needs to be bailed out by the insurance fund if it lends less than

$$L^C = \frac{E}{1-(1-\phi)(R-\Delta)} < L^{max}.$$

(d) Given the same distribution of $\tilde{L}$ as in the question (c), what is the expected net profit of the bank's owners? How does it depend on Δ and L? What general principle(s) does this example illustrate?

(e) Suppose the bank can choose the level of risk, Δ, and the volume of loans L, freely within the range permitted by the assumptions above. What levels would it choose if it starts with a given equity level E? What rate of return on equity would this choice result in? Show that the net rate of return is negative for some parameter values. Why do you think this can be the case?

(f) Will the size of ϕ affect risk taking? If so, in what way?

5 **When Salop meets Hellmann-Murdock-Stiglitz, based on Repullo (2004)**

Consider a banking economy whose market structure is similar to the Salop Salop (1979) model in Exercise 2, Chapter 4: the economy has N banks, indexed by $i = 1, 2, \ldots, N$, and a continuum of depositors whose population is normalized to 1. Both banks and depositors are symmetrically distributed along a circular street, as Figure 4.6 shows. The circumference of the street is normalized to 1. To reach a bank and deposit, a depositor must incur a transaction cost of c for each unit of distance between her location and the bank's office.

The time horizon is infinite over day t, $t = 0, 1, \cdots, +\infty$. Banks are infinitely lived, as long as they are not bankrupted; while in each day a generation of depositors, whose population is 1, are born in the morning and die in the night. Each depositor is born with one unit of endowment; depositors deposit in banks in the morning, hoping to withdraw in the evening for consumption. Every morning banks collect endowments from depositors and invest the deposits in one of the two assets; then in the evening the assets return so that banks collect the returns to repay depositors. Similar to the Hellmann-Murdock-Stiglitz model from Exercise 3, Chapter 4, two types of assets are available for banks:

- Prudent asset, with a net return α, and
- Gambling asset, with a net return of γ with probability θ and 0 with probability $1 - \theta$.

The prudent asset has higher expected return, $\alpha > \theta \gamma$, but if the gamble succeeds the bank earns higher private return, $\gamma > \alpha$. When the gamble fails, the bank will lose its license of banking from the next period onward. Banks' discount factor is $0 < \delta < 1$.

A bank is required to hold at least k_0 capital for each unit of deposits it collects. Capital providers, or, shareholders of banks are infinitely lived agents, and they require a return ρ, $\rho > \alpha$ on bank capital.

(a) Assume that each morning, a representative bank i chooses its capital ratio k_i, $k_i \geq k_0$ and deposit rate r_i. Then all banks invest in prudent asset.

   i. For a depositor located at distance x from bank i, towards bank $i+1$, what r_i makes the depositor indifferent between going to bank i and bank $i+1$? Given that all banks are symmetric in setting deposit rate r, compute the demand for deposits of bank i.

ii. Specify the optimization problem for bank *i* who aims to maximize its franchise value. What is the bank's optimal choice on *k*?
iii. What is the equilibrium deposit rate under such optimal *k*? What is the bank's franchise value?

(a) Assume that each morning, a representative bank *i* chooses its capital ratio k_i, $k_i \geq k_0$ and deposit rate r_i. Then all banks invest in gambling asset.

i. Specify the optimization problem for bank *i* who aims to maximize its franchise value. What is the bank's optimal choice on *k*?
ii. What is the equilibrium deposit rate under such optimal *k*? What is the bank's franchise value?

(c) Market equilibria and optimal capital requirement

i. Define a market equilibrium as prudent equilibrium, if all banks coordinate to choose prudent assets, and no bank has the incentive to deviate and choose gambling assets—even for just one day. Specify the condition under which prudent equilibrium exists.
ii. Define a market equilibrium as gambling equilibrium, if all banks coordinate to choose gambling assets, and no bank has the incentive to deviate and choose prudent assets—even for just one day. Specify the condition under which gambling equilibrium exists.
iii. Compute depositors' payoff under prudent/gambling equilibrium, as well as a bank's franchise value under prudent/gambling equilibrium. If the regulator aims to maximize social welfare as the sum of depositors' payoff and banks' franchise value, what is the regulator's optimal choice on capital requirement k_0?

NOTES

1 Modigliani and Miller (1958) show that if capital markets are perfect, information is complete and symmetric, and there are no taxes, bankruptcy costs or agency costs, a firm's value (i.e., the value of claims over the firm's income) is independent of its financial structure and only depends on the present value of future returns.
2 Although, in regulatory practice, bank capital includes other capital (so-called Tier 2 capital) than common equity (so-called Tier 1 capital), in this chapter, we mostly regard equity and capital as interchangeable terms for simplicity.

PART V
Appendix

Solutions to selected exercises

APPENDIX

CHAPTER 2

EXERCISE 1

Proof: It's known that $-\frac{cu''(c)}{u'(c)} > 1$, this is equivalent to $\frac{\partial [cu'(c)]}{\partial c} < 0$. Together with $c_1^* < c_2^*$ and $R > 1$, it implies that $1 \cdot u'(1) > Ru'(R)$. Further, (c_1^*, c_2^*) satisfies resource constraint $c_2^* = \frac{(1-pc_1^*)R}{1-p}$ and optimality condition $u'(c_1^*) = Ru'(c_2^*)$. Resource constraint implies either (a) $c_1^* > 1$ and $c_2^* < R$, or (b) $c_1^* \leq 1$ and $c_2^* \geq R$.

- If (a) is true, $1 \cdot u'(1) > c_1^* u'(c_1^*) > c_2^* u'(c_2^*) > Ru'(R)$, it goes through;
- If (b) is true, $u'(c_1^*) = Ru'(c_2^*) \leq Ru'(R) < 1 \cdot u'(1)$, which implies $c_1^* > 1$. A contradiction.

EXERCISE 2 RISK SHARING AND FINANCIAL INTERMEDIATION

(2a) $c_1^* = \dfrac{R}{(1-\pi)R^{\frac{1}{\gamma}} + \pi R}$, $c_2^* = \dfrac{R^{1+\frac{1}{\gamma}}}{(1-\pi)R^{\frac{1}{\gamma}} + \pi R}$, and $\lim_{\gamma \to +\infty} \dfrac{c_2^*}{c_1^*} = R^{\frac{1}{\gamma}} = 1$.

EXERCISE 3 COMPLETE MARKET AND CONSTRAINED EFFICIENCY, BASED ON ALLEN AND GALE (2007)

(3a) The budget constraint for a consumer in $t = 0$ is $q_1 p c_1 + q_2 s (1-p) c_2 \leq 1$.

(3b) The optimization problem for the consumer is

$$\max_{\{c_1, c_2\}} \quad pu(c_1) + (1-p)u(c_2),$$

$$\text{s.t.} \quad q_1 p c_1 + q_2 s (1-p) c_2 \leq 1.$$

First-order condition yields $\dfrac{u'(c_1)}{u'(c_2)} = \dfrac{q_1}{q_2 s}$.

(3c) To receive 1 unit t_1 consumption, one way is to invest 1 unit in the short asset in $t = 0$. Thus, non-arbitrage condition for investing in the short asset is $q_1 = 1$. Similarly, to receive 1 unit t_2 consumption, one way is to invest $\frac{1}{R}$ units in the long asset in $t = 0$. Thus, non-arbitrage condition for investing in the long asset requires $q_2 s = \frac{1}{R}$.

SOLUTIONS TO SELECTED EXERCISES

(3d) First-order condition thus becomes $\frac{u'(c_1)}{u'(c_2)} = \frac{q_1}{q_2 s} = R$, exactly the same as the planner's solution.

EXERCISE 4 BANK RUN AND FINANCIAL FRAGILITY

(4a) To make a profitable deviation from the run equilibrium, there must be resources left after the run, or, $\pi c_1^* + (1 - \pi c_1^*) \delta > c_1^*$, $\delta > \frac{(1-\pi)c_1^*}{1-\pi c_1^*}$. Notice that $c_1^* > 1$, $\delta > \frac{(1-\pi)c_1^*}{1-\pi c_1^*} > \frac{(1-\pi)c_1^*}{c_1^* - \pi c_1^*} = 1$. Therefore, eligible threshold $\overline{\delta} = \frac{(1-\pi)c_1^*}{1-\pi c_1^*}$ must be strictly higher than 1, while lower than R.

(4c) To push asset price until the liquidation value of illiquid assets is above $\overline{\delta}$, so that the run equilibrium is eliminated.

EXERCISE 5 PANDEMIC AND BANK RUN

With infected patient consumers, total demand for repayment is $(p+f)c_1^* > \alpha^*$, so that an amount L of long assets needs to be liquidated until $\alpha^* + \delta L = (p+f)c_1^*$, $L = \frac{fc_1^*}{\delta}$. For the uninfected, patient consumers, their expected return (if they wait until $t=2$) is $\tilde{c}_2 = \frac{1-\alpha^*-L}{1-p-f}R = \frac{1-\alpha^*-\frac{fc_1^*}{\delta}}{1-p-f}R$. A bank run only happens if f is large enough so that $\tilde{c}_2 < c_1^*$, incentivizing uninfected, patient consumers to mimic impatient consumers and withdraw early. Further, we can compute the threshold f from $\tilde{c}_2 = \frac{1-\alpha^*-\frac{fc_1^*}{\delta}}{1-p-f}R < c_1^*$, or, $f > \frac{R(1-\alpha^*)-(1-p)c_1^*}{(\frac{R}{\delta}-1)c_1^*} = \underline{f}$.

EXERCISE 6 NOMINAL DEPOSITS THAT ELIMINATE BANK RUNS, BASED ON SKEIE (2008)

Hint: the key is to show that as long as banks can recall the nominal loans, there is no need to liquidate the long assets. As long as the long assets are not prematurely liquidated, a bank run only makes patient consumers that withdraw early worse off, as they are only able to consume less than c_2^* real goods in any case.

APPENDIX

CHAPTER 3

EXERCISE 1 MARKET SEGMENTATION, LOANABLE FUNDS, AND REAL EFFECTS, BASED ON HOLMSTRÖM AND TIROLE (1997)

(1a) i. The aggregate demand for bank capital equals per capita demand times the bank borrowers' population, i.e.,

$$\left[F(\bar{A}(R)) - F(\underline{A}(\beta,R))\right] L_B^B = \left[F(\bar{A}(R)) - F(\underline{A}(\beta,R))\right] \frac{p_G C}{\beta \Delta p}$$

ii. Market equilibrium implies that

$$\left[F(\bar{A}(R)) - F(\underline{A}(\beta,R))\right] \frac{p_G C}{\beta \Delta p} = \overline{L_B}. \tag{A.1}$$

iii. Using implicit function theorem[1] to differentiate both sides of (A.1) with respect to $\overline{L_B}$,

$$-f(\underline{A}(\beta,R)) \frac{\partial \underline{A}(\beta,R)}{\partial \beta} \frac{\partial \beta}{\partial \overline{L_B}} \frac{p_G C}{\beta \Delta p} - \left[F(\bar{A}(R)) - F(\underline{A}(\beta,R))\right] \frac{p_G C}{\beta^2 \Delta p} \frac{\partial \beta}{\partial \overline{L_B}} = 1. \tag{A.2}$$

It is easily seen from (3.19) that $\frac{\partial \underline{A}(\beta,R)}{\partial \beta} > 0$; with $\left[F(\bar{A}(R)) - F(\underline{A}(\beta,R))\right] > 0$, (A.2) implies that $\frac{\partial \beta}{\partial \overline{L_B}} < 0$, or an exogenous "capital flight", i.e., a fall in $\overline{L_B}$, leads to higher equilibrium ROE β. This increases $\underline{A}(\beta,R)$ and reduces bank borrowers' population $F(\bar{A}(R)) - F(\underline{A}(\beta,R))$—a fall in bank funding.

(1b) i. The aggregate demand for consumers' funding includes the demand for direct lending and the demand for consumers' funding in bank lending, i.e.,

$$\int_{\underline{A}(\beta,R)}^{\bar{A}(R)} (I - L_B^B - A) dF(A) + \int_{\bar{A}(R)}^{I} (I - A) dF(A) = S(R). \tag{A.3}$$

ii. Equilibrium β and R are jointly determined by (A.1) and (A.3). **iii.** Using implicit function theorem to differentiate both sides of (A.3) with respect to $S(R)$. Applying the Leibniz's rule[2], similar to question **(1a) iii.**, it is not difficult to see that an exogenous "saving glut", i.e., an increase in S, leads to lower risk-free rate R and higher equilibrium ROE β. This reduces $\bar{A}(R)$, increases direct lending, and bank lending (if the bank's marginal gain from falling R outweighs its marginal loss from rising β).

EXERCISE 2 ASYMMETRIC INFORMATION, MONITORING, AND MARKET SEGMENTATION

(2a) The payoff for the good project is $p(G-R)$, while for the bad is $pq(B-R)$, as illustrated by Figure A.1. The kinked gray line shows the firm's actual choice under different R.

(2b) In a competitive credit market, (1) PCs of both borrowers and lenders hold, and (2) lenders make zero profit. Note that expected profit from bad projects is negative, lenders should induce borrowers to choose good projects, i.e., $R \leq \hat{R}$. Borrowers with good project must have $R \leq G$. Zero profit implies that $pR - 1 = 0$. The cutoff gross interest rate $\hat{R}$ is determined by the cross of two payoff functions, $p(G-\hat{R}) = pq(B-\hat{R})$ and $\hat{R} = \frac{G-qB}{1-q}$. Combining the constraints, $R = \frac{1}{p} \leq \hat{R} = \frac{G-qB}{1-q}$, or, $p \geq \frac{1-q}{G-qB}$.

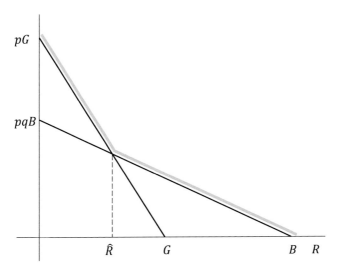

Figure A.1 *Payoffs of projects*

# APPENDIX

(2c) In competitive equilibrium, (1) PC implies that, for banks $\Pi^{bank} \geq 0$ (implying that they can only lend to good borrowers), for borrowers $\Pi^b = p(G-R^b) \geq 0$, and (2) banks make zero profit, $pR^b - 1 - c = 0$. Combining the conditions to get $R^b = \frac{1+c}{p} \leq G$, or, $p \geq \frac{1+c}{G}$.

(2d) Depending on the parameter values

1. If $\frac{1+c}{G} \leq \frac{1-q}{G-qB}$

   For the range $p \in \left[\frac{1-q}{G-qB}, 1\right)$, direct finance.

   For the range $p \in \left[\frac{1+c}{G}, \frac{1-q}{G-qB}\right)$, bank finance.

   For the range $p \in \left(0, \frac{1+c}{G}\right)$, no finance.

2. If $\frac{1+c}{G} > \frac{1-q}{G-qB}$

   For the range $p \in \left[\frac{1-q}{G-qB}, 1\right)$, direct finance, as banks can only offer higher rates so that they are dominated.

   For the range $p \in \left(0, \frac{1-q}{G-qB}\right)$, no finance.

EXERCISE 3

Starting from zero profit condition (3.24),

$$1+\delta = \frac{(1+r)\int_0^{\bar{p}(r)} p_i f(p_i) dp_i}{\int_0^{\bar{p}(r)} f(p_i) dp_i}.$$

Differentiating δ with respect to r,

$$\frac{d\delta}{dr} = \frac{\left[(1+r)\int_0^{\bar{p}(r)} p_i f(p_i) dp_i\right]\left[\int_0^{\bar{p}(r)} f(p_i) dp_i\right]}{\left[\int_0^{\bar{p}(r)} f(p_i) dp_i\right]^2}$$

$$-\frac{\left[\int_0^{\bar{p}(r)} f(p_i) dp_i\right](1+r)\int_0^{\bar{p}(r)} p_i f(p_i) dp_i}{\left[\int_0^{\bar{p}(r)} f(p_i) dp_i\right]^2}$$

$$= \frac{\left[\int_0^{\bar{p}(r)} p_i f(p_i)dp_i + (1+r)\left(\int_0^{\bar{p}(r)} p_i f(p_i)dp_i\right)'\right]\int_0^{\bar{p}(r)} f(p_i)dp_i}{\left[\int_0^{\bar{p}(r)} f(p_i)dp_i\right]^2}$$

$$-\frac{\left[\int_0^{\bar{p}(r)} f(p_i)dp_i\right](1+r)\int_0^{\bar{p}(r)} p_i f(p_i)dp_i}{\left[\int_0^{\bar{p}(r)} f(p_i)dp_i\right]^2}$$

$$= \frac{\left[\int_0^{\bar{p}(r)} p_i f(p_i)dp_i + (1+r)\bar{p}'(r)\bar{p}f(\bar{p})\right]\int_0^{\bar{p}(r)} f(p_i)dp_i}{\left[\int_0^{\bar{p}(r)} f(p_i)dp_i\right]^2}$$

$$-\frac{\bar{p}'(r)f(\bar{p})(1+r)\int_0^{\bar{p}(r)} p_i f(p_i)dp_i}{\left[\int_0^{\bar{p}(r)} f(p_i)dp_i\right]^2}$$

$$= \frac{\int_0^{\bar{p}(r)} p_i f(p_i)dp_i}{\int_0^{\bar{p}(r)} f(p_i)dp_i} - \frac{(1+r)\int_0^{\bar{p}(r)} p_i f(p_i)dp_i \bar{p}'(r)f(\bar{p})}{\left[\int_0^{\bar{p}(r)} f(p_i)dp_i\right]^2} + \frac{(1+r)\bar{p}'(r)\bar{p}f(\bar{p})}{\int_0^{\bar{p}(r)} f(p_i)dp_i},$$

using the Leibniz's rule (see Exercise 1).

EXERCISE 4 ADVERSE SELECTION AND CREDIT MARKET

(4b) Without knowing the types of borrowers, the bank can only offer loans with a uniform gross rate R. Whether it is accepted or not depends on borrowers' participation constraints, or, $p(G-R)\geq 0$ (PC-G), $q(B-R)\geq 0$ (PC-B).

For the range $R \in (-\infty, G]$ Both PC-G and PC-B hold so that the bank gets both types of borrowers. To maximize its profit, the bank should set $R=G$, and the expected return is $\Pi(G)=[\alpha p+(1-\alpha)q]G-1$. However, whether the bank is indeed willing to offer the loans depends on its participation constraint, i.e., $\Pi(G)\geq 0$. Then

1. If $\Pi(G) \geq 0$, the bank offers loan contracts $R = G$ and both types of borrowers accept;
2. If $\Pi(G) < 0$, the market is idle.

For the range $R \in (G, B)$ Only PC-B holds so that the bank only gets bad borrowers. The bank's optimal rate is $R = B$ with profit $\Pi(B) = (1-\alpha)(qB-1) > 0$. The bank's participation constraint holds so that the contract is valid.

For the range $R \in (B, +\infty)$ Neither PC-G nor PC-B holds. Nobody accepts the contract and the market is idle.

(4c) The only candidates are $R = G$ and $R = B$. Which one to choose depends on (1) the bank's participation constraint holds; (2) the bank makes higher profit. Suppose $\Pi(G) \geq 0$, the bank can offer either $R = G$ or $R = B$. If $R = G$, $\Pi(G) = [\alpha p + (1-\alpha)q]G - 1$; if $R = B$, $\Pi(B) = (1-\alpha)(qB-1)$. The bank offers $R = G$ if $\Pi(G) > \Pi(B)$, or, $\alpha(pG - 1) > (1-\alpha)q(B-G)$—the gain from including the good borrowers outweighs the loss from the information rent retained by the bad borrowers.

(4d) Again the bank has to offer uniform R. Borrowers participation constraints are $p(G-R) - W \leq 0$ (PC-G) and $q(B-R) - W \leq 0$ (PC-B), or, $R \leq \frac{pG-W}{p} = G - \frac{W}{q} = R_1$ (PC-G) and $R \leq \frac{qB-W}{q} = B - \frac{W}{q} = R_2$ (PC-B). The bank's participation constraint is $\Pi \geq 0$ (PC-Bank). Assumption $W < \frac{B-G}{\frac{1}{q}-\frac{1}{p}}$ implies $R_1 < R_2$:

For the range $R \in (-\infty, R_1)$ Both PC-G and PC-B hold so that the bank gets both types of borrowers. To maximize its profit, the bank should set $R_1 = G - \frac{W}{p}$, and the expected return is $\Pi(R_1) = [\alpha p + (1-\alpha)q]\left(G - \frac{W}{p}\right) - (1-W)$. However, whether the bank is indeed willing to offer the loans depends on its participation constraint, i.e., $\Pi \geq 0$. Then

1. If $\Pi(R_1) \geq 0$, the bank offers loan contracts $R = R_1$ and both types of borrowers accept;
2. If $\Pi(R_1) < 0$, the market is idle.

For the range $R \in (R_1, R_2]$ Only PC-B holds so that the bank only gets bad borrowers. The bank's optimal rate is R_2 with profit $\Pi(R_2) = (1-\alpha)(qB-1) > 0$. The bank's participation constraint holds so that the contract is valid.

For the range $R \in (R_2, +\infty)$ Neither PC-G nor PC-B holds. Nobody accepts the contract and the market is idle.

Assume that PC-Bank holds. The bank chooses R_1 if $\Pi(R_1) > \Pi(R_2)$, or, $\alpha(pG-1) + (1-\alpha)\left(1-\frac{q}{p}\right)W > (1-\alpha)q(B-G)$. Compared with the condition in **(4c)**, additional $(1-\alpha)\left(1-\frac{q}{p}\right)W > 0$ makes this inequality more likely to hold. The reason is, with borrowers' own stakes in the projects, the cost of failure is partially borne by the borrowers instead of totally by the bank. This makes the bank more likely to offer a lower rate R to attract all borrowers, with lower failure cost for the bad ones.

EXERCISE 5 COSTLY STATE VERIFICATION AND BANKING EQUILIBRIUM

(5a) An entrepreneur's expected profit is $p[R_H - (1+r)(k-W)]$, and a bank's expected profit is

$$p(1+r)(k-W) + (1-p)(R_L - C) - (1+\delta)(k-W).$$

(5b) Zero profit implies that

$$p(1+r)(k-W) + (1-p)(R_L - C) - (1+\delta)(k-W) = 0, \quad (A.4)$$

so that $r = \frac{1+\delta}{p} - \frac{(1-p)(R_L - C)}{p(k-W)} - 1$, and $\frac{\partial r}{\partial W} < 0$. Higher initial wealth reduces lending rate.

(5c) An entrepreneur is only willing to borrow if $p[R_H - (1+r)(k-W)] \geq (1+\delta)W$. Combining with $r = \frac{1+\delta}{p} - \frac{(1-p)(R_L - C)}{p(k-W)} - 1$, rearrange to get $E[R] - (1+\delta)k - (1-p)C \geq 0$ (participation constraint, PC-E).

(5d) Consider the alternative choices of an entrepreneur's reporting:

- It does not make sense for the entrepreneur to always report R_H, despite the true return;
- If she is honest and always reports the truth, her expected profit is $p[R_H - (1+r)(k-W)]$, and her bank makes a non-negative profit;
- However, "all entrepreneurs being honest" cannot be equilibrium, as one can deviate unilaterally and always report R_L, to earn a profit $p(R_H - R_L)$ that is higher than $p[R_H - (1+r)(k-W)]$, leaving her bank always suffering a loss;
- Therefore, the only equilibrium is to always report R_L, and knowing this, no bank is willing to lend.

(5e) Obviously, an entrepreneur has no incentive to be honest in the second period, so that her bank always receives R_L, should a second period loan is granted. If the entrepreneur is honest in the first period, the bank's expected profit is

$$-(1+\delta)(k-W) + (1-p)R_L + p(1+r)(k-W) + p\left[R_L - (1+\delta)(k-W)\right],$$

loan rate r can then be solved by zero profit condition,

$$r = \frac{(1+p)(1+\delta)}{p} - \frac{R_L}{p(k-W)} - 1. \tag{A.5}$$

However, to ensure that the entrepreneur is indeed honest in the first period, her profit from truth telling must exceed that from lying, if the true return is R_H, i.e.,

$$R_H - (1+r)(k-W) + pR_H + (1-p)R_L - R_L \geq R_H - R_L,$$

$$\frac{p(R_H - R_L) + R_L}{k-W} \geq 1+r,$$

so that the entrepreneur's rent from truth-telling (period 2's continuation return) must exceed loan interest, in which r is determined by (A.5).

CHAPTER 4

EXERCISE 2 TRANSACTION COST, MONOPOLISTIC COMPETITION, AND BANK ENTRY, BASED ON SALOP (1979)

(2a) The distance between two banks is $\frac{1}{N}$, for any depositor living between two neighboring banks, the maximum travel distance x is $\frac{1}{2N}$.

Total transaction cost of all depositors is thus $2ND\int_0^{\frac{1}{2N}} cx\,dx = \frac{cD}{4N}$, and banks' total fixed cost is fN.

(2b) The social planner's problem is $\min_N C = fN + \frac{cD}{4N}$, first-order condition $\frac{\partial C}{\partial N} = 0$ implies that the optimal $N^* = \frac{1}{2}\left(\frac{cD}{f}\right)^{\frac{1}{2}}$.

(2c) As Figure A.2 shows, with traveling distance $x_{i,i+1}$ to bank i, the marginal depositor is indifferent so that $r_D^i - cx_{i,i+1} = r_D^{i+1} - c\left(\frac{1}{N} - x_{i,i+1}\right)$, i.e., $x_{i,i-1} = \frac{1}{2N} + \frac{r_D^i - r_D^{i-1}}{2c}$. Applying the same method, for the marginal depositor between bank i and bank $i-1$, her distance to bank i is $x_{i,i-1} = \frac{1}{2N} + \frac{r_D^i - r_D^{i-1}}{2c}$. Total deposits for bank i are provided by depositors along $x_{i,i+1}$ and $x_{i,i-1}$, i.e., $D_i = D(x_{i,i+1} + x_{i,i-1}) = D\left(\frac{1}{N} + \frac{2r_D^i - r_D^{i+1} - r_D^{i-1}}{2c}\right)$.

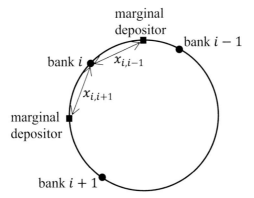

Figure A.2 Marginal depositors and suppliers of deposits

(2d) Bank i's problem is $\max_{r_D^i} \Pi_i = D(r - r_D^i)\left(\frac{1}{N} + \frac{2r_D^i - r_D^{i+1} - r_D^{i-1}}{2c}\right)$, first-order condition $\frac{\partial \Pi_i}{\partial r_D^i} = 0$ implies that $r - r_D^i = \frac{c}{N} + \frac{2r_D^i - r_D^{i+1} - r_D^{i-1}}{2}$. Under symmetry, $r_D = r - \frac{c}{N}$, and each bank's profit $\Pi = \frac{cD}{N^2}$.

(2e) Free-entry implies that $\Pi = \frac{cD}{N^2} = f$ so that $N = \left(\frac{cD}{f}\right)^{\frac{1}{2}} > N^*$.

EXERCISE 3 FINANCIAL LIBERALIZATION AND DYNAMIC MORAL HAZARD, BASED ON HELLMANN ET AL. (2000)

(3a) Profit on deposits is $m_P(r_i, k) = \alpha(1+k) - \rho k - r_i$ (prudent) or $m_G(r_i, k) = \theta[\gamma(1+k) - r_i] - \rho k$ (gambling).

(3b) No gambling condition implies that the payoff from one-period gambling is dominated by the payoff from staying prudent, i.e., $\pi_P(r_i, \mathbf{r}_{-i}, k) + \delta V_P(r_i, \mathbf{r}_{-i}, k) \geq \pi_G(r_i, \mathbf{r}_{-i}, k) + \theta \delta V_P(r_i, \mathbf{r}_{-i}, k)$ with $V_P(r_i, \mathbf{r}_{-i}, k) = \frac{1}{1-\delta} \pi_P(r_i, \mathbf{r}_{-i}, k)$. Solve to get $r \leq \frac{(1-\delta)(1+k)(\alpha - \theta \gamma)}{1-\theta} + \delta[\alpha(1+k) - \rho k] \equiv \hat{r}(k)$. The optimal r_P is achieved by $\max_{r_P} \pi_P(r_P, \mathbf{r}_P, k) = m_P(r_P, k) D(r_P, \mathbf{r}_P)$. First order condition requires that $\frac{\partial \pi_P}{\partial r_P} = \frac{\partial m_P}{\partial r_P} D(r_P, \mathbf{r}_P) + m_P(r_P, k)\frac{\partial D}{\partial r_P} = -D(r_P, \mathbf{r}_P) + m_P(r_P, k)\frac{\partial D}{\partial r_P} = 0$. Rearrange to get $m_P(r_P, k) = \frac{D(r_P, \mathbf{r}_P)}{\frac{\partial D(r_P, \mathbf{r}_P)}{\partial r_P}}$. Similarly, for gambling banks, $m_G(r_G, k) = \frac{D(r_G, \mathbf{r}_P)}{\frac{\partial D(r_G, \mathbf{r}_P)}{\partial r_G}}$.

(3c) Starting from $m_P(r_P, k) = \frac{D(r_P, \mathbf{r}_P)}{\frac{\partial D(r_P, \mathbf{r}_P)}{\partial r_P}}$, defining $\epsilon = \frac{\partial D(r_P, \mathbf{r}_P)}{\partial r_P} \frac{r_P}{D(r_P, \mathbf{r}_P)}$, rearrange to get $r_P = \frac{\epsilon}{1+\epsilon}[\alpha(1+k) - \rho k] \equiv f(\alpha, \rho, k, \epsilon)$. Similarly, one can get $r_G = \frac{\epsilon}{1+\theta\epsilon}[\theta\gamma(1+k) - \rho k]$.

(3d) Under r_P, the bank's franchise value is $V_P(r_P, \mathbf{r}_P, k) = \frac{1}{1-\delta} m_P(r_P, k) D(r_P, \mathbf{r}_P)$, and $\frac{\partial V_P}{\partial k} = \frac{D(r_P, \mathbf{r}_P)}{1-\delta}(\alpha - \rho) < 0$ (by applying the Envelope Theorem[3] on the value function V_P) implies that the optimal capital ratio to maximize its franchise value is $k = 0$.

(3e) As $\frac{\partial r_P}{\partial k} = \frac{\epsilon}{1+\epsilon}(\alpha - \rho) < 0$, r_P is declining with k. One can also see that $\frac{\partial r_G}{\partial k} = \frac{\epsilon}{1+\theta\epsilon}(\theta\gamma - \rho) < \frac{\partial r_P}{\partial k} < 0$. For $\hat{r}(k) = \frac{(1-\delta)(1+k)(\alpha - \theta\gamma)}{1-\theta} + \delta[\alpha(1+k) - \rho k]$, $\frac{\partial \hat{r}(k)}{\partial k} = \frac{(1-\delta)(\alpha - \theta\gamma)}{1-\theta} + \delta(\alpha - \rho)$, the sign is ambiguous. If $\frac{\partial \hat{r}(k)}{\partial k} < 0$, $\delta > \frac{\alpha - \theta\gamma}{\rho(1-\theta) + \theta(\alpha - \gamma)}$.

SOLUTIONS TO SELECTED EXERCISES

(3f) See Figure A.3. Gambling is the dominant strategy above $\hat{r}(k)$, and being prudent is the dominant strategy below $\hat{r}(k)$; the thick gray line thus delineates banks' optimal r. As is shown in (3e), $r_G(k)$ is steeper than $r_P(k)$, and the two lines cross at the same point on $\hat{r}(k)$, as at this point a bank is indifferent between being prudent and gambling. Therefore, for any $k > \underline{k}$, being prudent is an equilibrium outcome.

(3g) The outcomes under two policies are illustrated in Figure A.3. Policy 2 is obviously optimal. Although depositors are indifferent under the same deposit rate, banks have higher franchise value under the lower capital ratio.

EXERCISE 4 IMPERFECT SCREENING AND CREDIT RATING, BASED ON SHAFFER (1998)

(4a) The average loan loss rate based on common credit scores is

$$\frac{\zeta(H|\mathcal{H})a(1-\pi_H)+(1-\zeta(L|\mathcal{L}))(1-a)(1-\pi_L)}{\zeta(H|\mathcal{H})a+(1-\zeta(L|\mathcal{L}))(1-a)}.$$

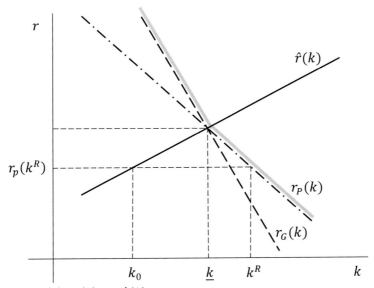

Figure A.3 $r_P(k)$, $r_G(k)$, and $\hat{r}(k)$

The minimum $\zeta(H|\mathcal{H})/\zeta(L|\mathcal{L})$ that achieves the same loan loss rate is given by

$$\frac{\zeta(H|\mathcal{H})}{1-\zeta(L|\mathcal{L})} = \frac{1-(1-p(H|\mathcal{H}))^n}{1-p(L|\mathcal{L})^n},$$

solve to get $\zeta(H|\mathcal{H}) = \zeta(L|\mathcal{L}) \approx 0.532$.

(4b) $\zeta(H|\mathcal{H}) = \zeta(L|\mathcal{L}) \approx 0.535$.

(4c) $\zeta(H|\mathcal{H}) = \zeta(L|\mathcal{L}) \approx 0.897$. Credit scores are likely to be preferred if default risk is higher and/or loss from default is higher.

CHAPTER 5

EXERCISE 1 MORTGAGE-BACKED SECURITIES

(1a) The probability that both loans are repaid is p^2, the probability that both loans default is $(1-p)^2$, and the probability that only one loan defaults is $1 - p^2 - (1-p)^2$. Therefore, the expected return of the senior tranche is

$$\left[p^2 + 1 - p^2 - (1-p)^2\right]R = 1 - (1-p)^2 = (2-p)pR,$$

and the expected return of the junior tranche is $p^2 R$.

(1b) The probability that both loans are repaid is $(1+\epsilon)p^2$, the probability that both loans default is $(1+\epsilon)(1-p)^2$, and the probability that only one loan defaults is $1-(1+\epsilon)p^2-(1+\epsilon)(1-p)^2$. Therefore, the expected return of the senior tranche is

$$\left[(1+\epsilon)p^2 + 1 - (1+\epsilon)p^2 - (1+\epsilon)(1-p)^2\right]R = 1-(1+\epsilon)(1-p)^2 < 1-(1-p)^2,$$

and the expected return of the junior tranche is $(1+\epsilon)p^2 R > p^2 R$.

EXERCISE 4 ORIGINATE-TO-DISTRIBUTE AND THE LIMIT OF ARBITRAGE, BASED ON SHLEIFER AND VISHNY (2010)

(4a) By (5.11), banks' demand for long assets is

$$D_b(P_2) = Nd - Nd\left(\frac{1-P_2}{P_2}\frac{1-h}{h}\right)$$

Together with market clearing condition, solve for P_2 as $P_2 = \frac{h+hd-d-h\sigma}{h-d}$. Condition $h > d > \sigma$ is needed to ensure $P_2 > 0$.

(4b) From the result for P_2, one can see that $\frac{\partial P_2}{\partial \sigma} < 0$. A demand shock from noise traders makes P_2 fall.

(4c) From the result for P_2, one can see that $\frac{\partial^2 P_2}{\partial \sigma \partial h} = \frac{d}{(d-h)^2} > 0$. Sensitivity of price to demand shock is higher when haircut is small.

CHAPTER 6

EXERCISE 3 STRATEGIC BANK OPACITY, BASED ON WAGNER (2007)

(3a) i. Investors will require R_H/R_L for state H/L. Investors' return is thus R_H/R_L for state H/L, and banker's return is 0. **ii.** Now investors cannot make any state-contingent request.

- Suppose investors require R_H: they will be fully repaid in state H but they have to run on the bank in state L. Their expected return is $pR_H + (1-p)\beta R_L$, and banker's expected return is 0;
- Suppose investors require R_L: they will be fully repaid in both states so that their expected return is $pR_L + (1-p)R_L$, and banker's expected return is $p(R_H - R_L) > 0$.

(3b) Investors will request R_L if $pR_L + (1-p)R_L > pR_H + (1-p)\beta R_L$, or, when $p < \frac{(1-\beta)R_L}{R_H - \beta R_L}$. It is straightforward to see that $\frac{(1-\beta)R_L}{R_H - \beta R_L} < \frac{(1-\beta)R_L}{R_L - \beta R_L} = 1$ so that such p exists. Therefore, in $t=0$, the banker will choose an opaque project with $p < \frac{(1-\beta)R_L}{R_H - \beta R_L}$, inducing the investors to request R_L and making a strictly positive expected return $p(R_H - R_L) > 0$.

(3c) Given the result in **(3b)**, the likelihood of bank run in $t=2$ is thus 0. As the banker's expected return is increasing with p, her optimal choice is setting $p \to \frac{(1-\beta)R_L}{R_H - \beta R_L}$.

CHAPTER 8

EXERCISE 1 OVERBORROWING AND SYSTEMIC RISK, BASED ON BIANCHI (2011)

(1a) The household's optimization problem is

$$\max_{\{c_0^T, c_0^N, b_1, c_1^T\}} u = \ln c_0^T + \ln c_0^N + \ln c_1^T,$$

$$\text{s.t.} \quad c_0^T + p_0^N c_0^N + b_1 = b_0 + y_0^T + p_0^N y_0^N,$$

$$c_1^T = b_1 + y_1^T,$$

$$b_1 \geq -\kappa \left(y_0^T + p_0^N y_0^N \right).$$

(1b) i. Set up the Lagrangian for the optimization problem as $\mathcal{L} = \ln c_0^T + \ln c_0^N + \ln c_1^T + \lambda_0 \left(b_0 + y_0^T + p_0^N y_0^N - c_0^T - p_0^N c_0^N - b_1 \right) + \lambda_1 \left(b_1 + y_1^T - c_1^T \right) + \nu \left[b_1 + \kappa \left(y_0^T + p_0^N y_0^N \right) \right]$, first-order conditions yield $\frac{c_0^T}{c_0^N} = p_0^N$. As non-tradables are not used for bond transactions, they have to be consumed, i.e., $c_0^N = y_0^N$, and $\frac{c_0^T}{y_0^N} = p_0^N$. **ii.** First-order conditions from the Lagrangian yield $\frac{1}{c_0^T} = \frac{1}{c_1^T} + \nu$. The value of ν is the shadow price of bonds, by Kuhn-Tucker condition

$$\nu \begin{cases} = 0 & \text{if } b_1 > -\kappa \left(y_0^T + p_0^N y_0^N \right) \\ \geq & \text{if } b_1 = -\kappa \left(y_0^T + p_0^N y_0^N \right). \end{cases}$$

Therefore, if the borrowing constraint is not binding, $\nu = 0$ and $\frac{1}{c_0^T} = \frac{1}{c_1^T}$ or $c_0^T = c_1^T$; if the borrowing constraint is binding, $\nu \geq 0$ and $\frac{1}{c_0^T} \geq \frac{1}{c_1^T}$ or $c_0^T \leq c_1^T$.

(1c) i. If the borrowing constraint is not binding, $c_0^T = c_1^T$. Combining budget constraints $c_0^T + p_0^N c_0^N + b_1 = b_0 + y_0^T + p_0^N y_0^N$ and $c_1^T = b_1 + y_1^T$ and using the fact that $c_0^N = y_0^N$, one can get $c_0^T = \frac{b_0 + y_0^T + y_1^T}{2}$.

That the borrowing constraint is not binding means $b_1 > -\kappa \left(y_0^T + p_0^N y_0^N \right)$, combing the budget constraints and the value of c_0^T to get

SOLUTIONS TO SELECTED EXERCISES

$b_1 = b_0 + y_0^T - c_0^T > -\kappa\left(y_0^T + p_0^N y_0^N\right) = -\kappa\left(y_0^T + c_0^T\right)$, rearrange to get $b_0 > \frac{-(3\kappa+1)y_0^T + (1-\kappa)y_1^T}{1+\kappa}$. That is, the borrowing constraint is not binding if the household does not start with too much debt. **ii.** When the borrowing constraint is binding, combine the binding borrowing constraint with the budget constraints and get $c_0^T = \frac{b_0 + (1+\kappa)y_0^T}{1-\kappa}$. In this case, $b_1 = b_0 + y_0^T - c_0^T = -\frac{\kappa b_0 + 2\kappa y_0^T}{1-\kappa}$.

(1d) i. Use the result from exercise **(1c) i.**, $c_0^T(\bar{y}) - c_0^T(\bar{y}-1) = \frac{1}{2}$. **ii.** Use the result from exercise **(1c) ii.**, $c_0^T(\bar{y}) - c_0^T(\bar{y}-1) = \frac{1+\kappa}{1-\kappa} > 1 > \frac{1}{2}$.

EXERCISE 2 VALUE-AT-RISK AND LEVERAGE CYCLE, BASED ON SHIN (2010)

(2a) It is a reverse case of Shin model in Section 8.5, as Figure A.4 shows. The new equilibrium corresponds to lower bank assets $\tilde{q}_A$ and asset price $\tilde{P}$.

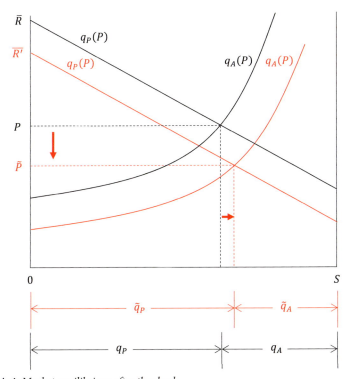

Figure A.4 *Market equilibrium after the shock*

APPENDIX

CHAPTER 9

EXERCISE 4 SWAP AGREEMENT AND DEMAND FOR RESERVES, BASED ON BRÄUNING AND IVASHINA (2020)

(4a) i. The firm's optimization problem is $\max_{\hat{H}} \ln(W - \hat{H}) + \frac{\ln(S_0 \hat{H})}{F_0}$, and first-order condition yields $\hat{H} = \frac{W}{1+F_0}$. **ii.** Using covered interest parity (9.38), rewrite $\hat{H}$ as $\hat{H} = \frac{1+r^f}{1+r^f + (1+r^h)S_0} W$, or, in home currency, $H = S_0 \hat{H} = \frac{1+r^f}{1+r^f + (1+r^h)S_0} WS_0$.

(4b) i. Rewrite $\hat{H}$ as $\hat{H} = \frac{1}{1 + \frac{1+r^h}{1+r^f} S_0} W$. Given that $\frac{1+r^h}{1+r^f} = 1 + \Delta r$ (taking logarithm on both sides, using $\lim_{x \to 0} \ln(1+x) = x$, it becomes $r^h - r^f = \Delta r$), $\hat{H} = \frac{1}{1+(1+\Delta r)S_0} W$. Then $\frac{\partial \hat{H}}{\partial \Delta r} = -\frac{S_0 W}{[1+(1+\Delta r)S_0]^2} < 0$. Given that $H = S_0 \hat{H}$, $\frac{\partial H}{\partial \Delta r} < 0$, too. **ii.** Differentiating the bank's budget constraint $H + U = (1+r^f)R^f + f(L^f)$ with respect to Δr, $\frac{\partial R^f}{\partial \Delta r} = \frac{1}{1+r^f}\left[\frac{\partial H}{\partial \Delta r} - f'(L^f)\frac{\partial L^f}{\partial \Delta r}\right] < 0$, using the results from **i.** and (9.41)/(9.42). Higher interest rate differential makes it less attractive to hold foreign reserves. **iii.** Differentiate budget constraint (9.20), $D^h + E = R^h + L^h + S_0 R^f + S_0 L^f$, with respect to Δr,

$$\frac{\partial R^h}{\partial \Delta r} = \frac{\partial D^h}{\partial \Delta r} - \frac{\partial L^h}{\partial \Delta r} - S_0 \frac{\partial L^f}{\partial \Delta r} - S_0 \frac{\partial R^f}{\partial \Delta r} > 0$$

—using (9.35), $\frac{\partial D^h}{\partial \Delta r} = \frac{\partial D^h}{\partial r^h} > 0$, and the fact that differentiating (9.18), $k(L^h + S_0 L^f) + k' S_0 U \le E$, leads to $\frac{\partial L^h}{\partial \Delta r} + S_0 \frac{\partial L^f}{\partial \Delta r} = 0$ when the capital constraint is binding. Higher interest rate differential makes it more attractive to hold home reserves.

CHAPTER 10

EXERCISE 1 CONTESTABLE ELECTION AND CREDIT CYCLES, BASED ON ENGLMAIER AND STOWASSER (2017)

(1a) Bank's efficient credit supply is defined as $\max_{L_t} \Pi_t(L_t) - C_t(L_t)$, and first-order condition yields $\Pi'_t(L_t) - C'_t(L_t) = 0$. A totally benevolent social planner's problem is

$$\max_{L_t} \psi(L_t) + \Pi_t(L_t) - C_t(L_t),$$

first-order condition yields $\Pi'_t(L_t) - C'_t(L_t) = -\psi'(L_t) < 0$, meaning L_t is higher than bank's solution.

(1b) A semi benevolent social planner's problem in election year is

$$\max_{L_t} \psi(L_t) + \iota_t \phi\big(\xi\big(\psi(L_t)\big)\big) + \Pi_t(L_t) - C_t(L_t),$$

with $\iota_t = 1$. First-order condition yields

$$\Pi'_t(L_t) - C'_t(L_t) = -\psi'(L_t) - \phi'(\xi)\xi'(\psi)\psi'(L_t) < -\psi'(L_t), \quad \text{(A.6)}$$

meaning L_t is higher than totally benevolent social planner's solution.

(1c) Rewrite (A.6) as

$$\Pi'_t(L_t) + \psi'(L_t) + \phi'(\xi)\xi'(\psi)\psi'(L_t) = C'_t(L_t),$$

that is, marginal cost $C'_t(L_t)$ increases with election induced distortion

$$\phi'(\xi)\xi'(\psi)\psi'(L_t)$$

which is the highest around the neighborhood of the threshold.

EXERCISE 2 PARTISAN CREDIT CYCLES, BASED ON ALESINA (1987) AND ALESINA (1988)

(2a) Party i's optimal decision problem is

$$\max_{l_t^i} \mathcal{L}_t^i = \frac{1}{2}(\delta_t^i - \bar{\delta}^i)^2 + \frac{\theta^i}{2}(l_t^i - \bar{l}^i)^2 + \beta\left[\frac{1}{2}(\delta_{t+1}^i - \bar{\delta}^i)^2 + \frac{\theta^i}{2}(l_{t+1}^i - \bar{l}^i)^2\right],$$

s.t. $\delta_t^i = l_t^i - l_t^e$.

Solve to get $(1+\theta^i)l_t^i = \bar{\delta}^i + \theta^i \bar{l}^i + l_t^e$. Given that in equilibrium $l_t^e = l_{t+1}^e = E_t[l_{t+1}^i]$, the equilibrium condition can be rewritten as $l_t^i = \bar{l}^i + \frac{\bar{\delta}^i}{\theta^i}$.

(2b) Solve the same optimization problem as in **(2a)** with an additional constraint $l_t^e = p^L l_t^L + (1-p^L) l_t^R$. Solve l_t^L and l_t^R simultaneously from

$$\begin{cases} \{l_t^L - [p^L l_t^L + (1-p^L) l_t^R] - \bar{\delta}^L\}(1-p^L) + \theta^L(l_t^L - \bar{l}^L) = 0, \\ \{l_t^R - [p^L l_t^L + (1-p^L) l_t^R] - \bar{\delta}^R\}p^L + \theta^R(l_t^R - \bar{l}^R) = 0. \end{cases}$$

CHAPTER 11

EXERCISE 1 ADVERSE SELECTION, "BUYERS' STRIKE", AND MARKET FREEZE

(1a) $p=\frac{1}{2}$, which attracts both good and bad sellers. In expectation on having both types of sellers, buyers are willing to pay $p=\frac{1}{2}$.

(1b) $p=0$, which attracts only bad sellers. In expectation on having bad sellers only, buyers are willing to pay $p=0$.

(1c) $p=0$, which attracts only bad sellers, and good sellers are driven out of the market. In expectation on having bad sellers only, buyers are willing to pay $p=0$.

EXERCISE 2 ILLIQUID BANKS AND PRIVATE LIQUIDITY INSURANCE, BASED ON DIAMOND AND RAJAN (2011)

(2a) If an investor buys in $t=0$ at P_0 for each unit of face value, the gross return is $\frac{1}{P_0}$. If she decides to wait and buy in $t=1$ at P_1, the expected gross return in $t=0$ is $q\frac{1}{P_1}+(1-q)$. If she is indifferent in the timing of buying, it must be that $P_0 = \frac{1}{\frac{q}{P_1}+1-q}$.

(2b) Given that a bank sells part of securities, she only liquidates a risky asset if one piece of liquidated asset yields no lower gross return than that from selling one piece of security, i.e., $l \geq P_1 Z$. Known that $l \sim U[0,Z]$, the probability of a risky asset being sold is $\text{Prob}(l \geq P_1 Z) = \frac{Z - P_1 Z}{Z} = 1 - P_1$. The mean gross return from sold risky assets is $E(l|l \geq ZP_1) = \frac{Z + P_1 Z}{2}$. To fulfill the depositors liquidity demand, η_1 must be so high that

$$\eta_1 \beta Z P_1 + (1-\beta)\text{Prob}(l \geq P_1 Z)E(l|l \geq ZP_1) = fD,$$

$$\eta_1 = \frac{fD}{\beta Z P_1} - \frac{(1-\beta)(1-P_1^2)}{2\beta P_1}.$$

(2c) Given that η_0 of security is sold at $t=0$, when a shock takes place at $t=1$, the bank can liquidate any risky asset with liquidation value not below P_1 so that she has no incentive to sell securities.

Known that $l \sim U[0,Z]$, the probability of a risky asset being sold is $\text{Prob}(l \geq P_1 Z) = \frac{Z - P_1 Z}{Z} = 1 - P_1$. The mean gross return from sold risky assets is $E(l \mid l \geq ZP_1) = \frac{Z + P_1 Z}{2}$. To fulfill the depositors liquidity demand, η_0 must be so high that

$$\eta_0 \beta Z P_0 + (1-\beta) \text{Prob}(l \geq P_1 Z) E(l \mid l \geq ZP_1) = fD,$$

$$\eta_0 = \frac{fD}{\beta Z P_0} - \frac{(1-\beta)(1-P_1^2)}{2\beta P_0}.$$

(2d) If the bank sells η_1 security in $t=1$, the profit in $t=2$ is

$$\Pi(\eta_1) = q\left[\beta(1-\eta_1)Z + (1-\beta)P_1 Z - (1-f)D\right] + (1-q)(Z-D).$$

If the bank sells η_0 security at $t=0$, the profit in $t=2$ is

$$\Pi(\eta_0) = (1-\eta_0)\beta Z + q\left[(1-\beta)P_1 Z - (1-f)D\right] + (1-q)\left[(1-\beta)Z + \beta \eta_0 Z P_0 - D\right].$$

It's easy to show that $\Pi(\eta_1) = \Pi(\eta_0)$ under $P_0 = \frac{1}{\frac{q}{P_1} + 1 - q}$. The bank is indeed indifferent.

EXERCISE 4 EXCESS MATURITY TRANSFORMATION AND SYSTEMIC LIQUIDITY RISK, BASED ON KASHYAP AND STEIN (2012)

(4a) A bank is distressed if its interim dividend is below αI. Given the interim dividend is uniformly distributed over $[0,K]$, the probability that the bank is distressed, conditional on crisis state, is $\frac{\alpha I}{K}$. The social planner's problem is to maximize a representative bank's profit Π by choosing I

$$\max_I \Pi = I(R - r + \alpha \Delta) - \frac{p\alpha IcI}{K}.$$

Solve the first-order condition $\frac{\partial \Pi}{\partial I} = 0$ for optimal investment

$$I^* = (R - r + \alpha \Delta)\frac{K}{2p\alpha c}.$$

(4b) A bank's problem is to maximize its profit Π by choosing I, taking the other banks' average $\bar{I}$ as given

$$\max_I \Pi = I(R-r+\alpha\Delta) - \frac{p\alpha Ic\bar{I}}{K}$$

Symmetricity implies that in equilibrium $\bar{I} = I^B$. Solve the first-order condition $\frac{\partial \Pi}{\partial I} = 0$ for optimal investment

$$I^B = (R-r+\alpha\Delta)\frac{K}{p\alpha c},$$

and $I^B > I^*$. This is because individual banks do not take other banks' decision into account, and the negative externality of I^B on the cost of distressed banks during crisis, $c\bar{I}$, implies over-investment in I^B.

(4c) With tax rate τ on short-term debt, a bank's problem becomes

$$\max_I \Pi = I[R-r+\alpha(\Delta-\tau)] - \frac{p\alpha Ic\bar{I}}{K}.$$

Solve the first-order condition $\frac{\partial \Pi}{\partial I} = 0$ for optimal investment

$$I^\tau = [R-r+\alpha(\Delta-\tau)]\frac{K}{p\alpha c},$$

and $I^\tau = I^*$ only if $\tau = \frac{R-r+\alpha\Delta}{2\alpha}$.

CHAPTER 12

EXERCISE 1 MORAL HAZARD, RISK-TAKING INCENTIVE OF BANKS, AND CAPITAL REGULATION

(1a) The payoff for the good project is $p_G(G-R)$, while for the bad is $p_B(B-R)$. The critical value of $\hat{R}$ makes $p_G(G-R) = p_B(B-R)$, solve to get $\hat{R} = \frac{p_G G - p_B B}{p_G - p_B}$.

(1b) To convince the depositors to participate in a bank running only the bad project, $p_B R \geq 1$. Depositors earn zero profit from deposits, $p_B R - 1 = 0$.

Therefore, $R = \frac{1}{p_B}$. Using the result of **(1a)**, a bank's running only the bad project implies $R > \hat{R} = \frac{p_G G - p_B B}{p_G - p_B}$, i.e., $\frac{1}{p_B} > \hat{R} = \frac{p_G G - p_B B}{p_G - p_B}$.

(1c) i. With capital holding k, to convince the depositors to participate in a bank running only the bad project, $p_B R \geq 1-k$; depositors earn zero profit from deposits, $p_B R - (1-k) = 0$. Therefore, $R = \frac{1-k}{p_B}$. A profit-maximizing bank running only the bad project chooses to $\max_k p_B \left(B - \frac{1-k}{p_B}\right) - (1+\rho)k$ which is linear in k. The optimal k is 0, call it k_B. **ii.** With capital holding k, to convince the depositors to participate in a bank running only the good project, $p_G R \geq 1-k$; depositors earn zero profit from deposits, $p_G R - (1-k) = 0$. Therefore, $R = \frac{1-k}{p_G}$. A profit-maximizing bank running only the good project chooses to $\max_k p_G \left(G - \frac{1-k}{p_G}\right) - (1+\rho)k$ which is linear in k. The optimal k should be as small as possible. On the other hand, the fact that the bank is only running the good project implies that $R \leq \hat{R}$. Now $\hat{R}$ is achieved under $p_G(G-R) - (1+\rho)k = p_B(B-R) - (1+\rho)k$, compute to get $\hat{R} = \frac{p_G G - p_B B}{p_G - p_B}$. Combining $R = \frac{1-k}{p_G}$ and $R \leq \hat{R}$ to get $k \geq 1 - \left(\frac{p_G G - p_B B}{p_G - p_B}\right) p_G$. The optimal capital level is thus $k = 1 - \left(\frac{p_G G - p_B B}{p_G - p_B}\right) p_G$, call it k_G. **iii.** A profit-maximizing bank will either (1) run the good project only, with k_G, or (2) run the bad project only, with k_B. If the bank chooses only the good project, she must earn higher profit, i.e., $p_G \left(G - \frac{1-k_G}{p_G}\right) - (1+\rho)k_G > p_B \left(B - \frac{1-k_B}{p_B}\right) - (1+\rho)k_B$. Solve to get $\rho < \frac{p_G G - p_B B}{k_G} = \frac{p_G G - p_B B}{1 - \left(\frac{p_G G - p_B B}{p_G - p_B}\right) p_G} = \hat{\rho}$, and $k^* = k_G = 1 - \left(\frac{p_G G - p_B B}{p_G - p_B}\right) p_G$.

EXERCISE 2 SKIN-IN-THE-GAME AND CAPITAL REQUIREMENT

(2a) The bank's expected profit from investing in project G is $\Pi_G = p_G \left[R_G - (1-k)R_D\right] - kR_E$, and the bank's expected profit from investing in project B is $\Pi_B = p_B \left[R_B - (1-k)R_D\right] - kR_E$. It is easy to see that

$$\Pi_G > R_E - (1-k)p_G R_D - kR_E = (1-k)(R_E - p_G R_D) > 0,$$

as long as $p_G R_G > R_E \geq R_D$.

(2b) Project B is more profitable than project G, even when project G is non-profitable if $\Pi_B > 0 > \Pi_G$, or,

$$p_B R_B - (1-k)p_B R_D > 0 > p_G R_G - (1-k)p_G R_D.$$

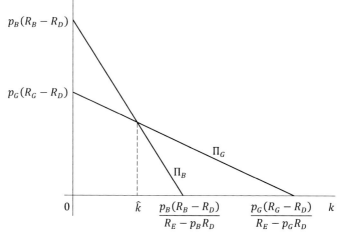

Figure A.5 *Incentive compatibility constraint and participation constraint*

(2c) Hint: to induce the bank to choose project G, using capital requirement k, the regulator has to meet (1) incentive compatibility constraint (IC), such that $\Pi_G > \Pi_B$, and (2) participation constraint (PC) such than $\Pi_G > 0$, as Figure A.5 illustrates, if $\Pi_G(k) > 0$, for any $0 \leq \hat{k} < k \leq 1$ (note that $\Pi_B(k)$ is steeper than $\Pi_G(k)$).

(2d) Hint: p_G and p_B now denote the probabilities of survival, and the bank's problem is now maximizing its expected value over the infinite time horizon, by choosing between two projects.

EXERCISE 3 EFFICIENT BANK CAPITALIZATION, BASED ON HOMAR AND VAN WIJNBERGEN (2017)

(3a) The bank chooses liquidation instead of rollover only if the expected return from the former is higher than that from the latter, i.e.,

$$R(1-q) + R\delta q - (1-k) > p[R - (1-k)],$$

implying that

$$k > 1 - \frac{R(1-p-q+\delta q)}{1-p} \equiv \underline{k}.$$

$\underline{k}$ increases with q and decreases with δ.

(3b) After the shock, the bank is only willing to liquidate bad projects if its actual equity ratio is no lower than the new threshold

$$\underline{k}' = 1 - \frac{R[1-p-(q+\epsilon)+\delta(q+\epsilon)]}{1-p} > \underline{k},$$

implying a minimum capital injection $\underline{k}' - \underline{k} = \frac{R\epsilon(1-\delta)}{1-p}$.

EXERCISE 4 BANK CAPITAL, DEPOSIT INSURANCE, AND BAILOUT

(4a) i. From the balance sheet at $t=0$, $L+P = D+E$. Given that $P = \phi D$, $D = \frac{L-E}{1-\phi}$. **ii.** The bank needs to be still solvent after paying insurance premiums, or, $E - P \geq 0$. Together with $L + P = D + E$ and $P = \phi D$, it's easy to see that $L^{max} = \frac{E}{\phi}$.

(4b) From the balance sheet at $t=1$, $\tilde{L} + \tilde{S} = D + \tilde{E}$. Then, if $\tilde{L} \geq D$, $\tilde{S} = 0$ and $\tilde{E} = \tilde{L} - D$; if $\tilde{L} < D$, $\tilde{S} = D - \tilde{L}$ and $\tilde{E} = 0$. Therefore, shareholders' return is

$$\tilde{\Pi} = \tilde{E} - E = \begin{cases} \tilde{L} - \dfrac{L-E}{1-\phi} - E & \text{if } \tilde{L} \geq D, \\ -E & \text{if } \tilde{L} < D. \end{cases}$$

(4c) The bank only needs bail out on the downside, or, $\tilde{L} = (R-\Delta)L$. No bailout condition implies that $\tilde{L} = (R-\Delta)L \geq D = \frac{L-E}{1-\phi}$, or, the maximum of loan supply is $L^C = \frac{E}{1-(1-\phi)(R-\Delta)} < L^{max}$, given that $R - \Delta < 1$, as illustrated in Figure A.6.

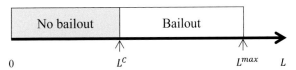

Figure A.6 Bank risk-taking and bailout

(4d) If $L \leq L^C$, there is no bailout so that shareholders' expected profit is

$$E[\Pi_1] = \frac{1}{2}(R+\Delta)L + \frac{1}{2}(R-\Delta)L - D - E = RL - \frac{L-E}{1-\phi} - E.$$

If $L > L^C$, there is bailout on the downside so that the bank's equity is wiped out in that case. Shareholders' expected profit is

$$E[\Pi_2] = \frac{1}{2}[(R+\Delta)L - D] - E = \frac{1}{2}\left[(R+\Delta)L - \frac{L-E}{1-\phi}\right] - E.$$

Obviously $E[\Pi_1]$ is independent on Δ, while $E[\Pi_2]$ is increasing with Δ, or, with insolvency risk limited liability encourages risk taking (and risk shifting in this case). In addition, the threshold $\frac{\partial L^C}{\partial \Delta} < 0$.

(4e) (1) If $L \leq L^C$, $\frac{\partial E[\Pi_1]}{\partial L} = R - \frac{1}{1-\phi}$, then if $R > \frac{1}{1-\phi}$, optimal $L = L^C$. Lower Δ increases L^C, hence increases $E[\Pi_1]$, implying the optimal $\Delta \to R-1$.

(2) If $L > L^C$, $\frac{\partial E[\Pi_2]}{\partial L} = \frac{1}{2}\left[R + \Delta - \frac{1}{1-\phi}\right]$, then if $R + \Delta > \frac{1}{1-\phi}$, optimal $L = L^{max}$. Given that $\frac{\partial E[\Pi_2]}{\partial \Delta} > 0$, optimal $\Delta \to 1$. Comparing $E[\Pi_1]|_{L^C, \Delta \to R-1}$ with $E[\Pi_2]|_{L^{max}, \Delta \to 1}$, it is easy to see that $E[\Pi_1]|_{L^C, \Delta \to R-1} < E[\Pi_2]|_{L^{max}, \Delta \to 1}$ as long as $R - 1 < \Delta < 1$. Choosing to be as risky as possible is always a dominant strategy. Since ROE of the riskiest bank is $\frac{R}{2\phi} - 1$: if $\phi > \frac{R}{2}$, no bank will be in operation; if $\phi \leq \frac{R}{2}$, all banks take the highest risk.

(4f) ϕ affects banks' risk exposure through loan supply, i.e., $\phi \uparrow$, $L^{max} \downarrow$.

NOTES

1 Implicit function is defined through equation $F(x,u) = 0$, $x, u \in \mathbb{R}$ and $u(x): \mathbb{R} \to \mathbb{R}$. Given $\frac{\partial F}{\partial u} \neq 0$, then

$$\frac{\partial u}{\partial x} = -\frac{\frac{\partial F}{\partial x}}{\frac{\partial F}{\partial u}}.$$

2 Differentiating function $\int_0^{x(t)} f(x,t)\,dx$ with respect to t gives

$$\frac{d}{dt}\int_0^{x(t)} f(x,t)\,dx = f(x(t),t)\,x'(t).$$

3 For a value function $m(a)$ that is defined as
$m(a) = \max_x f(x(a),a)$, the derivative of $m(a)$ with respect to a is given by

$$\frac{dm(a)}{da} = \frac{\partial f(x,a)}{\partial a}\bigg|_{x=x(a)}.$$

BIBLIOGRAPHY

Acemoglu, D., A. Ozdaglar, and A. Tahbaz-Salehi (2015): "Systemic risk and stability in financial networks," *American Economic Review*, 105, 564–608.

Acharya, V. V. (2009): "A theory of systemic risk and design of prudential bank regulation," *Journal of Financial Stability*, 5, 224–255.

Acharya, V. V., M. Crosignani, T. Eisert, and C. Eufinger (2020): "Zombie credit and (dis-) inflation: Evidence from Europe," Working Paper 27158, National Bureau of Economic Research.

Acharya, V. V., T. Eisert, C. Eufinger, and C. Hirsch (2019): "Whatever it takes: The real effects of unconventional monetary policy," *Review of Financial Studies*, 32, 3366–3411.

Acharya, V. V., D. Gale, and T. Yorulmazer (2011): "Rollover risk and market freezes," *Journal of Finance*, 66, 1177–1209.

Acharya, V. V. and O. Merrouche (2013): "Precautionary hoarding of liquidity and interbank markets: Evidence from the subprime crisis," *Review of Finance*, 17, 107–160.

Acharya, V. V., L. H. Pedersen, T. Philippon, and M. Richardson (2017): "Measuring systemic risk," *Review of Financial Studies*, 30, 2–47.

Admati, A. and M. Hellwig (2013): *The Bankers' New Clothes: What's Wrong with Banking and What to Do about It*, Princeton: Princeton University Press.

Adrian, T. and A. Ashcraft (2012): "Shadow banking: A review of the literature," *Federal Reserve Bank of New York Staff Report No. 580*.

Adrian, T. and M. K. Brunnermeier (2016): "CoVaR," *American Economic Review*, 106, 1705–1741.

Adrian, T. and H. S. Shin (2014): "Procyclical leverage and value-at-risk," *Review of Financial Studies*, 27, 373–403.

Affinito, M. and E. Tagliaferri (2010): "Why do (or did?) banks securitize their loans? Evidence from Italy," *Journal of Financial Stability*, 6, 189–202.

Agarwal, S., G. Amromin, I. Ben-David, S. Chomsisengphet, and D. D. Evanoff (2011): "The role of securitization in mortgage renegotiation," *Journal of Financial Economics*, 102, 559–578.

Agarwal, S., G. Amromin, I. Ben-David, and S. Dinç (2018): "The politics of foreclosures," *Journal of Finance*, 73, 2677–2717.

Agarwal, S., Y. Chang, and A. Yavas (2012): "Adverse selection in mortgage securitization," *Journal of Financial Economics*, 105, 640–660.

Agarwal, S., S. Chomsisengphet, C. Liu, C. Song, and N. S. Souleles (2018): "Benefits of relationship banking: Evidence from consumer credit markets," *Journal of Monetary Economics*, 96, 16–32.

Agarwal, S. and R. Hauswald (2010): "Distance and private information in lending," *Review of Financial Studies*, 23, 2757–2788.

Agarwal, S., B. Morais, C. Ruiz Ortega, and J. Zhang (2016): "The political economy of bank lending: Evidence from an emerging market," Policy Research Working Paper Series 7577, The World Bank.

Aiyar, S., C. W. Calomiris, and T. Wieladek (2016): "How does credit supply respond to monetary policy and bank minimum capital requirements?" *European Economic Review*, 82, 142–165.

Akerlof, G. A. (1970): "The market for lemons: Quality uncertainty and the market mechanism," *Quarterly Journal of Economics*, 84, 488–500.

Albertazzi, U., G. Eramo, L. Gambacorta, and C. Salleo (2015): "Asymmetric information in securitization: An empirical assessment," *Journal of Monetary Economics*, 71, 33–49.

Alesina, A. (1987): "Macroeconomic policy in a two-party system as a repeated game," *Quarterly Journal of Economics*, 102, 651–678.

——— (1988): "Credibility and policy convergence in a two-party system with rational voters," *American Economic Review*, 78, 796–805.

Allen, F. and D. Gale (1998): "Optimal financial crises," *Journal of Finance*, 53, 1245–1284.

——— (2000): "Financial contagion," *Journal of Political Economy*, 108, 1–33.

——— (2001): *Comparing Financial Systems*, Cambridge: The MIT Press.

——— (2007): *Understanding Financial Crises (Clarendon Lectures in Finance)*, New York: Oxford University Press.

Allen, F., J. Qian, and M. Qian (2005): "Law, finance, and economic growth in China," *Journal of Financial Economics*, 77, 57–116.

Altman, E. I. (1968): "Financial ratios, discriminant analysis and the prediction of corporate bankruptcy," *Journal of Finance*, 23, 589–609.

Angelini, P., S. Neri, and F. Panetta (2014): "The interaction between capital requirements and monetary policy," *Journal of Money, Credit and Banking*, 46, 1073–1112.

BIBLIOGRAPHY

Anginer, D., A. C. Bertay, R. J. Cull, A. Demirgüç-Kunt, and D. S. Mare (2019): "Bank regulation and supervision ten years after the Global Financial Crisis," Policy Research Working Paper Series 9044, The World Bank.

Anginer, D. and A. Demirgüç-Kunt (2019): "Bank runs and moral hazard: A review of deposit insurance," in *The Oxford Handbook of Banking, 3rd Edition*, ed. by A. N. Berger, P. Molyneux, and J. O. S. Wilson, New York: Oxford University Press, chap. 21, 685–706.

Ashcraft, A. (2006): "New evidence on the lending channel," *Journal of Money, Credit and Banking*, 38, 751–775.

Atkinson, A. and J. Stiglitz (2015): *Lectures on Public Economics, Updated Edition*, Princeton: Princeton University Press.

Auer, R. and S. Ongena (2019): "The countercyclical capital buffer and the composition of bank lending," CESifo Working Paper Series 7815, CESifo.

Avdjiev, S., B. Bogdanova, P. Bolton, W. Jiang, and A. Kartasheva (2020): "CoCo issuance and bank fragility," *Journal of Financial Economics*, 138, 593–613.

Avdjiev, S., W. Du, C. Koch, and H. S. Shin (2019): "The dollar, bank leverage, and deviations from covered interest parity," *American Economic Review: Insights*, 1, 193–208.

Bagehot, W. (1873): *Lombard Street: A Description of the Money Market*, London: Henry S. King & Co.

Bahaj, S. and F. Malherbe (2020): "The forced safety effect: How higher capital requirements can increase bank lending," *Journal of Finance*, 75, 3013–3053.

Bailey, W., W. Huang, and Z. Yang (2011): "Bank loans with Chinese characteristics: Some evidence on inside debt in a state-controlled banking system," *Journal of Financial and Quantitative Analysis*, 46, 1795–1830.

Banerjee, R. N. and H. Mio (2018): "The impact of liquidity regulation on banks," *Journal of Financial Intermediation*, 35, 30–44.

Barth, J. R., G. Caprio, and R. Levine (2013): "Bank regulation and supervision in 180 countries from 1999 to 2011," *Journal of Financial Economic Policy*, 5, 111–219.

Baskaya, Y. S., J. di Giovanni, Ş. Kalemli-Özcan, J.-L. Peydro, and M. F. Ulu (2017): "Capital flows and the international credit channel," *Journal of International Economics*, 108, 15–22.

Baumann, U. and E. W. Nier (2004): "Disclosure, volatility, and transparency: An empirical investigation into the value of bank disclosure," *Economic Policy Review*, 31–45.

Baumol, W. J., J. C. Panzar, and R. D. Willig (1982): *Contestable Markets and the Theory of Industry Structure*, New York: Harcourt Brace Jovanovich.

BCBS (2010): *An assessment of the long-term economic impact of stronger capital and liquidity requirements*, Basel Committee on Banking Supervision, August.

Beatty, A. and S. Liao (2014): "Financial accounting in the banking industry: A review of the empirical literature," *Journal of Accounting and Economics*, 58, 339–383.

Bech, M., J. Chapman, and R. Garratt (2010): "Which bank is the central bank?" *Journal of Monetary Economics*, 57, 352–363.

Bech, M. and T. Keister (2014): "On the economics of committed liquidity facilities," BIS Working Papers 439, Bank for International Settlements.

——— (2017): "Liquidity regulation and the implementation of monetary policy," *Journal of Monetary Economics*, 92, 64–77.

Beck, T., S. Da-Rocha-Lopes, and A. F. Silva (2020): "Sharing the pain? Credit supply and real effects of bank bail-ins," *Review of Financial Studies*, forthcoming.

Beck, T., H. Degryse, R. De Haas, and N. van Horen (2018): "When arm's length is too far: Relationship banking over the credit cycle," *Journal of Financial Economics*, 127, 174–196.

Beck, T., R. Levine, and A. Levkov (2010): "Big bad banks? The winners and losers from bank deregulation in the United States," *Journal of Finance*, 65, 1637–1667.

Behn, M., R. Haselmann, T. Kick, and V. Vig (2015): "The political economy of bank bailouts," IMFS Working Paper Series 86, Goethe University Frankfurt, Institute for Monetary and Financial Stability (IMFS).

Behn, M., R. Haselmann, and P. Wachtel (2016): "Procyclical capital regulation and lending," *Journal of Finance*, 71, 919–956.

Benmelech, E., J. Dlugosz, and V. Ivashina (2012): "Securitization without adverse selection: The case of CLOs," *Journal of Financial Economics*, 106, 91–113.

Berg, T. (2018): "Got rejected? Real effects of not getting a loan," *Review of Financial Studies*, 31, 4912–4957.

Berger, A. N., A. Demirgüç-Kunt, R. Levine, and J. G. Haubrich (2004): "Bank concentration and competition: An evolution in the making," *Journal of Money, Credit and Banking*, 36, 433–451.

Berger, A. N., I. Hasan, and M. Zhou (2009): "Bank ownership and efficiency in China: What will happen in the world's largest nation?" *Journal of Banking and Finance*, 33, 113–130.

Berger, A. N. and G. F. Udell (1992): "Some evidence on the empirical significance of credit rationing," *Journal of Political Economy*, 100, 1047–1077.

Bernanke, B. and M. Gertler (1989): "Agency costs, net worth, and business fluctuations," *American Economic Review*, 79, 14–31.

Bernanke, B., M. Gertler, and S. Gilchrist (1999): "The financial accelerator in a quantitative business cycle framework," in *Handbook of Macroeconomics*, ed. by J. B. Taylor and M. Woodford, Elsevier, vol. 1, Part C, chap. 21, 1341–1393.

Bernhardsen, T. and A. Kloster (2010): "Liquidity management system: Floor or corridor?" Staff Memo 4/2010, Norges Bank.

Bharath, S. T., S. Dahiya, A. Saunders, and A. Srinivasan (2011): "Lending relationships and loan contract terms," *Review of Financial Studies*, 24, 1141–1203.

Bianchi, J. (2011): "Overborrowing and systemic externalities in the business cycle," *American Economic Review*, 101, 3400–3426.

Bianchi, J. and S. Bigio (2020): "Banks, liquidity management and monetary policy," *Econometrica*, forthcoming.

Blickle, K., M. K. Brunnermeier, and S. Luck (2020): "Micro-evidence from a system-wide financial meltdown: The German crisis of 1931," mimeo, Federal Reserve Bank of New York and Princeton University.

Boissay, F., F. Collard, and F. Smets (2016): "Booms and banking crises," *Journal of Political Economy*, 124, 489–538.

Bolton, P., X. Freixas, L. Gambacorta, and P. E. Mistrulli (2016): "Relationship and transaction lending in a crisis," *Review of Financial Studies*, 29, 2643–2676.

Bonner, C. and S. C. W. Eijffinger (2016): "The impact of liquidity regulation on bank intermediation," *Review of Finance*, 20, 1945–1979.

Boone, J. (2008): "A new way to measure competition," *Economic Journal*, 118, 1245–1261.

Boot, A. W. (2000): "Relationship banking: What do we know?" *Journal of Financial Intermediation*, 9, 7–25.

Bord, V. M. and J. a. A. Santos (2015): "Does securitization of corporate loans lead to riskier lending?" *Journal of Money, Credit and Banking*, 47, 415–444.

Borio, C. (2003): "Towards a macroprudential framework for financial supervision and regulation?" BIS Working Papers 128, Bank for International Settlements.

Borio, C. and M. Drehmann (2009): "Assessing the risk of banking crises—revisited," *BIS Quarterly Review*, March, 29–46.

Borio, C. and H. Zhu (2012): "Capital regulation, risk-taking and monetary policy: A missing link in the transmission mechanism?" *Journal of Financial Stability*, 8, 236–251.

Bottero, M., C. Minoiu, J.-L. Peydró, A. Polo, A. F. Presbitero, and E. Sette (2019): "Negative monetary policy rates and portfolio rebalancing: Evidence from credit register data," IMF Working Papers 2019/044, International Monetary Fund.

Boyd, J. H. and G. De Nicolò (2005): "The theory of bank risk taking and competition revisited," *Journal of Finance*, 60, 1329–1343.

Braggion, F., N. Dwarkasing, and L. Moore (2017): "Nothing special about banks: Competition and bank lending in Britain, 1885-1925," *Review of Financial Studies*, 30, 3502–3537.

Bräuning, F. and V. Ivashina (2020): "Monetary policy and global banking," *Journal of Finance*, 75, 3055–3095.

Broecker, T. (1990): "Credit-worthiness tests and interbank competition," *Econometrica*, 58, 429–452.

Broner, F. and J. Ventura (2016): "Rethinking the effects of financial globalization," *Quarterly Journal of Economics*, 131, 1497–1542.

Brown, C. and I. S. Dinç (2005): "The politics of bank failures: Evidence from emerging markets," *Quarterly Journal of Economics*, 120, 1413–1444.

Brownlees, C. and R. F. Engle (2016): "SRISK: A conditional capital shortfall measure of systemic risk," *Review of Financial Studies*, 30, 48–79.

Brunnermeier, M. K., G. Gorton, and A. Krishnamurthy (2012): "Risk topography," *NBER Macroeconomics Annual 2011*, 26, 149–176.

Brunnermeier, M. K. and Y. Koby (2018): "The reversal interest rate," Working Paper 25406, National Bureau of Economic Research.

Brunnermeier, M. K. and M. Oehmke (2009): "Complexity in financial markets," mimeo, Princeton University.

——— (2013): "The maturity rat race," *Journal of Finance*, 68, 483–521.

Brunnermeier, M. K. and L. H. Pedersen (2009): "Market liquidity and funding liquidity," *Review of Financial Studies*, 22, 2201–2238.

Brunnermeier, M. K. and Y. Sannikov (2014): "A macroeconomic model with a financial sector," *American Economic Review*, 104, 379–421.

Bruno, V. and H. S. Shin (2015): "Capital flows and the risk-taking channel of monetary policy," *Journal of Monetary Economics*, 71, 119–132.

——— (2015): "Cross-border banking and global liquidity," *Review of Economic Studies*, 82, 535–564.

Bubb, R. and A. Kaufman (2014): "Securitization and moral hazard: Evidence from credit score cutoff rules," *Journal of Monetary Economics*, 63, 1–18.

Buch, C. M. and L. S. Goldberg (2017): "Cross-border prudential policy spillovers: How much? How important? Evidence from the International Banking Research Network," *International Journal of Central Banking*, 13, 505–558.

Bussière, M., J. Cao, J. de Haan, R. Hills, S. Lloyd, B. Meunier, J. Pedrono, D. Reinhardt, S. Sinha, R. Sowerbutts, and K. Styrin (2021): "The interaction between macroprudential policy and monetary policy: Overview," *Review of International Economics*, 29, 1–19.

Caballero, R. J., T. Hoshi, and A. K. Kashyap (2008): "Zombie lending and depressed restructuring in Japan," *American Economic Review*, 98, 1943–1977.

Calomiris, C. W., R. Fisman, and Y. Wang (2010): "Profiting from government stakes in a command economy: Evidence from Chinese asset sales," *Journal of Financial Economics*, 96, 399–412.

Calomiris, C. W. and C. Kahn (1991): "The role of demandable debt in structuring optimal banking arrangements," *American Economic Review*, 81, 497–513.

Calvo, G. A., L. Leiderman, and C. M. Reinhart (1993): "Capital inflows and real exchange rate appreciation in Latin America: The role of external factors," *Staff Papers (International Monetary Fund)*, 40, 108–151.

―――― (1996): "Inflows of capital to developing countries in the 1990s," *Journal of Economic Perspectives*, 10, 123–139.

Campello, M. (2002): "Internal capital markets in financial conglomerates: Evidence from small bank responses to monetary policy," *Journal of Finance*, 57, 2773–2805.

Cao, J. (2012): *Banking Regulation and the Financial Crisis*, Abingdon Oxford: Routledge.

Cao, J. and L. Chollete (2017): "Monetary policy and financial stability in the long run: A simple game-theoretic approach," *Journal of Financial Stability*, 28, 125–142.

Cao, J. and V. Dinger (2021): "Financial globalization and bank lending: The limits of domestic monetary policy," *Journal of Financial and Quantitative Analysis*, forthcoming.

Cao, J. and G. Illing (2011): "Endogenous exposure to systemic liquidity risk," *International Journal of Central Banking*, 7, 173–216.

―――― (2019): *Money: Theory and Practice (Springer Texts in Business and Economics)*, Cham: Springer Nature Switzerland AG.

―――― (2021): "Money in the equilibrium of banking," *Journal of Money, Credit and Banking*, forthcoming.

Cao, J. and R. E. Juelsrud (2020): "Opacity and risk-taking: Evidence from Norway," *Journal of Banking and Finance*, forthcoming.

Cardone-Riportella, C., R. Samaniego-Medina, and A. Trujillo-Ponce (2010): "What drives bank securitisation? The Spanish experience," *Journal of Banking and Finance*, 34, 2639–2651.

Carlin, B. I. (2009): "Strategic price complexity in retail financial markets," *Journal of Financial Economics*, 91, 278–287.

Carlin, B. I. and G. Manso (2010): "Obfuscation, learning, and the evolution of investor sophistication," *Review of Financial Studies*, 24, 754–785.

Carlson, M. A., S. Correia, and S. Luck (2019): "The effects of banking competition on growth and financial stability: Evidence from the National Banking Era," mimeo, Board of Governors of the Federal Reserve System and Federal Reserve Bank of New York.

Carlsson, H. and E. van Damme (1993): "Global games and equilibrium selection," *Econometrica*, 61, 989–1018.

Carvalho, D. (2014): "The real effects of government-owned banks: Evidence from an emerging market," *Journal of Finance*, 69, 577–609.

Casu, B., A. Clare, A. Sarkisyan, and S. Thomas (2013): "Securitization and bank performance," *Journal of Money, Credit and Banking*, 45, 1617–1658.

Célerier, C. and A. Matray (2019): "Bank-branch supply, financial inclusion, and wealth accumulation," *Review of Financial Studies*, 32, 4767–4809.

Cerutti, E., G. Dell'Ariccia, and M. S. Martínez Pería (2007): "How banks go abroad: Branches or subsidiaries?" *Journal of Banking and Finance*, 31, 1669–1692.

Cetorelli, N. and L. S. Goldberg (2012): "Banking globalization and monetary transmission," *Journal of Finance*, 67, 1811–1843.

Challe, E., B. Mojon, and X. Ragot (2013): "Equilibrium risk shifting and interest rate in an opaque financial system," *European Economic Review*, 63, 117–133.

Chen, K., J. Ren, and T. Zha (2018): "The nexus of monetary policy and shadow banking in China," *American Economic Review*, 108, 3891–3936.

Chen, Q., I. Goldstein, Z. Huang, and R. Vashishtha (2018): "Bank transparency and deposit flows," *available at SSRN 3212873*.

Chen, Y. (1999): "Banking panics: The role of the first-come, first-served rule and information externalities," *Journal of Political Economy*, 107, 946–968.

Claessens, S. and L. Laeven (2004): "What drives bank competition? Some international evidence," *Journal of Money, Credit and Banking*, 36, 563–83.

Cohen, B. H. and M. Scatigna (2016): "Banks and capital requirements: Channels of adjustment," *Journal of Banking and Finance*, 69, S56–S69.

Cole, S. (2009): "Fixing market failures or fixing elections? Agricultural credit in India," *American Economic Journal: Applied Economics*, 1, 219–250.

Cong, L. W., H. Gao, J. Ponticelli, and X. Yang (2019): "Credit allocation under economic stimulus: Evidence from China," *Review of Financial Studies*, 32, 3412–3460.

Dang, T. V., G. Gorton, B. Holmström, and G. Ordoñez (2017): "Banks as secret keepers," *American Economic Review*, 107, 1005–1029.

Daníelsson, J., P. Embrechts, C. Goodhart, C. Keating, F. Muennich, O. Renault, and H. S. Shin (2001): "An academic response to Basel II," FMG Special Papers 130, LSE Financial Markets Group.

d'Aspremont, C., J. Gabszewicz, and J. Thisse (1979): "On Hotelling's stability in competition," *Econometrica*, 47, 1145–1150.

Dávila, E. and A. Korinek (2018): "Pecuniary externalities in economies with financial frictions," *Review of Economic Studies*, 85, 352–395.

De Jonghe, O., H. Dewachter, and S. Ongena (2020): "Bank capital (requirements) and credit supply: Evidence from pillar 2 decisions," *Journal of Corporate Finance*, 60, 101518.

De Marco, F. and M. Macchiavelli (2016): "The political origin of home bias: The case of Europe," Finance and Economics Discussion Series 2016–060, Board of Governors of the Federal Reserve System (U.S.).

De Meza, D. and D. C. Webb (1987): "Too much investment: A problem of asymmetric information," *Quarterly Journal of Economics*, 102, 281–292.

De Nicolò, G. (2015): "Revisiting the impact of bank capital requirements on lending and real activity," *SSRN Electronic Journal*.

De Nicolò, G., A. Gamba, and M. Lucchetta (2012): "Capital regulation, liquidity requirements and taxation in a dynamic model of banking," IMF Working Papers 2012/72, International Monetary Fund.

Degryse, H., M. Kim, and S. Ongena (2009): *Microeconometrics of Banking: Methods, Applications, and Results*, Oxford: Oxford University Press.

Delis, M. D. and G. P. Kouretas (2011): "Interest rates and bank risk-taking," *Journal of Banking and Finance*, 35, 840–855.

Dell'Ariccia, G., D. Igan, and L. Laeven (2012): "Credit booms and lending standards: Evidence from the subprime mortgage market," *Journal of Money, Credit and Banking*, 44, 367–384.

Dell'Ariccia, G., L. Laeven, and R. Marquez (2014): "Real interest rates, leverage, and bank risk-taking," *Journal of Economic Theory*, 149, 65–99.

Demirgüç-Kunt, A. and E. Detragiache (2002): "Does deposit insurance increase banking system stability? An empirical investigation," *Journal of Monetary Economics*, 49, 1373–1406.

Demirgüç-Kunt, A., E. Detragiache, and T. Tressel (2008): "Banking on the principles: Compliance with Basel Core Principles and bank soundness," *Journal of Financial Intermediation*, 17, 511–542.

Demirgüç-Kunt, A., E. J. Kane, and L. Laeven (2008): "Determinants of deposit-insurance adoption and design," *Journal of Financial Intermediation*, 17, 407–438.

Demirgüç-Kunt, A. and V. Maksimovic (1998): "Law, finance, and firm growth," *Journal of Finance*, 53, 2107–2137.

Diamond, D. W. (1984): "Financial intermediation and delegated monitoring," *Review of Economic Studies*, 51, 393–414.

Diamond, D. W. and P. H. Dybvig (1983): "Bank runs, deposit insurance, and liquidity," *Journal of Political Economy*, 91, 401–419.

Diamond, D. W. and R. G. Rajan (2001): "Liquidity risk, liquidity creation, and financial fragility: A theory of banking," *Journal of Political Economy*, 109, 287–327.

―――― (2005): "Liquidity shortages and banking crises," *Journal of Finance*, 60, 615–647.

―――― (2011): "Fear of fire sales, illiquidity seeking, and credit freezes," *Quarterly Journal of Economics*, 126, 557–591.

Diamond, P. A. (1965): "National debt in a neoclassical growth model," *American Economic Review*, 55, 1126–1150.

Dick, A. (2006): "Nationwide branching and its impact on market structure, quality, and bank performance," *Journal of Business*, 79, 567–592.

Diebold, F. X. and K. Yilmaz (2015): *Financial and Macroeconomic Connectedness: A Network Approach to Measurement and Monitoring*, Oxford: Oxford University Press.

Dinç, I. S. and N. Gupta (2011): "The decision to privatize: Finance and politics," *Journal of Finance*, 66, 241–269.

Djankov, S., O. Hart, C. McLiesh, and A. Shleifer (2008): "Debt enforcement around the world," *Journal of Political Economy*, 116, 1105–1149.

Djankov, S., R. La Porta, F. Lopez-de Silanes, and A. Shleifer (2003): "Courts," *Quarterly Journal of Economics*, 118, 453–517.

Djankov, S., C. McLiesh, and A. Shleifer (2007): "Private credit in 129 countries," *Journal of Financial Economics*, 84, 299–329.

Downing, C., D. Jaffee, and N. Wallace (2009): "Is the market for mortgage-backed securities a market for lemons?" *Review of Financial Studies*, 22, 2257–2294.

Drazen, A. (2000): *Political Economy in Macroeconomics*, Princeton: Princeton University Press.

Du, W., J. Im, and J. Schreger (2018): "The U.S. treasury premium," *Journal of International Economics*, 112, 167–181.

Du, W., A. Tepper, and A. Verdelhan (2018): "Deviations from covered interest rate parity," *Journal of Finance*, 73, 915–957.

Duijm, P. and P. Wierts (2016): "The effects of liquidity regulation on bank assets and liabilities," *International Journal of Central Banking*, 12, 385–411.

Dungey, M., R. A. Fry, B. Gonzalez-Hermosillo, and V. L. Martin (2011): *Transmission of Financial Crises and Contagion: A Latent Factor Approach*, CERF Monographs on Finance and the Economy, Oxford: Oxford University Press.

Eggertsson, G. B., R. E. Juelsrud, L. H. Summers, and E. G. Wold (2019): "Negative nominal interest rates and the bank lending channel," Working Paper 25416, National Bureau of Economic Research.

Eisenberg, L. and T. Noe (2001): "Systemic risk in financial systems," *Management Science*, 47, 236–249.

Elliott, D. and A. O. Santos (2012): "Assessing the cost of financial regulation," International Monetary Fund Working Paper No. 12/233 12/233, International Monetary Fund.

Ellison, G. and S. F. Ellison (2009): "Search, obfuscation, and price elasticities on the internet," *Econometrica*, 77, 427–452.

Englmaier, F. and T. Stowasser (2017): "Electoral cycles in savings bank lending," *Journal of the European Economic Association*, 15, 296–354.

Fidrmuc, J. and R. Lind (2020): "Macroeconomic impact of Basel III: Evidence from a meta-analysis," *Journal of Banking and Finance*, 112, 105359.

Flannery, M. J. (2005): "No pain, no gain? Effecting market discipline via reverse convertible debentures," in *Capital Adequacy beyond Basel: Banking, Securities, and Insurance*, ed. by H. S. Scott, New York: Oxford University Press, Chapter 5.

Forbes, K., D. Reinhardt, and T. Wieladek (2017): "The spillovers, interactions, and (un) intended consequences of monetary and regulatory policies," *Journal of Monetary Economics*, 85, 1–22.

Fosu, S., C. G. Ntim, W. Coffie, and V. Murinde (2017): "Bank opacity and risk-taking: Evidence from analysts' forecasts," *Journal of Financial Stability*, 33, 81–95.

Freixas, X., L. Laeven, and J.-L. Peydró (2015): *Systemic Risk, Crises, and Macroprudential Regulation*, Cambridge: The MIT Press.

Freixas, X. and J.-C. Rochet (2008): *Microeconomics of Banking, 2nd Edition*, Cambridge: The MIT Press.

Fungáčová, Z., A. Shamshur, and L. Weill (2017): "Does bank competition reduce cost of credit? Cross-country evidence from Europe," *Journal of Banking and Finance*, 83, 104–120.

Fuster, A. and J. Vickery (2018): "Regulation and risk shuffling in bank securities portfolios," *Federal Reserve Bank of New York Staff Report No. 851*.

Gai, P., A. Haldane, and S. Kapadia (2011): "Complexity, concentration and contagion," *Journal of Monetary Economics*, 58, 453–470.

Gale, D. and M. Hellwig (1985): "Incentive-compatible debt contracts: The one-period problem," *Review of Economic Studies*, 52, 647–663.

Gale, D. and T. Yorulmazer (2013): "Liquidity hoarding," *Theoretical Economics*, 8, 291–324.

Galí, J. (2015): *Monetary Policy, Inflation, and the Business Cycle: An Introduction to the New Keynesian Framework and Its Applications, 2nd Edition*, Cambridge: The MIT Press.

Gambacorta, L. and H. S. Shin (2018): "Why bank capital matters for monetary policy," *Journal of Financial Intermediation*, 35, 17–29.

Gao, H., H. Ru, and D. Tang (2020): "Subnational debt of China: The politics-finance nexus," *Journal of Financial Economics*, forthcoming.

Gavalas, D. (2015): "How do banks perform under Basel III? Tracing lending rates and loan quantity," *Journal of Economics and Business*, 81, 21–37.

Geanakoplos, J. (2003): "Liquidity, default, and crashes: Endogenous contracts in general equilibrium," in *Advances in Economics and Econometrics: Theory and Applications, Econometric Society Monographs. Eighth World Conference, Volume 2*, ed. by M. Dewatripont, L. P. Hansen, and S. J. Turnovsky, New York: Cambridge University Press, 170–205.

⸻ (2010): "The leverage cycle," in *NBER Macroeconomics Annual 2009, Volume 24*, ed. by D. Acemoglu, K. Rogoff, and M. Woodford, Chicago: University of Chicago Press, 1–65.

⸻ (2010): "Solving the present crisis and managing the leverage cycle," *Economic Policy Review*, 101–131.

Gertler, M. and P. Karadi (2011): "A model of unconventional monetary policy," *Journal of Monetary Economics*, 58, 17–34.

Gertler, M. and N. Kiyotaki (2010): "Financial intermediation and credit policy in business cycle analysis," in *Handbook of Monetary Economics, Volume 3*, ed. by B. M. Friedman and M. Woodford, Amsterdam: Elsevier, chap. 11, 547–599.

——— (2015): "Banking, liquidity, and bank runs in an infinite horizon economy," *American Economic Review*, 105, 2011–2043.

Goldstein, I. and A. Pauzner (2005): "Demand–deposit contracts and the probability of bank runs," *Journal of Finance*, 60, 1293–1327.

Goncharenko, R., S. Ongena, and A. Rauf (2020): "The agency of CoCos: Why contingent convertible bonds are not for everyone," *Journal of Financial Intermediation*, forthcoming.

Goodhart, C. A. E. (1999): "Myths about the lender of last resort," *International Finance*, 2, 339–360.

Goodhart, C. A. E. and G. Illing (2002): "Introduction: Financial crises, contagion and the lender of last resort," in *Financial Crises, Contagion and the Lender of Last Resort: A Reader*, ed. by C. A. E. Goodhart and G. Illing, Oxford: Oxford University Press, 1–26.

Goodhart, C. A. E. and D. Schoenmaker (1995): "Should the functions of monetary policy and banking supervision be separated?" *Oxford Economic Papers*, 47, 539–560.

Gorton, G. (1985): "Bank suspension of convertibility," *Journal of Monetary Economics*, 15, 177–193.

——— (2008): "The panic of 2007," Working Paper 14358, National Bureau of Economic Research.

——— (2010): *Slapped by the Invisible Hand: The Panic of 2007*, New York: Oxford University Press.

Gorton, G. and A. Metrick (2009): "Haircuts," Yale ICF Working Paper No. 09–15.

——— (2012): "Securitized banking and the run on repo," *Journal of Financial Economics*, 104, 425–451.

Gorton, G. and G. Pennacchi (1995): "Banks and loan sales Marketing nonmarketable assets," *Journal of Monetary Economics*, 35, 389–411.

Gorton, G. and E. W. Tallman (2016): "How did pre-Fed banking panics end?" Working Paper 22036, National Bureau of Economic Research.

Gorton, G. and A. Winton (2003): "Financial intermediation," in *Handbook of the Economics of Finance*, ed. by G. M. Constantinides, M. Harris, and R. M. Stulz, Elsevier, vol. 1, Part 1, chap. 8, 431–552.

Griffin, J. M. and G. Maturana (2016): "Who facilitated misreporting in securitized loans?" *Review of Financial Studies*, 29, 384–419.

Gropp, R., C. Gruendl, and A. Guettler (2014): "The impact of public guarantees on bank risk-taking: Evidence from a natural experiment," *Review of Finance*, 18, 457–488.

Gropp, R., A. Guettler, and V. Saadi (2020): "Public bank guarantees and allocative efficiency," *Journal of Monetary Economics*, 116, 53–69.

Gropp, R., T. Mosk, S. Ongena, and C. Wix (2019): "Banks response to higher capital requirements: Evidence from a quasi-natural experiment," *Review of Financial Studies*, 32, 266–299.

Guiso, L., P. Sapienza, and L. Zingales (2004): "Does local financial development matter?" *Quarterly Journal of Economics*, 119, 929–969.

Hart, O. and J. Moore (1994): "A theory of debt based on the inalienability of human capital," *Quarterly Journal of Economics*, 109, 841–879.

Haselmann, R., K. Pistor, and V. Vig (2010): "How law affects lending," *Review of Financial Studies*, 23, 549–580.

Haselmann, R., D. Schoenherr, and V. Vig (2018): "Rent seeking in elite networks," *Journal of Political Economy*, 126, 1638–1690.

Haselmann, R. and P. Wachtel (2010): "Institutions and bank behavior: Legal environment, legal perception, and the composition of bank lending," *Journal of Money, Credit and Banking*, 42, 965–984.

He, Z. and A. Krishnamurthy (2013): "Intermediary asset pricing," *American Economic Review*, 103, 732–770.

Heider, F., M. Hoerova, and C. Holthausen (2015): "Liquidity hoarding and interbank market rates: The role of counterparty risk," *Journal of Financial Economics*, 118, 336–354.

Heider, F., F. Saidi, and G. Schepens (2019): "Life below zero: Bank lending under negative policy rates," *Review of Financial Studies*, 32, 3728–3761.

Hellmann, T. F., K. C. Murdock, and J. E. Stiglitz (2000): "Liberalization, moral hazard in banking, and prudential regulation: Are capital requirements enough?" *American Economic Review*, 90, 147–165.

Holmström, B. and J. Tirole (1997): "Financial intermediation, loanable funds, and the real sector," *Quarterly Journal of Economics*, 112, 663–691.

Homar, T. and S. J. G. van Wijnbergen (2017): "Bank recapitalization and economic recovery after financial crises," *Journal of Financial Intermediation*, 32, 16–28.

Huang, H. and C. A. E. Goodhart (1999): "A model of the lender of last resort," IMF Working Papers 1999/039, International Monetary Fund.

Huang, Y., M. Pagano, and U. Panizza (2020): "Local crowding-out in China," *Journal of Finance*, 75, 2855–2898.

Hughes, J. P., W. Lang, L. J. Mester, and C.-G. Moon (1996): "Efficient banking under interstate branching," *Journal of Money, Credit and Banking*, 28, 1045–1071.

Hung, C.-H. D., Y. Jiang, F. H. Liu, H. Tu, and S. Wang (2017): "Bank political connections and performance in China," *Journal of Financial Stability*, 32, 57–69.

IIF (2011): *The Cumulative Impact on the Global Economy of Changes in the Financial Regulatory Framework*, Institute of International Finance, September.

Imbens, G. and K. Kalyanaraman (2012): "Optimal bandwidth choice for the regression discontinuity estimator," *Review of Economic Studies*, 79, 933–959.

Imbens, G. and T. Lemieux (2008): "Regression discontinuity designs: A guide to practice," *Journal of Econometrics*, 142, 615–635.

International Monetary Fund (2014): "Risk taking, liquidity, and shadow banking: Curbing excess while promoting growth," Global Financial Stability Report, October 2014, International Monetary Fund.

Ioannidou, V., S. Ongena, and J.-L. Peydró (2015): "Monetary policy, risk-taking, and pricing: Evidence from a quasi-natural experiment," *Review of Finance*, 19, 95–144.

Ivashina, V., L. Laeven, and E. Moral-Benito (2020): "Loan types and the bank lending channel," Working Paper 27056, National Bureau of Economic Research.

Iyer, R. and J.-L. Peydró (2011): "Interbank contagion at work: Evidence from a natural experiment," *Review of Financial Studies*, 24, 1337–1377.

Iyer, R. and M. Puri (2012): "Understanding bank runs: The importance of depositor-bank relationships and networks," *American Economic Review*, 102, 1414–1445.

Iyer, R., M. Puri, and N. Ryan (2016): "A tale of two runs: Depositor responses to bank solvency risk," *Journal of Finance*, 71, 2687–2726.

Jayaratne, J. and P. E. Strahan (1998): "Entry restrictions, industry evolution, and dynamic efficiency: Evidence from commercial banking," *Journal of Law and Economics*, 41, 239–274.

Jeanne, O. and A. Korinek (2020): "Macroprudential regulation versus mopping up after the crash," *Review of Economic Studies*, 87, 1470–1497.

Jensen, M. C. and W. H. Meckling (1976): "Theory of the firm: Managerial behavior, agency costs and ownership structure," *Journal of Financial Economics*, 3, 305–360.

Jiang, L., R. Levine, and C. Lin (2016): "Competition and bank opacity," *Review of Financial Studies*, 29, 1911–1942.

Jiang, W., A. A. Nelson, and E. Vytlacil (2014): "Liar's loan? Effects of origination channel and information falsification on mortgage delinquency," *Review of Economics and Statistics*, 96, 1–18.

——— (2014): "Securitization and loan performance: Ex ante and ex post relations in the mortgage market," *Review of Financial Studies*, 27, 454–483.

Jiang, Z., A. Krishnamurthy, and H. Lustig (2020): "Foreign safe asset demand and the dollar exchange rate," *Journal of Finance*, forthcoming.

Jiménez, G., S. Ongena, J.-L. Peydró, and J. Saurina (2012): "Credit supply and monetary policy: Identifying the bank balance-sheet channel with loan applications," *American Economic Review*, 102, 2301–2326.

——— (2014): "Hazardous times for monetary policy: What do twenty-three million bank loans say about the effects of monetary policy on credit risk-taking?" *Econometrica*, 82, 463–505.

——— (2017): "Macroprudential policy, countercyclical bank capital buffers, and credit supply: Evidence from the Spanish dynamic provisioning experiments," *Journal of Political Economy*, 125, 2126–2177.

Juelsrud, R. E. and E. G. Wold (2020): "Risk-weighted capital requirements and portfolio rebalancing," *Journal of Financial Intermediation*, 41.

Kahn, C. M. and W. Wagner (2020): "Sources of liquidity and liquidity shortages," *Journal of Financial Intermediation*, forthcoming.

Kang, S., J. Dong, H. Yu, J. Cao, and V. Dinger (2021): "City commercial banks and credit allocation: Firm-level evidence," BOFIT Discussion Papers, 4/2021.

Kara, A., D. Marqués-Ibáñez, and S. Ongena (2016): "Securitization and lending standards: Evidence from the European wholesale loan market," *Journal of Financial Stability*, 26, 107–127.

Kashyap, A. K. and J. C. Stein (2000): "What do a million observations on banks say about the transmission of monetary policy?" *American Economic Review*, 90, 407–428.

——— (2012): "The optimal conduct of monetary policy with interest on reserves," *American Economic Journal: Macroeconomics*, 4, 266–282.

Kaufman, G. G. (1991): "Lender of last resort: A contemporary perspective," *Journal of Financial Services Research*, 5, 95–110.

Keeley, M. C. (1990): "Deposit insurance, risk, and market power in banking," *American Economic Review*, 80, 1183–1200.

Keynes, J. M. (1930): *A Treatise on Money*, New York: Harcourt, Brace and Company.

Keys, B., T. Mukherjee, A. Seru, and V. Vig (2010): "Did securitization lead to lax screening? Evidence from subprime loans," *Quarterly Journal of Economics*, 125, 307–362.

Keys, B., A. Seru, and V. Vig (2012): "Lender screening and the role of securitization: Evidence from prime and subprime mortgage markets," *Review of Financial Studies*, 25, 2071–2108.

Khwaja, A. I. and A. Mian (2005): "Do lenders favor politically connected firms? Rent provision in an emerging financial market," *Quarterly Journal of Economics*, 120, 1371–1411.

——— (2008): "Tracing the impact of bank liquidity shocks: Evidence from an emerging market," *American Economic Review*, 98, 1413–1442.

Kim, J., M. Kim, and Y. Kim (2020): "Bank transparency and the market's perception of bank risk," *Journal of Financial Services Research*, 58, 115–142.

Kimball, M. S. (1990): "Precautionary saving in the small and in the large," *Econometrica*, 58, 53–73.

Kiyotaki, N. and J. Moore (1997): "Credit cycles," *Journal of Political Economy*, 105, 211–248.

Klein, M. A. (1971): "A theory of the banking firm," *Journal of Money, Credit and Banking*, 3, 205–218.

Koetter, M. and A. Popov (2020): "Political cycles in bank lending to the government," *Review of Financial Studies*, forthcoming.

Kroszner, R. S. and P. E. Strahan (2014): "Regulation and deregulation of the U.S. banking industry: Causes, consequences, and implications for the future," in *Economic Regulation and Its Reform: What Have We Learned?*, ed. by N. L. Rose, Chicago: University of Chicago Press, 485–543.

Laeven, L. and F. Valencia (2018): "Systemic banking crises revisited," IMF Working Papers 18/206, International Monetary Fund.

La Porta, R., F. L. de Silanes, and A. Shleifer (2002): "Government ownership of banks," *Journal of Finance*, 57, 265–301.

La Porta, R., F. L. de Silanes, A. Shleifer, and R. W. Vishny (1999): "The quality of government," *Journal of Law, Economics, and Organization*, 15, 222–279.

——— (1997): "Legal determinants of external finance," *Journal of Finance*, 52, 1131–1150.

——— (1998): "Law and finance," *Journal of Political Economy*, 106, 1113–1155.

Lerner, A. P. (1934): "The concept of monopoly and the measurement of monopoly power," *Review of Economic Studies*, 1, 157–175.

Lucas, R. E. and N. L. Stokey (1987): "Money and interest in a cash-in-advance economy," *Econometrica*, 55, 491–513.

MacRae, C. D. (1977): "A political model of the business cycle," *Journal of Political Economy*, 85, 239–263.

MAG (2010): *Assessing the macroeconomic impact of the transition to stronger capital and liquidity requirements: Interim report*, Macroeconomic Assessment Group, August.

Malherbe, F. (2014): "Self-fulfilling liquidity dry-ups," *Journal of Finance*, 69, 947–970.

Martin, A., D. Skeie, and E.-L. von Thadden (2014): "Repo runs," *Review of Financial Studies*, 27, 957–989.

Martin, S. (2002): *Advanced Industrial Economics (2nd Edition)*, Oxford: Blackwell Publishers.

Martínez-Miera, D. and R. Repullo (2010): "Does competition reduce the risk of bank failure?" *Review of Financial Studies*, 23, 3638–3664.

Martynova, N. and E. Perotti (2018): "Convertible bonds and bank risk-taking," *Journal of Financial Intermediation*, 35, 61–80.

Mas-Colell, A., M. D. Whinston, and J. R. Green (1995): *Microeconomic Theory*, New York: Oxford University Press.

Matsuyama, K. (2008): *Aggregate Implications of Credit Market Imperfections: Notes for the Lectures at the University of Tokyo.*

Mian, A. and A. Sufi (2017): "Fraudulent income overstatement on mortgage applications during the credit expansion of 2002 to 2005," *Review of Financial Studies*, 30, 1832–1864.

Miles, D., J. Yang, and G. Marcheggiano (2013): "Optimal bank capital," *Economic Journal*, 123, 1–37.

Mishkin, F. S. and S. G. Eakin (2018): *Financial Markets and Institutions, 8th Edition*, Pearson Education.

Modigliani, F. and M. H. Miller (1958): "The cost of capital, corporation finance and the theory of investment," *American Economic Review*, 48, 261–297.

Moe, T. G., J. A. Solheim, and B. Vale (2004): *The Norwegian Banking Crisis*, Norges Bank.

Monti, M. (1972): "Deposit, credit, and interest rate determination under alternative bank objectives," in *Mathematical Methods in Investment and Finance*, ed. by G. P. Szego and K. Shell, Amsterdam: North-Holland.

Morais, B., J.-L. Peydró, J. Roldán-peña, and C. Ruiz-Ortega (2019): "The international bank lending channel of monetary policy rates and QE: Credit supply, reach-for-yield, and real effects," *Journal of Finance*, 74, 55–90.

Morris, S. and H. S. Shin (2002): "Social value of public information," *American Economic Review*, 92, 1521–1534.

⸻ (2003): "Global games: Theory and applications," in *Advances in Economics and Econometrics: Theory and Applications, Eighth World Congress*, ed. by M. Dewatripont, L. P. Hansen, and S. J. Turnovsky, Cambridge: Cambridge University Press, vol. 1 of *Econometric Society Monographs*, 56–114.

Myers, S. C. (1977): "Determinants of corporate borrowing," *Journal of Financial Economics*, 5, 147–175.

Myers, S. C. and N. S. Majluf (1984): "Corporate financing and investment decisions when firms have information that investors do not have," *Journal of Financial Economics*, 13, 187–221.

Nier, E. W. (2005): "Bank stability and transparency," *Journal of Financial Stability*, 1, 342–354.

Nordhaus, W. (1975): "The political business cycle," *Review of Economic Studies*, 42, 169–190.

Norges Bank (2020): *Monetary policy report with financial stability assessment 3/2020.*

Obstfeld, M. and K. S. Rogoff (1996): *Foundations of International Macroeconomics*, Cambridge: The MIT Press.

Ohls, J. (2017): "Moral suasion in regional government bond markets," Discussion Papers 33/2017, Deutsche Bundesbank.

Ongena, S., A. Popov, and N. van Horen (2019): "The invisible hand of the government: Moral suasion during the European Sovereign Debt Crisis," *American Economic Journal: Macroeconomics*, 11, 346–379.

Ongena, S., I. Schindele, and D. Vonnák (2021): "In lands of foreign currency credit, bank lending channels run through?" *Journal of International Economics*, 129, 103435.

Oxford Economics (2013): *Analyzing the impact of bank capital and liquidity regulations on US economic growth*, The Clearing House Association, April.

Panzar, J. C. and J. N. Rosse (1977): "Chamberlin vs. Robinson: An empirical test for monopoly rents," *Bell Laboratories Economic Discussion Paper*, 90.

——— (1987): "Testing for monopoly equilibrium," *Journal of Industrial Economics*, 35, 443–56.

Piskorski, T., A. Seru, and V. Vig (2010): "Securitization and distressed loan renegotiation: Evidence from the subprime mortgage crisis," *Journal of Financial Economics*, 97, 369–397.

Pozsar, Z., T. Adrian, A. Ashcraft, and H. Boesky (2012): "Shadow banking," *Federal Reserve Bank of New York Staff Report No. 458*.

Puri, M., J. Rocholl, and S. Steffen (2017): "What do a million observations have to say about loan defaults? Opening the black box of relationships," *Journal of Financial Intermediation*, 31, 1–15.

Purnanandam, A. (2011): "Originate-to-distribute model and the subprime mortgage crisis," *Review of Financial Studies*, 24, 1881–1915.

Qian, J. and P. E. Strahan (2007): "How laws and institutions shape financial contracts: The case of bank loans," *Journal of Finance*, 62, 2803–2834.

Qian, X., T. Cao, and W. Li (2011): "Promotion pressure, officials' tenure and lending behavior of the city commercial banks," *Economic Research Journal*, 2011, 72–85 (in Chinese).

Rajan, R. G. (1992): "Insiders and outsiders: The choice between informed and arm's-length debt," *Journal of Finance*, 47, 1367–1400.

——— (2006): "Has finance made the world riskier?" *European Financial Management*, 12, 499–533.

Rajan, R. G. and L. Zingales (1995): "What do we know about capital structure? Some evidence from international data," *Journal of Finance*, 50, 1421–1460.

Reinhart, C. M. and K. S. Rogoff (2009): *This Time Is Different: Eight Centuries of Financial Folly*, Princeton: Princeton University Press.

Repullo, R. (2004): "Capital requirements, market power, and risk-taking in banking," *Journal of Financial Intermediation*, 13, 156–182.

Repullo, R. and J. Saurina (2012): "The countercyclical capital buffer of Basel III: A critical assessment," in *The Crisis Aftermath: New Regulatory Paradigms*, ed. by M. Dewatripont and X. Freixas, London: Centre for Economic Policy Research (CEPR), 45–67.

Repullo, R. and J. Suarez (2013): "The procyclical effects of bank capital regulation," *Review of Financial Studies*, 26, 452–490.

Rice, T. and P. E. Strahan (2010): "Does credit competition affect small-firm finance?" *Journal of Finance*, 65, 861–889.

Rime, D., A. Schrimpf, and O. Syrstad (2017): "Segmented money markets and covered interest parity arbitrage," BIS Working Papers 651, Bank for International Settlements.

Ru, H. (2018): "Government credit, a double-edged sword: Evidence from the China Development Bank," *Journal of Finance*, 73, 275–316.

Salop, S. C. (1979): "Monopolistic competition with outside goods," *Bell Journal of Economics*, 10, 141–156.

Samuelson, P. A. (1958): "An exact consumption-loan model of interest with or without the social contrivance of money," *Journal of Political Economy*, 66, 467–482.

Sapienza, P. (2004): "The effects of government ownership on bank lending," *Journal of Financial Economics*, 72, 357–384.

Schenone, C. (2010): "Lending relationships and information rents: Do banks exploit their information advantages?" *Review of Financial Studies*, 23, 1149–1199.

Schiantarelli, F., M. Stacchini, and P. E. Strahan (2020): "Bank quality, judicial efficiency, and loan repayment delays in Italy," *Journal of Finance*, 75, 2139–2178.

Schularick, M. and A. M. Taylor (2012): "Credit booms gone bust: Monetary policy, leverage cycles, and financial crises, 1870–2008," *American Economic Review*, 102, 1029–1061.

Shaffer, S. (1998): "The winner's curse in banking," *Journal of Financial Intermediation*, 7, 359–392.

Sharpe, S. A. (1990): "Asymmetric information, bank lending and implicit contracts: A stylized model of customer relationships," *Journal of Finance*, 45, 1069–1087.

Shen, C.-H. and C.-Y. Lin (2012): "Why government banks underperform: A political interference view," *Journal of Financial Intermediation*, 21, 181–202.

Shin, H. S. (2010): *Risk and Liquidity (Clarendon Lectures in Finance)*, New York: Oxford University Press.

Shivdasani, A. and Y. Wang (2011): "Did structured credit fuel the LBO boom?" *Journal of Finance*, 66, 1291–1328.

Shleifer, A. and R. W. Vishny (1994): "Politicians and firms," *Quarterly Journal of Economics*, 109, 995–1025.

_____ (1997): "The limits of arbitrage," *Journal of Finance*, 52, 35–55.

_____ (2010): "Unstable banking," *Journal of Financial Economics*, 97, 306–318.

Skeie, D. (2008): "Banking with nominal deposits and inside money," *Journal of Financial Intermediation*, 17, 562–584.

Slovik, P. and B. Cournède (2011): "Macroeconomic impact of Basel III," OECD Economics Department Working Papers 844, OECD Publishing.

Stahl, D. (1989): "Oligopolistic pricing with sequential consumer search," *American Economic Review*, 79, 700–712.

Stiglitz, J. E. and A. Weiss (1981): "Credit rationing in markets with imperfect information," *American Economic Review*, 71, 393–410.

Temesvary, J., S. Ongena, and A. L. Owen (2018): "A global lending channel unplugged? Does U.S. monetary policy affect cross-border and affiliate lending by global U.S. banks?" *Journal of International Economics*, 112, 50–69.

Tirole, J. (1988): *The Theory of Industrial Organization*, Cambridge: The MIT Press.

Townsend, R. M. (1979): "Optimal contracts and competitive markets with costly state verification," *Journal of Economic Theory*, 21, 265–293.

Valencia, F. and L. Laeven (2012): "Systemic banking crises database: An update," IMF Working Papers 2012/163, International Monetary Fund.

van den Heuvel, S. J. (2002): "Does bank capital matter for monetary transmission?" *Economic Policy Review*, 8, 259–265.

Varian, H. (1980): "A model of sales," *American Economic Review*, 70, 651–59.

Wagner, W. (2007): "Financial development and the opacity of banks," *Economics Letters*, 97, 6–10.

_____ (2011): "Systemic liquidation risk and the diversity-diversification trade-off," *Journal of Finance*, 66, 1141–1175.

Walsh, C. E. (2017): *Monetary Theory and Policy, 4th Edition*, Cambridge: The MIT Press.

Wang, Y. and H. Xia (2014): "Do lenders still monitor when they can securitize loans?" *Review of Financial Studies*, 27, 2354–2391.

Woodford, M. (2004): *Interest and Prices: Foundations of a Theory of Monetary Policy*, Cambridge: The MIT Press.

Zheng, Y. (2020): "Does bank opacity affect lending?" *Journal of Banking and Finance*, 119, forthcoming.

INDEX

1997 Asian financial crisis 12
2007–2009 global financial crisis 139, 224; and bail-in 558; and banking regulation 18, 526; and banking sector 7; buyers' strike 493; and complexity in products 225, 227; and dynamic provisioning 556; fiscal cost 13; foreclosure 464; and international banking 400, 405; liquidity hoarding 531; and liquidity regulation 539; and macroprudential regulation 484; market freeze 531; monetary policy in 289; and monetary policy response 294; qualitative easing 293; quantitative easing (QE) 294; and relationship banking 128; repo run 187, 199; risk-taking channel 332; securitized banking in 186; sellers' strike 493; stimulus plan 470; and systemic expected shortfall (SES) 519; and systemic risk 481; targeted liquidity provision in 291

accumulated other comprehensive income (AOCI) 266
adverse selection: and credit rationing 92, 109; definition 90; and liquidity hoarding 531; and market liquidity 75; in securitization 215; in Stiglitz-Weiss model 115
agency cost 343, 351
Allen-Gale model 45; bank run solution under liquidity cost 56; bank run solution under zero liquidity cost 51; constrained efficiency under zero liquidity cost 50; social planner's solution under liquidity cost 54; social planner's solution under zero liquidity cost 47
Allen-Gale network model 238; banking solution 240; complete banking network 241; contagion 243; illiquid but solvent bank 244, 246; incomplete banking network 243; insolvency and contagion 247; insolvent, bankrupted bank 244, 247; liquid bank 244; liquidity buffer and solvency 244; liquidity shock 243; pecking order 245; preferences 238; regional setting 238; social planner's solution 240; technologies 239
American Community Survey (ACS) 212
asset-backed security (ABS) 176
asset-based loan 328
asset market 494
asset price: in Geanakoplos model 380; and Liquidity Coverage Ratio (LCR) 541; in Shin model 375
asymmetric information 90, 527, 543
auditing 97, 346
autarky solution: of Dang-Gorton-Holmström-Ordoñez model 253; of Diamond-Dybvig model 34; with international banking 412, 415
automatic teller machine (ATM) 227
available-for-sale (AFS) security 265, 266
average treatment effect (ATE) 216

Bagehot Rules 532; collateral in 532; credibility rule 532; illiquidity versus insolvency 533; no-free-lunch rule 532; regulatory capture 537; solvency rule 532; time consistency problem 534; too big to fail 534, 536
bail-in 558, 564
bailout: and moral suasion 469; and regulatory capture 537
balance sheet: assets 4; in Bianchi-Bigio model 296; in Bräuning-Ivashina model 419; of central bank 284; consolidated 419; in Diamond-Dybvig model 36; in Eisenberg-Noe model 235; global 402, 419; of a global bank 419; in Holmström-Tirole model 104; in Kashyap-Stein identification 329; in Khwaja-Mian identification 325; in Klein-Monti model 141; liabilities 4; liquid assets 5; in money creation 283; procyclicality 544; a stylized bank's 4
bank: branch 403; definition of 4; as delegated monitor 92; as financial intermediary 31; global 402; government-controlled 434; government-owned 434; as information producer 13, 91, 457; as liquidity provider 28; as liquidity service provider 13, 485; and money creation 277, 283; narrow definition of 4; as opaque financial institution 226, 249; subsidiary 403; in transmission of monetary policy 277, 340; as a veil 341
bank assets to GDP ratio 6
bank capital channel 557
bank funding versus market funding 8
bank holiday 40
bank lending: in Bernanke-Gertler model 354; co-existence with direct lending 100, 355; under countercyclical capital buffer (CCyB) 555; and creditor protection 459; cross-border 402; in Holmström-Tirole model 103; under interaction between capital regulation and monetary policy 558; and law enforcement 461; and legal rule 459; and moral hazard 359; and political connection 462

bank lending channel 18, 277, 296, 319; Bianchi-Bigio model 296; and discount window 305; and international banking 428; Kashyap-Stein identification 329, 330; Khwaja-Mian identification 324, 327; and liquidity management 296; identification 323; through cash-flow loans 329
bank performance: measures of 14; in securitized banking 214
bank resolution 464, 467, 558; in 2007–2009 global financial crisis 13
bank run 29, 37, 529; of Allen-Gale model 47, 54; Cao-Illing model 61; coordination failure in 40; under demand deposit contract 61, 66; and deposit insurance 41, 80; Diamond-Dybvig model 30; in Diamond-Rajan contagion model 504; empirical evidence 79; fundamental driven 38, 79; and lender-of-last-resort policy 42, 532; as market discipline 30, 62; and opacity 226; optimal 45; panic driven 38, 79; panic in 38; policy response of 40; rumor in 38; self-fulfilling 39; as self-fulfilling equilibrium 39; as a sunspot equilibrium 39; and suspension of convertibility 40
bank run equilibrium: of Diamond-Dybvig model 39
bank-oriented economy 9
bank-specific risk 481; and microprudential regulation 484
banking: in conventional macroeconomics 340; cross-border 400; fragility in 29; government control in 434; government ownership in 434; under government ownership 453; industrial organization in 138; under information frictions 90; and macro linkages 340; political economy in 434; under zero lower bound (ZLB) 334
banking competition: barrier to entry 164; Boone Indicator (BI) 162; in dynamic setting 149; effect identification 163; funding cost 166, 167; H-statistic

161; Herfindahl–Hirschman Index (HHI) 160; Lerner Index (LI) 161; measurement 159; N-bank concentration ratio (CRn) 160; and opacity 264, 265; price setting 141; risk-taking 139, 144, 149; in static setting 144; under winner's curse 154, 158
banking crisis 10, 12, 80, 243, 468, 526; and banking regulation 527
banking liberalization 438; and credit allocation 472; political economy in 472
banking-macro linkage 340, 341; and banking regulation 480; and bank-side friction 341, 359, 362; Bernanke-Gertler model 342; Bianchi model 365; and borrower-side friction 340, 341; business-driven credit cycles 341; credit-driven business cycles 341; financial accelerator 340–342; and financial friction 340, 341; Geanakoplos model 380; Gertler-Karadi-Kiyotaki model 359; leverage cycle 342; moral hazard 359; nonlinear behavior 370; overborrowing 365; principal-agent problem 340, 341; Shin model 371
banking network 226, 235; Allen-Gale network model 238; and banks' vulnerability 249; complete 241; connectedness 238; and contagion 226, 235; and domino effect 235; Eisenberg-Noe model 235; externality 484; incomplete 243; international 401; and risk-sharing 235, 238; simulation 262; strength 238; structure 238, 241, 249; as web of claims 226, 235, 483
banking regulation 17, 480, 526; bail-in 558; and banking-macro linkage 480; calibration of prudential controls 514; capital regulation 542, 550, 553, 554; common exposure 514; consumer protection 481; correlation 514; countercyclical capital buffer (CCyB) 544, 545; design 515, 526; empirical evidence 550, 539; and financial stability 480; and information friction 527; interaction with monetary policy 528; interconnection 514; liquidity regulation 528; lender-of-last-resort policy 532; Liquidity Coverage Ratio (LCR) 538; macroprudential perspective of 485, 512, 527; microprudential perspective of 484, 512, 527; microprudential versus macroprudential 513; and monetary policy 557; Net Stable Funding Ratio (NSFR) 538; price versus stability 480; proximate objective 513; as public good 480; regulatory arbitrage 527; regulatory capture 537; risk in modelling 514; and risk-taking 527; special features 480; systemically important bank (SIB) buffer 546; and systemic risk 481; taxpayer protection 481; ultimate objective 513
banking relationship 80
banking solution: of Cao-Illing model 71; of Diamond-Dybvig model 35
bankruptcy remote 182
Basel Committee on Banking Supervision (BCBS) 526
Basel I 526, 543
Basel II 544; internal rating based (IRB) approach 555; standard approach (SA) 555
Basel III 266, 484, 492, 501, 526, 528; empirical evidence 539, 550; Liquidity Coverage Ratio (LCR) 492, 501, 538; liquidity regulation 537; and macroprudential perspective of banking regulation 484; Net Stable Funding Ratio (NSFR) 492, 538; systemically important bank (SIB) buffer 546
Bernanke-Gertler model 342; agency cost 351; bank finance 354; capital formation 345; capital supply under asymmetric information 356; capital supply with no asymmetric information 348; costly state verification 346; depositor 353; direct finance 354; dead weight loss 356; financial accelerator 343; financial

intermediation 354; internal and external funding 352; long-run fluctuation 358; market equilibrium with asymmetric information 348; market equilibrium with no asymmetric information 347; moral hazard problem 351; no finance 355; optimal contract 350; production technology 345; revelation principle 349; short-run fluctuation 357; successful entrepreneur 353; swinging entrepreneur 353

Bianchi model 365; binding borrowing constraint 369; borrowing capacity 369; borrowing constraint 367; collateralized lending 367; downward spiral 370; Euler equation 369; moral hazard problem 367; non-*binding borrowing constraint* 369; occasionally binding constraint 365, 370

Bianchi-Bigio model 296, 329; balancing stage 298; bank lending and liquidity risk exposure 296; funding liquidity risk 303; lending stage 296; liquidity management and bank lending channel 299; marginal cost of lending 301; marginal return of lending 303; and Net Stable Funding Ratio (NSFR) 538

Boone Indicator (BI) 162

borrowed reserves (BR) 285, 287

Boyd-De Nicolò model 144; competition versus stability 144, 146; franchise value hypothesis 144; limited liability 145, 147; moral hazard hypothesis 146; and risk buffer 148

Bräuning-Ivashina model 418; balance sheet 419; covered interest rate parity (CIP) 422; cross-border credit supply 418; cross-border monetary policy spillover 423; currency mismatch 419; currency risk 419; exchange rate dynamics 418; exchange rate risk 419; global bank 418; hedging 419; international transmission of monetary policy 420; monetary policy 418; monetary policy spillover 418

Brexit 10, 19, 400

bribe 440, 445

Brunnermeier-Oehmke model 485, 530; debt contract 486; debt rollover 487, 488; liquidation cost 487; long-term debt contract 487; maturity rat race 487, 489; outcome under long-term contract 488; outcome under short-term contract 488; rollover externality 491; rollover risk 492; short-term debt contract 487; signal 487

business cycle: versus credit cycle 549

business-driven credit cycles 341

buyers' strike 493

Cao-Illing model 61, 305; banking solution 71; constrained efficiency 68, 307; contracting in frictional matching *market with hold-up problem* 64; contracting in frictionless matching market 64; contracting with banks subject to bank runs 66; contracting with banks subject to holdup problem 65; and Liquidity Coverage Ratio (LCR) 538; excess liquidity risk with money 314; for monetary economy 305; with nominal contract 305; social planner's solution 68; time consistency problem 534

capital: costly 542, 548; and debt overhang 543; in Holmström-Tirole model 100; and limited liability 542; and monetary policy transmission 557; and moral hazard problem 100, 106; regulatory 551; and resilience 542; and risk-taking 543, 547; as skin-in-the-game 542, 548, 550; and tax advantage 543; Tier 1 546, 553, 574; Tier 2 574

capital buffer 543; externality 365; loss absorbing 542, 543; for loss absorption 543

capital market 408

capital regulation 542; and banking outcome 553; Basel II 544; Basel III 546; cost on real economy 551; countercyclical capital buffer (CCyB) 544, 545; countercyclicality 545, 555; dynamic provisioning 555; empirical

628

evidence 550; and monetary policy 556; and portfolio rebalancing 554; procyclicality 544, 555; risk premium 553; and risk-taking 547, 550; systemically important bank (SIB) buffer 546
capital requirement: in Bianchi-Bigio model 297; and cost of capital 548; cost on real economy 551; countercyclical 545, 555; countercylicality 545; European Banking Authority (EBA) 553; in Gertler-Karadi-Kiyotaki model 365; of a global bank 420; and liquidity risk 550; and monetary policy transmission 557; procyclical 544, 555; and unconventional monetary policy transmission 558; on unhedged FX position 420
capital shortfall 519
Carlin model 227; cutoff value 233; informed investor 229; market power and product complexity 230; mixed strategy equilibrium 231; price dispersion 231; uninformed investor 229
case law 458
cash-flow loan 328
cash-in-advance constraint 305
cash in circulation 284
central bank 17, 276, 434; assets 285; balance sheet 284; discount rate 287; discount window 285, 287; and financial stability 276; interest rate paid on bank reserves 287; as the lender of last resort 18, 276, 285, 532; liabilities 284; liquidity facility 184, 276, 532, 542; as liquidity insurance provider 276; as maker of monetary policy 276; mandate 276; and maturity transformation 305; as monetary authority 276, 305; in qualitative easing 293; in quantitative easing (QE) 295; reserve account 284
central bank money 281
central banking 276, 279
China–United States trade war 19, 400
city commercial bank (CCB) 438, 457, 472

civil law 458; French 459; German 459; Scandinavian 459
clearing bank 184
collateral 75; in Bianchi model 367; in central bank liquidity facility 540, 541; in discount loan 313; and financial accelerator 357; in Geanakoplos model 380; high-quality liquid assets (HQLA) as 540; as insurance in securitized banking 184; and law enforcement 460; in lender-of-last-resort policy 532; and occasionally binding constraint 342; out of securitization 182; pledgeability rule 460; in repo 182, 285
collateralized debt obligation (CDO) 177, 181
collateralized loan obligation (CLO) 212
commercial and industrial (C&I) lending 331
commercial bank 466
commercial paper 177
common equity 546, 548, 559, 574; and contingent convertible (CoCo) conversion 559; versus contingent convertible (CoCo) 563
common law 458; complexity in banking 224; and arbitrage against regulation 225; by complexity in products 225, 227; computational complexity 225; and diversification 224; and economy of scope 224; by geographical location 224; international banking 401; and market liquidity 75; in multiple dimensions 224; by network complexity 226, 235; by opacity 226, 249; and operational efficiency 224; by organizational complexity 224
complexity in products 227; Carlin model 227; and obfuscation 227; and price dispersion 228
conditional, contingent, or contributing value-at-risk (CoVaR) 516
conflict of interest 543
constrained efficiency: of Allen-Gale model 50; of Allen-Gale network model 238; of Cao-Illing model 68, 307; of Diamond-Dybvig model 32

consumer: early 250; impatient 29, 31, 239; late 250; patient 29, 31, 239
consumption: with international banking 410
contagion 226, 247; Allen-Gale network model 238; and capital buffer 542; cross-border 402; empirical evidence 262; identification 262; statistical correlation 262; and systemic risk 484
contagion: Diamond-Rajan contagion model 502; in interbank market 502
contestable market 161
continental law 458
contingent convertible (CoCo) 559; conversion 559; empirical evidence 564; trigger criterion 559
control right 436, 441
cooperative equilibrium 444
core economy 401, 426
corridor system 288, 419
corruption 459
cost efficiency 456
cost of liquidation 54
costly state verification 342
countercyclical capital buffer (CCyB) 545; and bank lending 556; in COVID-19 pandemic 547; and credit cycle 545, 549; and credit-to-GDP gap 549; empirical evidence 555
counterparty risk: in financial crisis 289; liquidity risk 289; in repo 183; solvency risk 289
CoVaR 516; bank size adjusted 517; definition 516; difference of 516
covered interest rate parity (CIP) 422, 428; in Bräuning-Ivashina model 422; break-down 424; deviation 428
COVID-19 pandemic: and adjustment in countercyclical capital buffer (CCyB) 547; and international banking 400; monetary policy during 295; quantitative easing (QE) in 295
crawling peg 429
credit allocation 469; in banking liberalization 472; government-owned bank 434, 453; and government ownership 469; and information production 457; and political connection 462; and political economy 469; private and foreign ownership in 456; and public finance 471; and public guarantee 470; and reelection 435
credit crunch 530
credit cycle: and countercyclical capital buffer (CCyB) 546, 549; and election cycle 436, 448; political 436, 448; procyclical 544; versus business cycle 549
credit default swap (CDS) 212
credit rationing 93; definition 108; empirical evidence 129; persistent 108; as a result of adverse selection 109; Stiglitz-Weiss model 109; temporary 108; under internal rating 130
credit register 324, 328, 332, 335, 425, 429, 460, 462, 558
credit risk 17, 90, 527; in money creation 283; political 436; under currency appreciation 428
credit-driven business cycles 341
credit-to-GDP gap 549
creditor protection 460
cross-border banking 400, 429
cross-border funding 428
cross-border lending 428
currency crisis 401
currency mismatch 409, 419, 428
currency risk 409, 419
current account: balance 412; deficit 417

Dang-Gorton-Holmström-Ordoñez model 249; autarky solution 253; banking solution 251, 258; bond market solution 251; global concavity 257; global risk aversion 257; liquidity preferences 250; local risk neutrality 257; opacity 252, 258; social planner's solution 252
De Meza-Webb model 120; competitive equilibrium 123; demand for loans 120; excess lending 124; information friction 124; lending efficiency 123; loan supply 123; loan supply curve 123; positive selection 120, 121
dead weight loss 356

debt contract: long-term 485, 487, 530; short-term 485, 486, 530
debt overhang 76, 543; and funding liquidity 76
Dell'Ariccia-Laeven-Marquez model 315; leverage channel 321; leverage effect 320; monetary policy pass-through 319; monitoring 316; pass-through channel 321; pass-through effect 319; risk-shifting channel 321; risk-shifting effect 318; risk-taking channel 317, 321
demand deposit contract 30, 31, 66, 239, 503; and bank as delegated monitor 96; and bank run 66; as commitment device 66; as discipline device 62, 66
demandable, non-contingent debt 61
deposit insurance 41, 80, 184; coverage 81; design 81; empirical evidence 80; and likelihood of bank run 80; limited guarantee 42; moral hazard problem 42, 80; operator 81; and systemic banking crisis 81
deposit rate 185
deregulation 163, 164
development bank 437, 441
Diamond-Dybvig model 30, 239, 529, 532, 533; autarky solution 34; bank run equilibrium 37; banking solution 35; equilibrium selection 43; exchange market solution 34; policy implication 40; social planner's solution 32
Diamond model 93; auditing 97; bank as delegated monitor 96; costly monitoring under direct lending 95; demand deposit contract 97; information friction 94; participation constraint with bank 98
Diamond-Rajan contagion model 502; bank run 504; contagion 510; demand deposit contract 504; equilibrium outcomes in interbank market 505; market liquidity 506
Diamond-Rajan sellers' strike model 492, 530, 538
difference-in-differences 167
direct lending: in Bernanke-Gertler model 355; co-existence with bank lending 100, 355; in Holmström-Tirole model 102
discount loan 305, 310
discount rate 287
discount window 285, 287, 303
domestic currency 408
domino effect 235
Douglas Amendment to the 1956 Bank Holding Company (BHC) Act 10, 164
dynamic provisioning 555
dynamic stochastic general equilibrium (DSGE) 358, 395

early warning indicator 521
Eisenberg-Noe model 235; balance sheet 236; credit risk 236; fixed point 237; solution algorithm 237; stress test 262
election cycle 437, 448
equity ratio 16
European debt crisis 40, 400, 468
exchange market solution: of Diamond-Dybvig model 34
exchange rate 418; forward 420, 428; spot 420, 427
exchange rate regime 429
exchange rate risk 402, 409, 419
expected shortfall (ES) 517
exponential hazard model 465
external funding 351
externality: and coordination failure 484; and Liquidity Coverage Ratio (LCR) 541; and SRISK 519; and systemic expected shortfall (SES) 519; and systemic risk 482; capital buffer 365; from debt rollover 491; from fire sale 482; from interbank lending rate 502; liquidity buffer 501, 530; liquidity hoarding 531, 541; negative 482; network 483; positive 482; from public finance 471; from refinancing 485; screening under loan sales 187, 192; systemic liquidity shortage 541

Federal Deposit Insurance Corporation (FDIC) 41
federal funds market 286
federal funds rate 286
fiat money 305

FICO score 213
financial accelerator 340–342; Bernanke-Gertler model 342; and collateral 357
financial crisis 77, 289, 382, 395, 401, 515, 521
financial friction 20; and banking-macro linkage 340, 341; bank-side friction 341, 359, 362; borrower-side friction 340, 341; in conventional macroeconomics 340; in international banking 417; and nonlinear behavior 370; political origin of 436
financial hub 406
financial innovation 227, 515
financial intermediary 4
financial intermediation 4; modern 176; traditional 176
financial liberalization 515
financial stability 480; versus price stability 557
FinTech 19
fire sale 32, 77, 186, 394, 482; externality 482
first-order stochastic domination 487
floor system 419
foreclosure 464
foreign currency (FX) funding 427
foreign exchange (FX) swap 420, 427
foreign ownership 456
foreign-controlled bank 403
fractional reserve banking 36, 184, 277, 280
fragility 29; as market discipline 30; from maturity mismatch 529; as risk-sharing mechanism 29
franchise value hypothesis 140, 144; empirical evidence 163
funding cost: in financial crisis 289; under liquidity regulation 539; in securitized banking 185; in traditional banking 184
Funding for Lending Scheme (FLS) 558
funding liquidity: and business cycles 76; and corporate governance 76; under debt overhang 76; definition of 76; determinants 76; and funding structure 76; under maturity mismatch 76

funding liquidity risk 290, 528, 529, 530; in Bianchi-Bigio model 303; and lender-of-last-resort policy 292

GARCH model 521
Geanakoplos model 380; asset price 380, 387; borrower 385; collateral requirement 380, 385; general equilibrium effect 390; lender 385; leverage cycle 380, 391; leverage ratio 388; loan contract 385; market equilibrium with borrowing 385; market equilibrium without borrowing 383; optimistic investor 382; pessimistic investor 382; subjective expected utility 383; vicious spiral 394
Gertler-Karadi-Kiyotaki model 359; aggregate deposit demand under financial friction 362; aggregate deposit supply without financial friction 359; bank-side friction 359; information rent 364; moral hazard problem 362; social planner's solution 361
getting-ready-before-the-crisis 495; ask price 500; bid price 500; limited liability 501; liquidity buffer 495; liquidity externality 501; liquidity shock 494; market equilibrium with insolvency risk 499; market equilibrium without insolvency risk 497; systemic liquidity shortage 501; wait-and-see 495
Glass-Steagall Act of 1933 10
global bank 418; balance sheet 419; in Bräuning-Ivashina model 418, 419; and international transmission of monetary policy 418; portfolio adjustment 424; reserve 419
global currency 402, 408
global game 44
global solution method 371
Gorton-Pennacchi model 188; incentive compatibility constraint 190; inefficient screening 191; loan sales 189; screening technology 189

government control 434; and political credit cycle 466; versus government ownership 441
government-controlled bank 434, 454
government ownership 434, 437; and bank performance 456; and banking outcomes 453; and credit allocation 469; political economy view 439, 453; principal-agent view 439, 453; Shleifer-Vishny government ownership model 439; social view 439, 453, 455; versus government control 441
government sponsored enterprise (GSE) 211, 213
Gramm-Leach-Bliley Act of 1999 10
gross profit 14

haircut 75, 183; as insurance for lenders 184, 185; on non-subprime related products 493; and originate to distribute 188, 193; on structured products 493; on subprime-related securities 186, 493
hedge fund 177
hedging 409, 419, 427
held-to-maturity (HTM) security 266
Hellmann-Murdock-Stiglitz model 149; and cap on deposit rate 153; and capital requirement 153; under monopoly 152; no-gambling condition 150; under perfect competition 152; policy implication 152; prudent solution 152; short-run gain versus long-run loss 150; trigger strategy 151
Herfindahl–Hirschman Index (HHI) 160, 163; formular 160; limitation 160
high-powered money 281
high-quality liquid asset (HQLA) 538, 540
hold-up problem 64
Holmström-Tirole model 100; bank balance sheet 104; bank lending 104; bank lending in 103; direct lending 102; direct lending in 102; incentive compatibility constraint 102, 104; information friction 101; information rent 103; monitoring 104; moral hazard 102, 104; participation constraint 103, 105; social welfare 106; wealth constraint 103, 105
home bias 468
Home Mortgage Disclosure Act (HMDA) 210
housing boom 515
H-statistic 161, 166; formular 161; interpretation 161

illiquid asset 28, 32, 67; liquidation 28
illiquidity 533
implicit function theorem 580
inalienable human capital 32
incentive compatibility constraint: in Bernanke-Gertler model 349; in Diamond-Dybvig model 36; in Gorton-Pennacchi model 190; in Holmström-Tirole model 102, 103
incredible threat 534
indifference curve 411
industrial organization in banking 138; and asymmetric information 141; Boyd-De Nicolò model 144; competition versus stability 139; in dynamic setting 141, 149; empirical evidence 158; franchise value hypothesis 140, 144; Hellmann-Murdock-Stiglitz model 149; Klein-Monti model 141; limited liability 139; market concentration 138; market power 139; market structure 138; moral hazard hypothesis 140, 146; price setting 141; real effect 159; risk-taking 139; Shaffer model 153; in static setting 140, 144; under two-sided market 139; winner's curse 141, 153, 158
industrial policy 471
information asymmetry 90
information externality 43
information friction 91; in banking regulation 527; in Diamond model 94; in Holmström-Tirole model 101; in Stiglitz-Weiss model 110
information rent 103, 364

informed investor 229
initial public offering 128
insolvency 533
interbank lending: equilibrium market rate 286, 288; externality 502; freeze 531; in Klein-Monti model 142; under liquidity regulation 539
interbank market 226, 529; contagion 502; demand for bank reserves 286; Diamond-Rajan contagion model 502; freeze 531; and liquidity management 277; refinancing from 485; risk-sharing 502; supply of bank lending 287
interest expenses 14
interest income 14
interest rate paid on bank reserves 287, 419
intermediation chain: modern 176; *traditional* 176
internal funding 352
internal liquidity market 332
internal rating based (IRB) approach 555
international banking 400; and bank lending channel 428; Bräuning-Ivashina model 418; contagion 401; currency denomination 407; currency dimension 402, 407; currency mismatch 409; and domestic monetary policy transmission 426; global currency 402, 408; lending destination 405; location dimension 402, 405; offshore financial center 405; ownership dimension 402, 403; and resource allocation 410; and risk-sharing 400, 410, 413; risk-taking channel of 428; and spillover 400, 424; traditional view 410
international trade 418
interstate branching 164; deregulation 165; and diversification 166 and funding cost 167; and household 168; and risk-taking 166
intrastate branching 164; and bank performance 166; deregulation 164; and income distribution 167; and inequality 168
iso-utility curve 411

Jensen's inequality 489
joint-stock commercial bank (JCB) 457

Kashyap-Stein identification 329, 330, 426; endogeneity 330; instrumental variable 331; sensitivity to balance sheet liquidity 331
Khwaja-Mian identification 324, 327, 425, 470, 554, 565
Klein-Monti model 141; demand curve 142; elasticity of deposit supply 143; elasticity of loan demand 142; intensity of competition 143; monopolistic competition 143; perfect market competition 143; price setting 143; supply curve 142
Kuhn-Tucker condition 49, 368

laissez-faire 447
law enforcement 458, 461; and bank lending 460; and collateral 460; and credit allocation 460
Law of Large Numbers 504
lean against the wind 428
leasing 328
legal environment 461; and alternative financing channel 462; and credit allocation 461
legal origin 458; and creditor protection 458; and debt enforcement 459; and development of banking systems 459; and government ownership 459; and law enforcement 459; and quality of government 459
legal rule 459; and bank lending 459, 460; and banking development 460; bankruptcy rule 460; collateral pledgeability rule 460; and creditor protection 460; and economic growth 460; and information sharing 461; and informational friction 460
legal system 457; and creditor protection 458; and development of banking systems 459; and efficiency 458; and government ownership 459; law enforcement 459; legal origin 458; legal rule 459; and quality of government 459

Leibniz's rule 581
lender of last resort 18, 276, 285
lender-of-last-resort policy 42, 532; Bagehot Rules; too big to fail 534, 536; collateral 532; credibility rule 532; incredible threat 534; moral hazard problem 533; no-free-lunch rule 532; regulatory capture 537; solvency rule 532; time consistency problem 534
lending standard 333
Lerner Index (LI) 161
leverage cycle 342, 371, 380; and boom-bust cycle 371; Geanakoplos model 380; general equilibrium effect 342, 380; procyclicality 371; and risk management 342, 371; Shin model 371
leverage ratio 15
leveraged buyout (LBO) 212
limit of arbitrage 32, 77, 395
limited liability 5, 500, 542; in Bernanke-Gertler model 349; in Diamond-Rajan sellers' strike model 500; and industrial organization in banking 139, 145, 147; and liquidity risk 530; and risk-taking channel 322
liquid asset 28, 31, 67
liquidation 28, 32; cost of 32
liquidity buffer 528, 529; externality 482, 530
Liquidity Coverage Ratio (LCR) 492, 501, 538; and asset price 541; in Cao-Illing model 538; and central bank liquidity facility 540; definition 538; in Diamond-Rajan sellers' strike model 538; empirical evidence 539; and externality 541; and funding cost 539; and interbank lending 539; and liquidity hoarding 541; and market liquidity risk 541; and net interest margin (NIM) 539; and real economy 539; and systemic liquidity shortage 542
liquidity crisis 493
liquidity crunch 486, 492, 502, 531, 536
liquidity hoarding 531, 541; adverse selection 531; externality 531; and Liquidity Coverage Ratio (LCR) 541

liquidity insurance 28
liquidity management 16, 277, 282, 485; and bank lending channel 277, 282, 296, 329; through interbank market 278; and liquidity buffer 530; and monetary policy implementation 282
liquidity market: in Cao-Illing model 67
liquidity preference 28, 29
liquidity preference shock 31
liquidity regulation 528; lender-of-last-resort policy 532; Liquidity Coverage Ratio (LCR) 538; liquidity risk 528; and monetary policy implementation 540; Net Stable Funding Ratio (NSFR) 538; and systemic liquidity risk 541
liquidity risk 29, 37, 74, 289, 486, 527, 528; in banking network 235; and capital requirement 550; general equilibrium effect 541; idiosyncratic 528; liquidity regulation 528; and liquidity regulation 541; in money creation 283; systemic 486, 492, 529; and time consistency problem 536
liquidity shortage: in Diamond-Rajan sellers' strike model 501; and Liquidity Coverage Ratio (LCR) 501, 542; systemic 482, 530, 542
liquidity spiral: definition of 74; mechanism 74
loan loss provision (LLP) 263
loan sales: inefficient screening 191; risk shifting 192; screening 189
loanable fund 277, 280, 282, 471
London interbank offered rate (LIBOR) 289
long asset 32, 239
long-run marginal expected shortfall (LRMES) 520
Lucas critique 551

macroprudential perspective of banking regulation 485, 512; calibration of prudential controls 514; correlation and common exposure 514; proximate objective 513; risk in modelling 514; top-down approach 514; ultimate objective 513
macroprudential regulation 18

marginal expected shortfall (MES) 518
market concentration 138
market concentration index 159
market discipline: and opacity 261, 264
market for reserves 286; demand for reserves 286; equilibrium market rate 288; supply of reserves 287
market freeze 493, 531
market liquidity: under adverse selection 75; complexity and 75; definition of 75; determinants 75; under moral hazard 75
market liquidity risk 289, 528; and Liquidity Coverage Ratio (LCR) 541
market-oriented economy 8
market power 139
market segmentation 424
market structure: measurement of 159
marked-to-market 266
Martin-Skeie-von Thadden model 199; collateral 202; debt rollover by repo 202; haircut 202; non-run equilibrium 203; run on the repos 206
maturity 16
maturity mismatch 16, 37, 74, 529; Brunnermeier-Oehmke model 485; and CoVaR 517; excess 485; and funding liquidity 76; and Liquidity Coverage Ratio (LCR) 492; liquidity risk 485; and Net Stable Funding Ratio (NSFR) 492; and rollover risk 485
maturity rat race 485, 486, 491, 530
maturity transformation 16, 29, 485, 529; and central bank 305
McFadden Act of 1927 10, 164
microprudential perspective of banking regulation 484, 512, 527; bottom-up approach 514; calibration of prudential controls 514; correlation and common exposure 514; proximate objective 513; risk in modelling 514; ultimate objective 513
monetary policy: bank capital channel of 557; bank lending channel of 277, 296, 323, 329; and banking regulation 556; and capital regulation 557; and central bank's balance sheet management 286; contractionary 286; corridor system 288, 419; in COVID-19 pandemic 295; and credit risk 279, 316; cross-border spillover of 400; currency channel of 409; currency swap agreement 291; expansionary 286; in financial crisis 288; floor system 419; Funding for Lending Scheme (FLS) 558; implementation 284, 286, 288, 419, 540; interaction with banking regulation 527; and international banking 426; international transmission of 418, 420, 424; key policy rate 284; leverage channel 279, 321; and Liquidity Coverage Ratio (LCR) 540; and liquidity regulation 540; and liquidity risk 278, 304; too low for too long 332; *maturity extension* 292; *and maturity transformation* 278; in normal time 284; open market operation 286; pass-through 319, 334; pass-through channel 279, 321; price tool 277, 282, 284; qualitative easing 293; quantitative easing (QE) 294; quantity tool 277, 281; risk-shifting channel 279, 321; risk-taking channel of 277, 321; short-term interest rate 282; target 286; targeted liquidity provision 291; transmission mechanism of 277; unconventional 289; and zombie lending 336
monetary policy shock: aggregate 324; bank-specific 324; idiosyncratic 324
money: central bank 281; as medium for transaction 278, 306; as the most liquid asset 278, 306
money base (MB) 285
money creation 282; credit risk 283; limit 283; liquidity risk 283; and reserve requirement 284
money market: dollarized 429; domestic 408; international 408
money market fund 177
money multiplier 281
monitoring 17, 91; in Dell'Ariccia-Laeven-Marquez model 315; in Diamond model 95; in Holmström-Tirole

636

model 104; and opacity 262; under public guarantee 470
monopolistic competition: in Klein-Monti model 142
moral hazard: and bank capitalization 100; and bank lending 359; in Bernanke-Gertler model 351; in Bianchi model 367; and capital 100, 106; and capitalization 100; and deposit insurance 42, 80; definition 90; in Gertler-Karadi-Kiyotaki model 362; in Holmström-Tirole model 102, 103; in lender-of-last-resort policy 533, 534; in loan sales 192; and market liquidity 75; and misreporting 94; and monitoring 91, 95; in originate-to-distribute 210; and risk-taking channel 279; in securitization 215
moral hazard hypothesis 140, 144, 146
moral suasion 468; and bank bailout 469; in European debt crisis 468; and home bias 468; and political connection 469; in sovereign debt rollover 468; subnational 469
mortgage-backed security (MBS) 176, 294
multibank holding companies (MBHCs) 164

Nash bargaining solution 446
National Banking Era 163
N-bank concentration ratio (CRn) 160
negative monetary policy rate 294, 334
net interest margin (NIM) 15, 334, 456, 539
Net Stable Funding Ratio (NSFR) 492, 538; in Bianchi-Bigio model 538; definition 538
net worth 340, 357, 364, 365, 428; and financial accelerator 341, 343
network in banking 226, 235
New Keynesian macroeconomics 341
non-borrowed reserves (NBR) 285, 287
non-cooperative equilibrium 444
non-interest income 14
non-performing loan (NPL) 264, 331, 333, 456, 461, 467
non-run equilibrium: of Diamond-Dybvig model 40

Nordhaus-MacRae model 448; credit cycle 448; credit supply 448; empirical evidence 464; loss function 449; myopic and backward-looking voter 452; opportunistic politician 452; political cost 449; voters' expectation 448
Nordic banking crisis 438

occasionally binding constraint 342, 342
off-balance sheet 266; and opacity 266; and risk management 188; and risk-taking 266; in securitization 182
offshore financial center 405
on call deposit 14
one-share-one-vote principle 441
opacity 226, 249; balance sheet-based measurement of 265; and bank run 226, 261; and banking competition 264, 265; Dang-Gorton-Holmström-Ordoñez model 249; and efficiency 261; and fragility 261; and funding cost 265; and information disclosure 265; and information sensitivity 226, 249, 264; LLP-based measurement of 263; market analysts' forecast error-based measurement of 265; and market discipline 261, 264; market measure measurement of 263; measurement 263; and public information 261; and risk premium 265; and risk-taking 262, 264–267; as strategic choice 226, 261; as systematic discrepancy and inconsistency 263
open market operation 276, 286
operating expenses 14
operating expense (OE) ratio 15
originate to distribute: and haircut 188, 193
originate-to-distribute 192; definition 181; empirical evidence 210; and lending standard 210, 215; and loan quality 210; and moral hazard 210; and risk-taking 210; and screening 210, 215; Shleifer-Vishny model 192
Outright Monetary Transactions (OMT) 336
overlapping generation model 344

participation constraint: in Bernanke-Gertler model 349; in Dell'Ariccia-Laeven-Marquez model 316, 317; in Diamond model 98; in Holmström-Tirole model 102, 103
passporting 10
perfect market competition: in Hellmann-Murdock-Stiglitz model 152; in Klein-Monti model 143
personal connection: banker-politician 434
policy-oriented bank 438
political bank resolution cycle 464, 467
political connection 462; and bank lending 462; and bank performance 464; and credit misallocation 463; formation of 463; and government-owned bank 462; implicit 464; and moral suasion 469; and political credit cycle 466; and *preferential resource allocation 463*; and selective default 463
political credit cycle: in advanced economies 466; and agricultural credit 464; bank resolution cycle 465, 467; crowd-out 467; distortion 467; and election cycle 465; in emerging market economies 464; empirical evidence 464; and government control 467; Nordhaus-MacRae model 448; and political connection 466; and political party turnover 467; post-election contraction 467; and stimulation effect 467
political cycle 436
political economy 434; allocation efficiency 469; and bank performance 453; in banking 436; control right 436; credit policy 440; credit risk 436; empirical evidence 452; government ownership 436, 437, 453; home bias 468; legal system 457; moral suasion 468; political connection 462; political credit cycle 448; and real economy outcome 435; reciprocal reward 435; reelection 435; Shleifer-Vishny government ownership model 437; through personal connection 434

political tie 462
positive selection 93, 119, 121; in De Meza-Webb model 119, 121; and excess lending 123
pre-regulation era 163
price stability 276; versus financial stability 557
principal-agent problem 90; and banking-macro linkage 340, 341
profit-cost margin (PCM) 160, 161
profit efficiency 456
promotion pressure index (PPI) 473
propensity score 216
propensity score matching (PSM) 215; average treatment effect (ATE) 216; propensity score 216
property right 437
public finance: and credit allocation 471; and crowd-in 471; crowding-out effect 471; and moral suasion 468; through industrial policy 471
public goods 437, 480
public guarantee 464; for borrower 470; and credit allocation 470; and risk management 470; for state-owned firm 471
public–private partnership 438

qualitative easing 293
quantitative easing (QE) 294; and capital requirement 558; in COVID-19 pandemic 295; and monetary base 295; and spillover 425

real business cycle (RBC) 366
reelection 448
refinance 485
regression discontinuity design (RDD) 213
regulatory arbitrage 527
regulatory capital 551
regulatory capital ratio 520
regulatory capture 537
Reigle-Neal Interstate Banking and Branching Efficiency Act (IBBEA) of 1994 10, 165
relationship banking 125; and competitive advantage 126;

definition 125; discipline effect 126; empirical evidence 125; in financial crisis 128; lock-in effect 127; and monopoly of information 127; relationship measures 127; soft information in 126; versus initial public offering 128; versus market funding 127
relative profit differences (RPD) 162
repo 177, 182, 285, 493, 530; bi-party 183; haircut 183; and information sensitivity 186; rate 183; and securitization 192; structure 182; tri-party 184
repo market 177; buyers' strike 493; freeze 187; haircut 183; repo rate 183; repo run 187, 188; sellers' strike 493
repo rate 183, 185; September 2020 spike 295
repo run 187, 188; in the 2007–2009 financial crisis 199; Martin-Skeie-von Thadden model 199
repurchase agreement (repo) 177, 182
reserve 185, 280, 284, 419; excess 281, 286, 298
reserve account 284
reserve requirement 277, 281, 540; in Bianchi-Bigio model 297; as a limit to money creation 283
retail deposits 4; in total bank liabilities 5
retained earning 546
return on assets (ROA) 15, 456, 464
return on equity (ROE) 15, 317, 456, 543
revelation principle 349
reversal rate 335
risk allocation: in frictionless economy 179; in matching market 179; by securitization 180; in traditional banking 179
risk appetite 177, 400
risk aversion 31, 33
risk management 17, 90; and leverage cycle 342, 371; and public guarantee 470; Value-at-Risk (VaR) 372
risk premium 289; and capital regulation 553; and counterparty risk 289; in financial crisis 289; TED spread 289

risk shifting 81, 318; to central bank 541; in Dell'Ariccia-Laeven-Marquez model 318; under loan sales 192; and risk-taking channel 279
risk weight 543
risk-free rate 289, 316
risk-sharing: in bank runs 29; in banking network 226, 235; in banking network 238; in interbank market 502; in international banking 400, 410; of liquidity risk 29; in securitization 177
risk-taking 42; and banking competition 139; in banking deregulation 166; in banking dynamics 141; and banking regulation 527; and capital 543, 548; and capital regulation 547, 550; and fire sale externality 482; franchise value hypothesis 140, 144; and industrial organization in banking 139; and lending standard 333; and monetary policy 277, 279, 304, 315; moral hazard hypothesis 140, 146; and off-balance sheet 266; and opacity 262, 264–267; under originate-to-distribute model 210; in securitization 210, 213; short-run gain versus long-run loss 150; under winner's curse 141, 153, 158
risk-taking channel 277, 279; Cao-Illing model 304; credit risk 316; of currency appreciation 428; Dell'Ariccia-Laeven-Marquez model 315, 317; empirical evidence 332; international 428; liquidity risk 304
risk-weighted asset (RWA) 550, 554
rollover 70; with repo 188; sovereign debt 468
rollover risk 76, 485, 492
Roman law 458
Romano-Germanic law 458
run on the repos 187, 188; in the 2007–2009 financial crisis 199; Martin-Skeie-von Thadden model 199

safe-haven 424
saving: with international banking 411

savings bank 466
screening 17, 91; in Gorton-Pennacchi model 188; under loan sales 187, 189, 191; in originate-to-distribute 185, 210, 214; under public guarantee 470; in securitization 187; in Shaffer model 154
search for yield 316, 332
seasoned equity offering (SEO) 546, 548
securitization: and adverse selection 215; and bank performance 214; definition 177; in Europe 218; in Italy 217; and moral hazard 215; off-balance sheet 181; procedure 181; and repo 192; and risk-sharing 177; and risk-taking 210, 213; in Spain 218; tranching 181; and transfer of credit risk 218
securitization rule-of-thumb 213
securitized banking 19; *and bank fragility* 186, 188; and bank performance 214; definition 179; and financial stability 187; and information sensitivity 186; and regulatory cost 185; and repo run 188; and risk-sharing 185; Shleifer-Vishny model 192; structure 182; versus traditional banking 184
sellers' strike 492, 493; Diamond-Rajan sellers' strike model 492
shadow bank 16, 184, 527
shadow banking 184
Shaffer model 153; duopoly solution 155; market entry 157; under monopolistic competition 156; monopoly solution 155; screening 154; type-I error 155; type-II error 158
Shin model 371; asset price 375; excess volatility 378; leverage cycle 378; leveraged investor 373; non-leveraged investor 373; procyclicality 380, 544; risk aversion 373; Value-at-Risk (VaR) 372, 374
Shleifer-Vishny government ownership model 439; bargaining 440, 445; control rights 443, 446; cooperative equilibrium 444; credit policy 440; first-best solution 442; laissez-faire solution 447; Nash bargaining solution 446; non-cooperative equilibrium 444; political cost 440; political economy solution with bargaining 445; political economy solution without bribe 443; social welfare 441
Shleifer-Vishny model 192; financial instability 199; haircut 193, 195; leverage 195; leverage cycle 199; originate-to-distribute 192; securitization 192; securitization equilibrium with repo 195; securitization equilibrium without repo 193
short asset 31, 239
short-term funding 486, 491
skin-in-the-game 317, 320, 542, 548, 550
social planner's solution: of Allen-Gale model 47, 55; of Cao-Illing model 68; of Diamond-Dybvig model 30
soft information 126
solvency risk 289
sovereign bond 468
sovereign debt 468
sovereign debt crisis 401, 468
sovereign default 401
sovereign risk 418
special purpose vehicle (SPV) 181, 212
spillover 400, 424
SRISK 519; capital shortfall 519; definition 520; and externality 519
standard approach (SA) 555
state-owned bank 438, 456
state-owned enterprise (SOE) 464
Stiglitz-Weiss model 107; adverse selection effect 112; competitive equilibrium 114; credit rationing equilibrium 114; demand for loans 111; inefficiency 118; information friction 110; lending efficiency 115; loan supply 111; loan supply curve 114; undersupply of lending 118
stress test 261, 262, 514
subprime loan 186
subprime mortgage 186
sudden-stop 371
sunspot equilibrium 39

suspension of convertibility 40
syndicated loan 335
systemic bank failure 513
systemic banking crisis 81; cost of GDP 12; and deposit insurance 81; fiscal cost 13; in Germany, 1931 80; world map 11
systemic crisis 515
systemic event 513
systemic expected shortfall (SES) 517; definition 519; and externality 519
systemic risk 481; cascading bank failure 482, 502; common exposure 482, 502; comovement 482, 502; too connected to fail 483; and contagion 484, 502; as coordination failure 484; correlation 502; CoVaR 516; credit growth and 515; excess maturity mismatch 486; and externality 482; and fire sale externality 482; inefficient liquidity buffer 492; interconnection 482, 502; and macroprudential regulation 484, 512; measurement 515; network effect 483; source of 482; SRISK 519; systemic expected shortfall (SES) 517; systemic liquidity risk 486, 529; systemic liquidity shortage 482
systemically important bank (SIB) 533, 536, 546
systemically important bank (SIB) buffer 546
systemically important financial institution (SIFI) 290

targeted liquidity provision 291; currency swap agreement 293; maturity extension 292; for systemically important financial institution (SIFI) 293
tax advantage 543
tax deduction 442
TED rate 289

threat point 446
time consistency problem 534
time deposit 14
too big to fail 534, 536
too connected to fail 483
trade finance 328
tranching 181; bankruptcy remote tranche 182; equity tranche 182; junior tranche 182; mezzanine tranche 182; seniority in 181
transaction-oriented banking 126
transactional banking 126
transmission mechanism of monetary policy 277
trigger strategy 151
two-sided market 139
type-I error 155
type-II error 158

uncovered interest rate parity (UIP) 427; deviation 428; non-arbitrage condition 427
uninformed investor 229
unit banking 164
universal bank 19, 224

Value-at-Risk (VaR) 372, 516, 544

wholesale funding 5; and Liquidity Coverage Ratio (LCR) 539; and maturity rat race 491; and Net Stable Funding Ratio (NSFR) 535; in total bank liabilities 5
winner's curse 141, 154, 157

z-score 16, 265
zero lower bound (ZLB) 294; and balance sheet rebalancing 335; and banking outcome 334; and monetary policy pass-through 334; and net interest margin (NIM) 334; reversal rate 335
zombie lending 336; definition 336; empirical evidence 336; real effect 336